Lecture Notes in Computer Science 7797

Commenced Publication in 1973
Founding and Former Series Editors:
Gerhard Goos, Juris Hartmanis, and Jan van Leeuwen

Editorial Board

Andrei Voronkov
Christoph Weidenbach (Eds.)

Programming Logics

Essays in Memory of Harald Ganzinger

 Springer

Volume Editors

Andrei Voronkov
University of Manchester
Oxford Road
Manchester, M13 9PL, UK
E-mail: andrei.voronkov@manchester.ac.uk

Christoph Weidenbach
Max-Planck-Institut für Informatik
Campus E1 4
66123 Saarbrücken, Germany
E-mail: weidenbach@mpi-inf.mpg.de

ISSN 0302-9743   e-ISSN 1611-3349
ISBN 978-3-642-37650-4   e-ISBN 978-3-642-37651-1
DOI 10.1007/978-3-642-37651-1
Springer Heidelberg Dordrecht London New York

Library of Congress Control Number: 2013934837

CR Subject Classification (1998): F.4.1, I.2.2-4, D.1.6, F.3.1-2, D.3.1, F.1.0

LNCS Sublibrary: SL 1 – Theoretical Computer Science and General Issues

Typesetting: Camera-ready by author, data conversion by Scientific Publishing Services, Chennai, India

Printed on acid-free paper

Springer is part of Springer Science+Business Media (www.springer.com)

Preface

Harald Ganzinger died on June 3, 2004, after a long and serious illness. Exactly one year later, on June 3 and 4, 2005, Andreas Podelski, Andrei Voronkov, and Reinhard Wilhelm organized a workshop on "Programming Logics," the name of Ganzinger's department at the Max Planck Institute for Informatics. The workshop took place at the Max Planck Institute for Informatics and included leading scientists in the area of programming logics. The program of the workshop is presented in Table 1.

The idea for this volume was born out of the workshop . It was a long journey until it was finished. We are, in particular, indebted to our reviewers including among others Peter Baumgartner, Maria Alpuente Frasnedo, Silvio Ghilardi, Thomas Hillenbrand, Matthias Horbach, Laura Kovács, Herbert Kuchen, Ralf Lämmel, Nicolas Peltier, Stephan Schulz, Doitsa Swierstra, Dmitry Tishkovsky, and Patrick Wischnewski. Thanks to Krista Ames for proofreading the English. The EasyChair conference management system was a great help in dealing with all aspects of putting together this volume.

Some weeks before Harald Ganzinger passed away, a directors, board meeting at the Max Planck Institute for Informatics took place. All directors including Harald attended. One item on the agenda was to fix the date for an important event happening in autumn of 2004. It was during this discussion that everyone suddenly realized that Harald would already be gone by then. Silence. Harald smiled and said: "I'm available. I don't have any appointment at that time."

Andrei Voronkov
Christoph Weidenbach

Table 1. Program of the "Programming Logics" Workshop

Andrei Voronkov, Robert Nieuwenhuis	The Scientific Life of Harald Ganzinger
Christopher Lynch	Constructing Bachmair-Ganzinger Models
Nachum Dershowitz, Maria Paola Bonacina	Canonical Ground Horn Theories
Robert Nieuwenhuis	First-Order Theorem Proving by Constraint Propagation and by Local Search
David Plaisted, Swaha Miller	The Relative Power of Semantics and Unification
Deepak Kapur	Will Algebraic Geometry Rescue Program Verification?
Pierre Lescanne	Experiments in Higher-Order Epistemic Logic with Common Knowledge Using a Proof Assistant
Claude Kirchner, Hélène Kirchner, Fabrice Nahon	Narrowing-Based Inductive Proof Search
Uwe Waldmann	Modular Proof Systems for Partial Functions with Weak Equality
Viorica Sofronie-Stokkermans	On Reasoning in Local Theory Extensions
Renate Schmidt	First-Order Resolution Methods for Modal Logics
Witold Charatonik	Set Constraints
Neil Jones	Programs as Data Objects
Manfred Broy	Reasoning on Feedback Under Lack of Time
Frank Pfenning	Linear Logical Algorithms
David McAllester	Logical Algorithms and Generalized A$_*$ in Computer Vision and NLP
Moshe Y. Vardi	Alternation as an Algorithmic Construct
Jean-Pierre Jouannaud, Jean Goubault	Resolution, Paramodulation and Finite Semantics Trees
Amir Pnueli	Program Synthesis in Action: Solving a Doubly Exponential Hard Problem in Time N^3
Robert Giegerich	The Power of Abstraction in Biosequence Analysis
Alexander Bockmayr	Bio-Logics: Logic Modeling of Bioregulatory Networks
Gernot Stenz, Reinhold Letz	Advanced Pruning Concepts for Tableau Calculi
Hans de Nivelle, Ruzica Piskac	Verification of a Result Checker in Saturate
Andreas Podelski, Andrey Rybalchenko	Software Model Checking for Termination and Liveness

Table of Contents

Harald Ganzinger's Legacy: Contributions to Logics and Programming

Deepak Kapur[1], Robert Nieuwenhuis[2], Andrei Voronkov[3],
Christoph Weidenbach[4], and Reinhard Wilhelm[5]

[1] University of New Mexico
http://www.cs.unm.edu/~kapur/
[2] Technical University of Catalonia
http://www.lsi.upc.es/~roberto
[3] University of Manchester
http://www.voronkov.com
[4] Max Planck Institute for Informatics
http://www.mpi-inf.mpg.de/~weidenb
[5] Saarland University
http://rw4.cs.uni-saarland.de/people/wilhelm.shtml

Abstract. In 2004 Harald Ganzinger was nominated for the Herbrand Award, which he received only two months before he passed away on June 3, 2004. We describe Ganzinger's scientific achievements. We hope that this paper will also be useful as a reference guide to Ganzinger's most significant contributions and publications in many areas of computer science.

Je mehr du gedacht, je mehr du getan hast, desto länger hast du gelebt.[1]

Immanuel Kant

From Harald Ganziger's death notice.

1 Introduction

Harald Ganzinger's research career spanned over 3 decades during which he made numerous contributions to many areas of computer science, ranging from fundamental theory to low-level implementation techniques. During this time period, he also powerfully influenced many researchers' lives. He had publications with more than 35 different coauthors from many different countries. In this article, we briefly review Ganzinger's contributions to Logics and Programming with a special focus on automated theorem proving.

Among many other honors, Ganzinger received the Herbrand Award for Distinguished Contributions to Automated Deduction in March 2004. This award was created to honor individuals or groups for important contributions to this field. It is named after the famous French mathematician and logician Jacques

---

[1] The more you have thought, the more you have done, the longer you have lived.

A. Voronkov and C. Weidenbach (Eds.): Ganzinger Festschrift, LNCS 7797, pp. 1–18, 2013.

Herbrand [Her30] and is given at most once per year at the Conference on Automated Deduction (CADE).

The citation for the Herbrand Award for Harald Ganzinger states that it was to recognize

- his seminal work on the theory underlying modern theorem proving systems,
- the breadth of his research covering nearly all major areas of deduction, and the depth of his results in each one of them,
- his effective contributions to the development of systems and implementation techniques,
- his dedicated promotion of automated reasoning both inside and outside the community.

As a recipient of the Herbrand Award, Ganzinger ranks among the most influential people in automated deduction. All recipients of the award to date are Larry Wos (1992), Woody Bledsoe (1994), J. Alan Robinson (1996), Wu Wen-Tsun (1997), Gérard Huet (1998), Robert S. Boyer and J Strother Moore (1999), William W. McCune (2000), Donald W. Loveland (2001), Mark E. Stickel (2002), Peter B. Andrews (2003), Harald Ganzinger (2004), Martin Davis (2005), Wolfgang Bibel (2006), Alan Bundy (2007), Edmund Clarke (2008), Deepak Kapur (2009), David Plaisted (2010), Nachum Dershowitz (2011), and Melvin Fitting (2012).

2   From Compilers to Automated Deduction: Breadth and Depth of Ganzinger's Contributions

We summarize Ganzinger's contributions to numerous areas of computer science in chronological order.

2.1   Mid 70's to Mid 80's: Compiler Construction

Ganzinger started his scientific career working on the compilation of programming languages. He worked on a project funded by the Deutsche Forschungsgemeinschaft (German Research Foundation, DFG) in the "Sonderforschungsbereich 49" (Research Center 49) at the Technical University of Munich. The project's goal was the automatic generation of compilers from appropriate descriptions of compilation subtasks. Typical description mechanisms were regular expressions, context-free grammars, and attribute grammars. Generation methods for lexical analyzers from regular expressions and syntax analyzers from context-free grammars were already well-known at that time. Evaluators for attribute grammars, and even the attribute-grammar mechanism itself, were however topics of active research. The composition of the generated modules and their cooperation on intermediate program representations had not yet been adequately investigated.

Ganzinger's first publication [GW75], together with Wilhelm, concerned different ways compiler modules could cooperate and conditions under which such representations could be suppressed. The latter transformation became known as *deforestation* in the functional-language domain. A number of publications described the compiler-generating systems developed in the aforementioned project [WRC+76, GRW77]. Further publications dealt with particular problems in compilation, such as an algebraic view of type conversions [Gan76] and storage optimization for automatically generated compilers [Gan79b].

Ganzinger was not content with implementing a system that would do the generation job. He wanted to also reason about its correctness and, therefore, needed the connection of the descriptions of the compilation subtasks to programming language semantics [Gan79a]. As a next step, a language semantics was transformed into a description that was usable as input to a compiler generator [Gan80, GGMW82]. All this work led him to gain an algebraic view of compiler components, which he used again to pick up the topic of his first publication, namely how to structure compilers in a modular way [Gan83b, Gan83c, Gan83a]. These publications comprised Ganzinger's Habilitation thesis, submitted to the Technical University of Munich in 1983.

2.2 Mid 80's to Early 90's: Abstract Data Type Specifications, Reasoning, and Completion of Conditional Equations

Ganzinger began investigating abstract data types in order to develop methods for modularizing descriptions of compilers; this approach would allow compiler descriptions to be adapted to different related programming languages [Gan81]. In his efforts to support automated reasoning about parameterized algebraic specification of abstract data types, Ganzinger's work on algebraic specification emphasized proof-theoretic investigations [Gan83a, Gan83d].

A particular mention must be made of Ganzinger's work on investigating extensions of the Knuth-Bendix completion procedure to conditional equational specifications [Gan86, Gan87c, Gan87a]. Using complexity bounds on proofs, Ganzinger developed a technique for the completion of many-sorted conditional equations that declares conditional equations as either eliminable, non-operational, or contributing to proofs as reductive rewrite rules [Gan87b]. He was able to show the termination of completion on many nontrivial conditional equation specifications. These ideas could be viewed as precursor of related concepts, which would subsequently serve as the basis for Ganzinger's insightful work on optimizing proofs in the superposition calculus using proof orderings and redundancy.

As a part of the European project "Prospectra", Ganzinger and his colleagues at the University of Dortmund developed the software system CEC, supporting the completion of conditional equational specifications in order to generate software from it [BGB87, BGS88b].

Ganzinger also showed how the order-sorted completion of Goguen et al. could be improved by observing that order-sorted algebraic specifications can be transformed into equivalent many-sorted specifications using his earlier results on completion for many-sorted conditional equations [Gan89, Gan91b].

Motivated by his early work on compilers and algebraic specification, Ganzinger further developed a new theory for rewriting and completion of conditional equations [Gan87a] and applied it, among others, to deduction in order-sorted theories and termination proofs of logic programs [GW93].

2.3   90's Onwards: Superposition Calculus and Its Applications

Ganzinger generalized automated deduction from conditional equations to the full first-order setting. By combining ideas from Knuth Bendix completion, paramodulation, resolution, and other earlier work on first-order reasoning, he, together with Bachmair, developed the *superposition calculus* [BG90c]. It was revolutionary in the sense that it combined previously separately known concepts in a single calculus:

– ordering restrictions on inferences,
– an abstract redundancy criterion that relies on the same ordering,
– a model assumption that guides the search for relevant inferences, and
– the saturation concept that eventually leads to a proof or a model.

Using the superposition calculus, Ganzinger devised a new, cleaner way of giving semantics to logic programs with equality and negation. He showed that saturated programs have a unique perfect model for a given ordering, thus extending earlier notions of stratified logic programs [BG91a].

Ganzinger's search for practical techniques to include specialized procedures into the superposition calculus and refutational theorem provers started in the early nineties; he began with work on hierarchical first-order theories with sufficient completeness requirements [BGW92, BGW94], continued with results on the Shostak combination procedure [Gan02], and, finally, incorporated it in refutational provers [GHW03]. During the last two decades, Ganzinger showed how to design specialized inference systems for a large variety of domains, such as transitive relations and total orderings [BG94e, BG98a], commutative semigroups [BG94a], commutative rings [BGS94], and cancellative Abelian monoids [GW96]. Closely related to this, he contributed to a better understanding of the relationship between Buchberger's algorithm for computing Groebner Bases and saturation [BG94b]. Furthermore, he developed chaining techniques for deduction in many-valued logics [GSS00].

In addition to actually building theorem proving procedures, Ganzinger was keen on applying superposition to decision problems. He designed superposition-based decision procedures for several classes of formulas, such as the monadic class with equality (which he proved to be equivalent to a class of set constraints [BGW93a]), the two-variable guarded fragment with transitive relations [GMV99], the guarded fragment with equality [GdN99], and modal logics [GHMS98].

Concerning tableaux calculi, Ganzinger produced new results on rigid reachability [GJV00], which have been applied by others for proving new results on second-order unification [LV00]. He gave an equality elimination method with ordering constraints [BGV98].

Another completely different part of Ganzinger's research concerned deduction-based complexity analysis. Among several other results in this area,

Ganzinger showed how complexity classes can be characterized by the existence of sets of clauses that are saturated with respect to different term orderings [BG96, BG01b], and he showed that this technique can be made effective by means of the Saturate system which was first developed by Nieuwenhuis and Nivela and then continued by him [NN93, GNN99].

Ganzinger's research activities also included new ideas on instantiation-based theorem proving, which, among other applications, make it possible to incorporate decision procedures for propositional satisfiability into first-order theorem proving [GK03, GK04, GK06]. Other work includes saturation techniques with lazy clause normal form transformation, the Prolog implementation of which (in Saturate) Ganzinger showed to be superior to efficiently implemented CASC winning systems on a large class of problems [GS05]. Furthermore, he recognized the importance of theory combinations and, after his seminal paper on hierarchical superposition [BGW94], he did further work on combination frameworks [GHN⁺04, GSSW06].

3   Seminal Contribution to the Theory Underlying Modern Automated Reasoning Systems

In this section, we discuss Ganzinger's main contribution to the theory of automated reasoning: the *superposition* calculus. The superposition calculus has greatly influenced research in automated reasoning. Whereas we concentrated in the previous sections solely on Ganzinger's work, we now also explain the roots of the superposition calculus and its influence on other researchers work to the present day.

The origin of superposition can actually be found in the seminal paper of Robinson on resolution [Rob65]. The main contributions of Robinson's work were the dedication of the resolution calculus to a normal form of formulas (CNF, clause normal form) and the replacement of an explicit or implicit instantiation rule for first-order variables by unification. Although it was recognized that the resolution principle constituted a big step forward towards automation, looking at it from today's perspective, it lacked structure and simply generated too many inferences for almost any interesting problem. In particular, even simple problems, particularly including equality, generated enormous search spaces due to the axiomatic handling of the equality relation. In order to overcome this situation, the idea to replace the equality axiom system by an extra inference rule was born: paramodulation, mechanizing the principle of replacing equals by equals [WRCS67, RW69].

Purely equational theories, i.e., theories consisting of a set of equations, attracted particular attention. Sets of equations can represent computable functions in a natural way, so researchers became interested in how to represent and reason in this setting. The starting point here was Knuth and Bendix's seminal paper on completion [KB70]. In fact, the study of purely equational systems was Ganzinger's starting point in automated reasoning, see Section 2.2. The Knuth-Bendix completion procedure added another dimension to the work on paramodulation: replace equals by equals, but always replace complex structures by simpler ones. The idea of ordering was added, yielding in particular a model of computation via rewriting instead of exploring a search space.

Next, researchers started to combine the ideas of paramodulation-based first-order theorem proving for clauses and Knuth-Bendix completion for purely equational systems. Bachmair and Ganzinger established their theory of resolution and paramodulation-based theorem proving with abstract redundancy criteria [BG90c, BG94d] – the *superposition* calculus in the early 1990's, which was built on earlier work of Peterson on establishing paramodulation completeness [Pet83], Zhang and Kapur on model construction and clausal superposition [ZK88, ZK89, Zha88, ZK90], Kapur, Musser and Narendran [KMN88] as well as Bachmair and Dershowitz's work on redundancy of superpositions [BD88], and Lynch and Snyder's work on redundancy in constrained completion [LS95]. It was first developed as a sound and complete calculus for first-order logic with equality. Ganzinger provided a rigorous analysis of the partly noticed and exploited relationships between the rewriting theory and Knuth-Bendix completion on the one hand and paramodulation-based refutational theorem proving on the other hand.

The following four subsections explore the influence of this contribution on the area of automated deduction.

3.1   Incorporation of Theories

In the same way that Ganzinger built equational reasoning into the superposition calculus, he and other researchers extended the superposition calculus by specific inference mechanisms for various theories. Their motivation was always that inference rules dedicated to a particular theory are superior to applying standard superposition to an axiomatization of the theory.

The first class of structures they considered consisted of subtheories of equality. The main result for transitive relations and extensions thereof [BG94e, BG94c, BG98a, BGNR99] was that the ordering restrictions could be transferred to the arguments of a transitive relation. A particular application of the equational relation is the implementation of a unique name assumption that can also be handled more efficiently by specific inference rules [SB05]. For associative and commutative (AC) function symbols, AC superposition replaces the theory by AC unification, AC-constraints, or computes modulo the axioms but deletes AC-variants [BG94a, NR94, Hil08]. With respect to algebraic structures, specific superposition calculi have been developed for cancellative abelian monoids [GW96], for abelian groups and semigroups [Stu98a, GN00, GN01b, GN04], for commutative rings [Stu98b], and for totally ordered divisible abelian groups [Wal01].

The above-mentioned theories were all first-order logic expressible. Superposition extensions for combinations with other, not necessarily first-order, theories have been studied as well. The Shostak framework [GHW03] as well as the hierarchic framework [BGW92, BGW94] are superposition extensions that support the combination of a first-order clause set with some theory. The frameworks have in particular been instantiated and applied for modular proof systems for partial functions [GSSW06] as well as for linear [KV07, AKW09] and non-linear [EKK+11] arithmetic.

3.2 Superposition Extensions

The superposition calculus itself was also subject to further research. Forbidding paramodulation into variables is one of the ingredients of efficient equational reasoning and also part of the superposition calculus. Extending this idea to the terms instantiated for variables during a superposition derivation leads to the basic strategy [BGLS92, NR92a, BGLS95]. Keeping completeness, paramodulation into instantiated terms can be forbidden at the price of a restricted notion of redundancy. Already part of the implementation of the basic strategy in the superposition calculus, the idea occurred to attach constraints to clauses. This idea yielded another branch of superposition extensions, namely constraint superposition [KKR90, NR92b, NR95, GN01a, LAWRS07]. Information stored in the clause constraint ranged from instantiation information to ordering information, to bookkeeping information on the current derivation.

As do many automated reasoning calculi, superposition computes on clauses and hence requires the transformation of a first-order formula into clause normal form with the disadvantage that local formula structure information is eventually distributed over many clauses. The non-clausal superposition calculus [BG92, GS05] overcomes this potential drawback by interleaving normal form transformation steps and superposition steps.

Another core concept of superposition is saturation. A clause set is saturated if all inferences lead to redundant clauses. If such a clause set is satisfiable, it is a representation of a minimal model for the clauses. Since saturated clause sets enjoy better computational properties, several researchers took this as a starting point for reasoning with respect to the minimal model, i.e., to develop superposition-based inductive theorem proving techniques [GS93, CN00, HW10].

3.3 Decidability

The superposition calculus turned the paramodulation and resolution calculus, which were already successful for specific examples, into an effective decision procedure for many known decidable fragments of first-order logic. Superposition decides a clause fragment if any saturation is finite. Furthermore, the approach is successful in providing decidability results for fragments unknown until then. Since there are efficient implementations of the superposition calculus, there are now generic and effective decision procedures for various classes.

Regarding already known decidable fragments and extensions thereof, superposition turned out to be a decision procedure for the class of first-order clauses with an explicit finite domain [HW07], for the monadic class with equality [BGW93b], for set constraints [BGW93a], for the guarded fragment with equality [GdN99], for fluted logic [SH00], and for divisible torsion-free abelian groups [Wal99].

With respect to description and non-classical logics such as modal logics, as well as data structure theories, additional decidability results about superposition calculus for these logics were obtained [GHMS98, SH07, KM08, HMS08, ARR03, ABRS09].

Among the theories where superposition was the key technology to prove decidability were the two variable guarded fragment with transitive relations [GMV99], shallow clause theories [Nie96, JMW98], and theories related to bottom-up tree automata [Wei99, JRV06, SR12].

3.4   Computation

In addition to providing an effective means for establishing decidability results, the saturation concept can also serve as a notion of computability. In particular, saturated clause sets can represent any function of deterministic complexity classes such as polynomial or exponential time complexity classes [McA93, BG01b]. The actual evaluation of function calls is supported by specific forms of contextual rewriting that also serve as effective computation mechanisms for functions in general [ZR85, BG90c, Nip96, WW10].

3.5   Systems and Applications

There are efficient implementations of the superposition calculus by the theorem provers E [Sch02], SPASS [WSH+07], and Vampire [RV02]. These have been successfully applied on various domains such as reasoning on data structures [ABRS09], reasoning on large ontologies [SWW10], or interpolant generation [McM03, HKV10]. Superposition-based theorem proving systems have become a standard technology in the context of first-order logic problem solving.

Further applications are adaptions of the superposition technology to other domains such as tableaux with equality [BGV98], many-valued logics [GSS00], and temporal reasoning [DFK06, SW12].

4   Effective Contributions to the Development of Systems and Implementation Techniques

Ganzinger was on of a few influential theoretical researchers in automated deduction who also contributed to the development of new practical deduction systems and implementation techniques. A large part of Ganzinger's theoretical work was motivated by experiments with his early implementation CEC [BGB87] for the completion of equational Horn specifications [BGS88b]. Initially in collaboration with Nieuwenhuis and Nivela [NN93], Ganzinger developed the *Saturate* system, a toolkit implementation in Prolog for experimentation with inference systems, constraint solvers, and redundancy provers [GNN99]. Ganzinger implemented and tested almost all of his theoretical contributions in the Saturate system, including such sophisticated concepts as contextual rewriting, deduction modulo ordering constraints, deduction with lazy clause normal form transformation, deduction modulo theory constraints like AC operators, and basic superposition.

Although the Saturate system was Ganzinger's toolbox for testing all concepts developed in the superposition context, he was aware of the potential of high-performance implementations of superposition. One of the world's leading state-of-the-art systems, SPASS [Wei97, GMW97], was implemented in Ganzinger's group headed by Weidenbach at MPI-INF. SPASS was the archetype of a modern superposition-based prover and has influenced other leading automated reasoning systems, including E and Vampire. Among Ganzinger's contributions to high-performance implementation techniques is his research in term indexing: substitution trees [Gra95] were developed in his group, and he generalized this indexing approach to context trees. Context trees are still a leading indexing technique that requires least memory and supports the sharing of terms while being competitive in time [GNN01, GNN04].

5 Promotion of Automated Reasoning

Within the automated reasoning community, Ganzinger promoted the field of automated reasoning by his activities as the Programme Committee Chair of conferences like CADE, RTA, and LPAR, by organizing events at the MPI-INF such as the 2000 Summer Retreat in Automated Deduction, by his duties as FLoC (Associate) General Chair as well as in the German DFG Research Programme "Deduktion", and by inviting researchers to MPI-INF for talks and visits.

What is perhaps even more important, around the time Ganzinger was appointed as one of the Directors at the Max Planck Institute for Informatics (MPI-INF), he shifted his research area from Compilers and Algebraic Specification to the area of Automated Deduction, devoting to this field the large amount of resources available through his position. As a result, MPI-INF became the leading research center for automated deduction in the world in the late 1990's. Many junior researchers in automated deduction received a PhD or held a postdoc position in his group at MPI-INF; senior researchers were often visitors there. Among the scientists working in Ganzinger's group at MPI-INF were: Werner Backes, Peter Barth, David Basin, Hubert Baumeister, Peter Baumgartner, Alexander Bockmayr, Witold Charatonik, Giorgio Delzanno, Friedrich Eisenbrand, Detlef Fehrer, Matthias Fischmann, Stefan Friedrich, Jörn Freiheit, Lilia Georgieva, Peter Graf, Michael Hanus, Thomas Hillenbrand, Jörg Hoffmann, Malte Hübner, Sajjad Syed Hussain, Ullrich Hustadt, Carsten Ihlemann, Florent Jacquemard, Swen Jacobs, Manfred Jäger, David Nicolaas Jansen, Georg Jung, Thomas Kasper, Konstantin Korovin, Yevgeny Kazakov, Christoph Kirsch (formerly Meyer), Patrick Maier, Alexander Malkis, Peter Madden, Seán Matthews, Supratik Mukhopadhyay, Robert Nieuwenhuis, Hans de Nivelle, Andreas Nonnengart, Hans-Jürgen Ohlbach, Ruzica Piskac, Andreas Podelski, Virgile Prevosto, Solofo Ramangalahy, Madala R. K. Krishna Rao, Stefan Ratschan,

Anya Romina, Andrey Rybalchenko, Ina Schäfer, Renate A. Schmidt, Zhikun She, Viorica Sofronie-Stokkermans, Gernot Stenz, Georg Struth, Jürgen Stuber, Jean-Marc Talbot, Andreas Tönne, Leon van der Torre, Margus Veanes, Luca Viganò, Sergei Vorobyov, Andrei Voronkov, Silke Wagner, Uwe Waldmann, Christoph Weidenbach, Emil Weydert, Thomas Wies, Jinzhao Wu, and Frank Zartmann.

In addition to Ganzinger's work group there were regular, month-long visits by researchers from all over the world including Michael Adamczyk, Leo Bachmair, Philippe Balbiani, Clark Barrett, Henrik Bjorklund, Chris Brink, Alan Bundy, Evelyne Contejean, Véronique Cortier, Yannis Dimopoulos, Javier Esparza, Andrea Formisano, Dov Gabbay, Alberto Griggio, Nevin Heintze, Andreas Herzig, Ranjit Jhala, Deepak Kapur, Piotr Krysta, Andrzej Lukaszewski, Shilong Ma, Jerzy Marcinkowski, Laurent Mauborgne, Fleming Nielson, Pilar Nivela, Damian Niwinski, Frank Pfenning, David Plaisted, Ian Pratt, Shahid Rahman, Hans Rott, Rosa Ruggeri, Pawel Rzechonek, R. K. Shyamasunda, Anatol Slissenko, Andrzej Szalas, Evan Tick, Lincoln Wallen, Li Wei, and Bican Xia.

Ganzinger also promoted automated reasoning outside the community by developing numerous new applications of deduction-based methods applicable in other fields. He applied the theory of the model construction method for defining the semantics of logic programs [BG91a]; he used resolution-based methods for solving set constraints [BGW93a] (used in program analysis); and he developed saturation-based complexity analysis [BG96, BG01b], thus approximating deduction to the field of descriptive complexity; he developed deduction-based techniques for universal algebra [BGS94]. Indirectly, Ganzinger's theoretical results have also contributed to solving hard open problems in other areas. As an example, he made an important contribution the discovery of the basic strategy for paramodulation, which played a key role in the celebrated automatic proof of the Robbins algebra problem by the EQP prover developed by McCune [McC97].

Acknowledgements. We are particularly indebted to Uwe Waldmann for his comments on this paper and to Jennifer Müller for providing a complete account of Ganzinger's publications and group statistics.

References

[ABRS09]   Armando, A., Bonacina, M.P., Ranise, S., Schulz, S.: New results on rewrite-based satisfiability procedures. ACM Transactions on Computational Logic 10(1), 1–47 (2009)

[AKW09]   Althaus, E., Kruglov, E., Weidenbach, C.: Superposition Modulo Linear Arithmetic SUP(LA). In: Ghilardi, S., Sebastiani, R. (eds.) FroCoS 2009. LNCS, vol. 5749, pp. 84–99. Springer, Heidelberg (2009)

[ARR03]   Armando, A., Ranise, S., Rusinowitch, M.: A rewriting approach to satisfiability procedures. Information and Computation 183(2), 140–164 (2003)

[BD88]   Bachmair, L., Dershowitz, N.: Critical pair criteria for completion. Journal of Symbolic Computation 6(1), 1–18 (1988)

[BG89]   Bertling, H., Ganzinger, H.: Completion-time optimization of rewrite-time goal solving. In: Extended Abstracts of the Third International Workshop on Unification (Preliminary Version) (1989)

[BG90a]   Bachmair, L., Ganzinger, H.: Completion of first-order clauses with equality by strict superposition (abstract). In: Term Rewriting: Theory and Applications (Ext. Abstracts of the 2nd German Workshop) (1990)

[BG90b]   Bachmair, L., Ganzinger, H.: Completion of First-order Clauses with Equality by Strict Superposition (Extended Abstract). In: Okada, M., Kaplan, S. (eds.) CTRS 1990. LNCS, vol. 516, pp. 162–180. Springer, Heidelberg (1991)

[BG90c]   Bachmair, L., Ganzinger, H.: On Restrictions of Ordered Paramodulation with Simplification. In: Stickel, M.E. (ed.) CADE 1990. LNCS (LNAI), vol. 449, pp. 427–441. Springer, Heidelberg (1990)

[BG91a]   Bachmair, L., Ganzinger, H.: Perfect model semantics for logic programs with equality. In: Furukawa, K. (ed.) Proceedings of the Eighth International Conference on Logic Programming, Paris, France, June 24-28, pp. 645–659. The MIT Press (1991)

[BG91b]   Bachmair, L., Ganzinger, H.: Rewrite-based equational theorem proving with selection and simplification. Technical Report MPI-I-91-208, Max-Planck-Institut für Informatik, Saarbrücken (August 1991)

[BG92]   Bachmair, L., Ganzinger, H.: Non-clausal Resolution and Superposition with Selection and Redundancy Criteria. In: Voronkov, A. (ed.) LPAR 1992. LNCS, vol. 624, pp. 273–284. Springer, Heidelberg (1992)

[BG93]   Bachmair, L., Ganzinger, H.: Associative-commutative superposition. Technical Report MPI-I-93-267, Max-Planck-Institut für Informatik, Saarbrücken (December 1993)

[BG94a]   Bachmair, L., Ganzinger, H.: Associative-commutative Superposition. In: Lindenstrauss, N., Dershowitz, N. (eds.) CTRS 1994. LNCS, vol. 968, pp. 155–167. Springer, Heidelberg (1995)

[BG94b]   Bachmair, L., Ganzinger, H.: Buchberger's Algorithm: A Constraint-based Completion Procedure. In: Jouannaud, J.-P. (ed.) CCL 1994. LNCS, vol. 845, pp. 285–301. Springer, Heidelberg (1994)

[BG94c]   Bachmair, L., Ganzinger, H.: Ordered Chaining for Total Orderings. In: Bundy, A. (ed.) CADE 1994. LNCS (LNAI), vol. 814, pp. 435–450. Springer, Heidelberg (1994)

[BG94d]   Bachmair, L., Ganzinger, H.: Rewrite-based equational theorem proving with selection and simplification. Journal of Logic and Computation 4(3), 217–247 (1994)

[BG94e]   Bachmair, L., Ganzinger, H.: Rewrite techniques for transitive relations. In: Ninth Annual IEEE Symposium on Logic in Computer Science, Paris, France (July 1994)

[BG96]   Basin, D., Ganzinger, H.: Complexity Analysis Based on Ordered Resolution. In: Eleventh Annual IEEE Symposium on Logic in Computer Science (LICS). IEEE Computer Society Press, New Brunswick, New Jersey, USA, pp. 456–465. IEEE Computer Society Press (1996)

[BG98a]   Bachmair, L., Ganzinger, H.: Ordered chaining calculi for first-order theories of transitive relations. Journal of the ACM 45(6) (November 1998); Revised Version of MPI-I-95-2-009

[BG98b]   Bachmair, L., Ganzinger, H.: Equational reasoning in saturation-based theorem proving. In: Bibel, W., Schmitt, P. (eds.) Automated Deduction: A Basis for Applications. Kluwer (1998)

[BG98c]   Bachmair, L., Ganzinger, H.: Strict Basic Superposition. In: Kirchner, C.,
           Kirchner, H. (eds.) CADE 1998. LNCS (LNAI), vol. 1421, pp. 160–174.
           Springer, Heidelberg (1998)
[BG01a]   Bachmair, L., Ganzinger, H.: Resolution theorem proving. In: Robinson,
           A., Voronkov, A. (eds.) Handbook of Automated Reasoning, vol. I, ch. 2,
           pp. 19–99. Elsevier (2001)
[BG01b]   Basin, D.A., Ganzinger, H.: Automated complexity analysis based on or-
           dered resolution. Journal of the ACM 48(1), 70–109 (2001)
[BGB87]   Bertling, H., Ganzinger, H., Baumeister, H.: CEC (Conditional Equations
           Completion). In: Brandenburg, F.J., Vidal-Naquet, G., Wirsing, M. (eds.)
           STACS 1987. LNCS, vol. 247, p. 470. Springer, Heidelberg (1987)
[BGLS92]   Bachmair, L., Ganzinger, H., Lynch, C., Snyder, W.: Basic Paramodula-
           tion and Superposition. In: Kapur, D. (ed.) CADE 1992. LNCS (LNAI),
           vol. 607, pp. 462–476. Springer, Heidelberg (1992)
[BGLS95]   Bachmair, L., Ganzinger, H., Lynch, C., Snyder, W.: Basic paramodula-
           tion. Information and Computation 121(2), 172–192 (1995)
[BGNR99]   Bofill, M., Godoy, G., Nieuwenhuis, R., Rubio, A.: Paramodulation with
           non-monotonic orderings. In: 14th IEEE Symposium on Logic in Com-
           puter Science (LICS), Trento, Italy, July 2-5, vol. 5, pp. 225–233 (1999)
[BGS88a]   Bertling, H., Ganzinger, H., Schäfers, R.: CEC: A system for conditional
           equational completion — User manual, version 1.0 (1988)
[BGS88b]   Bertling, H., Ganzinger, H., Schäfers, R.: CEC: A system for the completion
           of conditional equational specifications. In: Ganzinger, H. (ed.) ESOP 1988.
           LNCS, vol. 300, pp. 378–379. Springer, Heidelberg (1988)
[BGS88c]   Bertling, H., Ganzinger, H., Schäfers, R.: A collection of specifications
           completed by the CEC-system, version 1.0 (1988)
[BGS94]   Bachmair, L., Ganzinger, H., Stuber, J.: Combining Algebra and Universal
           Algebra in First-order Theorem Proving: The Case of Commutative Rings.
           In: Reggio, G., Astesiano, E., Tarlecki, A. (eds.) Abstract Data Types
           1994 and COMPASS 1994. LNCS, vol. 906, pp. 1–29. Springer, Heidelberg
           (1995)
[BGV98]   Bachmair, L., Ganzinger, H., Voronkov, A.: Elimination of Equality via
           Transformation with Ordering Constraints. In: Kirchner, C., Kirchner,
           H. (eds.) CADE 1998. LNCS (LNAI), vol. 1421, pp. 175–190. Springer,
           Heidelberg (1998)
[BGW92]   Bachmair, L., Ganzinger, H., Waldmann, U.: Theorem Proving for Hier-
           archic First-order Theories. In: Kirchner, H., Levi, G. (eds.) ALP 1992.
           LNCS, vol. 632, pp. 420–434. Springer, Heidelberg (1992)
[BGW93a]   Bachmair, L., Ganzinger, H., Waldmann, U.: Set constraints are the
           monadic class. In: Eighth Annual IEEE Symposium on Logic in Computer
           Science (LICS), Montreal, Canada, pp. 75–83. IEEE Computer Society
           Press (1993)
[BGW93b]   Bachmair, L., Ganzinger, H., Waldmann, U.: Superposition with Simpli-
           fication as a Decision Procedure for the Monadic Class with Equality. In:
           Mundici, D., Gottlob, G., Leitsch, A. (eds.) KGC 1993. LNCS, vol. 713,
           pp. 83–96. Springer, Heidelberg (1993)
[BGW94]   Bachmair, L., Ganzinger, H., Waldmann, U.: Refutational theorem prov-
           ing for hierarchic first-order theories. Appl. Algebra Eng. Commun. Com-
           put. 5, 193–212 (1994)
[CN00]   Comon, H., Nieuwenhuis, R.: Induction = I-Axiomatization + First-Order
           Consistency. Information & Computation 159(1), 151–186 (2000)

[DFK06]   Degtyarev, A., Fisher, M., Konev, B.: Monodic temporal resolution. ACM
            Trans. Comput. Log. 7(1), 108–150 (2006)

[EKK+11]   Eggers, A., Kruglov, E., Kupferschmid, S., Scheibler, K., Teige, T.,
            Weidenbach, C.: Superposition Modulo Non-linear Arithmetic. In: Tinelli,
            C., Sofronie-Stokkermans, V. (eds.) FroCoS 2011. LNCS, vol. 6989,
            pp. 119–134. Springer, Heidelberg (2011)

[Gan76]   Ganzinger, H.: Darstellung der Artanpassung in höheren Programmier-
            sprachen durch Repräsentation von Gruppen. In: Schneider, H.J., Nagl, M.
            (eds.) Programmiersprachen, 4. Fachtagung der GI, Erlangen, Proceedings,
            März 8-10. Informatik-Fachberichte, vol. 1, pp. 194–202. Springer (1976)

[Gan79a]   Ganzinger, H.: An approach to the derivation of compiler description
            concepts from the mathematical semantics concept. In: Böhling, K.-H.,
            Spies, P.P. (eds.) GI - 9. Jahrestagung, Bonn, Proceedings, Oktober 1-5.
            Informatik-Fachberichte, vol. 19, pp. 206–217. Springer (1979)

[Gan79b]   Ganzinger, H.: On Storage Optimization for Automatically Generated
            Compilers. In: Weihrauch, K. (ed.) GI-TCS 1979. LNCS, vol. 67,
            pp. 132–141. Springer, Heidelberg (1979)

[Gan80]   Ganzinger, H.: Transforming denotational semantics into practical at-
            tribute grammars. In: Jones, N.D. (ed.) Semantics-Directed Compiler Gen-
            eration. LNCS, vol. 94, pp. 1–69. Springer, Heidelberg (1980)

[Gan81]   Ganzinger, H.: Description of parameterized compiler modules. In: Brauer,
            W. (ed.) GI - 11. Jahrestagung in Verbindung mit Third Conference of the
            European Co-operation in Informatics (ECI), München, Proceedings, Ok-
            tober 20.-23. Informatik-Fachberichte, vol. 50, pp. 11–19. Springer (1981)

[Gan83a]   Ganzinger, H.: Increasing modularity and language-independency in au-
            tomatically generated compilers. Sci. Comput. Program. 3(3), 223–278
            (1983)

[Gan83b]   Ganzinger, H.: Modular compiler descriptions based on abstract seman-
            tic data types. In: Proceedings 2nd Workshop on Abstract Data Types,
            University of Passau (1983)

[Gan83c]   Ganzinger, H.: Modular Compiler Descriptions Based on Abstract Se-
            mantic Data Types (Extended Abstract). In: Díaz, J. (ed.) ICALP 1983.
            LNCS, vol. 154, pp. 237–249. Springer, Heidelberg (1983)

[Gan83d]   Ganzinger, H.: Parameterized specifications: Parameter passing and im-
            plementation with respect to observability. ACM Transactions on Pro-
            gramming Languages and Systems 5(3), 318–354 (1983)

[Gan86]   Ganzinger, H.: Knuth-Bendix completion for parametric specifications
            with conditional equations. In: Workshop on Specification of Abstract
            Data Types, ADT (1986)

[Gan87a]   Ganzinger, H.: A completion procedure for conditional equations. In:
            Kaplan, S., Jouannaud, J.-P. (eds.) CTRS 1987. LNCS, vol. 308, pp. 62–83.
            Springer, Heidelberg (1988)

[Gan87b]   Ganzinger, H.: Completion with History-dependent Complexities for Gen-
            erated Equations. In: Sannella, D., Tarlecki, A. (eds.) Abstract Data Types
            1987. LNCS, vol. 332, pp. 73–91. Springer, Heidelberg (1988)

[Gan87c]   Ganzinger, H.: Ground Term Confluence in Parametric Conditional Equa-
            tional Specifications. In: Brandenburg, F.J., Wirsing, M., Vidal-Naquet,
            G. (eds.) STACS 1987. LNCS, vol. 247, pp. 286–298. Springer, Heidelberg
            (1987)

[Gan89]   Ganzinger, H.: Order-sorted Completion: The Many-sorted Way (Extended Abstract). In: Díaz, J., Yu, Y. (eds.) CAAP 1989 and TAPSOFT 1989. LNCS, vol. 351, pp. 244–258. Springer, Heidelberg (1989)

[Gan91a]   Ganzinger, H.: A Completion Procedure for Conditional Equations. Journal of Symbolic Computation 11, 51–81 (1991)

[Gan91b]   Ganzinger, H.: Order-sorted completion: the many-sorted way. Theoretical Computer Science 89, 3–32 (1991)

[Gan02]   Ganzinger, H.: Shostak Light. In: Voronkov, A. (ed.) CADE 2002. LNCS (LNAI), vol. 2392, pp. 332–346. Springer, Heidelberg (2002)

[GdN99]   Ganzinger, H., de Nivelle, H.: A superposition decision procedure for the guarded fragment with equality. In: 14th IEEE Symposium on Logic in Computer Science (LICS), Trento, Italy, July 2–5, pp. 295–305 (1999)

[GGMW82]   Ganzinger, H., Giegerich, R., Möncke, U., Wilhelm, R.: A truly generative semantics-directed compiler generator. In: SIGPLAN Symposium on Compiler Construction, pp. 172–184 (1982)

[GHBR87]   Ganzinger, H., Heeg, G., Baumeister, H., Rüger, M.: Smalltalk-80. Informationstechnik — IT 29(4), 241–251 (1987)

[GHMS98]   Ganzinger, H., Hustadt, U., Meyer, C., Schmidt, R.A.: A resolution-based decision procedure for extensions of K4. In: Zakharyaschev, M., Segerberg, K., de Rijke, M., Wansing, H. (eds.) Advances in Modal Logic 2, Papers from the Second Workshop on Advances in Modal Logic, Uppsala, Sweden, pp. 225–246. CSLI Publications (1998)

[GHN⁺04]   Ganzinger, H., Hagen, G., Nieuwenhuis, R., Oliveras, A., Tinelli, C.: DPLL(T): Fast Decision Procedures. In: Alur, R., Peled, D.A. (eds.) CAV 2004. LNCS, vol. 3114, pp. 175–188. Springer, Heidelberg (2004)

[GHW03]   Ganzinger, H., Hillenbrand, T., Waldmann, U.: Superposition Modulo a Shostak Theory. In: Baader, F. (ed.) CADE 2003. LNCS (LNAI), vol. 2741, pp. 182–196. Springer, Heidelberg (2003)

[GJV00]   Ganzinger, H., Jacquemard, F., Veanes, M.: Rigid reachability, the nonsymmetric form of rigid E-unification. Int. J. Found. Comput. Sci. 11(1), 3–27 (2000)

[GK03]   Ganzinger, H., Korovin, K.: New directions in instantiation-based theorem proving. In: Proc.18th IEEE Symposium on Logic in Computer Science (LICS 2003), pp. 55–64. IEEE Computer Society Press (2003)

[GK04]   Ganzinger, H., Korovin, K.: Integrating equational reasoning into instantiation-based theorem proving. In: Marcinkowski, J., Tarlecki, A. (eds.) CSL 2004. LNCS, vol. 3210, pp. 71–84. Springer, Heidelberg (2004)

[GK06]   Ganzinger, H., Korovin, K.: Theory Instantiation. In: Hermann, M., Voronkov, A. (eds.) LPAR 2006. LNCS (LNAI), vol. 4246, pp. 497–511. Springer, Heidelberg (2006)

[GMV99]   Ganzinger, H., Meyer, C., Veanes, M.: The two-variable guarded fragment with transitive relations. In: 14th IEEE Symposium on Logic in Computer Science (LICS), Trento, Italy, July 2-5, pp. 24–34 (1999)

[GMW97]   Ganzinger, H., Meyer, C., Weidenbach, C.: Soft Typing for Ordered Resolution. In: McCune, W. (ed.) CADE 1997. LNCS (LNAI), vol. 1249, pp. 321–335. Springer, Heidelberg (1997)

[GN00]   Godoy, G., Nieuwenhuis, R.: Paramodulation with built-in abelian groups. In: 15th IEEE Symp. Logic in Computer Science (LICS), Santa Barbara, USA, pp. 413–424. IEEE Computer Society Press (2000)

[GN01a]   Ganzinger, H., Nieuwenhuis, R.: Constraints and Theorem Proving. In:
            Comon, H., Marché, C., Treinen, R. (eds.) CCL 1999. LNCS, vol. 2002,
            pp. 159–201. Springer, Heidelberg (2001)
[GN01b]   Godoy, G., Nieuwenhuis, R.: Ordering Constraints for Deduction with
            Built-in Abelian Semigroups, Monoids and Groups. In: 16th IEEE Sym-
            posium on Logic in Computer Science (LICS), Boston, USA, June 16–20,
            pp. 38–47. IEEE Computer Society Press (2001)
[GN04]   Godoy, G., Nieuwenhuis, R.: Superposition with Completely Built-in
            Abelian Groups. Journ. Symbolic Computation 37(1), 1–33 (2004)
[GNN99]   Ganzinger, H., Nieuwenhuis, R., Nivela, P.: The Saturate System (1999),
            Software and documentation,
            http://www.mpi-inf.mpg.de/SATURATE/Saturate.html
[GNN01]   Ganzinger, H., Nieuwenhuis, R., Nivela, P.: Context trees. In: EuroGP 2001.
            LNCS (LNAI), vol. 2038, pp. 242–256, Siena, Italy (2001)
[GNN04]   Ganzinger, H., Nieuwenhuis, R., Nivela, P.: Fast term indexing with coded
            context trees. Journal of Automated Reasoning 32(2), 103–120 (2004)
[Gra95]   Graf, P.: Substitution Tree Indexing. In: Hsiang, J. (ed.) RTA 1995. LNCS,
            vol. 914, pp. 117–131. Springer, Heidelberg (1995)
[GRW77]   Ganzinger, H., Ripken, K., Wilhelm, R.: Automatic generation of optimiz-
            ing multipass compilers. In: IFIP Congress, pp. 535–540 (1977)
[GS93]   Ganzinger, H., Stuber, J.: Inductive Theorem Proving by Consistency for
            First-order Clauses. In: Rusinowitch, M., Remy, J.-L. (eds.) CTRS 1992.
            LNCS, vol. 656, pp. 226–241. Springer, Heidelberg (1993)
[GS05]   Ganzinger, H., Stuber, J.: Superposition with equivalence reasoning and
            delayed clause normal form transformation. Inf. Comput. 199(1-2), 3–23
            (2005)
[GSS00]   Ganzinger, H., Sofronie-Stokkermans, V.: Chaining techniques for auto-
            mated theorem proving in many-valued logics. In: 30th IEEE International
            Symposium on Multiple-Valued Logic (ISMV)L, pp. 337–344 (2000)
[GSSW06]   Ganzinger, H., Sofronie-Stokkermans, V., Waldmann, U.: Modular proof
            systems for partial functions with Evans equality. Inf. Comput. 204(10),
            1453–1492 (2006)
[GW75]   Ganzinger, H., Wilhelm, R.: Verschränkung von Compiler-Moduln. In:
            Mühlbacher, J.R. (ed.) GI 1975. LNCS, vol. 34, pp. 654–665. Springer,
            Heidelberg (1975)
[GW93]   Ganzinger, H., Waldmann, U.: Termination Proofs of Well-moded Logic
            Programs via Conditional Rewrite Systems. In: Rusinowitch, M., Remy,
            J.-L. (eds.) CTRS 1992. LNCS, vol. 656, pp. 430–437. Springer, Heidelberg
            (1993)
[GW96]   Ganzinger, H., Waldmann, U.: Theorem Proving in Cancellative Abelian
            Monoids. In: McRobbie, M.A., Slaney, J.K. (eds.) CADE 1996. LNCS
            (LNAI), vol. 1104, pp. 388–402. Springer, Heidelberg (1996)
[Her30]   Herbrand, J.: Recherches sur la théorie de la démonstration. Traveaux
            de la Societé des Sciences de Varsoria 33 (1930); Translation appeared in
            van Heijenoort, J.: From Frege to Gödel: A Source Book in Mathematical
            Logic, pp. 525–581. Harvard University Press (1967)
[Hil08]   Hillenbrand, T.: Superposition and Decision Procedures – Back and Forth.
            PhD thesis, Universität des Saarlandes (2008)
[HKV10]   Hoder, K., Kovács, L., Voronkov, A.: Interpolation and Symbol Elimi-
            nation in Vampire. In: Giesl, J., Hähnle, R. (eds.) IJCAR 2010. LNCS,
            vol. 6173, pp. 188–195. Springer, Heidelberg (2010)

[HMS08]   Hustadt, U., Motik, B., Sattler, U.: Deciding expressive description logics
          in the framework of resolution. Inf. Comput. 206(5), 579–601 (2008)
[HW07]   Hillenbrand, T., Weidenbach, C.: Superposition for finite domains. Re-
          search Report MPI-I-2007-RG1-002, Max-Planck Institute for Informatics,
          Saarbruecken, Germany (April 2007)
[HW10]   Horbach, M., Weidenbach, C.: Superposition for fixed domains. ACM
          Transactions on Computational Logic 11(4), 1–35 (2010)
[JMW98]   Jacquemard, F., Meyer, C., Weidenbach, C.: Unification in Extensions
          of Shallow Equational Theories. In: Nipkow, T. (ed.) RTA 1998. LNCS,
          vol. 1379, pp. 76–90. Springer, Heidelberg (1998)
[JRV06]   Jacquemard, F., Rusinowitch, M., Vigneron, L.: Tree Automata with
          Equality Constraints Modulo Equational Theories. In: Furbach, U.,
          Shankar, N. (eds.) IJCAR 2006. LNCS (LNAI), vol. 4130, pp. 557–571.
          Springer, Heidelberg (2006)
[KB70]   Knuth, D.E., Bendix, P.B.: Simple word problems in universal algebras. In:
          Leech, I. (ed.) Computational Problems in Abstract Algebra, pp. 263–297.
          Pergamon Press (1970)
[KKR90]   Kirchner, C., Kirchner, H., Rusinowitch, M.: Deduction with symbolic
          constraints. Revue Française d'Intelligence Artificielle 4(3), 9–52 (1990)
[KM08]   Kazakov, Y., Motik, B.: A resolution-based decision procedure for *shoiq*.
          Journal of Automated Reasoning 40(2-3), 89–116 (2008)
[KMN88]   Kapur, D., Musser, D.R., Narendran, P.: Only prime superpositions need
          be considered in the Knuth-Bendix completion procedure. Journal of Sym-
          bolic Computation 6(1), 19–36 (1988)
[KV07]   Korovin, K., Voronkov, A.: Integrating Linear Arithmetic into Superpo-
          sition Calculus. In: Duparc, J., Henzinger, T.A. (eds.) CSL 2007. LNCS,
          vol. 4646, pp. 223–237. Springer, Heidelberg (2007)
[LAWRS07] Lev-Ami, T., Weidenbach, C., Reps, T.W., Sagiv, M.: Labelled Clauses.
          In: Pfenning, F. (ed.) CADE 2007. LNCS (LNAI), vol. 4603, pp. 311–327.
          Springer, Heidelberg (2007)
[LS95]   Lynch, C., Snyder, W.: Redundancy criteria for constrained completion.
          Theoretical Compututer Science 142(2), 141–177 (1995)
[LV00]   Levy, J., Veanes, M.: On the undecidability of second-order unification.
          Inf. Comput. 159(1-2), 125–150 (2000)
[McA93]   McAllester, D.: Automatic recognition of tractability in inferences rela-
          tions. Journal of the ACM 40(2), 284–303 (1993)
[McC97]   McCune, W.: Solution of the Robbins problem. Journal of Automated
          Reasoning 19(3), 263–276 (1997)
[McM03]   McMillan, K.L.: Interpolation and SAT-based Model Checking. In: Hunt
          Jr., W.A., Somenzi, F. (eds.) CAV 2003. LNCS, vol. 2725, pp. 1–13.
          Springer, Heidelberg (2003)
[Nie96]   Nieuwenhuis, R.: Basic paramodulation and decidable theories. In:
          Eleventh Annual IEEE Symposium on Logic in Computer Science, New
          Brunswick, New Jersey, USA, pp. 473–482. IEEE Computer Society Press
          (1996)
[Nip96]   Nipkow, T.: More Church-Rosser Proofs (in Isabelle/HOL). In: McRobbie,
          M.A., Slaney, J.K. (eds.) CADE 1996. LNCS, vol. 1104, pp. 733–747.
          Springer, Heidelberg (1996)

[NN93]   Nivela, P., Nieuwenhuis, R.: Practical Results on the Saturation of Full
           First-order Clauses: Experiments with the Saturate System (System De-
           scription). In: Kirchner, C. (ed.) RTA 1993. LNCS, vol. 690, pp. 436–440.
           Springer, Heidelberg (1993)
[NR92a]   Nieuwenhuis, R., Rubio, A.: Basic Superposition is Complete. In: Krieg-
           Brückner, B. (ed.) ESOP 1992. LNCS, vol. 582, pp. 371–390. Springer,
           Heidelberg (1992)
[NR92b]   Nieuwenhuis, R., Rubio, A.: Theorem Proving with Ordering Constrained
           Clauses. In: Kapur, D. (ed.) CADE 1992. LNCS, vol. 607, pp. 477–491.
           Springer, Heidelberg (1992)
[NR94]   Nieuwenhuis, R., Rubio, A.: AC-Superposition with Constraints: No
           AC-unifiers Needed. In: Bundy, A. (ed.) CADE 1994. LNCS, vol. 814,
           pp. 545–559. Springer, Heidelberg (1994)
[NR95]   Nieuwenhuis, R., Rubio, A.: Theorem Proving with Ordering and Equality
           Constrained Clauses. Journal of Symbolic Computation 19(4), 321–351
           (1995)
[Pet83]   Peterson, G.E.: A technique for establishing completeness results in theo-
           rem proving with equality. SIAM J. on Computing 12(1), 82–100 (1983)
[Rob65]   Robinson, J.A.: A machine-oriented logic based on the resolution principle.
           Journal of the ACM 12(1), 23–41 (1965)
[RV02]   Riazanov, A., Voronkov, A.: The design and implementation of VAM-
           PIRE. AI Communications 15(91-110) (2002)
[RW69]   Robinson, G.A., Wos, L.T.: Paramodulation and theorem-proving in first
           order theories with equality. Machine Intelligence 4, 135–150 (1969)
[SB05]   Schulz, S., Bonacina, M.P.: On handling distinct objects in the superpo-
           sition calculus. In: Notes 5th IWIL Workshop on the Implementation of
           Logics, pp. 11–66 (2005)
[Sch02]   Stephan Schulz, E.: A Brainiac Theorem Prover. Journal of AI Commu-
           nications 15(2/3), 111–126 (2002)
[SH00]   Schmidt, R.A., Hustadt, U.: A Resolution Decision Procedure for Fluted
           Logic. In: McAllester, D. (ed.) CADE 2000. LNCS, vol. 1831, pp. 433–448.
           Springer, Heidelberg (2000)
[SH07]   Schmidt, R.A., Hustadt, U.: The axiomatic translation principle for modal
           logic. ACM Trans. Comput. Log. 8(4), 1–51 (2007)
[SR12]   Seidl, H., Reuß, A.: Extending $\mathcal{H}_1$-Clauses with Path Disequalities. In:
           Birkedal, L. (ed.) FOSSACS 2012. LNCS, vol. 7213, pp. 165–179. Springer,
           Heidelberg (2012)
[Stu98a]   Stuber, J.: Superposition theorem proving for abelian groups represented
           as integer modules. Theoretical Computer Science 208(1-2), 149–177
           (1998)
[Stu98b]   Stuber, J.: Superposition theorem proving for commutative rings. In:
           Bibel, W., Schmitt, P.H. (eds.) Automated Deduction - A Basis for Appli-
           cations, vol. III. Applications, ch.2, pp. 31–55. Kluwer, Dordrecht (1998)
[SW12]   Suda, M., Weidenbach, C.: A PLTL-Prover Based on Labelled Superposi-
           tion with Partial Model Guidance. In: Gramlich, B., Miller, D., Sattler, U.
           (eds.) IJCAR 2012. LNCS, vol. 7364, pp. 537–543. Springer, Heidelberg
           (2012)
[SWW10]   Suda, M., Weidenbach, C., Wischnewski, P.: On the Saturation of YAGO.
           In: Giesl, J., Hähnle, R. (eds.) IJCAR 2010. LNCS (LNAI), vol. 6173,
           pp. 441–456. Springer, Heidelberg (2010)

[Wal99]   Waldmann, U.: Cancellative Superposition Decides the Theory of Divisible
            Torsion-free Abelian Groups. In: Ganzinger, H., McAllester, D., Voronkov,
            A. (eds.) LPAR 1999. LNCS (LNAI), vol. 1705, pp. 131–147. Springer,
            Heidelberg (1999)

[Wal01]   Waldmann, U.: Superposition and Chaining for Totally Ordered Di-
            visible Abelian Groups. In: Goré, R., Leitsch, A., Nipkow, T. (eds.)
            EuroGP 2001. LNCS, vol. 2038, pp. 226–241. Springer, Heidelberg (2001),
            www.mpi-inf.mpg.de/~uwe/paper/IJCAR01-bibl.html

[Wei97]   Weidenbach, C.: SPASS—version 0.49. Journal of Automated Reason-
            ing 18(2), 247–252 (1997)

[Wei99]   Weidenbach, C.: Towards an Automatic Analysis of Security Protocols in
            First-Order Logic. In: Ganzinger, H. (ed.) CADE 1999. LNCS (LNAI),
            vol. 1632, pp. 314–328. Springer, Heidelberg (1999)

[WRC+76]   Wilhelm, R., Ripken, K., Ciesinger, J., Ganzinger, H., Lahner, W.,
            Nollmann, R.: Design evaluation of the compiler generating system MUGI.
            In: Yeh, R.T., Ramamoorthy, C.V. (eds.) Proceedings of the 2nd Inter-
            national Conference on Software Engineering, San Francisco, California,
            USA, 1976, October 13-15, pp. 571–576. IEEE Computer Society (1976)

[WRCS67]   Wos, L., Robinson, G.A., Carson, D.F., Shalla, L.: The concept of demod-
            ulation in theorem proving. Journal of the ACM 14(4), 698–709 (1967)

[WSH+07]   Weidenbach, C., Schmidt, R.A., Hillenbrand, T., Rusev, R., Topic, D.:
            System Description: SPASS Version 3.0. In: Pfenning, F. (ed.) CADE 2007.
            LNCS (LNAI), vol. 4603, pp. 514–520. Springer, Heidelberg (2007)

[WW10]   Weidenbach, C., Wischnewski, P.: Subterm contextual rewriting. AI Com-
            munications 23(2-3), 97–109 (2010)

[Zha88]   Zhang, H.: Reduction, superposition and induction: Automated reason-
            ing in an equational logic. Research Report 88–06, University of Iowa
            (November 1988)

[ZK88]   Zhang, H., Kapur, D.: First-order Theorem Proving using Conditional
            Rewrite Rules. In: Lusk, E.'., Overbeek, R. (eds.) CADE 1988. LNCS,
            vol. 310, pp. 1–20. Springer, Heidelberg (1988)

[ZK89]   Zhang, H., Kapur, D.: Consider only General Superpositions in Com-
            pletion Procedures. In: Dershowitz, N. (ed.) RTA 1989. LNCS, vol. 355,
            pp. 513–527. Springer, Heidelberg (1989)

[ZK90]   Zhang, H., Kapur, D.: Unnecessary inferences in associative-commutative
            completion procedures. Mathematical Systems Theory 23(3), 175–206
            (1990)

[ZR85]   Zhang, H., Remy, J.-L.: Contextual Rewriting. In: Jouannaud, J.-P. (ed.)
            RTA 1985. LNCS, vol. 202, pp. 46–62. Springer, Heidelberg (1985)

Bio-Logics: Logical Analysis
of Bioregulatory Networks

Alexander Bockmayr and Heike Siebert

DFG Research Center MATHEON,
Fachbereich Mathematik und Informatik, Freie Universität Berlin,
Arnimallee 6, D-14195 Berlin, Germany
{bockmayr,siebert}@mi.fu-berlin.de

Abstract. We discuss different ways of applying logic to analyze the structure and dynamics of regulatory networks in molecular biology. First, the structure of a bioregulatory network may be described naturally using propositional or multi-valued logic. Second, the resulting non-deterministic dynamics may be analyzed using temporal logic and model checking. Third, information on time delays may be incorporated using a refined modeling approach based on timed automata.

1 Introduction

The last decades have seen a tremendous progress in molecular biology. Current genome, transcriptome or proteome projects, whose goal is to determine completely all the genes, RNA or proteins in a given organism, produce an exponentially growing amount of data. A major challenge consists in exploiting all these data and in understanding how the various components of a biological system (i.e., genes, RNA, proteins etc.) interact in order to perform complex biological functions. This has lead to the new field of systems biology, which aims at a system-level understanding of biological systems [13]. While traditional biology examines single genes or proteins in isolation, system biology simultaneously studies the complex interaction of many levels of biological information (genomic DNA, mRNA, proteins, informational pathways and networks) to understand how they work together.

The development of computational models of biological systems plays a major role in systems biology, see e.g. [27]. A variety of formalisms for modeling, simulating, and analyzing different types of biological systems has been proposed during the last years. In this paper, we focus on the logical analysis of regulatory networks in biology. Bioregulatory networks form an important class of biological systems. The understanding of regulation is crucial for many applications in medicine and pharmacy.

Mathematical and computational modeling has long been recognized as an important tool for understanding the dynamical behavior of bioregulatory networks. Classically, such networks are modeled in terms of differential equations resulting in a fully quantitative description. However, experimental data is often

A. Voronkov and C. Weidenbach (Eds.): Ganzinger Festschrift, LNCS 7797, pp. 19–34, 2013.

of qualitative nature and thus not sufficient for deriving the required parameter values. In addition, detailed descriptions of the reaction mechanisms are needed for a complete kinetic model. The resulting systems of differential equations are mostly non-linear and thus cannot be solved analytically. Numerical methods can provide very accurate solutions. However, this accuracy may be misleading since it relies on parameter estimations based on insufficient data.

These difficulties led to the development of discrete modeling approaches aiming to grasp the essential character of a systems' behavior based on qualitative data. The logical analysis of bioregulatory networks was pioneered more than 30 years ago by the work of Sugita, Kauffman, Glass, and Thomas [26,11,9,28]. Thomas [28] introduced a purely logical formalism, which, over the years, has been further developed and successfully applied to different biological problems (see [31], [32] and references therein). The only information on a regulatory component required in this formalism is whether or not it has an activity level relevant for some interaction in the network. For example, in order to activate a certain gene, the concentration of some protein has to be above a given threshold. The two relevant activity levels then represent the concentration being below or above the threshold. Since a regulatory component can be involved in more than one interaction, more than two activity levels may be associated with it. A state of the network gives the current activity levels for each component. To derive the dynamical behavior of the system, discrete parameters are introduced that determine the strength of the different interactions in a given state. Parameter values can be specified, for instance, based on information on the ratio of production and decay rates of chemical substances. They are used to define a discrete function that determines the evolution of the system. However, rather than executing all indicated changes in the components at the same time, an asynchronous updating rule is employed to obtain a non-deterministic state transition graph. It has been shown that this approach captures essential qualitative features of the dynamical behavior of complex biological networks (again see [31] and [32]).

In this paper, we discuss how logical methods can be applied to the analysis of regulatory networks in molecular systems biology. We start in Sect. 2 by introducing a logical formalism for modeling bioregulatory networks based on the classical Thomas approach. In Sect. 3 we illustrate the method on a model of the mammalian cell cycle. Sect. 4 focusses on general principles relating the structure and the dynamics of bioregulatory networks. In Sect. 5, we discuss how temporal logic and model checking may be used to analyze the dynamics of bioregulatory networks. Finally, a refinement of the logic modeling approach based on the incorporation of time delays is presented in Sect. 6.

2   Network Structure and Dynamics

In this section we introduce a logical formalism that allows to capture structural properties and the dynamical behavior of a bioregulatory network. It is based on the classical modeling approach of Thomas (see for example [31] and [32]). As in [6], the structure of the network is represented by a directed multigraph, i.e., a directed graph that may contain parallel edges.

Definition 1. *Let $n \in \mathbb{N}$ denote the number of regulatory components. An interaction (multi-)graph (or bioregulatory (multi-)graph) $\mathcal{I}$ is a labeled directed multigraph with vertex set $V := \{\alpha_1, \ldots, \alpha_n\}$ and edge set E. Let $\mathcal{T}(\alpha_j)$ be the set of all edges whose tail is α_j, and $\mathcal{H}(\alpha_j)$ the set of edges whose head is α_j. Each edge e from α_j to α_i is labeled with a sign $\varepsilon_e \in \{+, -\}$ and a set $M_e \subseteq \{1, \ldots, d_j\}$, where d_j denotes the out-degree of α_j. Let p_j be the maximal value of the union of all sets M_e with $e \in \mathcal{T}(\alpha_j)$. We call $\{0, \ldots, p_j\}$ the range of α_j. For each $i \in \{1, \ldots, n\}$ we denote by $Pred(\alpha_i)$ the set of vertices α_j such that $\alpha_j \to \alpha_i$ is an edge in E.*

The vertices of this graph represent the components of the regulatory network, e. g. genes, the range of a vertex the different expression levels of the corresponding component affecting the behavior of the network. Thus, the vertices can be interpreted as variables that take values in the corresponding range. An edge e from α_j to α_i signifies that α_j influences α_i in a positive or negative way, depending on ε_e and provided that the current expression level of α_j is in M_e. The way α_j influences α_i may also depend on the context. For example, presence or absence of a co-factor may determine whether an activating or an inhibiting effect can be observed or how strong the influence is. Such effects can even occur in auto-regulation. Consider a gene α with low, intermediate and high activity level that remains quiescent at low level, but influences itself via its own product at an intermediate level leading to a strong increase of production. Once it reaches the high concentration level self-inhibition occurs, downregulating the level not necessarily to zero but to the intermediate level, resulting in an oscillation between intermediate and high concentrations. Such a situation can be captured in a graph with two edges leading from α to itself, one negative and one positive, labeled with appropriate disjoint sets M_e. The original Thomas formalism, where the network structure is represented by a directed graph not allowing for multiple edges, could capture the oscillation via a negative edge, but not the additional stable behavior at low activity level, since here an additional positive edge is needed.

Fig. 1(a) shows a simple interaction graph comprising two vertices. The two different edges leading from α_2 to α_1 signify that α_2 has an inhibiting influence on α_1 if its expression level is 1. However, on the higher expression level 2 the influence becomes activating. Furthermore, there are two edges, e_3 and e_4, from α_2 to itself. The corresponding sets M_{e_3} and M_{e_4} intersect. It is not clear from the interaction graph alone whether α_2 with expression level 1 inhibits or activates itself. The outcome depends on the interplay between the influence from α_2 on itself and the influence of α_1 on α_2. Thus, in order to determine the dynamical behavior of the system we need further information.

Definition 2. *Let $\mathcal{I}$ be an interaction graph. A state of the system described by $\mathcal{I}$ is a tuple $s \in S^n := \{0, \ldots, p_1\} \times \cdots \times \{0, \ldots, p_n\}$. The set of resource edges of α_i in state s is the set*

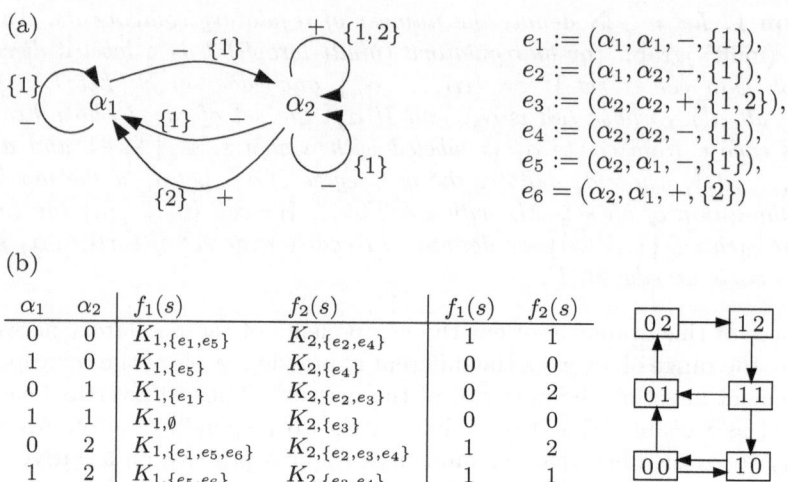

(a)

$$e_1 := (\alpha_1, \alpha_1, -, \{1\}),$$
$$e_2 := (\alpha_1, \alpha_2, -, \{1\}),$$
$$e_3 := (\alpha_2, \alpha_2, +, \{1, 2\}),$$
$$e_4 := (\alpha_2, \alpha_2, -, \{1\}),$$
$$e_5 := (\alpha_2, \alpha_1, -, \{1\}),$$
$$e_6 = (\alpha_2, \alpha_1, +, \{2\})$$

(b)

α_1	α_2	$f_1(s)$	$f_2(s)$	$f_1(s)$	$f_2(s)$
0	0	$K_{1,\{e_1,e_5\}}$	$K_{2,\{e_2,e_4\}}$	1	1
1	0	$K_{1,\{e_5\}}$	$K_{2,\{e_4\}}$	0	0
0	1	$K_{1,\{e_1\}}$	$K_{2,\{e_2,e_3\}}$	0	2
1	1	$K_{1,\emptyset}$	$K_{2,\{e_3\}}$	0	0
0	2	$K_{1,\{e_1,e_5,e_6\}}$	$K_{2,\{e_2,e_3,e_4\}}$	1	2
1	2	$K_{1,\{e_5,e_6\}}$	$K_{2,\{e_3,e_4\}}$	1	1

Fig. 1. In (a), interaction graph of a regulatory system comprising two components and six interactions. In (b), state table for general parameters with specific values, and the resulting state transition graph.

$$R_i(s) := \{e \in \mathcal{H}(\alpha_i) \mid e : \alpha_j \to \alpha_i, \ (\varepsilon_e = + \land s_j \in M_e) \lor (\varepsilon_e = - \land s_j \notin M_e)\}.$$

Given a set $K(\mathcal{I}) := \{K_{i,R_i(s)} \mid i \in \{1, \ldots, n\}, s \in S^n\}$ *of (logical)* parameters $K_{i,R_i(s)}$, *which take values in the range of* α_i, *we define* $f^{K(\mathcal{I})} = f : S^n \to S^n$, $s \mapsto (K_{1,R_1(s)}, \ldots, K_{n,R_n(s)})$. *We call* $(\mathcal{I}, f)$ *a* bioregulatory network.

In a given state s only the edges e labeled with a w.r.t. s suitable set M_e represent active influences. The set of edge resources $R_i(s)$ contains all active positive edges and all inactive negative edges reaching α_i. That is, we interpret the absence of an inhibiting influence as activating influence. The value of the parameter $K_{i,R_i(s)}$, and thus $f_i(s)$, then indicates how the expression level of α_i will evolve. It will increase (decrease) if the parameter value is greater (smaller) than s_i. The expression level stays the same if both values are equal. Thus the function f holds all the information necessary to determine the dynamical behavior of the network. In the table given in Fig. 1(b) we see in the second column the values $f(s)$. The third column provides a specification of the parameter values, and thus of f.

Typically, the set of resources $R_i(s)$, and with it the logical parameters, is defined as the set of predecessors of α_i (instead of edges reaching α_i) having an activating influence on α_i (see [4]). Since we introduced a more general framework allowing for parallel edges, knowledge of the current expression level of a predecessor of α_i is not enough to determine the character of the corresponding interaction. For an interaction graph without parallel edges, the notion of edge resources and vertex resources are equivalent.

The signs on the edges together with the sets M_e determine whether a component is an activator or an inhibitor of some other component in a given state. An activating influence, i.e., an effective activator or a non-effective inhibitor, cannot induce a decrease in expression level of the target component. This is reflected in the following parameter constraint:

$$\omega \subseteq \omega' \subseteq \mathcal{H}(\alpha_i) \Rightarrow K_{i,\omega} \leq K_{i,\omega'} \tag{1}$$

for all $i \in \{1, \ldots, n\}$ and ω, ω' resource edge sets of α_i. In the following we will always assume that this constraint is satisfied.

We have seen that the way the structure of the network influences its dynamics is captured in the specification of the logical parameters. Depending on their values, edges in the graph may or may not be *functional* in the following sense. Obviously, if there is an edge e from α_j to α_i and $K_{i,R} = K_{i,R\setminus\{e\}}$ for all suitable resource sets R, then the edge e has no influence on the dynamics of the system. In that case, deleting e from the interaction graph has no consequences regarding the dynamics of the network. Thus, in the following, we may assume for every $N := (\mathcal{I}, f)$ that whenever there is an edge $e : \alpha_j \to \alpha_i$ in $\mathcal{I}$, then there exists a suitable resource set R such that $K_{i,R} \neq K_{i,R\setminus\{e\}}$. Thus, there exist states $s, s^{(j)}$ satisfying $f_i(s) \neq f_i(s^{(j)})$, $s_j \neq s_j^{(j)}$, and $s_k = s_k^{(j)}$ for all $k \neq j$.

In the same way, we may infer the existence of an edge in $\mathcal{I}$ from the values of $f(s)$. It is easy to see that, if s is a state such that $f_i(s) \neq f_i(s^{(j)})$ with $s^{(j)}$ as defined above, then there is an edge from α_j to α_i.

Remark 1. If we consider a Boolean model the situation is easy to grasp. In addition to deriving the existence of edges from f, we can also easily deduce the sign of that edge. If s and $s^{(j)}$ are defined as above, then the value of $s_j^{(j)}$ is determined by the value of s_j. Furthermore, we know for every edge e that $M_e = \{1\}$. It is now not difficult to see that e is a positive edge if $s_j = f_i(s)$, and negative if $s_j^{(j)} = f_i(s)$. We say that $\mathcal{I}$ and f are *consistent*, if the edges in $\mathcal{I}$ coincide with those computed from f.

Consistency can also be defined for multi-valued models, however the definitions get more involved [14]. Often, a system is defined primarily by the function f, and its corresponding structure is derived locally, i.e., for a given state. Then, labeling edges simply by signs with no additional activity level sets is sufficient. A global representation of the network structure can be defined as a union of the local graphs (see e.g. [19]). The information inherent in such a global graph is naturally much coarser than that represented by the interaction graph of Def. 1, but it is still useful in highlighting dependencies of the network components and already allows interesting insights in the network characteristics.

The remainder of this section will deal with the representation of the dynamical behavior of the network in the state space S^n. Other than in continuous dynamics described by suitable differential equations, we have more than one possibility to derive the dynamical behavior of the system from the function f. The first possibility that comes to mind is to use the relation $\{(s, f(s)); s \in S^n\}$

to define state transitions. That is to say, we update all activity levels s_i of the regulatory components at the same time. This method of updating is called *synchronous update*. Much work has been done using this approach, often using stochastic methods to analyze systems for large n (see e.g. [10]). However, this method of updating the activity levels of different components is highly idealistic. The molecules and chemical reactions leading to the activation of different components differ. Thus it is reasonable to assume that although a given situation may provide the conditions for a change in the activity level of more than one regulatory component, it will evolve at first to a state that differs only in one component. This procedure is called *asynchronous update* and will be used in the remainder of this paper. We obtain the following definition.

Definition 3. *The* state transition graph $\mathcal{S}_N$ *corresponding to the bioregulatory network* $N = (\mathcal{I}, f)$ *is a directed graph with vertex set* S^n. *There is an edge* $s \to s'$ *if either* $s = f(s) = s'$ *or if there is* $i \in \{1, \dots, n\}$ *such that* $s'_i = s_i + sgn(K_{i, R_i(s)} - s_i) \neq s_i$ *and* $s_j = s'_j$ *for all* $j \in \{1, \dots, n\} \setminus \{i\}$.

If s is a state such that $f(s)$ differs from s in more than one component, then there will be more than one successor of s in $\mathcal{S}_N$. In Fig. 1(b) we see the state transition graph corresponding to the state table also given in the figure.

In the following, we introduce some basic structures in this graph that are of biological interest using standard terminology from graph theory, such as paths and cycles.

Definition 4. *Let* $\mathcal{S}_N$ *be a state transition graph. An infinite path* $(s^0, s^1, \dots)$ *in* $\mathcal{S}_N$ *is called* trajectory. *A nonempty set of states* D *is called* trap set *if every trajectory starting in* D *never leaves* D. *A trap set* A *is called* attractor *if for any* $s^1, s^2 \in A$ *there is a path from* s^1 *to* s^2 *in* $\mathcal{S}_N$. *A is called* cyclic attractor *if A contains at least two states.*

A state s^0 *is called* steady state, *if* s^0 *is a fixed point of* f, *that is, if there is an edge from* s^0 *to itself. A cycle* $C := (s^1, \dots, s^r, s^1)$, $r \geq 2$, *is called a* trap cycle *if every* s^j, $j \in \{1, \dots, r\}$, *has only one outgoing edge in* $\mathcal{S}_N$, *i. e., the trajectory starting in* s^1 *is unique.*

Let M *be an arbitrary set of states. The set of states* s, *such that there exists a path from* s *to some state in* M, *is called the* basin of attraction *of* M. *The* immediate basin of attraction *of* M *is the set of states* s *such that for every trajectory* $(s, s^1, \dots)$ *starting in* s *there exists* k_0 *with* $s^k \in M$ *for all* $k \geq k_0$.

In other words, the attractors of $\mathcal{S}_N$ correspond to the terminal strongly connected components of the graph. It is easy to see that steady states and trap cycles are attractors.

When analyzing the state transition graph, not only trap cycles but cycles in general are of interest. In the general case, a concise statement about the asymptotic behavior represented by the trajectories is not possible, since there may be trajectories traversing the cycle in question which leave it again at some point. As a consequence the immediate basin of attraction of a cycle may be empty. This illustrates that although a trajectory is an infinite path in a finite graph, it does not necessarily reach an attractor. However, it is easy to see that for each state there exists a trajectory starting in the state leading to an attractor.

Attractors represent regions of predictability and stability in the behavior of the system. It is not surprising that an attractor can often be associated with a meaningful aspect of the system's role in biological processes. A fixed point in a regulatory network associated with cell differentiation, for example, may represent the stable state reached at the end of a developmental process. Trap cycles can often be identified with homeostasis of sustained oscillatory activity, as can be found in the cell cycle or circadian rhythm.

3   The Mammalian Cell Cycle: An Example

To illustrate the methods introduced in Sect. 2, we consider a model of cell cycle control in eukaryotes. There is a number of different discrete models available, focussing on different aspects and research questions (see [8] for an overview). Here, we focus on a generic model of the mammalian cell cycle proposed by Fauré et al. in [7].

The cell cycle is a series of events allowing a cell to duplicate itself, which is important for many biological processes, such as differentiation, apoptosis and regeneration. It is divided in a series of well-defined phases that lead to replication of the genome of the cell and the division in two daughter cells.

Replication of DNA occurs in the *S phase*, while in the *M phase* replicated genetic material is separated. Usually, so-called gap phases occur between M and S phase, the G_1 *phase* following the M phase and set before the S phase, and the G_2 *phase* between S and M phase. Starting from the G_1 phase, the cell cycle has to pass a checkpoint, the so-called restriction point. Beyond this point the cell is committed to dividing, that is, the cell cycle is executed in its entirety. Regulation of the cell cycle may also prohibit the passing of the restriction point. The cell then enters a quiescent state, called the G_0 *phase*.

The Boolean model of the cell cycle as proposed in [7] is shown in Fig. 2. For a detailed explanation of the biological significance of the regulatory components, see [7] and references therein. Note that this interaction graph does not contain parallel edges. Thus each edge is defined by its head and tail. Furthermore, for each edge e we have $M_e = \{1\}$.

We begin the dynamical analysis by the following observation. Since the component $CycD$ is only influenced by itself, its value can be viewed as input in the system. Thus we can characterize the dynamics of the system in the presence of active $CycD$ and in its absence separately. This mirrors the biological situation since an extracellular signal eliciting cell division leads to activation of the protein Cyclin D as a first step. In the G_0 phase Cyclin D is not active. The logical model gives rise to one steady state. In this state $CycD$ is not activated. It can be reached from every other state lacking active $CycD$ in the state transition graph. In other words, the set of states lacking active $CycD$ is the basin of attraction of the unique steady state. The steady state represents the quiescent

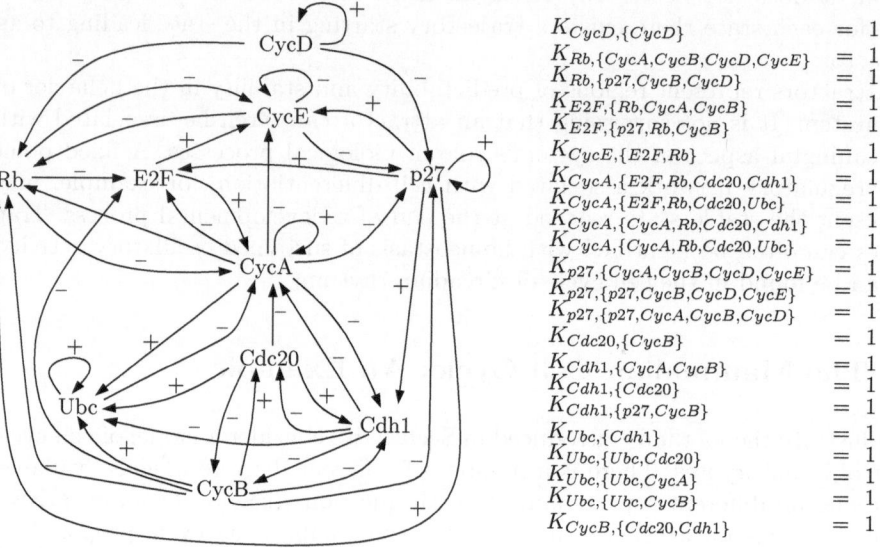

$$
\begin{aligned}
K_{CycD,\{CycD\}} &= 1 \\
K_{Rb,\{CycA,CycB,CycD,CycE\}} &= 1 \\
K_{Rb,\{p27,CycB,CycD\}} &= 1 \\
K_{E2F,\{Rb,CycA,CycB\}} &= 1 \\
K_{E2F,\{p27,Rb,CycB\}} &= 1 \\
K_{CycE,\{E2F,Rb\}} &= 1 \\
K_{CycA,\{E2F,Rb,Cdc20,Cdh1\}} &= 1 \\
K_{CycA,\{E2F,Rb,Cdc20,Ubc\}} &= 1 \\
K_{CycA,\{CycA,Rb,Cdc20,Cdh1\}} &= 1 \\
K_{CycA,\{CycA,Rb,Cdc20,Ubc\}} &= 1 \\
K_{p27,\{CycA,CycB,CycD,CycE\}} &= 1 \\
K_{p27,\{p27,CycB,CycD,CycE\}} &= 1 \\
K_{p27,\{p27,CycA,CycB,CycD\}} &= 1 \\
K_{Cdc20,\{CycB\}} &= 1 \\
K_{Cdh1,\{CycA,CycB\}} &= 1 \\
K_{Cdh1,\{Cdc20\}} &= 1 \\
K_{Cdh1,\{p27,CycB\}} &= 1 \\
K_{Ubc,\{Cdh1\}} &= 1 \\
K_{Ubc,\{Ubc,Cdc20\}} &= 1 \\
K_{Ubc,\{Ubc,CycA\}} &= 1 \\
K_{Ubc,\{Ubc,CycB\}} &= 1 \\
K_{CycB,\{Cdc20,Cdh1\}} &= 1
\end{aligned}
$$

Fig. 2. The interaction graph of the Boolean model of the mammalian cell cycle [7]. For each edge e we have $M_e = \{1\}$. Edges in the resource sets are denoted by the tail vertex of the edge. All parameters with value 1 of the regulatory network arise from those given above and the condition $\omega \subset \omega' \Rightarrow K_{\alpha,\omega} \le K_{\alpha,\omega'}$.

phase G_0. In the presence of active Cyclin D there is also a unique attractor. This attractor is a set of intertwined cycles. It comprises 112 states. The basin of attraction encompasses all states indicating the presence of active Cyclin D. In the cyclic attractor we can identify the different phases of the cell cycle. In both cases, presence and absence of $CycD$, the basin of attraction and the immediate basin of attraction do not coincide. That is due to the fact that there exist cycles in the state transition graph that do not belong to an attractor (see [7] for more details).

A more thorough analysis shows that some trajectories in the state transition graph are clearly unrealistic given the current biological knowledge. The data incorporated in the discrete model is simply not sufficient to yield a more precise representation. However, the qualitative aspects of the system's behavior were determined correctly, namely two attractors, a stable state representing the quiescent G_0 phase and a cyclic behavior representing the course of events in the cell division. A next step in the process of obtaining more information about the system is to analyze the influence of small changes in the structure of the network on the resulting behavior. Deleting certain edges or vertices, for example, can be interpreted as mutations in the original system. Comparison with experimental results of loss-of-function or gain-of-function mutations may thus lead to a refined model. In turn the predictions of such a model may be checked by suitable experiments, yielding new information on the real system.

4 Linking Structure and Dynamics

In the preceding section, we presented a practical application of the modeling formalism introduced in Sect. 2. An important issue, both from the theoretical and practical viewpoint, is to better understand the relationship between the structure and the dynamics of a bioregulatory network $N = (\mathcal{I}, f)$. Since the dynamics are derived from the function f, finding meaningful mathematical relations between dynamical and structural aspects is only possible if $\mathcal{I}$ and f are consistent (see Remark 1 in Sect. 2). In the following, we only consider consistent networks.

It has been shown that feedback circuits, i.e., sequences of consecutive edges $(e^0, \ldots, e^k)$ in the interaction graph such that the tail vertex of e^0 coincides with the head vertex of e^k, and all tail vertices of the involved edges are distinct, are of particular importance for the behavior of a system. Such a circuit is called positive if the number of positive edges in the cycle is even, and negative otherwise. Thomas [30] conjectured in 1981 that

- a positive circuit in the interaction graph is a necessary condition for multi-stationarity, i.e., multiple steady states.
- a negative circuit in the interaction graph is a necessary condition for stable periodic behavior.

During the last 25 years, these conjectures have been proven in various settings, for both discrete and continuous modeling formalisms, see e.g. [25] and the references therein. We can formulate them in the following way for our framework. The proofs can be found in [19,18]. Note that the notion of interaction graph used in these references is not the same as in our definition, but the results easily translate to our setting, and even allow for stronger statements using local interaction graphs (compare Remark 1).

Theorem 1. *Let $N = (\mathcal{I}, f)$ be a bioregulatory network. If there are two distinct attractors in the asynchronous state transition graph $\mathcal{S}_N$, then there exists a positive circuit in $\mathcal{I}$. If there is a cyclic attractor in $\mathcal{S}_N$, then there exists a negative circuit in $\mathcal{I}$.*

In general, the inverse statements of the results in the above theorem are not true. Fig. 3 shows a simple example clarifying this point. The network in the figure has only one attractor, the steady state $(0,0)$, but includes a positive as well as a negative circuit.

Finding sufficient conditions for positive resp. negative circuits to generate multiple attractors resp. cyclic attractors is an important problem, since it allows dynamical characterization of a given system based on investigation of the interaction graph rather than the exponentially larger state transition graph. In [15], the authors show that the asynchronous state transition graph has exactly two steady states and no other attractors, if the interaction graph is a single positive circuit. If $\mathcal{I}$ consists of only one negative cycle, then there is only one attractor in the asynchronous state transition graph, and this attractor is cyclic.

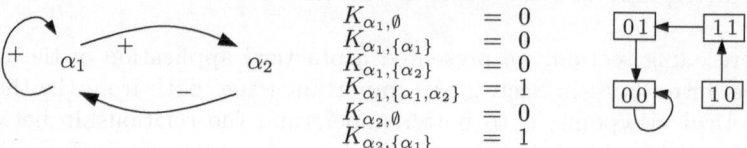

$$K_{\alpha_1,\emptyset} = 0$$
$$K_{\alpha_1,\{\alpha_1\}} = 0$$
$$K_{\alpha_1,\{\alpha_2\}} = 0$$
$$K_{\alpha_1,\{\alpha_1,\alpha_2\}} = 1$$
$$K_{\alpha_2,\emptyset} = 0$$
$$K_{\alpha_2,\{\alpha_1\}} = 1$$

Fig. 3. Interaction graph, parameters and state transition graph of a simple regulatory system. Since there are no parallel edges we again refer to edges in the resource sets by their tail vertex.

To obtain similar results for more complex networks, a purely structural analysis is clearly not sufficient, as the example in Fig. 3 shows. However, there exist different approaches supplementing structural observations with pinpoint dynamical information that allow for results about attractor characteristics based on circuits in the interaction graph [23,16,20]. Extending such results may lead to efficient analysis methods for bioregulatory networks, permitting an understanding of essential dynamical properties without having to generate the state transition graph in its entirety.

5 Model Checking for Biological Networks

In the previous sections, we have studied mathematical relationships between the interaction graph and the state transition graph. In this section, we discuss how the dynamics of a bioregulatory network, as represented by the state transition graph, can be analyzed in practice. Since the size of the state transition graph grows exponentially in the number of genes, the use of classical graph algorithms to determine shortest paths, elementary circuits, or strongly connected components is limited. A powerful alternative consists in using *model checking*: many non-trivial dynamic properties can be tested automatically by expressing them in a suitable temporal logic (e.g. *Computation Tree Logic* (CTL)) and applying model checking techniques from formal verification [4,5,3]. Model checking can also be used in reverse engineering of genetic networks. It allows finding values for the discrete parameters that are consistent with available biological knowledge [4].

Definition 5. *Given a set of atomic formulas AP, the set of CTL formulas (over AP) is inductively defined as follows:*

1. *Atomic formulas in AP are CTL formulas.*
2. *If φ and ψ are CTL formulas, then $\neg\varphi, \varphi\wedge\psi, \varphi\vee\psi, AX\varphi, EX\varphi, AF\varphi, EF\varphi, AG\varphi, EG\varphi, A[\varphi U\psi], E[\varphi U\psi]$ are CTL formulas.*

Each temporal operator in CTL consists of a path quantifier, A (for **A**ll paths) or E (there **E**xists a path), together with a linear time operator X (in the ne**X**t state), F (in some **F**uture state), G (in all future states, **G**lobally), or U (**U**ntil).

CTL formulas are interpreted over *Kripke structures* $M = (S, \rightarrow, L)$. Here, S is a finite set of states, $\rightarrow$ is a binary relation on S such that for each $s \in S$ there exists $s' \in S$ with $s \rightarrow s'$. The labeling function $L : S \rightarrow 2^{AP}$ defines for each state $s \in S$ the set $L(s)$ of atomic formulas valid in S.

Definition 6. *Given a Kripke model $M = (S, \rightarrow, L)$, a state $s \in S$, and a CTL formula φ, the satisfaction relation $M, s \models \varphi$ is inductively defined as follows:*

- $M, s \models p$ *iff* $p \in L(s)$.
- $M, s \models \neg\varphi$ *iff* $M, s \not\models \varphi$.
- $M, s \models \varphi \wedge \psi$ *iff* $M, s \models \varphi$ *and* $M, s \models \psi$.
- $M, s \models \varphi \vee \psi$ *iff* $M, s \models \varphi$ *or* $M, s \models \psi$.
- $M, s \models AX\varphi$ *iff for all* $s' \in S$ *with* $s \rightarrow s'$ *we have* $M, s' \models \varphi$.
- $M, s \models EX\varphi$ *iff for some* $s' \in S$ *with* $s \rightarrow s'$ *we have* $M, s' \models \varphi$.
- $M, s \models AF\varphi$ *iff for all paths* $s = s_1 \rightarrow s_2 \rightarrow \ldots$ *we have* $M, s_i \models \varphi$, *for some* $i \geq 1$.
- $M, s \models EF\varphi$ *iff for some path* $s = s_1 \rightarrow s_2 \rightarrow \ldots$ *we have* $M, s_i \models \varphi$, *for some* $i \geq 1$.
- $M, s \models AG\varphi$ *iff for all paths* $s = s_1 \rightarrow s_2 \rightarrow \ldots$ *we have* $M, s_i \models \varphi$, *for all* $i \geq 1$.
- $M, s \models EG\varphi$ *iff for some path* $s = s_1 \rightarrow s_2 \rightarrow \ldots$ *we have* $M, s_i \models \varphi$, *for all* $i \geq 1$.
- $M, s \models A[\varphi U \psi]$ *iff for all paths* $s = s_1 \rightarrow s_2 \rightarrow \ldots$ *there exists* $i \geq 1$ *such that* $M, s_i \models \psi$ *and* $M, s_j \models \varphi$, *for all* $1 \leq j < i$.
- $M, s \models A[\varphi U \psi]$ *iff for some path* $s = s_1 \rightarrow s_2 \rightarrow \ldots$ *there exists* $i \geq 1$ *such that* $M, s_i \models \psi$ *and* $M, s_j \models \varphi$, *for all* $1 \leq j < i$.

Given a state transition graph $\mathcal{S}_N = (S^n, \rightarrow)$ of a bioregulatory network $N = (\mathcal{I}, f)$, we may define a corresponding Kripke structure $M = (S, \rightarrow^0, L)$ by setting

- $S = S^n = \{0, \ldots, p_1\} \times \cdots \times \{0, \ldots, p_n\}$, $\rightarrow^0 = \rightarrow \cup \{s \rightarrow s \mid s$ is stable$\}$
- $AP = \{x_i = 0, x_i = 1, \ldots, x_i = p_i, x_i = f_i \mid i \in \{1, \ldots, n\}\}$, with new constant symbols $f_1, \ldots, f_n$, and
- $L(s) = \{x_i = s_i \mid i \in \{1, \ldots, n\}\} \cup \{x_i = f_i \mid f_i^{K(\mathcal{I})}(s) = s_i, i \in \{1, \ldots, n\}\}$.

Using this language, we may express various properties occurring in analyzing the dynamics of a bioregulatory network [17]. For example, the formula

$$state_s \equiv (x_1 = s_1 \wedge \cdots \wedge x_n = s_n)$$

is satisfied exactly in the state $s \in S^n$. Similarly, the formula

$$steady \equiv (x_1 = f_1 \wedge \cdots \wedge x_n = f_n)$$

is satisfied exactly by the steady states. The formula

$$state_s \rightarrow AF(steady)$$

expresses that on all paths starting in state s one eventually reaches a steady state. A periodic behavior is expressed by the formula

$$state_s \rightarrow AF(\neg state_s \wedge AF(state_s)),$$

which states that all paths starting from state s will reach a state different from s and then come back to s.

6   Incorporating Time Delays

The formalism introduced in the preceding sections requires only basic knowledge about the modeled system. In turn, the resulting representation of the network dynamics is high-level and non-deterministic. So far, we have no means to distinguish between different trajectories in the state transition graph, and thus must consider all possible cases. However, experimental data permitting a distinction may be available. This calls for suitable extensions of the formalism allowing for the incorporation of such data [29,31,12].

In this section, we focus on including temporal data concerning the network operations. Thus we introduce a time axis that allows to compare durations, or *time delays*, of different activity level changes of network components. The sole assumption about time delays inherent in the logical formalism is reflected in the asynchronous update rule introduced in Def. 3. We assume that different processes involved in activity level changes do not take the exact same amount of time, i. e., one is faster than the other. However, we do not know the ordering of the time delays involved and thus have to consider every possible outcome. This leads to the non-determinism of the state transition graph.

We now associate a time delay with every activity level change in the network. Then for each time delay we have to indicate the corresponding component and activity levels involved. Furthermore, we have to realize that in a biological system the processes governing activity level increase and decrease, e. g. production and decay of some substance, often differ in duration. So we introduce time delays $\tau_i^{k\varepsilon}$ associated with the process of activity level change of component α_i from k to $k+1$, if $\varepsilon = +$, or from k to $k-1$, if $\varepsilon = -$. Now, we can label each edge in the state transition graph with a time constraint identifying the value change of the corresponding state component as the fastest activity level change. Note that such a time constraint is not necessary if a state has only one outgoing edge, since there is no competition between processes in that case. Fig. 4(a) and (b) show the interaction graph and the labeled state transition graph of a simple network comprising two components.

In addition to time constraints corresponding to a single edge we can also calculate time constraints for paths in the state transition graph. However, these constraints may become more and more complex with increasing path length, because we have to keep in mind the history of each network component. For example in Fig. 4(c), the constraint for the path from (1,2) to (1,0) has to take into account that the process of activity level decrease for α_1 starts at the same time as that of α_2 and is not terminated when reaching the intermediate state

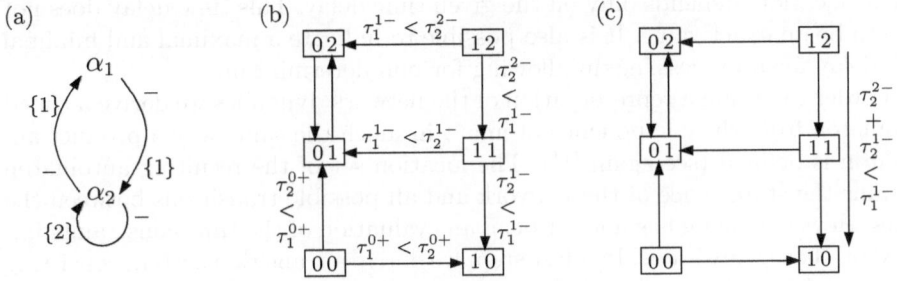

Fig. 4. In (a) interaction graph of a simple network. We use the logical parameters $K_{1,\emptyset} = K_{2,\emptyset} = K_{2,\{\alpha_2\}} = 0$, $K_{1,\{\alpha_2\}} = K_{2,\{\alpha_1\}} = 1$ and $K_{2,\{\alpha_1,\alpha_2\}} = 2$, where again edges in the resource sets are denoted by their tail vertex. In (b) and (c) corresponding state transition graph labeled with time constraints.

(1,1). Thus, in order to reach (1,0) the sum of both time delays τ_2^{2-} and τ_2^{1-} needs to be smaller than τ_1^{1-}.

If suitable data about the time delays is available, these should be incorporated in the structural description. Then an automated procedure should provide a representation of the dynamics taking into account all the given constraints. A possible framework that allows us to express the logical rules governing the network behavior as well as to measure time is the theory of timed automata (see e. g. [1]). Here the discrete changes in activity levels can be linked to conditions depending on the evolution of time. The details of the modeling procedure (see [21,22,24]) are beyond the scope of this paper, but in the following we explain the general idea. It can be divided in three steps:

- We model each network component separately, incorporating information on its range, interactions influencing the component, parameter values and time delays concerning the component.
- The local models are combined to a global model supplying information on the state space, state changes induced by the structure and parameter specification of the network, and constraints on time delays associates with state changes.
- The data inherent in the network model is evaluated to obtain a representation of the dynamical behavior in agreement with all given constraints.

Each network component is modeled as a timed automaton, equipped with a clock that measures time, and consists of discrete *locations* representing the different activity levels of the component. Such locations are called *regular*. Furthermore it contains so-called *intermediate* locations representing the process of activity level change, that is, the process we identify with a certain time delay. Changes from a regular location to an intermediate location are based on the system evolution determined by the logical function f introduced in Def. 2. However, a location change indicating the completion of an activity level change, represented by a change from an intermediate location to the corresponding regular location, depends only on the given time delay. This time delay does not have to be an exact value. It is also possible to indicate a maximal and minimal time delay for a process, again allowing for non-determinism.

In order to obtain a representation of the network dynamics we derive a timed automaton from the component automata in much the same way a product automaton is defined (see again [1]). The location set of the resulting automaton contains the state space of the network and all possible transitions between the states. However, there has not yet been an evaluation of the time constraints imposed on those transitions. In a last step, we derive a transition system consisting of states with a discrete part holding the activity level values and a continuous part holding the clock values. It represents the possible dynamical behavior of the network, all paths in the transition system are in agreement with the given constraints. Provided we have enough data on time delays, this representation allows for a much more refined analysis of the system's dynamics than the purely discrete state transition graph. Transitions and pathways appearing in the state transition graph can be ruled out if they violate the given time constraints. This can be of great advantage when modeling systems parts of which work on different time scales. Furthermore, it is possible to compare different trajectories regarding their feasibility with respect to the time constraints. For example, transitions depending on equality of time delays will occur less likely in biological systems than transitions allowing for perturbations in the time delays. The same considerations allow for the introduction of a stability concept for certain behaviors. Altogether we obtain a much more detailed picture of the network dynamics (see [21,22,24] for more information).

Of course, we have to make sure that there exist effective modeling and analysis methods for this framework. The theory of timed automata provides a suitable platform for our approach, since there are a variety of software packages for implementation, simulation and verification of such models. Concerning the analysis of the network behavior, model checking techniques can be applied. In particular, the CTL and LTL model checking problems are decidable for timed automata (see [2]).

7   Conclusion

During the last years, logic modeling has become a well established methodology in systems biology. It allows for the translation of working models of experimental biologists into a rigorous mathematical framework, requiring only basic qualitative information. Despite the high level of abstraction, analysis of such models can reveal characteristic patterns of the dynamical behavior, thus helping to understand biological function.

Linking the occurrence of certain dynamical patterns, regardless of their biological interpretation, to structural properties of the network is a task needing theoretical mathematical consideration. Already there have been interesting results, some of which were presented in Sect. 4. A more thorough understanding of the general rules governing the relation between structure and dynamics is not only of theoretical interest. It may also prove helpful in reverse engineering regulatory networks, i.e., discovering the structure underlying the experimentally observed dynamic behavior. For example, every bioregulatory system capable of reaching different stable states, representing different cell types in cell differentiation, necessarily contains a positive feedback circuit in its interaction graph, as can be deduced from Theorem 1. When logic modeling is applied to a regulatory network, a non-deterministic state transition graph is obtained, which can be further explored using temporal logic and model checking. Practical experience shows that model checking is also very useful for reverse engineering bioregulatory networks. Being able to build a model starting from very limited data is one of the strengths of the logical approach. However, if additional data is available, extensions of the formalism are needed to exploit this information and to enable a refined dynamical analysis. In Sect. 6 we introduced an extended approach incorporating data on time delays using timed automata. Further extensions may be needed, for example to include information on reaction mechanisms, thus providing a step by step enhancement of the model in accordance with the results of experimental biology.

References

1. Alur, R.: Timed Automata. In: Halbwachs, N., Peled, D.A. (eds.) CAV 1999. LNCS, vol. 1633, pp. 8–22. Springer, Heidelberg (1999)
2. Alur, R., Henzinger, T., Lafferriere, G., Pappas, G.: Discrete abstractions of hybrid systems. Proceedings of the IEEE 88, 971–984 (2000)
3. Batt, G., Ropers, D., de Jong, H., Geiselmann, J., Mateescu, R., Page, M., Schneider, D.: Analysis and verification of qualitative models of genetic regulatory networks: A model-checking approach. In: 19th International Joint Conference on Artificial Intelligence, IJCAI 2005, Edinburgh, pp. 370–375 (2005)
4. Bernot, G., Comet, J.-P., Richard, A., Guespin, J.: Application of formal methods to biological regulatory networks: extending Thomas' asynchronous logical approach with temporal logic. J. Theor. Biol. 229, 339–347 (2004)
5. Chabrier-Rivier, N., Chiaverini, M., Danos, V., Fages, F., Schächter, V.: Modeling and querying biomolecular interaction networks. Theoret. Comput. Sci. 325(1), 25–44 (2004)
6. Chaouiya, C., Remy, E., Mossé, B., Thieffry, D.: Qualitative Analysis of Regulatory Graphs: A Computational Tool Based on a Discrete Formal Framework. In: Bru, R., Romero-Vivó, S. (eds.) POSTA 2009. Lecture Notes in Control and Information Sciences, vol. 389, pp. 830–832. Springer, Heidelberg (2009)
7. Fauré, A., Naldi, A., Chaouiya, C., Thieffry, D.: Dynamical analysis of a generic Boolean model for the control of the mammalian cell cycle. Bioinform. 22, 124–131 (2006)
8. Fauré, A., Thieffry, D.: Logical modelling of cell cycle control in eukaryotes: a comparative study. Mol. BioSyst. 5, 1569–1581 (2009)
9. Glass, L., Kauffman, S.A.: The logical analysis of continuous, non-linear biochemical control networks. J. Theor. Biol. 39, 103–129 (1973)
10. Kauffman, S.: The Origins of Order. Oxford University Press (1993)
11. Kauffman, S.A.: Metabolic stability and epigenesis in randomly constructed genetic nets. J. Theor. Biol. 22, 437–467 (1969)

12. Kaufman, M., Andris, F., Leo, O.: A logical analysis of T cell activation and anergy. PNAS 96(7), 3894–3899 (1999)
13. Kitano, H.: Systems biology: A brief overview. Science 295, 1662–1664 (2002)
14. Naldi, A., Thieffry, D., Chaouiya, C.: Decision Diagrams for the Representation and Analysis of Logical Models of Genetic Networks. In: Calder, M., Gilmore, S. (eds.) CMSB 2007. LNCS (LNBI), vol. 4695, pp. 233–247. Springer, Heidelberg (2007)
15. Remy, É., Mossé, B., Chaouiya, C., Thieffry, D.: A description of dynamical graphs associated to elementary regulatory circuits. Bioinform. 19, 172–178 (2003)
16. Remy, E., Ruet, P.: Incorporating Time Delays into the Logical Analysis of Gene Regulatory Networks. Bioinform. 24, 220–226 (2008)
17. Richard, A.: Modèle formel pour les réseaux de régulation génétique et influence des circuits de rétroaction. PhD thesis, Univ. d'Evry, France (2006)
18. Richard, A.: Negative circuits and sustained oscillations in asynchronous automata networks. Advances in Applied Mathematics 44(4), 378–392 (2010)
19. Richard, A., Comet, J.-P.: Necessary conditions for multistationarity in discrete dynamical systems. Discrete Appl. Math. 155(18), 2403–2413 (2007)
20. Siebert, H.: Analysis of discrete bioregulatory networks using symbolic steady states. Bull. Math. Biol. 73, 873–898 (2011)
21. Siebert, H., Bockmayr, A.: Incorporating time delays into the logical analysis of gene regulatory networks. In: Priami, C. (ed.) CMSB 2006. LNCS (LNBI), vol. 4210, pp. 169–183. Springer, Heidelberg (2006)
22. Siebert, H., Bockmayr, A.: Context Sensitivity in Logical Modeling with Time Delays. In: Calder, M., Gilmore, S. (eds.) CMSB 2007. LNCS (LNBI), vol. 4695, pp. 64–79. Springer, Heidelberg (2007)
23. Siebert, H., Bockmayr, A.: Relating Attractors and Singular Steady States in the Logical Analysis of Bioregulatory Networks. In: Anai, H., Horimoto, K., Kutsia, T. (eds.) Ab 2007. LNCS, vol. 4545, pp. 36–50. Springer, Heidelberg (2007)
24. Siebert, H., Bockmayr, A.: Temporal constraints in the logical analysis of regulatory networks. Theor. Comput. Sci. 391(3), 258–275 (2008)
25. Soulé, C.: Mathematical approaches to gene regulation and differentiation. C.R. Paris Biolgies 329, 13–20 (2006)
26. Sugita, M.: Functional analysis of chemical systems in vivo using a logical circuit equivalent. J. Theor. Biol. 1, 415–430 (1961)
27. Szallasi, Z., Stelling, J., Periwal, V.: System modeling in cellular biology. MIT Press (2006)
28. Thomas, R.: Boolean formalisation of genetic control circuits. J. Theor. Biol. 42, 565–583 (1973)
29. Thomas, R.: Kinetic logic: a boolean approach to the analysis of complex regulatory systems. Lecture Notes in Biomathematics, vol. 29. Springer (1979)
30. Thomas, R.: On the relation between the logical structure of systems and their abilities to generate multiple steady states and sustained oscillations. In: Series in Synergetics, vol. 9, pp. 180–193. Springer (1981)
31. Thomas, R., d'Ari, R.: Biological Feedback. CRC Press (1990)
32. Thomas, R., Kaufman, M.: Multistationarity, the basis of cell differentiation and memory. II. Logical analysis of regulatory networks in terms of feedback circuits. Chaos 11, 180–195 (2001)

Canonical Ground Horn Theories

Maria Paola Bonacina[1,*] and Nachum Dershowitz[2]

[1] Dipartimento di Informatica, Università degli Studi di Verona,
Strada Le Grazie 15, I-37134 Verona, Italy
mariapaola.bonacina@univr.it
[2] School of Computer Science, Tel Aviv University, Ramat Aviv 69978, Israel
Nachum.Dershowitz@cs.tau.ac.il

Dedicated to the memory of **Harald Ganzinger,** friend and colleague.

Abstract. An abstract framework of canonical inference based on proof orderings is applied to ground Horn theories with equality. A finite presentation that makes all normal-form proofs available is called *saturated*. To maximize the chance that a saturated presentation be finite, it should also be *contracted*, in which case it is deemed *canonical*. We apply these notions to propositional Horn theories – or equivalently Moore families – presented as *implicational systems* or *associative-commutative rewrite systems*, and ground equational Horn theories, presented as *decreasing conditional rewrite systems*. For implicational systems, we study different notions of optimality and the completion procedures that generate them, and we suggest a new notion of *rewrite-optimality*, that takes contraction by simplification into account. For conditional rewrite systems, we show that reduced (fully normalized) is stronger than contracted (sans redundancy), and accordingly the *perfect* system – complete and reduced – is preferred to the canonical one – saturated and contracted. We conclude with a survey of approaches to normal-form proofs, saturated, or canonical, systems, and decision procedures based on them.

Keywords: Horn theories, conditional theories, Moore families, decision procedures, canonical systems, normal forms, saturation, redundancy.

> The first concept is ... the elimination of equations and rules. ...
> An equation $C \Rightarrow s = t$ can be discarded
> if there is also a proof of the same conditional equation,
> different from the one which led to the construction of the equation.
> In addition, this proof has to be simpler
> with respect to the complexity measure on proofs.
>
> – Harald Ganzinger (1991)

* Research supported in part by Ministero per l'Istruzione, l'Università e la Ricerca (grants no. 2003-097383 and 2007-9E5KM8) and by EU COST Action IC0901.

A. Voronkov and C. Weidenbach (Eds.): Ganzinger Festschrift, LNCS 7797, pp. 35–71, 2013.
© Springer-Verlag Berlin Heidelberg 2013

1   Motivation

We are interested in the study of presentations for theories in Horn logic with equality. We use the term "presentation" to mean a set of formulæ, reserving "theory" for a presentation with all its theorems. Thus, a *Horn presentation* is any set of Horn clauses, while a *Horn theory* is a deductively-closed set of formulæ that can be axiomatized by a Horn presentation. Since a Horn presentation can also be read naturally as a set of instructions for a computer, Horn theories are important in automated reasoning, artificial intelligence, declarative programming and deductive databases. The literature is vast; surveys include those by Apt [1] and Hodges [50]. More specifically, conditional rewriting (and unification) with equational Horn clauses has been proposed as a logic-based programming paradigm in [36,67,48,43,37]; see [49] for a survey.

On account of their double nature – computational and logical – Horn theories, and especially Horn theories with equality, presented by sets of *conditional equations* or *conditional rewrite rules*, played a special rôle in Harald Ganzinger's work (e.g. [47]). Harald's study of them represented the transition phase from his earlier work on compilers and programming languages to his later work in automated deduction.

From the perspective taken here, the quality of presentations depends on the quality of the proofs they make possible: the better are the proofs, the better is the presentation. Proofs are measured by *proof orderings*, and the most desirable ones are those that are minimal in the chosen ordering. Since a minimal proof in a certain presentation may not remain minimal in a presentation expanded by deduction, the best proofs are those that are minimal in deductively-closed presentations. These best proofs are called *normal-form proofs*. However, what is a deductively-closed presentation depends on the choice of *deduction mechanism*. Thus, the choices of notion of normal-form proof and deduction mechanism are intertwined.

One reason for deeming normal-form proofs to be best is their connection with decidability. The archetypal instance of this concept is rewriting for *equational theories*, where normal-form proofs are valley proofs. A *valley proof* of an equational theorem $\forall \bar{x} \ s \simeq t$, where $\bar{x}$ are the variables in $s \simeq t$, is a proof chain $\tilde{s} \xrightarrow{*} \circ \xleftarrow{*} \tilde{t}$, where $\tilde{s}$ and $\tilde{t}$ are s and t with their variables treated as Skolem constants, and equations only decrease terms. Given a presentation E of universally quantified equations, and a complete simplification ordering $\succ$, an equivalent *ground-convergent* presentation $E^\sharp$ offers a valley proof for every equational theorem $\forall \bar{x} \ s \simeq t$. If $E^\sharp$ is *finite*, it serves as a *decision procedure*, because validity can be decided by *rewriting* $\tilde{s}$ and $\tilde{t}$ "blindly" to their $E^\sharp$-normal forms and comparing the results. If $E^\sharp$ is also *reduced*, in the sense that as much as possible is in normal form, it is called *canonical*, and is unique for the given ordering $\succ$, a property first noticed by Mike Ballantyne (see [35]). Procedures to generate *canonical presentations*, which afford normal-form proofs and may be the basis for decision procedures, are called *completion procedures* (cf. [59,55,54,6,18,5]). For more on rewriting, see [32,38,71].

More generally, the notion of *canonicity* can be articulated into three properties of increasing strength, that were defined in the abstract framework of [33,13] as follows:

- A presentation is *complete* if it affords at least one normal-form proof for each theorem.
- A presentation is *saturated* if it supports all normal-form proofs for all theorems.
- A presentation is *canonical* if it is both saturated and contracted, in the sense of containing no redundancies.

If minimal proofs are unique, complete and saturated coincide. For equational theories, contracted means *reduced* and saturated means *convergent*. We call a system *perfect* when it is reduced but not saturated, only complete. A critical question is whether canonical, or perfect, presentations can be *finite* – possibly characterized by some quantitative bound – and/or *unique*. Viewed in this light, one purpose of studying these properties is to balance the strength of the "saturated," or "complete," requirement with that of the "contracted" requirement. On one hand, one wants saturation to be strong enough that a saturated presentation – when finite – yields a decision procedure for validity in the theory. On the other hand, one wants contraction to be as strong as possible, so as to maximize the possibility that the canonical presentation turns out to be finite. Furthermore, it is desirable that the canonical presentation be unique relative to the chosen ordering.

In this article, we present three main contributions:

- a study of canonicity in *propositional Horn theories* (Sect. 3);
- a study of canonicity in *conditional equational theories* in the ground case (Sect. 4);
- a survey of proof normalization and decision procedures based on saturated systems, primarily in Horn theories (Sect. 5).

Propositional Horn theories are the theories presented by sets of propositional Horn implications, known as *implicational systems*. The family of models of a theory of this kind is known as a *Moore family* and has the distinctive property of closure under intersection (see [11,10]). Moore families and implicational systems play a rôle in a variety of fields in computer science, including relational databases, data mining, artificial intelligence, logic programming, lattice theory and abstract interpretations. We refer to [22] and [10] for surveys, including applications, related formalisms and historical notes.

Since a Moore family may be presented by different implicational systems, it makes sense to define and generate implicational systems that are "optimal," or "minimal," or "canonical" in some suitable sense. Bertet and Nebut [11] proposed the notions of *directness* of implicational systems, optimizing computation by forward chaining, and *direct-optimality* of implicational systems, which adds an optimization step based on a symbol count. Bertet and Monjardet [10] considered other candidates and proved them all equal to direct-optimality, which, therefore, earned the appellation *canonical-directness*. Furthermore, they showed that given a Horn function, the Moore family of its models and its associated closure operator, the elements of the corresponding canonical-direct implicational system, read as disjunctions, give the *prime implicates* of the Horn function.

We investigate correspondences between "optimal" implicational systems (direct, direct-optimal) and canonical rewrite systems, by establishing an equivalence between implicational systems and associative-commutative rewrite systems, and by defining and comparing their respective deduction mechanisms and underlying proof orderings. We discover that direct-optimality can be simulated by normalization with respect to a different proof ordering than the one assumed by rewriting, and this discrepancy leads us to introduce a new notion of *rewrite-optimality*. Thus, while directness corresponds to saturation in an expansion-oriented deduction mechanism, rewrite-optimality corresponds to canonicity.

For conditional equational theories, we find that, unlike for equational theories, reduced implies contracted, but the two notions remain distinct. Thus, in the conditional case, perfect differs from canonical in two ways: complete is weaker than saturated, and reduced is stronger than contracted. Since complete/saturated determines how much expansion we need to do in completion, whereas reduced/contracted refers to how much simplification we should have, perfect is doubly preferable to canonical.

This article is organized as follows: Sect. 2 fixes notations and concepts; Sects. 3 and 4 are devoted to propositional Horn theories and to ground conditional equational theories, respectively; and Sect. 5 contains the survey of proof normalization and saturation-based systems. We conclude with a discussion.

2   Background

Horn clauses, the subject of this study, are an important subclass of logical formulæ.

2.1   Preliminaries

Let $\Sigma = \langle X, F, P \rangle$ be a vocabulary, consisting of variables X, function (and constant) symbols F, and predicate symbols P. Although this article is mainly concerned with the ground case, where there are no variables X, we keep basic definitions as general as possible. Let T be the set of atoms over Σ. Identity of terms and atoms will be denoted by $=$. A *context* is a term with a "hole" at some indicated position. The notation $l = t[s]_u$ indicates that term s occurs in term or atom l at position u within context t, and $Var(l)$ is the set of variables occurring in term or atom l. Positions u will henceforth be omitted from the notation.

A *Horn clause*,

$$\neg a_1 \vee \cdots \vee \neg a_n \quad \text{or} \quad \neg a_1 \vee \cdots \vee \neg a_n \vee c \,,$$

$(n \geq 0)$ is a clause (set of literals) with at most one positive literal, c, where $\vee$ (disjunction) is commutative and idempotent by nature, and $a_1, \ldots, a_n, c$ are atoms in T. Positive literals (c present and $n = 0$), sometimes called "facts", and negative clauses (c absent and $n > 0$), called "queries" or "goals," are special cases of Horn clauses. Horn clauses that are not queries are termed *definite* Horn clauses. A *Horn presentation* is a set of non-negative Horn clauses.

It is customary to write a Horn clause as the implication or *rule*

$$a_1 \cdots a_n \Rightarrow c .$$

A Horn clause is *trivial* if the *conclusion* c is the same as one of the *premises* a_i. The same clause also has n *contrapositive* forms

$$a_1 \cdots a_{j-1} a_{j+1} \cdots a_n \neg c \Rightarrow \neg a_j ,$$

for $1 \leq j \leq n$. Facts are written simply as is,

$$c ,$$

and queries as

$$a_1 \cdots a_n \Rightarrow \text{FALSE} ,$$

or just

$$a_1 \cdots a_n \Rightarrow .$$

The main inference rules for Horn-theory reasoning are *forward chaining* and *backward chaining*:

$$\frac{a_1 \cdots a_n \Rightarrow c \quad b_1 \cdots b_m c \Rightarrow d}{a_1 \cdots a_n b_1 \cdots b_m \Rightarrow d} \qquad \frac{a_1 \cdots a_n c \Rightarrow \quad b_1 \cdots b_m \Rightarrow c}{a_1 \cdots a_n b_1 \cdots b_m \Rightarrow} .$$

Another way to present a Horn theory is as an "implicational" system (see [11,10]). An *implicational system* S is a binary relation $S \subseteq \mathcal{P}(T) \times \mathcal{P}(T)$, read as a set of implications

$$a_1 \cdots a_n \Rightarrow c_1 \cdots c_m ,$$

for $a_i, c_j \in T$, with both sides understood as conjunctions. If all right-hand sides are singletons, S is a *unary* implicational system. Clearly, any definite Horn clause is such a unary implication and vice-versa, and any non-unary implication can be decomposed into a set of m unary implications, or, equivalently, Horn clauses, one for each c_i. Empty sets correspond to TRUE. Conjunctions of facts are written just as

$$c_1 \cdots c_m ,$$

instead of as $\emptyset \Rightarrow c_1 \ldots c_m$.

If we focus on propositional logic, atoms are propositional variables, that evaluate to either TRUE or FALSE. A propositional implication $a_1 \cdots a_n \Rightarrow c_1 \cdots c_m$ is equivalent to the bi-implication $a_1 \cdots a_n c_1 \cdots c_m \Leftrightarrow a_1 \cdots a_n$, again with both sides understood as conjunctions. Since one side is greater than the other in any monotonic well-founded ordering, it can also be translated into a rewrite rule

$$a_1 \cdots a_n c_1 \cdots c_m \;\rightarrow\; a_1 \cdots a_n \;,$$

where juxtaposition stands for the associative-commutative-idempotent (ACI) conjunction operator, and the arrow $\rightarrow$ has the operational semantics of rewriting and the logical semantics of *equivalence* (see, for instance, [27,28,17]).

When dealing with theories with equality, we presume the underlying axioms of equality (which are Horn), and use the predicate symbol $\simeq$ (in P) symmetrically: $l \simeq r$ stands for both $l \simeq r$ and $r \simeq l$. If one views atoms as terms and phrases an atom $r(t_1, \ldots, t_n)$ as an equation $r(t_1, \ldots, t_n) \simeq \text{TRUE}$, where r is a predicate symbol other than $\simeq$, $t_1, \ldots, t_n$ are terms, and TRUE is a special symbol, not in the original vocabulary, then any equational Horn clause can be written interchangeably as a *conditional equation*,

$$p_1 \simeq q_1, \cdots, p_n \simeq q_n \Rightarrow l \simeq r \;,$$

or as an equational clause

$$p_1 \not\simeq q_1 \vee \cdots \vee p_n \not\simeq q_n \vee l \simeq r \;,$$

where $p_1, q_1, \ldots, p_n, q_n, l, r$ are terms, and $p \not\simeq q$ stands for $\neg(p \simeq q)$.

A *conjecture* $C \Rightarrow l \simeq r$ is valid in a theory with presentation S, where C is some set (conjunction) of equations, if $l \simeq r$ is valid in $S \cup C$, or, equivalently, $S \cup C \cup \{l \not\simeq r\}$ is unsatisfiable, where $l \not\simeq r$ is the *goal*. A conjecture $p_1 \simeq q_1 \ldots p_n \simeq q_n$ is valid in S if $S \cup \{p_1 \not\simeq q_1 \vee \ldots \vee p_n \not\simeq q_n\}$ is unsatisfiable, in which case $p_1 \not\simeq q_1 \vee \ldots \vee p_n \not\simeq q_n$ is the *goal*.

The purely equational ground case, where all conditions are empty, the propositional case (with rules in the form $a_1 \simeq \text{TRUE}, \ldots, a_n \simeq \text{TRUE} \Rightarrow c \simeq \text{TRUE}$), and the intermediate case $a_1 \simeq \text{TRUE}, \ldots, a_n \simeq \text{TRUE} \Rightarrow l \simeq r$ (where $a_1, \ldots, a_n, c$ are propositional variables and l, r are ground terms), are all covered by the general ground equational Horn presentation case.

2.2   Canonical Systems

In this paper, we apply the framework of [33,13] to proofs made of ground Horn clauses. Let $\mathbb{A}$ be the set of all *ground conditional equations* and $\mathbb{P}$ the set of all *ground Horn proofs*, over signature Σ. Formulæ $\mathbb{A}$ and proofs $\mathbb{P}$ are linked by two functions $Pm \colon \mathbb{P} \rightarrow \mathcal{P}(\mathbb{A})$, that takes a proof p and gives its premises, denoted $[p]^{Pm}$, and $Cl \colon \mathbb{P} \rightarrow \mathbb{A}$, that takes a proof p and gives its conclusion, denoted $[p]_{Cl}$. Both are extended to sets of proofs – termed *justifications* – in the usual fashion. Proofs in $\mathbb{P}$ are ordered by two *well-founded* partial orderings: a *subproof relation* $\unrhd$ and a *proof ordering* $\geq$, which, for convenience, is assumed to compare only proofs with the same conclusion (that is, $p \geq q \Rightarrow [p]_{Cl} = [q]_{Cl}$).

In addition to standard inference rules of the form

$$\frac{A_1 \quad \ldots \quad A_n}{B_1 \quad \ldots \quad B_m}$$

that add inferred formulæ $B_1, \ldots, B_m$ to the set of known theorems, which already include the premises $A_1, \ldots, A_n$, we are interested in rules that delete or simplify already-inferred theorems. We use a "double-ruled" inference rule of the form

$$\frac{A_1 \quad \cdots \quad A_n}{B_1 \quad \cdots \quad B_m}$$

meaning that the formulæ (A_i) above the rule are *replaced* by those below (B_j). It is a *deletion* rule if the consequences are a proper subset of the premises; otherwise, it is a *simplification* rule. The challenge is incorporating such rules without endangering completeness of the inference system.

Given a presentation S, the set of all proofs using premises of S is denoted by $Pf(S)$ and defined by[1]

$$Pf(S) \stackrel{!}{=} \{p \in \mathbb{P} : [p]^{Pm} \subseteq S\}.$$

A proof is *trivial* if it proves only its single premise $([p]^{Pm} = \{[p]_{Cl}\})$ and has no subproofs other than itself $(p \trianglerighteq q \Rightarrow p = q)$. A trivial proof of $a \in \mathbb{A}$ is denoted by $\widehat{a}$. The theory of S is denoted by $Th\, S$ and defined by

$$Th\, S \stackrel{!}{=} [Pf(S)]_{Cl},$$

that is, the conclusions of all proofs using any number of premises from S.

Three basic assumptions on $\trianglerighteq$ and $\geq$ are postulated, for all proofs p, q, r and formulæ a:

1. Proofs use their premises:

$$a \in [p]^{Pm} \Rightarrow p \trianglerighteq \widehat{a}.$$

2. Subproofs do not use non-extant premises:

$$p \trianglerighteq q \Rightarrow [p]^{Pm} \supseteq [q]^{Pm}.$$

3. Proof orderings are monotonic with respect to subproofs:[2]

$$p \trianglerighteq q > r \Rightarrow \exists v \in Pf([p]^{Pm} \cup [r]^{Pm}).\, p > v \trianglerighteq r.$$

(Recall that $p \geq q \Rightarrow [p]_{Cl} = [q]_{Cl}$.)

Since $>$ is well-founded, there exist *minimal* proofs. The set of minimal proofs in a given justification P is defined as

$$\mu P \stackrel{!}{=} \{p \in P : \forall q \in P.\, q \not< p\},$$

while the *normal-form proofs* of a presentation S are the minimal proofs in the *theory* of S, that is,

$$Nf(S) \stackrel{!}{=} \mu Pf(Th\, S).$$

---

[1] We use $\stackrel{!}{=}$ to signify definitions.
[2] This is weakened in [21].

This definition is not trivial, because it is not necessarily the case that for all proofs p, $p > \widehat{[p]}_{Cl}$. For instance, for equational theories, and a standard choice of proof ordering (e.g., [5]), $\tilde{s} \to \circ \leftarrow \tilde{t} \not\succ \tilde{s} \simeq \tilde{t}$. In other words, trivial proofs are not normal-form proofs in general.

With these notions in place, the characterizations of presentations introduced in Sect. 1 can be defined formally: The *canonical presentation* is the set of premises of normal-form proofs, or

$$ S^{\sharp} \overset{!}{=} [Nf(S)]^{Pm} , $$

and a presentation S is *canonical* if $S = S^{\sharp}$. Since trivial proofs are not normal-form proofs in general, $S^{\sharp}$ is not $Th\,S$. Furthermore, $(S^{\sharp})^{\sharp} = S^{\sharp}$.

By lifting the proof ordering to justifications and presentations, canonicity can be characterized directly in terms of the ordering. We say that presentation B is *simpler* than a logically equivalent presentation A, denoted by $A \succsim B$, when B provides better proofs than does A, in the sense that

$$ \forall p \in Pf(A). \exists q \in Pf(B). \; p \geq q . $$

Thus, canonicity is characterized in terms of this quasi-ordering, by proving that the canonical presentation is the simplest, or, in other words, that $A \succsim A^{\sharp}$ [33,13].

In addition to canonical, a presentation S can be:

- *contracted*, if it is made of the premises of minimal proofs, or $S = [\mu Pf(S)]^{Pm}$;
- *saturated*, if its minimal proofs are exactly the normal-form proofs, or $\mu Pf(S) = Nf(S)$; or
- *complete*, if its set of minimal proofs contains a normal-form proof for every theorem, or $Th\,S = [Pf(S) \cap Nf(S)]_{Cl}$.

A clause is *redundant* in a presentation if adding it – or removing it – does not affect minimal proofs, and a presentation is *irredundant* if it does not contain anything redundant. A presentation is contracted if and only if it is irredundant, and canonical if and only if it is saturated and contracted [33,13].

A *(one-step) deduction mechanism* $\leadsto$ is a binary relation over presentations. A deduction step $S \leadsto S \cup S'$ is an *expansion* provided $S' \subseteq Th\,S$. A deduction step $S \cup S' \leadsto S$ is a *contraction* provided $S \cup S' \succsim S$. A sequence of deductions $S_0 \leadsto S_1 \leadsto \cdots$ is a *derivation*, whose result, or *limit*, is the set of *persisting* formulæ: $S_\infty \overset{!}{=} \bigcup_j \bigcap_{i \geq j} S_i$. Since [55], a fundamental requirement of derivations is *fairness*, doing all inferences that are needed to achieve the desired degree of proof normalization. A *fair* derivation generates a complete set in the limit, a *uniformly fair* derivation generates a saturated limit, and a *contracting* derivation generates a contracted limit. We refer to [13] for these definitions and results, as well as historical notes and references on fairness.

2.3   A Clausal Ordering

Modern theorem provers employ orderings to control and limit inference. Let $\succ$ be a *complete simplification ordering* on atoms and terms over Σ, by which we mean that the ordering is total (on ground terms), monotonic (with respect to term structure), stable (with respect to substitutions), and includes the subterm ordering, meaning that $t[s] \succ s$ for any non-empty context t (hence, $\succ$ is well-founded [26]). See [32], for example, for basic definitions.

Various orderings on Horn clause proofs are possible. Suppose we express atoms as equations and let $t \succ$ TRUE for all terms t over Σ. Literals may be ordered by an ordering $\succ_L$ that measures an equation $l \simeq r$ by the multiset $\{\!\{l, r\}\!\}$ and a disequation $l \not\simeq r$ by the multiset $\{\!\{l, r, l, r\}\!\}$, and compares such multisets by the multiset extension [34] of $\succ$. It follows that $l \not\simeq r \succ_L l \simeq r$, because $\{\!\{l, r, l, r\}\!\}$ is a bigger multiset than is $\{\!\{l, r\}\!\}$, which is desirable, so as to allow $l \simeq r$ to simplify $l \not\simeq r$.

Given this ordering on literals, an ordering $\succ_C$ on clauses is obtained by another multiset extension. An equational clause e of the form $p_1 \simeq q_1, \cdots, p_n \simeq q_n \Rightarrow l \simeq r$, regarded as a multiset of literals, is measured by

$$M(e) \;\overset{!}{=}\; \{\!\{ \{\!\{p_1, q_1, p_1, q_1\}\!\}, \ldots, \{\!\{p_n, q_n, p_n, q_n\}\!\}, \{\!\{l, r\}\!\} \}\!\}$$

and these multisets are compared by the multiset extension of $\succ_L$. Under this ordering, a clause $C \vee p \not\simeq q \vee l \simeq r$ is smaller than a clause $C \vee f[p] \not\simeq f[q] \vee l \simeq r$, because the multiset $M(C) \cup \{\!\{ \{\!\{p, q, p, q\}\!\}, \{\!\{l, r\}\!\} \}\!\}$ is smaller than the multiset $M(C) \cup \{\!\{ \{\!\{f[p], f[q], f[p], f[q]\}\!\}, \{\!\{l, r\}\!\} \}\!\}$. Similarly, a clause $C \vee l \simeq r$ is smaller than a clause $C \vee f[l] \simeq f[r]$, because the multiset $M(C) \cup \{\!\{ \{\!\{l, r\}\!\} \}\!\}$ is smaller than $M(C) \cup \{\!\{ \{\!\{f[l], f[r]\}\!\} \}\!\}$. A clause $C \Rightarrow l \simeq r$ is smaller than a clause $B \Rightarrow l \simeq r$, such that $C \subsetneq B$, because the multiset $M(C) \cup \{\!\{ \{\!\{l, r\}\!\} \}\!\}$ is smaller than the multiset $M(B) \cup \{\!\{ \{\!\{l, r\}\!\} \}\!\}$.

Example 1. If e_1 is $a \simeq b \Rightarrow c \simeq d$, $M(e_1) = \{\!\{ \{\!\{a, b, a, b\}\!\}; \{\!\{c, d\}\!\} \}\!\}$. If e_2 is $f(a) \simeq f(b) \Rightarrow c \simeq d$, $M(e_2) = \{\!\{ \{\!\{f(a), f(b), f(a), f(b)\}\!\}, \{\!\{c, d\}\!\} \}\!\}$. Since $f(a) \succ a$ and $f(b) \succ b$ in any ordering with the subterm property, $e_2 \succ_C e_1$.   □

If S is a set of clauses, we write $M(S)$ also for the multiset of their measures, and $\succ_M$ for the multiset extension of $\succ_C$. Let $>_P$ be the usual proof ordering where proofs are compared by comparing the multisets of their premises: $p >_P q$ if $[p]^{Pm} \succ_M [q]^{Pm}$.

Example 2. Consider the equational theory $\{a \simeq b, b \simeq c, a \simeq c\}$. Different proof orderings induce different canonical presentations.

a. If all proofs are minimal, the canonical saturated presentation is the whole theory, while any pair of equations, like $a \simeq b$ and $b \simeq c$, is sufficient to form a complete presentation, because, in this example, the proof of $a \simeq c$ by transitivity from $\{a \simeq b, b \simeq c\}$ is minimal. Since minimal proofs are not unique, saturated and complete indeed differ.

b. Suppose $a \succ b \succ c$. If all valley proofs are minimal, the whole theory is again the saturated presentation, while the only other complete presentation is $\{a \simeq c, b \simeq c\}$, which gives $a \to c \leftarrow b$ as minimal proof of $a \simeq b$.

c. If $a \succ b \succ c$ and the proof ordering is $>_P$, then minimal proofs are unique. The complete presentation $\{a \simeq c, b \simeq c\}$ is also saturated. The proof of $a \simeq b$ is again $a \to c \leftarrow b$, which is smaller than $a \to b$, since $\{\{\{a, c\}, \{b, c\}\}\} \prec_M \{\{\{a, b\}\}\}$.

d. If a and b are incomparable, that is, $a \neq b \wedge a \not\succ b \wedge b \not\succ a$, and all valley proofs are minimal, $a \leftrightarrow b$ is not a minimal proof, and $\{a \simeq c, b \simeq c\}$ is both complete and saturated.

e. On the other hand, if only trivial proofs are minimal, it is the whole theory $\{a \simeq b, b \simeq c, a \simeq c\}$ that is both saturated and complete.   □

3   Implicational Systems

In this section we study canonicity for propositional Horn theories. We consider propositional implicational systems, that are sets of implications $A \Rightarrow B$, whose antecedent A and consequent B are conjunctions of distinct propositional variables. The notation $A \Rightarrow_S B$ specifies that $A \Rightarrow B \in S$, for given implicational system S.

Let V be a set of propositional variables. A subset $X \subseteq V$ represents the propositional interpretation that assigns the value TRUE to all elements in X and FALSE to all those in $V \setminus X$. Accordingly, a set X is said to *satisfy* an implication $A \Rightarrow B$ over V if either $B \subseteq X$ or else $A \not\subseteq X$. Similarly, we say that X *satisfies* an implicational system S, or is a *model* of S, denoted by $X \models S$, if X satisfies all implications in S.

3.1   Moore Families

A *Moore family* on a given set V is a family $\mathcal{F}$ of subsets of V that contains V and is closed under intersection [12]. Moore families are in one-to-one correspondence with closure operators, where a *closure operator* on V is an operator $\varphi \colon \mathcal{P}(V) \to \mathcal{P}(V)$ that is

- *isotone*, that is, $X \subseteq X'$ implies $\varphi(X) \subseteq \varphi(X')$,
- *extensive*, that is, $X \subseteq \varphi(X)$, and
- *idempotent*, that is, $\varphi(\varphi(X)) = \varphi(X)$.

The Moore family $\mathcal{F}_\varphi$ associated with a given closure operator φ is the set of all fixed points of φ:

$$\mathcal{F}_\varphi \overset{!}{=} \{X \subseteq V : X = \varphi(X)\} .$$

The closure operator $\varphi_{\mathcal{F}}$ associated with a given Moore family $\mathcal{F}$ maps any $X \subseteq V$ to the least element of $\mathcal{F}$ that contains X:

$$\varphi_{\mathcal{F}}(X) \overset{!}{=} \bigcap \{Y \in \mathcal{F} : X \subseteq Y\} .$$

The Moore family $\mathcal{F}_S$ associated with a given implicational system S is the family of the *propositional models* of S, in the sense given above:

$$\mathcal{F}_S \overset{!}{=} \{X \subseteq V : X \models S\}\,.$$

In turn, every Moore family $\mathcal{F}$ can be presented at least by one implicational system, for instance $\{X \Rightarrow \varphi_{\mathcal{F}}(X) : X \subseteq V\}$. Combining the notions of closure operator for a Moore family, and Moore family associated with an implicational system, the closure operator φ_S for implicational system S maps any $X \subseteq V$ to the least model of S that satisfies X [11]:

$$\varphi_S(X) \overset{!}{=} \bigcap\{Y \subseteq V : Y \supseteq X \wedge Y \models S\}\,.$$

Example 3. If $S = \{a \Rightarrow b,\ ac \Rightarrow d,\ e \Rightarrow a\}$ and writing sets as strings, then $\mathcal{F}_S = \{\emptyset, b, c, d, ab, bc, bd, cd, abd, abe, bcd, abcd, abde, abcde\}$ and $\varphi_S(ae) = abe$.
□

As noted in Sect. 2.1, there is an obvious syntactic correspondence between Horn presentations and implicational systems. At the semantic level, there is a correspondence between Horn theories and Moore families, since Horn theories are those theories whose models are closed under intersection, a fact due to McKinsey [65] and later Horn himself [51, Lemma 7]. This result is rephrased in [10] in terms of Boolean functions and Moore families: if a Horn function is defined as a Boolean function whose conjunctive normal form is a conjunction of Horn clauses, a Boolean function is Horn if and only if the set of its true points (equivalently, the set of its models) is a Moore family.[3]

Different implicational systems can describe the same Moore family, like different presentations can describe the same theory. Two implicational systems S and S' are said to be *equivalent* if they have the same Moore family, $\mathcal{F}_S = \mathcal{F}_{S'}$.

3.2   Direct Systems

In this section we investigate the relation between the notion of *direct* implicational system and that of *saturated* presentation with respect to an appropriately chosen deduction mechanism. Directness appeared in [11], motivated by finding an implicational system that allows one to compute $\varphi_S(X)$ efficiently for any X:

Definition 1 (Directness [11, Def. 1]). *An implicational system S is direct if $\varphi_S(X) = S(X)$, where $S(X) \overset{!}{=} X \cup \bigcup\{B : A \Rightarrow_S B \wedge A \subseteq X\}$.*

In other words, a direct implicational system allows one to compute $\varphi_S(X)$ in one single round of forward chaining. In general, $\varphi_S(X) = S^*(X)$, where

$$S^0(X) = X$$
$$S^{i+1}(X) = S(S^i(X))$$
$$S^*(X) = \bigcup_i S^i(X)\,.$$

---

[3] For enumerations of Moore families and related structures, see [31] and Sequences A102894–7 and A108798–801 in [69].

Since S, X and V are all finite, $S^*(X) = S^k(X)$ for the smallest k such that $S^{k+1}(X) = S^k(X)$.

Example 4. The implicational system $S = \{ac \Rightarrow d, e \Rightarrow a\}$ is not direct. Indeed, for $X = ce$, the computation of $\varphi_S(X) = \{acde\}$ requires two rounds of forward chaining, because only after a has been added by $e \Rightarrow a$, can d be added by $ac \Rightarrow d$. That is, $S(X) = \{ace\}$ and $\varphi_S(X) = S^2(X) = S^*(X) = \{acde\}$. □

Generalizing this example, it is sufficient to have two implications $A \Rightarrow_S B$ and $C \Rightarrow_S D$ such that $A \subseteq X$, $C \not\subseteq X$ and $C \subseteq X \cup B$, for $\varphi_S(X)$ to require more than one iteration of forward chaining. Since $A \subseteq X$, but $C \not\subseteq X$, the first round adds B, but not D; since $C \subseteq X \cup B$, D is added in a second round. In the above example, $A \Rightarrow B$ is $e \Rightarrow a$ and $C \Rightarrow D$ is $ac \Rightarrow d$. The conditions $A \subseteq X$ and $C \subseteq X \cup B$ are equivalent to $A \cup (C \setminus B) \subseteq X$, because $C \subseteq X \cup B$ means that whatever is in C and not in B must be in X. Thus, to collapse the two iterations of forward chaining into one, it is sufficient to add the implication $A \cup (C \setminus B) \Rightarrow_S D$. In the example $A \cup (C \setminus B) \Rightarrow_S D$ is $ce \Rightarrow d$. This mechanism can be defined in more abstract terms as the following inference rule:

Implicational overlap

$$\frac{A \Rightarrow BO \quad CO \Rightarrow D}{AC \Rightarrow D} \quad B \cap C = \emptyset \neq O$$

Intuitively, the consequent of the first implication "overlaps" with the antecedent of the second one, whence the conclusion. The condition $O \neq \emptyset$ says that the overlap is non-trivial, and the condition $B \cap C = \emptyset$ says that it is as large as possible. Indeed, if $O = \emptyset$, the conclusion $AC \Rightarrow D$ is subsumed by $C \Rightarrow D$, and if $B \cap C \neq \emptyset$, then an alternate inference is more general. One inference step of this rule will be denoted by $\vdash_I$. Thus, directness can be characterized as follows:

Definition 2 (Generated direct system [11, Def. 4]). *Given an implicational system S, the direct implicational system $I(S)$ generated from S is the smallest implicational system containing S and closed with respect to implicational overlap.*

A main theorem of [11] shows that indeed $\varphi_S(X) = I(S)(X)$. What we call "overlap" is called "exchange" in [10], where a system closed with respect to implicational overlap is said to satisfy an "exchange condition."

As we saw in Sect. 2.1, an implicational system can be rewritten as a unary system or a set of Horn clauses, and vice-versa. Recalling that an implication $A \Rightarrow B$ is equivalent to the bi-implication $AB \Leftrightarrow A$, and using juxtaposition for ACI conjunction, we can view the bi-implication as a rewrite rule $AB \rightarrow A$, where $AB \succ A$ in any well-founded ordering with the subterm property. Accordingly, we have the following:

Definition 3 (Associated rewrite system). *The rewrite system R_X associated to a set $X \subseteq V$ of variables is $R_X = \{x \rightarrow \text{TRUE} : x \in X\}$. The rewrite system R_S associated with an implicational system S is $R_S = \{AB \rightarrow A : A \Rightarrow_S B\}$. Given S and X we can also form the rewrite system $R_X^S = R_X \cup R_S$.*

Example 5. If $S = \{a \Rightarrow b, ac \Rightarrow d, e \Rightarrow a\}$, then $R_S = \{ab \to a, acd \to ac, ae \to e\}$. If $X = ae$, then $R_X = \{a \to \text{TRUE}, e \to \text{TRUE}\}$. Thus, $R_X^S = \{a \to \text{TRUE}, e \to \text{TRUE}, ab \to a, acd \to ac, ae \to e\}$. □

We show that there is a correspondence between implicational overlap and the classical notion of overlap between monomials in Boolean rewriting that was developed for theorem proving in both propositional and first-order logic (e.g. [52,53,4,73]) and applied also to declarative programming (e.g. [28,37,17]). Here we are concerned only with its propositional version:

Equational overlap

$$\frac{AO \to B \quad CO \to D}{M \to N} \quad A \cap C = \emptyset \neq O, \; M \succ N$$

where M and N are the normal forms of BC and AD with respect to $\{AO \to B, CO \to D\}$, and $\succ$ is some ordering on sets of propositions (with the subterm property).

Intuitively, the left hand sides of the two rules "overlap," yielding the proof $BC \leftarrow AOC \to AD$, which justifies the conclusion. One inference step of this rule will be denoted by $\vdash_E$. We observe the correspondence first on the implicational system of Example 4:

Example 6. For $S = \{ac \Rightarrow d, e \Rightarrow a\}$, we have $R_S = \{acd \to ac, ae \to e\}$, and the overlap of the two rewrite rules gives $ace \leftarrow acde \to cde$. Hence, the proof $ce \leftarrow ace \leftarrow acde \to cde$ yields the rewrite rule $cde \to ce$, which corresponds to the implication $ce \Rightarrow d$ generated by implicational overlap. □

Note how an implicational overlap between consequent and antecedent corresponds to an equational overlap between left hand sides, since both antecedent and consequent appears on the left hand sides of rewrite rules representing bi-implications.

Lemma 1. *If $A \Rightarrow B$ and $C \Rightarrow D$ are two non-trivial Horn clauses ($|B| = |D| = 1$, $B \not\subseteq A$, $D \not\subseteq C$), then if $A \Rightarrow B, C \Rightarrow D \vdash_I E \Rightarrow D$ by implicational overlap, then $AB \to A, CD \to C \vdash_E DE \to E$ by equational overlap, and vice-versa. Furthermore, all other equational overlaps are trivial.*

This result reflects the fact that implicational overlap is designed to produce a direct system $I(S)$, which, once fed with a set X, yields its image $\varphi_{I(S)}(X)$ in a single round of forward chaining. Hence, implicational overlap unfolds the forward chaining in the implicational system. Since forward chaining is complete for Horn logic, it is coherent to expect that the only non-trivial equational overlaps are those corresponding to implicational overlaps.

Proof. (If direction.) Assume $A \Rightarrow B, C \Rightarrow D \vdash_I E \Rightarrow D$. Since B is a singleton by hypothesis, it must be that the consequent of the first implication and the antecedent of the second one overlap on B. Thus, $C \Rightarrow D$ is $BF \Rightarrow D$ and the implicational overlap of $A \Rightarrow B$ and $BF \Rightarrow D$ generates $AF \Rightarrow D$. The corresponding rewrite rules are $AB \to A$ and $BFD \to BF$, which also overlap on B yielding the equational overlap

$$AFD \leftarrow ABFD \to ABF \to AF ,$$

which generates the corresponding rule $AFD \to AF$.

(Only if direction.) If $AB \to A, CD \to C \vdash_E DE \to E$, the rewrite rules $AB \to A$ and $CD \to C$ can overlap in four ways: $B \cap C \neq \emptyset$, $A \cap D \neq \emptyset$, $A \cap C \neq \emptyset$ and $B \cap D \neq \emptyset$, which we consider in order.

1. $B \cap C \neq \emptyset$: Since B is a singleton, it must be $B \cap C = B$, hence $C = BF$ for some F. Thus, $CD \to C$ is $BFD \to BF$, and the overlap of $AB \to A$ and $BFD \to BF$ is the same as above, yielding $AFD \to AF$. The corresponding implications $A \Rightarrow B$ and $BF \Rightarrow D$ generate $AF \Rightarrow D$ by implicational overlap.
2. $A \cap D \neq \emptyset$: Since D is a singleton, it must be $A \cap D = D$ or $A = DF$ for some F. Thus, $AB \to A$ is $DFB \to DF$ and the overlap is

$$CF \leftarrow CDF \leftarrow CDFB \to CFB ,$$

   so that $CFB \to CF$ is generated. The corresponding implications $C \Rightarrow D$ and $DF \Rightarrow B$ overlap on D and generate $CF \Rightarrow B$ by implicational overlap.
3. $A \cap C \neq \emptyset$: Let $A = FO$ and $C = OG$, so that the rules are $FOB \to FO$ and $OGD \to OG$, with $O \neq \emptyset$ and $F \cap G = \emptyset$. The resulting equational overlap is trivial: $FOG \leftarrow FOGD \leftarrow FBOGD \to FBOG \to FOG$.
4. $B \cap D \neq \emptyset$: Since B and D are singletons, it must be $B \cap D = B = D$, and rules $AB \to A$ and $CB \to C$ produce the trivial overlap $AC \leftarrow ABC \to AC$.

$\square$

The "if" direction holds also for non-Horn clauses: suppose $A \Rightarrow FO, OG \Rightarrow D \vdash_I AG \Rightarrow D$ by implicational overlap, with $O \neq \emptyset = F \cap G$. The corresponding rewrite rules $AFO \to A$ and $OGD \to OG$ also overlap on O, yielding

$$AGD \leftarrow AFOGD \to AFOG \to AG ,$$

which generates the rule $AGD \to AG$ corresponding to $AG \Rightarrow D$.

Let $\leadsto_I$ be the deduction mechanism of implicational overlap: $S \leadsto_I S'$ if $S' = S \cup \{A \Rightarrow B\}$ and $A \Rightarrow B$ is generated by implicational overlap from implications in S. Clearly, such a deduction mechanism only features expansion. For propositional Horn theories, it is reasonable to assume that minimal proofs are unique, so that complete and saturated, and fair and uniformly fair, coincide. If minimal proofs are not unique, all our results still hold, provided the hypothesis of fairness of derivations is replaced by uniform fairness. For an expansion-only mechanism such as $\leadsto_I$, fairness simply means performing all applicable implicational overlaps eventually. If we apply these concepts to implicational systems and the $\leadsto_I$ deduction mechanism, we have:

Proposition 1. *Given an implicational system S, for all fair derivations $S = S_0 \leadsto_I S_1 \leadsto_I \cdots$, $S_\infty = I(S)$.*

Proof. By fairness, S_∞ is saturated, and therefore closed with respect to implicational overlap. Since $\leadsto_I$ deletes nothing, S_∞ contains S. Since $\leadsto_I$ adds nothing beside implicational overlaps, S_∞ is equal to the smallest system with these properties, that is, $S_\infty = I(S)$. □

Let $\leadsto_E$ be the deduction mechanism of equational overlap: $R \leadsto_E R'$ if $R' = R \cup \{M \to N\}$ and $M \to N$ is generated by equational overlap from rewrite rules in R. Equational overlap combines expansion, in the form of the generation of $BC \leftrightarrow AD$, with contraction – its normalization to $M \to N$, where $M \succ N$. This sort of contraction applied to normalize a newly generated formula, before it is inserted in the database, is called *forward contraction*, while the contraction applied to reduce an equation that was already established is called *backward contraction*. Thus, $\leadsto_E$ features expansion and forward contraction, and therefore is expansion-oriented, since contraction is limited to forward contraction. Similar to $\leadsto_I$, fairness means performing all applicable equational overlaps eventually. Lemma 1 yields the following correspondence between deduction mechanisms:

Lemma 2. *For all implicational systems S, $S \leadsto_I S'$ if and only if $R_S \leadsto_E R_{S'}$.*

Proof

- If $S \leadsto_I S'$ then $R_S \leadsto_E R_{S'}$ follows from the if direction of Lemma 1.
- If $R_S \leadsto_E R'$ then $S \leadsto_I S'$ and $R' = R_{S'}$ follows from the only-if direction of Lemma 1. □

The next theorem shows that for fair derivations the process of completing S with respect to implicational overlap, and turning the result into a rewrite system, is equivalent to the process of translating S into the rewrite system R_S, and then completing it with respect to equational overlap. In other words, completion and translation commute. For the sake of expressivity, we abuse the notation slightly, and use $(R_S)_\infty$ in lieu of R_∞ for the limit of a derivation $R_0 \leadsto_E R_1 \leadsto_E \cdots$ where $R_0 = R_S$.

Theorem 1. *For every implicational system S and for all fair derivations $S = S_0 \leadsto_I S_1 \leadsto_I \cdots$ and $R_S = R_0 \leadsto_E R_1 \leadsto_E \cdots$, we have*

$$R_{(S_\infty)} = (R_S)_\infty .$$

Proof

(a) $R_{(S_\infty)} \subseteq (R_S)_\infty$: for any $AB \to A \in R_{(S_\infty)}$, $A \Rightarrow B \in S_\infty$ by Definition 3; then $A \Rightarrow B \in S_j$ for some $j \geq 0$. Let j be the smallest such index. If $j = 0$, or $S_j = S$, $AB \to A \in R_S$ by Definition 3, and $AB \to A \in (R_S)_\infty$, because $\leadsto_E$ features no backward contraction. If $j > 0$, $A \Rightarrow B$ is generated at stage j by implicational overlap. By Lemma 2 and by fairness of $R_0 \leadsto_E R_1 \leadsto_E \cdots$, $AB \to A \in R_k$ for some $k > 0$. Then $AB \to A \in (R_S)_\infty$, since $\leadsto_E$ features no backward contraction.

(b) $(R_S)_\infty \subseteq R_{(S_\infty)}$: for any $AB \to A \in (R_S)_\infty$, $AB \to A \in R_j$ for some $j \geq 0$. Let j be the smallest such index. If $j = 0$, or $R_j = R_S$, $A \Rightarrow B \in S$ by Definition 3, and $A \Rightarrow B \in S_\infty$, because $\leadsto_I$ features no backward contraction. Hence $AB \to A \in R_{(S_\infty)}$. If $j > 0$, $AB \to A$ is generated at stage j by equational overlap. By Lemma 2 and by fairness of $S_0 \leadsto_I S_1 \leadsto_I \cdots$, $A \Rightarrow B \in S_k$ for some $k > 0$. Then $A \Rightarrow B \in S_\infty$, since $\leadsto_I$ features no backward contraction, and $AB \to A \in R_{(S_\infty)}$ by Definition 3.   □

Since the limit of a fair $\leadsto_I$-derivation is $I(S)$, it follows that:

Corollary 1. *For every implicational system S, and for all fair derivations $S = S_0 \leadsto_I S_1 \leadsto_I \cdots$ and $R_S = R_0 \leadsto_E R_1 \leadsto_E \cdots$, we have*

$$R_{(I(S))} = (R_S)_\infty .$$

3.3 Computing Minimal Models

The motivation for generating $I(S)$ from S is to be able to compute, for any subset $X \subseteq V$, its minimal S-model $\varphi_S(X)$ in one round of forward chaining. In other words, one envisions a two-stage process: in the first stage, S is saturated with respect to implicational overlap to generate $I(S)$; in the second stage, forward chaining is applied to $I(S) \cup X$ to generate $\varphi_{I(S)}(X) = \varphi_S(X)$. In the rewrite-based framework, these two stages can be replaced by one. For any $X \subseteq V$ we can compute $\varphi_S(X) = \varphi_{I(S)}(X)$, by giving as input to a completion procedure the rewrite system R_X^S and extracting the rules in the form $x \to \text{TRUE}$. For this purpose, the deduction mechanism is enriched with contraction rules, as follows:

Simplification

$$\frac{AC \to B \quad C \to D}{AD \to B \quad C \to D} \, AD \succ B \qquad \frac{AC \to B \quad C \to D}{B \to AD \quad C \to D} \, B \succ AD$$

$$\frac{B \to AC \quad C \to D}{B \to AD \quad C \to D} \, ,$$

where A can be empty, and

Deletion

$$\frac{A \leftrightarrow A}{} \, ,$$

which eliminates trivial equalities.

Let $\leadsto_R$ denote the deduction mechanism that extends $\leadsto_E$ with simplification and deletion. Thus, in addition to the simplification applied as forward contraction within equational overlap, there is simplification applied as backward contraction to any rule. Accordingly, we consider derivations that are both fair and contracting, meaning that both expansion and contraction are applied systematically.

The following theorem shows that the completion of R_X^S with respect to $\rightsquigarrow_R$ generates a limit that includes the least S-model of X. As before, we use $(R_X^S)_\infty$ in lieu of R_∞ for the limit of a derivation $R_0 \rightsquigarrow_R R_1 \rightsquigarrow_R \cdots$ where $R_0 = R_X^S$.

Theorem 2. *For all $X \subseteq V$, implicational systems S, and fair and contracting derivations $R_X^S = R_0 \rightsquigarrow_R R_1 \rightsquigarrow_R \cdots$, if $Y = \varphi_S(X) = \varphi_{I(S)}(X)$, then*

$$R_Y \subseteq (R_X^S)_\infty .$$

Proof. By Definition 3, $R_Y = \{x \rightarrow \text{TRUE} : x \in Y\}$. The proof is by induction on the construction of $Y = \varphi_S(X)$.
Base case: If $x \in Y$ because $x \in X$, then $x \rightarrow \text{TRUE} \in R_X$, $x \rightarrow \text{TRUE} \in R_X^S$ and $x \rightarrow \text{TRUE} \in (R_X^S)_\infty$, since a rule in the form $x \rightarrow \text{TRUE}$ is persistent.
Inductive case: If $x \in Y$ because for some $A \Rightarrow_S B$, $B = x$ and $A \subseteq Y$, then $AB \rightarrow A \in R_S$ and $AB \rightarrow A \in R_X^S$. By the induction hypothesis, $A \subseteq Y$ implies that, for all $z \in A$, $z \in Y$ and $z \rightarrow \text{TRUE} \in (R_X^S)_\infty$. Let $j > 0$ be the smallest index in the derivation $R_0 \rightsquigarrow_E R_1 \rightsquigarrow_E \cdots$ such that for all $z \in A$, $z \rightarrow \text{TRUE} \in R_j$. Then there is an $i > j$ such that $x \rightarrow \text{TRUE} \in R_i$, because the rules $z \rightarrow \text{TRUE}$ simplify $AB \rightarrow A$ to $x \rightarrow \text{TRUE}$. It follows that $x \rightarrow \text{TRUE} \in (R_X^S)_\infty$, since a rule in the form $x \rightarrow \text{TRUE}$ is persistent. $\square$

Then, the least S-model of X can be extracted from the saturated set:

Corollary 2. *For all $X \subseteq V$, implicational systems S, and fair and contracting derivations $R_X^S = R_0 \rightsquigarrow_R R_1 \rightsquigarrow_R \cdots$, if $Y = \varphi_S(X) = \varphi_{I(S)}(X)$, then*

$$R_Y = \{x \rightarrow \text{TRUE} : x \rightarrow \text{TRUE} \in (R_X^S)_\infty\} .$$

Proof. If $x \rightarrow \text{TRUE} \in (R_X^S)_\infty$, then $x \rightarrow \text{TRUE} \in R_Y$, and $x \in Y$, by the soundness of equational overlap and simplification. The other direction was established in Theorem 2. $\square$

Example 7. Let $S = \{ac \Rightarrow d, e \Rightarrow a, bd \Rightarrow f\}$ and $X = ce$. Then $Y = \varphi_S(X) = acde$, and $R_Y = \{a \rightarrow \text{TRUE}, c \rightarrow \text{TRUE}, d \rightarrow \text{TRUE}, e \rightarrow \text{TRUE}\}$. On the other hand, for $R_S = \{acd \rightarrow ac, ae \rightarrow e, bdf \rightarrow bd\}$ and $R_X = \{c \rightarrow \text{TRUE}, e \rightarrow \text{TRUE}\}$, completion gives $(R_X^S)_\infty = \{c \rightarrow \text{TRUE}, e \rightarrow \text{TRUE}, a \rightarrow \text{TRUE}, d \rightarrow \text{TRUE}, bf \rightarrow b\}$, where $a \rightarrow \text{TRUE}$ is generated by simplification of $ae \rightarrow e$ with respect to $e \rightarrow \text{TRUE}$, $d \rightarrow \text{TRUE}$ is generated by simplification of $acd \rightarrow ac$ with respect to $c \rightarrow \text{TRUE}$ and $a \rightarrow \text{TRUE}$, and $bf \rightarrow b$ is generated by simplification of $bdf \rightarrow bd$ with respect to $d \rightarrow \text{TRUE}$. Thus, $(R_X^S)_\infty$ includes R_Y, which is made exactly of the rules in the form $x \rightarrow \text{TRUE}$ of $(R_X^S)_\infty$. The direct system $I(S)$ contains the implication $ce \Rightarrow d$, generated by implicational overlap from $e \Rightarrow a$ and $ac \Rightarrow d$. The corresponding equational overlap of $acd \rightarrow ac$ and $ae \rightarrow e$ gives $ce \leftarrow ace \leftarrow acde \rightarrow cde$ and, hence, generates the rule $cde \rightarrow ce$. However, this rule is redundant in the presence of $\{c \rightarrow \text{TRUE}, e \rightarrow \text{TRUE}, d \rightarrow \text{TRUE}\}$ and simplification. $\square$

3.4   Direct-Optimal Systems

Bertet and Nebut [11] refined the notion of direct implicational system into that of *direct-optimal* implicational system. In this subsection, we disprove the conjecture that the direct-optimal implicational system corresponds to the canonical rewrite system with respect to equational overlap and contraction.

Optimality is defined with respect to a measure $|S|$ that counts the sum of the number of occurrences of symbols on each of the two sides of each implication in a system S:

Definition 4 (Optimality [11, Section 2]). *An implicational system S is optimal if, for all equivalent implicational system S', $|S| \leq |S'|$ where*

$$|S| \stackrel{!}{=} \sum_{A \Rightarrow_S B} |A| + |B|$$

and $|A|$ is the cardinality of set A.

From an implicational system S, one can generate an equivalent implicational system $D(S)$ that is direct, optimal, and has the following properties, shown to be necessary and sufficient for directness and optimality (cf. [11, Thm. 2]):

- *extensiveness*: for all $A \Rightarrow_{D(S)} B$, $A \cap B = \emptyset$;
- *isotony*: for all $A \Rightarrow_{D(S)} B$ and $C \Rightarrow_{D(S)} D$, if $C \subset A$, then $B \cap D = \emptyset$;
- *premise property*: for all $A \Rightarrow_{D(S)} B$ and $A \Rightarrow_{D(S)} B'$, $B = B'$;
- *non-empty conclusion property*: for all $A \Rightarrow_{D(S)} B$, $B \neq \emptyset$.

This leads to the following characterization:

Definition 5 (Direct-optimal system [11, Def. 5]). *Given a direct system S, the* direct-optimal *system $D(S)$ generated from S contains precisely the implications*

$$A \Rightarrow \bigcup \{B : A \Rightarrow_S B\} \setminus \{C : D \Rightarrow_S C \wedge D \subsetneq A\} \setminus A,$$

for each set A of propositions – provided the conclusion is non-empty.

From the above four properties, we can deduce an *optimization* procedure, applying – in order – the following rules:

Premise

$$\frac{A \Rightarrow B, \ A \Rightarrow C}{A \Rightarrow BC},$$

Isotony

$$\frac{A \Rightarrow B, \ AD \Rightarrow BE}{A \Rightarrow B, \ AD \Rightarrow E},$$

Extensiveness

$$\frac{AC \Rightarrow BC}{AC \Rightarrow B},$$

Definiteness

$$\frac{A \Rightarrow \emptyset}{}.$$

The first rule merges all rules with the same antecedent A into one and implements the *premise* property. The second rule removes from the consequent thus generated those subsets B that are already implied by subsets A of AD, to enforce *isotony*. The third rule makes sure that antecedents C do not themselves appear in the consequent to enforce *extensiveness*. Finally, implications with empty consequent are eliminated. This latter rule is called *definiteness*, because it eliminates negative clauses, which, for Horn theories, represent queries and are not "definite" clauses.

Clearly, the changes wrought by the optimization rules do not affect the theory. Application of this optimization to the direct implicational system $I(S)$ yields the direct-optimal system $D(S)$ of S.

The following example shows that this notion of optimization does *not* correspond to elimination of redundancies by contraction in completion:

Example 8. Let $S = \{a \Rightarrow b, ac \Rightarrow d, e \Rightarrow a\}$. Then, $I(S) = \{a \Rightarrow b, ac \Rightarrow d, e \Rightarrow a, e \Rightarrow b, ce \Rightarrow d\}$, where $e \Rightarrow b$ is generated by implicational overlap of $e \Rightarrow a$ and $a \Rightarrow b$, and $ce \Rightarrow d$ is generated by implicational overlap of $e \Rightarrow a$ and $ac \Rightarrow d$. Next, optimization replaces $e \Rightarrow a$ and $e \Rightarrow b$ by $e \Rightarrow ab$, so that $D(S) = \{a \Rightarrow b, ac \Rightarrow d, e \Rightarrow ab, ce \Rightarrow d\}$. If we consider the rewriting side, we have $R_S = \{ab \to a, acd \to ac, ae \to e\}$. Equational overlap of $ae \to e$ and $ab \to a$ generates $be \to e$, and equational overlap of $ae \to e$ and $acd \to ac$ generates $cde \to ce$, corresponding to the two implicational overlaps. Thus, $(R_S)_\infty = \{ab \to a, acd \to ac, ae \to e, be \to e, cde \to ce\}$. The rule corresponding to $e \Rightarrow ab$, namely $abe \to e$, would be redundant if added to $(R_S)_\infty$, because it would be reduced to a trivial equivalence by $ae \to e$ and $be \to e$. Thus, the optimization consisting of replacing $e \Rightarrow a$ and $e \Rightarrow b$ by $e \Rightarrow ab$ does not correspond to a rewriting inference. $\square$

The reason for this discrepancy is the different choice of ordering. The procedure of [11] optimizes the overall size of the system. For the above example, we have $|\{e \Rightarrow ab\}| = 3 < 4 = |\{e \Rightarrow a, e \Rightarrow b\}|$. The corresponding proof ordering measures a proof of a from a set X and an implicational system S by a multiset of pairs $\langle |B|, \#_B S \rangle$, for each $B \Rightarrow_S aC$ such that $B \subseteq X$, where $\#_B S$ is the number of implications in S with antecedent B. A proof of a from $X = \{e\}$ and $\{e \Rightarrow ab\}$ will have measure $\{\!\{\langle 1, 1\rangle\}\!\}$, which is smaller than the measure $\{\!\{\langle 1, 2\rangle\}\!\}$ of a proof of a from $X = \{e\}$ and $\{e \Rightarrow a, e \Rightarrow b\}$.

Completion, on the other hand, optimizes with respect to a complete simplification ordering $\succ$. For $\{abe \to e\}$ and $\{ae \to e, be \to e\}$, we have $ae \prec abe$ and $be \prec abe$ by the subterm property of $\succ$, so $\{\!\{ae, e\}\!\} \prec_L \{\!\{abe, e\}\!\}$ and $\{\!\{be, e\}\!\} \prec_L \{\!\{abe, e\}\!\}$ in the multiset extension $\succ_L$ of $\succ$, and $\{\!\{\{\!\{ae, e\}\!\}, \{\!\{be, e\}\!\}\}\!\} \prec_C \{\!\{\{\!\{abe, e\}\!\}\}\!\}$ in the multiset extension $\succ_C$ of $\succ_L$. Indeed, from a rewriting point of view, it is better to have $\{ae \to e, be \to e\}$ than $\{abe \to e\}$, since rules with smaller left-hand side are more applicable.

3.5   Rewrite Optimality

It is apparent that the differences between direct optimality and completion arise because of the application of the *premise* rule. Accordingly, we propose an alternative definition of optimality, one that does not require the *premise* property, because symbols in repeated antecedents are counted only once:

Definition 6 (Rewrite optimality). *An implicational system S is* rewrite-optimal *if $\| S \| \leq \| S' \|$ for all equivalent implicational system S', where the measure $\| S \|$ is defined by:*

$$\| S \| \stackrel{!}{=} |Ante(S)| + |Cons(S)| ,$$

for $Ante(S) \stackrel{!}{=} \{c \in A : \ A \Rightarrow_S B\}$, the set of symbols occurring in antecedents, and $Cons(S) \stackrel{!}{=} \{\!\!\{c \in B : \ A \Rightarrow_S B\}\!\!\}$, the multiset *of symbols occurring in consequents.*

Unlike Definition 4, where antecedents and consequents contribute equally, here symbols in antecedents are counted only once, because $Ante(S)$ is defined as a set – hence, without repetitions – while symbols in consequents are counted as many times as they appear, since $Cons(S)$ is a multiset.

Rewrite optimality appears to be an appropriate choice to work with Horn clauses, because the *premise* property conflicts with the decomposition of non-unary implications (e.g., $a_1 \cdots a_n \Rightarrow c_1 \cdots c_m$) into Horn clauses (e.g., $a_1 \cdots a_n \Rightarrow c_i$ for $1 \leq i \leq n$) that we saw in Sect. 2.1. Indeed, if S is a non-unary implicational system, and S_H is the equivalent Horn system obtained by decomposing non-unary implications, the application of the *premise* rule to S_H undoes the decomposition.

Example 9. Applying rewrite optimality to $S = \{a \Rightarrow b, ac \Rightarrow d, e \Rightarrow a\}$ of Example 8, we have $\|\{e \Rightarrow ab\}\| = 3 = \|\{e \Rightarrow a, e \Rightarrow b\}\|$, so that replacing $\{e \Rightarrow a, e \Rightarrow b\}$ by $\{e \Rightarrow ab\}$ is no longer justified. Thus, $D(S) = I(S) = \{a \Rightarrow b, ac \Rightarrow d, e \Rightarrow a, e \Rightarrow b, ce \Rightarrow d\}$, and the rewrite system associated with $D(S)$ is $(R_S)_\infty = \{ab \to a, acd \to ac, ae \to e, be \to e, cde \to ce\}$. A proof ordering corresponding to rewrite optimality would measure a proof of a from a set X and an implicational system S by the set of the cardinalities $|B|$, for each $B \Rightarrow_S aC$ such that $B \subseteq X$. Accordingly, a proof of a from $X = \{e\}$ and $\{e \Rightarrow ab\}$ will have measure $\{\!\!\{1\}\!\!\}$, which is the same as the measure of a proof of a from $X = \{e\}$ and $\{e \Rightarrow a, e \Rightarrow b\}$. $\qquad\square$

Thus, we deem *canonical* the result of optimization without *premise* rule:

Definition 7 (Canonical system). *Given an implicational system S, the* canonical *implicational system $O(S)$ generated from S is the closure of S with respect to implicational overlap, isotony, extensiveness and definiteness.*

Let $\leadsto_O$ denote the deduction mechanism that features implicational overlap as expansion rule and the optimization rules except *premise*, namely *isotony*, *extensiveness* and *definiteness*, as contraction rules. Then, we have:

Proposition 2. *Given an implicational system S, for all fair and contracting derivations $S = S_0 \leadsto_O S_1 \leadsto_O \cdots$, $S_\infty = O(S)$.*

Proof. If the derivation is fair and contracting, both expansion and contraction rules are applied systematically. Hence, the result. □

The following lemma shows that every inference by $\leadsto_O$ is covered by an inference in $\leadsto_R$:

Lemma 3. *For all implicational systems S, if $S \leadsto_O S'$, then $R_S \leadsto_R R_{S'}$.*

Proof. We consider four cases, corresponding to the four inference rules in $\leadsto_O$:

1. *Implicational overlap:* If $S \leadsto_O S'$ by an implicational overlap step, then $R_S \leadsto_R R_{S'}$ by equational overlap, by Lemma 2.
2. *Isotony:* For an application of this rule, $S = S'' \cup \{A \Rightarrow B, AD \Rightarrow BE\}$ and $S' = S'' \cup \{A \Rightarrow B, AD \Rightarrow E\}$. Then, $R_S = R_{S''} \cup \{AB \to A, ADBE \to AD\}$. Simplification applies to R_S using $AB \to A$ to rewrite $ADBE \to AD$ to $ADE \to AD$, yielding $R_{S''} \cup \{AB \to A, ADE \to AD\} = R_{S'}$.
3. *Extensiveness:* When this rule applies, $S = S'' \cup \{AC \Rightarrow BC\}$ and $S' = S'' \cup \{AC \Rightarrow B\}$. Then, $R_S = R_{S''} \cup \{ACBC \to AC\}$. By mere idempotence of juxtaposition, $R_S = R_{S''} \cup \{ABC \to AC\} = R_{S'}$.
4. *Definiteness:* If $S = S' \cup \{A \Rightarrow \emptyset\}$, then $R_S = R_{S'} \cup \{A \leftrightarrow A\}$ and an application of deletion eliminates the trivial equation, yielding $R_{S'}$. □

However, the other direction of this lemma does not hold. Although every equational overlap is covered by an implicational overlap and deletions correspond to applications of the definiteness rules, there are simplifications by $\leadsto_R$ that do not correspond to inferences in $\leadsto_O$:

Example 10. Assume that the implicational system S includes $\{de \Rightarrow b, b \Rightarrow d\}$. Accordingly, R_S contains $\{deb \to de, bd \to b\}$. A simplification inference applies $bd \to b$ to reduce $deb \to de$ to $be \leftrightarrow de$, which is oriented into $be \to de$, if $b \succ d$, and into $de \to be$, if $d \succ b$. (Were $\leadsto_R$ equipped with a cancellation inference rule, $be \leftrightarrow de$ could be rewritten to $b \leftrightarrow d$, whence $b \to d$ or $d \to b$.) The deduction mechanism $\leadsto_O$ can apply implicational overlap to $de \Rightarrow b$ and $b \Rightarrow d$ to generate $de \Rightarrow d$. However, $de \Rightarrow d$ is reduced to $de \Rightarrow \emptyset$ by the extensiveness rule, and $de \Rightarrow \emptyset$ is deleted by the definiteness rule. Thus, $\leadsto_O$ does not generate anything that corresponds to $be \leftrightarrow de$. □

This example can be generalized to provide a simple analysis of simplification steps, one that shows which steps correspond to $\leadsto_O$-inferences and which do not. Assume we have two rewrite rules $AB \to A$ and $CD \to C$, corresponding to non-trivial Horn clauses ($|B| = 1$, $B \not\subseteq A$, $|D| = 1$, $D \not\subseteq C$), and such that $CD \to C$ simplifies $AB \to A$. We distinguish three cases:

1. In the first one, CD appears in AB because CD appears in A. In other words, $A = CDE$ for some E. Then, the simplification step is

$$\frac{CDEB \to CDE,\ CD \to C}{CEB \to CE,\ CD \to C}$$

(where simplification is actually applied to both sides). The corresponding implications are $A \Rightarrow B$ and $C \Rightarrow D$. Since $A \Rightarrow B$ is $CDE \Rightarrow B$, implicational overlap applies to generate the implication $CE \Rightarrow B$ that corresponds to $CEB \rightarrow CE$:

$$\frac{C \Rightarrow D,\ CDE \Rightarrow B}{CE \Rightarrow B}.$$

The isotony rule applied to $CE \Rightarrow B$ and $CDE \Rightarrow B$ reduces the latter to $CDE \Rightarrow \emptyset$, which is then deleted by the definiteness rule. Thus, a combination of implicational overlap, isotony and definiteness simulates the effects of simplification.

2. In the second case, CD appears in AB because C appears in A, that is, $A = CE$ for some E, and $D = B$. Then, the simplification step is

$$\frac{CEB \rightarrow CE,\ CB \rightarrow C}{CE \leftrightarrow CE,\ CB \rightarrow C},$$

and there is an isotony inference

$$\frac{C \Rightarrow B,\ CE \Rightarrow B}{C \Rightarrow B,\ CE \Rightarrow \emptyset},$$

which generates the trivial implication $CE \Rightarrow \emptyset$ corresponding to the trivial equation $CE \leftrightarrow CE$. Both are deleted by definiteness and deletion, respectively.

3. The third case is the generalization of Example 10: CD appears in AB because D appears in A, and C is made of B and some F that also appears in A, that is, $A = DEF$ for some E and F, and $C = BF$. The simplification step is

$$\frac{DEFB \rightarrow DEF,\ BFD \rightarrow BF}{BFE \leftrightarrow DEF,\ BFD \rightarrow BF}.$$

Implicational overlap applies

$$\frac{DEF \Rightarrow B,\ BF \Rightarrow D}{DEF \Rightarrow D}$$

to generate an implication that is first reduced by extensiveness to $DEF \Rightarrow \emptyset$ and then eliminated by definiteness. Thus, nothing corresponding to $BFE \leftrightarrow DEF$ is generated.

It follows that whatever is generated by $\leadsto_{\mathrm{O}}$ is generated by $\leadsto_{\mathrm{R}}$, but may become redundant eventually:

Theorem 3. *For every implicational system S, for all fair and contracting derivations $S = S_0 \leadsto_{\mathrm{O}} S_1 \leadsto_{\mathrm{O}} \cdots$ and $R_S = R_0 \leadsto_{\mathrm{R}} R_1 \leadsto_{\mathrm{R}} \cdots$, for all $FG \rightarrow F \in R_{(S_\infty)}$, either $FG \rightarrow F \in (R_S)_\infty$ or $FG \rightarrow F$ is redundant in $(R_S)_\infty$.*

Proof. For all $FG \to F \in R_{(S_\infty)}$, $F \Rightarrow G \in S_\infty$ by Definition 3, and $F \Rightarrow G \in S_j$ for some $j \geq 0$. Let j be the smallest such index. If $j = 0$, or $S_j = S$, $FG \to F \in R_S = R_0$ by Definition 3. If $j > 0$, $F \Rightarrow G$ was generated by an application of implicational overlap, the isotony rule or extensiveness. By Lemma 3 and the assumption that the $\leadsto_R$-derivation is fair and contracting, $FG \to F \in R_k$ for some $k > 0$. In both cases, $FG \to F \in R_k$ for some $k \geq 0$. If $FG \to F$ persists, then $FG \to F \in (R_S)_\infty$. Otherwise, $FG \to F$ is rewritten by simplification and is therefore redundant in $(R_S)_\infty$. $\qquad\square$

Since the limit of a fair and contracting $\leadsto_O$-derivation is $O(S)$, it follows that:

Corollary 3. *For every implicational system S, for all fair and contracting derivations $S = S_0 \leadsto_O S_1 \leadsto_O \cdots$ and $R_S = R_0 \leadsto_R R_1 \leadsto_R \cdots$, and for all $FG \to F \in R_{O(S)}$, either $FG \to F \in (R_S)_\infty$ or $FG \to F$ is redundant in $(R_S)_\infty$.*

4   Conditional Rewrite Systems

In this section we investigate canonicity in *conditional equational theories*, focusing on the ground case. We study conditional reduction and we propose a notion of *reducedness*, where also conditions themselves are subject to reduction, so that it may be possible to "reduce" overly-complex conditions, without affecting the equality relation. It follows that for conditional equational theories, unlike for equational ones, being *reduced* and being *contracted* are distinct. As a consequence, perfect systems – complete and reduced – and canonical systems – saturated and contracted – also differ.

4.1   Decreasing Systems

To use conditional equations for simplification, one needs to establish that the conditions hold. If testing the validity of the conditions yields a problem that is as difficult as the one we would like to solve by applying conditional equations, conditional simplification becomes unpractical. In other words, the complexity of conditions should be bounded. Therefore, we start with a notion of *decreasing-ness*, which appeared in [29] and ensures that testing conditions does not yield bigger problems:

Definition 8 (Decreasing conditional equation). *A ground conditional equation $p_1 \simeq q_1, \cdots, p_n \simeq q_n \Rightarrow l \simeq r$ is decreasing if $l \succ r, p_1, q_1, \ldots, p_n, q_n$; a conditional equation is decreasing if all its ground instances are.*

A *decreasing inference* is an application of the following inference rule:

$$\frac{C \Rightarrow l \simeq r \quad w_1 \quad \cdots \quad w_n}{C \setminus \{w_1, \ldots w_n\} \Rightarrow f[l] \simeq f[r]} \qquad f[l] \simeq f[r] \succ_C C$$

where f is any context and $w_1 \ldots w_n$ are equations. If $C \setminus \{w_1, \ldots w_n\} = \emptyset$, an equation is deduced; otherwise, a conditional equation is deduced, where those conditions that are not discharged remain part of the conclusion. Condition $f[l] \simeq f[r] \succ_C C$ characterizes the inference as *decreasing*. Since $\succ$ is a simplification ordering and therefore has the subterm property, $f[l] \simeq f[r] \succ_C l \simeq r$ also holds. Thus, $f[l] \simeq f[r] \succ_C (C \Rightarrow l \simeq r)$ follows. On the other hand, the subproofs of the w_i may contain larger premises.

The *depth of a decreasing inference* is 0 if $f[l] = f[r]$ (a trivial equation is deduced) or $n = 0$ (no subproofs). Otherwise, it is 1. The *depth of a proof* is the sum of the depth of its inferences, that is, the number of non-trivial inferences where a conditional equation is applied and some if its conditions are discharged. Thus, purely equational proofs have depth 0, because they do not have conditions.

Definition 9 (Equivalence). *Given a presentation S of a theory, two terms s and t are S-equivalent, written $s \equiv_S t$, if there is a proof p, such that $[p]_{Cl} = s \simeq t$ and $[p]^{Pm} \subseteq S$, made of decreasing inferences.*

We can use minimal elements of S-equivalence classes as their representatives:

Definition 10 (Normal form). *The S-normal form of a term t is the $\succ$-minimal element of its S-equivalence class.*

By the same token, a term t is in *normal form* with respect to S, if it is its own S-normal form.

4.2   Reduced Systems

Given a set S of conditional equations, we are interested in a reduced version of S. Computing a reduced system involves deletion of trivial conditional equations, subsumption and simplification, as defined by the following inference rules:

Deletion

$$\frac{C \Rightarrow r \simeq r}{} \qquad \frac{C, l \simeq r \Rightarrow l \simeq r}{}$$

Subsumption

$$\frac{C, D \Rightarrow u[l] \simeq u[r] \quad C \Rightarrow l \simeq r}{C \Rightarrow l \simeq r}$$

Simplification

$$\frac{C, p \simeq q \Rightarrow l[p] \simeq r}{C, p \simeq q \Rightarrow l[q] \simeq r} \quad p \succ q \qquad \frac{C, p \simeq q, u[p] \simeq v \Rightarrow l \simeq r}{C, p \simeq q, u[q] \simeq v \Rightarrow l \simeq r} \quad p \succ q$$

$$\frac{C, D \Rightarrow l[u] \simeq r \quad C \Rightarrow u \simeq v}{C, D \Rightarrow l[v] \simeq r \quad C \Rightarrow u \simeq v} \quad u \succ v,$$

where the first two simplification rules use a condition to simplify the consequence or another condition of the same conditional equation, while the third one applies a conditional equation $C \Rightarrow u \simeq v$ to simplify another conditional equation whose conditions include C. Inferences shown on the left-hand side of $\simeq$ apply also to the right-hand side, since $\simeq$ is symmetric.

These inference rules produce a reduced system according to the following definition:

Definition 11 (S-reduced). *Let $S = S' \uplus \{e\}$ be a presentation, where $e = (C \Rightarrow l \simeq r)$ is a conditional equation, $C = \{p_i \simeq q_i\}_{i=1}^n$, and, for convenience, $l \succ r$ and $p_i \succ q_i$, for all i, $1 \leq i \leq n$. Then, e is S-reduced if*

1. *e is not trivial,*
2. *no conditional equation in S' subsumes e,*
3. *l is in $(S' \cup C)$-normal form,*
4. *r is in $(S \cup C)$-normal form,*
5. *for all i, $1 \leq i \leq n$,*
   (a) p_i is in $(S' \cup (C \setminus \{p_i \simeq q_i\}))$-normal form and
   (b) q_i is in $(S' \cup C)$-normal form.

The difference between Item 3 and Item 4 is designed to prevent $C \Rightarrow l \simeq r$ from simplifying itself. In Item 5, a condition $p \simeq q \in C$ is normalized also with respect to the other equalities in C, because all equalities in C must be true to apply a conditional equation e. Thus, the notion of reducedness incorporates the notion of reduction with respect to a context as in the *conditional contextual rewriting* proposed by Zhang [74]. The difference between Item 5a and Item 5b is meant to prevent $p_i \simeq q_i$ from simplifying itself. Thus, we can safely define the following:

Definition 12 (Self-reduced). *A conditional equation e is self-reduced, if it is $\{e\}$-reduced. The self-reduced form of e is denoted $e^\flat$.*

Example 11. For $S = \{e_1, e_2\}$, where e_1 is $a \simeq b \Rightarrow c \simeq d$, and e_2 is $f(a) \simeq f(b) \Rightarrow c \simeq d$, as in Example 1, both e_1 and e_2 are S-reduced. $\qquad\square$

Definition 13 (Reduced). *A presentation S is reduced, if all its elements are S-reduced.*

Definition 14 (Perfect). *A presentation S is perfect, if it is complete and reduced.*

Example 12. Let $S = \{e_1, e_2\}$, where e_1 is $a \simeq b \Rightarrow f(a) \simeq c$ and e_2 is $a \simeq b \Rightarrow f(b) \simeq c$, with $f > a > b > c$. The presentation S is not reduced, because clause e_1 is not. Indeed, the normal form of $f(a)$ with respect to $(S \setminus \{e_1\}) \cup \{a \simeq b\}$ is c, and the reduced form of e_1 is the trivial clause $a \simeq b \Rightarrow c \simeq c$. Clause e_2 is reduced. $\qquad\square$

Proposition 3. *If S is reduced, then it is contracted.*

Proof. Assume that S is not contracted. Then, there exists an $e \in S$, such that $e \notin [\mu Pf(S)]^{Pm}$ (see Sect. 2.2). In other words, if $e \in [p]^{Pm}$, then $p \notin \mu Pf(S)$. For each such p, there is a $q \in \mu Pf(S)$, such that $p > q$ and $e \notin [q]^{Pm}$. By monotonicity of the proof ordering with respect to subproofs (cf. Property 3 in Sect. 2.2), proof p must contain a subproof involving e, possibly consisting of e itself, which is replaced by a smaller subproof in q. Thus, proof p and premise e must contain at least a term that is not in S-normal form. Hence, e is not in S-reduced form, and S is not reduced.   □

On the other hand, a presentation can be contracted but not reduced, as shown in the following example:

Example 13. If $a > b > c$, neither $a \simeq b \Rightarrow b \simeq c$ nor $a \simeq b \Rightarrow a \simeq c$ is decreasing. The presentations $S_1 = \{a \simeq b \Rightarrow b \simeq c\}$, $S_2 = \{a \simeq b \Rightarrow a \simeq c\}$, and $S_3 = \{a \simeq b \Rightarrow b \simeq c, \ a \simeq b \Rightarrow a \simeq c\}$ are equivalent. However, S_1 is reduced, whereas S_2 is not, since the S_2-reduced form of $a \simeq b \Rightarrow a \simeq c$ is $a \simeq b \Rightarrow b \simeq c$. Neither is S_3 reduced, although it is contracted. Indeed, while $a \simeq b \Rightarrow b \simeq c$ is S_3-reduced, the S_3-reduced form of $a \simeq b \Rightarrow a \simeq c$ is the trivial clause $a \simeq c \Rightarrow a \simeq c$.   □

Unlike the ground equational case, where contracted and canonical collapse to reduced, because all inferences consist of rewriting, in the conditional case contracted and reduced are different (like S_3 in Example 13). Furthermore, decreasing simplification is "incomplete" with respect to Definition 11, because non-reduced presentations may not be reducible by decreasing simplification, as the clauses are not decreasing (like S_2 and S_3 in Example 13). The following lemma and theorem follow from the definitions.

Lemma 4. *A conditional equation e has a normal-form proof in presentation S, if the S-reduced form of e^b is subsumed by a conditional equation in S.*

Theorem 4. *If S is canonical, then S subsumes the S-reduced form of every theorem of S.*

Example 14. Consider again the three presentations of Example 13, $e_1 = a \simeq b \Rightarrow b \simeq c$ and $e_2 = a \simeq b \Rightarrow a \simeq c$. We have $e_1^b = a \simeq b \Rightarrow b \simeq c = e_2^b$. Thus, both S_1 and S_3 are complete (and saturated), because they contain $a \simeq b \Rightarrow b \simeq c$. On the other hand, S_2 does not, and therefore it is not complete. In summary, S_1 is perfect (reduced and complete), S_3 is canonical (contracted and saturated), whereas S_2 is neither.   □

In summary, in the conditional case, a perfect system – complete and reduced – and a canonical system – saturated and contracted – differ in two ways: complete is weaker than saturated, and reduced is stronger than contracted. Since complete/saturated determines how much expansion is required in completion, whereas reduced/contracted refers to how much simplification completion should feature, both discrepancies hint that the perfect system is really the best system, as the name suggests.

5   Horn Normal Forms

In this section, we survey proof normalization and decision procedures, based on canonical systems, in Horn theories and beyond. Since $Th\,S$ is defined based on proofs (cf. Sect. 2.2), the choice of normal-form proofs is intertwined with the choice of the deduction mechanism that generates the proofs. This double choice is guided by the purpose of ensuring that $S^\sharp$ forms the basis for a decision procedure. To achieve decidability, the various notions of normal-form proof aim at minimizing non-deterministic choice-points that require search. Then, Horn proofs may have the following qualities:

- *Linear*: in *linear resolution proofs* at each step a *center clause* is resolved with a *side clause*, to generate the next center clause (see, for instance, Chapter 7 in the book by Chang and Lee [23]). The first center clause, or *top clause*, is the goal given by the problem. Linearity eliminates one choice point, because the main premise of the next step must be whatever was generated by the previous step.
- *Linear input*: the choice of side clauses is restricted to input clauses [23].
- *Reducing*: a linear proof is reducing if each center clause is smaller than its predecessor in the ordering $\succ_C$ – this implies termination [18].
- *Unit-resulting*: each step must generate a unit clause; thus, all literals but one must be resolved away, which eliminates the choice of literal in the center clause, but may require multiple side clauses (traditionally called *satellites* or *electrons* as in the *unit-resulting resolution* of McCharen, Overbeek and Wos [64]).
- *Confluent*: whatever choices are left, such as choice of side premise(s) or choice of subterm, are irrelevant for finding or not finding a proof, which means they will never need to be undone by backtracking.

Valley proofs for purely equational theories satisfy all these properties, some vacuously (like unit-resulting). In this section we survey different choices of normal-form proofs for Horn theories, and we examine how they yield different requirements on canonical presentations, and on the completion procedures that generate them at the limit.

5.1   Trivial Proofs

If trivial proofs are assumed to be normal-form proofs, closure with respect to *forward chaining* gives the canonical presentation. Canonical, saturated and complete coincide. Given a Horn presentation S, $S^\sharp$ is made of all ground facts that follow from S and the axioms of equality by forward chaining. In other words, $S^\sharp$ is the least Herbrand model of S, and, equivalently, the least fixed-point of the mapping associated to program S and the axioms of equality in the fixed point semantics of logic programming (see the aforementioned surveys [1,50] or Lloyd's book [62]).

Existence of the least Herbrand model is a consequence of the defining property of Horn theories, namely closure of the family of models with respect to intersection. This is also the basis upon which to draw a correspondence between Horn clauses with *unary* predicate symbols and certain tree automata, called *two-way alternating tree automata* (cf. [24, Sec. 7.6.3]). Tree automata are automata that accept trees, or, equivalently, terms. Given a Horn presentation S, the predicate symbols in S are the states of the automaton. As usual, a subset of states is defined to be *final*. Then, the essence of the correspondence is that a ground term t is accepted by the automaton if the atom $r(t)$ is in $S^{\sharp}$ and r is final. The deduction mechanism for computing the accepted terms is still *forward chaining*. It is sufficient to have unary predicate symbols, because the notion of being accepted applies to *one* term at a time. This restriction is advantageous because many properties in the *monadic fragment* are decidable. For the class of two-way alternating tree automata, clauses are further restricted to have one of the following forms:

1. $a_1(x_1), \ldots, a_n(x_n) \Rightarrow c(u)$, where $x_1, \ldots, x_n$ are (not necessarily distinct) variables, u is a linear, non-variable term, and $x_1, \ldots, x_n \in Var(u)$;
2. $a(u) \Rightarrow c(x)$, where u is a linear term and x is a variable; and
3. $a_1(x), \ldots, a_n(x) \Rightarrow c(x)$.

We refer the interested reader to [24] for more details and results.

5.2   Ground-Preserving Linear Input Proofs

According to Kounalis and Rusinowitch [60], normal-form proofs for Horn theories with equality are *linear input* proofs by ordered resolution and ordered superposition, where only maximal literals are resolved upon, and only maximal sides of maximal literals are superposed into and from. Furthermore, in order to have a normal-form proof, all side clauses $p_1 \simeq q_1, \cdots, p_n \simeq q_n \Rightarrow l \simeq r$ in the proof must be *ground-preserving*: $Var(p_i \simeq q_i) \subseteq Var(l \simeq r)$, for all i, $1 \leq i \leq n$, and either $l \succ r$ or $r \succ l$, or $Var(l) = Var(r)$.

A conjecture is a conjunction $\forall \bar{x} \; u_1 \simeq v_1, \ldots, u_k \simeq v_k$, whose negation is a ground (Skolemized) negative clause $\tilde{u}_1 \not\simeq \tilde{v}_1 \vee \cdots \vee \tilde{u}_k \not\simeq \tilde{v}_k$. If all side clauses are ground-preserving and the top clause is ground, all center clauses will also be ground. This, together with the ordering restrictions on resolution and superposition and the assumption that the ordering is a complete simplification ordering – hence, is total on ground terms, literals and clauses – imply that every center clause is smaller than its parent center clause, so that proofs are *reducing*.

Therefore, a finite presentation that features such a normal-form proof for every conjunction of positive literals is a *decision procedure*. The *Horn completion procedure* of [60], with ordered resolution, superposition, simplification by conditional equations, and subsumption, generates at the limit a *saturated* presentation, which is such a decision procedure, if it is finite and all its clauses are ground-preserving.

5.3   Linear Input Unit-Resulting Proofs

An approach for Horn logic without equality was studied by Baumgartner in his book on *theory reasoning* [9]. Here normal-form proofs of conjunctions of positive literals are *linear input unit-resulting* (UR) resolution proofs. A completion procedure, called *Linearizing Completion*, applies selected resolution inferences and additions of contrapositives to compile the given presentation into one that offers normal-form proofs for all conjunctions of positive literals. The name "Linearizing" evokes the transformation of UR-resolution proofs (not in normal form) into linear UR-resolution proofs (in normal form).

If finite, the resulting saturated presentation is used as a decision procedure for the Horn theory in the context of *partial theory model elimination*. Similar to *partial theory resolution* of Stickel [70], a *decision procedure* that generates conditions for the unsatisfiability of a set of literals in the theory, as opposed to deciding unsatisfiability, suffices. The saturated presentation generated by Linearizing Completion is a decision procedure in this weaker sense.

5.4   Valley Proofs

If the notion of normal-form proof of the unconditional case is generalized to the conditional case, normal-form proofs are valley proofs of depth 0, where all conditions have been solved away. The *Maximal Unit Strategy* of [30] achieves this effect by restricting expansion inferences to have at least one unit premise: it applies superposition between unconditional equations and to superpose unconditional equations into maximal terms of conditions.

In the limit, the saturated set contains all positive unit theorems, or, equivalently, all conditional equations are redundant [18], so that there is a normal-form proof for every theorem. However, such a presentation will be infinite in most cases, so that the *Maximal Unit Strategy* is better seen as a *semi-decision procedure* for forward-reasoning theorem proving, rather than as a generator of decision procedures [29].

5.5   Nested Valley Proofs

In [29,30], a normal-form proof of $s \simeq t$ is a valley proof, in which each subproof is also in normal form, and each term in a subproof is smaller than the greater of s and t. To enforce the latter constraint, only *decreasing instances of conditional equations* are applied. The *Decreasing Strategy* of [29,30] simplifies by *decreasing instances* of conditional equations and applies ordered paramodulation/superposition of decreasing instances, to generate at the limit a saturated presentation that features normal-form proofs for all theorems. Our analysis in Sect. 4 started from this point to develop the notions of reduced and perfect system, showing the incompleteness of decreasing simplification with respect to reducedness and the difference between canonical and perfect system.

If we compare this notion of normal-form proof based on decreasingness with the conditional valley proofs of null depth of Sect. 5.4, we see that decreasingness allows *nested* valley proofs, or, equivalently, it does not require that normal-form proofs have depth 0: this means renouncing linearity.

To compare with the ground-preserving linear input proofs of Sect. 5.2, consider a conditional equation that is not ground-preserving, such as

$p_1 \simeq q_1, \cdots, p_n \simeq q_n \Rightarrow l \simeq r$, where $l \succ r$ and either r, or one of the p_i's, or one of the q_i's, for some i, $1 \leq i \leq n$, contains a variable that does not occur in l. Such a conditional equation cannot be decreasing. However, the motivations for the two conditions are different. The motivation for the ground-preserving property is to ensure that proofs are reducing. The motivation for decreasingness, which improved upon previous suggestions in [57,56], is to capture exactly the finiteness of recursive evaluation of terms.

Another significant difference between decreasingness, on one hand, and earlier requirements, on the other, including the ground-preserving condition and the requirements studied by Kaplan and Rémy [58] or Ganzinger [47], is that they are static properties of conditional rewrite rules or equations, whereas decreasingness is tested dynamically on the applied instances. This difference resembles the one between Knuth-Bendix completion [59], where all equations must be oriented, and Unfailing, or Ordered, Completion, that applies oriented instances of unoriented equations [20,61,54,6,5,18].

5.6   Quasi-Horn Theories

A generalization of the approach of Sect. 5.2 was given by Bachmair and Ganzinger in [7], by considering *quasi-Horn clauses* and replacing the ground-preserving property with the *universally reductive* property.

A clause C is *quasi-Horn* if it has at most one positive equational literal, and, if there is one – say $l \simeq r$, then $(l \simeq r)\sigma$ is maximal in $C\sigma$ for all ground instances $C\sigma$ of C. A general clause C is *universally reductive* if it contains a literal L such that (i) $Var(C) \subseteq Var(L)$, (ii) for all ground substitutions σ, $L\sigma$ is strictly maximal in $C\sigma$, (iii) if L is an equational literal, it is a positive equation $s \simeq t$, such that $Var(s \simeq t) \subseteq Var(s)$ and for all ground substitutions σ, $s\sigma \succ t\sigma$. Clause C is said to be universally reductive for L. Clearly, if a quasi-Horn clause that contains a positive equation is universally reductive, it is universally reductive for the positive equation.

A quasi-Horn clause is more general than a Horn clause, because it allows more than one positive literal, provided they are not equations: if there is a positive equation, then it must be unique and maximal. A quasi-Horn clause C that contains a positive equation $l \simeq r$ will be involved only in superposition inferences into, or from, $l \simeq r$: ordered resolution does not apply to C, because its non-equational literals are not maximal; ordered factoring and equality resolution,[4] are not applicable either, because C has only one positive literal and its negative literals are not maximal. Furthermore, superposition of C into a clause without positive equations will produce another clause without positive equations. In essence, the notion of quasi-Horn clause serves the purpose of making sure that the equational part of the problem is Horn, and can be dealt with separately with respect to the non-equational part, which may be non-Horn and require ordered resolution and ordered factoring.

---

[4] Equality resolution is ordered resolution with $x \simeq x$.

The notion of goal is generalized from ground negative clause to ground clause without positive equations, and the notion of normal-form proof for such a goal is weakened accordingly: the equational reasoning part by ordered superposition is *linear*, whereas the ordered resolution and ordered factoring part for the non-equational component is not necessarily linear. A finite saturated set of universally-reductive quasi-Horn clauses is a *decision procedure* in that it provides a normal-form proof for all goals in this form.

5.7 Beyond Quasi-Horn

It is well known that the restrictions of general inferences that are complete for Horn logic (including *linear input resolution, unit resolution, forward chaining*) are not complete for full first-order logic (see [23]). In the non-equational case, linear input proofs must be replaced by linear proofs, involving also *factoring* and *ancestor-resolution* inferences. In the presence of equality, one needs to deal with the interplay of the equational and non-equational parts in its full generality. Nevertheless, completion procedures to generate saturated or canonical presentations have been investigated also in the unrestricted first-order context. One purpose is to find whether inference systems or strategies that are not complete for first-order logic, may become complete if a canonical, or at least saturated, presentation is given.

An example is the classical *resolution with set of support* of Wos et al. [72], where the set of support initially contains the goal clauses (those resulting from the negation of the conjecture), its complement contains the presentation, and all generated clauses are added to the set of support. This is complete for resolution in first-order logic, but it is not complete for ordered resolution and superposition in first-order logic with equality. However, it is well known that, if the presentation is saturated, then the set of support strategy is complete also for first-order logic with equality and ordered inferences, for the simple reason that all inferences from the saturated presentation are redundant.

For first-order theories, in general, there is no finite canonical presentation that forms the basis for a decision procedure. Obtaining decision procedures for fragments of first-order logic rests on some combination of saturation by completion and syntactic constraints on the presentation. A survey can be found in [42]. More recent results based on syntactic constraints include those of Comon-Lundh and Courtier in [25]. In [40], Dowek studied proof normalization in the context of a sequent calculus modulo a congruence on terms, where normal-form proofs are cut-free proofs.

Another thread of research on decision procedures is that of *satisfiability modulo a theory* (SMT), where T-*satisfiability* is the problem of deciding satisfiability of a set of ground literals in theory T. Armando et al. [3,2] proved that a rewrite-based inference system for first-order logic with equality is guaranteed to generate finitely many clauses when applied to T-satisfiability problems in several theories of data structures, and any of their combinations. Thus, such an inference system equipped with a fair search plan yields a decision procedure for T-satisfiability in those theories. Bonacina and Echenim generalized this approach to T-satisfiability in theories of *recursive data structures* [14], extended it to decide T-satisfiability of arbitrary ground formulæ [15], and investigated how using a rewrite-based inference system as a pre-processor for an SMT-solver yields decision procedures [16]. Lynch and Morawska [63] combined the approach of [3] with syntactic constraints to obtain complexity bounds for some theories. Bonacina, Lynch and de Moura obtained more decision procedures by equipping a theorem prover that integrates superposition into an SMT-solver with *speculative inferences* [19].

5.8   Knowledge Representation

In the context of knowledge representation, various forms of *knowledge compilation* have been studied to transform a given knowledge base into a normal form that enables efficient reasoning. Roussel and Mathieu [68] investigated the problem of "completing" a knowledge base, so that forward chaining becomes complete also in the first-order case (without equality). An *achieved* knowledge base corresponds to a saturated presentation, and the process that generates it is called *achievement*.

Clearly, in many instances an achieved knowledge base that is equivalent to the original one will be infinite, so that one has to resort to either *partial achievement* or *total achievement* techniques. Partial achievement produces a finite knowledge base by setting a limit on either the depth of instances, or the length of chains of literals, that may be produced. Total achievement relaxes, in a controlled way, the requirement that the achieved base be equivalent to the original one. More recently, Furbach and Obermaier [44] considered knowledge compilation in description logics.

6   Discussion

Knuth-Bendix completion [59,55,54,6,5,18] was designed to derive decision procedures for validity in algebraic theories. Its outstanding feature is the use of inferred rules to continuously reduce equations and rules during the inference process. As a byproduct, the resulting reduced convergent system is unique – given a well-founded ordering of terms for orienting equations into rules [35] – and appropriately viewed as *canonical*.

In the ground equational case, reduction and completion are one and the same [61,45,66,8,13]. The natural next step up is to consider what canonical ground Horn presentations might look like. Here, we take a new look at ground Horn theories from the point of view of the theory of canonical inference initiated in [33,13]. Of course, entailment of equational Horn clauses is also easily decidable in the propositional [41] and ground [46] cases. However, it turns out that reduced and canonical – hence, reduction and completion – are distinct in this case.

For implicational systems, we analyzed the notions of direct and direct-optimal implicational system in terms of completion and canonicity. We compared implicational systems with inference mechanisms featuring implicational overlap and optimization, and rewrite systems with inference mechanisms featuring equational overlap and simplification. We found that a direct implicational system corresponds to the canonical limit of a derivation by completion that features expansion by equational overlap and contraction by forward simplification. When completion also features backward simplification and is given a subset of the alphabet as input, together with the implicational system, it computes the image of the subset with respect to the closure operator associated with the implicational system. In other words, it computes the minimal model that satisfies both the implicational system and the subset. On the other hand, a direct-optimal implicational system does not correspond to the limit of a derivation by completion, because the underlying proof orderings are different and therefore normalization induces two different notions of optimization. Accordingly, we introduced a new notion of optimality for implicational systems, termed *rewrite optimality*, that corresponds to canonicity defined by completion up to redundancy.

Although limited to the propositional level, our analysis is complementary to those of [28,37,17,39] in a few ways. First, previous studies primarily compared answering a query with respect to a program of definite clauses, interpreted by SLD-resolution, as in Prolog, with answering a query with respect to a program of rewrite rules, interpreted by linear completion, with equational overlap, with or without simplification. Thus, from an operational point of view, those analyses focused on *backward reasoning* from the query, whereas ours concentrates on optimizing and completing presentations by *forward reasoning*. Second, SLD-resolution involves no contraction, so that earlier comparisons placed an inference mechanism with contraction (linear completion) side-by-side with one without. The treatment in [17] included the case where the Prolog interpreter is enriched with subsumption, but it was only subsumption between goals, with no contraction of the presentation. Here we have also compared different forms of contraction, putting optimization of implicational systems and simplification of rewrite systems in parallel. The present analysis agrees with prior ones in indicating the role of simplification in differentiating reasoning by completion about equivalences from reasoning about implications. Indeed, as we have seen, the canonical rewrite system can be more reduced than the rewrite-optimal implicational system (cf. Theorem 3).

Future work includes generalizing this analysis to non-ground Horn theories, similar to what was done in [21] to extend the application of the abstract framework of [33,13] from ground completion to standard completion of equational theories. Other directions may be opened by exploring new connections between canonical systems and decision procedures.

Acknowledgements. We thank Andreas Podelski, Andrei Voronkov and Reinhard Wilhelm for organizing the workshop in Harald's memory in Saarbrücken in June 2005.

References

1. Apt, K.R.: Logic programming. In: van Leeuwen, J. (ed.) Handbook of Theoretical Computer Science. Formal Methods and Semantics, vol. B, ch. 10, pp. 493–574. North-Holland, Amsterdam (1990)
2. Armando, A., Bonacina, M.P., Ranise, S., Schulz, S.: New results on rewrite-based satisfiability procedures. ACM Transactions on Computational Logic 10(1), 129–179 (2009)
3. Armando, A., Ranise, S., Rusinowitch, M.: A rewriting approach to satisfiability procedures. Information and Computation 183(2), 140–164 (2003)
4. Bachmair, L., Dershowitz, N.: Inference rules for rewrite-based first-order theorem proving. In: Proceedings of the Second Annual IEEE Symposium on Logic in Computer Science, pp. 331–337. IEEE Computer Society Press (1987)
5. Bachmair, L., Dershowitz, N.: Equational inference, canonical proofs, and proof orderings. Journal of the Association for Computing Machinery 41(2), 236–276 (1994)
6. Bachmair, L., Dershowitz, N., Plaisted, D.A.: Completion without failure. In: Aït-Kaci, H., Nivat, M. (eds.) Resolution of Equations in Algebraic Structures. Rewriting Techniques, vol. II, pp. 1–30. Academic Press (1989)
7. Bachmair, L., Ganzinger, H.: Rewrite-based equational theorem proving with selection and simplification. Journal of Logic and Computation 4, 217–247 (1994)
8. Bachmair, L., Tiwari, A., Vigneron, L.: Abstract congruence closure. Journal of Automated Reasoning 31(2), 129–168 (2003)
9. Baumgartner, P. (ed.): Theory Reasoning in Connection Calculi. LNCS (LNAI), vol. 1527. Springer, Heidelberg (1998)
10. Bertet, K., Monjardet, B.: The multiple facets of the canonical direct implicational basis. Cahiers de la MSE No. b05052, Maison des Sciences Economiques, Université Paris Panthéon-Sorbonne (June 2005), http://ideas.repec.org/p/mse/wpsorb/b05052.html
11. Bertet, K., Nebut, M.: Efficient algorithms on the Moore family associated to an implicational system. Discrete Mathematics and Theoretical Computer Science 6, 315–338 (2004)
12. Birkhoff, G.: Lattice Theory. Revised edn. American Mathematical Society, New York (1948)
13. Bonacina, M.P., Dershowitz, N.: Abstract canonical inference. ACM Transactions on Computational Logic 8(1) (2007)
14. Bonacina, M.P., Echenim, M.: Rewrite-based satisfiability procedures for recursive data structures. In: Cook, B., Sebastiani, R. (eds.) Proceedings of the Fourth Workshop on Pragmatics of Decision Procedures in Automated Reasoning (PDPAR), Fourth Federated Logic Conference (FLoC). Electronic Notes in Theoretical Computer Science, vol. 174(8), pp. 55–70. Elsevier, Amsterdam (2007)
15. Bonacina, M.P., Echenim, M.: On variable-inactivity and polynomial T-satisfiability procedures. Journal of Logic and Computation 18(1), 77–96 (2008)
16. Bonacina, M.P., Echenim, M.: Theory decision by decomposition. Journal of Symbolic Computation 45(2), 229–260 (2010)
17. Bonacina, M.P., Hsiang, J.: On rewrite programs: Semantics and relationship with Prolog. Journal of Logic Programming 14(1 & 2), 155–180 (1992)
18. Bonacina, M.P., Hsiang, J.: Towards a foundation of completion procedures as semidecision procedures. Theoretical Computer Science 146, 199–242 (1995)

19. Bonacina, M.P., Lynch, C.A., de Moura, L.: On deciding satisfiability by theorem proving with speculative inferences. Journal of Automated Reasoning 47(2), 161–189 (2011)
20. Brown Jr., T.C.: A Structured Design-Method for Specialized Proof Procedures. PhD thesis, California Institute of Technology, Pasadena, CA (1975)
21. Burel, G., Kirchner, C.: Completion Is an Instance of Abstract Canonical System Inference. In: Futatsugi, K., Jouannaud, J.-P., Meseguer, J. (eds.) Goguen Festschrift 2006. LNCS, vol. 4060, pp. 497–520. Springer, Heidelberg (2006)
22. Caspard, N., Monjardet, B.: The lattice of Moore families and closure operators on a finite set: A survey. Electronic Notes in Discrete Mathematic, vol. 2 (1999)
23. Chang, C.L., Lee, R.C.T.: Symbolic Logic and Mechanical Theorem Proving. Academic Press (1973)
24. Comon, H., Dauchet, M., Gilleron, R., Jacquemard, F., Lugiez, D., Tison, S., Tommasi, M.: Tree Automata Techniques and Applications (2005), http://www.grappa.univ-lille3.fr/tata
25. Comon-Lundh, H., Courtier, V.: New Decidability Results for Fragments of First-order Logic and Application to Cryptographic Protocols. In: Nieuwenhuis, R. (ed.) RTA 2003. LNCS, vol. 2706, pp. 148–164. Springer, Heidelberg (2003)
26. Dershowitz, N.: A note on simplification orderings. Information Processing Letters 9(5), 212–215 (1979)
27. Dershowitz, N.: Equations as programming language. In: Proceedings of the Fourth Jerusalem Conference on Information Technology, Jerusalem, Israel, pp. 114–124. IEEE Computer Society Press (May 1984)
28. Dershowitz, N.: Computing with rewrite systems. Information and Control 64(2/3), 122–157 (1985)
29. Dershowitz, N.: Canonical Sets of Horn Clauses. In: Leach Albert, J., Monien, B., Rodríguez-Artalejo, M. (eds.) ICALP 1991. LNCS, vol. 510, pp. 267–278. Springer, Heidelberg (1991)
30. Dershowitz, N.: Ordering-based strategies for Horn clauses. In: Proceedings of the Twelfth International Joint Conference on Artificial Intelligence, Sydney, Australia, pp. 118–124 (1991)
31. Dershowitz, N., Huang, G.S., Harris, M.A.: Enumeration problems related to ground Horn theories (2008), http://arxiv.org/abs/cs/0610054
32. Dershowitz, N., Jouannaud, J.P.: Rewrite systems. In: van Leeuwen, J. (ed.) Handbook of Theoretical Computer Science. Formal Methods and Semantics, vol. B, ch. 6, pp. 243–320. North-Holland, Amsterdam (1990)
33. Dershowitz, N., Kirchner, C.: Abstract canonical presentations. Theoretical Computer Science 357, 53–69 (2006)
34. Dershowitz, N., Manna, Z.: Proving termination with multiset orderings. Communications of the ACM 22(8), 465–476 (1979)
35. Dershowitz, N., Marcus, L., Tarlecki, A.: Existence, uniqueness, and construction of rewrite systems. SIAM Journal of Computing 17(4), 629–639 (1988)
36. Dershowitz, N., Plaisted, D.A.: Logic programming cum applicative programming. In: Proceedings of the 1985 Symposium on Logic Programming, Boston, MA, pp. 54–66 (1985)
37. Dershowitz, N., Plaisted, D.A.: Equational programming. In: Hayes, J.E., Michie, D., Richards, J. (eds.) Machine Intelligence 11: The Logic and Acquisition of Knowledge, ch. 2, pp. 21–56. Oxford University Press, Oxford (1988)
38. Dershowitz, N., Plaisted, D.A.: Rewriting. In: Robinson, A., Voronkov, A. (eds.) Handbook of Automated Reasoning, vol. I, ch. 9, pp. 535–610. Elsevier, Amsterdam (2001)

39. Dershowitz, N., Reddy, U.: Deductive and inductive synthesis of equational programs. Journal of Symbolic Computation 15, 467–494 (1993)
40. Dowek, G.: Confluence as a Cut Elimination Property. In: Nieuwenhuis, R. (ed.) RTA 2003. LNCS, vol. 2706, pp. 2–13. Springer, Heidelberg (2003)
41. Dowling, W.F., Gallier, J.H.: Linear-time algorithms for testing the satisfiability of propositional Horn formulæ. Journal of Logic Programming 1(3), 267–284 (1984)
42. Fermüller, C., Leitsch, A., Hustadt, U., Tammet, T.: Resolution decision procedures. In: Robinson, A., Voronkov, A. (eds.) Handbook of Automated Reasoning, vol. II, ch. 25, pp. 1793–1849. Elsevier, Amsterdam (2001)
43. Fribourg, L.: SLOG—Logic Interpreter for Equational Clauses. In: Choffrut, C., Lengauer, T. (eds.) STACS 1990. LNCS, vol. 415, pp. 479–480. Springer, Heidelberg (1990)
44. Furbach, U., Obermaier, C.: Knowledge compilation for description logics. In: Dershowitz, N., Voronkov, A. (eds.) Proceedings of the Fourteenth International Conference on Logic for Programming, Artificial Intelligence and Reasoning (LPAR), Short Papers Session (2007)
45. Gallier, J., Narendran, P., Plaisted, D.A., Raatz, S., Snyder, W.: Finding canonical rewriting systems equivalent to a finite set of ground equations in polynomial time. Journal of the Association for Computing Machinery 40(1), 1–16 (1993)
46. Gallier, J.H.: Fast algorithms for testing unsatisfiability of ground Horn clauses with equations. Journal of Symbolic Computation 4, 233–254 (1987)
47. Ganzinger, H.: A completion procedure for conditional equations. Journal of Symbolic Computation 11(1 & 2), 51–81 (1991)
48. Goguen, J.A., Meseguer, J.: Eqlog: Equality, types, and generic modules for logic programming. In: DeGroot, D., Lindstrom, G. (eds.) Logic Programming: Functions, Relations, and Equations, pp. 295–363. Prentice-Hall, Englewood Cliffs (1986)
49. Hanus, M.: The integration of functions into logic programming: From theory to practice. Journal of Logic Programming 19&20, 583–628 (1994)
50. Hodges, W.: Logical features of Horn clauses. In: Gabbay, D.M., Hogger, C.J., Robinson, J.A. (eds.) Handbook of Logic in Artificial Intelligence and Logic Programming. Logical Foundations, vol. I, pp. 449–503. Oxford University Press, Oxford (1993)
51. Horn, A.: On sentences which are true in direct unions of algebras. Journal of Symbolic Logic 16, 14–21 (1951)
52. Hsiang, J.: Refutational theorem proving using term rewriting systems. Artificial Intelligence 25, 255–300 (1985)
53. Hsiang, J.: Rewrite method for theorem proving in first order theories with equality. Journal of Symbolic Computation 3, 133–151 (1987)
54. Hsiang, J., Rusinowitch, M.: On Word Problems in Equational Theories. In: Ottmann, T. (ed.) ICALP 1987. LNCS, vol. 267, pp. 54–71. Springer, Heidelberg (1987)
55. Huet, G.: A complete proof of correctness of the Knuth–Bendix completion algorithm. Journal of Computer and System Sciences 23(1), 11–21 (1981)
56. Jouannaud, J.P., Waldmann, B.: Reductive conditional term rewriting systems. In: Proceedings of the Third IFIP Working Conference on Formal Description of Programming Concepts, Ebberup, Denmark (1986)
57. Kaplan, S.: Simplifying conditional term rewriting systems: Unification, termination, and confluence. Journal of Symbolic Computation 4(3), 295–334 (1987)

58. Kaplan, S., Rémy, J.L.: Completion algorithms for conditional rewriting systems. In: Aït-Kaci, H., Nivat, M. (eds.) Resolution of Equations in Algebraic Structures. Rewriting Techniques, vol. II, pp. 141–170. Academic Press (1989)
59. Knuth, D.E., Bendix, P.B.: Simple word problems in universal algebras. In: Leech, J. (ed.) Computational Problems in Abstract Algebra, pp. 263–297. Pergamon Press, Oxford (1970)
60. Kounalis, E., Rusinowitch, M.: On word problems in Horn theories. Journal of Symbolic Computation 11(1 & 2), 113–128 (1991)
61. Lankford, D.S.: Canonical inference. Memo ATP-32, Automatic Theorem Proving Project, University of Texas, Austin, TX (1975)
62. Lloyd, J.W.: Foundations of Logic Programming, 2nd extended edn. Symbolic Computation Series. Springer, Berlin (1987)
63. Lynch, C., Morawska, B.: Automatic decidability. In: Plotkin, G. (ed.) Proceedings of the Seventeenth IEEE Symposium in Logic in Computer Science. IEEE Computer Society Press (2002)
64. McCharen, J.D., Overbeek, R.A., Wos, L.: Complexity and related enhancements for automated theorem proving programs. Computers and Mathematics with Applications 2(1), 1–16 (1976)
65. McKinsey, J.C.C.: The decision problem for some classes of sentences without quantifiers. Journal of Symbolic Logic 8, 61–76 (1943)
66. Plaisted, D.A., Sattler-Klein, A.: Proof lengths for equational completion. Information and Computation 125(2), 154–170 (1996)
67. Reddy, U.S.: Narrowing as the operational semantics of functional languages. In: Proceedings of the Symposium on Logic Programming, pp. 138–151. IEEE Computer Society Press (1985)
68. Roussel, O., Mathieu, P.: Exact Knowledge Compilation in Predicate Calculus: The Partial Achievement Case. In: McCune, W. (ed.) CADE 1997. LNCS, vol. 1249, pp. 161–175. Springer, Heidelberg (1997)
69. Sloane, N.J.A.: The On-Line Encyclopedia of Integer Sequences (2006), http://www.research.att.com/~njas/sequences
70. Stickel, M.E.: Automated deduction by theory resolution. Journal of Automated Reasoning 1, 333–355 (1985)
71. Bezem, M., Klop, J.W., de Vrijer, R.: TeReSe: Term Rewriting Systems. Cambridge University Press, Cambridge (2003)
72. Wos, L., Carson, D.F., Robinson, G.A.: Efficiency and completeness of the set of support strategy in theorem proving. Journal of the Association for Computing Machinery 12, 536–541 (1965)
73. Zhang, H.: A new method for the boolean ring based theorem proving. Journal of Symbolic Computation 17(2), 189–211 (1994)
74. Zhang, H.: Contextual rewriting in automated reasoning. Fundamenta Informaticae 24, 107–123 (1995)

A Generic Functional Representation of Sorted Trees Supporting Attribution
(Haskell Can Do It)

Jean-Marie Gaillourdet, Patrick Michel,
Arnd Poetzsch-Heffter, and Nicole Rauch

University of Kaiserslautern
{jmg,poetzsch,p_michel,rauch}@cs.uni-kl.de

Abstract. Many important tasks and algorithms in computer science build on sorted trees. Typical examples are the translation of programs represented by syntax trees or the processing of (recursive) data structures following some XML schema. In purely functional programming, sorted trees are usually implemented by terms of recursive data types such that a term represents a tree node and the subterms represent its children. The drawback of this representation is that the context of a tree node is not accessible and has to be managed by different means, e.g., by additional arguments of the functions working on the tree.

In this paper, we present a pattern for the realization of sorted trees that overcomes this drawback. The technique is fully declarative. In contrast to competing patterns for trees such as Zippers, it supports pattern matching on the tree data structure. Functions on tree nodes can be used to express the decoration of trees by attribute values in a flexible way. In particular, links between tree nodes can easily be defined and attributions can be modularized into phases with clear interfaces. Techniques adapted from the "Scrap your boilerplate" approach allow for the high-level specification of contextual constraints. We show how our approach can be realized in Haskell and discuss tool support.

1 Introduction

Many important tasks and algorithms in computer science build on sorted trees. Typical examples are the translation of programs represented by syntax trees or the processing of (recursive) data structures following some XML schema. A *sorted tree* is an ordered directed acyclic labeled graph where the labeling follows some application specific rules. Except for the root node, every tree node has a parent node and possibly sibling nodes, i.e., it has a so-called *context*. In purely functional programming, sorted trees are usually implemented by terms of recursive data types such that a term represents a tree node and the subterms represent its children. The drawback of this representation is that the context of a tree node is not accessible and has to be managed by different means, e.g., by additional arguments of the functions working on the tree. The drawback in particular appears in two application scenarios:

A. Voronkov and C. Weidenbach (Eds.): Ganzinger Festschrift, LNCS 7797, pp. 72–89, 2013.
© Springer-Verlag Berlin Heidelberg 2013

- the *editing* scenario in which one can freely navigate in trees (up and down, left and right) and update the tree at a current cursor position
- the *decoration* scenario in which tree nodes are decorated with attribute values that might depend on the context

Zippers [10] and Web Weavers [9] are functional programming patterns developed for the editing scenario. In this paper, we develop a technique for the generic functional representation of sorted trees for the decoration scenario. More precisely, the technique addresses the following requirements:

- Pattern matching on the tree representation should be available in the same way as for the term representation of trees.
- After a first visit of the tree, navigation should be possible without memory allocation.
- The representation should be optimized towards the decoration scenario. In particular, efficient memoization of functions on tree nodes should be possible (whereas modifications of the tree might be more expensive).
- Generic programming techniques on trees should be supported.

In our solution, every node has an additional component to access the upper context. As we use a cyclic realization to represent the context, we obtain a tree representation that needs no memory allocation during navigation in the tree. This is different from Zippers where every navigation step causes the call of constructors.

Our implementation takes the data types of an abstract syntax as input and generates a module with input-dependent declarations. Together with a (fixed) library module, programmers obtain an expressive API to handle trees that are sorted according to the abstract syntax. In particular, they can design attributions as functions on tree nodes. We use the term *attribution* for the decoration of a (possibly already attributed) tree with attribute values, independent of the technique for specifying the decoration.

We implemented our approach for Haskell 98 using several standard extensions[1]. To understand the conceptual aspects of the approach, the reader should be familiar with functional programming. Some of the technical aspects assume knowledge of Haskell.

Overview. The rest of the paper is structured as follows. Section 2 describes how programmers can use our approach. Section 3 discusses the motivation underlying the approach and related work. Section 4 presents our realization of trees in Haskell in detail. Section 5 contains furhter technical implementation aspects. Section 6 concludes.

2   The Programmer's Side of the Approach

This section introduces and motivates our technique along with an example from semantic analysis of programs. We show:

---

[1] We use multi-parameter type classes with functional dependencies, rank2types, existential types, and undecidable instances.

- what our technique offers to programmers, and
- how the technique can be used to decorate syntax trees by attribute values and to implement semantic analysis.

We use typed lambda expressions as programs and check that all used variables are bound and all expressions are well-typed. The type information is given together with the variable binding in λ-abstractions. Types are either the primitive type Ind for individuals or function types. In Haskell, the data types to represent such programs could be defined as in Fig. 1. Our tool takes such data type defini-

```
data Program =   Program { ast::LExp }
data LExp    =   Var { uv::UsedVar }
             |   Abs { dv::String, tp::Type, body::LExp }
             |   App { fun::LExp, arg::LExp }
data UsedVar =   UsedVar { str::String }
data Type    =   Ind | Fun { dom::Type, rng::Type }
```

Fig. 1. A recursive data type to represent simply typed lambda expressions

tions[2] and the root type of the trees we are interested in as input and generates data types for the tree positions and functions to navigate in the tree. In the example, the type of the root is Program, the types generated for tree positions include P.Program, P.LExp, P.UsedVar, and P.Type. Similarly, there are constructors P.Abs, etc. for tree positions. Compared to the term constructors, they take an additional argument capturing the upper tree context. From a programmers point of view, such constructors are only used in pattern matching. For example, the following function isAbs checks whether an LExp position is an abstraction:

```
isAbs :: P.LExp → Bool
isAbs (P.Abs _ _ _ _) = True
isAbs _               = False
```

The function P.pos :: Program → P.Program allows to access the root position of the tree corresponding to a term of type Program; here is an example application:

```
progp = P.pos (Program (Abs "x" Ind (Var (UsedVar "x"))))
```

Starting from the root position, we can navigate in the tree both in a typed and an untyped way. For example in P.body (P.ast progp), we first select the outer most lambda expression and then its body. Whereas the selector P.ast :: P.Program → P.LExp never fails, the selector P.body fails if applied to a variable or application. Untyped navigation abstracts from the types of the tree positions. Our framework provides the generic functions parent yielding the parent of a position and child yielding the n-th child of a position. As they are partial functions, we support monadic treatment for undefined cases and casts. Here is an example expression with the Maybe monad:

```
(P.asProgram =<< parent (P.ast progp)  ==  Just progp
```

---

[2] As described in Sect. 5 our tool uses a different, slightly more flexible input syntax.

As the type of the expression parent (P.ast progp) cannot be inferred, the cast by P.asProgram is necessary. In undefined cases, tree navigation functions and casts would yield the value Nothing. Another important generic function is the function term that yields for a given position the corresponding term; in particular, term (P.dv (P.ast progp)) is equal to the string "x".

Now we have all technical prerequisites to illustrate how the tree representation can be used for the flexible solution of semantic analysis problems. As example problem, we want to check that all used variables in a lambda expression are bound and then decorate the expression and their subexpression by their types. Following ideas from [23,6], we solve this problem in a nonstandard way. In a first step, we define a function decl :: P.UsedVar → P.LExp that yields for a used variable the abstraction where it is bound; for this function, the upper context of tree nodes has to be available. Then, we compute the decoration with type information bottom up. Along with the example, we explain further features of our framework.

The helper function lkupBd searches bottom up for the binding of a variable v starting at a position lp in a lambda expression. If lp is an abstraction binding v, it yields lp; otherwise, it continues the search at the parent position:

```
lkupBd :: String → P.LExp → Maybe P.LExp
lkupBd v lp@(P.Abs dvp _ _ _)
 | v == term dvp =  Just lp
lkupBd v lp      =  lkupBd v =<< P.asLExp =<< parent lp

declMaybe :: P.UsedVar → Maybe P.LExp
declMaybe  uvp@(P.UsedVar sp _) =
   lkupBd (term sp) =<< P.asLExp =<< parent uvp
```

The function declMaybe looks up the binding for the used variable and returns Nothing if such a binding does not exist.

Similar to the programming techniques described in [17], our framework supports generic queries. For example, we could be interested to check that for all used variables in a program declMaybe is defined. The forall query (defined in the library, see Sect. 4) applies the predicate isJust.declMaybe to all positions of its argument type, i.e., of type P.UsedVar, and conjoins the results:

```
allDeclared :: P.Program → Bool
allDeclared = forall (isJust . declMaybe)
```

Checking that all used variables are declared is a typical example of a context condition. Expressing such context conditions by generic queries is a nice declarative mechanism resembling informal formulations of context conditions in language reports.

```
decl :: P.UsedVar → P.LExp
decl = fromJust . declMaybe
```

Assuming allDeclared, we can use a function decl in later phases of the semantic analysis. That is, for such phases developers can use a simplified API to the syntax tree in which lkupBd and declMaybe are hidden. Here, we show a simple type analysis as an example of a subsequent analysis phase:

```
typeMaybe :: P.LExp → Maybe Type
typeMaybe(P.Var uvp _)     = Just $ term $ P.tp $ decl uvp
typeMaybe(P.Abs _ tp bd _) = Fun (term tp) <$> typeMaybe bd
typeMaybe(P.App fn arg _)
  | (domM =<< typeMaybe fn) == typeMaybe arg
                           =   rngM =<< typeMaybe fn
  | otherwise              =   Nothing
```

The type of a variable uvp is obtained by just taking the term of the type of the abstraction expression in which uvp is bound. The type of an abstraction is the obvious function type. The type of an application is the range type of the function argument. typeMaybe yields Nothing for wrongly typed lambda expressions. To support monadic exception handling, our framework provides monadic selectors for terms and positions, e.g., domM and P.domM. Thus, the expression domM =<< typeMaybe fn evaluates to the domain type of the type of fn if the type of fn is defined and is a function type.

3   Motivation and Related Work

Our approach provides a middle ground between functional programs without support of sorted trees and full-fledged attribute grammar systems. This section discusses our motivations and related work.

3.1   Motivational Background

Language processing phases are usually defined over the structure of the syntax tree. Conceptually, there are two central patterns to combine such phases:

- *Functional Pattern*: A phase is specified as a function taking the syntax tree plus additional arguments as input and returning a tuple of results. The results are used for the input of subsequent phases. In particular, one of the results might be a new or restructured tree according to the same or a different syntax (e.g., an intermediate representation of a program).
- *Decoration Pattern*: A phase is specified as a process decorating a tree by attribute values. The input is a possibly partially decorated syntax tree; the output is the same tree with additional attributes.

Let us revisit the semantic analysis problem of Sect. 2. According to the functional pattern, it is difficult to separate name and type analysis into two phases. Typically, one would realize it as one phase declared as a function

```
semAnalysis :: Program → Maybe TypedProgram
```

that takes a program term p as input and returns a term of type TypedProgram in which every lambda expression has its type as an additional component (if p satisfies the context conditions, otherwise Nothing). The realization in Sect. 2 follows the decoration pattern with two phases. The first takes the raw syntax tree as input and decorates it with the attribute decl. The second phase takes this output as input and computes the type information for all (sub-)expressions. It is important to notice that the interfaces between the language processing phases heavily depend on the pattern used. According to our experience, the decoration pattern simplifies the decoupling of phases. It allows for more declarative interfaces between phases. In particular, the construction of additional data structures such as symbol tables can often be avoided or simplified. Of course, both patterns can be combined.

Whereas the decoration pattern is well-supported by attribute grammars or similar techniques, it is difficult to be directly used in purely functional programming. A main motivation for our work was to decrease this burden and to support the application of the decoration pattern without having to use an attribute grammar systems.

3.2 Related Work

Our work is related to techniques for specifying the decoration of trees with attribute values in functional settings. For the language embedding, it is related to tree representations in purely functional generic programming.

Attribution of Trees. During the last forty years, a number of specification and implementation techniques have been developed for tree attribution (see e.g. [14,7,12,6,1]). Attribute grammars, developed by D. Knuth in [15], are among the best investigated techniques in the area (cf. [2] for an overview).

Here, we focus our discussion on the attribution mechanisms in *declarative* settings. With the design of MUG2 [5], Ganzinger and his coauthors were among the first looking for more declarative specification support in compiler generation (see also [3]). Further work resulted in the development of attribute coupling [4] and higher-order techniques [25]. They allowed the direct use of parts of the syntax tree to compute attribute values.

In the example of Sect. 2, we used the attribute decl to link used variable occurrences to their binding. To our knowledge, this technique was first realized in the Synthesizer Generator [23]. In a more general form, it is supported by the Door Attribute Grammars [6].

Starting in the nineties, attribute grammars were investigated as a specification method (see e.g. [13]) and as a functional programming paradigm (see e.g. [11]). We developed the MAX system [21]. It is built on positions in order-sorted terms and their attribution. A very interesting related work is the embedding of AGs as a domain-specific language into Haskell [24].

Attribute grammars have two potential advantages over our approach. First, most classes of attribute grammars allow to check statically that attribute dependencies are acyclic, i.e., one reason of non-termination can be avoided. Secondly, AG systems typically generate implementations that are more efficient than a straightforward implementation with our approach. In particular, they store attribute values for later use. To achieve the latter, one has to combine techniques

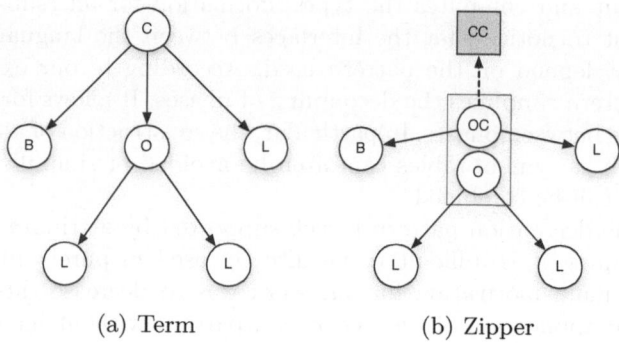

(a) Term   (b) Zipper

Fig. 2. Different representations of the same term structure

for function memoization with our approach (cf. [20,8]). Our experience is that for a functional programmer who only knows his language, our approach is easier to learn and allows for more flexibility than an attribute grammar system.

Purely Functional Tree Representations. In [10], Huet describes the so-called *Zipper* approach to representing positions within a term in a purely functional setting. Its main application area is the *editing* scenario (see Sect. 1). Zippers are based on pointer reversal. To represent a term position p in a term t, the Zipper consists of the subterm at p and the path from p to the root, containing the context of the subterm. If p is the root position, the path is empty. Otherwise, it consists of the term siblings of p and the path of p's parent. Figure 2 illustrates the situation for typed terms. The Zipper is a pair of the subterm with constructor O and a path with constructor OC. The path consists of the left sibling B, the right sibling L, and the path to root (here only CC). Every navigation operation in a Zipper entails several constructor calls and thus memory allocations. Thus, navigation is more expensive than just selecting subterms. On the other hand, modifications of the tree at the "current" positions is relatively cheap.

The programming technique "Weaving a Web" [9] addresses the same requirements as the Zipper and shares many of its characteristics. Like our approach, it uses cyclic structures to represent positions. Zippers and Weavers address a similar problem than ours, but have other runtime characteristics and provide a different programming API for trees. In particular, our approach supports pattern matching on the position structure that is almost the same as for the term structure (see function `typeMaybe` in Sect. 2 as an example). Most notably, the variables bound by the matching are positions again. Pattern matching in the other two approaches needs more knowledge from the programmer and does not yield positions as result of the matching. For example matching on a Zipper to bind a position in a subtree would yield a term representation of the subtree.

Another challenge that we addressed is to enable typed and untyped operations on the trees. Typing is nice for pattern matching, but for navigation (cf. function **parent**) and for generic queries (cf. function **allDeclared**) it can be a burden. That is why we adopted the generic techniques from the "Scrap your boilerplate" design pattern (cf. [17,18,16]).

4   Trees in Purely Functional Programming

This section describes how our approach is realized in the lazy functional programming language Haskell98 with the extensions described in Sect. 1.[3] First, we explain the representation of trees and show how they are realized in a typed way. Then, we describe the type classes for positions and their instantiation. Finally, we explain some of the generic programming features. As said above, the input to our tool is essentially a set of first-order recursive data type definitions and the root type of the trees we are interested in (cf. Sect. 5 for more details). The Haskell code for the trees consists of a *library* file that is independent of the input and of a *generated output* file containing input-dependent data types. We use the example from Fig. 1 to illustrate our technique.

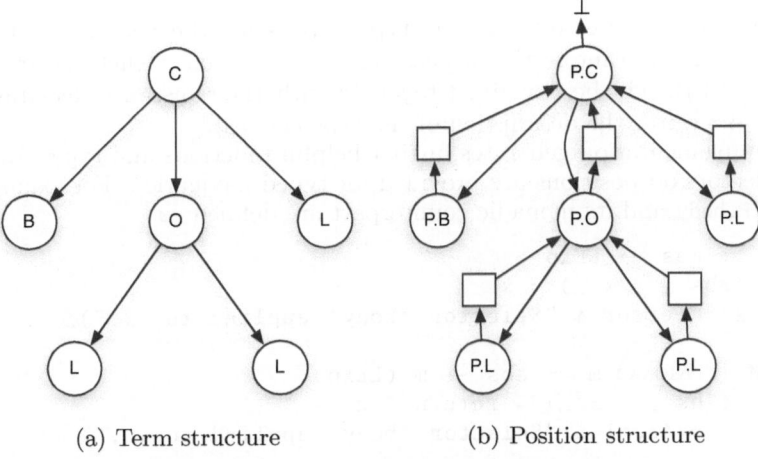

(a) Term structure   (b) Position structure

Fig. 3. Two representations of the same tree

4.1   Typed Tree Positions

The basic idea of how typed trees are represented is illustrated in Fig. 3. In addition to the term representation as shown in Fig. 3(a), we provide a typed tree representation. For each term constructor K, there is a corresponding constructor *P.K* for *(tree) positions*. As demonstrated in Fig. 3(b), this constructor takes a *context* as an additional argument. For example for type **LExp** of Fig. 1, we get the following *position type* and *context type* (similar types are generated for **Program**, **Type**, **UsedVar**, and **String**):

---

[3] To realize our approach in an eager functional language, one could adapt the technique described in [9] to represent cyclic graph structures.

```
data LExp = Var UsedVar LExpContext
          | Abs String Type LExp LExpContext
          | App LExp LExp LExpContext

data LExpContext = Absbody LExp
                 | Appfun LExp
                 | Apparg LExp
                 | Programast Program
```

When these types and their constructors are used together with the term data types or to stress that they are position types and constructors, we use the prefix P. as shown in Sect. 2. Type P.LExp differs from LExp only by the context component. The context of a position p captures its parent position pp and expresses how to select p from pp. Note that if a position type occurs only at the root, we get an empty data declaration for the corresponding context type. For example for type Program, the following is generated:

```
data Program = Program LExp ProgramContext
data ProgramContext
```

Position types are instances of the type classes for the generic treatment of positions. The most interesting aspect, namely how cyclic structures are created (see Fig. 3(b)), will be explained together with their instance declarations in Subsect. 4.3 (after the description of the type classes).

The implementation generates further helpful functions and types. In particular, selectors on positions are provided for typed navigation. For example, the selector P.body and its monadic counterpart are defined as:

```
body :: Abs → LExp
body (Abs _ _ x _) = x
body x = (error $ "Selector 'body' applied to ...")

bodyM :: MONAD m ⇒ Abs → m (LExp)
bodyM (Abs _ _ x _) = return $ x
bodyM x = (fail $ "Selector 'body' applied to ...")
```

4.2   Type Classes for Positions

The next step is to describe the library containing the input-independent type classes and generic functions for positions. We focus here on the central construction and leave out the treatment of selectors and the relations to type classes of the Haskell library (SHOW, EQ, TYPEABLE, ORD). Further features will be described in Sect. 5.

Let us recall that our approach supports two related representations of a tree structure, the term representation and the representation by positions in the tree. The type classes provide us with overloaded functions for navigating in the tree, relating the tree and term representation, accessing the context of a position, and creating positions. We designed the type classes POSITIONS and TERMPOSITIONS for these functions such that

```
type Index = Int

class POSITIONS pos root | pos → root
  where
    parent  :: MONAD m ⇒ pos → m (Position root)
    size    :: pos → Index
    child   :: MONAD m ⇒ Index → pos → m (Position root)
    root    :: pos → root
    rootM   :: MONAD m ⇒ pos → m root
    ...


class (POSITIONS pos root) ⇒ TERMPOSITIONS pos root term ctx
    | pos → root, pos → term, term → ctx
  where
    term    :: pos → term
    context :: pos → ctx
    create  :: term → ctx → pos


data Position root =  forall pos term ctx .
              TERMPOSITIONS pos root term ctx ⇒ Position pos


instance POSITIONS (Position root) root
  where
    parent     (Position p)  = parent p
    size       (Position p)  = size p
    child idx  (Position p)  = child idx p
    root       (Position p)  = root p
```

Fig. 4. Type classes and type for positions

- POSITIONS can be instantiated without knowing the term types,
- TERMPOSITIONS is built on POSITIONS and includes the relation to terms.

The type class POSITIONS uses a data type `Position` to express the range type of `parent` and `child`.

The overall construction is given in Fig. 4. Both type classes are multi-parameter type classes with functional dependencies[4]. The type class POSITIONS states that a position type `pos` (e.g., `P.LExp`) and the corresponding type of the tree `root` (e.g., `P.Program`) are in that class if the listed functions are provided (`size` returns the number of children). The type class TERMPOSITIONS states that a position type `pos` with its corresponding root type `root`, term type `term`, and context type `ctx` are in that class if there are the functions:

- `term` yielding the subterm at the given position,
- `context` yielding the context of the given position,

---

[4] At the time of submission of this paper, type families, an alternative approach to type classes, were still under development.

```
instance POSITIONS LExp Program  where
  parent x = case context x of
     Absbody y     → return $ Position y
     Appfun y      → return $ Position y
     Apparg y      → return $ Position y
     Programast y → return $ Position y
  size (Var _uv _ctx)           = 1
  size (Abs _dv _tp _body _ctx) = 3
  size (App _fun _arg _ctx)     = 2
  ...


instance TERMPOSITIONS LExp Program T.LExp LExpContext where
  term (Var _uv _c)      = T.Var (term _uv)
  term (Abs _d _t _b _c) = T.Abs (term _d) (term _t) (term _b)
  term (App _fn _ag _c)  = T.App (term _fn) (term _ag)
  context (Var _uv _ctx)           = _ctx
  context (Abs _dv _tp _body _ctx) = _ctx
  context (App _fun _arg _ctx)     = _ctx
  create (T.Var _uv) p =
     let x = Var _uvp p
         _uvp = (create _uv $ Varuv x)
     in x
  create (T.Abs _dv _tp _body) p =
     let x = Abs _dvp _tpp _bodyp p
         _dvp = (create _dv $ Absdv x)
         _tpp = (create _tp $ Abstp x)
         _bodyp = (create _body $ Absbody x)
     in x
  create (T.App _fun _arg) p =
     let x = App _funp _argp p
         _funp = (create _fun $ Appfun x)
         _argp = (create _arg $ Apparg x)
     in x
```

Fig. 5. Instances of the type classes POSITIONS and TERMPOSITIONS

– create taking a term t and a context c and yielding the position that represents a node with context c and subterm t. We have `term (create t c) = t` and `context (create t c) = c`.

The data type `Position` is parametric in the root type of a tree. Its constructor takes a value of a position type. The type `Position` plays the role of a "supertype" of all position types. In particular, the untyped navigation functions `parent` and `child` need `Position` to express the range type. Although it is not a concrete position type, we would like to apply our position API, or at least a part of it, also to values of `Position`. Because there is no equivalent term type, `Position` cannot be an element of TermPositions. However, the pair (`Position root`) and `root` is an instance of class Positions (see Fig. 4). The realization of the functions is taken from the position instance. Next, we describe the instantiation of the generated position types.

4.3   Instantiating the Type Classes for Positions

All pairs of term types and position types are instances of class TermPositions. Figure 5 illustrates the construction by showing the instance declarations for type `P.LExp`. As these declarations are part of the module where the position types are defined, `P.LExp` is denoted by `LExp` in this module (similarly for the constructors). To distinguishing them from their position counterparts, the term types and constructors of Fig. 1 are imported with the prefix `T.`; e.g., `T.App` is the binary constructor for an application expression.

The type `P.LExp` together with its root type `P.Program` is an instance of class Positions. The parent of a position x of type `P.LExp` is obtained via the context of x. The size of a position is simply determined by pattern matching. The rest of the instance declaration is omitted here, as it is not of interest for understanding the overall construction and as it uses parts of the implementation that are beyond the presentation in the paper.

The type `P.LExp`, together with `P.Program`, with the corresponding term type `T.LExp`, and with the context type `P.LExpContext`, form an instance of class TermPositions. The term corresponding to a position is constructed recursively by applying the term constructor to the terms of the child positions. The recursion ends when an external or basic type is encountered or when a term constructor has zero arguments. The context of a position is its last component. The most interesting part is the creation of positions. As explained in Sect. 2, positions are created top down starting with a function `pos`. Here is its definition in the generated module for the position declarations:

```
pos :: T.Program → Program
pos x = create x (undefined :: ProgramContext)
```

I.e., the root position has an undefined context. As illustrated in Fig. 5, other positions are created by using the upper context and by lazily creating the positions of the children with the newly created position in their contexts. That is, the position structure is created incrementally when it is visited.

4.4   Generic Programming with Positions

Based on the techniques of [17,18], we support generic programming for positions. Our tool generates instance declarations for type class DATA for all defined term and position types. The library module provides generally useful declarations, in particular for handling generic queries. In the following, we sketch part of the supported functionality and explain the adaptation of the "Scrap your boilerplate" technique to positions.

As a matter of convenience, "cast" functions are generated with descriptive names. The underlying cast functionality is taken from class TYPEABLE, introduced in [18]. For every position type T there is a function asT :: Position → Maybe T. Furthermore, we provide predicates checking the type of a position. Here are the corresponding declarations for type LExp:

```
asLExp :: forall root . Position root → Maybe LExp
asLExp (Position p) = (cast p :: Maybe LExp)
isLExp :: Position root → Bool
isLExp = (maybe False $ const True) . asLExp
```

In Sect. 2, we considered the generic query that checks that all variables are bound:

```
allDeclared :: P.Program → Bool
allDeclared = forall (isJust . declMaybe)
```

It uses the forall query. Figure 6 shows the definition of forall and the used combinators for recursive traversals. The design adapts the approach of [17]. To handle the cyclic structure caused by the context components, we have to avoid to follow these components in a query. This is realized in the combinator everythingBut[5] that uses the predicate isContext to exclude the context components. Combinator everythingBut is used to define the combinators everythingDown and everythingUp that apply a query to all positions of the subtree rooted by a given position or all positions in the context. In addition to the forall query, the framework provides a query all to collect all positions satisfying a predicate and the dual queries exists and some.

5   Implementation Aspects

This section discusses the implementation of the approach in our tool Katja[6]. Katja is a code generator translating specifications of a order-sorted data types to different target languages. There exist backends for Java, Isabelle/HOL and Haskell. For Java, the order between sorts is reflected by the generated subtype hierarchy. In the following, we provide more details on Katja and discuss memoization.

---

[5] Note that such a combinator was also introduced in a recent version of the DATA. Generics library, yet it has a different meaning and is not usable for our application.

[6] http://softech.cs.uni-kl.de/Homepage/Katja

```
data UndefinedTypeCase = UTC deriving (TYPEABLE, DATA)

everythingBut :: GenericQ Bool → (r→r→r)
                                → GenericQ r → GenericQ r
everythingBut q k f x
  | q x       = f UTC -- neutral element
  | otherwise = gmapQl k (f x) (everythingBut q k f) x

type GenericQP r = forall a root .
                   (DATA a, POSITIONS a root ) ⇒ a → r

everythingDown :: (r → r → r) → GenericQ r → GenericQP r
everythingDown join q qp =
  everythingBut (isContext(root p)) join q qp

forall :: TERMPOSITIONS a root ctx term ⇒
                   (a → Bool) → GenericQP Bool
forall pq = everythingDown (&&) (True 'mkQ' pq)

all :: TERMPOSITIONS a root sel ctx term ⇒
                   (a → Bool) → GenericQP [a]
all pq = everythingDown (++) ([] 'mkQ' collect)
    where collect x = if pq x then [x] else []
```

Fig. 6. A glimpse of the generic programming facilities

5.1 Generator

Because Haskell does not support full order-sortedness, the Haskell backend restricts the permissible input to specifications which have a direct translation to Haskell. The specification of the example of Fig. 1 is given in Fig. 7.

The specification line indicates a name for the whole specification. It is comparable to a module name. Then, there is a backend block. It contains declarations which apply to only one of Katja's backends. Here, it contains imports for external sorts and the declaration of the Haskell module name to use for the generated code. The root line declares that tree position types for terms of sort Program should be generated. Pos is an identifier used to differentiate between term types and tree position types, here it is the name of the module containing the tree position definitions. The Haskell backend also generates a module with that name and puts all the corresponding tree position types in it. Then, String is declared to be a sort provided by the environment. The remaining lines declare sorts either as constructors or as variants, i.e., as super sort of a set of other sorts. As said above, the Haskell backend restricts sort declarations to the subset which can be expressed directly in Haskell, i.e., a constructor has to be part of at most one variant.

Katja generates three Haskell modules from the specification of Fig. 7, an input-independent library module DATA.POSITIONS, a module containing term data type definitions Lambda.Term and a module containing tree position data

```
specification Lambda

backend haskell {
  module Lambda
  import String from Prelude
}

root Program Pos

external String

Program ( LExp ast )

LExp      = Var | Abs | App
Var       ( UsedVar uv )
Abs       ( String dv, Type tp, LExp body )
App       ( LExp fun, LExp arg )

UsedVar ( String str )

Type      = Ind | Fun
Fun       ( Type dom, Type rng )
Ind       ()
```

Fig. 7. The example of Fig. 1 using the concrete syntax of Katja

type definitions Lambda.Pos. Each of the last two modules contains type definitions for every sort and selector functions for every declared selector.

Java Backend. The Java backend generates a jar file, that contains compiled interfaces and classes which realize the type hierarchy specified in the input file (see [19] for details). The partial type order is reflected by subtyping between interfaces in the Java target. In addition to the core functions and types for term positions, the Java implementation provides a rich set of declarations to work with positions and terms. In particular, it supports selectors, visitors, iterators, and substitution methods. Similar to the Haskell implementation, the generated Java types are immutable and the construction of tree positions is performed lazily. In contrast to the Haskell backend it uses smart constructors to maximally share all term and tree position objects.

Isabelle/HOL Backend. The Isabelle/HOL backend generates a theory that contains an embedding of the tree position data types and functions into higher-order logic. The encoding resembles term positions, i.e., the embedding represents positions in a structure that is dual to the term structure (see [22]). On positions, constructor functions are used to access subpositions, while "selectors" are used to access to the upper context of a position. To express partiality on the related position constructors, a construction by inductive sets is used that only contain the defined cases. In addition to the core data types, the Isabelle/HOL theory contains most of the generic functions explained for Haskell above as well as helper lemmas that make the application of these functions more convenient.

5.2 Memoized Attribute Functions

Other than Zippers, the cyclic structure underlying tree positions allows navigation without allocation. This opens up the possibility to do pointer-based hashing in order to realize memoization of functions on tree positions, e.g., attribute functions. In [20], Peyton-Jones et. al. discuss the support for pointer-based hashing in GHC. This is not applicable to Zippers, because the allocation during navigation leads to constantly changing memory representations of equal zipper terms.

We performed preliminary experiments comparing attribute functions applied to tree nodes in different representations and memoized with different underlying data structures. These showed that pointer-based hashing using GHC's `StableName` abstraction with hash maps perform better than Zippers memoized with a map using the path from the current node to the root as key in a map. In order to quantify these benefits, further investigations are necessary.

6   Conclusions

We presented an approach to realize sorted trees in purely functional programming languages. Nodes/positions in these trees have an upper context. The tree representation is optimized towards the specification of attributions as functions on tree nodes in two ways. It supports

- pattern matching, similar to the term representation
- memoization using stable names

Such a direct support allows to combine attribution patterns with the full power and flexibility of higher-order functional programming. We demonstrated in particular the use of type classes to realize generic functions and applied the technique of "Scrap your boilerplate" to provide a convenient way to formulate context conditions. As all needed declarations can be generated from the data type representing the abstract syntax, the overhead for the programmer is negligible.

Having attributes as functions on tree positions provides a rich interface to an attributed tree. The attribution process can be structured into phases where phase $n+1$ takes the attributed tree of phase n as input, not just the results of the synthesized attributes at the root of the tree. In our example, the type analysis phase used the result of the name analysis phase in form of the function `decl`. By this modularization, language processing becomes a stepwise attribution and enrichment of the tree structure in which auxiliary attributes and functions for one phase can be hidden from other phases. E.g., helper functions such as `lkupBd` can be hidden in subsequent phases. This enrichment process can of course include transformation of tree parts. Altogether the approach can help:

- to make programming patterns known from attribute grammars available in functional programming and
- to overcome the dichotomy of programs into tree structure and declaration table that is found in many declarative approaches to language processing.

The approach follows goals of Ganzinger's earlier works in two ways. First, it presents a very flexible attribution technique with an additional modularization possibility. Second, it describes how this technique can be realized in a declarative framework that allows its automatic embedding into formal reasoning.

Future work includes the improvement of the memoization support and the realization of the technique with type families.

Acknowledgments. Many thanks go to Ralf Lämmel and an anonymous reviewer for their patient and elaborate comments on an earlier version of this paper.

References

1. Augusteijn, L.: The Elegant Compiler Generator System. In: Deransart, P., Jourdan, M. (eds.) Attribute Grammars and their Applications. LNCS, vol. 461, pp. 238–254. Springer, Heidelberg (1990)
2. Deransart, P., Jourdan, M., Lorho, B. (eds.): Attribute Grammars. LNCS, vol. 323. Springer, Heidelberg (1988)
3. Ganzinger, H.: Increasing modularity and language-independency in automatically generated compilers. Science of Computer Programming (1983)
4. Ganzinger, H., Giegerich, R.: Attribute coupled grammars. In: SIGPLAN 1984 Symposium on Compiler Construction, SIGPLAN Notices, vol. 19(6), pp. 157–170. ACM Press (1984)
5. Ganzinger, H., Giegerich, R., Möncke, U., Wilhelm, R.: A truly generative semantics-directed compiler generator. In: SIGPLAN 1982: Proceedings of the 1982 SIGPLAN Symposium on Compiler Construction, pp. 172–184. ACM Press (1982)
6. Hedin, G.: An Overview of Door Attribute Grammars. In: Fritzson, P.A. (ed.) CC 1994. LNCS, vol. 786, pp. 31–51. Springer, Heidelberg (1994)
7. Hendriks, P.R.H.: ASF system user's guide. Technical Report CS-R8823, CWI (1988)
8. Hinze, R.: Memo functions, polytypically! In: Proceedings of the 2nd Workshop on Generic Programming, pp. 17–32 (2000)
9. Hinze, R., Jeuring, J.: Weaving a web. J. Funct. Program. 11(6), 681–689 (2001)
10. Huet, G.: The Zipper. Journal of Functional Programming 7(5), 549–554 (1997)
11. Johnson, T.: Attribute Grammars as a Functional Programming Paradigm. In: Kahn, G. (ed.) FPCA 1987. LNCS, vol. 274, pp. 154–173. Springer, Heidelberg (1987)
12. Jourdan, M., Parigot, D.: The FNC-2 system: Advances in attribute grammars technology. Technical Report No. 834, INRIA (April 1988)
13. Kastens, U.: Attributed Grammars as a Specification Method. In: Alblas, H., Melichar, B. (eds.) SAGA School 1991. LNCS, vol. 545, pp. 16–47. Springer, Heidelberg (1991)
14. Kastens, U., Hutt, B., Zimmermann, E. (eds.): GAG: A Practical Compiler Generator. LNCS, vol. 141. Springer, Heidelberg (1982)

15. Knuth, D.E.: The semantics of context-free languages. Mathematical Systems Theory (1968)
16. Lämmel, R.: Scrap your boilerplate with XPath-like combinators. In: POPL 2007, Proceedings. ACM Press (January 2007)
17. Lämmel, R., Peyton Jones, S.: Scrap your boilerplate: a practical design pattern for generic programming. In: ACM SIGPLAN Notices, Proceedings of the ACM SIGPLAN Workshop on Types in Language Design and Implementation TLDI, vol. 38(3), pp. 26–37 (2003)
18. Lämmel, R., Peyton Jones, S.: Scrap more boilerplate: reflection, zips, and generalised casts. In: Proceedings of the ACM SIGPLAN International Conference on Functional Programming (ICFP 2004), pp. 244–255. ACM Press (2004)
19. Michel, P.: Adding position structures to Katja. Technical Report 353/06, University of Kaiserslautern (June 2005)
20. Peyton Jones, S., Marlow, S., Elliott, C.: Stretching the Storage Manager: Weak Pointers and Stable Names in Haskell. In: Koopman, P., Clack, C. (eds.) IFL 1999. LNCS, vol. 1868, pp. 37–58. Springer, Heidelberg (2000)
21. Poetzsch-Heffter, A.: Prototyping realistic programming languages based on formal specifications. Acta Informatica 34, 737–772 (1997)
22. Poetzsch-Heffter, A., Rauch, N.: Application and Formal Specification of Sorted Term-Position Algebras. In: Fiadeiro, J.L., Mosses, P.D., Yu, Y. (eds.) WADT 2004. LNCS, vol. 3423, pp. 201–217. Springer, Heidelberg (2005)
23. Reps, T., Marceau, C., Teitelbaum, T.: Remote attribute updating for language-based editors. In: ACM-SIGPLAN ACM-SIGACT (ed.) Thirteenth Annual ACM Symposium on Principles of Programming Languages, pp. 1–13. ACM Press (January 1986)
24. Viera, M., Swierstra, S.D., Swierstra, W.: Attribute grammars fly first-class: how to do aspect oriented programming in haskell. In: Proceedings of the 14th ACM SIGPLAN International Conference on Functional Programming, ICFP 2009, pp. 245–256. ACM, New York (2009)
25. Vogt, H., Swierstra, S., Kuiper, M.: Higher order attribute grammars. In: SIGPLAN 1989 Conference on Progamming Language Design and Implementation, SIGPLAN Notices, vol. 24(7), pp. 131–145. ACM Press (1989)

The Blossom of Finite Semantic Trees

Jean Goubault-Larrecq[1],[*] and Jean-Pierre Jouannaud[2],[**],[***]

[1] ENS Cachan
61 avenue du président Wilson, F-94230 Cachan
goubault@lsv.ens-cachan.fr
http://www.lsv.ens-cachan.fr/~goubault/
[2] École Polytechnique, F-91400 Palaiseau
jouannaud@lix.polytechnique.fr
http://www.lix.polytechnique.fr/Labo/Jean-Pierre.Jouannaud/

This paper is dedicated to the memory of Harald Ganzinger.

1 Introduction

Automated deduction in first-order logic finds almost all its roots in Herbrand's work, starting with Herbrand's interpretations, a clausal calculus, and rules for unification. J.A. Robinson's key contribution was the formulation of resolution and its completeness proof, in which semantic trees were semi-apparent. Robinson and Wos introduced the specific treatment of equality commonly called paramodulation. The systematic introduction of orderings to cut the search space is due to Lankford. Kowalski studied in more details the case of Horn clauses, while Peterson gave the first proof that paramodulation inside variables was superfluous, assuming a term ordering order-isomorphic to the natural numbers. Knuth studied the case of equality unit clauses, under the name of completion. All these works were done by using standard proof techniques, including semantic trees [Kow69].

Further progress required more powerful proof techniques.

The first was proposed by Huet with Noetherian orderings on terms, allowing the use of the powerful noetherian induction principle to establish a strong theory of abstract and concrete rewriting, another name for the case of equality unit clauses. The method was then extended by Jouannaud and Kirchner who introduced induction on proofs abstracted by multisets of terms. Bachmair, Dershowitz and Hsiang made the last step with the proof reduction method [BD94].

[*] Partially supported by the RNTL project Prouvé and the ACI Rossignol.
[**] Project LogiCal, Pôle Commun de Recherche en Informatique du Plateau de Saclay, CNRS, École Polytechnique, INRIA, Université Paris-Sud. Now at LIAMA, INRIA and Tsinghua University, Beijing, China.
[***] Harald Ganzinger and I had the opportunity to closely collaborate within the European projects *COMPASS* and *Combination of Computational Logics*. As a member of the Fachbeirat of the Max Planck Institute für Informatik in Saarbrücken for 6 years from the beginning, I had also the privilege to closely collaborate with Harald Ganzinger in his dedication to make the institute stronger. He will stay for ever in my memory as a genuine friend.

A. Voronkov and C. Weidenbach (Eds.): Ganzinger Festschrift, LNCS 7797, pp. 90–122, 2013.
© Springer-Verlag Berlin Heidelberg 2013

This tool allowed this subfield to make very fast progress until a new bottleneck was encountered with constrained equality unit clauses.

The second proof method was proposed by Hsiang and Rusinowitch [HR86], who invented transfinite semantic trees, a generalization of semantic trees generated from a transfinite ordering on the Herbrand base. They were able to generalize Peterson's result to arbitrary well-founded orderings. Considering again the case of equality unit clauses, they showed the completeness of ordered completion, an old conjecture of Lankford, which was found to have many theoretical applications by providing us with a true semi-decision procedure for equality based on computing normal forms. Being conceptually complex constructions, transfinite semantic trees did not make their way through in the community.

The third was proposed by Bachmair and Ganzinger, which allowed to make tremendous progress in all directions ever since, to a point that people did not find the need to look for new methods. Bachmair and Ganzinger's model generation technique [BG01a] is based on *forcing* a specific interpretation which can be seen as characterizing the satisfiability property of a given set of clauses. Many groups throughout the world studied and used this method, which was found a bit mysterious at first. Our goal here is to shed a new light on this important approach, by adopting a presentation based on semantic trees which we think is easy to grasp.

As transfinite semantic trees, Bachmair and Ganzinger's model generation technique is based on a well-founded ordering on terms which can be transfinite. It aims at showing the refutation-completeness property of a set of inference rules $\mathcal{I}$ used for generating the empty clause from a given unsatisfiable set $\mathcal{S}$ of clauses. The ordering is used to restrict the possible inferences to those involving maximal atoms.

Our first problem was to construct finite semantic trees with transfinite orderings. The answer is provided by Gödel and Maltsev's compactness theorem[1]: only finitely many ground instances of $\mathcal{S}$ suffice. These ground instances generate finitely many atoms which define interpretations which are finitely refuted, hence a finite semantic tree. A consequence of this construction is that the ordering need not be total, nor well-founded: it needs only be strict. It can then be completed into a total strict ordering on the finite set of atoms. The well-foundedness assumption however becomes necessary in the presence of an equality predicate.

Our second problem was to guess which node in the semantic tree of an unsatisfiable set of ground clauses would allow us to make an inference. The answer is easy: the model generation technique builds an interpretation which defines indeed a path in the semantic tree ending in an inference node.

The third problem was to show that this inference decreases the semantic tree in some well-founded ordering, allowing us to conclude by induction that the tree could be reduced in finite time to its root, hence showing that the empty clause had been generated. Building well-founded orderings on the semantic tree

---

[1] The solution was hinted at by Michael Rusinowitch in a discussion with the first author.

is much easier than on the set of clauses itself, allowing us again to slightly improve over the existing literature in some cases.

We do not think that our contribution lies in any improvement over the current literature. Our first main contribution, as we feel, is to show that all these concepts elaborated by Ganzinger and his collaborators are *intrinsic* to the entire field of automated deduction, rather than *specific* to his model generation proof method as one might have thought. The second contribution is the use of a single proof method to obtain them all, suggesting that some of these restrictions may be combined. We will treat here a few basic results only: ordered resolution, ordered resolution with selection, ordered linear resolution, and ordered resolution and paramodulation. We consider the systematic use of our technique as an exercice which will allow the reader to better grasp the subtleties of Ganzinger's work.

2   Ordered Resolution with Selection

The semantic tree technique makes it relatively clear that not only resolution is complete, but also *ordered* resolution, where only literals that are maximal in their respective clauses are resolved upon [CL73]. This is a very effective restriction of resolution. We recall the completeness argument for ordered resolution in Section 2.1. We also improve it, by showing that ordered resolution is complete for any stable ordering (even, say, not well-founded).

Another very effective restriction is ordered resolution with *selection*, where a selection function is used to denote selected exceptions to the ordering restriction. This refinement of resolution generalizes both ordered resolution and positive resolution (where one of the premise is constrained to contain only positive literals). It has been known for a long time to resist semantic tree arguments, and Bachmair and Ganzinger's forcing technique [BG01a] provided an elegant completeness argument. We show how the two techniques blend naturally together in Section 2.2. In Section 2.3, we deal briefly with redundancy elimination strategies, an important part of Bachmair and Ganzinger's work in automated deduction. We sketch how our technique generalizes to the completeness of linear resolution in Section 2.4, a refinement of resolution whose completeness was traditionally thought to require different arguments.

2.1   Ordered Resolution

A *literal* is an atom or its negation. We write $+A$ for the atom A seen as an atom, and $-A$ for its negation. We shall usually write $\pm A$ for a literal, obtained by taking A with a sign, either $+$ or $-$. A *clause* is a finite set of literals separated by $\vee$.

Let $\succsim$ be any stable quasi-ordering on atoms which restricts to an ordering on ground atoms. By *stable*, we mean that for any two atoms A, B, if $A \succsim B$, then $A\sigma \succsim B\sigma$ for every substitution σ. Let $\precsim$ be the converse of $\succsim$, $\succ$ be the strict part of $\succsim$, and $\prec$ be the converse of $\succ$. The rule of *ordered resolution* is as follows, where the two premises are assumed renamed, without loss of generality, so as to have no variable in common.

$$\frac{+A_1 \vee \ldots + A_m \vee C \quad - A_1' \vee \ldots \vee -A_{m'}' \vee C'}{C\sigma \vee C'\sigma} \quad \begin{array}{l} m \geq 1, n \geq 1, \\ \sigma = mgu(A_1 = A_2 = \ldots = A_m = \\ \qquad A_1' = \ldots = A_{m'}'), \\ \forall B \in C\sigma \vee C'\sigma, A_1\sigma \not\succsim B \\ \qquad 1 \leq i \leq m, 1 \leq i' \leq m' \end{array}$$

We write $mgu(E)$ the most general unifier of any given set of term equations. As usual, we let σ be *more general than* θ if and only if $\theta = \sigma\sigma'$ for some substitution σ', and we write $\sigma \sqsubseteq \theta$.

Ordered resolution is sound and complete, in the sense that, starting from a set S of clauses, we may deduce the empty clause $\square$ by finitely many applications of the above rule if and only if S is unsatisfiable. We may in fact restrict m' to be 1 (no negative factoring), or m to be 1 (no positive factoring) without breaking completeness, but not both. Alternative presentations split this rule in one binary ordered resolution rule, and additional positive/negative factoring rules. We shall do this in later sections. For now, the current presentation will be more practical.

Soundness is trivial. Completeness is, of course, harder, so let's start by showing how semantic trees can be used to show that ordered resolution is complete when $\succsim$ is *enumerable*, i.e., when it satisfies the following property:

(∗) there is an enumeration $A_1^0, A_2^0, \ldots, A_i^0, \ldots$ of ground atoms such that $i > j$ whenever $A_i^0 \succ A_j^0$.

This much had been known since [Joy76]. Plain, unordered resolution, will in particular be complete, since this is the case where $\succsim$ is just the equality relation on atoms, which is clearly enumerable. We shall show that property (∗) is not required later.

Let $A_1^0, A_2^0, \ldots, A_i^0, \ldots$ be any given enumeration of ground atoms satisfying (∗). A *partial interpretation* I on this enumeration is a finite list $\pm_1 A_1^0, \pm_2 A_2^0, \ldots, \pm_k A_k^0$. If A_i^0 occurs under the $+$ sign, then A_i^0 is *true* in I; A_i^0 is *false* if it occurs under the $-$ sign, and *undefined* otherwise.

The *Herbrand tree* is the binary tree whose vertices are partial interpretations. The partial interpretation $I = \pm_1 A_1^0, \pm_2 A_2^0, \ldots, \pm_k A_k^0$ has two successors $\pm_1 A_1^0, \pm_2 A_2^0, \ldots, \pm_k A_k^0, -A_{k+1}^0$ and $\pm_1 A_1^0, \pm_2 A_2^0, \ldots, \pm_k A_k^0, +A_{k+1}^0$—provided A_{k+1}^0 exists, otherwise I is a leaf. The root of the tree is the empty partial interpretation ϵ.

The maximal paths of the Herbrand tree are naturally in bijection with Herbrand interpretations., i.e., sets of ground atoms. If I_H is a Herbrand interpretation, we follow the maximal path going through ϵ, then $\pm_1 A_1^0$, then $\pm_1 A_1^0, \pm_2 A_2^0$, $\ldots$, where $\pm_i$ is $+$ if $A_i^0 \in I_H$, $-$ otherwise. Conversely, any path goes through vertices that mention each atom A with a unique sign; collect those that occur with the $+$ sign, thus defining a Herbrand interpretation.

Figure 1 shows a (finite) semantic tree on the three atoms r, q, p in this order. I.e., $A_1^0 = r$, $A_2^0 = q$, $A_3^0 = p$. Vertex **1** is the empty partial interpretation ϵ, vertex **2** is $-r$, **3** is $+r$, **4** is $-r, -q$, etc.

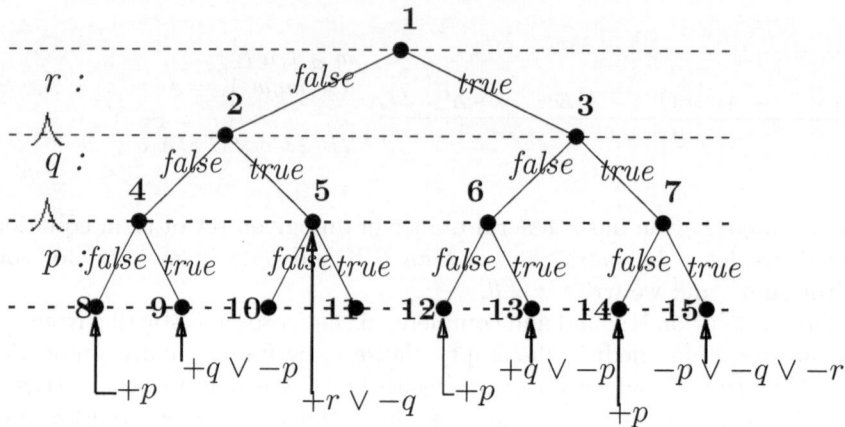

Fig. 1. A semantic tree

Let us say that a ground clause C is *false* at vertex $I = \pm_1 A_1^0, \pm_2 A_2^0, \ldots,$ $\pm_k A_k^0$ if and only if, for every literal $\pm A$ of C, the opposite literal $\mp A$ is listed in I. In Figure 1, the clause $+r \vee -q$ is false at $-r, +q$ (vertex **5**), and also, say, at $-r, +q, -p$ (vertex **10**).

Let S be an unsatisfiable set of clauses: for every Herbrand interpretation I_H, there is a ground instance $C\theta$ of a clause $C \in S$ such that I_H makes $C\theta$ false. Since the value of $C\theta$ depends on the truth value of only finitely many atoms, there is a partial interpretation, i.e., a vertex along I_H where $C\theta$ is false—e.g., vertex **10** makes $+r \vee -q$ false, assuming $+r \vee -q$ is a ground instance of some clause in S. A *failure node* is any highest vertex in the Herbrand tree that makes some ground instance $C\theta$ of some clause $C \in S$ false.

By König's Lemma, if S is unsatisfiable, then the *closed tree* T_S obtained from the Herbrand tree by cutting it at failure nodes is finite. The compactness theorem for first-order logic follows easily: only finitely elements of S account for the finitely many leaves of T_S.

Given a finite closed tree T_S, either the root ϵ is a failure node, so that S must contain the empty clause $\square$; or there must be a lowest non-failure vertex I, called an *inference node*. For example, $-r, -q$ (vertex **4**) in Figure 1 is an inference node. Its two successors, which must be of the form $I, -A$ and $I, +A$ respectively, must be failure nodes for some ground instances of first-order clauses C_+ and C_- respectively, in S, say $C_+\theta_+$ and $C_-\theta_-$. By the definition of failure nodes, $C_+\theta_+$ must be a disjunction of $+A$ with some literals above A (i.e., appearing before A in the enumeration $A_1^0, A_2^0, \ldots$), and $C_-\theta_-$ must be a disjunction of $-A$ with some literals above A again. Write C_+ as $+A_1 \vee \ldots + A_m \vee C$, where $+A_1, \ldots, +A_m$ are the literals L in C_+ such that $L\theta_+ = +A$, and write C_- as $-A_1' \vee \ldots \vee -A_{m'}' \vee C'$, where $-A_1', \ldots, -A_{m'}'$ are the literals L' in C_- such that $L'\theta_- = -A$. Renaming apart the free variables of C_+ and C_-, in particular,

$A_1, \ldots, A_m, A'_1, \ldots, A'_n$ are unifiable. Call σ their most general unifier; since $\gtrsim$ is stable, and using assumption $(*)$ above, $A_i\sigma \not\gtrsim B$ and $A'_{i'}\sigma \not\gtrsim B$ for every atom B in $C\sigma \vee C'\sigma$, $1 \leq i \leq m$, $1 \leq i \leq m'$. So the ordered resolution rule applies, and we may generate the resolvent $C\sigma \vee C'\sigma$. E.g., in Figure 1, the inference node $-r, -q$ (vertex **4**) allows one to resolve between the two clauses whose respective ground instances decorate the failure nodes below it, namely $+p$ and $+q \vee -p$, yielding a clause with $+q$ as ground instance.

Let S' be S union $C\sigma \vee C'\sigma$. Since $C\sigma \vee C'\sigma$ is now false at the inference node I, $T_{S'}$ is a closed tree with strictly less vertices than T_S. This process must therefore terminate; then ϵ will be a failure node, at which point $\Box$ has been inferred: completeness follows.

There are several degrees of freedom that we can exploit in this argument. First, the usual argument goes by considering the ground instances of clauses in S (which form an unsatisfiable set), showing that propositional ordered resolution is complete for the latter, then lifting propositional resolution refutations to the first-order level by so-called *lifting*. The argument above shows that we can reason directly at the level of first-order clauses, considering ground instances on the fly. While this makes no difference in ordered resolution, this is definitely needed when selection functions are introduced (Section 2.2), because nothing like stability will be required of selection functions.

Second, assumption $(*)$ can be completely dispensed with, as we promised, using compactness: if S is unsatisfiable, then some finite set of ground instances of S is already unsatisfiable. Clearly, this finite set uses only finitely many ground atoms $A_1^0, \ldots, A_n^0$, and we can replay the argument above by using only these atoms. Now it is easy to enumerate them in such a way that $A_i^0 \succ A_j^0$ implies $i > j$, whether $(*)$ holds or not: just find a topological sort of the A_i^0 with respect to the ordering $\succ$. (This is where we are using that $\gtrsim$ restricts to an ordering on ground atoms.)

Third, the way we pick interesting vertices (here, inference nodes) in the tree clearly dictates what constraints we may add to the resolution rule while retaining completeness. Picking inference nodes is a good match for ordered resolution. Other forms of resolution will require us to find other vertices in T_S. In the context of semantic trees, the import of the Bachmair-Ganzinger forcing method can be seen as a clever way of finding alternative vertices in T_S. This is simple and elegant: any vertex I is just a partial interpretation, and we shall find it by constructing I as a partial interpretation, alternatively as specifying which ground atoms should be true and which should be false while going down the closed tree T_S.

Fourth, and finally, we are free to apply alternative termination arguments. Taking the notations above, we have argued that we could produce a finite ordered resolution refutation by showing that we could rewrite T_S into another closed tree $T_{S'}$ by generating the right ordered resolvent. This terminates because the size $|T_S|$ of T_S is greater than that of $T_{S'}$. However, any well-founded measure of finite closed trees T_S would work equally well. This is precisely what we shall exploit next.

2.2   Ordered Resolution with Selection

Let *sel* be any fixed *selection function*, by which we mean any function that maps each clause C to a possibly empty subset of the negative literals in C—the *selected* literals in C. The idea is that, if *sel* (C) is non-empty, then we require to resolve on all selected literals; if *sel* $(C) = \emptyset$, then we revert to resolving upon $\succ$-maximal literals. On the other hand, we additionally require that the other premise $+A_1 \vee \ldots + A_m \vee C$ contains no selected literal at all.

Again assume a given stable quasi-ordering $\succsim$ whose restriction to ground atoms is an ordering, and assume additionally that $\succ$ is also stable: $A \succ B$ implies $A\sigma \succ B\sigma$ for every atoms A, B, and substitution σ. In case all these conditions are satisfied, we say that $\succsim$ is *strongly stable*. E.g., any reflexive closure $\succeq$ of a strict stable ordering $\succ$—the traditional setting for ordered resolution—is a strongly stable quasi-ordering.

The rule of *ordered resolution with selection* is

$$\frac{\overbrace{C_i \vee +A_{i1} \vee \ldots \vee +A_{in_i}}^{1 \leq i \leq \ell} \quad C' \vee -A'_1 \vee \ldots \vee -A'_\ell}{C_1\sigma \vee \ldots \vee C_\ell\sigma \vee C'\sigma}$$

with the following side-conditions:

(i) $n_i \geq 1$ for every i, $1 \leq i \leq \ell$;

(ii) $\sigma = mgu\{A_{ij} = A'_i | 1 \leq i \leq \ell, 1 \leq j \leq n_i\}$;

(iii) $sel(C_i \vee +A_{i1} \vee \ldots \vee +A_{in_i}) = \emptyset$ and $A_{i1}\sigma \not\precsim B$ for every atom B in $C_i\sigma$, for every i, $1 \leq i \leq \ell$;

(iv) $sel(C' \vee -A'_1 \vee \ldots \vee -A'_\ell) = \{-A'_1, \ldots, -A'_\ell\}$ and $\ell \geq 1$, or no literal is selected, $\ell = 1$ and $A'_1\sigma \not\prec B$ for every atom B in $C'\sigma$.

Note that *sel* is *arbitrary*. In particular, imagine that we select $\{-p(X)\}$ in $+q(X) \vee -p(X) \vee -r(X)$. While it would be natural to also select $\{-p(a)\}$ in its instance $+q(a) \vee -p(a) \vee -r(a)$, selection functions are not required in any way to do so, and we may perfectly well choose to select $\{-r(a)\}$, or $\{-p(a), -r(a)\}$, or nothing instead. This fact alone ruins any hope of proving completeness by lifting a completeness argument from the propositional to the first-order case.

Note also that, while we still require positive factoring (in general $n_i \neq 1$) in the *side clauses* $C_i \vee +A_{i1} \vee \ldots \vee +A_{in_i}$, we dispense with negative factoring in the *main clause* $C' \vee -A'_1 \vee \ldots \vee -A'_\ell$.

Theorem 1. *Ordered resolution with selection is complete: for any strongly stable quasi-ordering $\succsim$, for any selection function sel, for any set of clauses S, S is unsatisfiable if and only if we can derive $\square$ from S by ordered resolution with selection.*

Proof. We spend the rest of this section proving this.

The "if" direction is obvious. Conversely, fix a finite enumeration $A^0_1, \ldots, A^0_n$ of all ground atoms in the finite unsatisfiable set of ground instances of clauses in S secured by the compactness theorem. Sort them so that $A^0_i \succ A^0_j$ implies

$i > j$. A closed tree T_S is *adequate* if and only if its vertices are of the form $\pm_1 A_1^0, \ldots, \pm A_k^0$ with $k \leq n$. By construction, there is an adequate closed tree T_S. Also, for each failure node I of T_S, there is a clause C_I in S and a substitution θ_I such that $C_I \theta_I$ is ground and false at I.

Given any set S' of clauses, call a *decorated tree* any tuple $(T, C_\bullet, \theta_\bullet)$, where T is an adequate closed tree, $C_\bullet$ maps each leaf I of T to a clause C_I of S', and $\theta_\bullet$ maps each leaf I to a substitution θ_I such that $C_I \theta_I$ is ground and false at I. The discussion above shows that S has a decorated tree.

Given a decorated tree $(T, C_\bullet, \theta_\bullet)$ for S', either the root ϵ is a leaf, then C_ϵ is necessarily the empty clause $\square$, and we are done. Or we find a path through T as follows. Define the ground atom H_I and the sign $\pm_I$, for each leaf I, so that $\pm_I H_I$ is the literal $\pm A_i^0$ in $C_I \theta_I$ with the highest index i; i.e., the lowest (largest) literal on the path leading to I.

Definition 1 (Generative). *Let us say that C_I, and by extension $C_I \theta_I$, is generative if and only if $\pm_I$ is the $+$ sign, and no literal is selected: $\mathrm{sel}\,(C_I) = \emptyset$.*

This is our version of Bachmair and Ganzinger's notion of *productive* clauses. Any clause C_I can be written uniquely as $\pm_I H_I \vee +\mathcal{P}_I \vee -\mathcal{N}_I$, where $\mathcal{P}_I$ is the set of atoms occurring under the $+$ sign in C_I (except H_I), and $\mathcal{N}_I$ is the set of atoms occurring under the $-$ sign in C_I. (We write $+\mathcal{P}$ for the disjunction of all $+B$, $B \in \mathcal{P}$, and $-\mathcal{N}$ for the disjunction of all $-B$, $B \in \mathcal{N}$.) Generative clauses are those where $\pm_I$ is the $+$ sign, and no literal is selected in $-\mathcal{N}_I$.

Now build a specific interpretation by Bachmair-Ganzinger forcing. Intuitively, each productive clause can be written as a Horn-like clause $H_I \Leftarrow -\mathcal{P}_I \wedge +\mathcal{N}_I$, stating that H_I should be set to true whenever all atoms in $\mathcal{P}_I$ are false and all atoms in $\mathcal{N}_I$ are true. We say that $-\mathcal{P}_I \wedge +\mathcal{N}_I$ is *true*, and that H_I is *forced* whenever this happens; otherwise, H_I will be set to the default value "false". We shall do so while traveling downwards inside T. E.g., look at Figure 1. The clause $+p$ is necessarily generative. The clause $+q \vee -p$ cannot be generative, because the only positive atom is not maximal, and similarly for $+r \vee -q$. Then, starting from vertex **1**, we let r be set to the default value false—no generative clause forces it to true. So we must go down left, and arrive at vertex **2**. Then we let q be false, go to **4**, and finally force p to true, arriving at **9**. Formally:

Definition 2. *Let $(T, C_\bullet, \theta_\bullet)$ be a decorated tree. Define a failure node I in T as follows. Let $I_0 = \epsilon$ be the root of T. Then define I_k, $k \geq 1$, by induction on k as follows. Let I_k be given. If I_k is a failure node, then stop, and let $I = I_k$. Otherwise, if there is a generative clause $C_{I'} = +H_{I'} \vee +\mathcal{P}_{I'} \vee -\mathcal{N}_{I'}$ such that $-\mathcal{P}_{I'}\theta_{I'} \wedge +\mathcal{N}_{I'}\theta_{I'}$ is true in I_k and $H_{I'}\theta_{I'} = A_{k+1}^0$, then force A_{k+1}^0 to true: define I_{k+1} as $I_k, +A_{k+1}^0$. Otherwise, let I_{k+1} be I_k.*

Alternatively, the failure node I is obtained by traveling down T, starting from the root. At each non-leaf vertex, we prefer to take the left branch, unless the left successor I' is already a failure node and $C_{I'}$ has no selected atom (in which case $C_{I'}$ is the generative clause indicated in Definition 2). This stops at a leaf I. Either the last direction we took was left, and then there must be a selected atom in I (this will ensure the left alternative in condition (iv)), or the last direction we took was right, in which case the maximal atom in $C_I \theta_I$ will have the $-$ sign (ensuring the right alternative in condition (iv)). We prove this in Lemma 2 below.

Clearly,

Lemma 1. *The partial interpretation I of Definition 2 satisfies the following two properties:*

(I.1) *For every generative clause $C_{I'}$ such that $-\mathcal{P}_{I'}\theta_{I'} \wedge +\mathcal{N}_{I'}\theta_{I'}$ is true in I, $H_{I'}\theta_{I'}$ is true in I.*

(I.2) *If H is a true atom in I, then there is a generative clause $C_{I'}$ such that $H_{I'}\theta_{I'} = H$. Moreover, $-\mathcal{P}_{I'}\theta_{I'} \wedge +\mathcal{N}_{I'}\theta_{I'}$ is true in I.*

These properties crucially depend on the fact that once an atom has been forced to true, resp. false, in I_k, it will remain so in all subsequent $I_{k'}$, $k' \geq k$. (Whence the name of forcing.)

The failure node I will be the place where resolution takes place, much as inference nodes were the places where resolution took place in Section 2.1. Let us see how I provides us with the main clause $C' \vee -A'_1 \vee \ldots \vee -A'_\ell$, so that condition (iv) is satisfied:

Lemma 2. *If there is at least one selected literal in C_I, C_I can be written as $C' \vee -A'_1 \vee \ldots \vee -A'_\ell$, where $-A'_1, \ldots, -A'_\ell$ are exactly the selected literals of C_I, and $\ell \geq 1$. Otherwise, let σ be any substitution that is more general than θ_I. Then, C_I is necessarily of the form $C' \vee -A'_1$, where $-A'_1\sigma$ is maximal in $C_I\sigma$, i.e., where $-A'_1\sigma \not\succ B$ for every atom B in $C'\sigma$.*

Proof. If $sel(C_I)$ is non-empty, this is clear. So assume $sel(C_I) = \emptyset$. Consider $\pm_I H_I$. If $\pm_I$ were $+$, C_I would be generative. But since $C_I\theta_I$ is false at I, $-\mathcal{P}_I\theta_I \wedge +\mathcal{N}_I\theta_I$ is true in I. By $(I.1)$ $H_I\theta_I$ would be true in I, too. This would make $C_I\theta_I$ true at I, contradiction. So $\pm_I$ is $-$. Let $-A'_1$ be H_I. Clearly, $A'_1\theta_I$ is below or equal to $A\theta_I$ for any A in C'. So $A'_1\sigma \not\succ A\sigma$, since $\succ$ is stable and $\sigma \sqsubseteq \theta_I$. $\square$

We now show that the other conditions (i), (ii), (iii) on the rule of ordered resolution with selection also apply:

Lemma 3. *Let $A'_1, \ldots, A'_\ell$ be defined as in Lemma 2. For each i, $1 \leq i \leq \ell$, there is a generative clause $C_{I'_i}$ such that $H_{I'_i}\theta_{I'_i} = A'_i\theta_I$.*

Write $C_{I'_i}$ as $C_i \vee +A_{i1} \vee \ldots \vee +A_{in_i}$, where $+A_{i1}, \ldots, +A_{in_i}$ are all the literals L in $C_{I'_i}$ such that $L\theta_{I'_i} = +A'_i\theta_I$. Then:

(i) $n_i \geq 1$;

(ii) *the mgu $\sigma = mgu\{A_{ij} = A'_i | 1 \leq i \leq \ell, 1 \leq j \leq n_i\}$ exists, and $\sigma \sqsubseteq \theta$, where*
$\theta = \theta_I \cup \theta_{I'_1} \cup \theta_{I'_2} \cup \ldots \cup \theta_{I'_\ell}$;

(iii) $sel(C_i \vee +A_{i1} \vee \ldots \vee +A_{in_i}) = \emptyset$ *and $A_{i1}\sigma \not\succ B$ for every atom B in $C_i\sigma$, for every i, $1 \leq i \leq \ell$;*

Proof. Since $C_I \theta_I$ is false at I, all the atoms $A'_i \theta_I$ are true in I. By $(I.2)$, first part, there is a generative clause $C_{I'_i}$ such that $H_{I'_i} \theta_{I'_i} = A'_i \theta_I$. Necessarily, $C_{I'_i} \theta_{I'_i}$ contains the literal $+A'_i \theta_I$.

Let therefore $+A_{i1}, \ldots, +A_{in_i}$, $n_i \geq 1$, be all the literals L in $C_{I'_i}$ such that $L\theta_{I'_i} = +A'_i \theta_I$, and let C_i be the disjunction of the remaining literals of $C_{I'_i}$. (Note that there may be *several* such literals L, whence n_i may be different from 1, requiring positive factoring.) We have just found the side premise $C_{I'_i} = C_i \vee +A_{i1} \vee \ldots \vee +A_{in_i}$. Since $n_i \geq 1$, *(i)* follows.

Then, $A_{ij}\theta_{I'_i} = A'_i \theta_I$. Since without loss of generality, A_{ij} and $A_{i'j'}$ have no free variable in common whenever $i \neq i'$, and since A_{ij} and $A'_{i'}$ have no free variable in common (for all i, i', j), the substitution $\theta_I \cup \theta_{I'_1} \cup \theta_{I'_2} \cup \ldots \cup \theta_{I'_\ell}$ makes sense, and unifies all A_{ij}s and A'_is: *(ii)* follows.

Since $C_{I'_i}$ is generative, no literal is selected in it. Assume that $A_{ij}\sigma \precsim B\sigma$ for some $B \in C_i$; by stability, using $\sigma \sqsubseteq \theta_{I'_i}$, $A_{ij}\theta_{I'_i} \precsim B\theta_{I'_i}$, that is, $H_{I'_i}\theta_{I'_i} \precsim B\theta_{I'_i}$. This is impossible, since $H_{I'_i}\theta_{I'_i}$ is the largest literal in $C_{I'_i}\theta_{I'_i}$, since by construction $B\theta_{I'_i} \neq H_{I'_i}\theta_{I'_i}$, and since $\succsim$ restricts to an ordering on ground atoms. So *(iii)* follows. $\qquad\square$

Therefore $C_1\sigma \vee \ldots \vee C_\ell\sigma \vee C'\sigma$ is indeed inferable by the rule of ordered resolution with selection.

We now turn to termination. Let S' be the set of clauses of which $(T, C_\bullet, \theta_\bullet)$ is a decorated tree, and let S'' be S' union the resolvent $C_1\sigma \vee \ldots \vee C_\ell\sigma \vee C'\sigma$. We shall build a new decorated tree $(T', C'_\bullet, \theta'_\bullet)$, for S'' this time, in Definition 3 below, in such a way that $(T', C'_\bullet, \theta'_\bullet)$ is less than $(T, C_\bullet, \theta_\bullet)$ in some well-founded ordering.

This ordering must be more sophisticated than the natural ordering on sizes $|T|$ of trees T that we used in Section 2.1. To use this ordering, we should show that the resolvent is false at some vertex I' strictly above I, which would allow us to define T' as T, with the subtree rooted at I' chopped out. But I' may well be I itself in our new setting. This is mainly because we do not implement negative factoring.

As a consolation, we check that the resolvent $(C_1\sigma \vee \ldots \vee C_\ell\sigma \vee C'\sigma)\theta = C_1\theta_{I'_1} \vee \ldots \vee C_\ell\theta_{I'_\ell} \vee C'\theta_I$ is false at I itself. In the problematic case where the highest vertex I' where this is false is I itself (and the chopping described above would not decrease the size of the tree), this will allow us to redecorate I with $C_1\sigma \vee \ldots \vee C_\ell\sigma \vee C'\sigma, \theta$ instead of C_I, θ_I. We shall see that the new decoration is then smaller than the old one in a suitable ordering.

So let us check that $C_1\theta_{I'_1} \vee \ldots \vee C_\ell\theta_{I'_\ell} \vee C'\theta_I$ is false at I. $C'\theta_I$ is false at I, since $C'\theta_I$ is a sub-clause of $C_I\theta_I$, which is false at I. And each $C_i\theta_{I'_i}$, $1 \leq i \leq \ell$, is false at I, by the following argument. The generative clause $C_{I'_i}$ equals $+H_{I'_i} \vee +\mathcal{P}_{I'_i} \vee -\mathcal{N}_{I'_i}$. By construction of $C_{I'_i}$ and by $(I.2)$, second part, $-\mathcal{P}_{I'_i}\theta_{I'_i} \wedge +\mathcal{N}_{I'_i}\theta_{I'_i}$ is true at I. By construction, $C_i\theta_{I'_i}$ is exactly the sub-clause $+\mathcal{P}_{I'_i}\theta_{I'_i} \vee -\mathcal{N}_{I'_i}\theta_{I'_i}$, which is false at I. So $(C_1\sigma \vee \ldots \vee C_\ell\sigma \vee C'\sigma)\theta$ is indeed false at I. Since it only contains atoms not lower than the atoms in the premises, it is false at I.

Therefore, we define:

Definition 3. *Let I' be the highest vertex in T, above I, where the resolvent $(C_1\sigma \vee \ldots \vee C_\ell\sigma \vee C'\sigma)\theta$ is false. Define the new decorated tree $(T', C'_\bullet, \theta'_\bullet)$ as follows:*

(a) *If I' is strictly higher than I in T, then let T' be the closed tree whose leaves are I' plus all the leaves of T that are not below I'. ("Chop at I'.") Let $C'_{I'}$ be the resolvent $C_1\sigma \vee \ldots \vee C_\ell\sigma \vee C'\sigma$, and $\theta'_{I'}$ be θ. Let $C'_{I''}$ be $C_{I''}$ and $\theta'_{I''}$ be $\theta_{I''}$ for every $I'' \neq I'$.*
(b) *If $I' = I$, let T' be just T, C'_I be the resolvent $C_1\sigma \vee \ldots \vee C_\ell\sigma \vee C'\sigma$, θ'_I be θ; let $C'_{I''}$ be $C_{I''}$ and $\theta'_{I''}$ be $\theta_{I''}$ for every $I'' \neq I$.*

The latter case can only happen when the lowest atom of $(C_1\sigma \vee \ldots \vee C_\ell\sigma \vee C'\sigma)\theta$ is the same as that of $C_I\theta_I$, i.e., $H_I\theta_I$. Consider the other literals of $(C_1\sigma \vee \ldots \vee C_\ell\sigma \vee C'\sigma)\theta = C_1\theta_{I'_1} \vee \ldots \vee C_\ell\theta_{I'_\ell} \vee C'\theta_I$. The literals in $C_i\theta_{I'_i}$, $1 \leq i \leq \ell$, are, by definition of C_i, strictly higher than $H_{I'_i}\theta_{I'_i} = A'_i\theta_I$, which is an atom of $C_I\theta_I$, and is therefore higher than or equal to H_I. The literals of $C_i\theta_{I'_i}$ are then always strictly higher than H_I. The only reason why H_I can occur in $(C_1\sigma \vee \ldots \vee C_\ell\sigma \vee C'\sigma)\theta = C_1\theta_{I'_1} \vee \ldots \vee C_\ell\theta_{I'_\ell} \vee C'\theta_I$ is therefore that it occurs in $C'\theta_I$. What matters here is that by replacing $C_I\theta_I$ by $C_1\theta_{I'_1} \vee \ldots \vee C_\ell\theta_{I'_\ell} \vee C'\theta_I$ as the clause at leaf I, we have replaced large literals $H_I\theta_I$ by clauses $C_i\theta_{I'_i}$ which contain an arbitrary number of strictly smaller literals.

This suggests defining a measure based on multiset extensions. Formally:

Definition 4. *Define $A_i^0 \succ' A_j^0$ if and only if $i > j$. For every failure node I' in a decorated tree $(T, C_\bullet, \theta_\bullet)$, let $\mu_1(C_{I'}, \theta_{I'})$ be the multiset of all $A\theta_{I'}$, where $\pm A$ ranges over the literals of $C_{I'}$. This is ordered by the multiset extension $\succ'_{mul}$ of $\succ'$.*

(Note that $A \succ B$ implies $A \succ' B$, but the converse implication fails in general, unless $\succ$ is total on ground atoms, which we do not assume.)

In case (b), where $I' = I$, we therefore obtain $\mu_1(C_I, \theta_I) \succ'_{mul} \mu_1(C'_I, \theta'_I)$.

Definition 5. *Define $\mu^-(T, C_\bullet, \theta_\bullet)$ as the multiset of all measures $\mu_1(C_{I'}, \theta_{I'})$, when I' ranges over the failure nodes of T.*

In case (b), $\mu_1(C_I, \theta_I)$ decreases strictly, while $\mu_1(C_{I''}, \theta_{I''})$ remains unchanged for the other leaves I''. So $\mu^-(T, C_\bullet, \theta_\bullet)$ $(\succ'_{mul})_{mul}$ $\mu^-(T', C'_\bullet, \theta'_\bullet)$ in case (b). Let $|T|$ denote the size of T, and note that $|T| = |T'|$ in this case. In case (a), clearly $|T| > |T'|$, so in any case $\mu(T, C_\bullet, \theta_\bullet)$ $(>, (\succ'_{mul})_{mul})_{lex}$ $\mu(T', C'_\bullet, \theta'_\bullet)$, where:

Definition 6. *The measure $\mu(T, C_\bullet, \theta_\bullet)$ is defined as the pair $(|T|, \mu^-(T, C_\bullet, \theta_\bullet))$.*

Since $>$ is well-founded, and since $\succ'$, which is an ordering on a *finite* set of atoms $A_1^0, \ldots, A_n^0$, is also well-founded, we conclude:

Lemma 4. *The reduction relation that replaces $(T, C_\bullet, \theta_\bullet)$ by $(T', C'_\bullet, \theta'_\bullet)$, as defined in Definition 3, terminates.*

We now terminate the proof of Theorem 1. Assume S unsatisfiable. Starting from a decorated tree for S, we build a derivation by ordered resolution with selection of $S = S_0$, S_1, ..., S_k, ..., each mapped to a decorated tree $(T_0, C_{0\bullet}, \theta_{0\bullet})$, $(T_1, C_{1\bullet}, \theta_{1\bullet})$, ..., $(T_k, C_{k\bullet}, \theta_{k\bullet})$, ..., where each decorated tree is obtained from the previous one by the reduction defined in Definition 3. By Lemma 4, this terminates, say at step k. Then the root of T_k must be a failure node, so S_k contains the empty clause $\square$. $\square$

This proof clearly takes its roots in both the semantic tree technique and Bachmair and Ganzinger forcing. Note that we only require $\succsim$ to be strongly stable. We don't need it to be a reduction ordering, or to be total on ground atoms, or even to be well-founded.

2.3   Redundancy Elimination and Games

An important component of every automated deduction system is a set of *redundancy elimination* rules. Classic redundant clauses include tautologies and subsumed clauses [BG01a]. Other useful redundancy elimination rules include simplification rules. A crucial import of Bachmair and Ganzinger's approach to resolution was to define standard redundancy criteria, a unified approach justifying which redundant clauses can be eliminated, and which simplification rules can be applied while preserving completeness.

We may see the subtle interaction between resolution and redundancy rules as a two-player game [dN95] between a *player* P and an *opponent* O. At each turn, either the empty clause $\square$ has been derived, and P wins, or P chooses a resolvent to produce, then O applies any finite number of redundancy rules. Completeness is then equivalent to the existence of a winning strategy for P, starting from any unsatisfiable set S of clauses.

For simplicity, and without loss of generality, we shall assume that O can only add clauses, or remove clauses. Replacing and simplifying clauses will be implemented by adding the replacement clauses and removing the replaced clauses.

The proof of Theorem 1 shows what resolvent P should play at each turn; this resolvent is the one we constructed, which makes $\mu(T, C_\bullet, \theta_\bullet)$ decrease strictly. Completeness in the presence of redundancy elimination rules follows, as soon as, whatever O does, it can only make the chosen measure $\mu(T, C_\bullet, \theta_\bullet)$ decrease or stay the same. This is obvious when O adds a clause: $(T, C_\bullet, \theta_\bullet)$ stays the same. This is trickier when O removes a clause. We need to make sure that: (†) whatever clause C is removed by O from the current clause set S', for any leaf I' of T such that $C = C_{I'}$ (note that there might be 0, 1, or several such leaves), there is another clause $C'_{I'}$ in S such that some ground instance $C'_{I'}\theta'_{I'}$ of $C'_{I'}$ is false at I', and $\mu_1(C_{I'}, \theta_{I'}) \succeq'_{mul} \mu_1(C'_{I'}, \theta'_{I'})$, where $\succeq'_{mul}$ is the reflexive closure of $\succ'_{mul}$. If so, we shall change $(T, C_\bullet, \theta_\bullet)$ into $(T', C'_\bullet, \theta'_\bullet)$, where $T' = T$, $C'_{I'}$ and $\theta'_{I'}$ are as given above for all leaves I' such that $C = C_{I'}$ (note that $C'_{I'}\theta'_{I'}$ cannot be false strictly above I', since I' is a failure node, whence $T' = T$), and $C'_{I'} = C_{I'}$, $\theta'_{I'} = \theta_{I'}$ for all other leaves I'. It is clear that $\mu(T, C_\bullet, \theta_\bullet)$ will be larger than $\mu(T', C'_\bullet, \theta'_{I'})$ in the reflexive closure of $(>, (\succ'_{mul})_{mul})_{lex}$, whence completeness is preserved.

Let us find a more readable criterion than condition (†) above. Recall that $C_1, \ldots, C_k \models C$ if and only if every Herbrand interpretation that makes all ground instances of $C_1, \ldots, C_k$ true also makes every ground instance of C true. Equivalently, every Herbrand interpretation that makes some ground instance of C false must make some ground instance of some C_i, $1 \leq i \leq k$, false. By analogy, let us say that $C_1 \ldots, C_k \models^* C$ if and only if every *partial* interpretation that makes some ground instance of C false must make some ground instance of some C_i false, too, $1 \leq i \leq k$.

Imitating Bachmair and Ganzinger's standard redundancy criterion, we may enforce the above condition (†) by requiring the stronger property that $C_1, \ldots, C_k \models^* C$, for some clauses $C_1, \ldots, C_k$ in the current clause set S such that $C \succ_{mul} C_1, \ldots, C \succ_{mul} C_k$. Here $\succ_{mul}$ makes sense provided we see clauses as multisets of literals, ignoring signs. Let us show that indeed (†) must hold. For each leaf I' where $C = C_{I'}$, since $C_1, \ldots, C_k \models^* C$, there is a clause $C_i, 1 \leq i \leq k$, having a ground instance that is false at I'. Let $C'_{I'}$ be C_i, and $C'_{I'}, \theta'_{I'}$ be the corresponding ground instance. We must show that $\mu_1(C_{I'}, \theta_{I'}) \succeq'_{mul} \mu_1(C'_{I'}, \theta'_{I'})$. Since $C_{I'} = C \succ_{mul} C_i = C'_{I'}$, we may obtain $C'_{I'}$ from $C_{I'}$ by repetitively replacing atoms by finitely many smaller ones in the $\succ$ strict ordering. Since $\succ$ is stable, we may reproduce this at the ground level, and obtain $C'_{I'} \theta'_{I'}$ from $C_{I'} \theta_{I'}$ by repetitively replacing ground atoms by smaller ones in the $\succ$ strict ordering. These are in particular smaller in $\succ'$ as well. So $\mu_1(C_{I'}, \theta_{I'}) \succeq'_{mul} \mu_1(C'_{I'}, \theta'_{I'})$, and (†) follows.

To recap, the natural standard redundancy criterion in our case reads as:

> If $C \in S$, and $C_1 \ldots, C_k \models^* C$ for some clauses $C_1, \ldots, C_k$ in S such that $C \succ_{mul} C_1, \ldots, C \succ_{mul} C_k$, then erase C.

We have shown that applying this criterion at any time during ordered resolution with selection preserves completeness. This is close to Bachmair and Ganzinger's standard redundancy criterion, which uses $\models$ instead of $\models^*$.

We illustrate this on a few well-known redundancy elimination rules.

In case C is a tautology $C_0 \vee +A \vee -A$, k is zero, and the criterion is vacuously satisfied: we can always eliminate tautologies without breaking completeness in ordered resolution with selection.

In case $C = C_{I'}$ is subsumed by some clause $C_1 = C'_{I''}$ ($k = 1$), it is not necessarily the case that $C \succ_{mul} C_1$, or even that $\mu_1(C_{I'}, \theta_{I'}) \succeq'_{mul} \mu_1(C'_{I''}, \theta'_{I''})$. E.g., take $C = +P(x)$, $C_1 = +P(x) \vee +P(y)$, which subsume each other, while $C \not\succ_{mul} C_1$. This suggests that eliminating subsumed clauses is fraught with danger. And indeed, it is well-known that eliminating backward-subsumed clauses may break completeness. We shall let the reader check that we indeed obtain $\mu_1(C_{I'}, \theta_{I'}) \succeq'_{mul} \mu_1(C'_{I''}, \theta'_{I''})$ as soon as $C'_{I''}$ subsumes C *linearly*, i.e., C is of the form $C'_{I''} \sigma \vee C''$, where σ does not unify any distinct literals in $C'_{I''}$ (i.e., $C'_{I''} \sigma$ is not a factor of $C'_{I''}$). This justifies that eliminating linearly subsumed clauses (whether backward or forward) does not break completeness. Eliminating linearly subsumed clauses is implemented in SPASS [WBH+02]. The linearity restriction is also implicit in work by Bachmair and Ganzinger, who define clauses as multisets, not sets (we shall do so as well in Section 3).

Our argument shows that completeness is in fact preserved if we remove $C = C'_{I''}\sigma \vee C''$, when both C and $C'_{I''}$ are in S, whatever σ is (i.e., even when C is subsumed non-linearly by $C'_{I''}$), provided C'' contains an atom A such that $A \succ B$ for every B in $C'_{I''}\sigma$: indeed in this case C can only be false at a vertex strictly below I'', hence C cannot be of the form $C_{I'}$ for any failure node I'.

Many other redundancy elimination rules are listed in [BG01a], on which the arguments above apply. We would like to end this section by examining the subtle case of the splitting-with-naming rule of [RV01a] (which was called *splittingless splitting* in [GLRV04], by analogy with inductionless induction). This will in particular show where using $\models^*$ instead of $\models$ makes a difference. Assume we are given an initial set of clauses on a set $\mathcal{P}$ of predicates. Call these $\mathcal{P}$-clauses. For each equivalence class of $\mathcal{P}$-clauses C modulo renaming, let $\ulcorner C \urcorner$ be a fresh nullary predicate symbol not in $\mathcal{P}$. Call these fresh symbols the *splitting symbols*. The splittingless splitting rule allows one to replace a clause of the form $C \vee C'$, where C and C' are non-empty clauses that have no variable in common, where C' is a $\mathcal{P}$-clause, and where C contains at least one atom $P(t_1, \ldots, t_n)$ with $P \in \mathcal{P}$, by the two clauses $C \vee -q$ and $+q \vee C'$, where $q = \ulcorner C' \urcorner$. This rule is not only effective in practice [RV01a], it is also an important tool in proving certain subclasses of first-order logic decidable, and to obtain optimal complexity bounds (see e.g., [GL05]). Take $\succ$ so that $P(t_1, \ldots, t_n) \succ q$ for every $P \in \mathcal{P}$ and for any splitting symbol q. Then it is easy to see that the standard redundancy criterion is satisfied, and we can indeed *replace* $C \vee C'$ by the smaller clauses $C \vee -q$ and $+q \vee C'$. So completeness is preserved, as shown by Bachmair and Ganzinger, as soon as $\succ$ is a well-founded reduction ordering that is total on ground terms.

Our approach, as it is, does *not* apply here. We are paying the dues for all the benefits that our use of compactness brought us. Indeed, remember our proof started by taking a finite subset of ground atoms $A_1^0, \ldots, A_n^0$ that are required for finding a contradiction. While P is only required to play clauses with ground instances among the latter, O is not limited in any such way. Here, O may indeed produce $C \vee -q$ and $+q \vee C'$, where q is *not* among $A_1^0, \ldots, A_n^0$. Then we cannot remove $C \vee C'$. Assume that $C \vee C'$ is $C_{I'_i}$, for some leaves I'_i, $1 \leq i \leq k$. There is no reason why $C \vee -q$ or $+q \vee C'$ should be false at any I'_i: indeed q is *undecided*. In other words, while $(C \vee -q), (+q \vee C') \models C \vee C'$, we do *not* get $(C \vee -q), (+q \vee C') \models^* C \vee C'$. Bachmair and Ganzinger's standard redundancy criterion applies, but our variant does not.

This can be repaired easily if O can only generate finitely many splitting symbols. In this case, just assume they are all among $A_1^0, \ldots, A_n^0$, and completeness again follows. E.g., in [GL05], the only splitting symbols we ever need are of the form $\ulcorner B(X) \urcorner$, where $B(X)$ is any disjunction of literals $-P(X)$, where P is taken from a finite set. So there are finitely many splitting symbols, and we can without loss of generality assume they are all among $A_1^0, \ldots, A_n^0$.

Despite these difficulties, completeness still holds in the general case. However, this is more complex: first, we need to assume a form of our old condition (∗), namely that the ordering $\succ$ on splitting symbols can be extended to a total ordering on the splitting symbols $q_1, q_2, \ldots, q_i, \ldots$ (a similar condition is used in [SV05, Theorem 4]); second, we need to consider transfinite semantic trees [HR91] based on the transfinite (indexed by the ordinal $\omega + n$) enumeration $q_1, q_2, \ldots, q_i, \ldots, A_1^0, \ldots, A_n^0$, where $A_1^0, \ldots, A_n^0$ are the ground atoms $P(t_1, \ldots, t_n)$, $P \in \mathcal{P}$, given by the compactness theorem... but this is Bachmair and Ganzinger's usual forcing argument in disguise.

2.4   Where Trees Matter: Completeness of Linear Resolution

Until now, we have only used semantic trees as a convenient way of organizing paths, i.e., Herbrand interpretations. Similarly, Bachmair and Ganzinger's forcing argument builds an interpretation. One might therefore ask whether the use of *trees* brings any additional benefit than just reasoning on paths.

We claim that *linear resolution* can be shown complete using a semantic tree technique. This appears to be new by itself: the standard proof of completeness of linear resolution is by Anderson and Bledsoe's excess literal argument, applied to so-called minimally unsatisfiable sets of clauses. Furthermore, our semantic tree technique will really use trees, not just the paths inside the trees.

The rule of *linear resolution* can be explained as follows. Start from a clause set S_0, and pick a clause C_0 in S_0, non-deterministically. Find a resolvent of C_0 (the *center* clause) with some clause in S_0 (the *side* clause). Name this resolvent C_1; this is the *top* clause. The current clause set is now $S_1 = S_0 \cup \{C_1\}$. Then find a resolvent of the top clause C_1 (now the new center clause) with some side clause in S_1, call it C_2 (the new top clause). Proceed, getting a sequence of successive resolvents C_i, $i \geq 0$, until (hopefully) the empty clause $\square$ is obtained. Observe that this is a non-deterministic procedure. The point in linear resolution is that the only allowed center clause at the next step is the previous top clause.

That linear resolution is complete means that, if S_0 is unsatisfiable, then there is a sequence of choices, first of C_0, then of each side clause, so that the empty clause $\square$ eventually occurs as the top clause. Our technique will establish a more general result: linear *ordered* resolution, where each resolvent is constrained to be ordered (see Section 2.1), is complete again. This holds even if we only allow factoring in center clauses but disallow it in side clauses.

This refinement of linear resolution can be formalized as follows. The only deduction rule is:

$$\frac{\mp A_1' \vee C' \quad \pm A_1 \vee \ldots \pm A_m \vee C}{C\sigma \vee C'\sigma} \quad \begin{array}{l} m \geq 1, \\ \sigma = mgu(A_1 = A_2 = \ldots = A_m = A_1'), \\ \forall B \in C\sigma, A_i\sigma \not\precsim B \\ 1 \leq i \leq m \end{array}$$

where $\pm$ is the same sign throughout, and $\mp$ is its opposite. The left premise is meant to be the side clause, and the right premise is the center clause.

The process of linear resolution is then defined through a transition relation. A *state* of the linear resolution procedure is a pair (S, C), where C is a clause in S. The *transition relation* of linear resolution) is given by

$$(S, C) \rightsquigarrow (S \cup \{C'\}, C')$$

where

$$\frac{C''\quad C}{C'}$$

by the ordered linear resolution rule above, for some $C'' \in S$. Remember that C is the center clause, C'' is the side clause, and C' is the top clause.

Completeness means that, if S is unsatisfiable, then $(S, C) \rightsquigarrow^* (S', \Box)$ for some $C \in S$ and some clause set S'.

We prove this by modifying the notion of semantic tree slightly. E.g., consider the example of Figure 1, this time with the ordering $q \prec r \prec p$, see Figure 2.

Now look at vertex **2**. The choice on r here is irrelevant: there is no clause decorating any failure node below **2** that depends on the truth value of r. It is therefore tempting to reduce the semantic tree to the one shown in Figure 3, where vertex **2** has been replaced by the subtree rooted at vertex **5**. This reduction process is similar to that used in BDDs [Ake78].

We now allow paths in semantic trees to skip over some atoms, as in Figure 3, where r is skipped in the paths on the left: r is a *don't care*. But atoms will still be enumerated in the same ordering on each path. Call the resulting modified notion a *lax semantic tree* for S. Each path, hence each leaf (failure node) defines a *lax* partial interpretation, defined as a finite list $\pm_1 A_{i_1}^0, \pm_2 A_{i_2}^0, \ldots, \pm_k A_{i_k}^0$ of signed ground atoms, $1 \le i_1 < i_2 < \ldots < i_k$. We define *decorated* lax trees (for S) in the expected way, as a triple $\mathcal{T} = (T, C_\bullet, \theta_\bullet)$, where $C_I \in S$ and θ_I are such that $C_I \in S$, $C_I \theta_I$ is ground and false at leaf I.

We shall fix an unsatisfiable S and an enumeration $A_1^0, A_2^0, \ldots, A_n^0$ guaranteed by the compactness theorem in the rest of the section.

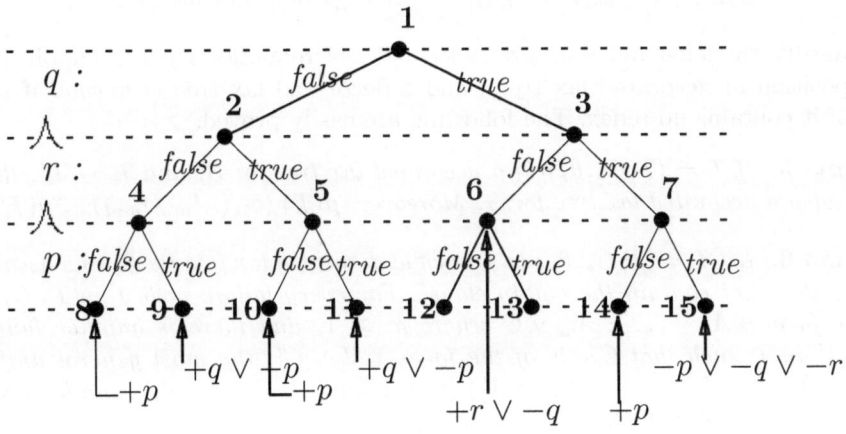

Fig. 2. Another semantic tree, based on a different ordering

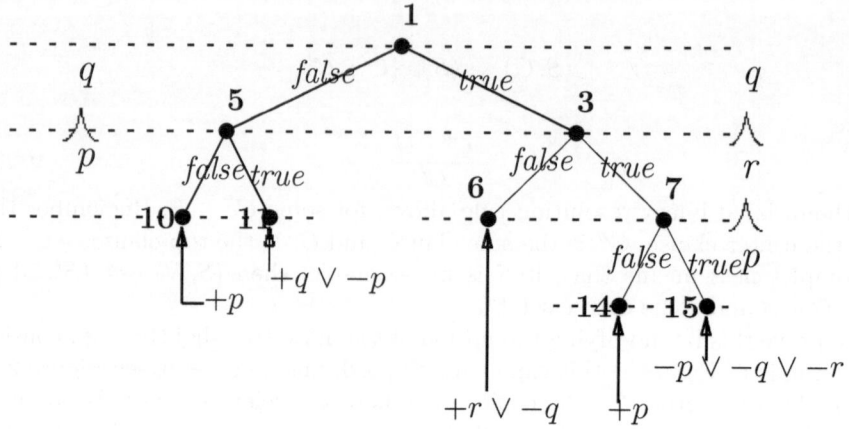

Fig. 3. A normal decorated lax tree

We now define *reduction* on decorated lax trees $\mathcal{T}$ as follows. It will be helpful to denote a decorated lax subtree of $\mathcal{T}$ of the form shown on the right as $A(\mathcal{T}_{left}, \mathcal{T}_{right})$. We say that a subtree *uses* A if and only if it has a failure node I such that A occurs as a ground atom in $C_I \theta_I$.

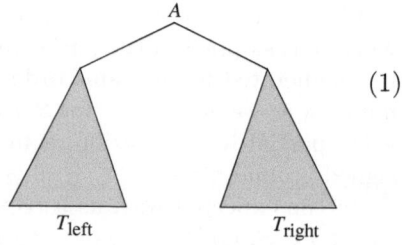

(1)

We use the following two reduction rules:

$$A(\mathcal{T}_{left}, \mathcal{T}_{right}) \rightsquigarrow \mathcal{T}_{right} \qquad \text{if } \mathcal{T}_{right} \text{ does not use } A$$
$$A(\mathcal{T}_{left}, \mathcal{T}_{right}) \rightsquigarrow \mathcal{T}_{left} \qquad \text{if } \mathcal{T}_{left} \text{ does not use } A$$

Standardly, the left-hand sides are called *redexes*, reduction rules are applied at any position in decorated lax trees, and a decorated lax tree is *normal* if and only if it contains no redex. The following are easily proved.

Lemma 5. *If $\mathcal{T} = (T, C_\bullet, \theta_\bullet)$ is a decorated lax tree for S, and $\mathcal{T} \rightsquigarrow \mathcal{T}'$, then $\mathcal{T}'$ is also a decorated lax tree for S. Moreover, $\mu(\mathcal{T}) \ (>, (\succ'_{mul})_{mul})_{lex} \ \mu(\mathcal{T}')$.*

Lemma 6. *Let $\mathcal{T} = (T, C_\bullet, \theta_\bullet)$ be a normal decorated lax tree for S, and assume that S does not contain the empty clause. For every failure node I in T, C_I is of the form $\pm A_1 \vee \ldots \pm A_m \vee C$ where $m \geq 1$, and there is another failure node I' in T such that $C_{I'}$ is of the form $\mp A'_1 \vee C'$, the most general unifier $\sigma = mgu(A_1 = A_2 = \ldots = A_m = A'_1)$ is well-defined, $\sigma \sqsubseteq \theta_I \cup \theta_{I'}$, and for every atom B in $C\sigma$, $A_i \sigma \not\succeq B$.*

Moreover, letting θ be such that $\sigma\theta = \theta_I \cup \theta_{I'}$, the ground instance $(C\sigma \vee C'\sigma)\theta$ of the linear resolvent $C\sigma \vee C'\sigma$ is false at I', and for every atom B in C, $A'_1 \theta_{I'} \succ' B\theta_I$.

Proof. Since the empty clause is not in S, C_I cannot be the empty clause.

Let A be the ground atom A_i^0 with the largest index i that occurs in $C_I\theta_I$, i.e., the last ground atom labeling an internal vertex occurring on the branch I. As a leaf, I may be the left successor of its parent, or its right successor. The following picture displays the case where I is left.

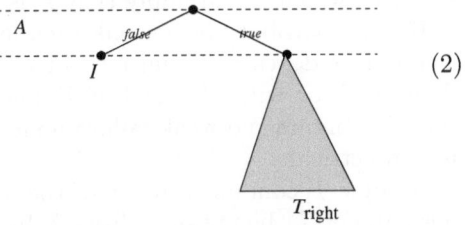

$$(2)$$

Assume I is left, as in the picture. The other case is symmetrical. So C_I is of the form $+A_1 \vee \ldots + A_m \vee C$, where $A_1, \ldots, A_m$ enumerate those atoms B in C_I such that $B\theta_I = A$. Since $\mathcal{T}$ is normal, (2) is not a redex, so $\mathcal{T}_{right}$ uses A: there is a failure node I' in $\mathcal{T}_{right}$ such that $C_{I'}\theta_{I'}$ contains the atom A. Because this clause must be false at I', A must occur negatively. So $C_{I'}$ is of the form $-A'_1 \vee C'$, where $A'_1\theta_{I'} = A$.

In particular, $\theta_I \cup \theta_{I'}$ is a unifier of $A_1, \ldots, A_m, A'_1$. Let σ be their mgu, and θ be such that $\sigma\theta = \theta_I \cup \theta_{I'}$.

Note that the atoms B that occur in C are such that $B\theta_I = A_j^0$ with $j < i$, so $A'_1\theta_{I'} = A_i^0 \succ' B\theta_I$. In particular, for every atom $B = B'\sigma$ that occurs in $C\sigma$, $A_i\theta_I = A_i^0 \succ' B\theta$, whence $A_i\sigma \not\precsim B$ since $\precsim$ is stable. It also follows that $(C\sigma \vee C'\sigma)\theta = C\theta_I \vee C'\theta_{I'}$ is false at I'. $\qquad\square$

Contrarily to ordered resolution, where we had to find an inference node, here *any* failure node will enable us to apply a resolution step. This is a consequence of the fact that $\mathcal{T}$ is normal.

Since reduction clearly terminates, if S is unsatisfiable, then it has a *normal* decorated lax tree. The reduction rules are not confluent, and in general normal forms are not unique. But there is only one normal form in the following special case, which is the only one we shall require.

Lemma 7. *Let $\mathcal{T} = (T, C_\bullet, \theta_\bullet)$ be a decorated lax tree for S. Say that a failure node I' in $\mathcal{T}$ is weak if and only if there is a ground atom A in I' (seen as a partial Herbrand interpretation, i.e., as a set of ground atoms) that does not occur in $C_{I'}\theta_{I'}$.*

Let I be a partial Herbrand interpretation, and assume that the only weak failure nodes I' in $\mathcal{T}$ are such that $I' \subseteq I$. Then $\mathcal{T}$ has a unique normal form $\mathcal{T}'$ for $\rightsquigarrow$. Moreover, (C_I, θ_I) still decorates some failure node I' in $\mathcal{T}'$, with $I' \subseteq I$.

Proof. For short, say that $\mathcal{T}$ is *good* if and only if its only weak failure nodes I' are such that $I' \subseteq I$. If $\mathcal{T}$ is good, then it can have at most one weak failure node: either it is normal, and there is nothing to prove, or one finds the weak failure node I' by following the unique branch from the root that goes to the left of A_i^0 if $-A_i^0 \in I$, or to the right if $+A_i^0 \in I$; since $-A_i^0$ or $+A_i^0$ is in $I' \subseteq I$, one of the two cases must happen.

Note that any subtree $\mathcal{T}'$ of $\mathcal{T}$ whose failure nodes are not weak is normal. Indeed, assume that $\mathcal{T}'$ contained a redex, say $A(\mathcal{T}_l, \mathcal{T}_r)$ where $\mathcal{T}_r$ does not use A.

Then any failure node I' in $\mathcal{T}_r$ is such that A does not occur in $C_{I'}\theta_{I'}$, although $+A \in I'$, which would imply that I' is weak.

If $\mathcal{T}$ is good but not normal, then let $I' \subseteq I$ be its unique weak failure node. The only redexes in $\mathcal{T}$ must be of the form $A(\mathcal{T}_l, \mathcal{T}_r)$ with I' a leaf of $\mathcal{T}_l$ and $\mathcal{T}_r$ normal, or with I' a leaf of $\mathcal{T}_r$ and $\mathcal{T}_l$ normal. Indeed, if I' is a leaf of $\mathcal{T}_l$, then $\mathcal{T}_r$ contains no weak failure node, and is therefore normal. The other case is symmetrical.

Assume $\mathcal{T}$ contains a redex of the form $A(\mathcal{T}_l, \mathcal{T}_r)$ with I' a leaf of $\mathcal{T}_l$, and $\mathcal{T}_r$ normal. Let $\mathcal{T}'$ be obtained from $\mathcal{T}$ by contracting this redex, necessarily to $\mathcal{T}_l$. Let I'' be the partial Herbrand interpretation obtained from I' by deleting $-A$. Clearly, I'' is a failure node in $\mathcal{T}'$, and is decorated with $(C_{I'}, \theta_{I'})$. We claim that I'' is the only weak failure node in $\mathcal{T}'$, if any. Indeed, for any other weak failure node I''' in $\mathcal{T}'$, either I''' or $I''' \cup \{-A\}$ was a failure node in $\mathcal{T}$. But either case implies $I''' \subseteq I$, since $\mathcal{T}$ is good, and I'' is the only failure node such that $I'' \subseteq I$.

In particular, if a good tree rewrites to another tree, then the latter is good. Among good trees, the relation $\leadsto$ has no critical pair: a critical pair would be a subtree of the form $A(\mathcal{T}_l, \mathcal{T}_r)$ that we could rewrite both as $\mathcal{T}_l$ and as $\mathcal{T}_r$; this would imply that $\mathcal{T}_l$ does not use A, hence that the unique weak failure node I' is in $\mathcal{T}_l$, and also, symmetrically, that I' is in $\mathcal{T}_r$, contradiction.

So $\leadsto$ is convergent on good trees. Since (C_I, θ_I) decorates the only possible weak failure node in $\mathcal{T}$, and any decoration of the unique weak failure node in a tree still decorates some failure node in any of its redexes, we conclude.   □

Completeness follows. Let S_0 be an unsatisfiable set of clauses. It has a decorated lax tree $\mathcal{T} = (T, C_\bullet, \theta_\bullet)$, which we may assume normal by Lemma 5. If the root of the tree is a failure node, then S_0 contains the empty clause. Otherwise, let C_0 be any clause in S_0 that decorates some failure node I in $\mathcal{T}$. Taking C_0 as the center clause, Lemma 6 guarantees that we can resolve C_0 with some side clause C_0' using the rule of linear resolution; C_0' decorates some other failure node I' in $\mathcal{T}$. Let C_1 be the resolvent. Lemma 6 also guarantees us that $C_1\theta$ is false at I' for some θ. We modify $\mathcal{T}$ by redecorating I' with the pair C_1, θ: we obtain another decorated lax tree $\mathcal{T}'$, which may fail to be good, as now the failure node I' may be weak. But this is the only failure node in $\mathcal{T}'$ that can be weak. So Lemma 7 applies: $\mathcal{T}'$ has a unique normal form $\widehat{\mathcal{T}'}$ for $\leadsto$, which is a decorated lax tree for $S_0 \cup \{C_1\}$. Moreover, C_1 still decorates some failure node in $\widehat{\mathcal{T}'}$, so that we can take C_2 as new center clause, and repeat the process.

Theorem 2. *Linear ordered resolution is complete: given any stable quasi-ordering $\succsim$, for any set of clauses S, S is unsatisfiable if and only if we can derive $\square$ by linear ordered resolution.*

Proof. It only remains to prove termination, which reduces to showing that $\mu(\mathcal{T})\ (>, (\succ'_{mul})_{mul})_{lex}\ \mu(\widehat{\mathcal{T}'})$, using the above notations. By Lemma 5, $\mu(\mathcal{T}')$ is larger than or equal to $\mu(\widehat{\mathcal{T}'})$ in $(>, (\succ'_{mul})_{mul})_{lex}$, so it remains to show $\mu(\mathcal{T})\ (>, (\succ'_{mul})_{mul})_{lex}\ \mu(\mathcal{T}')$. In turn, this follows from the fact that $\mu_1(C_{I'}, \theta_{I'}) \succ'_{mul} \mu_1(C_1, \theta)$, where we write $C_0' = C_{I'}$ as $\mp A_1' \vee C'$, C_0 as

$\pm A_1 \vee \ldots \pm A_m \vee C$, and we let σ, θ be as in Lemma 6, so that the resolvent is $C_1 = C\sigma \vee C'\sigma$. This fact is proved as in the ordered resolution with selection case: $\mu_1(C_1, \theta)$ is obtained from the multiset $\mu_1(C_{I'}, \theta_{I'})$ by replacing one occurrence of $A = A'_1\theta_{I'}$ by the multiset of atoms $B\theta_I$, $B \in C$. But $A'_1\theta_{I'} \succ' B\theta_I$ (Lemma 6). □

A nice consequence of this new completeness proof is, as for any other proof obtained by semantic trees, that completeness is easily seen to be retained in the presence of redundancy elimination techniques.

E.g., we can remove tautologies, because tautologies cannot decorate any failure node. But this should be understood in a slightly different manner as for ordinary resolution, because linear resolution is a non-deterministic process. The completeness argument above shows that *there is* a way of doing linear resolution that leads to the empty clause without deriving any tautology as top clause. So, whenever we use linear resolution and derive a tautology as top clause, we can immediately stop deriving new clauses and backtrack.

Similarly, we can eliminate linearly subsumed clauses. Backward subsumption is not an issue here. Forward subsumption is as subtle as tautology elimination: if the top clause is subsumed, then we can stop and backtrack. Alternately, the completeness argument shows that we can *replace* C' by C'_1, and continue with C'_1 as the new top clause, thus restarting a proof.

We would like to stress that the tree structure is important here: the above proof crucially rests on reduction $\rightsquigarrow$, which cannot be defined by just considering the paths of the tree T.

3   Ordered Resolution, Paramodulation and Factoring

We now move to clauses involving the equality predicate.

3.1   Inference Rules

Inference Rules. First, we give inference rules applying to clauses defined as multisets of atoms: the same atom may appear several times in a clause. A ground instance of a clause is a true instance, there is no need to apply contractions. We use also an ordering on atoms extending an ordering $\succ$ on terms that will be defined later.

Reflexivity is also called *equality resolution* in the literature, because it appears to be a resolution between the clause $-u = v \vee C$ and the reflexivity axiom $x = x$.

This inference system is known to be complete when the ordering is a stable ordering, which is monotonic, total and well-founded on ground terms, in which case it must have the subterm property as well. Relaxing any one of these properties raises the question of what the new inference rule should be. Some authors [BG01b, BGNR99] keep the same inference rule for paramodulation, but we prefer another formulation which pinpoints the needed properties of the ordering in use. This is why we have renamed the paramodulation inference rule

Resolution

$$\frac{+A \vee C \quad -A' \vee D}{C\sigma \vee D\sigma} \qquad \sigma = mgu(A = A'); \forall B \in C\sigma \vee D\sigma, A\sigma \not\prec B$$

Monotonic Paramodulation

$$\frac{C \vee l = r \qquad D \vee \pm A[u]}{C\sigma \vee D\sigma \vee \pm A\sigma[r\sigma]} \qquad \begin{cases} \sigma = mgu(l = u); \forall B \in C\sigma, (l\sigma = r\sigma) \not\prec B \\ r\sigma \not\prec l\sigma; \forall B \in D\sigma, A\sigma \not\prec B \end{cases}$$

Factoring

$$\frac{+A \vee +A' \vee C}{+A\sigma \vee C\sigma} \qquad \sigma = mgu(A = A'); \forall B \in C\sigma, A\sigma \not\prec B$$

Reflexivity

$$\frac{-u = v \vee C}{C\sigma} \qquad \sigma = mgu(u = v); \forall B \in C\sigma, (u\sigma = v\sigma) \not\prec B$$

Fig. 4. $\mathcal{ORMP}$: Ordered versions of Resolution, Monotonic Paramodulation, Factoring and Reflexivity

Ordered Paramodulation

$$\frac{C \vee l = r \qquad D \vee \pm A[u]}{C\sigma \vee D\sigma \vee \pm A\sigma[r\sigma]} \qquad \begin{cases} \sigma = mgu(l = u); \forall B \in C\sigma, (l\sigma = r\sigma) \not\prec B \\ A\sigma \not\prec A\sigma[r\sigma]; \forall B \in D\sigma, A\sigma \not\prec B \end{cases}$$

Fig. 5. Ordered Paramodulation Revisited

as *monotonic paramodulation*. We introduce now our version of paramodulation, *ordered paramodulation* and compare both rules by means of a few examples.

In ordered paramodulation, checking the rule instance has been replaced by checking the whole rewritten atom: ordered paramodulation coincides with monotonic paramodulation when the ordering is monotonic, total and well-founded. We call $\mathcal{ORP}$ the set of inference rules made of ordered resolution, ordered paramodulation, (ordered) factoring and (ordered) reflexivity.

Violating Monotonicity. $\mathcal{ORP}$ is incomplete when the ordering on terms does not satisfy monotonicity. Consider the following unsatisfiable set of ground clauses

$$\{gb = b, \ fg^2b \neq fb\} \text{ with } fg^3b \succ fgb \succ fb \succ fg^2b \succ gb \succ b.$$

Assuming that the ordering on terms is extended to atoms considered as multisets by taking its multiset extension, this set of ground unit clauses is closed under the inference rules in $\mathcal{ORP}$. Note that the ordering can be easily completed so as to satisfy the subterm property on the whole set of ground terms.

Using monotonic ordered paramodulation instead of ordered paramodulation yields the following set of clauses:

$$\{gb = b, \ fg^2b \neq fb \ , fgb \neq fb, \ fb \neq fb, \ \square\}$$

and $\mathcal{ORMP}$ is indeed again complete [BG01b]. Note however that monotonic ordered paramodulation can be interpreted as ordered paramodulation with an ordering which is the monotonic extension of the ordering on ground instances of equality atoms. This ordering is therefore essentially monotonic.

Violating Subterm. $\mathcal{ORP}$ turns out to be again incomplete when the ordering on terms does not satisfy the subterm property. Consider the following unsatisfiable set of ground clauses

$$\{a \neq fa, \ fb \neq fa, \ b = fb, \ a = fb\}, \text{ with } a \succ b \succ fa \succ fb.$$

This set is closed under ordered paramodulation, resolution, factoring and reflexivity, assuming that the ordering on terms is extended to atoms considered as multisets by taking its multiset extension.

In [BGNR99], the authors show completeness of $\mathcal{ORMP}$ for Horn clauses when using a well-founded ordering which does not have the subterm property (with a proof which is quite intricate). To compute the set of clauses generated, we first need to extend the ordering into a well-founded ordering on the whole set of atoms:

$$f^n a \succ f^n b \succ \ldots \succ f^2 a \succ f^2 b \succ a \succ b \succ fa \succ fb.$$

$\mathcal{ORMP}$ then yields the following infinite set of clauses:

$$\{a \neq fa, \ fb \neq fa, \ a = fb\} \cup$$
$$\{f^n b = f^m b, \ a \neq f^m b, \ f^{n+1} b \neq f^{m+1} b \mid n \geq 0, m > 0\} \cup$$
$$\{\Box\}.$$

Indeed, any extension of the ordering would yield the same result, because the lefthand and righthand sides of equations are compared instead of the atoms themselves. Therefore, the equations $a = fb$ and $b = fb$ suffice for generating the whole set.

Subterm Monotonicity Does Not Suffice. We thought for a while that monotonicity could be restricted to the subterm relationship. Here is an example showing that this restriction of monotonicity does not ensure completeness:

$$\{fa \neq b, \ a = b, \ gb = b, fga = b\}$$
$$\text{with}$$
$$f^2 b \succ f^2 a \succ fgb \succ fga \succ ga \succ gb \succ fb \succ fa \succ a \succ b.$$

Indeed, we need to paramodulate $fga = b$ by $a = b$ as if fga were bigger than fgb. In other words, the ordering $\succ$ must be monotonic on the rewrite relation induced by the equality atoms $s = t$ generated from the clauses $s = t \vee C$ in which $s = t$ is maximal.

3.2   Ordering Terms, Atoms and Clauses

From now on, we assume that $\succeq$ is a stable, partial quasi-ordering on terms which restricts to a total strict ordering on ground terms which is monotonic and satisfies the subterm property. As a consequence, it is a simplification ordering, and is therefore well-founded on any set of terms which is generated from a finite signature. As another straightforward consequence, ordered paramodulation and monotonic ordered paramodulation coincide.

We assume further that $\succ$ is extended to atoms so as to satisfy the following two properties:

(monotonicity) $s \succ t$ implies $A[s] \succ A[t]$ for any atom $A[s]$;
(*) $s \succ t$ implies $A[s] \succ (s = t)$ if A is not an equality atom;
(†) $\succ$ is total on ground equalities.

Note that monotonicity extends monotonicity from terms to atoms. It also implies that $(u[s] = u[t]) \succ (s = t)$ if $u[\ ] \neq [\ ]$ by the subterm property of $\succ$ applied twice and transitivity.

An example of ordering satisfying these properties can be obtained by extending the ordering $\succ$ from terms to atoms by letting

$$P(\overline{u}) \succ Q(\overline{u}) \text{ iff } (\max(\overline{u}), P, \overline{u})(\succ_{mul}, >_{\mathcal{P}}, \succ_{stat(P)})_{lex} (\max(\overline{v}), Q, \overline{v})$$

where the *precedence* $>_{\mathcal{P}}$ is a well-founded ordering on the set of predicate symbols in which the equality predicate is minimal and *stat* is a function from $\mathcal{P}$ to $\{lex, mul\}$ such that $stat(P) = mul$ iff P is the equality predicate.

3.3   Herbrand Equality Interpretations

Our goal is now to construct all Herbrand equality interpretations over a finite set $\mathcal{A}$ of ground atoms, which we suppose without loss of generality to be *closed under reflexivity*, that is, to contain all atoms $s = s$ such that $(s = t) \in \mathcal{A}$ for some t. The total well-founded ordering $\succ$ allows us to order the finite set of ground atoms, hence $\mathcal{A} = \{A_j\}_{j<n}$ such that $A_i \succ A_j$ if and only if $i > j$ (remember that we do not distinguish $s = t$ from $t = s$). The enumeration of the set of ground atoms based on the ordering $\succ$ provides us with a convenient characterization of Herbrand equality interpretations, which are then organized as a finitely branching tree whose vertices at a given depth assign a truth value to the same ground atom. Interpretations are in one-to-one correspondence with the branches of the tree.

Unlike the previous usual formulation of Herbrand interpretations, we assume here for convenience a set of three truth values $\{U, T, F\}$ where U stands for the *undefined* truth value and is used to consider partial interpretations as total functions over $\{U, T, F\}$.

Definition 7. *A (partial) Herbrand interpretation I of a finite set $\mathcal{A} = \{A_i\}_{i<n}$ of ground atoms is a mapping $[\_]_I$ from $\mathcal{A}$ to the set of truth values $\{U, T, F\}$. I is said to be* total *whenever its target is the subset $\{T, F\}$.*

Note that Herbrand interpretations are defined with respect to a given finite vocabulary of ground atoms closed under reflexivity. As usual, a *partial interpretation* I of an initial segment $\{A_i\}_{i<j\leq n}$ of $\mathcal{A}$ satisfies $[A_k]_I = U$ for all $j \leq k < n$. This is used in particular to represent all total interpretations assigning the same truth value among $\{T, F\}$ to the ground atoms in the initial segment, in the sense that if a formula ϕ takes value $x \in \{T, F\}$ in I, it takes the same value x in all total extensions of I. Here, undefined values may occur anywhere.

The logical connectives are classically extended to the third truth value by setting $T \vee U = T$, $F \vee U = U$, $T \wedge U = U$, $F \wedge U = F$ and $\neg U = U$. Interpretations are then extended to propositional formulae over $\mathcal{A}$ by taking their homomorphic extension. Let $U < T, U < F$ be the usual order on truth values, and $<$ be its natural pointwise extension to partial Herbrand interpretations. The intuition is that a partial Herbrand interpretation I of $\mathcal{A}$ stands for all total Herbrand interpretations H bigger than I in the order on interpretations.

We now turn our attention to Herbrand equality interpretations. Let E_I be the subset of equalities in $\mathcal{A}$ interpreted by T in some Herbrand interpretation I. Our goal is to define partial Herbrand equality interpretations in a way that specializes to the total case.

Definition 8. *A Herbrand equality interpretation is a Herbrand interpretation I that is compatible with the axioms of equality, that is:*
  (i) for any term s, $[s = s]_I = T$;
  (ii) for any two atoms A, B such that $A \longleftrightarrow^*_{E_I} B$, then $[A]_I = [B]_I$;
  (iii) for any two terms s, t such that $s \longleftrightarrow^*_{E_I} t$ and any term u such that $u[s] = u[t] \in \mathcal{A}$, then $[u[s] = u[t]]_I = T$.

Note that the proof from A to B may involve atoms not in $\mathcal{A}$. A similar phenomenon may occur with the proof from s to t. Indeed, the first two conditions suffice to characterize Herbrand equality interpretations under our assumptions on $\succ$ and $\mathcal{A}$:

Lemma 8. *A Herbrand interpretation I of $\mathcal{A}$ is a Herbrand equality interpretation of $\mathcal{A}$ iff*
  (i) for any ground atom $s = s \in \mathcal{A}$, $[s = s]_I = T$,
  (ii) for any two different ground atoms $A, B \in \mathcal{A}$ such that $B \succ A$, $[A]_I, [B]_I \in \{T, F\}$ and $A \longleftrightarrow^*_{E_I} B$, then $[B]_I = [A]_I$.

Note that no constraint at all is imposed on A, B when $[A]_I = U$ or $[B]_I = U$. In case of a total interpretation, we obtain the usual characterization.

Proof. Clearly, if I is a partial Herbrand equality interpretation, (i) and (ii) must be satisfied. We need to show the converse.

Assume that $s \longleftrightarrow^*_{E_I} t$ and $u[s] = u[t] \in \mathcal{A}$ for some $u[]$. If s and t are identical, then $[u[s] = u[s]]_I = T$ by (i). Otherwise, let $s \succ t$. Then, $u[s] = u[t] \longleftrightarrow^*_{E_I} u[t] = u[t]$ which belongs to $\mathcal{A}$ by closure assumption and is smaller than $u[s] = u[t]$ by property of the ordering. By (ii) and (i), $[u[s] = u[t]]_I = [u[t] = u[t]]_I = T$. $\square$

We now verify our intuition that partial Herbrand equality interpretations represent total ones:

Lemma 9. *Let ϕ be an arbitrary propositional formula over the vocabulary $\mathcal{A}$, I be a partial Herbrand equality interpretation, and $H > I$ be a total Herbrand equality interpretation. Then $[\phi]_H = [\phi]_I$ iff $[\phi]_I \neq U$.*

We finally capture the idea that there are enough Herbrand equality interpretations on the one hand, and that a set of ground atoms becomes unsatisfiable in presence of the axioms of equality:

Definition 9. *A set $\mathcal{E}$ of Herbrand equality interpretations is* complete *if every Herbrand equality interpretation in $\{T, F\}^{\mathcal{A}}$ is smaller than some interpretation in $\mathcal{E}$ in the order of interpretations.*

Definition 10. *A set S of clauses is said to be* E-unsatisfiable *if S augmented with the axioms of equality is unsatisfiable.*

The following property of complete sets of Herbrand equality interpretations is the basis of our completeness proof:

Lemma 10. *A set $\mathcal{G}$ of ground clauses built from a set $\mathcal{A}$ of ground atoms closed under reflexivity is E-unsatisfiable iff $\mathcal{G}$ refutes a complete set of Herbrand equality interpretations over $\mathcal{A}$.*

Proof. Because the axioms of equality cannot refute Herbrand equality interpretations on the one hand, and a ground clause C refuting a partial interpretation I refutes all total interpretations bigger than I by Lemma 9 on the other hand.   □

We now consider the problem of extending a complete set $\mathcal{E}$ of partial Herbrand equality interpretations over a finite set $\mathcal{A}$ of ground atoms into a complete set $\mathcal{E}'$ of partial Herbrand equality interpretations over $\mathcal{A} \cup \{B\}$. The new set of ground atoms should of course contain the ground atoms $s = s$ and $t = t$ whenever B is the ground equality atom $s = t$. We will assume that $s = s$ and $t = t$ are added one by one before $s = t$. The flexibility of partial interpretations allows us to extend each interpretation in $\mathcal{E}$ by exactly one interpretation in $\mathcal{E}'$:

Definition 11. *Given a partial Herbrand equality interpretation I over $\mathcal{A}$, we define its extension I' to $\mathcal{A} \cup \{B\}$ as follows:*

1. *If $B \in \mathcal{A}$, $I' = I$. Otherwise,*
2. *If B is a ground atom $s = s$, then $[B]_{I'} = T$.*
3. *If $B \longleftrightarrow^{*}_{E_I} A_i \in \mathcal{A}$ with $[A_i]_I \in \{T, F\}$, then $[B]_{I'} = [A_i]_I$.*
4. *If B is a ground atom $s = t$ such that there exists $A_i \neq A_j$ with $[A_i]_I = T$, $[A_j]_I = F$ and $A_i \longleftrightarrow^{*}_{E_I \cup \{s=t\}} A_j$, then $[s = t]_{I'} = F$.*
5. *Otherwise, $[B]_{I'} = U$.*

Note that Case 4 does not apply when B is strictly bigger than any ground atom in $\mathcal{A}$ since $\succ$ contains subterm.

It is clear that the set of branches of $T_{\mathcal{E}}$ is in one-to-one correspondance with the set $\mathcal{E}$. This property will be exploited without saying in the rest of the paper.

Definition 13. *The tree $T_{\mathcal{E}}$ of Herbrand equality interpretations over $\mathcal{A}$ is narrow iff every internal vertex I has either one successor assigning a truth value among $\{U, T, F\}$ to the ground atom $A_{|I|+1}$, or else two assigning the truth values among T and F respectively to the ground atom $A_{|I|+1}$. The set $\mathcal{E}$ of interpretations will be called* narrow *as well.*

Lemma 12. *Every complete set $\mathcal{E}$ of Herbrand equality interpretations over $\mathcal{A}$ contains a narrow complete set $\mathcal{E}'$.*

Proof. Let I be a internal vertex of $T_{\mathcal{E}}$ with a successor J such that $[A_{|I|+1}]_J = U$. Then, the other successors of I, if any, may be deleted without compromising completeness. □

Using narrow sets of interpretations makes the undefined truth value useless: if I has J for single successor assigning the truth value U to the ground atom $A_{|I|+1}$, then we can collapse the vertices I and J and omit this ground atom. We prefer however to keep undefined values because they allow us the possibility of having a given ground atom interpreted at a given depth in the tree of Herbrand equality interpretations, all branches therefore having the same length. In other words, all branches of the tree give a truth value in $\{U, T, F\}$ to all ground atoms in $\mathcal{A}$, rather than a truth value in $\{T, F\}$ to a subset of ground atoms in $\mathcal{A}$ as it is the case in Section 2.4.

3.4   Semantic Trees and Generating Interpretations

In this section, we assume given:

- a finite set of ground atoms $\mathcal{A} = \{A_I\}_{i<n}$ closed under reflexivity such that $A_i \succ A_j$ iff $i > j$;
- an E-unsatisfiable set $\mathcal{G}$ of ground clauses built from the ground atoms in $\mathcal{A}$ which is closed under positive factoring;
- a complete narrow set $\mathcal{E}$ of partial Herbrand equality interpretations over $\mathcal{A}$, or equivalently, its associated narrow tree $T_{\mathcal{E}}$.

We will say that the triple $(\mathcal{A}, \mathcal{G}, \mathcal{E})$ (or equivalently $(\mathcal{A}, \mathcal{G}, T_{\mathcal{E}})$ or even $(\mathcal{A}, \mathcal{G}, T_{\mathcal{G}})$ satisfies assumption (*). Note that the two closure properties that we assume can be enforced without extending the set of ground terms, as would closure of $\mathcal{G}$ under ordered paramodulation.

Definition 14. *Given $(\mathcal{A}, \mathcal{G}, T_{\mathcal{E}})$ satisfying (*), we call* failure node *any vertex J of $T_{\mathcal{E}}$ for which there exists $C \in \mathcal{G}$ such that $[C]_J = F$ and $[C]_I = U$ for any ancestor I of J. We call* semantic tree *associated with $(\mathcal{A}, \mathcal{G}, T_{\mathcal{E}})$ any tree obtained from $T_{\mathcal{E}}$ by replacing a failure node J on each branch of the tree by a leaf decorated with the associated clause C. We denote it by $T_{\mathcal{G}}$.*

Note that $T_{\mathcal{G}}$ is not defined uniquely. This is on purpose, since it will be convenient to consider non-minimal semantic trees in our completeness proof. However, our definition forces the ground atom enumerated at a failure node to be either T or F.

Since C is a ground clause, $[C]_J$ is defined iff all its atoms are assigned a truth value in $\{T, F\}$ by J. Hence, the failure node cannot assign the undefined truth value U to the last ground atom enumerated at a failure node. Another consequence, since $\mathcal{G}$ is E-unsatisfiable, is that the semantic tree is *closed*, that is, all its branches end up in a failure node. As usual, the only clause refuting the root of the tree is the empty clause.

We now define a specific interpretation G (actually, a class of interpretations) ending up in a failure node at which an ordered resolution or paramodulation will always be possible. The idea is that a ground equality atom $l = r$ should belong to E_G, that is, be interpreted in T by G, iff it stems from a ground instance of a clause $l = r \vee C$ that can be used to perform a ground ordered paramodulation. The generating interpretation is of course directly related to the notion of *generated equality* of Bachmair and Ganzinger. It pops up very naturally in the context of semantic trees.

Definition 15. *The set of generating interpretations G of a narrow closed semantic tree associated with the triple $(\mathcal{A}, \mathcal{G}, T_{\mathcal{E}})$ satisfying (*) is defined inductively as follows. Assume some vertex I in the semantic tree is the generating interpretation constructed so far. If I is a leaf, we are done. Otherwise, let A be $A_{|I|+1}$.*

1. *If I has a unique successor I' in the semantic tree, we choose I'. Otherwise, let L be its left successor ($[A]_L = F$) and K be its right successor.*
2. *If A is a ground equality atom and L is not a failure node, then we choose L.*
3. *If A is a ground equality atom $s = t$ and L is a failure node, then we choose K. In this case, the clause $s = t \vee C\theta$ decorating L is called a generating clause and $s = t$ is a generated equation.*
4. *Otherwise, we choose L or K in an arbitrary way, provided that if the chosen one is a failure node, then the other one must also be a failure node (i.e., we prefer internal vertices over failure nodes).*

We denote by G an arbitrary generating interpretation, and by Gen_G the set of generating clauses.

Notice that we need not make any particular choice when the enumerated ground atom A is not an equality (Case 4), therefore leaving room for improvement. For example, we could superimpose a selection function as in Section 2. Note also that we could define generating interpretations for non-narrow trees. The above definition then shows that we would always need taking the successor J such that $[A]_J = U$ whenever there is one.

In Bachmair and Ganzinger's work, the generating interpretation is unique, as well as the set of generating clauses. This is so because they encode predicates as

Boolean functions. Here, the generating interpretation is not unique, but the set of generating clauses does not depend upon the choice of a particular generating interpretation: it is easy to see that a clause $s = t \vee C\theta$ generates the equation $s = t$ with $s \succ t$ if $s = t$ is maximal in the clause and is irreducible by the previously generated equations. (Irreducibility is by the definition of Herbrand equality interpretations, and the fact that the successor of I is not unique in this case.) The definition by Bachmair and Ganzinger is slightly different, since they allow the right hand side t of the equation $s = t$ to be reducible. We could do that as well, since this becomes important for showing completeness of the superposition paramodulation strategy. This would not need changing the definition of generating interpretations: we would only have to collect more equations along them.

As is standard, we interpret each equation $u = v$ in E_G as a rewrite rule $u \to v$ if $u \succ v$, or as $v \to u$ if $v \succ u$ (and as any one rule if $u = v$, which will not happen).

Lemma 13. *Assume that G is a generating interpretation of a narrow closed semantic tree. Then E_G is a canonical set of rewrite rules.*

Proof. All the equations $s = t$ in E_G must be generated, i.e., produced in Case 3 of Definition 15. Let us use the notations given there. By definition of the tree of Herbrand equality interpretations, and since I has two successors, $s = t$ is neither true nor false in E_I, in particular $s \neq t$. Since $\succ$ is total on ground terms, $s \succ t$ or $t \succ s$. Let us assume $s \succ t$.

Let now $u = v$ be another equation in E_G. We have just seen that we could assume $u \succ v$. Moreover, by our assumption (†) that $\succ$ is total on ground equalities, $(u = v) \succ (s = t)$, or the converse inequality. By properties of $\succ$, $u \succ s$ and $u \succ t$, hence u is not a subterm of s or of t. It follows that $s = t$ cannot be reduced by $u \to v$.

Therefore, $s = t$ is irreducible with respect to $E_G \setminus \{s = t\}$. Since E_G is clearly terminating, the result follows. $\square$

Lemma 14. *Assume that G is a generating interpretation of a narrow closed semantic tree associated with the triple $(\mathcal{A}, \mathcal{G}, T_\mathcal{E})$ satisfying (*). Assume further that A_i is reducible by some equation $s = t$ of E_G, $s \succ t$, meaning that s occurs as a subterm of A_i. Then there exists a generating clause $s = t \vee C\theta$ in $\mathcal{G}$ such that:*
   (i) $A_i \longrightarrow_{s=t} B$, with $A_i \succ B$,
   (ii) $(s = t) \succ A$ for every atom A of $C\theta$,
   (iii) $[C\theta]_G = F$.

This happens notably when $A_i \longleftrightarrow^*_{E_G} A_j$ for some $j < i$: since E_G is a canonical set of rules (Lemma 13), $A_i \longrightarrow^*_G A' \; ^*_G \longleftarrow A_j$ for some A', and $A_i \succeq A'$, $A_j \succeq A'$. Since $A_i \succ A_j$, it is impossible that $A_i = A'$, so A_i must rewrite in at least one E_G step to A', and the lemma applies.

In case the ordering $\succ$ is not monotonic, the lemma does not hold anymore, and reducible atoms may not be reducible by (irreducible) generated equations.

Our example violating subterm monotonicity shows this behavior for the atom $fga = b$ which is reducible by $ga = a$ and $ga = b$, but not by $a = b$ although $a = b$ reduces ga. It is easy to see that monotonicity is only needed for equations reducing other equations, that is, for the equations in $\mathcal{E}$.

Proof. (i) is the assumption, plus the fact that $\succ$ is monotonic. Beware that B may fail to belong to $\mathcal{A}$.

We are left with (ii) and (iii). Since $s = t$ is in E_G, look at the first time it was added to the generating interpretation in the process of Definition 15. This must be by Case 3 of this definition, at a point where the current vertex was I, with two successors K and L, such that $[s = t]_L = F$ and L is a failure node for some generating clause $s = t \vee C\theta$.

Since $s = t$ is the last ground atom enumerated by L, it is maximal in the clause. Since $\mathcal{G}$ is closed under positive factoring, we can assume without loss of generality that $(s = t) \notin C\theta$, hence $[C\theta]_G = [C\theta]_I = F$ and $s = t$ is strictly bigger than any ground atom in $C\theta$.   □

3.5   Refutational Completeness of $\mathcal{ORP}$

Let S be a set of clauses which is E-unsatisfiable. Our purpose is to show that $\mathcal{ORP}$ is refutationally complete, that is, the empty clause is generated in finite time from S. To do this, we will reason at the ground level, and use a lifting argument to relate the ground level with the non-ground level. Lifting is simple because a ground instance $C\theta$ of a clause is a multiset of ground atoms, therefore eliminating any need for contraction.

Theorem 3. *A set of clauses S is E-unsatisfiable iff the empty clause belongs to the closure of $\mathcal{G}$ under $\mathcal{ORP}$.*

Proof. By compactness and Lemma 10, we first choose a finite E-unsatisfiable set of ground instances of S. Let $\mathcal{A}$ be the set of ground atoms occurring in $\mathcal{G}$. We add to $\mathcal{A}$ all ground atoms of the form $s = s$ whenever $s = t \in \mathcal{A}$, and close $\mathcal{G}$ under positive factoring. We then compute the set $\mathcal{E}$ of Herbrand equality interpretations over $\mathcal{A}$ and organize it as a narrow tree $T_{\mathcal{E}}$. Therefore, the triple $(\mathcal{A}, \mathcal{G}, T_{\mathcal{E}})$ satisfies (*). We finally compute the narrow closed semantic tree T_G. This ends up the initialization phase.

We define the complexity of a semantic tree $T_{\mathcal{G}}$ to be the multiset of clauses in $T_{\mathcal{G}}$ that decorate its leaves. Complexities are compared in the multiset extension of $\succ$. Since the last ground atom enumerated at a failure node cannot be undefined, the smallest semantic tree in this order is therefore the empty tree, decorated by the empty clause.

During the course of the proof, we will perform an operation on the current triple $(\mathcal{A}, \mathcal{G}, T_{\mathcal{E}})$ called *extension*, each time a new clause is added to $\mathcal{G}$; let us call $\mathcal{G}'$ the new set. First, we recompute the set of ground atoms, let us call it $\mathcal{A}'$, and complete it as before with the necessary ground atoms $s = s$. As before, we also close $\mathcal{G}$ under positive factoring. We then extend the complete set of interpretations $\mathcal{E}$ over $\mathcal{A}$ into a new complete set $\mathcal{E}''$ by adding the ground atoms in $\mathcal{A}' \setminus \mathcal{A}$ one by one, in increasing order, thanks to Definition 11. By Lemma 11, $\mathcal{E}''$ is complete. By Lemma 12, we now compute $\mathcal{E}' \subseteq \mathcal{E}''$ such that $\mathcal{E}'$ is narrow. Therefore, the new triple $(\mathcal{A}', \mathcal{G}', T_{\mathcal{E}'})$ satisfies (*). By Lemma 11, the interpretations in $\mathcal{E}'$ are refuted by a subset of the clauses in $\mathcal{G} \subseteq \mathcal{G}'$ that refute the interpretations in $\mathcal{E}$. Since the interpretations in $\mathcal{E}'$ are in one-to-one correspondence with those of $\mathcal{E}$, it follows that extensions do not increase the complexity of the semantic tree.

We now reason by induction on the semantic tree $T_{\mathcal{G}}$. If $T_{\mathcal{G}}$ is empty, we are done. Otherwise, we choose an arbitrary generating interpretation ending up in a leaf J of $T_{\mathcal{G}}$. By non-emptiness, J has a parent vertex I. By definition of the semantic tree, J is decorated by a ground clause in $\mathcal{G}$ of the form $\pm P(\overline{u}\theta) \vee C\theta$, where $\pm P(\overline{u}) \vee C$ is in S. In it, $A = P(\overline{u}\theta)$ is the last ground atom enumerated by J, hence is larger than or equal to any ground atom in C. And A is assigned either the value T or the value F in J. Let us assume that there exists some clause in $\mathcal{ORP}(\mathcal{G})$ that refutes some extension J' of J to be defined next, and is strictly smaller than $\pm P(\overline{u}\theta) \vee C\theta$. This clause may involve new ground atoms (because of paramodulation inferences). We therefore apply finitely many completion steps resulting in a set of clauses $\mathcal{G}'$ containing $\mathcal{G}$ and the new clause and a semantic tree $T_{\mathcal{G}'}$. By our assumption, we can replace the clause $\pm P(\overline{u}\theta) \vee C\theta$ refuting the vertex J' extending J by the inferred clause which is strictly smaller, therefore decreasing the complexity of the semantic tree. We conclude by induction hypothesis.

It remains to show that our assumption can be fulfilled. By definition of the generated interpretation, there are four cases:

1. $P(\overline{u}\theta)$ is of the form $s = s$, in which case I has J as single successor decorated by $\neg s = s \vee C\theta \succ C\theta$. By reflexivity, $C\theta$ belongs to $\mathcal{ORP}(\mathcal{G})$ and refutes the interpretation J.

2. $P(\overline{u}\theta)$ is irreducible by E_I. Then, I has two successors, L (left) and K (right), by definition of Herbrand equality interpretations. We claim that both are failure nodes. If $P(\overline{u}\theta)$ is not an equality atom, then we are in Case 4 of Definition 15, and the claim is immediate. Otherwise, either Case 2 or Case 3 applies. In Case 2, we must have chosen $J = L$, contradicting the fact that J is a failure node. In Case 3, L is a failure node, and we must have chosen $J = K$, and we conclude since J is a failure node.

   So I has two successors, which are both failure nodes. Both are decorated by clauses in both of which the ground atom $P(\overline{u}\theta)$ is maximal. Let these clauses be $+P(\overline{u}\theta) \vee C\theta$ and $-P(\overline{u}\theta) \vee D\theta$, in which $P(\overline{u}\theta)$ is strictly bigger than any ground atom occurring in $C\theta$. So the resolvent $C\theta \vee D\theta$ refutes the interpretation I.

3. $A = P(\overline{u}\theta)$ is reducible by E_I at a non-variable position p of $P(\overline{u})$ by an equation $s = t \in E_I$ such that $s \succ t$, yielding the ground atom $A[t]_p$. By Lemma 14, $s = t$ is generated by a clause $s = t \vee D\theta$ such that $s = t$ is strictly larger than any ground atom in $D\theta$. Therefore, there is an ordered paramodulation between $s = t \vee D\theta$ and the clause $\pm A \vee C\theta$, yielding $A[t]_p \vee C\theta \vee D\theta$, which therefore belongs to $\mathcal{ORP}(\mathcal{G})$. Consider now the tree of

Herbrand equality interpretations extended from the previous one to the set of ground atoms $\mathcal{A} \cup \{A[t]_p\}$. Let I', J' be the respective extensions of I, J. Since $[s = t]_J = T$, $[A[t]_p]_{J'} = [A[s]_p]_{J'} = [A]_{J'} = [A]_J = F$, and since $A = A[s]_p \succ A[t]_p$, $[A[t]_p]_{I'} = F$. By Lemma 11, $[C\theta]_{J'} = [D\theta]_{J'} = F$, hence $[C\theta \vee D\theta]_{J'} = F$, and by the same token as previously $[C\theta \vee D\theta]_{I'} = F$. Therefore $[A[t]_p \vee C\theta \vee D\theta]_{I'} = F$.

4. $P(\overline{u}\theta)$ is reducible by E_I at a position in θ, hence $x\theta \longrightarrow_{E_I} x\theta'$ for some variable that occurs in $\overline{u}$. We now consider the clause instance $+P(\overline{u}\theta') \vee C\theta'$, which is strictly smaller than the previous one. This case is similar to the previous one, except that there may be several new ground atoms in $+P(\overline{u}\theta') \vee C\theta'$. $\qquad\qquad\square$

4   Conclusion

Recasting Ganzinger's work into the framework of finite semantic trees was an enriching experience. The logical next step is to consider basic ordered resolution and paramodulation together with selection strategies via term selection, as done in [BGLS].

To conclude, we must compare the model generation model with semantic trees. The implicit answer we give here is that there is no significant difference between the two. The former does not construct all interpretations, only a *relevant* one, while the latter describes the relevant one as a maximal branch in the tree of all interpretations. One main difference is the use of the compactness argument to make the semantic tree finite. The same could probably be done with model generation. A second difference is that semantic trees fit our own intuition better.

Acknowledgments. The authors thank Sergiu Bursuc, Yevgueny Kazarov from MPI, as well as Michaël Lienhardt, Bruno Marnette, Muriel Roger and Kumar Neeraj Verma from ENS Cachan for their remarks. Thanks also go to the anonymous referees.

References

[Ake78]   Akers, S.B.: Functional testing with binary decision diagrams. In: Eighth Annual Conference on Fault-Tolerant Computing, pp. 75–82 (1978)

[BD94]   Bachmair, L., Dershowitz, N.: Equational inference, canonical proofs and proof orderings. Journal of the ACM 41(2), 236–276 (1994)

[BG01a]   Bachmair, L., Ganzinger, H.: Resolution Theorem Proving, vol. I, ch. 2, pp. 19–99. North-Holland (2001), [RV01b]

[BG01b]   Bofill, M., Godoy, G.: On the Completeness of Arbitrary Selection Strategies for Paramodulation. In: Yu, Y., Spirakis, P.G., van Leeuwen, J. (eds.) ICALP 2001. LNCS, vol. 2076, pp. 951–962. Springer, Heidelberg (2001)

[BGLS]   Bachmair, L., Ganzinger, H., Lynch, C., Snyder, W.: Basic Paramodulation and Superposition. In: Kapur, D. (ed.) CADE 1992. LNCS (LNAI), vol. 607, pp. 462–476. Springer, Heidelberg (1992)

[BGNR99]   Bofill, M., Godoy, G., Nieuwenhuis, R., Rubio, A.: Paramodulation with non-monotonic orderings. In: Proc. 14th IEEE Symposium on Logics in Computer Science (LICS 1999), pp. 225–233. IEEE Computer Society Press (1999)

[CL73]   Chang, C.-L., Lee, R.C.-T.: Symbolic Logic and Mechanical Theorem Proving. Computer Science Classics. Academic Press (1973)

[dN95]   de Nivelle, H.: Ordering Refinements of Resolution. PhD thesis, Technische Universiteit Delft (1995)

[GL05]   Goubault-Larrecq, J.: Deciding $\mathcal{H}_1$ by resolution. Information Processing Letters (2005) (to appear)

[GLRV04]   Jean Goubault-Larrecq, Muriel Roger, and Kumar Neeraj Verma. Abstraction and resolution modulo AC: How to verify Diffie-Hellman-like protocols automatically. J. Logic and Algebraic Programming (2004) (to appear)

[HR86]   Hsiang, J., Rusinowitch, M.: A New Method for Establishing Refutational Completeness in Theorem Proving. In: Siekmann, J.H. (ed.) CADE 1986. LNCS, vol. 230, pp. 141–152. Springer, Heidelberg (1986)

[HR91]   Hsiang, J., Rusinowitch, M.: Proving refutational completeness of theorem-proving strategies: The transfinite semantic tree method. Journal of the ACM 38(3), 559–587 (1991)

[Joy76]   Joyner Jr., W.H.: Resolution strategies as decision procedures. Journal of the ACM 23(3), 398–417 (1976)

[Kow69]   Kowalski, R.: Semantic trees in automatic theorem-proving. Machine Intelligence 4, 86–101 (1969)

[RV01a]   Riazanov, A., Voronkov, A.: Splitting without backtracking. In: Nebel, B. (ed.) Proc. 17th Intl. Joint Conf. Artificial Intelligence, vol. 1, pp. 611–617. Morgan Kaufmann (August 2001)

[RV01b]   Alan Robinson, J., Voronkov, A. (eds.): Handbook of Automated Reasoning. North-Holland (2001)

[SV05]   Seidl, H., Verma, K.N.: Flat and One-Variable Clauses: Complexity of Verifying Cryptographic Protocols with Single Blind Copying. In: Baader, F., Voronkov, A. (eds.) LPAR 2004. LNCS (LNAI), vol. 3452, pp. 79–94. Springer, Heidelberg (2005)

[WBH+02]   Weidenbach, C., Brahm, U., Hillenbrand, T., Keen, E., Theobald, C., Topic, D.: SPASS Version 2.0. In: Voronkov, A. (ed.) CADE 2002. LNCS (LNAI), vol. 2392, pp. 275–279. Springer, Heidelberg (2002)

Functional Logic Programming: From Theory to Curry[*]

Michael Hanus

Institut für Informatik, CAU Kiel, D-24098 Kiel, Germany
mh@informatik.uni-kiel.de

Abstract. Functional logic programming languages combine the most important declarative programming paradigms, and attempts to combine these paradigms have a long history. The declarative multi-paradigm language Curry is influenced by recent advances in the foundations and implementation of functional logic languages. The development of Curry is an international initiative intended to provide a common platform for the research, teaching, and application of integrated functional logic languages. This paper surveys the foundations of functional logic programming that are relevant for Curry, the main features of Curry, and extensions and applications of Curry and functional logic programming.

1 Introduction

Compared to traditional imperative languages, functional as well as logic languages provide a higher and more abstract level of programming that leads to reliable and maintainable programs. Although the motivations are similar in both paradigms, the concrete languages differ due to their different foundations, namely the lambda calculus and first-order predicate logic. Thus, it is a natural idea to combine these worlds of programming into a single paradigm, and attempts for doing so have a long history. However, the interactions between functional and logic programming features are complex in detail so that the concrete design of an integrated functional logic language is a non-trivial task. This is demonstrated by a lot of research work on the semantics, operational principles, and implementation of functional logic languages since more than two decades. Fortunately, recent advances in the foundation and implementation of functional logic languages have shown reasonable principles that lead to the design of practically applicable programming languages. The declarative multi-paradigm language Curry[1] [69,92] is based on these principles. It is developed by an international initiative of researchers in this area and intended to provide a common platform for the research, teaching, and application of integrated functional logic languages. This paper surveys the foundations of functional logic programming that are relevant for Curry, design decisions and main features of

[*] This work was partially supported by the German Research Council (DFG) under grants Ha 2457/5-1 and Ha 2457/5-2 and the NSF under grant CCR-0218224.
[1] http://www.curry-language.org

A. Voronkov and C. Weidenbach (Eds.): Ganzinger Festschrift, LNCS 7797, pp. 123–168, 2013.

Curry, implementation techniques, and extensions and applications of functional logic programming.

Since this paper is intended to be a compact survey, not all of the numerous papers in this area can be mentioned and the relevant topics are only sketched. Interested readers might look into the cited references for more details. In particular, there exist other surveys on particular topics related to this paper. [66] is a survey on the development and the implementation of various evaluation strategies for functional logic languages that have been explored until more than a decade ago. [15] contains a good survey on more recent evaluation strategies and classes of functional logic programs. The survey [119] is more specialized but reviews the efforts to integrate constraints into functional logic languages.

The rest of this paper is structured as follows. The next main section introduces and reviews the foundations of functional logic programming that are used in current functional logic languages. Section 3 discusses important aspects of the language Curry. Section 4 surveys the efforts to implement Curry and related functional logic languages. Sections 5 and 6 contain references to further extensions and applications of functional logic programming, respectively. Finally, Section 7 contains our conclusions with notes about related languages.

2   Foundations of Functional Logic Programming

2.1   Basic Concepts

Functional logic languages are intended to combine the most important features of functional languages (algebraic data types, polymorphic typing, demand-driven evaluation, higher-order functions) and logic languages (computing with partial information, constraint solving, nondeterministic search for solutions). A *functional program* is a set of *functions* or *operations* defined by *equations* or *rules*. A *functional computation* consists of replacing subexpressions by equal (w.r.t. the defining equations) subexpressions until no more replacements (or *reductions*) are possible and a value or normal form is obtained. For instance, consider the operation `double` defined by[2]

```
double x = x + x
```

The expression "`double 1`" is replaced by 1+1. The latter can be replaced by 2 if we interpret the operator "+" to be defined by an infinite set of equations, e.g., 1+1 = 2, 1+2 = 3, etc (we will discuss the handling of such operations later). In a similar way, one can evaluate nested expressions (where the replaced subexpression is underlined):

$$\underline{\texttt{double (1+2)}} \quad \rightarrow \quad \underline{\texttt{(1+2)}}\texttt{+(1+2)} \quad \rightarrow \quad \texttt{3+}\underline{\texttt{(1+2)}} \quad \rightarrow \quad \underline{\texttt{3+3}} \quad \rightarrow \quad 6$$

---

[2] For concrete examples in this paper, we use the Curry syntax which is very similar to the syntax of Haskell [117], i.e., (type) variables and function names usually start with lowercase letters and the names of type and data constructors start with an uppercase letter. The application of an operation f to an expression e is denoted by juxtaposition ("$f\ e$"). Moreover, binary operators like "+" are written infix.

There is also another order of evaluation if we replace the arguments of operators from right-to-left:

double (1+2) → (1+2)+(1+2) → (1+2)+3 → 3+3 → 6

In this case, both derivations lead to the same result. This indicates a fundamental property of declarative languages: the value of a computed result does not depend on the order or time of evaluation due to the absence of side effects. This simplifies the reasoning about and maintenance of declarative programs.

Obviously, these are not all possible evaluation orders. Another one is obtained by evaluating the argument of double before applying its defining equation:

double (1+2) → double 3 → 3+3 → 6

In this case, we obtain the same result with less evaluation steps. This leads to questions about appropriate *evaluation strategies*, where a strategy can be considered as a function that determines for an expression the next subexpression to be replaced: Which strategies are able to compute values for which classes of programs? As we will see, there are important differences in case of recursive programs. If there are several strategies, which strategies are better w.r.t. the number of evaluation steps, implementation effort, etc? Many works in the area of functional logic programming have been devoted to finding appropriate evaluation strategies. A detailed account of the development of such strategies can be found in [66]. In the following, we will only survey the strategies that are relevant for current functional logic languages.

Although functional languages are based on the lambda calculus that is purely based on function definitions and applications, modern functional languages offer more features for convenient programming. In particular, they support the definition of algebraic data types by enumerating their *constructors*. For instance, the type of Boolean values consists of the constructors True and False that are declared as follows:

    data Bool = True | False

Operations on Booleans can be defined by pattern matching, i.e., by providing several equations for different argument values:

    not True = False
    not False = True

The principle of replacing equals by equals is still valid provided that the actual arguments have the required form, e.g.:

not (not False) → not True → False

More complex data structures can be obtained by recursive data types. For instance, a list of elements, where the type of elements is arbitrary (denoted by the type variable a), is either the empty list "[]" or the non-empty list "x:xs" consisting of a first element x and a list xs. Hence, lists can be defined by

    data List a = [] | a : List a

For conformity with Haskell, the type "List a" is usually written as [a] and finite lists $e_1 : e_2 : \ldots : e_n : []$ are written as $[e_1, e_2, \ldots, e_n]$. We can define operations on recursive types by inductive definitions where pattern matching supports the convenient separation of the different cases. For instance, the concatenation operation "++" on polymorphic lists can be defined as follows (the optional type declaration in the first line specifies that "++" takes two lists as input and produces an output list, where all list elements are of the same unspecified type):

```
(++) :: [a] -> [a] -> [a]
[]      ++ ys = ys
(x:xs) ++ ys = x : xs++ys
```

Beyond its application for various programming tasks, the operation "++" is also useful to specify the behavior of other operations on lists. For instance, the behavior of an operation last that yields the last element of a list can be specified as follows: for all lists l and elements e, last $l = e$ iff $\exists xs : xs \,\texttt{++}\, [e] = l$.[3] Based on this specification, one can define an operation and verify that this definition satisfies the given specification (e.g., by inductive proofs as shown in [34]). This is one of the situations where functional logic languages become handy. Similarly to logic languages, functional logic languages provide search for solutions for existentially quantified variables. In contrast to pure logic languages, they support equation solving over nested functional expressions so that an equation like $xs \,\texttt{++}\, [e] = [\texttt{1,2,3}]$ is solved by instantiating xs to the list [1,2] and e to the value 3. For instance, in Curry one can define the operation last as follows:

```
last l | xs++[e] =:= l = e    where xs,e free
```

Here, the symbol "=:=" is used for *equational constraints* in order to provide a syntactic distinction from defining equations. Similarly, *extra variables* (i.e., variables not occurring in the left-hand side of the defining equation) are explicitly declared by "where...free" in order to provide some opportunities to detect bugs caused by typos. A *conditional equation* of the form $l \mid c = r$ is applicable for reduction if its condition c has been solved. In contrast to purely functional languages where conditions are only evaluated to a Boolean value, functional logic languages support the *solving* of conditions by guessing values for the unknowns in the condition. As we have seen in the previous example, this reduces the programming effort by reusing existing operations and allows the direct translation of specifications into executable program code. The important question to be answered when designing a functional logic language is: How are conditions solved and are there constructive methods to avoid a blind guessing of values for unknowns? This is the purpose of narrowing strategies that are discussed next.

---

[3] The exact meaning of the equality symbol is omitted here since it will be discussed later.

2.2   Narrowing

Techniques for goal solving are well developed in the area of logic programming. Since functional languages advocate the equational definition of operations, it is a natural idea to integrate both paradigms by adding an equality predicate to logic programs, leading to *equational logic programming* [93,115,116]. On the operational side, the resolution principle of logic programming must be extended to deal with replacements of subterms. *Narrowing*, originally introduced in automated theorem proving [125], is a constructive method to deal with such replacements. For this purpose, defining equations are interpreted as rewrite rules that are only applied from left to right (as in functional programming). In contrast to functional programming, the left-hand side of a defining equation is *unified* with the subterm under evaluation. In order to provide more detailed definitions, some basic notions of term rewriting [31,48] are briefly recalled. Although the theoretical part uses notations from term rewriting, its mapping into the concrete programming language syntax should be obvious.

Since we ignore polymorphic types in the theoretical part of this paper, we consider a many-sorted *signature* Σ partitioned into a set $\mathcal{C}$ of *constructors* and a set $\mathcal{F}$ of (defined) *functions* or *operations*. We write $c/n \in \mathcal{C}$ and $f/n \in \mathcal{F}$ for n-ary constructor and operation symbols, respectively. Given a set of variables $\mathcal{X}$, the set of *terms* and *constructor terms* are denoted by $\mathcal{T}(\mathcal{C} \cup \mathcal{F}, \mathcal{X})$ and $\mathcal{T}(\mathcal{C}, \mathcal{X})$, respectively. The set of variables occurring in a term t is denoted by $\mathcal{V}ar(t)$. A term t is *ground* if $\mathcal{V}ar(t) = \varnothing$. A term is *linear* if it does not contain multiple occurrences of one variable. A term is *operation-rooted* (*constructor-rooted*) if its root symbol is an operation (constructor). A *head normal form* is a term that is not operation-rooted, i.e., a variable or a constructor-rooted term.

A *pattern* is a term of the form $f(d_1, \ldots, d_n)$ where $f/n \in \mathcal{F}$ and $d_1, \ldots, d_n \in \mathcal{T}(\mathcal{C}, \mathcal{X})$. A *term rewriting system* (TRS) is set of rewrite rules, where an (unconditional) *rewrite rule* is a pair $l \to r$ with a linear pattern l as the *left-hand side* (*lhs*) and a term r as the *right-hand side* (*rhs*). Note that this definition reflects the specific properties of functional logic programs. Traditional term rewriting systems [48] differ from this definition in the following points:

1. We have required that the left-hand sides must be linear patterns. Such rewrite systems are also called *constructor-based* and exclude rules like

    $$(\text{xs ++ ys}) \text{ ++ zs} \ = \ \text{xs ++ (ys ++zs)} \qquad (assoc)$$
    $$\text{last (xs ++ [e])} \ = \ \text{e} \qquad (last)$$

    Although this seems to be a restriction when one is interested in writing equational specifications, it is not a restriction from a programming language point of view, since functional as well as logic programming languages enforces the same requirement (although logic languages do not require linearity of patterns, this can be easily obtained by introducing new variables and adding equations for them in the condition; conditional rules are discussed below). Often, non-constructor-based rules specify properties of operations rather than providing a constructive definition (compare rule *assoc* above that specifies the associativity of "++"), or they can be transformed into constructor-based rules by moving non-constructor terms in left-hand side arguments into the condition (e.g., rule *last*). Although there exist narrowing strategies for non-constructor-based rewrite rules (see [66,116,125] for more details), they often put requirements on the rewrite system that are too strong or difficult to check in universal programming languages, like termination or confluence. An important insight from recent works on functional logic programming is that the restriction to constructor-based programs is quite reasonable since this supports the development of efficient and practically useful evaluation strategies (see below). Although narrowing has been studied for more general classes of term rewriting systems, those extensions are often applied to areas like theorem proving rather than programming (e.g., [52]).

2. Traditional rewrite rules $l \to r$ require that $Var(r) \subseteq Var(l)$. A TRS where all rules satisfy this restriction is also called a *TRS without extra variables*.[4] Although this makes sense for rewrite-based languages, it limits the expressive power of functional logic languages (see the definition of `last` in Section 2.1). Therefore, functional logic languages usually do not have this variable requirement, although some theoretical results have only been proved under this requirement.

In order to formally define computations w.r.t. a TRS, we need a few further notions. A *position* p in a term t is represented by a sequence of natural numbers. Positions are used to identify particular subterms. Thus, $t|_p$ denotes the *subterm* of t at position p, and $t[s]_p$ denotes the result of *replacing the subterm* $t|_p$ by the term s (see [48] for details). A *substitution* is an idempotent mapping $\sigma : \mathcal{X} \to \mathcal{T}(\mathcal{C} \cup \mathcal{F}, \mathcal{X})$ where the *domain* $Dom(\sigma) = \{x \in \mathcal{X} \mid \sigma(x) \neq x\}$ is finite. Substitutions are obviously extended to morphisms on terms. We denote by $\{x_1 \mapsto t_1, \ldots, x_n \mapsto t_n\}$ the *substitution* σ with $\sigma(x_i) = t_i$ $(i = 1, \ldots, n)$ and $\sigma(x) = x$ for all other variables x. A substitution σ is *constructor* (*ground constructor*), if $\sigma(x)$ is a constructor (ground constructor) term for all $x \in Dom(\sigma)$.

A *rewrite step* $t \to_{p,R} t'$ (in the following, p and R will often be omitted in the notation of rewrite and narrowing steps) is defined if p is a position in t, $R = l \to r$ is a rewrite rule with fresh variables,[5] and σ is a substitution with $t|_p = \sigma(l)$ and $t' = t[\sigma(r)]_p$. The instantiated lhs $\sigma(l)$ is also called a *redex* (*reducible expression*). A term t is called *irreducible* or in *normal form* if there is no term s with $t \to s$. $\overset{*}{\to}$ denotes the reflexive and transitive closure of a relation $\to$.

Rewrite steps formalize functional computation steps with pattern matching as introduced in Section 2.1. The goal of a sequence of rewrite steps is to compute

---

[4] In case of conditional rules, which are discussed later, the condition is considered as belonging to the right-hand side so that variables occurring in the condition but not in the left-hand side are also extra variables.

[5] In classical traditional term rewriting, fresh variables are not used when a rule is applied. Since we consider also rules containing extra variables in right-hand sides, it is important to replace them by fresh variables when the rule is applied.

a normal form. A *rewrite strategy* determines for each rewrite step a rule and a position for applying the next step. A *normalizing strategy* is one that terminates a rewrite sequence in a normal form, if it exists. Note, however, that normal forms are not necessarily the interesting results of functional computations, as the following example shows.

Example 1. Consider the operation

```
idNil [] = []
```

that is the identity on the empty list but undefined for non-empty lists. Then, a normal form like "`idNil [1]`" is usually considered as an error rather than a result. Actually, Haskell reports an error for evaluating the term "`idNil [1+2]`" rather than delivering the normal form "`idNil [3]`". □

Therefore, the interesting results of functional computations are *constructor terms* that will be also called *values*. Evaluation strategies used in functional programming, such as lazy evaluation, are not normalizing, as the previous example shows.

Functional logic languages are able to do more than pure rewriting since they instantiate variables in a term (also called *free* or *logic variables*) so that a rewrite step can be applied. The combination of variable instantiation and rewriting is called *narrowing*. Formally, $t \leadsto_{p,R,\sigma} t'$ is a *narrowing step* if p is a non-variable position in t (i.e., $t|_p$ is not a variable) and $\sigma(t) \to_{p,R} t'$. Since the substitution σ is intended to instantiate the variables in the term under evaluation, one often restricts $\mathcal{Dom}(\sigma) \subseteq \mathcal{Var}(t)$. We denote by $t_0 \leadsto^*_\sigma t_n$ a sequence of narrowing steps $t_0 \leadsto_{\sigma_1} \ldots \leadsto_{\sigma_n} t_n$ with $\sigma = \sigma_n \circ \cdots \circ \sigma_1$ (where $\sigma = \{\}$ in the case of $n = 0$). Since in functional logic languages we are interested in computing *values* (constructor terms) as well as *answers* (substitutions), we say that the narrowing derivation $t \leadsto^*_\sigma c$ *computes the value c with answer σ* if c is a constructor term.

The above definition of narrowing is too general for a realistic implementation since it allows arbitrary instantiations of variables in the term under evaluation. Thus, all possible instantiations must be tried in order to compute all possible values and answers. Obviously, this does not lead to a practical implementation. Therefore, older narrowing strategies (see [66] for a detailed account) were influenced by the resolution principle and required that the substitution used in a narrowing step must be a most general unifier of $t|_p$ and the left-hand side of the applied rule. As shown in [19], this condition prevents the development of optimal evaluation strategies. Therefore, most recent narrowing strategies relax this traditional requirement but provide another constructive method to compute a small set of unifiers in narrowing steps, as we will see below. The next example shows the non-optimality of narrowing with most general unifiers.

Example 2. Consider the following program containing a declaration of natural numbers in Peano's notation and two operations for addition and a "less than or equal" test (the pattern "`_`" denotes an unnamed *anonymous variable*):

```
data Nat = 0 | S Nat
```

```
add 0     y = y
add (S x) y = S (add x y)

leq 0     _   = True                                    (leq₁)
leq (S _) 0   = False                                   (leq₂)
leq (S x) (S y) = leq x y                               (leq₃)
```

Consider the initial term "leq v (add w 0)" where v and w are free variables. By applying rule leq_1, v is instantiated to 0 and the result True is computed:

$$\text{leq v (add w 0)} \quad \rightsquigarrow_{\{v \mapsto 0\}} \quad \text{True}$$

Further answers can be obtained by instantiating v to (S...). This requires the evaluation of the subterm (add w 0) in order to allow the application of rule leq_2 or leq_3. For instance, the following narrowing derivation computes the value False with answer $\{v \mapsto S\ z, w \mapsto 0\}$:

$$\text{leq v (add w 0)} \quad \rightsquigarrow_{\{w \mapsto 0\}} \quad \text{leq v 0} \quad \rightsquigarrow_{\{v \mapsto S\ z\}} \quad \text{False}$$

However, we can also apply rule leq_1 in the second step of the previous narrowing derivation and obtain the following derivation:

$$\text{leq v (add w 0)} \quad \rightsquigarrow_{\{w \mapsto 0\}} \quad \text{leq v 0} \quad \rightsquigarrow_{\{v \mapsto 0\}} \quad \text{True}$$

Obviously, the last derivation is not optimal since it computes the same value as the first derivation with a less general answer and needs one more step. This derivation can be avoided by instantiating variable v to S z in the first narrowing step:

$$\text{leq v (add w 0)} \quad \rightsquigarrow_{\{v \mapsto S\,z,\ w \mapsto 0\}} \quad \text{leq (S z) 0}$$

Now, rule leq_1 is no longer applicable, as intended. However, this first narrowing step contains a substitution that is not a most general unifier between the evaluated subterm (add w 0) and the left-hand side of some rule for add.   □

Needed Narrowing. The first narrowing strategy that advocated the use of non-most general unifiers and for which optimality results have been shown is needed narrowing [19]. Furthermore, needed narrowing steps can be efficiently computed. Therefore, it has become the basis of modern functional logic languages.[6]

Needed narrowing is based on the idea to perform only narrowing steps that are in some sense necessary to compute a result (such strategies are also called *lazy* or *demand-driven*). For doing so, it analyzes the left-hand sides of the rewrite rules of an operation under evaluation (starting from an outermost operation). If there is an argument position where all left-hand sides are constructor-rooted, the corresponding actual argument must be also rooted by one of the constructors in order to apply a rewrite step. Thus, the actual argument is evaluated to head

---

[6] Concrete languages and implementations add various extensions in order to deal with larger classes of programs that will be discussed later.

normal form if it is operation-rooted and, if it is a variable, nondeterministically instantiated with some constructor.

Example 3. Consider again the program of Example 2. Since the left-hand sides of all rules for `leq` have a constructor-rooted first argument, needed narrowing instantiates the variable v in "`leq v (add w 0)`" to either `0` or `S z` (where z is a fresh variable). In the first case, only rule leq_1 becomes applicable. In the second case, only rules leq_2 or leq_3 become applicable. Since the latter rules have both a constructor-rooted term as the second argument, the corresponding subterm (`add w 0`) is recursively evaluated to a constructor-rooted term before applying one of these rules.   □

Since there are TRSs with rules that do not allow such a reasoning, needed narrowing is defined on the subclass of *inductively sequential* TRSs. This class can be characterized by definitional trees [12] that are also useful to formalize and implement various narrowing strategies. Since only the left-hand sides of rules are important for the applicability of needed narrowing, the following characterization of definitional trees [13] considers patterns partially ordered by subsumption (the *subsumption ordering* on terms is defined by $t \leq \sigma(t)$ for a term t and substitution σ).

A *definitional tree* of an operation f is a non-empty set T of linear patterns partially ordered by subsumption having the following properties:

Leaves property: The maximal elements of T, called the *leaves*, are exactly the (variants of) the left-hand sides of the rules defining f. Non-maximal elements are also called *branches*.

Root property: T has a minimum element, called the *root*, of the form $f(x_1, \ldots, x_n)$ where $x_1, \ldots, x_n$ are pairwise distinct variables.

Parent property: If $\pi \in T$ is a pattern different from the root, there exists a unique $\pi' \in T$, called the *parent* of π (and π is called a *child* of π'), such that $\pi' < \pi$ and there is no other pattern $\pi'' \in \mathcal{T}(\mathcal{C} \cup \mathcal{F}, \mathcal{X})$ with $\pi' < \pi'' < \pi$.

Induction property: All the children of a pattern π differ from each other only at a common position, called the *inductive position*, which is the position of a variable in π.[7]

An operation is called inductively sequential if it has a definitional tree and its rules do not contain extra variables. A TRS is inductively sequential if all its defined operations are inductively sequential. Intuitively, inductively sequential functions are defined by structural induction on the argument types. Purely functional programs and the vast majority of operations in functional logic programs are inductively sequential. Thus, needed narrowing is applicable to most operations, although extensions are useful for particular operations (see below).

It is often convenient and simplifies the understanding to provide a graphic representation of definitional trees, where each inner node is marked with a pattern, the inductive position in branches is surrounded by a box, and the leaves

---

[7] There might be more than one potential inductive position when constructing a definitional tree. In this case one can select any of them since the results about needed narrowing do not depend on the selected definitional tree.

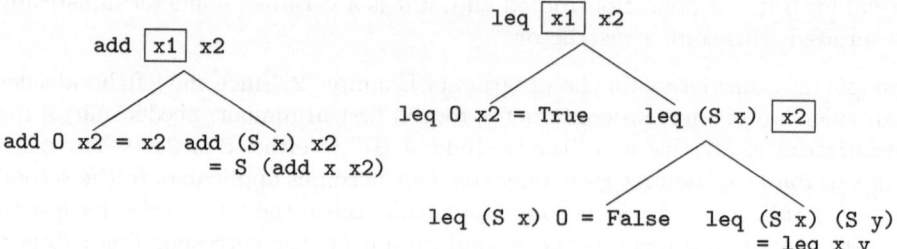

Fig. 1. Definitional trees of the operations `add` and `leq`

contain the corresponding rules. For instance, the definitional trees of the operations `add` and `leq`, defined in Example 2, are illustrated in Figure 1. Definitional
trees have also a strong correspondence to traditional pattern matching by case
expressions in functional languages, as we will see later.

The formal definition of needed narrowing is based on definitional trees and
can be found in [19]. A definitional tree can be computed at compile time (see
[15,69] for algorithms to construct definitional trees) and contains all information
for the efficient implementation of the decisions to be made at run time (compare
Example 3). Intuitively, a needed narrowing step is applied to an operation-
rooted term t by considering a definitional tree (with fresh variables) for the
operation at the root. The tree is recursively processed from the root until one
finds a maximal pattern that unifies with t. Thus, to compute a needed narrowing
step, one starts with the root pattern of the definitional tree and performs at
each level with pattern π the following case distinction:

- If π is a leaf, we apply the corresponding rule.
- If π is a branch and p its inductive position, we consider the corresponding
  subterm $t|_p$:
  1. If $t|_p$ is rooted by a constructor c and there is a child π' of π having c at
     the inductive position, we proceed by examining π'. If there is no such
     child, we fail, i.e., no needed narrowing step is applicable.
  2. If $t|_p$ is a variable, we nondeterministically instantiate this variable by
     the constructor term at the inductive position of a child π' of π and
     proceed with π'.
  3. If $t|_p$ is operation-rooted, we recursively apply the computation of a
     needed narrowing step to $\sigma(t|_p)$, where σ is the instantiation of the vari-
     ables of t performed in the previous case distinctions.

As discussed above, the failure to compute a narrowing step in case (1) is not
a weakness but advantageous when we want to compute values. For instance,
consider the term $t = $ `idNil [1+2]` where the operation `idNil` is as defined
in Example 1. A normalizing strategy performs a step to compute the normal
form `idNil [3]` whereas needed narrowing immediately fails since there exists
no value as a result. Thus, the early failure of needed narrowing avoids wasting
resources.

As a consequence of the previous behavior, the properties of needed narrowing are stated w.r.t. constructor terms as results. In particular, the equality symbol "=:=" in goals is interpreted as the *strict equality* on terms, i.e., the equation $t_1 =:= t_2$ is satisfied iff t_1 and t_2 are reducible to the same ground constructor term. In contrast to the mathematical notion of equality as a congruence relation, strict equality is not reflexive. Similarly to the notion of result values, this is intended in programming languages where an equation between functional expressions that do not have a value, like "idNil [1] =:= idNil [1]", is usually not considered as true. Furthermore, normal forms or values might not exist (note that we do not require terminating rewrite systems) so that reflexivity is not a feasible property of equational constraints (see [60] for a more detailed discussion on this topic).

Strict equality can be defined as a binary operation by the following set of (inductively sequential) rewrite rules. The constant Success denotes a solved (equational) constraint and is used to represent the result of successful evaluations.[8]

$$c =:= c = \text{Success} \qquad \forall c/0 \in C$$
$$c\, x_1 \ldots x_n =:= c\, y_1 \ldots y_n = x_1=:=y_1 \,\&\ldots\&\, x_n=:=y_n \qquad \forall c/n \in C, n > 0$$
$$\text{Success} \,\&\, \text{Success} = \text{Success}$$

Thus, it is sufficient to consider strict equality as any other operation. Concrete functional logic languages provide more efficient implementations of strict equality where variables can be bound to other variables instead of instantiating them to ground terms (see also Section 3.2).

Now we can state the main properties of needed narrowing. A (correct) *solution* for an equation $t_1 =:= t_2$ is a constructor substitution σ (note that constructor substitutions are desired in practice since a broader class of solutions would contain unevaluated or undefined expressions) if $\sigma(t_1) =:= \sigma(t_2) \overset{*}{\to} \text{Success}$. Needed narrowing is sound and complete, i.e., all computed solutions are correct and for each correct solution a possibly more general one is computed, and it does not compute redundant solutions in different derivations:

Theorem 1 ([19]). *Let $\mathcal{R}$ be an inductively sequential TRS and c an equation.*

1. *(Soundness) If $e \leadsto^*_\sigma$ Success is a needed narrowing derivation, then σ is a solution for e.*
2. *(Completeness) For each solution σ of e, there exists a needed narrowing derivation $e \leadsto^*_{\sigma'}$ Success with $\sigma'(x) \le \sigma(x)$ for all $x \in Var(e)$.*
3. *(Minimality) If $e \leadsto^*_\sigma$ Success and $e \leadsto^*_{\sigma'}$ Success are two distinct needed narrowing derivations, then σ and σ' are independent on $Var(e)$, i.e., there is some $x \in Var(e)$ such that $\sigma(x)$ and $\sigma'(x)$ are not unifiable.*

Furthermore, in successful derivations, needed narrowing computes only steps that are necessary to obtain the result and, consequently, it computes the *shortest*

---

[8] Since narrowing is used to solve equations, it does not compute solutions such that an equation is *not* satisfied. This is the motivation to use the specific constant Success rather than the Boolean values True and False as the outcome of equation solving.

of all possible narrowing derivations if derivations on common subterms are shared (a standard implementation technique in non-strict functional languages) [19, Corollary 1]. Needed narrowing is currently the only narrowing strategy with such strong results. Therefore, it is an adequate basis for modern functional logic languages, although concrete implementations support extensions that are discussed next.

Weakly Needed Narrowing. Inductively sequential TRS are a proper subclass of (constructor-based) TRSs. Although the majority of function definitions is inductively sequential, there are also operations where it is more convenient to relax this requirement. The next interesting superclass are *weakly orthogonal TRSs*. These are rewrite systems where left-hand sides can overlap in a semantically trivial way. Formally, a TRS without extra variables (recall that we consider only left-linear constructor-based rules) is *weakly orthogonal* if $\sigma(r_1) = \sigma(r_2)$ for all (variants of) rules $l_1 \to r_1$ and $l_2 \to r_2$ and substitutions σ with $\sigma(l_1) = \sigma(l_2)$.

Example 4. A typical example of a weakly orthogonal TRS is the *parallel-or*, defined by the rules:

or True _	= True	(or_1)
or _ True	= True	(or_2)
or False False	= False	(or_3)

A term like "or s t" could be reduced to True whenever one of the arguments s or t evaluates to True. However, it is not clear which of the arguments should be evaluated first, since any of them could result in a nonterminating rewriting or narrowing derivation. or has no definitional tree and, thus, needed narrowing cannot be applied.   □

In rewriting, several normalizing strategies for weakly orthogonal TRSs have been proposed, such as parallel outermost [114] or weakly needed [122] rewriting that are based on the idea to replace several redexes in parallel in one step. Since strategies for functional logic languages already support nondeterministic evaluations, one can exploit this feature to extend needed narrowing to a *weakly needed narrowing* strategy. The basic idea is to generalize the notion of definitional trees to include *or-branches* which conceptually represent a union of definitional trees [12,18,100]. If such an or-branch is encountered during the evaluation of a narrowing step, weakly needed narrowing performs a nondeterministic guess and proceeds with the subtrees below the or-branches.

Example 5. Consider again the rules for the operation or shown in Example 4 and the operation f defined by

    f 0 = True

One can construct separate definitional trees for the rule sets $\{or_1, or_3\}$ and $\{or_2\}$ and join them by an or-branch. Then there are the following different weakly needed narrowing derivations based on this *generalized definitional tree* for the term "or (f x) (f x)":

or (f x) (f x) $\leadsto_{\{x \mapsto 0\}}$ or True (f 0) $\leadsto_{\{\}}$ True
or (f x) (f x) $\leadsto_{\{x \mapsto 0\}}$ or True (f 0) $\leadsto_{\{\}}$ or True True $\leadsto_{\{\}}$ True
or (f x) (f x) $\leadsto_{\{x \mapsto 0\}}$ or (f 0) True $\leadsto_{\{\}}$ or True True $\leadsto_{\{\}}$ True
or (f x) (f x) $\leadsto_{\{x \mapsto 0\}}$ or (f 0) True $\leadsto_{\{\}}$ True

□

Obviously, weakly needed narrowing is no longer optimal in the sense of needed narrowing. However, it is sound and complete for weakly orthogonal TRS in the sense of Theorem 1 [18].

Weakly needed narrowing can be improved by computing weakly needed narrowing steps in parallel, discarding steps with non-minimal substitutions and replacing several outermost redexes in parallel. The resulting strategy, called *parallel narrowing* [18], computes only one derivation for Example 5 and has the general property (beyond soundness and completeness) that it behaves deterministically (i.e., without choices) on ground terms. However, the computation of parallel narrowing steps is quite complex (see [18] for details) so that it has not been integrated in existing functional logic languages, in contrast to weakly needed narrowing that is implemented in languages such as Curry [69,92] or TOY [101].

Overlapping Inductively Sequential Systems. Inductively sequential and weakly orthogonal TRSs are *confluent*, i.e., each term has at most one normal form. This property is sensible for functional languages since it ensures that operations are well defined (partial) functions in the mathematical sense. Since the operational mechanism of functional logic languages is more powerful due to its built-in search mechanism, in this context it makes sense to consider also operations defined by non-confluent TRSs. Such operations are also called *nondeterministic*. The prototype of such a nondeterministic operation is a binary operation "?" that returns one of its arguments:

    x ? y = x
    x ? y = y

Thus, the expression "0 ? 1" has two possible results, namely 0 or 1.

Since functional logic languages already handle nondeterministic computations, they are also capable of dealing with such nondeterministic operations. To provide a reasonable semantics for functional logic programs, constructor-based rules are sufficient but confluence is not required [62]. If operations are interpreted as mappings from values into sets of values (actually, due to the presence of recursive non-strict operations, algebraic structures with cones of partially ordered sets are used instead of sets, see [62] for details), one can provide model-theoretic and proof-theoretic semantics with the usual properties (minimal term models, equivalence of model-theoretic and proof-theoretic solutions, etc). Thus, functional logic programs with nondeterministic operations are still in the design space of declarative languages. Moreover, nondeterministic operations have advantages w.r.t. demand-driven evaluation strategies so that they became a standard feature of current functional logic languages, whereas older languages, like ALF [65], Babel [109], K-Leaf [60], or SLOG [58], put confluence requirements on their programs. The following example discusses this in more detail.

Example 6. Based on the binary operation "?" introduced above, one can define an operation `insert` that nondeterministically inserts an element at an arbitrary position in a list:

```
insert e []      = [e]
insert e (x:xs) = (e : x : xs) ? (x : insert e xs)
```

Exploiting this operation, one can define an operation `perm` that returns an arbitrary permutation of a list:

```
perm []      = []
perm (x:xs) = insert x (perm xs)
```

One can already see an important property when reasoning about nondeterministic operations: the computation of results is arbitrary, i.e., one result is as good as any other. For instance, if one evaluates `perm [1,2,3]`, any permutation (e.g., `[3,2,1]` as well as `[1,3,2]`) is an acceptable result. If one puts specific conditions on the results, the completeness of the underlying computational model (e.g., INS, see below) ensures that the appropriate results meeting these conditions are selected.

For instance, one can use `perm` to define an operation `psort` to sort a list based on a "partial identity" function `sorted` that returns its input list if it is sorted:

```
sorted []                            = []
sorted [x]                           = [x]
sorted (x1:x2:xs) | leq x1 x2 =:= True = x1 : sorted (x2:xs)

psort xs = sorted (perm xs)
```

Thus, `psort xs` returns only those permutations of `xs` that are sorted. The advantage of this definition of `psort` in comparison to traditional "generate-and-test" solutions becomes apparent when one considers the demand-driven evaluation strategy (note that one can apply the weakly needed narrowing strategy to such kinds of programs since this strategy is only based on the left-hand sides of the rules but does not exploit confluence). Since in an expression like `sorted (perm xs)` the argument of `sorted` is only evaluated as demanded by `sorted`, the permutations are not fully computed at once. If a permutation starts with a non-ordered prefix, like `S 0 : 0 : perm xs`, the application of the third rule of `sorted` fails and, thus, the computation of the remaining part of the permutation (which can result in $n!$ different permutations if n is the length of the list `xs`) is discarded. The overall effect is a reduction in complexity in comparison to the traditional generate-and-test solution.   □

This example shows that nondeterministic operations allow the transformation of "generate-and-test" solutions into "test-of-generate" solutions with a lower complexity since the demand-driven narrowing strategy results in a demand-driven construction of the search space (see [13,62] for further examples). Antoy [13] shows that desirable properties of needed narrowing can be transferred to programs with nondeterministic operations if one considers *overlapping inductively sequential systems*. These are TRSs with inductively sequential rules where each rule can have multiple right-hand sides (basically, inductively sequential TRSs with occurrences of "?" in the top-level of right-hand sides), possibly containing extra variables. For instance, the rules defining `insert` form an overlapping inductively sequential TRS if the second rule is interpreted as a single rule with two right-hand sides ("`e:x:xs`" and "`x : insert e xs`"). The corresponding strategy, called *INS* (*inductively sequential narrowing strategy*), is defined similarly to needed narrowing but computes for each narrowing step a set of replacements. INS is a conservative extension of needed narrowing and optimal modulo nondeterministic choices of multiple right-hand sides, i.e., if there are no multiple right-hand sides or there is an oracle for choosing the appropriate element from multiple right-hand sides, INS has the same optimality properties as needed narrowing (see [13] for more details).

A subtle aspect of nondeterministic operations is their treatment if they are passed as arguments. For instance, consider the nondeterministic operation `coin` defined by

```
coin = 0 ? 1
```

and the expression "`double coin`" (where `double` is defined as in Section 2.1). If the argument `coin` is evaluated (to 0 or 1) before it is passed to `double`, we obtain the possible results 0 and 2. However, if the argument `coin` is passed unevaluated to `double`, we obtain after one rewrite step the expression `coin+coin` which has four possible further rewrite derivations resulting in the values 0, 1, 1, and 2. The former behavior is referred to as *call-time choice* semantics [94] since the choice for the desired value of a nondeterministic operation is made at call time, whereas the latter is referred to as *need-time choice* semantics. There are arguments for either of these semantics depending on the programmer's intention (see [15] for more examples).

Although call-time choice suggests an eager or call-by-value strategy, it fits well into the framework of demand-driven evaluation where arguments are shared to avoid multiple evaluations of the same subterm. For instance, the actual subterm (e.g., `coin`) associated to argument x in the rule "`double x = x+x`" is not duplicated in the right-hand side but a reference to it is passed so that, if it is evaluated by one subcomputation, the same result will be taken in the other subcomputation. This technique, called *sharing*, is essential to obtain efficient (and optimal) evaluation strategies. If sharing is used, the call-time choice semantics can be implemented without any further machinery. Furthermore, in many situations call-time choice is the semantics with the "least astonishment". For instance, consider the reformulation of the operation `psort` in Example 6 to

```
psort xs = idOnSorted (perm xs)

idOnSorted xs | sorted xs =:= xs = xs
```

Then, for the call `psort xs`, the call-time choice semantics delivers only sorted permutations of `xs`, as expected, whereas the need-time choice semantics delivers all permutations of `xs` since the different occurrences of `xs` in the rule of `idOnSorted` are not shared. For instance, to evaluate the call `psort [3,2,1]`, one has to verify that the condition

```
sorted (perm [3,2,1]) =:= perm [3,2,1]
```

of `idOnSorted` is satisfied (see below for more details about conditional rules). This can be shown by reducing both occurrences of "`perm [3,2,1]`" to the list `[1,2,3]`. Since the condition is satisfied, the call `idOnSorted (perm [3,2,1])` will be reduced to `perm [3,2,1]` w.r.t. the need-time choice semantics. Thus, one finally obtains all permutations of the input list.

Due to these reasons, current functional logic languages usually adopt the call-time choice semantics.

Conditional Rules. The narrowing strategies presented so far are only defined for rewrite rules without conditions, although some of the concrete program examples indicate that conditional rules are convenient in practice. Formally, a *conditional rewrite rule* has the form $l \to r \Leftarrow C$ where l and r are as in the unconditional case and the condition C consists of finitely many equational constraints of the form $s =:= t$. Due to the interpretation of equational constraints as strict equalities, one can define a rewrite step with a conditional rule similar to the unconditional case with the additional requirement that each equational constraint in the condition of an applicable rule must be *joinable*, i.e., both sides of the equation must be reducible to the same ground constructor term.[9] A more precise definition will be provided in Section 2.3.

To extend narrowing to conditional rules, one can define narrowing steps on *equational goals*, i.e., (multi)sets of equations, where an application of a conditional rule adds new conditions to the equational goal. However, to obtain an efficient implementation, functional logic languages often use another technique. As discussed before, efficient narrowing strategies exploit the structure of the left-hand sides of rewrite rules to decide its applicability. In order to do the same for conditional rules, one can consider conditions as part of the right-hand side. This can be achieved by transforming a conditional rule of the form

$$l \to r \Leftarrow s_1 =:= t_1 \& \ldots \& s_n =:= t_n$$

into an unconditional rule

$$l \to cond(s_1 =:= t_1 \& \ldots \& s_n =:= t_n, \ r)$$

where the "*conditional*" is defined by $cond(\texttt{Success}, x) \to x$. Since overlapping inductively sequential TRSs allow rules with multiple right-hand sides, one can transform also sets of conditional rules with identical left-hand sides, in contrast to pure term rewriting with confluence requirements where only

---

[9] The recursion in this intuitive definition of conditional rewriting can be avoided by an iterative definition using levels for rewriting conditions, see [33].

restricted subsets of conditional rules can be transformed into unconditional ones (e.g., [33]). Actually, Antoy [14] has shown a systematic method to translate any conditional constructor-based TRS into an overlapping inductively sequential TRS performing equivalent computations.

For restricted subsets of conditional rules, other transformations that allow the application of more sophisticated narrowing strategies are possible. For instance, in [17] it is shown how to transform any weakly orthogonal conditional TRS into an unconditional TRS so that the weakly needed and parallel narrowing strategies are sound and complete on the transformed programs. The application of parallel narrowing to the transformed programs has the effect that conditions are evaluated in parallel so that nondeterministic evaluation steps are completely avoided on ground terms.

Further Works. Although weakly needed narrowing or INS are reasonable narrowing strategies for rather general classes of functional logic programs, further works investigated improvements for specific classes of TRSs. For instance, [97] proposes a refinement of definitional trees if there is more than one inductive position (e.g., in operations like "=:=" and "&" defined above). This is exploited to implement needed narrowing in a way that reduces the number of nondeterministic choices. [50,51] proposes natural narrowing as a refinement of weakly needed narrowing by incorporating a better treatment of demandedness properties.

Since the formal reasoning about sophisticated narrowing strategies could be fairly complex, *narrowing calculi* have been studied. Usually, such calculi are defined by a set of inference rules on equational goals so that properties like soundness and completeness can be shown by proving invariants w.r.t. the application of inference rules. This simplifies the proof of properties of narrowing techniques but has the disadvantage that a connection to efficient implementations required for real languages is more difficult to establish. Examples for such narrowing calculi are LNC [107] for confluent TRSs, OINC [95] for orthogonal TRSs and goals with ground normal forms as right-hand sides, or CLNC [62] as the narrowing equivalent to CRWL (see below). LNC and OINC do not require constructor-based TRSs. This has useful applications for applicative TRSs [111] in order to study narrowing calculi for programs with higher-order operations.

2.3   Constructor-Based Rewriting Logic

As discussed in the previous section on overlapping inductively sequential TRS, sharing becomes important for the semantics of nondeterministic operations. This has the immediate consequence that traditional equational reasoning is no longer applicable. For instance, the expressions `double coin` and `coin+coin` are not equal since the latter can reduce to 1 while this is impossible for the former w.r.t. a call-time choice semantics. In order to provide a semantical basis for such general functional logic programs, González-Moreno et al. [62] have proposed the rewriting logic *CRWL* (Constructor-based conditional ReWriting Logic) as a logical (execution- and strategy-independent) foundation for declarative programming with non-strict and nondeterministic operations and call-time choice semantics. This logic has been also used to link a natural model theory as an extension of the traditional theory of logic programming and to establish soundness and completeness of narrowing strategies for rather general classes of TRSs [47].

To deal with non-strict operations, CRWL considers signatures $\Sigma_\perp$ that are extended by a special symbol $\perp$ to represent *undefined values*. For instance, $\mathcal{T}(\mathcal{C} \cup \{\perp\}, \mathcal{X})$ denotes the set of partial constructor terms, e.g., $1 : 2 : \perp$ denotes a list starting with elements 1 and 2 and an undefined rest. Such *partial terms* are considered as finite approximations of possibly infinite values. CRWL defines the deduction of two kinds of basic statements: *approximation statements* $e \to t$ with the intended meaning "the partial constructor term t approximates the value of e", and *joinability statements* $e_1 = := e_2$ with the intended meaning that e_1 and e_2 have a common *total* approximation $t \in \mathcal{T}(\mathcal{C}, \mathcal{X})$ with $e_1 \to t$ and $e_2 \to t$, thus modeling strict equality with terms containing variables. To model call-time choice semantics, rewrite rules are only applied to partial *values*. Hence, the following notation for *partial constructor instances* of a set of (conditional) rules $\mathcal{R}$ is useful:

$$[\mathcal{R}]_\perp = \{\sigma(l \to r \Leftarrow C) \mid l \to r \Leftarrow C \in \mathcal{R}, \sigma : \mathcal{X} \to \mathcal{T}(\mathcal{C} \cup \{\perp\}, \mathcal{X})\}$$

Then CRWL is defined by the following set of inference rules (where the program is represented by a TRS $\mathcal{R}$):

Bottom: $e \to \perp$ $e \in \mathcal{T}(\mathcal{C} \cup \mathcal{F} \cup \{\perp\}, \mathcal{X})$

Restricted
reflexivity: $x \to x$ $x \in \mathcal{X}$

Decomposition: $\dfrac{e_1 \to t_1 \ \cdots \ e_n \to t_n}{c(e_1, \ldots, e_n) \to c(t_1, \ldots, t_n)}$ $c/n \in \mathcal{C},\, t_i \in \mathcal{T}(\mathcal{C} \cup \{\perp\}, \mathcal{X})$

Function
reduction: $\dfrac{e_1 \to t_1 \ \cdots \ e_n \to t_n \quad C \quad r \to t}{f(e_1, \ldots, e_n) \to t}$ $\begin{array}{l} f(t_1, \ldots, t_n) \to r \Leftarrow C \in [\mathcal{R}]_\perp \\ \text{and } t \neq \perp \end{array}$

Joinability: $\dfrac{e_1 \to t \quad e_2 \to t}{e_1 = := e_2}$ $t \in \mathcal{T}(\mathcal{C}, \mathcal{X})$

Rule (Bottom) specifies that $\perp$ approximates any expression. The condition $t \neq \perp$ in rule (Function reduction) avoids unnecessary applications of this rule since this case is already covered by the first rule. The restriction to partial constructor instances in this rule formalizes non-strict operations with a call-time choice semantics. Operations might have non-strict arguments that are not evaluated since the corresponding actual arguments can be derived to $\perp$ by rule (Bottom). If the value of an argument is required to evaluate the right-hand side of a rule, it must be evaluated to a partial constructor term before it is passed to the right-hand side (since $[\mathcal{R}]_\perp$ contains only partial constructor instances), which corresponds to a call-time choice semantics. Note that this does not prohibit the use of lazy implementations since this semantical behavior can be enforced by sharing unevaluated expressions. Actually, [62] defines a lazy narrowing calculus that reflects this behavior.

Fapp	$f(\sigma(t_1), \ldots, \sigma(t_n)) \rightarrow_l \sigma(r)$	$f(t_1, \ldots, t_n) \rightarrow r \in \mathcal{R}, \sigma : \mathcal{X} \rightarrow \mathcal{T}(\mathcal{C}, \mathcal{X})$
LetIn	$g(\ldots, e, \ldots) \rightarrow_l$ $\texttt{let } x = e \texttt{ in } g(\ldots, x, \ldots)$	$e = f(\ldots) \ (f \in \mathcal{F}) \text{ or } e = \texttt{let} \ldots$ $g \in \mathcal{C} \cup \mathcal{F}, x \in \mathcal{X}$ fresh variable
Flat	$\texttt{let } x = (\texttt{let } y = e_1 \texttt{ in } e_2) \texttt{ in } e_3 \rightarrow_l$ $\texttt{let } y = e_1 \texttt{ in } (\texttt{let } x = e_2 \texttt{ in } e_3)$	y does not appear free in e_3
Bind	$\texttt{let } x = t \texttt{ in } e \rightarrow_l \sigma(e)$	$t \in \mathcal{T}(\mathcal{C}, \mathcal{X}), \sigma = \{x \mapsto t\}$
Elim	$\texttt{let } x = e_1 \texttt{ in } e_2 \rightarrow_l e_2$	x does not appear free in e_2
Contx	$e[e_1]_p \rightarrow_l e[e_2]_p$	$e_1 \rightarrow_l e_2$ and p position in e

Fig. 2. Rules for let-rewriting [103]

CRWL can be used as the logical foundation of functional logic languages with non-strict nondeterministic operations. It is a basis for the verification of functional logic programs [45] and has been extended in various directions, e.g., higher-order operations [63], algebraic types [30], polymorphic types [61], failure [104], constraints [102] etc. An account on CRWL and its applications can be found in [119].

As discussed in [103], a disadvantage of CRWL is its high level of abstraction: CRWL relates expressions to computed (partial) results but misses a one-step evaluation mechanism similarly to rewriting for functional programs or narrowing for functional logic programs. Thus, it is sometimes difficult to use CRWL to reason about computations in functional logic languages. To overcome this drawback, López-Fraguas et al. [103] proposed specific reduction relations conform with CRWL (for simplicity, we consider here only rules without conditions). The following reduction relation $\rightarrowtail$ is similarly to standard rewriting but restricts the reduction of operations to situations where the arguments are partial terms. Furthermore, any expression can be approximated by $\bot$.

$$e[f(t_1, \ldots, t_n)]_p \rightarrowtail e[r]_p \quad \text{if } f(t_1, \ldots, t_n) \rightarrow r \in [\mathcal{R}]_\bot \text{ and } p \text{ position in } e$$

$$e \rightarrowtail e[\bot]_p \quad \text{if } p \text{ is a position in } e$$

CRWL and the relation $\rightarrowtail$ are equivalent in the sense that CRWL and $\rightarrowtail$ relates the same partial terms to each expression [103].

This reduction relation is more appropriate to reason about computations. For instance, it has been applied in [79] to approximate call patterns in functional logic computations. On the negative side, this reduction relation allows a nondeterministic choice between reducing or approximating a call to some operation which leads to a large computation space. Furthermore, the order of reduction steps does not reflect the typical demand-driven order of evaluation steps. Therefore, López-Fraguas et al. [103] proposed *let-rewriting*, i.e., rewriting on expressions containing let-bindings which denote arguments that need to be evaluated in order to reduce some operation. For this purpose, *let-expressions* are expressions where the extended form "$\texttt{let } x = e_1 \texttt{ in } e_2$" is also permitted ($x$ is visible in e_2 but not in e_1, i.e., lets are not recursive). The let-rewriting relation $\rightarrow_l$ is defined by the rules in Figure 2 (we omit the precise definition of free variable occurrences and substitutions on let-expressions since they are standard). In contrast to CRWL, let-rewriting does not use $\bot$ to approximate expressions that are not demanded. Instead, such expressions are moved from an argument position to a let-binding (LetIn) which can be eliminated (Elim) if they are not demanded. Thus, a function call is reduced if the arguments do not contain any operation (Fapp) which reflects the call-time choice semantics. The equivalence of CRWL and let-rewriting is shown in [103]. There it is also shown that let-rewriting is equivalent to standard rewriting for deterministic programs. Let-rewriting does not enforce any reduction strategy. This will be considered in Section 2.5 where a more strategy-oriented semantics will be discussed.

2.4   Residuation

Although narrowing extends soundness and completeness results of logic programming to the general framework of functional logic programming, it is not the only method that has been proposed to integrate functions into logic programs. An alternative technique, called *residuation*, is based on the idea to delay or suspend function calls until they are ready for deterministic evaluation. The residuation principle is used, for instance, in the languages Escher [99], Le Fun [2], Life [1], NUE-Prolog [110], and Oz [126]. Since the residuation principle evaluates function calls by deterministic reduction steps, nondeterministic search must be encoded by predicates [1,2,110] or disjunctions [99,126]. Moreover, if some part of a computation might suspend, one needs a primitive to execute computations concurrently. For instance, the conjunction of constraints "&" needs to evaluate both arguments to Success so that it is reasonable to do it concurrently, i.e., if the evaluation of one argument suspends, the other one is evaluated.

Example 7. Consider Example 2 together with the operation

```
nat 0     = Success
nat (S x) = nat x
```

If the operation add is evaluated by residuation, i.e., suspends if the first argument is a variable, the expression "add y 0 =:= S 0 & nat y" is evaluated as follows:

$$
\begin{aligned}
\text{add y 0 =:= S 0 \& } \underline{\text{nat y}} \;\; &\rightarrow_{\{y\mapsto S\,x\}} && \underline{\text{add (S x) 0}} \text{ =:= S 0 \& nat x} \\
&\rightarrow_{\{\}} && \text{S (add x 0) =:= S 0 \& nat x} \\
&\rightarrow_{\{\}} && \text{add x 0 =:= 0 \& } \underline{\text{nat x}} \\
&\rightarrow_{\{x\mapsto 0\}} && \underline{\text{add 0 0}} \text{ =:= 0 \& Success} \\
&\rightarrow_{\{\}} && \underline{\text{0 =:= 0}} \text{ \& Success} \\
&\rightarrow_{\{\}} && \underline{\text{Success \& Success}} \\
&\rightarrow_{\{\}} && \text{Success}
\end{aligned}
$$

Thus, the solution $\{y \mapsto S\,0\}$ is computed by switching between the residuating operation add and the constraint nat that instantiates its argument to natural numbers.   □

Narrowing and residuation are quite different approaches to integrate functional and logic programming. Narrowing is sound and complete but requires the nondeterministic evaluation of function calls if some arguments are unknown. Residuation might not compute some result due to the potential suspension of evaluation but avoids guessing on operations. From an operational point of view, there is no clear advantage of one of the strategies. One might have the impression that the deterministic evaluation of operations in the case of residuation is more efficient, but there are examples where residuation has an infinite computation space whereas narrowing has a finite one (see [67] for more details). On the other hand, residuation offers a concurrent evaluation principle with synchronization on logic variables (sometimes also called *declarative concurrency* [128]) and a conceptually clean method to connect *external operations* to declarative programs [35] (note that narrowing requires operations to be explicitly defined by rewrite rules). Therefore, it is desirable to integrate both principles in a single framework. This has been proposed in [69] where residuation is combined with weakly needed narrowing by extending definitional trees with branches decorated with a *flexible/rigid* tag. Operations with flexible tags are evaluated as with narrowing whereas operations with rigid tags suspend if the arguments are not sufficiently instantiated. The overall strategy is similar to weakly needed narrowing with the exception that a rigid branch with a free variable in the corresponding inductive position results in the suspension of the operation under evaluation. For instance, if the branch of add in Figure 1 has a rigid tag, then add is evaluated as shown in Example 7.

2.5   Flat Programs

The constructor-based rewriting logic defines the meaning of functional logic programs without referring to a concrete evaluation strategy. However, reasoning about the behavior of programs (e.g., program analysis), optimizing programs (e.g., partial evaluation), or building language specific tools (e.g., debuggers, profilers) demands for a more detailed description of the operational semantics of programs. On the one hand, such a description should reflect all details of the program execution, like pattern matching, sharing, binding logic variables, etc. On the other hand, it should be high level so that properties of programs can be formally derived.

It has been shown that such a description can be better based on an intermediate *flat representation of programs* rather than on the source-level functional logic programs. Figure 3 shows the syntax of such a flat language which has been successfully applied for this purpose. Flat programs contain an explicit representation of pattern matching (*case/fcase* corresponds to branches in definitional trees, *or* represents a choice between definitional trees in the case of rules with overlapping left-hand sides). The difference between *case* and *fcase* corresponds to residuation and narrowing: when the argument e evaluates to a free variable, *case* suspends whereas *fcase* nondeterministically binds this variable to a pattern in a branch of the case expression.

$$
\begin{array}{lll}
P & ::= D_1 \ldots D_m & \text{(program)} \\
D & ::= f(x_1, \ldots, x_n) = e & \text{(function definition)} \\
e & ::= x & \text{(variable)} \\
  & \quad | \quad c(e_1, \ldots, e_n) & \text{(constructor call)} \\
  & \quad | \quad f(e_1, \ldots, e_n) & \text{(function call)} \\
  & \quad | \quad case\ e\ of\ \{p_1 \to e_1; \ldots; p_n \to e_n\} & \text{(rigid case)} \\
  & \quad | \quad fcase\ e\ of\ \{p_1 \to e_1; \ldots; p_n \to e_n\} & \text{(flexible case)} \\
  & \quad | \quad e_1\ or\ e_2 & \text{(disjunction)} \\
  & \quad | \quad let\ \{x_1 = e_1, \ldots, x_n = e_n\}\ in\ e & \text{(let binding)} \\
p & ::= c(x_1, \ldots, x_n) & \text{(pattern)}
\end{array}
$$

Fig. 3. Syntax for flat programs

Let bindings as shown in Figure 3 are in principle not required for translating functional logic programs into flat programs. However, they can be used to translate extended classes of programs containing circular data structures and are convenient to express sharing without the use of complex graph structures [49,64]. Operationally, let bindings introduce new structures in memory that are updated after evaluation, which is essential for lazy computations [98]. Furthermore, let bindings are also useful to represent free variables in expressions by a direct circular binding of the form "*let* $\{x = x\}$ *in* e".

For instance, the operations add and "?" defined in Section 2.2 have the following flat representations:

```
add x y  =  fcase x of { 0 → y; S z → S (add z y) }
x ? y    =  x or y
```

[87] defines a mapping between definitional trees and flat programs and shows the equivalence of needed narrowing and outermost narrowing on flat programs. A precise description of (weakly needed) narrowing and residuation with sharing is given in [3] as an extension of Launchbury's natural semantics for lazy evaluation [98]. For this purpose, one considers only *normalized* flat programs, i.e., programs where the arguments of constructor and function calls are always variables. Any flat program can be normalized by introducing new variables by let expressions [3]. For instance, the expression "double coin" is normalized into "*let* $\{x = coin\}$ *in* double x". In order to model sharing, the variables are interpreted as references into a heap where new let bindings are stored and function calls are updated with their evaluated results.

To be more precise, a *heap*, denoted by Γ, Δ, or Θ, is a partial mapping from variables to expressions (the *empty heap* is denoted by $[]$). The value associated to variable x in heap Γ is denoted by $\Gamma[x]$. $\Gamma[x \mapsto e]$ denotes a heap Γ' with $\Gamma'[x] = e$ and $\Gamma'[y] = \Gamma[y]$ for all $x \neq y$. We use this notation either as a condition or as an update of a heap. A logic variable x that is unbound in Γ is represented by a circular binding of the form $\Gamma[x] = x$.

VarCons $\Gamma[x \mapsto t] : x \Downarrow \Gamma[x \mapsto t] : t$ where t is constructor-rooted

VarExp $$\frac{\Gamma[x \mapsto e] : e \Downarrow \Delta : v}{\Gamma[x \mapsto e] : x \Downarrow \Delta[x \mapsto v] : v} \qquad \begin{array}{l} \text{where } e \text{ is not constructor-rooted} \\ \qquad \text{and } e \neq x \end{array}$$

Val $\Gamma : v \Downarrow \Gamma : v \qquad \begin{array}{l} \text{where } v \text{ is constructor-rooted} \\ \qquad \text{or a variable with } \Gamma[v] = v \end{array}$

Fun $$\frac{\Gamma : \rho(e) \Downarrow \Delta : v}{\Gamma : f(\overline{x_n}) \Downarrow \Delta : v} \quad \text{where } f(\overline{y_n}) = e \in P \text{ and } \rho = \{\overline{y_n \mapsto x_n}\}$$

Let $$\frac{\Gamma[\overline{y_k \mapsto \rho(e_k)}] : \rho(e) \Downarrow \Delta : v}{\Gamma : let\ \{\overline{x_k = e_k}\}\ in\ e \Downarrow \Delta : v} \quad \begin{array}{l} \text{where } \rho = \{\overline{x_k \mapsto y_k}\} \\ \text{and } \overline{y_k} \text{ are fresh variables} \end{array}$$

Or $$\frac{\Gamma : e_i \Downarrow \Delta : v}{\Gamma : e_1\ or\ e_2 \Downarrow \Delta : v} \quad \text{where } i \in \{1, 2\}$$

Select $$\frac{\Gamma : e \Downarrow \Delta : c(\overline{y_n}) \qquad \Delta : \rho(e_i) \Downarrow \Theta : v}{\Gamma : (f)case\ e\ of\ \{\overline{p_k \to e_k}\} \Downarrow \Theta : v} \quad \begin{array}{l} \text{where } p_i = c(\overline{x_n}) \\ \text{and } \rho = \{\overline{x_n \mapsto y_n}\} \end{array}$$

Guess $$\frac{\Gamma : e \Downarrow \Delta : x \qquad \Delta[x \mapsto \rho(p_i), \overline{y_n \mapsto y_n}] : \rho(e_i) \Downarrow \Theta : v}{\Gamma : fcase\ e\ of\ \{\overline{p_k \to e_k}\} \Downarrow \Theta : v}$$

where $p_i = c(\overline{x_n})$, $\rho = \{\overline{x_n \mapsto y_n}\}$, and $\overline{y_n}$ are fresh variables

Fig. 4. Natural semantics of normalized flat programs [3]

Using heap structures, one can provide a high-level description of the operational behavior of residuation and demand-driven narrowing with call-time choice in form of a natural semantics (also called big-step semantics). The natural semantics uses judgements of the form "$\Gamma : e \Downarrow \Delta : v$" with the meaning that in the context of heap Γ the expression e evaluates to value (head normal form) v and produces a modified heap Δ. Figure 4 shows the rules defining this semantics w.r.t. a given normalized flat program P ($\overline{o_k}$ denotes a sequence of objects $o_1, \ldots, o_k$). The rules VarCons and VarExp retrieve expressions from the heap: VarCons retrieves values whereas the expressions retrieved by VarExp are further evaluated. In order to avoid the reevaluation of the same expression, VarExp updates the heap with the computed value, which models sharing. Values (i.e., head normal forms) are just returned by rule Val. Fun unfolds function calls by evaluating the right-hand side after binding the formal parameters to the actual ones. Let introduces new bindings in the heap and renames the variables in the expressions with the fresh names introduced in the heap. Or nondeterministically evaluates one of its arguments. Finally, Select and Guess deal with *case* expressions. If the first argument of *case* evaluates to a constructor-rooted term, Select evaluates the corresponding branch of the *case* expression, otherwise (if the argument evaluates to an unbound variable), Guess nondeterministically binds the argument to one of the patterns of the *case* expression and continues with the corresponding branch.

By introducing a stack to model the context of a computation, one can also define an equivalent small-step semantics which can be enriched with more details of realistic implementations, such as search strategies, concurrency, external operations etc (see [3] for details).

The flat representation of programs and its operational semantics has been used for various language-oriented tools (e.g., compilers [20,27], partial evaluators [4,5], trace-oriented debuggers [40], profilers [39]) and extended in various ways (e.g., higher-order functions [87], memoization [53], encapsulated search [38], computation costs [39]).

Flat programs can be considered as a kernel language for functional logic programming since programs written in concrete functional logic languages like Curry with all its syntactic sugar can be automatically translated into flat programs. It is interesting to note that the language of flat programs is *not* minimal since it contains two concepts that can be simulated by each other: logic variables and overlapping rules (i.e., disjunctions expressed by *or*). For instance, a rule like

$$\text{x ? y } = \text{ x } or \text{ y}$$

can be expressed without *or* by introducing a logic variable z that ranges over two data constructors I0 and I1:

$$\text{x ? y } = \text{ } let \text{ }\{z = z\} \text{ } in \text{ } fcase \text{ } z \text{ } of \text{ } \{ \text{ I0 } \rightarrow \text{ x; } \text{ I1 } \rightarrow \text{ y } \}$$

On the other hand, logic variables can be eliminated by defining *nondeterministic generator operations* for each type. For instance, a generator for type Nat defined in Example 2 is the operation genNat defined by

$$\text{genNat } = \text{ 0 ? S genNat}$$

so that genNat evaluates to all possible values of type Nat. Now each occurrence of a logic variable can be replaced by a corresponding generator, e.g., the expression

$$let \text{ }\{x = x\} \text{ } in \text{ leq x (S 0)}$$

can be transformed into

$$let \text{ }\{x = \text{genNat}\} \text{ } in \text{ leq x (S 0)}$$

without changing the computed results. These equivalences have been used in implementations of functional logic languages [41,42]. Further details can be found in [24].

3   Language Concepts: Curry

After the review of recent results and techniques for functional logic programming, this section shows how they influenced the design of a concrete programming language. For this purpose, we consider Curry [69,92] (the relation to other languages will be briefly discussed in Section 7), a functional logic language based on many of the concepts introduced so far. The development of Curry is the outcome of an international initiative of researchers in the area of functional logic programming with the goal to provide a common standard for the research, teaching, and application of integrated functional logic languages.

The syntax of Curry is very similar to the syntax of Haskell [117] and has been already introduced in an informal manner. Curry is a polymorphically typed language with a Hindley/Milner-like type system supporting type inference [46]. Since the type concept is fairly standard and orthogonal to the other issues of the language, it is not explicitly addressed in the following. Therefore, this section is devoted to discuss concepts and design decisions that are unique to Curry.

3.1   Semantics

A Curry program is formally a constructor-based TRS. Thus, its *declarative semantics* is given by the rewriting logic CRWL, i.e., operations and constructors are non-strict with a call-time choice semantics for nondeterministic operations.

The *operational semantics* is based on an extension of needed narrowing on generalized definitional trees with sharing and residuation. The precise description is based on normalized flat programs as already shown in Section 2.5. Thus, for (flexible) inductively sequential operations, which form the vast majority of operations in application programs, the evaluation strategy is optimal w.r.t. the length of derivations and number of computed solutions and always computes a value if it exists (in case of nondeterministic choices only if the underlying implementation is fair w.r.t. such choices, as [26,27,88]). Therefore, the programmer can concentrate on the declarative meaning of programs and needs less attention to the consequences of the particular evaluation strategy (see [73] for a more detailed discussion). The following example shows that Curry is an improvement compared to Haskell which does not have a similar behavior for all inductively sequential operations.

Example 8. Consider the inductively sequential operation f defined by

```
f 0 []     = 0
f x (y:ys) = y
```

and a nonterminating operation ⊥. Then the expression "f ⊥ [1]" has the value 1, but Haskell does not terminate on this expression due to the strict left-to-right top-down pattern matching strategy. Furthermore, if the operation g is defined by

```
g x = 0
g 1 = 1
```

in Haskell the expression "g 1" is evaluated to 0 although the second equation indicates that 1 is also an acceptable result. As a consequence, program rules in Haskell cannot be interpreted as equations but all the rules defining an operation in a Haskell program must be passed through a complex pattern-matching compiler [129] in order to understand their meaning.   □

As discussed above, *external operations* not implemented by explicit rules, like basic arithmetic operators or I/O operations, cannot be handled by narrowing. Therefore, Curry exploits *residuation* to connect external operations in a conceptually clean way (see also [35]). Since external operations can not usually deal with unevaluated arguments possibly containing logic variables, the arguments of external operations are reduced to a ground value before the operation is evaluated. If some arguments are not ground but contain logic variables, the function call is suspended until the variables are bound to ground values. The *concurrent conjunction* "&" on constraints is the basic concurrency operator that evaluates both arguments in a non-specified order to success.

The discussion of residuation-based languages (see Section 2.4) might give the impression that residuation is useful for user-defined operations. Therefore, previous versions of Curry had also the possibility to define operations as "rigid". However, it turned out that this is unnecessary in practice, since the suspension of operations often caused more complications than their active application through narrowing (exceptions are related to concurrent objects and ports for distributed programming, see below). Moreover, the optimality of needed narrowing ensures that the argument guessing is restricted to a minimal part. Therefore, all user-defined operations are evaluated by narrowing and only external operations and conditionals like "if-then-else" or "case-of" are evaluated by residuation. The latter is motivated by the fact that conditionals are often used as guards to prevent infinite recursion. A useful primitive to define general "suspension" combinators for concurrent programming is the predefined operation ensureNotFree that returns its argument evaluated to head normal form but suspends as long as the result is a logic variable.

3.2   Constraints

Functional logic languages are able to solve equational constraints. As shown in Section 2.2, such constraints occur in conditions of conditional rules and are intended to restrict the applicability of the rewrite rule, i.e., a replacement with a conditional rule is only performed if the condition has been shown to be satisfied (e.g., compare the definition of last in Section 2.1). Thus, constraints are solved when conditional rules are applied. In terms of concurrent constraint programming languages [121], solving constraints in conditions corresponds to *tell* constraints. The dual operation, *ask*, is used in conditionals like "if-then-else". Curry distinguishes these different uses by different types: Success and Bool.

Equational constraints are expressions of type Success. Since constraints are ordinary expressions, they are first-class values that can be passed in arguments or data structures. For instance, the following "constraint combinator" takes a list of constraints as input and creates a new constraint that is satisfied if all constraints in the input list are satisfied:

```
allValid :: [Success] -> Success
allValid []     = success
allValid (c:cs) = c & allValid cs
```

Here, `success` is not a constructor but denotes the trivial constraint that is always satisfied. Exploiting the higher-order features of Curry (see below), one can define it also by

```
allValid = foldr (&) success
```

Note that the constructor `Success` was introduced in Section 2.2 only to provide a rewrite-based definition of strict equality. It is not available in Curry where a more efficient implementation of strict equality is used. The main difference shows up when an equational constraint "x =:= y" between two logic variables x and y is solved. Solving it with the rewrite rules shown in Section 2.2, x and y are nondeterministically bound to ground constructor terms which usually results in an infinite search space. This is avoided in Curry by binding one variable to the other, similar to logic programming.

Hence, the type `Success` is a type without constructors but with a few basic constraints like `success` and "=:=" and a concurrent conjunction "&" to combine constraints into larger units. Actually, one can consider `Success` as equivalent to the functional type "*ConstraintStore* → *ConstraintStore*" mapping a constraint store into a new constraint store. Then, the trivial constraint `success` is the identity mapping and a constraint like x=:=2 maps a constraint store into a new one which is extended by the binding of x to 2. Constraint stores are implicitly chained through a derivation, cloned in nondeterministic steps, and extended when evaluating a condition of a rule. This view has been used in [106] to connect a solver for real arithmetic constraints to a Curry implementation. By adding basic constraints that deal with other constraint domains, like real arithmetic or finite domain constraints, typical applications of constraint logic programming can be covered and combined with features of lazy higher-order programming [20,54,55,102,106,119].

The condition of a rule is any expression of type `Success`, i.e., it is not only a conjunction of equational constraints but can also be constructed by constraint combinators like `allValid`. By contrast, the condition in an "if-then-else" must be an expression of type `Bool` since two different values (`True` and `False`) are required to select the `then` or `else` branch according to the result of the Boolean test. For this purpose, Curry also supports a *test equality* predicate "==" of type "a->a->Bool" to check the equality of two *ground* constructor terms. In contrast to "=:=", a call to "==" is suspended if an argument contains logic variables so that the equality cannot be decided without instantiating these variables. Hence, one can consider "==" as a rigid operation defined by the rules

$$
\begin{aligned}
c == c &= \text{True} & \forall c/0 \in \mathcal{C} \\
c\ x_1 \ldots x_n == c\ y_1 \ldots y_n &= x_1{==}y_1\ \&\&\ldots\&\&\ x_n{==}y_n & \forall c/n \in \mathcal{C}, n > 0 \\
c\ x_1 \ldots x_n == d\ y_1 \ldots y_m &= \text{False} & \forall c/n \neq d/m \in \mathcal{C} \\
\text{True}\ \&\&\ x &= x \\
\text{False}\ \&\&\ x &= \text{False}
\end{aligned}
$$

As an alternative to the distinction between equational constraints in conditions and Boolean tests in conditionals, one might also use equational constraints in conditionals, as, for instance, done in the purely narrowing-based language TOY [101]. This demands for the negation of constraints so that a conditional "if c then e_1 else e_2" is evaluated by nondeterministically evaluating $c \wedge e_1$ or $\neg c \wedge e_2$. Actually, this is implemented in TOY by the use of *disequality constraints*. However, the complexity of the handling of disequality constraints puts more demands on the implementation side.

3.3 Higher-Order Operations

The use of higher-order operations, i.e., operations that take other operations as arguments or yield them as results, is an important programming technique in functional languages so that it should be covered also by functional logic languages. Typical examples are the mapping of an operation to all elements of a list (`map`) or a generic accumulator for lists (`foldr`):

```
map :: (a->b) -> [a] -> [b]
map _ []     = []
map f (x:xs) = f x : map f xs

foldr :: (a->b->b) -> b -> [a] -> b
foldr _ z []     = z
foldr f z (x:xs) = f x (foldr f z xs)
```

Logic languages often provide higher-order features through a transformation into a first-order program [131] by defining a predicate *apply* that implements the application of an arbitrary operation of the program to an expression. This technique is also known as "defunctionalization" [118] and enough to support the higher-order features of current functional languages (e.g., lambda abstractions can be replaced by new function definitions). Therefore, this solution is also used in Curry.

As an example, consider a program containing the unary operation **not** and the binary operations **add** and **leq**. Then, one can define the meaning of *apply* by the following rules:

$$
\begin{aligned}
apply\ \text{not} \quad & x = \text{not}\ x & (apply_1) \\
apply\ \text{add} \quad & x = \text{add}\ x & (apply_2) \\
apply\ (\text{add}\ x)\ & y = \text{add}\ x\ y & (apply_3) \\
apply\ \text{leq} \quad & x = \text{leq}\ x & (apply_4) \\
apply\ (\text{leq}\ x)\ & y = \text{leq}\ x\ y & (apply_5)
\end{aligned}
$$

Thus, a *partially applied function call*, i.e., a n-ary operation called with less than n arguments, is considered as a constructor-rooted, i.e., not further evaluable, term (one can also make this distinction clear by introducing new constructor symbols for such partial applications). Thus, the first argument in each rule for *apply* is always a constructor-rooted term. If an n-ary function call with $n-1$ arguments is applied to its final argument, the operation is evaluated (e.g., as in the rules $apply_1$, $apply_3$, $apply_5$). This explicit definition has been used in Prolog-based implementations of functional logic languages [20].

An important difference to purely functional languages shows up when the operation to be applied (i.e., the first argument of *apply*) is a logic variable. In this case, one can instantiate this variable to all possible operations occurring in the program [63]. Since this might result also in instantiations that are not intended w.r.t. the given types, one can restrict these instantiations to well-typed ones which requires to keep type information at run time [29,61]. Another option is the instantiation of variables denoting functions to (well-typed) lambda terms in order to cover programs that can reason about bindings and block structure [87]. Since all these options might result in huge search spaces due to function instantiation, and the feasibility and usefulness for larger application programs is not clear, Curry chooses a more pragmatic solution: function application *apply* is rigid, i.e., it suspends if the first functional argument is a logic variable. For this behavior, we can avoid the explicit introduction of rules for *apply*: it can be considered as a primitive operation with a meaning that is specified by extending the natural semantics of Figure 4 with the following rule (where partially applied function calls are considered as constructor-rooted terms in the rules VarCons and Val):

$$\text{Apply} \quad \frac{\Gamma : x \Downarrow \Delta : \varphi(\overline{x_k}) \qquad \Delta : \varphi(\overline{x_k}, y) \Downarrow \Theta : v}{\Gamma : apply\ x\ y \Downarrow \Theta : v}$$

where φ is either a constructor or an n-ary operation with $k < n$.

3.4 Encapsulated Search

An essential difference between functional and logic computations is their determinism behavior. Functional computations are deterministic. This enables a reasonable treatment of I/O operations by the monadic approach where I/O actions are considered as transformations on the outside world [130]. The monadic I/O approach is also taken in Curry. However, logic computations might cause (don't know) nondeterministic choices, i.e., a computation can be cloned and continued in two different directions. Since one can not clone the entire outside world, nondeterministic choices during monadic I/O computations are not allowed and lead to a run-time error in Curry. Since this might restrict the applicability of logic programming techniques in larger applications, there is a clear need to *encapsulate nondeterministic search* between I/O actions. For this purpose, [89] proposes the addition of a primitive search operator

```
try :: (a->Success) -> [a->Success]
```

that takes a constraint abstraction, e.g., (\x->x=:=coin), as input, evaluates it until the first nondeterministic step occurs, and returns the result: the empty list in case of failure, a list with a single element in case of success, or a list with at least two elements representing a nondeterministic choice. For instance, try (\x->x=:=coin) evaluates to [\x->x=:=0, \x->x=:=1]. Based on this primitive, one can define various search strategies to explore the search space and return its solutions. [105] shows an implementation of this primitive.

Although typical search operators of Prolog, like findall, once, or negation-as-failure, can be implemented using the primitive try, it became also clear that the combination with demand-driven evaluation and sharing causes further complications. For instance, in an expression like

```
let y = coin in try (\x->x=:=y)
```

it is not obvious whether the evaluation of coin (introduced outside but demanded inside the search operator) should be encapsulated or not. Hence, the result of this expression might depend on the evaluation order. For instance, if coin is evaluated before the try expression, it results in two computations where y is bound to 0 in one computation and to 1 in the other computation. Hence, try does not encapsulate the nondeterminism of coin (this is also the semantics of try implemented in [105]). However, if coin is evaluated inside the capsule of try (because it is not demanded before), then the nondeterminism of coin is encapsulated. These and more peculiarities are discussed in [38]. Furthermore, the order of the solutions might depend on the textual order of program rules or the evaluation time (e.g., in parallel implementations). Therefore, [38] contains a proposal for another primitive search operator:

```
getSearchTree :: a -> IO (SearchTree a)
```

Since getSearchTree is an I/O action, its result (in particular, the order of solutions) depends on the current environment, e.g., time of evaluation. It takes an expression and delivers a search tree representing the search space when evaluating the input:

```
data SearchTree a = Or [SearchTree a] | Val a | Fail
```

Based on this primitive, one can define various concrete search strategies as tree traversals. To avoid the complications w.r.t. shared variables, getSearchTree implements a *strong encapsulation view*, i.e., conceptually, the argument of getSearchTree is cloned before the evaluation starts in order to cut any sharing with the environment. Furthermore, the structure of the search tree is computed lazily so that an expression with infinitely many values does not cause the non-termination of the search operator if one is interested in only one solution. More details about search trees and their operational semantics can be found in [38,41].

Although these concepts are sufficient to encapsulate nondeterministic computations to avoid nondeterminism in I/O operations, it is often also desired to collect all the values of an expression in some data structure at arbitrary computation points, e.g., to accumulate all values, to compute a minimal value, or to check whether some constraint has no solution (similarly to "negation as failure" in logic programming). As mentioned above, the initial concepts for encapsulation in functional logic languages have the drawback that their result might depend on the degree of evaluation of the argument (which is difficult to grasp in non-strict languages). A solution to this problem is presented in [25] by the introduction of *set functions*. For each defined operation f, f_S denotes its corresponding set function. In order to be independent of the evaluation order, f_S encapsulates only the nondeterminism caused by evaluating f except for the nondeterminism caused by evaluating the arguments to which f is applied. For instance, consider the operation decOrInc defined by

```
decOrInc x = (x-1) ? (x+1)
```

Then "decOrInc$_S$ 3" evaluates to (an abstract representation of) the set $\{2, 4\}$, i.e., the nondeterminism originating from decOrInc is encapsulated into a set. However, "decOrInc$_S$ (2?5)" evaluates to two different sets $\{1, 3\}$ and $\{4, 6\}$ due to its nondeterministic argument, i.e., the nondeterminism originating from the argument is not encapsulated but produces different sets. It is shown in [25] that the results of set functions do not depend on the evaluation order so that the disadvantages of the earlier approaches are avoided. [104,120] contain similar proposals but with the restriction to test only the failure of expressions. There, an operation fails computes the set of all values of its argument expression and returns true, if this set is empty, or false, otherwise.

4   Implementation

The definition of needed narrowing and its extensions shares many similarities with pattern matching in functional or unification in logic languages. Thus, it is reasonable to use similar techniques to implement functional logic languages. Due to the coverage of logic variables and nondeterministic search, one could try to translate functional logic programs into Prolog programs in order to exploit the implementation technology available for Prolog. Actually, there are various approaches to implement functional logic languages with demand-driven evaluation strategies in Prolog (e.g., [11,20,44,68,96,100]). A common idea is the translation of source operations into predicates that compute only the *head normal form* (i.e., a constructor-rooted term or a variable) of a call to this operation. Thus, an n-ary operation could be translated into a predicate with $n + 1$ arguments where the last argument contains the head normal form of the evaluated call. For instance, the list concatenation "++" defined in Section 2.1 can be translated into the following Prolog predicate conc:

```
conc(Xs,Ys,H) :- hnf(Xs,HXs), conc_1(HXs,Ys,H).
conc_1([],Ys,H) :- hnf(Ys,H).
conc_1([X|Xs],Ys,[X|conc(Xs,Ys)]).
```

Since the first argument of "++" is an inductive position, its value is needed and, hence, computed by the predicate hnf before it is passed to the predicate conc_1 implementing the pattern matching on the first argument. Since the right-hand side of the second rule of "++" is already in head normal form, no further evaluation is necessary. In the first rule of `conc_1`, it is unknown at compile time whether the second argument `Ys` is already in head normal form. Therefore, the evaluation to head normal form is enforced by the predicate `hnf`. The goal `hnf`(t, h) evaluates any term t to its head normal form h. Some of the clauses defining `hnf` are:

```
hnf(V,V) :- var(V), !.
hnf([],[]).
hnf([X|Xs],[X|Xs]).
...
hnf(conc(Xs,Ys),H) :- conc(Xs,Ys,H).
...
```

Using this scheme, there is a straightforward transformation of needed narrowing and its extensions into Prolog. However, this scheme does not implement sharing where it is required that each function call should be evaluated at most once. This can be achieved by representing function calls as "suspensions" that contain two further arguments: one indicates whether the suspension has been already evaluated and the other contains the head normal form. Thus, the second rule of `conc_1` has then the form

```
conc_1([X|Xs],Ys,[X|susp(conc(Xs,Ys),E,H)]).
```

and the definition of `hnf` has the additional clause

```
hnf(susp(Call,E,H),H) :- var(E) -> hnf(Call,H), E=ready ; true.
```

Another implementation of sharing is proposed in [20] where only variables with multiple occurrences in right-hand sides are shared instead of function calls. In order to implement residuation, coroutining features of modern Prolog implementation can be exploited (see [20] for details).

The transformation of functional logic programs into Prolog programs has many advantages. It is fairly simple to implement, one can use constraint solvers available in many Prolog implementations in application programs, and one can exploit the advances made in efficient implementations of Prolog (depending on the Prolog implementation, one can improve the efficiency of the above code by a couple of minor transformations). Thus, one obtains with a limited effort an implementation that can be used for larger applications with a comparable efficiency than other more low-level implementations (e.g., [81,101]).

Despite these advantages, the transformation into Prolog has the drawback that one is fixed to Prolog's backtracking strategy to implement nondeterministic search. This hampers the implementation of encapsulated search or fair search strategies. Therefore, there are also various approaches to use other target languages than Prolog. For instance, [27] presents techniques to compile Curry programs into Java programs that implement a fair search for solutions. A translation of Curry programs into Haskell programs is proposed in [41,42] which offers a primitive operator to encapsulate search, similarly to `getSearchTree` introduced in Section 3.4. **Virtual machines** to compile Curry programs are proposed in [26,88,105]. In particular, [26,88] implement a fair (global) search for solutions, and [105] covers the implementation of encapsulated search.

Beyond the compilation of programs into particular target languages or virtual machines, the implementation of programming languages has many other facets that have been considered also for functional logic languages. For instance, **partial evaluation** is a powerful compile-time technique to optimize source-level programs. [9] contains a general framework for the partial evaluation of functional logic programs. It has been specialized to the case of needed narrowing in [10] where the superiority of needed narrowing has been shown also for partial evaluation. To provide a practical implementation of a partial evaluator covering all features of Curry, [5] shows that this is possible if the partial evaluator is based on the flat representation introduced in Section 2.5.

To understand the run-time behavior of functional logic programs, specific tools are required since it is well known that even the operational behavior of purely functional programs with lazy evaluation is difficult to understand [112]. This demands for tools specifically designed to show operational aspects of functional logic programs. Thus, a few activities into this direction have started. Since traditional tracing tools, although provided in practical systems, are often not helpful, the objective of **debugging tools** is usually a representation of operational aspects that are more oriented towards the program text rather than execution steps. For instance, COOSy [36] is a tool to observe the evaluation of individual expressions, operations, or logic variables in a program. It records the observable events during run time and presents the corresponding results (computed values, variable bindings etc) with a separate viewer. TeaBag [28] provides another view that connects the activities of virtual machine with the source program under execution. Other debugging tools are more oriented towards the semantics of functional logic programs. For instance, [40] describes a formal semantics for a trace-based debugging tool, [39] proposes a profiling tool based on a cost-augmented semantics of functional logic programs, [113] proposes a debugging approach based on dynamic slicing, and [6,43] contain approaches to declarative debugging based on the ideas developed in the area of logic programming [123].

5   Extensions

The language Curry described so far is based on the theoretical foundations on functional logic programming surveyed in Section 2. Thus, it is a basis to show the feasibility and usefulness of these concepts in practice. Nevertheless, various extensions to this base language have been explored in recent years. In this section, we review some of them: constraints, functional patterns, and support for distributed programming. Other aspects, which are not discussed below, are default rules [108], failure [104,120], inductive programming [56], tabling and memoization [16,53], connecting databases [57,75], or proof tools for the verification of functional logic programs [45].

5.1   Constraints

The integration of constraints has been already mentioned. Curry provides equational constraints that are solved in conditions. Further constraint domains, like real arithmetic, Boolean, or finite domains, can be supported by adding basic constraints for these domains (e.g., see [20,32,54,55,102,106,119] for some examples). It has been shown [54,55] that functional logic languages are good frameworks to solve constraint problems in a high-level and maintainable way.

As an example demonstrating the compactness obtained by combining constraint programming and higher-order features, consider a solver for SuDoku puzzles[10] with finite domain constraints. If we represent the SuDoku matrix m as a list of lists of finite domain variables, the "SuDoku constraints" can be easily specified by

```
allValid (map allDifferent m) &
allValid (map allDifferent (transpose m)) &
allValid (map allDifferent (squaresOfNine m))
```

where `allDifferent` is the usual constraint stating that all variables in its argument list must have different values, `transpose` is the standard matrix transposition, and `squaresOfNine` computes the list of 3×3 sub-matrices. Then, a SuDoku puzzle can be solved with these constraints by adding the usual domain and labeling constraints (see [77] for more details).

5.2   Functional Patterns

We have discussed in Section 2.2 the fundamental requirement of functional languages for *constructor-based* rewrite systems. This requirement is the key for practically useful implementations and excludes rules like

```
last (xs ++ [e])  =  e                                          (last)
```

The non-constructor pattern `(xs ++ [e])` in this rule can be eliminated by moving it into the condition part (see Section 2.1):

```
last l | xs++[e] =:= l = e    where xs,e free              (lastc)
```

However, the strict equality used in (*lastc*) has the disadvantage that all list elements are completely evaluated. Hence, an expression like `last [failed,3]` (where `failed` is an expression that has no value) leads to a failure. This disadvantage can be avoided by allowing *functional patterns*, i.e., expressions containing defined functions, in arguments of a rule's left-hand side so that (*last*) becomes a valid rule. In order to base this extension on the existing foundations of functional logic programming as described so far, a functional pattern is interpreted as an abbreviation of the set of constructor terms that is the result of evaluating (by narrowing) the functional pattern. Thus, rule (*last*) abbreviates the following (infinite) set of rules:

---

[10] A SuDoku puzzle consists of a 9×9 matrix of digits between 1 and 9 so that each row, each column, and each of the nine 3×3 sub-matrices contain pairwise different digits. The challenge is to find the missing digits if some digits are given.

```
last [x] = x
last [x1,x] = x
last [x1,x2,x] = x
...
```

Hence, the expression `last [failed,3]` reduces to 3 w.r.t. these rules. In order to provide a constructive implementation of this concept, [23] proposes a specific demand-driven unification procedure for functional pattern unification that can be implemented similarly to strict equality. Functional patterns are a powerful concept to express transformation problems in a high-level way. Concrete programming examples and syntactic conditions for the well-definedness of rules with functional patterns can be found in [23]. [80] exploits functional patterns for a declarative approach to process XML documents.

5.3 Distributed Programming

Distributed systems are of great importance but programming them is a non-trivial task. Since Curry has already features for concurrent programming via residuation, it provides a good basis that can be extended for distributed programming. For this purpose, [70] proposes *port constraints*. Conceptually, a *port* is a constraint between a multiset (of messages) and a list that is satisfied if all elements in the multiset occur in the list and vice versa. Clients use a primitive constraint `send m p` that extends a port p by an element (message) m. A server is just a recursive operation that processes the list of messages of a port and waits until the tail of the list is instantiated with the next message, i.e., it is rigid w.r.t. the message list. By sending messages containing logic variables, the server can instantiate them so that answers can be easily returned without explicit return channels. By making ports accessible through symbolic names similar to URLs, clients can send messages to servers running on an arbitrary host. As shown in [70], the use of ports provides a high-level concept to implement distributed systems and to integrate existing declarative programs fairly easy into distributed environments.

The port concept can be also used to implement *distributed objects* in Curry. It is well known from concurrent logic programming [124] that objects can be easily implemented as predicates processing a stream of incoming messages. The object's internal state is a parameter that may change in each recursive call that processes a message. By creating such object predicates with their own ports, one immediately obtains distributed objects that can reside on various hosts. To avoid the explicit modeling of objects by the programmer, [85] proposes ObjectCurry, a syntactic extension of Curry which allows the direct definition of templates that play the role of classes in conventional object-oriented languages. A template defines a local state and messages that modify the state and send messages to other objects. Templates can be directly transformed into standard Curry code by a preprocessor. To provide inheritance between templates, the preprocessor implements an extended type system that includes subtyping.

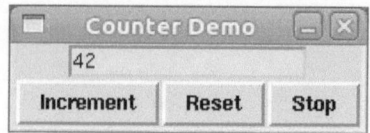

Fig. 5. A simple counter GUI

6   Applications

Although most of the published work on functional logic programming is related to foundational aspects, functional logic languages, in particular Curry, have been used in various applications in order to demonstrate the feasibility and advantages of functional logic programming. A summary of design patterns exploiting combined functional and logic features for application programming can be found in [21]. These patterns are unique to functional logic programming and cannot be directly applied in other paradigms. For instance, the *constraint constructor* pattern exploits the fact that functional logic languages can deal with failure so that conditions about the validity of data represented by general structures can be encoded directly in the data structures rather than in applications programs. This frees the application programs from dealing with complex conditions on the constructed data. Another pattern, called *locally defined global identifier*, has been used to provide high-level interfaces to libraries dealing with complex data, like programming of dynamic web pages or graphical user interfaces (GUIs) (see below). This pattern exploits the fact that functional logic data structures can contain logic variables which are globally unique when they are introduced. This is helpful to create local structures with globally unique identifiers and leads to improved abstractions in application programs. Further design patterns and programming techniques are discussed in [21,22].

The combination of functional and logic language features are exploited in [71] for the high-level programming of GUIs. The hierarchical structure of a GUI (e.g., rows, columns, or matrices of primitive and combined widgets) is represented as a data term. This term contains call-back functions as event handlers, i.e., the use of functions as first-class objects is natural in this application. Since event handlers defined for one widget should usually influence the appearance and contents of other widgets (e.g., if a slider is moved, values shown in other widgets should change), GUIs have also a logical structure that is different from its hierarchical structure. To specify this logical structure, logic variables in data structures are handy, since a logic variable can specify relationships between different parts of a data term. As a concrete example, consider the simple counter GUI shown in Figure 5. Using a Curry library designed with these ideas, one can specify this GUI by the following data term:

```
Col [Entry [WRef val, Text "0", Background "yellow"],
     Row [Button (updateValue incrText val) [Text "Increment"],
          Button (setValue val "0")         [Text "Reset"],
          Button exitGUI                    [Text "Stop"]]]
    where val free
```

The hierarchical structure of the GUI (a column with two rows) is directly reflected in the tree structure of this term. The first argument of each Button is the corresponding event handler. For instance, the invocation of exitGUI terminates the GUI, and the invocation of setValue assigns a new value to the referenced widget. For this purpose, the logic variable val is used. Since the attribute WRef of the entry widget defines its origin and it is used in various event handlers, it appropriately describes the logical structure of the GUI, i.e., the dependencies between different widgets. Note that other (more low level) GUI libraries or languages (e.g., Tcl/Tk) use strings or numbers as widget references which is potentially more error prone.

Similar ideas are applied in [72] to provide a high-level programming interface for web applications (dynamic web pages). There, HTML terms are represented as data structures containing event handlers associated to submit buttons and logic variables referring to user inputs in web pages that are passed to event handlers. These high-level APIs have been used in various applications, e.g., to implement web-based learning systems [84], constructing web-based interfaces for arbitrary applications [77,78], graphical programming environments [76], documentation tools [74], and web frameworks [86] for Curry. Furthermore, Curry has also been used for embedded systems programming [82,83] with specific libraries and application-specific compilers.

7   Conclusions and Related Languages

In this paper we surveyed foundations of functional logic programming and their practical realization in the declarative multi-paradigm language Curry. Curry is currently the only functional logic language which is based on such strong foundations (e.g., soundness and completeness and optimal evaluation on inductively sequential programs) and that has been also used to develop larger applications. Nevertheless, there exist languages with similar goals. We briefly discuss some of them and relate them to Curry.

The language **TOY** [101] has strong connections to Curry since it is based on similar foundations (rewriting logic CRWL, demand-driven narrowing). In contrast to Curry, it is purely narrowing-based and does not cover residuation or concurrency. As a consequence, there is no distinction between constraints and Boolean expressions, but disequality constraints are used to implement the negation of equations in conditional expressions. Similarly to some implementations of Curry, TOY supports constraints over finite domains or real numbers. In addition to Curry, TOY allows higher-order patterns in the left-hand sides of proram rules. Since residuation is not included in TOY, the connection with external operations is rather ad hoc. Furthermore, TOY does not provide a concept to encapsulate search.

Escher [99] is a residuation-based functional logic language. Nondeterminism is expressed by explicit disjunctions. The operational semantics is given by a set of reduction rules to evaluate operations in a demand-driven manner and simplify logical expressions. Due to its different computation model, the conditions under which completely evaluated answers can be computed are not clear.

The language **Oz** [126] is based on a computation model that extends the concurrent constraint programming paradigm [121] with features for distributed programming and stateful computations. Similarly to Escher, nondeterministic computations must be explicitly represented as disjunctions so that operations used to solve equations require different definitions than operations to rewrite expressions. In contrast to Escher and Curry, the base semantics is strict so that optimal evaluations are not directly supported.

The functional logic language **Mercury** [127] restricts logic programming features in order to provide a highly efficient implementation. In particular, predicates and functions must have distinct modes so that their arguments are either ground or unbound at call time. This inhibits the application of typical logic programming techniques, like computation with partially instantiated structures, so that some programming techniques for functional logic programming [21,71,72] cannot be applied in Mercury. This condition has been relaxed in the language **HAL** [59]. However, both languages are based on a strict operational semantics that does not support optimal evaluations.

Although many encouraging results have been obtained in recent years, the development of functional logic languages is ongoing and there are many topics for future work:

Semantics and Language Concepts: The notion of strict equality, although similar to functional languages, is for some applications too restrictive so that a more flexible handling is often desirable. Are more powerful higher-order features useful, and how can they be treated (from a semantical and implementation point of view)? Are there other concepts for concurrency and distribution together with a formal model? How can existing constraint solvers be integrated in a generic way, and which kinds of constraint domains and solvers are useful? More powerful type systems (e.g., type classes, subtypes, dependent types) and concepts for object-orientation beyond existing ones can be considered. Is the incorporation of modes useful? Are there appropriate concepts for meta-programming beyond existing approaches (e.g., libraries of the PAKCS distribution [81])?

Implementation: More efficient implementations, in particular, of advanced concepts such as encapsulated search, concurrency, fair scheduling, parallelism. Compilation into various target languages or target architectures, e.g., multi-core or embedded processors. Implementation of useful concepts from related languages, like Haskell's type classes, genericity, memoization. Program optimization, e.g., by powerful transformations or for restricted classes of programs. Domain-specific compilation for particular application domains (e.g., constraints, web programming, embedded or pervasive systems). Better environments for program development. More domain-specific libraries and APIs, standardization of libraries (e.g., for Curry) to improve compatibility of different implementations, standard interfaces to external operations.

Analysis and Transformation: Only a few approaches exist for the analysis of functional logic programs (e.g., [7,8,37,67,79,90,91,132]) so that this area deserves more studies, like termination analyses, abstract interpretation frameworks, analysis of particular properties (e.g., determinism, suspension, modes). Similarly, more powerful and practically applicable methods for transforming programs are required, like optimizing source and intermediate programs, more advanced program specialization, refactoring, and also general transformation frameworks.

Debugging: Some works done in this area have been already mentioned, but more work is required to provide practically useful support tools, like tracers, declarative debuggers, program slicers, or profilers for functional logic programs, integrated debugging environments, techniques and strategies for program correction and program verification.

Results and advances in these areas are also useful to support the development of more applications implemented with functional logic languages.

Acknowledgments. I am grateful to Harald Ganzinger who put me on this research track and created a productive research environment in his group that lead to my most important contributions in this area. Furthermore, I would like to thank Sergio Antoy, Bernd Braßel, Germán Vidal, and the anonymous reviewers for their constructive remarks on a previous version of this paper.

References

1. Aït-Kaci, H.: An Overview of LIFE. In: Schmidt, J.W., Stogny, A.A. (eds.) EWDW 1990. LNCS, vol. 504, pp. 42–58. Springer, Heidelberg (1991)
2. Aït-Kaci, H., Lincoln, P., Nasr, R.: Le Fun: Logic, equations, and Functions. In: Proc. 4th IEEE Internat. Symposium on Logic Programming, San Francisco, pp. 17–23 (1987)
3. Albert, E., Hanus, M., Huch, F., Oliver, J., Vidal, G.: Operational Semantics for Declarative Multi-Paradigm Languages. Journal of Symbolic Computation 40(1), 795–829 (2005)
4. Albert, E., Hanus, M., Vidal, G.: Using an Abstract Representation to Specialize Functional Logic Programs. In: Parigot, M., Voronkov, A. (eds.) LPAR 2000. LNCS (LNAI), vol. 1955, pp. 381–398. Springer, Heidelberg (2000)
5. Albert, E., Hanus, M., Vidal, G.: A Practical Partial Evaluator for a Multi-Paradigm Declarative Language. Journal of Functional and Logic Programming 2002(1) (2002)
6. Alpuente, M., Correa, F.J., Falaschi, M.: A Debugging Scheme for Functional Logic Programs. Electronic Notes in Theoretical Computer Science, vol. 64 (2002)

7. Alpuente, M., Falaschi, M., Manzo, F.: Analyses of Unsatisfiability for Equational Logic Programming. Journal of Logic Programming 22(3), 223–254 (1995)
8. Alpuente, M., Falaschi, M., Vidal, G.: A Compositional Semantic Basis for the Analysis of Equational Horn Programs. Theoretical Computer Science 165(1), 133–169 (1996)
9. Alpuente, M., Falaschi, M., Vidal, G.: Partial Evaluation of Functional Logic Programs. ACM Transactions on Programming Languages and Systems 20(4), 768–844 (1998)
10. Alpuente, M., Hanus, M., Lucas, S., Vidal, G.: Specialization of Functional Logic Programs Based on Needed Narrowing. Theory and Practice of Logic Programming 5(3), 273–303 (2005)
11. Antoy, S.: Non-Determinism and Lazy Evaluation in Logic Programming. In: Proc. Int. Workshop on Logic Program Synthesis and Transformation (LOPSTR 1991), pp. 318–331. Springer (1991)
12. Antoy, S.: Definitional Trees. In: Kirchner, H., Levi, G. (eds.) ALP 1992. LNCS, vol. 632, pp. 143–157. Springer, Heidelberg (1992)
13. Antoy, S.: Optimal Non-Deterministic Functional Logic Computations. In: Hanus, M., Heering, J., Meinke, K. (eds.) ALP 1997 and HOA 1997. LNCS, vol. 1298, pp. 16–30. Springer, Heidelberg (1997)
14. Antoy, S.: Constructor-based Conditional Narrowing. In: Proc. of the 3rd International ACM SIGPLAN Conference on Principles and Practice of Declarative Programming (PPDP 2001), pp. 199–206. ACM Press, New York (2001)
15. Antoy, S.: Evaluation Strategies for Functional Logic Programming. Journal of Symbolic Computation 40(1), 875–903 (2005)
16. Antoy, S., Ariola, Z.M.: Narrowing the Narrowing Space. In: Hartel, P.H., Kuchen, H. (eds.) PLILP 1997. LNCS, vol. 1292, pp. 1–15. Springer, Heidelberg (1997)
17. Antoy, S., Braßel, B., Hanus, M.: Conditional Narrowing without Conditions. In: Proceedings of the 8th ACM SIGPLAN International Conference on Principles and Practice of Declarative Programming (PPDP 2003), pp. 20–31. ACM Press (2003)
18. Antoy, S., Echahed, R., Hanus, M.: Parallel Evaluation Strategies for Functional Logic Languages. In: Proc. of the Fourteenth International Conference on Logic Programming (ICLP 1997), pp. 138–152. MIT Press (1997)
19. Antoy, S., Echahed, R., Hanus, M.: A Needed Narrowing Strategy. Journal of the ACM 47(4), 776–822 (2000)
20. Antoy, S., Hanus, M.: Compiling Multi-Paradigm Declarative Programs into Prolog. In: Kirchner, H. (ed.) FroCos 2000. LNCS, vol. 1794, pp. 171–185. Springer, Heidelberg (2000)
21. Antoy, S., Hanus, M.: Functional Logic Design Patterns. In: Hu, Z., Rodríguez-Artalejo, M. (eds.) FLOPS 2002. LNCS, vol. 2441, pp. 67–87. Springer, Heidelberg (2002)
22. Antoy, S., Hanus, M.: Concurrent Distinct Choices. Journal of Functional Programming 14(6), 657–668 (2004)
23. Antoy, S., Hanus, M.: Declarative Programming with Function Patterns. In: Hill, P.M. (ed.) LOPSTR 2005. LNCS, vol. 3901, pp. 6–22. Springer, Heidelberg (2006)
24. Antoy, S., Hanus, M.: Overlapping Rules and Logic Variables in Functional Logic Programs. In: Etalle, S., Truszczyński, M. (eds.) ICLP 2006. LNCS, vol. 4079, pp. 87–101. Springer, Heidelberg (2006)
25. Antoy, S., Hanus, M.: Set Functions for Functional Logic Programming. In: Proceedings of the 11th ACM SIGPLAN International Conference on Principles and Practice of Declarative Programming (PPDP 2009), pp. 73–82. ACM Press (2009)

26. Antoy, S., Hanus, M., Liu, J., Tolmach, A.: A Virtual Machine for Functional Logic Computations. In: Grelck, C., Huch, F., Michaelson, G.J., Trinder, P. (eds.) IFL 2004. LNCS, vol. 3474, pp. 108–125. Springer, Heidelberg (2005)

27. Antoy, S., Hanus, M., Massey, B., Steiner, F.: An Implementation of Narrowing Strategies. In: Proc. of the 3rd International ACM SIGPLAN Conference on Principles and Practice of Declarative Programming (PPDP 2001), pp. 207–217. ACM Press (2001)

28. Antoy, S., Johnson, S.: TeaBag: A Functional Logic Language Debugger. In: Proc. 13th International Workshop on Functional and (Constraint) Logic Programming (WFLP 2004), pp. 4–18, Aachen (Germany). Technical Report AIB-2004-05, RWTH Aachen (2004)

29. Antoy, S., Tolmach, A.: Typed Higher-Order Narrowing without Higher-Order Strategies. In: Middeldorp, A., Sato, T. (eds.) FLOPS 1999. LNCS, vol. 1722, pp. 335–352. Springer, Heidelberg (1999)

30. Arenas-Sánchez, P., Rodríguez-Artalejo, M.: A Semantic Framework for Functional Logic Programming with Algebraic Polymorphic Types. In: Bidoit, M., Dauchet, M. (eds.) CAAP 1997, FASE 1997, and TAPSOFT 1997. LNCS, vol. 1214, pp. 453–464. Springer, Heidelberg (1997)

31. Baader, F., Nipkow, T.: Term Rewriting and All That. Cambridge University Press (1998)

32. Berghammer, R., Fischer, S.: Implementing Relational Specifications in a Constraint Functional Logic Language. Electronic Notes in Theoretical Computer Science, vol. 177, pp. 169–183 (2007)

33. Bergstra, J.A., Klop, J.W.: Conditional Rewrite Rules: Confluence and Termination. Journal of Computer and System Sciences 32(3), 323–362 (1986)

34. Bird, R.S., Wadler, P.: Introduction to Functional Programming. Prentice-Hall (1988)

35. Bonnier, S., Maluszynski, J.: Towards a Clean Amalgamation of Logic Programs with External Procedures. In: Proc. 5th Conference on Logic Programming & 5th Symposium on Logic Programming (Seattle), pp. 311–326. MIT Press (1988)

36. Braßel, B., Chitil, O., Hanus, M., Huch, F.: Observing Functional Logic Computations. In: Jayaraman, B. (ed.) PADL 2004. LNCS, vol. 3057, pp. 193–208. Springer, Heidelberg (2004)

37. Braßel, B., Hanus, M.: Nondeterminism Analysis of Functional Logic Programs. In: Gabbrielli, M., Gupta, G. (eds.) ICLP 2005. LNCS, vol. 3668, pp. 265–279. Springer, Heidelberg (2005)

38. Braßel, B., Hanus, M., Huch, F.: Encapsulating Non-Determinism in Functional Logic Computations. Journal of Functional and Logic Programming 2004(6) (2004)

39. Brassel, B., Hanus, M., Huch, F., Silva, J., Vidal, G.: Run-Time Profiling of Functional Logic Programs. In: Etalle, S. (ed.) LOPSTR 2004. LNCS, vol. 3573, pp. 182–197. Springer, Heidelberg (2005)

40. Braßel, B., Hanus, M., Huch, F., Vidal, G.: A Semantics for Tracing Declarative Multi-Paradigm Programs. In: Proceedings of the 6th ACM SIGPLAN International Conference on Principles and Practice of Declarative Programming (PPDP 2004), pp. 179–190. ACM Press (2004)

41. Braßel, B., Huch, F.: On a Tighter Integration of Functional and Logic Programming. In: Shao, Z. (ed.) APLAS 2007. LNCS, vol. 4807, pp. 122–138. Springer, Heidelberg (2007)

Lemma 11. *Assume $\mathcal{E}$ is a complete set of partial Herbrand equality interpretations with respect to $\mathcal{A}$. Then the set $\mathcal{E}'$ obtained from $\mathcal{E}$ by replacing each partial Herbrand equality interpretation I by its extension I' to $\mathcal{A} \cup \{B\}$ is a complete set of partial Herbrand equality interpretations with respect to $\mathcal{A} \cup \{B\}$.*

Assume moreover that some interpretation $I \in \mathcal{E}$ is refuted by a ground clause C. Then, its extension I' in $\mathcal{E}'$ is refuted by the same clause C.

Proof. For the first statement, we need to show that every total Herbrand equality interpretation extending I extends I'. This follows from Definition 8 and Lemma 8. The second statement follows from Lemma 9.   □

Example 1. Let $\mathcal{A}$ be the set $\{A(a), a = c, A(b), a = b, A(c)\}$ in increasing order, A being a predicate and a, b, c constants. We give from left to right: the 12 total Herbrand equality interpretations over the subset $\{A(a), a = c, A(b), A(c)\}$ of $\mathcal{A}$; a complete set of 4 partial Herbrand equality interpretations; its extension to $\mathcal{A}$.

A(a)	a=c	A(b)	A(c)
T	T	T	T
T	T	F	T
T	F	T	T
T	F	T	F
T	F	F	T
T	F	F	F
F	T	T	F
F	T	F	F
F	F	T	T
F	F	T	F
F	F	F	T
F	F	F	F

A(a)	a=c	A(b)	A(c)
T	U	U	U
F	T	U	F
F	F	T	U
U	F	F	U

A complete set of four partial Herbrand equality interpretations.

A(a)	a=c	A(b)	a=b	A(c)
T	U	U	U	U
F	T	U	U	F
F	F	T	F	U
U	F	F	U	U

Its extension with the atom $a = b$.

As usual, it is convenient to view a given set of Herbrand equality interpretations as a tree.

Definition 12. *Given a set $\mathcal{E}$ of partial Herbrand equality interpretations over the set of ground atoms $\mathcal{A} = \{A_i\}_{i<n}$ ordered by $\succ$, we construct the tree of Herbrand equality interpretations $T_{\mathcal{E}}$ by induction on $\succ$. Each vertex I in the tree defines a partial Herbrand equality interpretation I of an initial segment $\{A_i\}_{i<j<n}$ of ground atoms enumerated so far and a set E_I of equalities interpreted by T in I. The vertex I has:*

1. *a single successor J such that $[A_j]_J = x$ in case all interpretations in $\mathcal{E}$ whose restriction coincide on $\{A_i\}_{i<j}$ assign the same value x to A_j;*
2. *two or three successors otherwise, depending on the different values assigned to A_i by the interpretations in $\mathcal{E}$ whose restriction coincide on $\{A_i\}_{i<j<n}$.*

Case 1 applies in particular when A_i is a ground atom of the form $s = s$ for some term s, in which case $[A_i]_J = T$, or when $A_j \longleftrightarrow^*_{E_I} A_k$ for some $k < j$, in which case $[A_j]_J = [A_k]_I$.

42. Braßel, B., Huch, F.: The Kiel Curry System KICS. In: Seipel, D., Hanus, M., Wolf, A. (eds.) INAP 2007. LNCS (LNAI), vol. 5437, pp. 195–205. Springer, Heidelberg (2009)

43. Caballero, R., Rodríguez-Artalejo, M.: DDT: a Declarative Debugging Tool for Functional-Logic Languages. In: Kameyama, Y., Stuckey, P.J. (eds.) FLOPS 2004. LNCS, vol. 2998, pp. 70–84. Springer, Heidelberg (2004)

44. Cheong, P.H., Fribourg, L.: Implementation of Narrowing: The Prolog-Based Approach. In: Apt, K.R., de Bakker, J.W., Rutten, J.J.M.M. (eds.) Logic Programming Languages: Constraints, Functions, and Objects, pp. 1–20. MIT Press (1993)

45. Cleva, J.M., Leach, J., López-Fraguas, F.J.: A logic programming approach to the verification of functional-logic programs. In: Proceedings of the 6th International ACM SIGPLAN Conference on Principles and Practice of Declarative Programming, pp. 9–19. ACM Press (2004)

46. Damas, L., Milner, R.: Principal type-schemes for functional programs. In: Proc. 9th Annual Symposium on Principles of Programming Languages, pp. 207–212 (1982)

47. del Vado Virseda, R.: A Demand-Driven Narrowing Calculus with Overlapping Definitional Trees. In: Proceedings of the 8th ACM SIGPLAN International Conference on Principles and Practice of Declarative Programming (PPDP 2003), pp. 253–263. ACM Press (2003)

48. Dershowitz, N., Jouannaud, J.-P.: Rewrite Systems. In: van Leeuwen, J. (ed.) Handbook of Theoretical Computer Science, vol. B, pp. 243–320. Elsevier (1990)

49. Echahed, R., Janodet, J.-C.: Admissible Graph Rewriting and Narrowing. In: Proc. Joint International Conference and Symposium on Logic Programming (JICSLP 1998), pp. 325–340 (1998)

50. Escobar, S.: Refining Weakly Outermost-Needed Rewriting and Narrowing. In: Proceedings of the 8th ACM SIGPLAN International Conference on Principles and Practice of Declarative Programming (PPDP 2003), pp. 113–123. ACM Press (2003)

51. Escobar, S.: Implementing Natural Rewriting and Narrowing Efficiently. In: Kameyama, Y., Stuckey, P.J. (eds.) FLOPS 2004. LNCS, vol. 2998, pp. 147–162. Springer, Heidelberg (2004)

52. Escobar, S., Meseguer, J., Thati, P.: Narrowing adn Rewriting Logic: from Foundations to Applications. Electronic Notes in Theoretical Computer Science 177, 5–33 (2007)

53. España, S., Estruch, V.: A Memoizing Semantics for Functional Logic Languages. In: Schmidt, D. (ed.) ESOP 2004. LNCS, vol. 2986, pp. 109–123. Springer, Heidelberg (2004)

54. Fernández, A.J., Hortalá-González, T., Sáenz-Pérez, F.: Solving Combinatorial Problems with a Constraint Functional Logic Language. In: Dahl, V. (ed.) PADL 2003. LNCS, vol. 2562, pp. 320–338. Springer, Heidelberg (2002)

55. Fernández, A.J., Hortalá-González, M.T., Sáenz-Pérez, F., del Vado-Vírseda, R.: Constraint Functional Logic Programming over Finite Domains. Theory and Practice of Logic Programming 7(5), 537–582 (2007)

56. Ferri-Ramírez, C., Hernández-Orallo, J., Ramírez-Quintana, M.J.: Incremental Learning of Functional Logic Programs. In: Kuchen, H., Ueda, K. (eds.) FLOPS 2001. LNCS, vol. 2024, pp. 233–247. Springer, Heidelberg (2001)

57. Fischer, S.: A Functional Logic Database Library. In: Proc. of the ACM SIGPLAN 2005 Workshop on Curry and Functional Logic Programming (WCFLP 2005), pp. 54–59. ACM Press (2005)

58. Fribourg, L.: SLOG: A Logic Programming Language Interpreter Based on Clausal Superposition and Rewriting. In: Proc. IEEE Internat. Symposium on Logic Programming, Boston, pp. 172–184 (1985)

59. García de la Banda, M.J., Demoen, B., Marriott, K., Stuckey, P.J.: To the Gates of HAL: A HAL Tutorial. In: Hu, Z., Rodríguez-Artalejo, M. (eds.) FLOPS 2002. LNCS, vol. 2441, pp. 47–66. Springer, Heidelberg (2002)

60. Giovannetti, E., Levi, G., Moiso, C., Palamidessi, C.: Kernel LEAF: A Logic plus Functional Language. Journal of Computer and System Sciences 42(2), 139–185 (1991)

61. Gonzáles-Moreno, J.C., Hortalá-González, M.T., Rodríguez-Artalejo, M.: Polymorphic Types in Functional Logic Programming. Journal of Functional and Logic Programming 2001(1) (2001)

62. González-Moreno, J.C., Hortalá-González, M.T., López-Fraguas, F.J., Rodríguez-Artalejo, M.: An approach to declarative programming based on a rewriting logic. Journal of Logic Programming 40, 47–87 (1999)

63. González-Moreno, J.C., Hortalá-González, M.T., Rodríguez-Artalejo, M.: A Higher Order Rewriting Logic for Functional Logic Programming. In: Proc. of the Fourteenth International Conference on Logic Programming (ICLP 1997), pp. 153–167. MIT Press (1997)

64. Habel, A., Plump, D.: Term Graph Narrowing. Mathematical Structures in Computer Science 6(6), 649–676 (1996)

65. Hanus, M.: Compiling Logic Programs with Equality. In: Deransart, P., Małuszyński, J. (eds.) PLILP 1990. LNCS, vol. 456, pp. 387–401. Springer, Heidelberg (1990)

66. Hanus, M.: The Integration of Functions into Logic Programming: From Theory to Practice. Journal of Logic Programming 19&20, 583–628 (1994)

67. Hanus, M.: Analysis of Residuating Logic Programs. Journal of Logic Programming 24(3), 161–199 (1995)

68. Hanus, M.: Efficient Translation of Lazy Functional Logic Programs into Prolog. In: Proietti, M. (ed.) LOPSTR 1995. LNCS, vol. 1048, pp. 252–266. Springer, Heidelberg (1996)

69. Hanus, M.: A Unified Computation Model for Functional and Logic Programming. In: Proc. of the 24th ACM Symposium on Principles of Programming Languages (Paris), pp. 80–93 (1997)

70. Hanus, M.: Distributed Programming in a Multi-Paradigm Declarative Language. In: Nadathur, G. (ed.) PPDP 1999. LNCS, vol. 1702, pp. 376–395. Springer, Heidelberg (1999)

71. Hanus, M.: A Functional Logic Programming Approach to Graphical User Interfaces. In: Pontelli, E., Santos Costa, V. (eds.) PADL 2000. LNCS, vol. 1753, pp. 47–62. Springer, Heidelberg (2000)

72. Hanus, M.: High-Level Server Side Web Scripting in Curry. In: Ramakrishnan, I.V. (ed.) PADL 2001. LNCS, vol. 1990, pp. 76–92. Springer, Heidelberg (2001)

73. Hanus, M.: Reduction Strategies for Declarative Programming. Electronic Notes in Theoretical Computer Science 57 (2001)

74. Hanus, M.: CurryDoc: A Documentation Tool for Declarative Programs. In: Proc. 11th International Workshop on Functional and (Constraint) Logic Programming (WFLP 2002), Research Report UDMI/18/2002/RR, pp. 225–228, University of Udine (2002)

75. Hanus, M.: Dynamic Predicates in Functional Logic Programs. Journal of Functional and Logic Programming 2004(5) (2004)

76. Hanus, M.: A Generic Analysis Environment for Declarative Programs. In: Proc. of the ACM SIGPLAN 2005 Workshop on Curry and Functional Logic Programming (WCFLP 2005), pp. 43–48. ACM Press (2005)

77. Hanus, M.: Type-Oriented Construction of Web User Interfaces. In: Proceedings of the 8th ACM SIGPLAN International Conference on Principles and Practice of Declarative Programming (PPDP 2006), pp. 27–38. ACM Press (2006)

78. Hanus, M.: Putting Declarative Programming into the Web: Translating Curry to JavaScript. In: Proceedings of the 9th ACM SIGPLAN International Conference on Principles and Practice of Declarative Programming (PPDP 2007), pp. 155–166. ACM Press (2007)

79. Hanus, M.: Call Pattern Analysis for Functional Logic Programs. In: Proceedings of the 10th ACM SIGPLAN International Conference on Principles and Practice of Declarative Programming (PPDP 2008), pp. 67–78. ACM Press (2008)

80. Hanus, M.: Declarative Processing of Semistructured Web Data. Technical Report 1103, Christian-Albrechts-Universität Kiel (2011)

81. Hanus, M., Antoy, S., Braßel, B., Engelke, M., Höppner, K., Koj, J., Niederau, P., Sadre, R., Steiner, F.: PAKCS: The Portland Aachen Kiel Curry System (2010), http://www.informatik.uni-kiel.de/~pakcs/

82. Hanus, M., Höppner, K.: Programming Autonomous Robots in Curry. Electronic Notes in Theoretical Computer Science 76 (2002)

83. Hanus, M., Höppner, K., Huch, F.: Towards Translating Embedded Curry to C. Electronic Notes in Theoretical Computer Science 86(3) (2003)

84. Hanus, M., Huch, F.: An Open System to Support Web-based Learning. In: Proc. 12th International Workshop on Functional and (Constraint) Logic Programming (WFLP 2003), pp. 269–282. Technical Report DSIC-II/13/03, Universidad Politécnica de Valencia (2003)

85. Hanus, M., Huch, F., Niederau, P.: ObjectCurry: An Object-Oriented Extension of the Declarative Multi-Paradigm Language Curry. In: Mohnen, M., Koopman, P. (eds.) IFL 2000. LNCS, vol. 2011, pp. 89–106. Springer, Heidelberg (2001)

86. Hanus, M., Koschnicke, S.: An ER-Based Framework for Declarative Web Programming. In: Carro, M., Peña, R. (eds.) PADL 2010. LNCS, vol. 5937, pp. 201–216. Springer, Heidelberg (2010)

87. Hanus, M., Prehofer, C.: Higher-Order Narrowing with Definitional Trees. Journal of Functional Programming 9(1), 33–75 (1999)

88. Hanus, M., Sadre, R.: An Abstract Machine for Curry and its Concurrent Implementation in Java. Journal of Functional and Logic Programming 1999(6) (1999)

89. Hanus, M., Steiner, F.: Controlling Search in Declarative Programs. In: Palamidessi, C., Meinke, K., Glaser, H. (eds.) ALP 1998 and PLILP 1998. LNCS, vol. 1490, pp. 374–390. Springer, Heidelberg (1998)

90. Hanus, M., Steiner, F.: Type-based Nondeterminism Checking in Functional Logic Programs. In: Proc. of the 2nd International ACM SIGPLAN Conference on Principles and Practice of Declarative Programming (PPDP 2000), pp. 202–213. ACM Press (2000)

91. Hanus, M., Zartmann, F.: Mode Analysis of Functional Logic Programs. In: LeCharlier, B. (ed.) SAS 1994. LNCS, vol. 864, pp. 26–42. Springer, Heidelberg (1994)

92. Hanus, M. (ed.): Curry: An Integrated Functional Logic Language (2011), http://www.curry-language.org

93. Hölldobler, S.: Foundations of Equational Logic Programming. In: Hölldobler, S. (ed.) Foundations of Equational Logic Programming. LNCS, vol. 353, Springer, Heidelberg (1989)

94. Hussmann, H.: Nondeterministic Algebraic Specifications and Nonconfluent Term Rewriting. Journal of Logic Programming 12, 237–255 (1992)
95. Ida, T., Nakahara, K.: Leftmost outside-in narrowing calculi. Journal of Functional Programming 7(2), 129–161 (1997)
96. Jiménez-Martin, J.A., Marino-Carballo, J., Moreno-Navarro, J.J.: Efficient Compilation of Lazy Narrowing into Prolog. In: Proc. Int. Workshop on Logic Program Synthesis and Transformation (LOPSTR 1992). Springer Workshops in Computing Series, pp. 253–270 (1992)
97. Julián Iranzo, P., Villamizar Lamus, C.: Analysing Definitional Trees: Looking for Determinism. In: Kameyama, Y., Stuckey, P.J. (eds.) FLOPS 2004. LNCS, vol. 2998, pp. 55–69. Springer, Heidelberg (2004)
98. Launchbury, J.: A Natural Semantics for Lazy Evaluation. In: Proc. 20th ACM Symposium on Principles of Programming Languages (POPL 1993), pp. 144–154. ACM Press (1993)
99. Lloyd, J.: Programming in an Integrated Functional and Logic Language. Journal of Functional and Logic Programming (3), 1–49 (1999)
100. Loogen, R., López Fraguas, F., Rodríguez Artalejo, M.: A Demand Driven Computation Strategy for Lazy Narrowing. In: Penjam, J., Bruynooghe, M. (eds.) PLILP 1993. LNCS, vol. 714, pp. 184–200. Springer, Heidelberg (1993)
101. Fraguas, F.J.L., Hernández, J.S.: TOY: A Multiparadigm Declarative System. In: Narendran, P., Rusinowitch, M. (eds.) RTA 1999. LNCS, vol. 1631, pp. 244–247. Springer, Heidelberg (1999)
102. López-Fraguas, F.J., Rodríguez-Artalejo, M., del Vado Virseda, R.: A lazy narrowing calculus for declarative constraint programming. In: Proceedings of the 6th International ACM SIGPLAN Conference on Principles and Practice of Declarative Programming, pp. 43–54. ACM Press (2004)
103. López-Fraguas, F.J., Rodríguez-Hortalá, J., Sánchez-Hernández, J.: A Simple Rewrite Notion for Call-time Choice Semantics. In: Proceedings of the 9th ACM SIGPLAN International Conference on Principles and Practice of Declarative Programming (PPDP 2007), pp. 197–208. ACM Press (2007)
104. López-Fraguas, F.J., Sánchez-Hernández, J.: A Proof Theoretic Approach to Failure in Functional Logic Programming. Theory and Practice of Logic Programming 4(1), 41–74 (2004)
105. Lux, W.: Implementing Encapsulated Search for a Lazy Functional Logic Language. In: Middeldorp, A., Sato, T. (eds.) FLOPS 1999. LNCS, vol. 1722, pp. 100–113. Springer, Heidelberg (1999)
106. Lux, W.: Adding Linear Constraints over Real Numbers to Curry. In: Kuchen, H., Ueda, K. (eds.) FLOPS 2001. LNCS, vol. 2024, pp. 185–200. Springer, Heidelberg (2001)
107. Middeldorp, A., Okui, S., Ida, T.: Lazy Narrowing: Strong Completeness and Eager Variable Elimination. Theoretical Computer Science 2(1,2), 95–130 (1996)
108. Moreno-Navarro, J.J.: Default Rules: An Extension of Constructive Negation for Narrowing-based Languages. In: Proc. Eleventh International Conference on Logic Programming, pp. 535–549. MIT Press (1994)
109. Moreno-Navarro, J.J., Rodríguez-Artalejo, M.: Logic Programming with Functions and Predicates: The Language BABEL. Journal of Logic Programming 12, 191–223 (1992)
110. Naish, L.: Adding Equations to NU-Prolog. In: Małuszyński, J., Wirsing, M. (eds.) PLILP 1991. LNCS, vol. 528, pp. 15–26. Springer, Heidelberg (1991)

111. Nakahara, K., Middeldorp, A., Ida, T.: A Complete Narrowing Calculus for Higher-Order Functional Logic Programming. In: Swierstra, S.D. (ed.) PLILP 1995. LNCS, vol. 982, pp. 97–114. Springer, Heidelberg (1995)
112. Nilsson, H., Fritzson, P.: Algorithmic debugging for lazy functional languages. Journal of Functional Programming 4(3), 337–370 (1994)
113. Ochoa, C., Silva, J., Vidal, G.: Dynamic Slicing Based on Redex Trails. In: Proc. of the ACM SIGPLAN 2004 Symposium on Partial Evaluation and Program Manipulation (PEPM 2004), pp. 123–134. ACM Press (2004)
114. O'Donnell, M.J. (ed.): Computing in Systems Described by Equations. LNCS, vol. 58. Springer, Heidelberg (1977)
115. O'Donnell, M.J.: Equational Logic as a Programming Language. MIT Press (1985)
116. Padawitz, P.: *Computing in Horn Clause Theories*. EATCS Monographs on Theoretical Computer Science, vol. 16. Springer (1988)
117. Peyton Jones, S. (ed.): Haskell 98 Language and Libraries—The Revised Report. Cambridge University Press (2003)
118. Reynolds, J.C.: Definitional Interpreters for Higher-Order Programming Languages. In: Proceedings of the ACM Annual Conference, pp. 717–740. ACM Press (1972)
119. Rodríguez-Artalejo, M.: Functional and Constraint Logic Programming. In: Comon, H., Marché, C., Treinen, R. (eds.) CCL 1999. LNCS, vol. 2002, pp. 202–270. Springer, Heidelberg (2001)
120. Sánchez-Hernández, J.: Constructive Failure in Functional-Logic Programming: From Theory to Implementation. Journal of Universal Computer Science 12(11), 1574–1593 (2006)
121. Saraswat, V.A.: Concurrent Constraint Programming. MIT Press (1993)
122. Sekar, R.C., Ramakrishnan, I.V.: Programming in Equational Logic: Beyond Strong Sequentiality. Information and Computation 104(1), 78–109 (1993)
123. Shapiro, E.: Algorithmic Program Debugging. MIT Press, Cambridge (1983)
124. Shapiro, E., Takeuchi, A.: Object Oriented Programming in Concurrent Prolog. In: Shapiro, E. (ed.) Concurrent Prolog: Collected Papers, vol. 2, pp. 251–273. MIT Press (1987)
125. Slagle, J.R.: Automated Theorem-Proving for Theories with Simplifiers, Commutativity, and Associativity. Journal of the ACM 21(4), 622–642 (1974)
126. Smolka, G.: The Oz Programming Model. In: van Leeuwen, J. (ed.) Computer Science Today. LNCS, vol. 1000, pp. 324–343. Springer, Heidelberg (1995)
127. Somogyi, Z., Henderson, F., Conway, T.: The execution algorithm of Mercury, an efficient purely declarative logic programming language. Journal of Logic Programming 29(1-3), 17–64 (1996)
128. Van Roy, P., Haridi, S.: Concepts, Techniques, and Models of Computer Programming. MIT Press (2004)
129. Wadler, P.: Efficient Compilation of Pattern-Matching. In: Peyton Jones, S.L. (ed.) The Implementation of Functional Programming Languages, pp. 78–103. Prentice Hall (1987)
130. Wadler, P.: How to Declare an Imperative. ACM Computing Surveys 29(3), 240–263 (1997)
131. Warren, D.H.D.: Higher-order extensions to Prolog: are they needed? In: Machine Intelligence, vol. 10, pp. 441–454 (1982)
132. Zartmann, F.: Denotational Abstract Interpretation of Functional Logic Programs. In: Van Hentenryck, P. (ed.) SAS 1997. LNCS, vol. 1302, pp. 141–156. Springer, Heidelberg (1997)

From Search to Computation: Redundancy Criteria and Simplification at Work

Thomas Hillenbrand[1], Ruzica Piskac[2],
Uwe Waldmann[1], and Christoph Weidenbach[1]

[1] Max-Planck-Institut für Informatik
Campus E1.4, 66123 Saarbrücken, Germany
[2] Max-Planck-Institut für Softwaresysteme,
Campus E1.4, 66123 Saarbrücken, Germany

Abstract. The concept of redundancy and simplification has been an ongoing theme in Harald Ganzinger's work from his first contributions to equational completion to the various variants of the superposition calculus. When executed by a theorem prover, the inference rules of logic calculi usually generate a tremendously huge search space. The redundancy and simplification concept is indispensable for cutting down this search space to a manageable size. For a number of subclasses of first-order logic appropriate redundancy and simplification concepts even turn the superposition calculus into a decision procedure. Hence, the key to successfully applying first-order theorem proving to a problem domain is to find those simplifications and redundancy criteria that fit this domain and can be effectively implemented.

We present Harald Ganzinger's work in the light of the simplification and redundancy techniques that have been developed for concrete problem areas. This includes a variant of contextual rewriting to decide a subclass of Euclidean geometry, ordered chaining techniques for Church-Rosser and priority queue proofs, contextual rewriting and history-dependent complexities for the completion of conditional rewrite systems, rewriting with equivalences for theorem proving in set theory, soft typing for the exploration of sort information in the context of equations, and constraint inheritance for automated complexity analysis.

1 Introduction

Theorem proving methods such as resolution or superposition aim at deducing a contradiction from a set of formulae by recursively deriving new formulae from given ones according to some logic calculus. A theorem prover computes one of the possible inferences of the current set of formulae and adds its conclusion to the current set, until a contradiction is found, or until a "closed" (or "saturated") set is reached, where the conclusion of every inference is already contained in the set.

Usually the inference rules of the calculus generate an infinite search space. For any serious application of saturation theorem provers, it is therefore indispensable to cut down the search space, and preferably, to turn undirected

A. Voronkov and C. Weidenbach (Eds.): Ganzinger Festschrift, LNCS 7797, pp. 169–193, 2013.

search into goal-directed computation. Simplification and redundancy detection are the key techniques to reduce the search space of a saturation-based prover. Abstractly stated, a redundant formula is a formula that is known to be unnecessary for deriving a contradiction and can be discarded, and a simplification is a process that makes a formula redundant, possibly by adding other (simpler) formulas. To be useful in practice, however, these abstract properties have to be approximated by concrete simplifications and redundancy criteria that fit the given problem domain and can be effectively and preferably also efficiently implemented. The importance of efficiency should not be underestimated here: current theorem provers can easily spend more than 90 % of their runtime on simplification and redundancy detection.

The concept of redundancy and simplification has been an ongoing theme in Harald Ganzinger's work from his first contributions to equational completion in the mid 1980's to the various variants of the superposition calculus. We give examples of the work of Harald Ganzinger, his students, and members of his group, that illustrate simplification and redundancy techniques and their application for concrete problem areas. This includes a variant of contextual rewriting to decide a subclass of Euclidean geometry, ordered chaining techniques for Church-Rosser and priority queue proofs, contextual rewriting and history-dependent complexities for the completion of conditional rewrite systems, rewriting with equivalences for theorem proving in set theory, soft typing for the exploration of sort information in the context of equations, and constraint inheritance for automated complexity analysis.

2   Preliminaries

We start this section by briefly summarizing the foundations of first-order logic, term rewriting, and refutational theorem proving. For a more detailed presentation we refer to [2] and [9].

We consider terms and formulas over a set of function symbols Σ, a set of predicate symbols Π, and a set of variables X, where Σ, Π, and X are disjoint. Every function and predicate symbol comes with a unique arity $n \geq 0$. The set of terms over Σ and X is the least set containing x whenever $x \in X$, and containing $f(t_1, \ldots, t_n)$ whenever each t_i is a term and $f \in \Sigma$ has arity n. The set of atoms over Π, Σ, and X contains $P(t_1, \ldots, t_n)$ whenever each t_i is a term and $P \in \Pi$ has arity n. We assume that Π contains a binary predicate symbol $\approx$ (equality), written in infix notation. An atom $t \approx t'$ is also called an equation. Formulas are constructed from atoms and the constants $\top$ (true) and $\bot$ (false) using the usual connectives $\neg$, $\vee$, $\wedge$, $\Rightarrow$, $\Leftrightarrow$ and the quantifiers $\forall$ and $\exists$. Throughout this survey we assume that function and predicate symbols are declared appropriately such that all syntactic objects (terms, atoms, etc.) are well-formed.

The set of variables occurring in a syntactic object Q is denoted by $\mathrm{Var}(Q)$. If $\mathrm{Var}(Q)$ is empty, then Q is called ground. We require that there exists at least one ground term.

A literal is either an atom A (also called a positive literal) or a negated atom $\neg A$ (also called a negative literal). A clause is either the symbol $\bot$ (empty clause) or a disjunction of literals. We identify clauses with finite multiset of literals. The symbol $[\neg]\, A$ denotes either A or $\neg A$. Instead of $\neg t \approx t'$, we sometimes write $t \not\approx t'$. If no explicit quantifiers are specified, variables in a clause are implicitly universally quantified.

A substitution σ is a mapping from X into the set of terms over Σ and X. Substitutions are homomorphically extended to terms, and likewise to atoms, literals, or clauses. We use postfix notation for substitutions and write $t\sigma$ instead of $\sigma(t)$; $\sigma\sigma'$ is the substitution that maps every x to $(x\sigma)\sigma'$. A syntactic object Q' is called an instance of an object Q, if $Q\sigma = Q'$ for some substitution σ. For a set N of clauses, the set of all ground instances of clauses in N is denoted by $\bar{N}$. A substitution that maps the variables $x_1, \ldots, x_n$ to the terms $t_1, \ldots, t_n$, respectively, is denoted by $\{x_1 \mapsto t_1, \ldots, x_n \mapsto t_n\}$.

An interpretation $\mathcal{A}$ for Σ and Π consists of a non-empty set U, called the domain of $\mathcal{A}$, and a mapping that assigns to every n-ary function symbol $f \in \Sigma$ a function $f^{\mathcal{A}} : U^n \to U$ and to each n-ary predicate symbol $P \in \Pi$ an n-ary relation $P^{\mathcal{A}} \subseteq U^n$. An $\mathcal{A}$-assignment α is a mapping from the set of variables X into the domain of $\mathcal{A}$. Assignments can be homomorphically extended to terms over Σ and X. An atom $P(t_1, \ldots, t_n)$ is called true with respect to $\mathcal{A}$ and α if $(\alpha(t_1), \ldots, \alpha(t_n)) \in P^{\mathcal{A}}$, otherwise it is called false.

The extension to arbitrary formulas happens in the usual way. In particular, a negative literal $\neg A$ is true with respect to $\mathcal{A}$ and α if and only if A is not true, and a clause C is true with respect to $\mathcal{A}$ and α if at least one of its literals is true. An interpretation $\mathcal{A}$ is a model of a formula, if it is true with respect to $\mathcal{A}$ and α for every $\mathcal{A}$-assignment α. It is a model of a set N of formulas, if it is a model of every formula in N. If $\mathcal{A}$ is a model of N, we also say that it satisfies N. A set of formulas is called satisfiable if it has a model. Obviously every set of formulas containing $\bot$ is unsatisfiable.

In refutational theorem proving, one is primarily interested in the question whether or not a given set of universally quantified clauses is satisfiable. For this purpose we may confine ourselves to term-generated interpretations, that is, to interpretations $\mathcal{A}$ where every element of U is the image of some ground term.[1] We may even confine ourselves to Herbrand interpretations, that is, to term-generated interpretations whose domain is the set of ground terms, and where every ground term is interpreted by itself: A set of clauses has a model, if and only if it has a term-generated model, if and only if it has a Herbrand model.

As long as we restrict ourselves to term-generated models we may think of a non-ground clause as a finite representation of the set of all its ground instances: A term-generated interpretation is a model of a clause C if and only it is a model of all ground instances of C.

When one uses the equality symbol $\approx$ in a logical language, one is commonly interested in interpretations $\mathcal{A}$ in which $\approx^{\mathcal{A}}$ is not an arbitrary binary relation

---

[1] Recall that we require that there is at least one ground term.

but actually the equality relation on the domain of $\mathcal{A}$. We refer to such interpretations as normal. If we want to recover the intuitive semantics of the equality symbol while working with Herbrand interpretations, we have to encode the intended properties of the equality symbol explicitly using the equality axioms reflexivity, symmetry, transitivity, and congruence. If N is a set of clauses, then an interpretation that is a model of N and of the equality axioms is called an equality model of N. A set of clauses has a normal model, if and only if it has a term-generated normal model, if and only if it has an equality Herbrand model. If N and N' are sets of clauses and every equality Herbrand model of N is a model of N', we say that N entails N' modulo equality and denote this by $N \models N'$.

For simplicity, we will usually assume that equality is the only predicate symbol. This does not restrict the expressivity of the logic: A predicate P different from $\approx$ can be coded using function symbols p and *true*, so that $P(t_1, \ldots, t_n)$ is to be taken as an abbreviation for $p(t_1, \ldots, t_n) \approx true$. Under these circumstances, every Herbrand interpretation is completely characterized by the interpretation $\approx^{\mathcal{A}}$ of the equality predicate. For any set $E_{\mathcal{A}}$ of ground equations there is exactly one Herbrand interpretation $\mathcal{A}$ in which the equations in $E_{\mathcal{A}}$ are true and all other ground equations are false. We will usually identify $\mathcal{A}$ and $E_{\mathcal{A}}$. A positive ground literal A is thus true in $E_{\mathcal{A}}$, if $A \in E_{\mathcal{A}}$; a negative ground literal $\neg A$ is true in $E_{\mathcal{A}}$, if $A \notin E_{\mathcal{A}}$.

In the rest of the paper, we will almost exclusively work with (equality) Herbrand interpretations and models, or more precisely, with the set $E_{\mathcal{A}}$ of equations corresponding to a Herbrand interpretation $\mathcal{A}$. For simplicity, we will usually drop the attribute "Herbrand".

We describe theorem proving calculi using inference rules of the form

$$\mathcal{I} \ \frac{C_1 \ \ldots \ C_n}{D_1}$$
$$\vdots$$
$$D_m$$

and reduction rules of the form

$$\mathcal{R} \ \frac{C_1 \ \ldots \ C_n}{D_1}$$
$$\vdots$$
$$D_m$$

Both kinds of rules are used to derive new formulas $D_1, \ldots, D_m$ (conclusions) from given formulas $C_1, \ldots, C_n$ (premises) that are contained in some set N; an application of an inference rule *adds* the conclusions to N; an application of a reduction rule *replaces* the premises by the conclusions in N. (The list of conclusions can be empty; in this case the reduction rule simply deletes the premises.)

To prove the completeness of calculi, we have to construct Herbrand interpretations and to check whether a given equation is contained in such an interpretation. Rewriting techniques are our main tool for this task. The rest of this subsection serves mainly to fix the necessary notation; for more detailed information about rewrite systems we refer the reader to [2].

As usual, positions (also known as occurrences) of a term are denoted by strings of natural numbers. $t[t']_o$ is the result of the replacement of the subterm at the position o in t by t'. We write $t[t']$ if o is clear from the context.

A binary relation $\to$ is called a rewrite relation, if it is stable under substitutions and contexts, that is, if $t_1 \to t_2$ implies $t_1\sigma \to t_2\sigma$ and $s[t_1]_o \to s[t_2]_o$ for all terms t_1, t_2, and s, and for all substitutions σ.

A rewrite rule is a pair (t, t') of terms, usually written as $t \to t'$. A rewrite system is a set of rewrite rules. If R is a rewrite system, then the rewrite relation $\to_R$ associated with R is the smallest rewrite relation containing $t \to_R t'$ for every rule $t \to t' \in R$.

For a binary relation $\to$, we commonly use the symbol $\leftarrow$ for its inverse relation, $\leftrightarrow$ for its symmetric closure, $\to^+$ for its transitive closure, and $\to^*$ for its reflexive-transitive closure (and thus $\leftrightarrow^*$ for its reflexive-symmetric-transitive closure).

A binary relation $\to$ is called noetherian (or terminating), if there is no infinite chain $t_1 \to t_2 \to t_3 \to \cdots$. We say that t is a normal form (or irreducible) with respect to $\to$ if there is no t' such that $t \to t'$; t is called a normal form of s if $s \to^* t$ and t is a normal form. We say that $\to$ is confluent if for every t_0, t_1, t_2 such that $t_1 \leftarrow^* t_0 \to^* t_2$ there exists a t_3 such that $t_1 \to^* t_3 \leftarrow^* t_2$. A terminating and confluent relation is called convergent.

A transitive and irreflexive binary relation $\succ$ is called an ordering. An ordering on terms is called a reduction ordering, if it is a noetherian rewrite relation. Well-known examples of reduction orderings are polynomial orderings, lexicographic path orderings (LPO), recursicve path orderings (RPO), and Knuth-Bendix orderings (KBO) [2].

A well-founded ordering on a set S generates a well-founded ordering on finite multisets over S. We use this construction to lift a term ordering $\succ$ to a literal and a clause ordering: We assign the multiset $\{s, t\}$ to a positive literal $s \approx t$ and the multiset $\{s, s, t, t\}$ to a negative literal $s \not\approx t$. The literal ordering $\succ_L$ compares these multisets using the multiset extension of $\succ$. The clause ordering $\succ_C$ compares clauses by comparing their multisets of literals using the multiset extension of $\succ_L$. (The subscripts L and C are often omitted.)

We use the symbol $\succeq$ to denote the reflexive closure of an ordering $\succ$. If $(S_0, \succ)$ is an ordered set, $S \subseteq S_0$, and $s \in S_0$, then $S^{\prec s}$ is an abbreviation for $\{t \in S \mid t \prec s\}$.

3   CEC – Conditional Equational Completion

After having worked on compiler generation and abstract data types for about ten years, Harald Ganzinger started to work on term rewriting and completion of algebraic specification in the mid 1980's. From 1986 to 1990, most of his work [20–24, 27] centered around the CEC system, serving both as a testbed to evaluate the usefulness of theoretical results and as an inspiration for further developments.

Knuth-Bendix completion [34] is a method that attempts to convert a set of equations into an equivalent convergent rewrite system. The completion procedure is based on two main operations. The first one is orientation: Equations $s \approx t$ are turned into rewrite rules $s \rightarrow t$ if s is larger than t according to some reduction ordering $\succ$. The second one is critical pair computation: If two rewrite rules $s \rightarrow t$ and $l \rightarrow r$ overlap, that is, if a non-variable subterm u of s at the position o can be unified with l, these two rewrite rules generate a new equation $(s[r]_o)\sigma \approx t\sigma$ (where σ is the most general unifier of u and l). These two main operations are supplemented by techniques to simplify (or discard) equations and rules.

The CEC ("Conditional Equational Completion") system [13], implemented in Prolog by Hubert Bertling, Harald Ganzinger and Renate Schäfers, generalizes Knuth-Bendix completion to conditional equations of the form

$$u_1 \approx v_1 \wedge \ldots \wedge u_n \approx v_n \Rightarrow s \approx t.$$

In previous approaches to completion of conditional equations, one had only considered *reductive* equations e, that is, conditional equations where the left-hand side s of the conclusion is larger than every other term occurring in e and, in particular, contains all variables of e. It is clear that this condition is quite restrictive and in fact makes most applications of conditional equations impossible. CEC, on the other side, does not require reductivity, and in fact even permits conditional equations containing extra variables, that is, variables that appear in the conditions or in the right-hand side of the conclusion, but not in the left-hand side.

One method CEC uses to deal with such conditional equations is to declare them as non-operational [20, 23]. This is the predecessor of a technique that should later become known as selection of negative literals in the superposition calculus: Instead of computing overlaps with the term s of a conditional equation $\Gamma \Rightarrow s \approx s'$, conditional rewrite rules are superposed on one selected equation of Γ, yielding new conditional equations. If the resulting conditional equations can be proved to be convergent, then the non-operational conditional equation is also convergent; it is irrelevant for the computation of normal forms (unless the specification is extended).

Moreover, CEC makes it possible to use quasi-reductive conditional equations in a Prolog-like manner. A conditional rewrite rule $u_1 \approx v_1 \wedge \ldots \wedge u_n \approx v_n \Rightarrow s \rightarrow t$ is called *quasi-reductive* [24], if it is deterministic, that is, $\mathrm{Var}(t) \subseteq \mathrm{Var}(s) \cup \bigcup_{j=1}^{n}(\mathrm{Var}(u_j) \cup \mathrm{Var}(v_j))$ and $\mathrm{Var}(u_i) \subseteq \mathrm{Var}(s) \cup \bigcup_{j=1}^{i-1}(\mathrm{Var}(u_j) \cup \mathrm{Var}(v_j))$ for every $1 \leq i \leq n$, and if $u_j\sigma \succeq v_j\sigma$ for $1 \leq j \leq i$ implies $s\sigma \succ_{\mathrm{st}} u_{i+1}\sigma$ and $u_j\sigma \succeq v_j\sigma$ for all $1 \leq j \leq n$ implies $s\sigma \succ t\sigma$.[2] Intuitively, this condition means that the instantiation of s yields the instantiation of u_1, normalizing any

---

[2] $\succ_{\mathrm{st}}$ is the transitive closure of the union of $\succ$ and the strict subterm ordering.

instantiated u_i and matching the result against v_i yields the instantiation of u_{i+1}, and normalizing every u_i yields the instantiation of t.

CEC also implements rewriting and completion modulo AC to deal with associative and commutative operators. An interesting feature from the user perspective is the ability to specify the term ordering incrementally during the completion process.

In contrast to an automated theorem prover, a completion procedure like CEC may fail if it encounters a conditional equation that can neither be oriented nor discarded. Powerful techniques for simplifying critical pair peaks are therefore extremely important for a successful completion procedure, and CEC contains a large repertoire of such techniques. A conditional equation $\Gamma \Rightarrow s \approx s'$ can be eliminated if there exists a proof of $\Gamma \Rightarrow s \approx s'$ that is simpler than $\Gamma \Rightarrow s \approx s'$ itself. Rewriting in contexts is a method to simplify conditional equations, where skolemized oriented condition equations are employed to reduce terms in the conclusion. CEC also uses non-reductive equations $\Gamma \Rightarrow s \rightarrow s'$ for simplification: if $\Gamma\sigma$ is a subset of Δ, then $s\sigma \rightarrow s'\sigma$ is available to simplify $\Delta \Rightarrow t \approx t'$. Finally, CEC makes it possible to make the complexity of a conditional equation history-dependent: complexities of input formulas can be arbitrarily chosen, whereas the origin of a derived conditional equation determines the complexity of the latter [21].

The completeness proof for the procedure implemented in CEC extends the proof ordering technique of Leo Bachmair, Nachum Dershowitz and Jieh Hsiang [4]: while Bachmair, Dershowitz and Hsiang use linear proofs and define an ordering on them as the multiset extension of the ordering of proof steps, one needs now tree-like proofs, represented as proof terms, which are compared using an RPO with an ordering on proof operators as precedence. As in [4], completion inferences lead to smaller proof terms.

CEC has been used, for instance, for the correctness proof for a code generator (Giegerich [29]) and for semi-functional translation of modal logics (Ohlbach [43]). It is able to deal with order-sorted specifications [24], including specifications with non-sort-decreasing rules, for which the procedure of Gnaedig, Kirchner and Kirchner [30] fails. Other examples include the specification of a maximum function over a total ordering, including the transitivity axiom [23].

4   Saturate

Among all techniques developed to deal with equality in first-order theorem proving, the paramodulation calculus of George Robinson and Larry Wos [47] has been the most influential. The paramodulation rule embodies the ideas of the resolution calculus and the operation of "replacing equals by equals" that is fundamental for term rewriting. Whenever a clause contains a positive literal $t \approx t'$, the paramodulation rule permits to rewrite a subterm t occurring in some literal $[\neg]\, A[t]$ of another clause to t'. For non-ground clauses, equality is replaced by unifiability, so that the resulting rule is essentially a combination of non-ground resolution and Knuth-Bendix completion.[3]

$$\mathcal{I} \; \frac{D' \vee t \approx t' \qquad\qquad C' \vee [\neg]\, s[w] \approx s'}{(D' \vee C' \vee [\neg]\, s[t'] \approx s')\sigma}$$

where σ is a most general unifier of t and w.[4]

Both resolution and completion are (or can be) subject to ordering restrictions with respect to some syntactical ordering $\succ$ on atoms or terms: In the Knuth-Bendix completion procedure,[5] only overlaps at non-variable positions between the maximal sides of two rewrite rules produce a critical pair. Similarly, the resolution calculus remains a semidecision procedure if inferences are computed only if each of the two complementary literals is maximal in its premise. It is natural to ask whether paramodulation may inherit the ordering restrictions of both its ancestors. More precisely: Let a paramodulation inference between clauses $D = D' \vee t \approx t'$ and $C = C' \vee [\neg]\, s[w] \approx s'$ be given as above, and let $\succ$ be a reduction ordering that is total on ground terms. Does the calculus remain refutationally complete if we require, as in completion, that (i) w is not a variable, (ii) $t\sigma \not\preceq t'\sigma$, (iii) $(s[w])\sigma \not\preceq s'\sigma$, and, as in ordered resolution, that (iv) $(t \approx t')\sigma$ is maximal in $D\sigma$, and (v) $(s[w] \approx s')\sigma$ is maximal in $C\sigma$?

A first result in this direction was obtained by Gerald Peterson [44], who showed the admissibility of restrictions (i) and (ii). It was extended to (i), (ii), (iii) for positive literals, and (v) by Michaël Rusinowitch [48], and to (i), (ii), (iv), and (v) by Jieh Hsiang and Michaël Rusinowitch [31]. The final answer was given by Leo Bachmair and Harald Ganzinger [5–7]: All five restrictions may be imposed on the paramodulation rule (which is named *superposition* then), however, an additional inference rule becomes necessary to cope with certain non-Horn clauses: either the *merging paramodulation* rule, which appeared first in (Bachmair and Ganzinger [5, 6]), or the *equality factoring* rule, which is due to Robert Nieuwenhuis [36]. The resulting inference system is the basis of the superposition calculus; it consists of the rules *superposition, equality resolution* (i. e., ordered resolution with the reflexivity axiom), and either *equality factoring* or *ordered factoring* and *merging paramodulation*.

The "model construction" technique developed by Bachmair and Ganzinger to prove the refutational completeness of superposition is based on an earlier idea by Zhang and Kapur [56]. Let N be saturated and let $\bar{N}$ be the set of all ground instances of clauses in N. We inspect all clauses in $\bar{N}$ in ascending order and construct a sequence of interpretations, starting with the empty interpretation. If a clause $C \in \bar{N}$ is false in the current interpretation $\mathcal{I}_C$ generated by clauses

---

[3] Essentially the same rule (usually restricted to equational unit or Horn clauses) occurs in narrowing calculi (Fay [18]) used for theory unification.

[4] We use the letters $\mathcal{I}$ and $\mathcal{R}$ to distinguish between *inference rules*, whose premises are kept after the conclusions have been added to the given set of clauses, and *reduction rules*, whose premises are replaced by the conclusions.

[5] Or rather: in its unfailing variant (Bachmair [3]), which is a semidecision procedure for unit equational logic.

smaller than C and has a positive and strictly maximal literal A, and if some additional conditions are satisfied, then a new interpretation is created extending the current one in such a way that A becomes true. We say that the clause is productive. Otherwise, the current interpretation is left unchanged. One can then show that, if N is saturated and does not contain the empty clause $\bot$, then every clause C is either true in $\mathcal{I}_C$ or productive, so that every clause of N becomes true in the limit interpretation $\mathcal{I}_N$ (also known as the perfect model of N).

The model construction method is the foundation of general notion of redundancy [7]. Essentially, every ground formula C that is true in $\mathcal{I}_C$ is useless to show that a set of formulas is not saturated. We call such formulas *weakly redundant*. Unfortunately, a formula that is weakly redundant in a set of formulas N may lose this property if we compute inferences from formulas in N and add the conclusions to N. For this reason, it is usually better to work with (strong) redundancy: Let $\bar{N}^{\prec C}$ be the set of all formulas in $\bar{N}$ that are smaller than C. We say that the formula C is *(strongly) redundant* with respect to N if $\bar{N}^{\prec C} \models C$, and that an inference with conclusion C is redundant with respect to N if $\bar{N}^{\prec D} \models C$, where D is the maximal premise of the inference.[6] Non-ground formulas and inferences are called redundant, if all their ground instances are redundant. Usual strategies for resolution-like calculi such as tautology deletion or clause subsumption are encompassed by this definition, just as the simplification steps and critical-pair criteria [3] that can be found in completion procedures. Superposition can also be enhanced by selection functions, so that hyperresolution-like strategies become applicable.

The SATURATE system [26] has been the first superposition-based theorem prover. The implementation was originally started by Robert Nieuwenhuis and Pilar Nivela and later continued by Harald Ganzinger. Written in Prolog, it lacks the inference speed of later superposition provers, such as E, SPASS, or VAMPIRE; it is still remarkable, though, for the huge number of calculi it uses, such as constraint superpostion, chaining, and lazy CNF transformation, and the sophisticated redundancy checks and simplification techniques enabled in this way. In the rest of this section we present four concrete applications of these simplification techniques.

4.1   Automatic Complexity Analysis

The automated complexity analysis technique of David Basin and Harald Ganzinger [12] is based on the concept of order locality. A set of clauses (without equality) is called local with respect to a term ordering $\succ$ if, for every ground clause C, $N \models C$ implies that there is a proof of C from those instances of N in which every term is smaller than or equal to some term of C. As a special case, defining $\succ$ as the subterm ordering yields the notion of subterm locality that had been previously investigated by David McAllester [35].

---

[6] Note that "redundancy" is called "compositeness" in [7]. In later papers the standard terminology has changed.

If the ordering $\succ$ has the property that for every ground term there are only finitely many smaller terms, then locality with respect to $\succ$ implies complexity bounds for the decision problem $N \models C$. More precisely, if for every clause of size n there exist $O(f(n))$ terms that are smaller than or equal to some term in the clause and that can be enumerated in time $g(n)$, and if a set N of Horn clauses is local with respect to $\succ$, then $N \models C$ is decidable in time $O(f(m)^k + g(m))$, where m is the size of C. The constant k depends only on N, it is at most the maximum of the number of variables of each clause in N. For instance, one obtains polynomial complexity bounds if one takes the subterm ordering as $\succ$; a Knuth-Bendix ordering yields exponential bounds and a polynomial ordering doubly exponential bounds.

Order locality is closely related to saturation with respect to ordered resolution: If N is a saturated set of clauses with respect to an atom ordering $\succ'$, then N is local with respect to some term ordering $\succ$, provided that certain compatibility requirements for $\succ$ and $\succ'$ are satisfied.

The SATURATE system [26] has been used both to prove saturation (and hence locality) and to transform sets of clauses into equivalent saturated and local sets. Formulas like the transitivity axiom show up rather frequently in such clause sets, and for such clauses, inheritance of ordering constraints is useful to show saturation. The technique is due to Nivela and Nieuwenhuis [41]: In contrast to a normal clause C, which can be taken as a representative of all its ground instances, a constrained clause $\Theta \parallel C$ represents only those ground instances of C that satisfy the constraint Θ, where Θ may be a conjunction of ordering and equality literals between terms or atoms. In particular, a clause whose constraint Θ is unsatisfiable is redundant, since it does not represent any ground instance.

Both the ordering restrictions of an inference and the constraints of its premises are propagated to its conclusion, so we obtain inference rules like the following for constraint resolution:

$$\mathcal{I} \ \frac{\Theta_1 \parallel D \vee A \qquad\qquad \Theta_2 \parallel C \vee \neg B}{\Theta_1 \wedge \Theta_2 \wedge A = B \wedge \Theta \parallel D \vee C}$$

Here, Θ_1 and Θ_2 are the constraints of the premises which are propagated to the conclusion, $A = B$ is the equality constraint of the inference, and Θ is the ordering constraint of the inference stating that the literals A and B are (strictly) maximal in their respective clauses.

Examples of theories that have been successfully saturated using the SATURATE system are the congruence closure axioms, the theory of tree embedding, and the theory of partial orderings.

4.2   Church–Rosser Theorems for the λ-Calculus

The λ-calculus, originally conceived by Alonzo Church and Stephen Kleene [16, 33] around 1935, is a model of computability that is based on the notions of function definition, function application, and recursion. It operates on λ-terms, which are the closure of a given set of variables $x, y, \ldots$ under application $(t_1 \, t_2)$

and abstraction $\lambda x.t$. A notion of variable substitution is defined recursively over the term structure. Since free variables in a substituted expression must not be bound after substitution, renaming of variables may become necessary. The result of replacing x in t by s this way is denoted by $t[s/x]$.

The calculus comes with conversion rules which capture when two λ-terms denote the same function: α-conversion models that the actual names of bound variables do not matter; β-conversion $(\lambda x.t)s \leftrightarrow_\beta t[s/x]$ corresponds to function application; and η-conversion covers extensional equality of functions: $\lambda x.(tx) \leftrightarrow_\eta t$ unless x is free in t. In order to ease the management of variables when manipulating λ-terms, Nicolaas Govert de Bruijn [15] suggested to consider, instead of $x, y, \ldots$, natural numbers in a fixed order, thereby getting rid of names altogether, and of α-conversion as well. The remaining conversions, if applied in left-to-right direction only, constitute reduction systems. A key property of the λ-calculus is that β-reduction $\rightarrow_\beta$ enjoys a Church–Rosser theorem: Any two $\leftrightarrow_\beta^*$-convertible terms are $\rightarrow_\beta^*$-reducible to a common successor. The same applies to $\rightarrow_\eta$, and to the union of the two reduction systems.

Tobias Nipkow [39] formalized this family of Church–Rosser theorems within the Isabelle/HOL system [40], which is a proof assistant for higher-order logic. Though interactive, Isabelle also features automation of subproofs via a term rewriting engine and a tableaux prover for predicate logic. Nipkow reported that the success of the latter depended on the right selection of lemmas supplied as parameters. For arithmetic goals arising from de Bruijn indices, he added a special tactic based on Fourier–Motzkin elimination. The proof development followed the lines of [15, Chapter 3], with an excursus to the approach of [51] via parallel reductions.

Each of the propositions that Nipkow showed with Isabelle/HOL encapsulates a single induction or is already deductive, at least modulo the arithmetic reasoning in the background; and in the former case the induction scheme was explicitly given. Therefore the question whether these propositions could be demonstrated automatically with a first-order theorem prover constituted a real challenge, and would set a landmark for the applicability of such systems if answered in the affirmative. This is what Harald Ganzinger and his student Sebastian Winkel set out for at the end of the 1990's. Their key idea was to integrate a fragment of arithmetic into the first-order axiomatization itself. They used a Peano-style formulation, postulated a total ordering, and related the latter to the successor and to the predecessor operation. Such theories fall into the domain of the chaining calculus [8], which specializes resolution and superposition for transitive resolution, and which is implemented in the SATURATE system [26]. Notably SATURATE managed to prove all the propositions, within the scope of some minutes.

Just to give an impression of the kind of reasoning in this domain, the first-order axiomatization on top of the approximation of numbers is shown now. A variable with de Bruijn number i is denoted by $\mathrm{var}(i)$; furthermore $\mathrm{abs}(s)$ denotes an abstraction, and $\mathrm{app}(s, t)$ an application. In formalizing substitutions, a function $\mathrm{lift}(t, i)$ is needed that increments all free variables in t that are greater than i or equal to i. SATURATE is supplied with a case-split definition according to the structure of t. This definition corresponds to the usual recursive one, but its semantics for SATURATE is purely first-order. All variables are universally quantified.

$$\neg(i < k) \vee \mathrm{lift}(\mathrm{var}(i), k) \approx \mathrm{var}(i)$$
$$\neg(k \leq i) \vee \mathrm{lift}(\mathrm{var}(i), k) \approx \mathrm{var}(s(i))$$
$$\mathrm{lift}(\mathrm{app}(s, t), k) \approx \mathrm{app}(\mathrm{lift}(s, k), \mathrm{lift}(t, k))$$
$$\mathrm{lift}(\mathrm{abs}(s), k) \approx \mathrm{abs}(\mathrm{lift}(s, \mathrm{succ}(k)))$$

In a similar fashion, SATURATE is provided with a definition of $\mathrm{subst}(t, s, k)$, which shall amount to $t[s/k]$. Note that within $t[s/k]$, all free variables of t above k are decremented, for application within β-reduction and η-reduction.

$$\neg(k < i) \vee \mathrm{subst}(\mathrm{var}(i), s, k) \approx \mathrm{var}(\mathrm{pred}(i))$$
$$\mathrm{subst}(\mathrm{var}(k), s, k) \approx s$$
$$\neg(i < k) \vee \mathrm{subst}(\mathrm{var}(i), s, k) \approx \mathrm{var}(i)$$
$$\mathrm{subst}(\mathrm{app}(t, u), s, k) \approx \mathrm{app}(\mathrm{subst}(t, s, k), \mathrm{subst}(u, s, k))$$
$$\mathrm{subst}(\mathrm{abs}(t), s, k) \approx \mathrm{abs}(\mathrm{subst}(t, \mathrm{lift}(s, 0), \mathrm{succ}(k)))$$

One of the inductive propositions that Nipkow proved in Isabelle about substitution is the identity $t[i/i] = t[i/i + 1]$. As to SATURATE, Harald Ganzinger and Sebastian Winkel first introduced a predicate for the induction hypothesis:

$$\mathrm{P}(t, i) \equiv \neg(0 \leq i) \vee \mathrm{subst}(t, \mathrm{var}(i), i) \approx \mathrm{subst}(t, \mathrm{var}(i), \mathrm{succ}(i))$$

Then SATURATE was able to discharge the conjunction of the following proof obligations in a single run, which correspond to the base case respectively the two step cases of the induction:

$$\mathrm{P}(\mathrm{var}(j), i)$$
$$\neg \mathrm{P}(t, k) \vee \mathrm{P}(\mathrm{abs}(t), i)$$
$$\neg \mathrm{P}(t, i) \vee \neg \mathrm{P}(u, i) \vee \mathrm{P}(\mathrm{app}(t, u), i)$$

The following clauses correspond to the base case respectively the two step cases of the induction:

$$\mathrm{P}(\mathrm{var}(j), i)$$
$$\neg \mathrm{P}(t, k) \vee \mathrm{P}(\mathrm{abs}(t), i)$$
$$\neg \mathrm{P}(t, i) \vee \neg \mathrm{P}(u, i) \vee \mathrm{P}(\mathrm{app}(t, u), i)$$

In the end SATURATE discharged the conjunction of these proof obligations in a single run, retaining no more than 57 clauses as non-redundant. The standard parameter setting was employed.

Transitivity and other ordering axioms play a vital role in the problem description. Transitive relations are known to be detrimental to the efficiency of standard theorem provers. SATURATE contains an implementation of the chaining calculus (Bachmair and Ganzinger [8]) with makes it possible to avoid explicit inferences with transitivity axioms.

Given a transitive relation R and a well-founded ordering $\succ$ on ground terms and literals, the chaining calculus has the following inference rules:

$$\mathcal{I} \; \frac{C \vee R(s,t) \qquad\qquad D \vee R(u,v)}{(C \vee D \vee R(s,v))\sigma}$$

$$\mathcal{I} \; \frac{C \vee R(t,s) \qquad\qquad D \vee \neg R(u,v)}{(C \vee D \vee \neg R(s,v))\sigma}$$

$$\mathcal{I} \; \frac{C \vee R(s,t) \qquad\qquad D \vee \neg R(v,u)}{(C \vee D \vee \neg R(s,v))\sigma}$$

where, for all rules, σ is an mgu of t and u. Moreover, the chaining rules are equipped with ordering restrictions similar to the superposition calculus; in particular the inferences only need to be performed if positive R-literals are strictly maximal in the respective premises, negative R-literals are maximal in the respective premises, and $s\sigma \not\succeq t\sigma$ and $v\sigma \not\succeq u\sigma$.

In order to assess the merits of the chaining calculus for this proof problem, one may want to compare the 57 clauses kept by SATURATE with the corresponding number for a theorem prover like SPASS that implements the standard superposition calculus without chaining. With default setting and the same reduction ordering, SPASS has to develop 947 non-redundant clauses until a proof is found. If splitting is turned off, then this number reduces to 342. Seemingly the presence of the two intertwined transitive relations $<$ and $\leq$ is a menace to SPASS. If the axiomatization is rephrased in terms of $<$ only, then with a set-of-support strategy and increased variable weight one gets down to 184 clauses. Starting with version SPASS 3.7 it now also supports chaining.

Via `http://isabelle.in.tum.de/dist/library/HOL/Lambda` the proof development within Isabelle is available. The SATURATE distribution can be obtained from `http://www.mpi-inf.mpg.de/SATURATE/Saturate.html` and contains all the mentioned first-order proof formulations.

4.3   Lazy CNF Transformation

Practically all automated theorem provers in use today are based on clausal logic. The input is preprocessed to obtain clause normal form (CNF), this includes the replacement of equivalences by conjunctions of implications and the elimination of existential quantifiers by Skolemization.

Very often it is useful to already exploit properties at the formula level via appropriate deduction mechanisms. Consider the following example: Suppose we have an equivalence $P \Leftrightarrow (Q \wedge Q')$, where P, Q, Q' are propositional formulas. Translation to CNF yields the three clauses $P \Rightarrow Q$, $P \Rightarrow Q'$, $Q \wedge Q' \Rightarrow P$. If $P \succ Q, Q'$ and C is a clause $R \vee R' \vee P$, then the two resolution steps deriving $R \vee R' \vee Q$ and $R \vee R' \vee Q'$ from C constitute a simplification of C: C follows from the three smaller clauses $Q \wedge Q' \Rightarrow P$, $R \vee R' \vee Q$ and $R \vee R' \vee Q'$. This fact is somewhat hidden within the set of clauses, though, whereas it was rather obvious considering the original equivalence. The situation is even worse if one side of the equivalence contains additional quantified variables, which are skolemized away during the clausification of one of the two directions of the equivalence. For example,

$$\forall A. \forall B. (A \subseteq B \iff \forall x. (x \in A \implies x \in B))$$

is turned into

$$\neg A \subseteq B \lor \neg x \in A \lor x \in B$$
$$f(A, B) \in A \lor A \subseteq B$$
$$\neg f(A, B) \in B \lor A \subseteq B.$$

To overcome this problem, Harald Ganzinger and Jürgen Stuber [28] introduced a variant of the superposition calculus with equivalences between formulas and lazy quantifier elimination. Its positive superposition rule

$$\mathcal{I} \frac{D \lor u \approx v \qquad C \lor s[u'] \approx t}{(D \lor C \lor s[v] \approx t)\sigma}$$

where σ is a most general unifier of u and u' is applicable both to term equations and to equivalences, that is, equations between formulas. This allows reasoning with equivalences as they usually arise from definitions in a natural way: If the larger side of an equivalence is an atomic formula, it can be used in a positive superposition; such an inference is a simplification for instance if D is empty and $u'\sigma = u$. If the larger side of an equivalence $u \approx v$ is not atomic, the equivalence can be eliminated using rules like

$$\mathcal{R} \frac{C \lor u \approx v}{C \lor u \approx \bot \lor v \approx \top} \qquad\qquad \mathcal{R} \frac{C \lor u \approx v}{C \lor u \approx \top \lor v \approx \bot}$$

whose results are then simplified by tableau-like expansion rules such as

$$\mathcal{R} \frac{C \lor (u_1 \land u_2 \approx \top)}{C \lor u_1 \approx \top} \qquad\qquad \mathcal{R} \frac{C \lor (u_1 \land u_2 \approx \top)}{C \lor u_2 \approx \top}.$$

Bound variables are encoded by de Bruijn indices, so a formula $\exists x \forall y \, f(x, y) \approx y$ is written as $(\exists \forall (p(2, 1) \approx 1)) \approx \top$, and quantified formulas are handled by γ and δ expansion rules

$$\mathcal{R} \frac{C \lor (\exists u \approx \top)}{C \lor u(f(x_1, \ldots, x_n)) \approx \top}$$

where $x_1, \ldots, x_n$ are the free variables in u and f is a fresh Skolem function, and

$$\mathcal{R} \frac{C \lor (\forall u \approx \top)}{C \lor u(z) \approx \top}$$

where z is a fresh variable. Since de Bruijn indices may be replaced by arbitrarily large terms, they must have greater precedence than all other function symbols in the recursive path ordering used to compare terms and formulas.

The calculus is implemented in the SATURATE system [26]. In applications like set theory, that are dominated by complex definitions, the number of inferences that SATURATE performs can be several orders of magnitude smaller compared to more conventional provers, such as VAMPIRE, or E. Motivated by the experiments with SATURATE, in SPASS a definition detection and expansion algorithm has been integrated that can simulate the above reasoning for many practical cases [1]. The fact that many equivalence transformations are now simplifications reduces the search space significantly; for certain examples the derivation of SATURATE is completely deterministic and terminates after few steps whereas other provers do not find a solution within any reasonable time limit.

4.4 Priority Queues

Runtime result checking is a method to ensure software reliability that has been proposed by Hal Wasserman and Manuel Blum [52]. In this approach, a checker program runs in parallel to the program to be checked and monitors its inputs and outputs. The checker either confirms correctness of the program's output or reports an error. It does not verify the correctness of the program, though; in fact it does not look into the program code at all. It only verifies that the output was correct on a given input.

A priority queue is a data structure that maintains a set of real numbers under the operations *insert_element* and *delete_and_return_minimal_element*. It can be implemented in such a way that each operation needs logarithmic time. A checker for priority queues has been developed by Ulrich Finkler and Kurt Mehlhorn [19]. It runs in parallel to the original priority queue algorithm and associates a lower bound with every member of the priority queue. The lower bound of an element e is defined as the maximum of all values that the priority queue returned as minimal since e was inserted. In the case that the priority queue would return a non-minimal element, the lower bound of the current minimal element will be greater than the element itself. When this element will be retrieved, the checker will report an error. The checker is time-efficient, but an off-line checker; this means that, when the priority queue is incorrectly implemented, i.e. returns a non-minimal element, this error will not be noticed immediately, but only at the moment when one of the smaller elements is returned in a later step.

A formal correctness proof for Finkler's and Mehlhorn's priority queue checker has been given by Ruzica Piskac using the SATURATE system. She showed that, if during the run of the priority queue the checker does not report any error until the queue is empty, then all returned minimal elements are correct [45]. The verification was done in two stages: in the first stage the correctness of the algorithm used for the checker was proved, while in the second stage a framework following more closely the concrete implementation and data structures was developed (de Nivelle and Piskac [42]).

The problem description defining the behavior of priority queues and of the checker contained more than 50 formulas (cf. Figure 1). In order to find the proof, SATURATE needed some additional lemmas (which again needed to be proved by the theorem prover, sometimes making further lemmas necessary). At the end more than 80 lemmas were used for the complete proof.

quasi-ordered set with bottom element:

$$p_1 \leq p_2 \wedge p_2 \leq p_3 \Rightarrow p_1 \leq p_3.$$
$$p_1 \leq p_2 \vee p_2 \leq p_1.$$
$$p \leq p.$$
$$\text{bottom} \leq p.$$
$$(p_1 < p_2) \Leftrightarrow (p_1 \leq p_2 \wedge \neg p_2 \leq p_1).$$

priority queues:

$$\neg\text{contains\_pq}(\text{create\_pq}, p).$$
$$\text{contains\_pq}(\text{insert\_pq}(pq, p_1), p_2) \Leftrightarrow (\text{contains\_pq}(pq, p_2) \vee p_1 \approx p_2).$$
$$\text{remove\_pq}(\text{insert\_pq}(pq, p), p) \approx pq.$$
$$\neg p_1 \approx p_2 \wedge \text{contains\_pq}(pq, p_2)$$
$$\Rightarrow \text{remove\_pq}(\text{insert\_pq}(pq, p_1), p_2) \approx \text{insert\_pq}(\text{remove\_pq}(pq, p_2), p_1).$$
$$\text{contains\_pq}(pq, p) \wedge (\forall p_1.\text{contains\_pq}(pq, p_1) \Rightarrow p \leq p_1)$$
$$\Rightarrow \text{find\_min\_pq}(pq, p) \approx p.$$
$$\text{contains\_pq}(pq, p) \wedge (\forall p_1.\text{contains\_pq}(pq, p_1) \Rightarrow p \leq p_1)$$
$$\Rightarrow \text{remove\_min\_pq}(pq, p) \approx \text{remove\_pq}(pq, p).$$

lower bounds:

$$\neg\text{contains\_s}(\text{create\_s}, p).$$
$$\text{contains\_s}(\text{assign\_s}(s, \text{pair}(p_1, r)), p_2)$$
$$\Leftrightarrow (\text{contains\_s}(s, p_2) \vee p_1 \approx p_2).$$
$$\neg\text{pair\_in\_s}(\text{create\_s}, p, r).$$
$$\text{pair\_in\_s}(\text{assign\_s}(s, \text{pair}(p_1, r_1)), p_2, r_2)$$
$$\Leftrightarrow (\text{pair\_in\_s}(s, p_2, r_2) \vee (p_1 \approx p_2 \wedge r_1 \approx r_2)).$$
$$\text{remove\_s}(\text{assign\_s}(s, \text{pair}(p, r)), p) \approx s.$$
$$\neg p_1 \approx p_2 \wedge \text{contains\_s}(s, p_2)$$
$$\Rightarrow \text{remove\_s}(\text{assign\_s}(s, \text{pair}(p_1, r)), p_2)$$
$$\approx \text{assign\_s}(\text{remove\_s}(s, p_2), \text{pair}(p_1, r)).$$
$$\text{lookup\_s}(\text{assign\_s}(s, \text{pair}(p, r)), p) \approx r.$$
$$\neg p_1 \approx p_2 \wedge \text{contains\_s}(s, p_2)$$
$$\Rightarrow \text{lookup\_s}(\text{assign\_s}(s, \text{pair}(p_1, r)), p_2)$$
$$\approx \text{lookup\_s}(s, p_2).$$
$$\text{update\_s}(\text{create\_s}, p) \approx \text{create\_s}.$$
$$r < p_2$$
$$\Rightarrow \text{update\_s}(\text{assign\_s}(s, \text{pair}(p_1, r)), p_2)$$
$$\approx \text{assign\_s}(\text{update\_s}(s, p_2), \text{pair}(p_1, p_2)).$$
$$p_2 \leq r$$
$$\Rightarrow \text{update\_s}(\text{assign\_s}(s, \text{pair}(p_1, r)), p_2)$$
$$\approx \text{assign\_s}(\text{update\_s}(s, p_2), \text{pair}(p_1, r)).$$

Fig. 1. Excerpt of the problem description

Six of the formulas to be proved make heavy use of ordering axioms, and, as in Sect. 4.2, the chaining inference rule was crucial for the success of SATURATE for these formulas. Being implemented in Prolog, SATURATE is in general much slower than provers like SPASS, VAMPIRE, or E. In those cases, however, where the chaining rule makes it possible to avoid explicit inferences with the transitivity axiom, SATURATE can be orders of magnitude faster. We have repeated the experiments with the same lemmas using SPASS, version 3.0, where chaining is not implemented. The running times of both theorem provers are shown in Figure 2.

benchmark	SATURATE	SPASS
lemma_not_min_elem_not_check	00:07.98	03:31.46
lemma_not_ok_persistence	00:03.24	–
lemma_contains_s_I_remove	00:06.50	–
remove_min_02_1	00:03.55	03:08.31
tmp_not_check_02	00:02.92	–
tmp_not_check_03	00:04.50	59:21.52

Fig. 2. Table shows time in format min:sec that SATURATE and SPASS spent on the problem. The symbol "−" indicates that a prover did not terminate after two hours of running.

All the experiments with SATURATE were done using the standard settings. It includes tautology deletion, forward subsumption, forward and backward reduction, and simplification by totality resolution.

5   Spass

The development of the theorem prover SPASS started in 1994 (Weidenbach et al. [54, 55]). Using memory-efficient data structures and specific indexing techniques, SPASS has been the first high speed implementation of the superposition calculus, followed by E [49] and VAMPIRE [46]. SPASS also features an advanced CNF transformation module, equivalence-based definition extraction and expansion technology, a large collection of simplification methods, a special treatment of monadic predicates ("sorts"), and a tableau-like splitting rule for dealing with clauses that can be written as disjunctions of variable-disjoint subclauses.

5.1   Euclidean Geometry

Philippe Balbiani [10, 11] introduced a convergent and terminating conditional term rewriting system for a subtheory of Euclidean geometry. Lacking a powerful general proof procedure, Balbiani developed a Prolog-based proof procedure just in order to establish the properties of this term rewriting system. Christof Brinker and Christoph Weidenbach showed that SPASS plus a specific form of contextual rewriting can also be used to produce a complete system for the Balbiani rule set [14].

The conditional equations in Figure 3 formalize properties of Euclidean geometry on the basis of straight lines, indicated by the letter d, and points, indicated by the letter p. For convenience, uppercase variable letters represent points and lowercase variable letters straight lines (sets of points). Then $d(X, Y)$ formalizes the line through X and Y and in case $X = Y$ an arbitrary but fixed line through X, $f_{dp}(x, X)$ the line parallel to x through X, $f_{pd}(X, x)$ the projection from X to x, $f_{dd}(x, y)$ the perpendicular in the intersection of x and y and, in case x and y are parallel, an arbitrary but fixed perpendicular on y, and $p(X, x)$ the perpendicular from X on x.

$$d(X, Y) \approx d(Y, X) \quad (\text{RGO}_0)$$
$$f_{dp}(x, f_{pd}(X, x)) \approx x \quad (\text{RGO}_1)$$
$$f_{pd}(X, f_{dp}(x, X)) \approx X \quad (\text{RGO}_2)$$
$$f_{dd}(y, f_{dd}(x, y)) \approx y \quad (\text{RGO}_3)$$
$$f_{dp}(p(X, x), X) \approx p(X, x) \quad (\text{RGO}_4)$$
$$f_{dd}(p(X, x), x) \approx p(X, x) \quad (\text{RGO}_5)$$
$$f_{pd}(X, d(X, Y)) \approx X \quad (\text{RGO}_6)$$
$$p(f_{pd}(X, x), f_{dd}(y, x)) \approx x \quad (\text{RGO}_7)$$

$$f_{pd}(f_{pd}(X, x), x) \approx f_{pd}(X, x) \quad (\text{RGO}_8)$$
$$f_{pd}(X, p(X, x)) \approx X \quad (\text{RGO}_9)$$
$$f_{dp}(f_{dp}(x, X), X) \approx f_{dp}(x, X) \quad (\text{RGO}_{10})$$
$$f_{dp}(d(X, Y), X) \approx d(X, Y) \quad (\text{RGO}_{11})$$
$$f_{dd}(f_{dd}(x, y), y) \approx f_{dd}(x, y) \quad (\text{RGO}_{12})$$
$$f_{dd}(x, p(X, x)) \approx x \quad (\text{RGO}_{13})$$
$$p(X, f_{dd}(x, f_{dp}(y, X))) \approx f_{dp}(y, X) \quad (\text{RGO}_{14})$$
$$p(X, f_{dd}(x, p(X, y))) \approx p(X, y) \quad (\text{RGO}_{15})$$
$$p(X, f_{dd}(x, d(X, Y))) \approx d(X, Y) \quad (\text{RGO}_{16})$$
$$p(f_{pd}(X, f_{dd}(x, y)), y) \approx f_{dd}(x, y) \quad (\text{RGO}_{17})$$
$$p(f_{pd}(X, p(Y, x)), x) \approx p(Y, x) \quad (\text{RGO}_{18})$$
$$p(f_{pd}(X, x), p(Y, x)) \approx x \quad (\text{RGO}_{19})$$
$$p(X, p(Y, f_{dp}(x, X))) \approx f_{dp}(x, X) \quad (\text{RGO}_{20})$$
$$p(X, p(Y, p(X, x))) \approx p(X, x) \quad (\text{RGO}_{21})$$
$$p(X, p(Y, d(X, Z))) \approx d(X, Z) \quad (\text{RGO}_{22})$$

$$f_{pd}(X, x) \not\approx f_{pd}(Y, x) \Rightarrow d(f_{pd}(X, x), f_{pd}(Y, x)) \approx x \quad (\text{RGO}_{23})$$

$$X \not\approx f_{pd}(Y, f_{dp}(x, X)) \Rightarrow d(X, f_{pd}(Y, f_{dp}(x, X))) \approx f_{dp}(x, X) \quad (\text{RGO}_{24})$$
$$X \not\approx f_{pd}(Y, p(X, x)) \Rightarrow d(X, f_{pd}(Y, p(X, x))) \approx p(X, x) \quad (\text{RGO}_{25})$$
$$X \not\approx f_{pd}(Y, d(X, Z)) \Rightarrow d(X, f_{pd}(Y, d(X, Z))) \approx d(X, Z) \quad (\text{RGO}_{26})$$

Fig. 3. Euclidean Conditional Rewrite System

In its general form, *Contextual Rewriting* is the reduction rule between a clauses C and D from a clause set N given below. The notion $\bar{N}^{\tau \prec C\tau}$ for a substitution τ grounding C denotes the set of all ground clauses generated from

N by instantiating variables with ground terms from the range of τ that are smaller than $C\tau$.

Let $C = C' \vee s \approx t$, $D = D' \vee [\neg]\, u[s']_p \approx v$ be two clauses in N. The reduction

$$\mathcal{R} \ \frac{C' \vee s \approx t \qquad\qquad D' \vee [\neg]\, u[s']_p \approx v}{\begin{array}{c} C' \vee s \approx t \\ D' \vee [\neg]\, u[t\sigma]_p \approx v \end{array}}$$

where (i) $s\sigma = s'$, (ii) $s\sigma \succ t\sigma$, (iii) $D \succ C\sigma$, (iv) τ is a Skolem substitution replacing the variables in $C\sigma$ and D by new Skolem constants, (v) $\bar{N}^{\tau \prec C\tau} \models D''\tau \vee \neg A\tau$ for all negative equations A in $C'\sigma$ where D'' are the negative equations in D', and (vi) $\bar{N}^{\tau \prec C\tau} \models \neg A\tau \vee D'''\tau$ for all positive equations A in $C'\sigma$ where D''' are the positive equations in D' is called *contextual rewriting*.

This general form of contextual rewriting can be effectively computed, but is very expensive. For example, given the Skolem constants for $C\sigma$ and D there are exponentially many possibilities in the number of variables to instantiate a clause from N eventually smaller than $C\sigma\tau$ by these constants. Furthermore, Harald Ganzinger implemented the rule in the SATURATE system [41] and his experiments revealed that the complexity shows up in practice. There were examples where the prover spent hours on the applicability of a single contextual rewriting application of the above form.

A detailed study of Balbiani's conditional rewrite system and proof procedure yielded that considering the context $\bar{N}^{\tau \prec C\tau}$ is not needed for termination of the saturation process. It is sufficient to study contextual rewriting with respect to the involved clauses and standard reduction of the generated clauses $D''\tau \vee \neg A\tau$ and $\neg A\tau \vee D'''\tau$. The result is the below *local* contextual rewriting rule.

Let $C = C' \vee s \approx t$, $D = D' \vee [\neg]\, u[s']_p \approx v$ be two clauses in N. The reduction

$$\mathcal{R} \ \frac{C' \vee s \approx t \qquad\qquad D' \vee [\neg]\, u[s']_p \approx v}{\begin{array}{c} C' \vee s \approx t \\ D' \vee [\neg]\, u[t\sigma]_p \approx v \end{array}}$$

where (i) $s\sigma = s'$, (ii) $s\sigma \succ t\sigma$, (iii) $D \succ C\sigma$, (iv) τ is a Skolem substitution replacing the variables in $C\sigma$ and D by new Skolem constants, (v) $\models D''\tau \vee \neg A\tau$ for all negative equations A in $C'\sigma$ where D'' are the negative equations in D', and (v) $\models \neg A\tau \vee D'''\tau$ for all positive equations A in $C'\sigma$ where D''' are the positive equations in D' is called *Local Contextual Rewriting*.

The applicability of local contextual rewriting can be decided in polynomial time[7], because the semantic tautology checks for $\models D''\tau \vee \neg A\tau$ and $\models \neg A\tau \vee D'''\tau$ can be decided by the well-known congruence closure algorithm [17].

We get the *Semantic Tautology Rule*

$$\mathcal{R} \ \frac{C}{\ \ }$$

if $\models C$ for free, because we need to decide semantic tautologies for the applicability of local contextual rewriting anyway.

---

[7] If the used ordering $\prec$ is decidable in polynomial time.

Now with these two extra rules local contextual rewriting and semantic tautology deletion the Balbiani system can be finitely saturated. SPASS needs less than one second to generate the saturated system consisting of 40 conditional equations. Except for the commutativity of $d(X, Y)$, all clauses have a single maximal oriented equation containing all variables in the left-hand side of the equation. Therefore, the saturated system can be effectively used to decide any ground query, i.e., universally quantified conjecture.

5.2   Soft Typing

The general redundancy notion of superposition is given with respect to the perfect, minimal (Herbrand) model $\mathcal{I}_N$, generated by a (saturated) clause set N. Any clause C such that $C\tau$ is true in the perfect model generated by all clauses of the actual clause set $\bar{N}$ smaller than $C\tau$ for all grounding τ, written $\mathcal{I}_C \models C$, is weakly redundant (see Section 4). One consequence of this result is that actually any clause C that is implied by smaller clauses from N can be deleted, i.e., if $N^{\prec C} \models C$ then C can be deleted. This is the foundation for most of all practically used redundancy and simplification notions, e.g., rewriting or subsumption.

The model-based redundancy notion poses two challenges in practice. First, it is dynamic. As long as the set N is not saturated and new clauses are derived the interpretation $\mathcal{I}_N$ changes and therefore, clauses must not be deleted but can only be blocked for inferences (see Section 4). Second, the properties $\mathcal{I}_N \models C$ and $\mathcal{I}_C \models C$ are undecidable in general, because they constitute a second-order property by considering validity in a minimal model of a set of first-order clauses from N.

One solution to this problem is to define an upper approximation $\mathcal{I}_N'$ of $\mathcal{I}_N$ that is (i) stable under inferences in N and for which (ii) the problem $\mathcal{I}_N' \models C$ becomes decidable. An (Herbrand) interpretation $\mathcal{I}_N'$ is an upper approximation of $\mathcal{I}_N$, written $\mathcal{I}_N \subseteq \mathcal{I}_N'$, if for all predicates P: $P^{\mathcal{I}_N} \subseteq P^{\mathcal{I}_N'}$ and the two interpretations agree on the interpretation of all function symbols. Then such an approximation can be used to simplify reasoning on N. A first application is the detection and deletion of redundant clauses. Consider a clause $\neg A_1 \vee \ldots \vee \neg A_n \vee C$ out of a clause set N such that for any grounding substitution σ the atoms $A_i\sigma$ are false in the approximation: $\mathcal{I}_N' \not\models A_1\sigma \wedge \ldots \wedge A_n\sigma$. Then the clause $\neg A_1 \vee \ldots \vee \neg A_n \vee C$ is a tautology and can be deleted. This technique is called *soft typing*. There are applications where soft typing is key to finitely saturate clause sets [25].

In order to effectively obtain an upper approximation $\mathcal{I}_N'$ the idea is to actually approximate the clause set N by a (consistent) clause set N' such that eventually $\mathcal{I}_N \subseteq \mathcal{I}_{N'}$ and N' belongs to a decidable clause class. This way, a second application of soft typing becomes available. Proving properties of N by considering N'. If Φ is a universally closed conjunction of atoms and $N' \models \Phi$, then $N \models \Phi$. Thus, if Φ is provable from N', which is decidable by construction, then we need not to consider validity with respect to N, which is undecidable, in general.

So we need to find an expressive, decidable sublanguage of first-order clause logic that can serve as the range class for an upper approximation. Monadic Horn clause sets are a natural and powerful candidate [32, 37, 53]. There exist several decidability results and we will show in this section that there also exist natural and powerful approximations into the class. Monadic Horn clause classes are typically used to describe sorts or types and serve as a theoretical basis in other contexts like programming languages or abstract interpretation, supporting the name *soft typing*. In order to keep this section simple, we do assume that clause sets do not contain equations. This is even not a restriction, because the equality relation can be encoded by explicitly providing the needed axioms.

The theoretical background for the application of approximation functions given below was developed by Harald Ganzinger, Christoph Meyer, and Christoph Weidenbach [25]. It was implemented by Enno Keen via the DFG2DFG tool, part of the SPASS distribution since 2001. All rules can be applied separately but exhaustively and can be actually composed to obtain different overall approximations. Note that application of the rules may turn a consistent clause set into an inconsistent one due to the upper approximation of predicates. So checking consistency of the approximated clause set is mandatory for the approach to work.

The *Horn Rule* transforms a non-Horn clause into a set of Horn clauses:

$$\mathcal{R} \ \frac{C \vee A_1 \vee \ldots \vee A_n}{C \vee A_1}$$

$$\vdots$$

$$C \vee A_n$$

where $n \geq 2$ and $A_1 \vee \ldots \vee A_n$ and no more positive atoms are in C.

The next two rules constitute alternative transformations from non-monadic literals into monadic literals.

The *Monadic Term Encoding Rule* transforms an n-ary predicate into a monadic atom by replacing predicate symbols with function symbols and thus moving non-monadic atoms to the term level.

$$\mathcal{R} \ \frac{C \vee [\neg]P(t_1, \ldots, t_n)}{C \vee [\neg]T(p(t_1, \ldots, t_n))}$$

where $n \geq 2$, p is a new function corresponding to the predicate P and T is a special fixed predicate. Applied to a given clause set, all occurrences of P in the clause set are transformed into the same function p. For all applications the same predicate T is used.

The *Monadic Projection Encoding Rule* transforms an n-ary predicate into several monadic atoms by argument projection:

$$\mathcal{R} \ \frac{C \vee [\neg]P(t_1, \ldots, t_n)}{C \vee [\neg]P_1(t_1)}$$

$$\vdots$$

$$C \vee [\neg]P_n(t_n)$$

where $n \geq 2$, and $P_1, \ldots, P_n$ are new monadic predicates. All occurrences of P in the clause set are transformed into the same predicates $P_1, \ldots, P_n$.

So far a combination of the rules enables the transformation from an arbitrary clause set into a monadic Horn clause set. From now on we assume all clause sets to be Horn and monadic. The following rules approximate a monadic Horn clause set into a monadic Horn clause set with a decidable entailment problem by relaxing the term structure. There are several candidates for such clause sets, relying on linearity and shallowness. A term is called *linear* if it contains no repeated variables. A term is called *shallow* if it is of the form $f(x_1, \ldots, x_n)$. The *Linear Approximation Rule* given below reduces the number of non-linear variable occurrences in a Horn clause by replacing a variable x repeated within an atom by some new variable x'. Note that the transformation is not applicable to clauses containing non-monadic literals.

The *Linear Approximation Rule* eliminates non-linear variable occurrences in atoms of monadic Horn clauses:

$$\mathcal{R} \ \frac{C \vee P(t)[x]_p[x]_q}{C\{x \mapsto x'\} \vee C \vee P(t)[x']_p[x]_q}$$

where $p \neq q$, and x' is a new variable.

Finally, nested terms are transformed into shallow terms by the *Shallow Approximation Rule*

$$\mathcal{R} \ \frac{C \vee P(t[s]_p)}{\neg S(x) \vee C \vee P(t[x]_p)}$$
$$C \vee S(s)$$

where s is a complex term at non-top position p in t, and x is a new variable and S a new predicate.

The rule can be further refined by considering all occurrences of s in t simultaneously and by filtering C with respect to variable dependencies with s.

The transformation rules Horn Transformation, Monadic Projection Encoding, Linear Approximation, Shallow and Relaxed Shallow produce upper approximations of the original clause set.

Eventually the rules can be combined to obtain a decidable approximation for a given clause set N. A typical sequence is the transformation to Horn clauses, transformation to monadic literals, linear transformation, and finally shallow transformation resulting in an approximation Horn clause set N' in the above sense. In practice, the challenge is to find approximations that lead to consistent and non-trivial upper approximations.

6 Conclusions

Simplification and redundancy detection are the key techniques to reduce the search space of a theorem prover. Harald Ganzinger has developed the fundamental abstract concept of redundancy and simplification for superposition-like calculi together with Leo Bachmair. His theoretical work, however, has always been supplemented by the urge to make it practically useful – by developing concrete, effective redundancy and simplification criteria to be implemented in current theorem provers in order to make them beneficial for various application domains. In this survey, we have tried to give a few representative examples of this practical side of his scientific work.

References

1. Afshordel, B., Hillenbrand, T., Weidenbach, C.: First-Order Atom Definitions Extended. In: Nieuwenhuis, R., Voronkov, A. (eds.) LPAR 2001. LNCS (LNAI), vol. 2250, pp. 309–319. Springer, Heidelberg (2001)
2. Baader, F., Nipkow, T.: Term rewriting and all that. Cambridge University Press, New York (1998)
3. Bachmair, L.: Canonical Equational Proofs. Birkhäuser, Boston (1991)
4. Bachmair, L., Dershowitz, N., Hsiang, J.: Orderings for equational proofs. In: [First Annual] Symposium on Logic in Computer Science, June 16–18, pp. 346–357. IEEE Computer Society Press, Cambridge (1986)
5. Bachmair, L., Ganzinger, H.: Completion of First-Order Clauses with Equality by Strict Superposition (extended abstract). In: Okada, M., Kaplan, S. (eds.) CTRS 1990. LNCS, vol. 516, pp. 162–180. Springer, Heidelberg (1991)
6. Bachmair, L., Ganzinger, H.: On Restrictions of Ordered Paramodulation with Simplification. In: Stickel, M.E. (ed.) CADE 1990. LNCS, vol. 449, pp. 427–441. Springer, Heidelberg (1990)
7. Bachmair, L., Ganzinger, H.: Rewrite-based equational theorem proving with selection and simplification. Journal of Logic and Computation 4(3), 217–247 (1994)
8. Bachmair, L., Ganzinger, H.: Ordered chaining calculi for first-order theories of transitive relations. Journal of the ACM 45(6), 1007–1049 (1998)
9. Bachmair, L., Ganzinger, H.: Resolution theorem proving. In: Robinson, A., Voronkov, A. (eds.) Handbook of Automated Reasoning, vol. 1, ch. 2, pp. 19–99. Elsevier (2001)
10. Balbiani, P.: Equation Solving in Geometrical Theories. In: Lindenstrauss, N., Dershowitz, N. (eds.) CTRS 1994. LNCS, vol. 968, Springer, Heidelberg (1995)
11. Balbiani, P.: Mécanisation de la géométrie: incidence et orthogonalité. Revue d'Intelligence Artificielle 11, 179–211 (1997)
12. Basin, D., Ganzinger, H.: Automated complexity analysis based on ordered resolution. Journal of the ACM 48(1), 70–109 (2001)
13. Bertling, H., Ganzinger, H., Schäfers, R.: CEC: A System for the Completion of Conditional Equational Specifications. In: Ganzinger, H. (ed.) ESOP 1988. LNCS, vol. 300, pp. 378–379. Springer, Heidelberg (1988)
14. Brinker, C.: Geometrisches Schließen mit SPASS. Diplomarbeit, Universität des Saarlandes and Max-Planck-Institut für Informatik, Saarbrücken, Germany (2000); Supervisors: Ganzinger, H., Weidenbach, C.
15. de Bruijn, N.G.: Lambda calculus notation with nameless dummies, a tool for automatic formula manipulation, with application to the Church–Rosser theorem. Indagationes Mathematicae 34(5), 381–392 (1972)
16. Church, A.: An unsolvable problem of elementary number theory. American Journal of Mathematics 58, 345–363 (1936)
17. Downey, P.J., Sethi, R., Tarjan, R.E.: Variations on the common subexpression problem. Journal of the ACM 27(4), 758–771 (1980)

18. Fay, M.: First-order unification in an equational theory. In: Fourth Workshop on Automated Deduction, pp. 161–167. Academic Press, Austin (1979)
19. Finkler, U., Mehlhorn, K.: Checking priority queues. In: Proceedings of the 10th Annual ACM-SIAM Symposium on Discrete Algorithms (SODA 1999). Society for Industrial and Applied Mathematics, pp. 901–902 (1999)
20. Ganzinger, H.: A Completion Procedure for Conditional Equations. In: Kaplan, S., Jouannaud, J.-P. (eds.) CTRS 1987. LNCS, vol. 308, pp. 62–83. Springer, Heidelberg (1988)
21. Ganzinger, H.: Completion with History-Dependent Complexities for Generated Equations. In: Sannella, D., Tarlecki, A. (eds.) Abstract Data Types 1987. LNCS, vol. 332, pp. 73–91. Springer, Heidelberg (1988)
22. Ganzinger, H.: Ground Term Confluence in Parametric Conditional Equational Specifications. In: Brandenburg, F.J., Vidal-Naquet, G., Wirsing, M. (eds.) STACS 1987. LNCS, vol. 247, pp. 286–298. Springer, Heidelberg (1987)
23. Ganzinger, H.: A completion procedure for conditional equations. Journal of Symbolic Computation 11, 51–81 (1991)
24. Ganzinger, H.: Order-sorted completion: the many-sorted way. Theoretical Computer Science 89, 3–32 (1991)
25. Ganzinger, H., Meyer, C., Weidenbach, C.: Soft Typing for Ordered Resolution. In: McCune, W. (ed.) CADE 1997. LNCS (LNAI), vol. 1249, pp. 321–335. Springer, Heidelberg (1997)
26. Ganzinger, H., Nieuwenhuis, R., Nivela, P.: The Saturate system (1994), http://www.mpi-sb.mpg.de/SATURATE
27. Ganzinger, H., Schäfers, R.: System support for modular order-sorted horn clause specifications. In: 12th International Conference on Software Engineering, pp. 150–159. IEEE Computer Society Press, Nice (1990)
28. Ganzinger, H., Stuber, J.: Superposition with equivalence reasoning and delayed clause normal form transformation. Information and Computation 199, 3–23 (2005)
29. Giegerich, R.: Specification and correctness of code generators – an experiment with the CEC-system. In: Müller, J., Ganzinger, H. (eds.) 1st German Workshop "Term Rewriting: Theory and Applications", SEKI-Report 89/02. Universität Kaiserslautern (1989)
30. Gnaedig, I., Kirchner, C., Kirchner, H.: Equational completion in order-sorted algebras. Theoretical Computer Science 72(2&3), 169–202 (1990)
31. Hsiang, J., Rusinowitch, M.: Proving refutational completeness of theorem-proving strategies: The transfinite semantic tree method. Journal of the ACM 38(3), 559–587 (1991)
32. Jacquemard, F., Meyer, C., Weidenbach, C.: Unification in Extensions of Shallow Equational Theories. In: Nipkow, T. (ed.) RTA 1998. LNCS, vol. 1379, pp. 76–90. Springer, Heidelberg (1998)
33. Kleene, S.: A theory of positive integers in formal logic. American Journal of Mathematics 57, 153–173, 219–244 (1935)
34. Knuth, D.E., Bendix, P.B.: Simple word problems in universal algebras. In: Leech, J. (ed.) Computational Problems in Abstract Algebra, pp. 263–297. Pergamon Press, Oxford (1970); Reprinted in Siekmann and Wrightson [50], pp. 342–376
35. McAllester, D.A.: Automatic recognition of tractability in inference relation. Journal of the ACM 40(2), 284–303 (1993)
36. Nieuwenhuis, R.: First-order completion techniques. Technical report, UPC-LSI, Cited in Nieuwenhuis and Rubio [38] (1991)

37. Nieuwenhuis, R.: Basic paramodulation and decidable theories (extended abstract). In: Proceedings 11th IEEE Symposium on Logic in Computer Science (LICS 1996), pp. 473–482. IEEE Computer Society Press (1996)
38. Nieuwenhuis, R., Rubio, A.: Basic Superposition is Complete. In: Krieg-Brückner, B. (ed.) ESOP 1992. LNCS, vol. 582, Springer, Heidelberg (1992)
39. Nipkow, T.: More Church–Rosser proofs (in Isabelle/HOL). Journal of Automated Reasoning 26, 51–66 (2001)
40. Nipkow, T., Paulson, L.C., Wenzel, M.: Isabelle/HOL. LNCS, vol. 2283. Springer, Heidelberg (2002)
41. Nivela, P., Nieuwenhuis, R.: Saturation of First-Order (constrained) Clauses with the Saturate System. In: Kirchner, C. (ed.) RTA 1993. LNCS, vol. 690, pp. 436–440. Springer, Heidelberg (1993)
42. de Nivelle, H., Piskac, R.: Verification of an off-line checker for priority queues. In: Aichernig, B.K., Beckert, B. (eds.) Third IEEE International Conference on Software Engineering and Formal Methods (SEFM 2005), pp. 210–219. IEEE, Koblenz (2005)
43. Ohlbach, H.J.: Translation methods for non-classical logics – an overview. Bulletin of the IGPL 1(1), 69–90 (1993)
44. Peterson, G.E.: A technique for establishing completeness results in theorem proving with equality. SIAM Journal on Computing 12(1), 82–100 (1983)
45. Piskac, R.: Formal correctness of result checking for priority queues. Master's thesis, Universität des Saarlandes (February 2005)
46. Riazanov, A., Voronkov, A.: The design and implementation of Vampire. AI Communications 15(2-3), 91–110 (2002)
47. Robinson, G., Wos, L.: Paramodulation and theorem-proving in first-order theories with equality. In: Meltzer, B., Michie, D. (eds.) Machine Intelligence, vol. 4, ch. 8, pp. 298–313. Edinburgh University Press, Edinburgh (1969); Reprinted in Siekmann and Wrightson [50], pp. 298–313
48. Rusinowitch, M.: Theorem-proving with resolution and superposition. Journal of Symbolic Computation 11(1&2), 21–49 (January/February 1991)
49. Schulz, S.: E – A Brainiac Theorem Prover. Journal of AI Communications 15(2/3), 111–126 (2002)
50. Siekmann, J., Wrightson, G.: Automation of Reasoning: Classical Papers on Computational Logic 1967-1970, vol. 2. Springer, Berlin (1983)
51. Takahashi, M.: Parallel reductions in λ-calculus. Information and Computation 118(1), 120–127 (1995)
52. Wasserman, H., Blum, M.: Software reliability via run-time result-checking. Journal of the ACM 44(6), 826–849 (1997)
53. Weidenbach, C.: Towards an Automatic Analysis of Security Protocols in First-Order Logic. In: Ganzinger, H. (ed.) CADE 1999. LNCS (LNAI), vol. 1632, pp. 314–328. Springer, Heidelberg (1999)
54. Weidenbach, C., Brahm, U., Hillenbrand, T., Keen, E., Theobald, C., Topic, D.: SPASS Version 2.0. In: Voronkov, A. (ed.) CADE 2002. LNCS (LNAI), vol. 2392, pp. 275–277. Springer, Heidelberg (2002)
55. Weidenbach, C., Gaede, B., Rock, G.: SPASS & FLOTTER, version 0.42. In: McRobbie, M.A., Slaney, J.K. (eds.) CADE 1996. LNCS (LNAI), vol. 1104, pp. 141–145. Springer, Heidelberg (1996)
56. Zhang, H., Kapur, D.: First-Order Theorem Proving using Conditional Rewrite Rules. In: Lusk, E., Overbeek, R. (eds.) CADE 1988. LNCS, vol. 310, pp. 1–20. Springer, Heidelberg (1988)

Elimination Techniques for Program Analysis[*]

Deepak Kapur

Department of Computer Science
University of New Mexico
Albuquerque, NM
kapur@cs.unm.edu

Dedicated to Harald Ganzinger

Abstract. Key ideas in our recent work on automatically generating polynomial equalities and inequalities as invariants/inductive assertions for imperative programs are reviewed. Two approaches based on elimination techniques are briefly discussed. The first approach is algebraic and is based on giving the semantics of programming language constructs in terms of polynomial ideals. The second approach is based on assuming a priori the shapes of inductive assertions of interest and then using quantifier elimination techniques to generate constraints on parameters specifying the shape. The key ideas of these approaches are illustrated through examples.

1 Introduction

This paper is an attempt to summarize research in our group on automatically generating loop invariants using algebraic and logical methods from 2003-2006. As will be clear later from several examples and the results, it is indeed possible to automatically generate polynomial equalities and inequalities as loop invariants for programs operating on numbers. Further, input-output specifications or postconditions of programs are not needed.

Consider a few examples for which loop invariants can be automatically generated using the techniques discussed in the paper. Let us begin with the following simple loop for computing the floor of the square root of a natural number.

Example 1. **function SquareRoot**(N: integer) **returns** a: integer
    var a, s, t: integer **end var**
    $a := 0, \ s := 1, \ t := 1$;
    while $s \leq N$ **do**
        $a := a + 1; \ t := t + 2; \ s := s + t$;
    end while

---

[*] This paper is based on a talk given at the Ganzinger Memorial Symposium held at the Max Planck Institute in May 2005. Most of this paper was written in the summer of 2006. This research was partially supported by NSF awards CCF-0541315 and CCF-0729097.

A. Voronkov and C. Weidenbach (Eds.): Ganzinger Festschrift, LNCS 7797, pp. 194–215, 2013.
© Springer-Verlag Berlin Heidelberg 2013

Using the approach discussed in [29], a conjunction of two polynomial equations, $t = 2a + 1$, $s = (a + 1)^2$, can be automatically generated as an invariant. In fact, this formula can be shown to be the strongest invariant expressed in terms of polynomial equations. There is no need to provide a postcondition to drive invariants or give a priori shapes of the desired invariants. The second polynomial equation, $s = (a + 1)^2$, though an invariant, is not an inductive invariant by itself; in other words, it is not the case that $s = (a + 1)^2 \implies (((s = (a + 1)^2)|_{s+t}^s)|_{t+2}^t)_{a+1}^a$.[1] In contrast, each conjunct in an equivalent strongest formula $t = 2a + 1 \wedge s = -a^2 + at - a + t \wedge t^2 = 2a + 4s - 3t$ is an invariant as well as an inductive invariant.

Here is a somewhat meaningless but historical example taken from a paper of Cousot and Halbwachs [6], where a method for generating linear inequalities as invariants was discussed using the abstract interpretation approach [5].

Example 2. **var** i, j: integer **end var**
    $\langle i, j \rangle := \langle 2, 0 \rangle;$
    while b_1 **do**
        if b_2 **then** $i := i + 4;$
                else $i := i + 2, \ \ j := j + 1;$
        end if
    end while

Polynomial methods discussed in [29,32,33] cannot be used to automatically generate an invariant for this example. However, methods based on quantifier-elimination [16] and Farkas' lemma [4] can generate an invariant for this example. Using the quantifier elimination approach illustrated in [16], the conjunction of inequalities

$$-j \leq 0 \wedge -i + 2j + 2 \leq 0$$

can be deduced as an invariant.

The following third example written in the language of guarded commands, taken from [30] models an Illinois cache coherence protocol.[2] The safety of the

---

[1] The notation $\alpha|_t^x$ stands for replacing all free occurrences of a variable x in a formula α by an expression t.

[2] In this paper, we use a simple side-effect free programming language for writing programs; evaluation of expressions has no side effects. The language consists of (multiple) assignments, guarded commands, and a looping construct such as **while**. A multiple assignment of the form $(x, y) := (a, b)$, for example, has the effect of simultaneously evaluating a, b and then assigning the results to x, y. The semantics of a guarded command is that it is executed only if the guard evaluates to **true**; otherwise, it has no effect. In case of multiple guards in a conditional statement, any guard that evaluates to **true** is nondeterministically chosen. If the body of a loop is a guarded command and no guard in it evaluates to **true**, then the loop terminates. A while loop also terminates if its test fails. A conditional statement of the form, **if** b **then** S_1 **else** S_2, is equivalent to $b \rightarrow S_1 \ [] \ \neg b \rightarrow S_2$; similarly, **if** b **then** S_1 is equivalent to $b \rightarrow S_1 \ [] \ \neg b \rightarrow skip$, where the *skip* statement has no effect on the program state.

protocol is expressed as $(y = 0 \lor u = 0) \land (0 \le y \le 1)$. This example illustrates many interesting aspects: (i) certain bounded integer inequalities such as the one above can be expressed as a disjunction of equalities (e.g., $y = 0 \lor y = 1$), and (ii) a disjunction of equalities can be expressed as an equality (e.g., $uy = 0$ is equivalent to $u = 0 \lor y = 0$).

Example 3.   var x, y, u, v: natural end var
$(x, y, u):=(0, 0, 0);$
   while *true* do
$$x = y = u = 0 \land v \ne 0 \to (v, x):=(v - 1, x + 1);$$
$$[] \; v \ne 0 \land y \ne 0 \to (v, y, u):=(v - 1, y - 1, u + 2);$$
$$[] \; v \ne 0 \land u \ne 0 \to (v, u, x):=(v - 1, u + x + 1, 0);$$
$$[] \; v \ne 0 \land x \ne 0 \to (v, u, x):=(v - 1, u + x + 1, 0);$$
$$[] \; x \ne 0 \to (x, y):=(x - 1, y + 1);$$
$$[] \; u \ne 0 \to (v, y, u):=(v + u - 1, y + 1, 0);$$
$$[] \; v \ne 0 \to (v, x, u, y):=(v + x + y + u - 1, 0, 0, 1);$$
$$[] \; y \ne 0 \to (y, v):=(y - 1, v + 1);$$
$$[] \; u \ne 0 \to (u, v):=(u - 1, v + 1);$$
$$[] \; x \ne 0 \to (x, v):=(x - 1, v + 1);$$
  end while

The above property is not an inductive invariant either; instead a stronger property, $(y = 0 \lor u = 0) \land (0 \le y \le 1) \land (0 \le x \le 1) \land (x = 0 \lor u = 0) \land (x = 0 \lor y = 0)$, which is equivalent to $yu = 0 \land y^2 = y \land x^2 = x \land xu = 0 \land xy = 0$, can be automatically generated as an invariant from which the safety property follows. This example also illustrates that often, a stronger property of a loop is needed to establish a property of a program.

In this paper, we discuss static methods for automatically generating loop invariants. The first method uses results from algebraic geometry to generate conjunctions of polynomial equations as invariants. There is no restriction imposed on the degree of polynomials appearing in the invariants. Restrictions on programs are identified for which this method automatically generates polynomial invariants of arbitrary degree.

In the second approach, candidate formulas for invariants are restricted to have a certain shape, which is specified using parameters associated with a formula on program variables. Program variables are then eliminated from verification conditions generated, using quantifier elimination techniques, to get constraints on parameter values. This approach was first introduced in a technical report in [15]. Subsequently, it has also been called constraint solving based method in the literature. It has been found effective in many aspects of formal methods research – in program analysis, program verification, program synthesis, invariant generation and controller synthesis for hybrid systems, as well as in termination of programs, particularly for generating polynomial interpretations and well-founded polynomial orderings. Consequently, it has become an active research topic.

As stated earlier, the focus in this paper is on research in our group, particularly, the key ideas in the approaches we have investigated. We will not have space to do comparisons with related approaches or to do a comprehensive literature survey of the advances made subsequently. An interested reader can consult [4,3,33,24,25] for related approaches. We apologize to other researchers working on related topics for not citing their work properly and duly crediting them. Further, the paper will not attempt to provide all the details for a curious reader to use it to generate invariants of even the examples discussed here. For that, the reader should consult the papers cited above.

2 An Approach Based on Polynomial Ideal Theory

Loop invariants are the key ingredient of the axiomatic approach towards program semantics, also called the Floyd-Hoare inductive assertion approach. The concept of invariant has been used in abstract algebra, particularly algebraic geometry, for nearly 200 years. However, in computer science, the use of invariants first appeared in a paper by Hoare on a proof of the program FIND. Since then, the use of invariants is ubiquitous in understanding the behavior of programs. Because of my interest in elimination methods in algebraic geometry since the mid 1980s, it was extremely gratifying to find a close connection between the concept of loop invariants with algebraic concepts of invariants in invariant theory, as the reader would observe from the discussion in this section.

In a seminal paper dating back to the early 1970s, Webgreit et al. [37,11] proposed that the semantics of the body of a loop can be expressed as a recurrence relation over the program state after the $(i + 1)$-th iteration in terms of the program state after the i-th iteration.

For example 1 in the introduction, the value of program variables a_{i+1}, s_{i+1}, and t_{i+1} after the $(i + 1)$-th iteration can be specified in terms of their values in previous iterations as

$$a_{i+1} = a_i + 1, \quad s_{i+1} = s_i + t_i + 2, \quad t_{i+1} = t_i + 2,$$

with the initial values $a_0 = 0, s_0 = 1, t_0 = 1$; furthermore, $a_i = i$, the loop index. These recurrences can be solved in many cases in terms of the loop index. If the loop index can also be eliminated from these solutions (using a Gröbner basis algorithm or related elimination methods), relations among program variables can be computed which do not depend upon the loop index. In this way, loop behavior can be characterized independently of the loop index. However, Wegbreit et al. were unable to carry the idea much further, i.e., they were unable to derive invariants of any nontrivial programs.

In [28], significant progress was made in deriving loop invariants automatically using related ideas. Below, we discuss the key ideas and present results; more details can be found in [28,29,31]. Since the following subsection uses algebraic terminology, the reader is strongly advised to consult [7].

It was proved in [29] that if one just considers polynomial equations (of any degree) as atomic formulas for specifying invariant properties of programs, then these polynomial invariants have a nice algebraic structure, called a *radical ideal* of polynomials. Given two invariants at a program location, expressed as polynomial equations $p_1 = 0$ and $p_2 = 0$, the following are also invariants:

1. $p_1 + p_2 = 0$,
2. $q p_1 = 0$ for any polynomial q, and
3. if $p_1 = p_3{}^k$ for some p_3 and $k > 0$, then $p_3 = 0$ is also an invariant.

The above are precisely the defining properties of a radical ideal of polynomials. In [29], this radical ideal associated with a program location was called the *polynomial invariant ideal.*

Theorem 1. *The set of invariants expressed as polynomial equations in $Q[x_1, \ldots, x_n]$ at a given program location constitute a radical ideal, called polynomial invariant ideal. Further, any elimination ideal of this radical ideal is also a polynomial invariant ideal.*[3]

From a logical perspective, the first property above follows from the fact that if formulas f_1 and f_2 are invariants, then so is their conjunction $f_1 \wedge f_2$.[4] The second property is a weaker version of the fact that if f_1 is in an invariant, then so is any formula f_2 implied by f_1 (a disjunction of f_1 with any arbitrary formula f_2 is obviously implied by f_1). The third property trivially follows from the idempotency of disjunction.

If f_1 is an invariant and it includes a constant, then that constant can be abstracted by a variable that can be existentially quantified. This is a constructive existential formula.

By Hilbert's basis theorem, every ideal over a Noetherian ring has a finite basis. So a polynomial invariant ideal has a finite basis as well. From this finite basis, a formula which has the structure of a conjunction of disjunctions of polynomial equations can be generated, from which every polynomial invariant follows. Interestingly, disjunctive polynomial invariants can be easily expressed in the language using a polynomial equation since $pq = 0$ is equivalent to $p = 0 \vee q = 0$. Disjunctive invariants are usually not as easy to express in other frameworks, particularly those based on abstract interpretation. Example 3 in the introduction about the Illinois cache coherence protocol is an excellent illustration of the expressive power of conjunctions of disjunctions of polynomial equations as inductive assertions.

The problem of discovering invariants at a program location thus reduces to computing the associated polynomial invariant ideal at the location. If this cannot be achieved, our goal is to find the closest possible approximation to this polynomial invariant ideal, which in ideal-theoretic terms, means computing a subideal, to this ideal, including the zero ideal, which corresponds to the formula true.

---

[3] Given an ideal I over a polynomial ring $Q[x_1, \ldots, x_n]$, its j-th elimination ideal I_j is the set of polynomials only in variables $x_{j+1}, \ldots x_n$ in I.

[4] The polynomial invariant $p_1 + p_2 = 0$ is however not equivalent to $p_1 = 0 \wedge p_2 = 0$.

The reader would observe that negation of polynomial equations is not allowed. It is an open problem how this approach can incorporate negated equations as a part of an invariant.[5]

Assuming that a significant component of program states at a program location constitutes an algebraic variety (i.e., polynomials characterizing program states form a radical ideal), many properties of such states can be characterized by a conjunction of a finite set of polynomial equations. The approach discussed in [29] is based on the following ideas:

1. Under certain conditions, semantics of programming language constructs can be given in terms of ideal-theoretic operations. So a program becomes a computation on ideals. This is further discussed in the next subsection.
2. The polynomial invariant ideal associated to a loop entry in a program can be computed as a fixed point. The challenge is to determine conditions under which this fixed point computation terminates in a finite number of steps, or can be approximated so that the approximation can be computed in finitely many steps. Below such conditions are given by imposing restrictions on programs (see [29] for precise definitions).

In Subsection 2.3, we identify key concepts and results of algebraic geometry used in obtaining the results reported in the next subsections. It is hoped that these insights can inspire others to investigate similar properties of logical theories of other data structures for generalizing our results.

2.1 Semantics as Ideal Operations

In [29], we gave a procedure for computing the polynomial invariant ideal of a simple loop in a program. The semantics of programming language constructs is given in terms of manipulating radical ideals (equivalently, algebraic varieties) characterizing program states [32]. As stated above, states are assumed to be specified as a conjunction of polynomial equations, where each polynomial equation is really a disjunction of equations, corresponding to basis elements of a radical ideal.

Similar to every Hoare triple $\{P\}\ S\ \{Q\}$ (assuming termination), we have an input radical ideal I characterizing states before the execution of S, and an output radical ideal J characterizing states after the execution of S. Thus P is a conjunction of polynomial equations corresponding to a finite basis of I and Q similarly corresponds to J. For the forward propagation semantics, we would like to derive the strongest possible postcondition Q for any given P, which

---

[5] The reader should however note that a negated equation, say $p \neq 0$, can be expressed as a polynomial equation $pz = 1$, where z is a new variable. It is unclear how such variables can be systematically introduced to generate invariants which have negated equations. A quantifier free formula that is a conjunction of polynomial equations and inequations defines a *quasi-variety*, which have been studied in automated geometry theorem proving [38]. It will be interesting to generalize the method of [29] to work on algebraic quasi-varieties instead of algebraic varieties.

translates to generating maximal nontrivial radical ideal J from a given radical input ideal I. For the backward semantics, we would like the weakest possible precondition P from any given Q. In ideal-theoretic terms, this is equivalent to generating minimal nonzero radical ideal I from a given radical ideal J.[6]

For an assignment statement of the form $x := e$, the strongest postcondition corresponding to a precondition P is $\exists x'(x = e|_{x'}^{x} \land P|_{x'}^{x})$, whereas the strongest precondition corresponding to a postcondition Q is $Q|_{e}^{x}$. Thus $Q|_{e}^{x}$ is equivalent to substituting e for x in the ideal basis corresponding to Q and then recomputing its radical ideal. If the assignment is invertible, then strongest postcondition semantics is also relatively easy to compute by substituting for variables, otherwise a new variable x' must be introduced to stand for the previous values of x before the assignment, and the elimination ideal is computed after eliminating x' from the radical ideal corresponding to $P|_{x'}^{x}$ and the polynomial equation $x = e|_{x'}^{x}$.[7]

The initial ideal is determined by the input state.

The semantics of a conditional statement is often approximated due to the condition in the statement. If a condition c is expressed as boolean combination of polynomial equations, then its effect can be expressed using ideal-theoretic operations. Otherwise, the condition c can be approximated by another condition d such that $c \implies d$ and d is a boolean combination of polynomial conditions. The coarsest approximation is where d is true (the corresponding ideal is the trivial zero ideal). Since merging of different control paths in a program (due to a conditional statement or a while statement) leads to the union of states corresponding to each path, this is represented logically as a disjunction of formulas corresponding to each path. In ideal-theoretic terms, it amounts to the intersection of the corresponding ideals. For example, if one path leads to $x = 0$ and the other path leads to $x = 1$, when these path merge, states are characterized by $x = 0 \lor x = 1$. For the first path, the ideal is $< x >$, and the ideal for the second path is $\langle x - 1 \rangle$. The intersection of these ideals is $\langle x(x - 1) \rangle$, which captures the disjunction.

In case of a location where program control can pass arbitrarily many times, we would like to conclude that the ideal corresponding to the states at that control point eventually stabilizes, i.e., the fixed point is reached approximating the polynomial invariant ideal. There are potentially infinitely many intersections of ideals corresponding to each iteration. The main issue is thus whether conditions can be identified under which this indeed happens.

2.2   Termination of Polynomial Invariant Ideal Computation

In [29,31], we gave a procedure for computing an approximation of the polynomial invariant ideal and proved that the procedure terminates under certain

---

[6] It might be useful to recall relationship between formulas and the associated ideals. If a formula $f \implies g$, then the ideal associated with g is a subideal of the ideal associated with f.

[7] This suggests that e appearing on the right side of an assignment can be an arbitrary polynomial.

technical conditions, particularly if assignment mappings are solvable with their eigenvalues as rational numbers (see [28] for precise details and proofs). This procedure uses a Gröbner basis algorithm for computing various ideal-theoretic operations. Instead of computing arbitrarily many intersections of ideals corresponding to the number of times a loop is executed, recurrence relations induced by the loop body on the values of program variables are solved. The condition of assignment mappings being solvable ensures that (i) recurrence corresponding to such an assignment can indeed be solved and (ii) program variables can be polynomially expressed in terms of the loop counter and some auxiliary variables standing for exponentials of eigenvalues. In this way, an invariant ideal corresponding to the multiple visits of a path is captured using program variables and the counter standing for the number of times the path is visited. The termination of the fixed point computation is established under these conditions by making use of a beautiful result in algebraic geometry that every algebraic variety can be decomposed into finitely many irreducible components [7]. This result is used to show that the algebraic variety of the states at the loop entry has irreducible components such that the dimension of at least one component goes up in every iteration of the procedure or the variety stabilizes, leading to the termination of the procedure. Since the dimension of a polynomial invariant ideal is bounded by the number of program variables, termination of the fixed point computation is guaranteed in steps bounded by the number of program variables in a program. Because of approximations made in the semantics of programming constructions (e.g. tests in conditional statements and loops) , invariants generated by this approach are strongest relative to these assumptions/approximations.

The following three results about simple loops are proved in [29].

Theorem 2. *If the procedure for computing polynomial invariant ideals terminates, then it indeed computes a polynomial invariant ideal of a given simple loop. In that sense, the approach of computing polynomial invariant ideals is complete and semidecidable for generating the strongest possible polynomial invariants of a simple loop.*

Theorem 3. *If sequences of assignment statements along different branches in a simple loop body can be executed in any order without affecting the semantics of the body (i.e., different sequences of assignments commute with each other), then the polynomial invariant ideal generation procedure terminates in as many iterations as the number of branches. In other words, the termination does not depend upon the number of program variables changing in the loop, but rather on the number of different sequences of assignments which must be considered.*

An immediate corollary of the above theorem is:

Corollary 1. *If a simple loop body is branch-free, i.e., it is a sequence of assignment statements, the procedure for computing its polynomial invariant ideal terminates in a fixed number of iterations.*

Theorem 4. *If sequences of assignments along different branches in a simple loop body do not commute and assignments are solvable mappings with rational* *numbers as their eigenvalues, then the procedure terminates in at most $m + 1$ iterations, where m is the number of program variables that change in the loop body.*

As the reader would notice, in certain cases, it is possible to precisely capture the semantics of a program in ideal-theoretic terms. In that sense, the semantics of a program can be derived without needing any postcondition or, for that matter, the input/output specification of a program.

2.3   Structural Properties of Logical Theories

We list below some key results of algebraic geometry about polynomial ideals over an algebraically closed field that were used to obtain the above results. It is hoped that this discussion will provide some guidance about what needs to be done to extend the above results to other data structures.

- Hilbert's basis theorem: Every ideal over a Noetherian ring has a finite basis. If we restrict the invariants to be characterized by a radical ideal, we get using Hilbert's basis theorem that there exists a strongest possible invariant obtained from a basis of the polynomial invariant ideal.
- Every algebraic variety (that corresponds to program states) can be decomposed into finitely many irreducible algebraic subvarieties.
- For solvable mappings with rational eigenvalues, progress in computing a polynomial invariant ideal is ensured because the dimension of at least one irreducible component of the variety corresponding to the approximating polynomial invariant ideal increases in every iteration of the fixed point algorithm. This argument appears to be a generalization of the argument used by Cousot and Halbwachs [6] in case of linear inequalities as loop invariants.
- If assignment mappings are restricted to have an invertible mapping (which is the case for solvable mappings), then the primality property of ideals is preserved under inverses of such assignment mappings. This result is used in the proof of termination.
- Ideal-theoretic operations, including intersections of ideals, elimination ideals, radical ideals, quotient ideals, can be algorithmically performed using Gröbner basis algorithms.

It will be interesting to see how many of the above stated properties generalize to decidable fragments of theories over other data structures.

A structural property on logical theories that is equivalent to Hilbert's basis theorem for polynomial invariant ideals is likely to require that a subtheory closed under conjunction and implication has a finite axiomatization. It can be easily shown that propositional calculus satisfies this property. This is not surprising since an equivalent characterization of propositional calculus is a boolean ring, which is Noetherian. In [18], an algebraic characterization of quantifier-free first-order predicate calculus with equality is presented. It is shown there that in general, not every subtheory has a finite basis.

3   A Quantifier Elimination Based Approach

"Soft" verification techniques have become popular and effective, of late. Such techniques include type checking, absence of memory leaks, absence of null pointers, array range-bound techniques, shape analysis of container data structures. Perhaps the main reason for their effectiveness is that efficient incomplete techniques can be developed for such limited kind of static program analysis in contrast to full program verification. Another reason for the popularity of such analyses is that programs can be analyzed as they are, instead of requiring additional annotations or a formal specification of their behavior.

The approach discussed in this section has similar advantages. It is assumed that the shape of possible invariant properties of programs of interest is known. Perhaps, the shape information can be determined from the postcondition associated with the program or by doing an a priori analysis of the program body. This requirement is similar in spirit to the design of an abstract domain required in the abstract interpretation framework introduced by Cousot [5].

In this section, we give an overview of an approach that (i) hypothesizes parameterized assertions at appropriate control points in a program, (ii) generates verification conditions from them, (iii) uses quantifier elimination techniques to generate constraints on parameters such that (iv) parameter values satisfying these constraints lead to valid verification conditions. The hypothesized assertions instantiated with these parameter values are then invariants. It will become evident that it is not necessary to do full quantifier-elimination; instead it suffices to generate a quantifier-free formula equivalent to $\forall \mathbf{X} \; \Gamma(\mathbf{P}, \mathbf{X})$, where Γ is also quantifier-free, $\mathbf{P}$ are the parameters in hypothesized assertions, and $\mathbf{X}$ are the program variables.

3.1   Parameterized Polynomial Relations for Expressing Shapes

A program is annotated at a sufficient number of control points (such as the entry of every loop, entry and exit of a procedure body, etc.) with formulas expressed using program variables and unknown parameters, with the specific values of the parameters determining the invariant.

Example 2 Continued.: Let us assume that the quantifier-free theory of parameterized Presburger arithmetic is used for specifying invariants. I.e., an invariant $I(i, j)$ is hypothesized at the loop entry to be an inequality of the form $c_1 i + c_2 j + d \leq 0$, where c_1, c_2, d are unknown parameters. Values of c_1, c_2, d determine the shape of the invariant. That is, for example, if $c_1 = 0$, then i will not appear in the invariant.[8]

The following verification conditions are generated using the hypothesized parameterized formula. As in [6], it is assumed that the boolean test b_2 in the conditional statement is not an inequality; so it is abstracted to be **true**; if it

---

[8] Of course, if $c_1 = 0, c_2 = 0, d = 0$, then the above formula simplifies to **true**, a trivial invariant.'

was a linear inequality, it could have been used to further refine the verification conditions. These conditions are given by

$(c_1 i + c_2 j + d \leq 0) \Rightarrow ((c_1 i + c_2 j + d) + 4c_1 \leq 0)$ and
$(c_1 i + c_2 j + d \leq 0) \Rightarrow ((c_1 i + c_2 j + d) + 2c_1 + c_2 \leq 0)$.

And, from the initial values of program variables i, j, the condition on the parameters c, d is that $2c_1 + d \leq 0$.

There are two technical problems to address: (i) Does a given program location of interest satisfy a nontrivial invariant of the given shape? (ii) If it does, what is such an invariant, i.e., can parameter values be found so that when instantiated with these specific values, the formula is indeed an invariant associated with the program location? Both of these questions are answered using quantifier-elimination by generating constraints on parameters from the verification conditions. The first problem is solved by checking the validity of a formula $\exists\, \mathbf{P}\, \forall\, \mathbf{X}\, \Gamma(\mathbf{P}, \mathbf{X})$, where $\Gamma(\mathbf{P}, \mathbf{X})$ is a conjunction of quantifier-free verification conditions. The second problem is solved by finding a quantifier-free formula only in $\mathbf{P}$ equivalent to $\forall\, \mathbf{X}\, \Gamma(\mathbf{P}, \mathbf{X})$. Elimination techniques and related heuristics are used to get constraints on these parameters, so that for any value of parameters satisfying these constraints, the instantiated hypothesized parameterized formula is indeed an invariant. To get the strongest possible invariant of the hypothesized form, a complete quantifier-elimination method is required. However, incomplete elimination heuristics can also be useful in deriving invariants.

For the above example 2, for an invariant of the above shape to exist,

$\Phi = \exists c_1, c_2, d \quad [\forall i, j, \quad \Gamma(c_1, c_2, d, i, j)]$, where
$\Gamma(c_1, c_2, d, i, j) = [(2c_1 + d \leq 0)$
$\qquad \wedge ((c_1 i + c_2 j + d \leq 0) \Rightarrow ((c_1 i + c_2 j + d) + 4c_1 \leq 0))$
$\qquad \wedge ((c_1 i + c_2 j + d \leq 0) \Rightarrow ((c_1 i + c_2 j + d) + 2c_1 + c_2 \leq 0))]$

needs to be valid over the integers, which is indeed the case. Had Φ not been valid, the invariant of the form $c_1 i + c_2 j + d \leq 0$ would not exist.[9]

It should be noted that these formulas fall outside the language of standard Presburger arithmetic. However, it is from the theory of parameterized Presburger arithmetic, in which coefficients of variables can be linear polynomials in parameters [16].

To generate an invariant, values of c_1, c_2, d that make $\forall i, j, \quad \Gamma(c_1, c_2, d, i, j)$ valid need to be computed. After eliminating i, j, the following equivalent quantifier-free formula can be generated:

$[(2c_1 + d \leq 0) \wedge (c_1 = 0 \vee c_1 < 0) \wedge ((c_1 = 0 \wedge c_2 \leq 0) \vee (c_1 \neq 0 \wedge (2c_1 + 2c_2) \leq 0))].$

The above constraints can be simplified to

$\Psi = [(d \leq 0 \wedge c_1 = 0 \wedge c_2 \leq 0) \vee (2c_1 + d \leq 0 \wedge c_1 < 0 \wedge 2c_1 + c_2 \leq 0)].$

For any values c_1, c_2, d that satisfy the above formula, $c_1 i + c_2 j + d \leq 0$ is an invariant. As an example, $c_1 = -2$, $c_2 = 0, d = 0$ satisfies the above constraints.

---

[9] In certain cases, the trivial invariant, true, e.g., obtained by making each of c_1, c_2, d to be 0, always exists. We are however interested in nontrivial invariants of the hypothesized shape.

Substituting for these values of parameters in the above template leads to $-2i \leq 0$ being an invariant. In fact, there are infinitely many values of c_1, c_2, d satisfying the above constraints.

Infinitely many solutions of Ψ can be obtained in terms of a generator set consisting of $\langle c_1 = 0, c_2 = -1, d = 0 \rangle$, $\langle c_1 = -1, c_2 = 2, d = 2 \rangle$ [34], such that every linear combination of these vectors is a solution of Ψ. Corresponding to each generator, there is an invariant obtained by substituting for these values of parameters into the above template. The conjunction of the invariants corresponding to these generators is $(-j \leq 0 \wedge -i + 2j + 2 \leq 0)$. This formula can be shown to be the strongest invariant expressed as a conjunction of linear inequalities for the above loop. The invariant $-2i \leq 0$, for example, is implied by it.

Note also that the above verification condition Γ can be augmented with additional constraints on parameters to get more specific invariants; in particular, to eliminate the trivial invariant, it can be augmented with $\neg(c_1 = 0 \wedge c_2 = 0 \wedge d = 0)$.

To generate a strongest possible invariant, there are two conditions which must be satisfied. Firstly, it should be possible for the subtheory from which parameterized formulas are drawn, to admit full quantifier-elimination. Secondly, in the generation of verification conditions, no approximation is made about the behavior of programming constructs. Both of these requirements can however be relaxed, but then the proposed approach may not generate the strongest possible invariant for a program. Further, even if the proposed approach declares that there does not exist any nontrivial invariant of the hypothesized shape because of approximations made, an invariant of the hypothesized shape may still exist.

Neither of these two conditions were met for the above example. Even then the strongest invariant expressed as linear inequalities is generated. This suggests that these conditions do not always have to be satisfied to derive the strongest possible invariants.

It is not essential for the subtheory to admit "complete" quantifier-elimination in order to extract useful information. Incomplete heuristics can be used instead. The semantics of a programming construct can be approximated to ensure that the resulting verification conditions are expressible in the underlying subtheory. As was the case in the above example, if a boolean test in a conditional statement or a loop cannot be expressed in the underlying subtheory, then it can be approximated with a weaker condition implied by the original test. In the worst case, it can always be approximated by **true**. Similarly for assignment statements, their effect can be approximated as well.

If an invariant for the above loop in Example 2 is hypothesized to be an nontrivial linear equation, the reader can verify that there does not exist such an nontrivial invariant (e.g., if $I(i, j) = (c_1 i + c_2 j + d = 0)$), since eliminating i, j, d from the verification condition results in $c_1 = 0, c_2 = 0, d = 0$, which simplifies I to the trivial invariant **true**).

As stated earlier, the above example was done using the theory of parameterized Presburger arithmetic. In [16], we discussed two additional subtheories to illustrate this approach: (i) the theory of algebraically closed fields (with $+, *, =$ as the primitive operations), and (iii) the theory of real-closed fields (with $+, *, =, \leq$ as the primitive operations). For each of these subtheories, parameterized invariants restricting the shape can be expressed. An example illustrating the use of (i) is discussed below. Even though the theory of real closed fields admits quantifier-elimination and formulas in this theory are an excellent candidate for specifying properties of programs, quantifier-elimination methods are quite impractical, even though they happen to be of the similar complexity as quantifier-elimination methods on other theories, including parameterized Presburger arithmetic and theory of algebraically closed fields. An interesting research problem is whether the special structure of formulas arising as verification conditions can be exploited to develop specialized heuristics for (incomplete) quantifier-elimination to generate useful nontrivial invariants expressed as nonlinear inequalities over the reals. An interested reader may consult [28] for some such attempts.

The approach discussed in this section can be used to automatically generate invariants for programs with nested loops and procedure calls, as illustrated in [16]. Below we discuss example 1 to illustrate how nonlinear invariants can be generated using this approach.

Example 1 continued: Example 1 in the introduction can also be handled by hypothesizing an invariant of the loop to have a shape of a polynomial equation where the degree of each term is ≤ 2. That is,

$$I(a, s, t) \Leftrightarrow u_1\, a^2 + u_2\, s^2 + u_3\, t^2 + u_4\, as + u_5\, at + u_6\, st + u_7 a + u_8 s + u_9 t + u_{10} = 0,$$

where $u_1, \ldots, u_{10}$ are parameters. As discussed in detail in [16], constraints on parameters are generated using a heuristic for simplifying parametric polynomials (over the theory of an algebraically closed field), from which a basis for parameter values is generated, leading to multiple independent invariants. Parametric Gröbner basis [14] constructions can also be used for this purpose. Below, we briefly review the derivation.

After eliminating program variables a, s, t from the verification condition, the following constraints on parameters are generated. Each of u_2, u_4, u_6 becomes 0, implying that the hypothesized shape of polynomial invariants can be further restricted by dropping out terms s^2, as, st. The following relations among other parameters are generated:

1. $u_1 = -u_5$, 2. $u_7 = -2u_3 - u_5 + 2u_{10}$, 3. $u_8 = -4u_3 - u_5$, 4. $u_9 = 3u_3 + u_5 - u_{10}$.

The above set of constraints has infinitely many solutions. However, this infinite solution set can be finitely described [34]. Each solution can be obtained from an independent set of 3 solutions obtained by making exactly one of the independent parameters, u_3, u_5 and u_{10}, to be 1, generating three invariants

$$t = 2a + 1, \quad s = -a^2 + at - a + t, \quad 4s = t^2 - 2a + 3t.$$

The reader would have noticed that these invariants are somewhat different from the ones given in the introduction. They are however logically equivalent. In fact, each of the above three invariants is also an inductive invariant. Whereas $s = (a+1)^2$ is a loop invariant, it is not an inductive invariant, as stated earlier. This invariant can be derived by combining $t = 2a+1$ and $s = -a^2 + at - a + t$. Further, the first invariant is independent. The second invariant is independent of first one but not of the third one: It can be derived from the first one and third one. Similarly, the third invariant can be derived from the first and second. Even though these invariants were generated from independent solutions of a linear system of equations, variables standing for various power products in the linear system are related (particularly, a, at and t are related). To get a set of independent invariants, it thus becomes necessary to check derivability of one from the others.

It is even possible to show termination of the loop in Example 1 using templates. Assuming a linear polynomial in the program variables a, s, and t can be used to show the termination of the loop, a template in a, s, and t can be hypothesized which takes values over the integers bounded from below (e.g., nonnegative integers or integers ≥ -20) and with the condition that every time, the loop body is executed, its values goes down.

3.2   Specifying Shape by Restricting Polynomial Degree

In [30], we proposed a method based on the framework of abstract interpretation [5] for generating polynomial equations of a certain degree as invariants. Restricting the degree of a polynomial is another way of generically specifying the shape of invariants.

In Section 2, we defined the semantics of programming language constructs ideal-theoretically. Tests expressed as disequalities in conditional statements and loops can be handled as well. For giving the semantics of a loop that can be executed arbitrarily many times, a widening operator á la abstract interpretation framework was exploited for approximating the semantics.

As an example, consider the loop with a single assignment statement of the form:

$$x := x+1.$$

Depending upon the initial value of x, say i, after the loop body has been executed two times, we have: $x = i \lor x = i+1 \lor x = i+2$, which is equivalent to the polynomial equation $(x-i)*(x-(i+1))*(x-(i+2)) = 0$. Assuming that there is no a priori restriction on the number of times the loop body is executed, it is easy to see that there is no polynomial invariant (of any degree) involving just x. However, if a loop test restricts x to take a finite value, then there is a polynomial invariant of the degree bounded by the maximum value of x (minus i). If the shape of polynomial invariants is restricted to be of a certain fixed degree, then depending upon the number of times the loop body is executed, this approach may or may not generate a polynomial invariant.

In [30], we defined a widening operator based on the degree of polynomial invariants of interest. Using this widening operator and exploiting the property that any finite-dimensional vector space has a finite basis, we proved that the algorithm for computing invariants will reach a fixed point in finitely many steps using the proposed widening operator. This also gives us a completeness result, namely that if tests in conditional statements and loops are ignored, and if all right hand sides of assignments are linear, then the approach finds all polynomial invariants of degree $\leq d$ for any given d.

The experimental results of this method are given in Table 1 below; the method was implemented by Carbonell in the Macaulay system, and timings were obtained using the software running a Pentium 4, 2.5 GHZ pc running Linux. More details can be found in [28]. This approach is able to automatically generate polynomial invariants for a large class of programs involving nested loops and computing number-theoretic functions.

3.3   Non-numeric Theories

The proposed approach seems quite promising since a number of theories and their combination admit quantifier-elimination [17]. Even if a quantifier-elimination procedure is too expensive or is incomplete, a number of useful heuristics can be developed to generate constraints on parameters and thus obtain useful invariants automatically.

We enumerate below requirements on a theory for this approach to succeed.

1. It should be possible to specify interesting program properties in parametric form in the theory.
2. It should be possible to approximate the semantics of programming language constructs so as to capture nontrivial properties of programs as well as generate verification conditions in the theory.
3. It should be possible to "easily" generate constraints on parameters which ensure that the verification conditions generated using the program semantics and the parametric hypothesized invariants are valid.
4. These constraints on parameters should be solvable, preferably in most general form. Each such solution of constraints on parameters instantiates a parameterized formula, resulting in an invariant.

Combination of Theories. In this subsection, we show how parameterized formulas over a combination of theories can be used as templates for invariants. A useful combination of theories is that of Presburger arithmetic and quantifier-free theory of equality over uninterpreted symbols [36,26]. This combination of theories is well-supported in SMT solvers along with other theories for which tremendous progress in their implementation has been reported recently. An uninterpreted symbol could be used to model a function call about which nothing can be assumed, or to model memory access, or could stand for a number theoretic function, such as $*, exp$, not expressible in Presburger arithmetic. Consider a simple program from [12], in which f has been used to model memory.

Table 1. Examples

Program	It Computes	Source	No. of Loops	No. of Variables	No. of Invariants	Time
cohencu	cube	[2]	5	1	3	0.94s
cohendiv	division	[2]	6	2	1-3	0.65s
wensley	division	[37]	6	1	3	0.99s
divbin	division	[13]	5	2	2-1	0.99s
mannadiv	division	[22]	6	2	1-3	1.12s
hard	division	[33]	6	2	3-3	1.31s
euclidex1	extended gcd	[20]	10	2	3-4	5.63s
euclidex3	extended gcd	[20]	12	3	2-3-5	8.53s
fermat1	divisor	[1]	5	3	1-1-1	0.89s
fermat2	divisor	[1]	5	1	1	0.92s
knuth	divisor	[20]	7	1	1	2.61s
lcm1	lcm	[33]	6	3	1-1-1	1.22s
lcm2	lcm	[9]	6	1	1	1.21s
sqrt	square root	[22]	3	1	2	0.46s
z3sqrt	square root	[35]	4	1	1	0.82s
dijkstra	square root	[9]	5	2	2-1	1.31s
freire1	square root	[10]	3	1	1	0.38s
freire2	cubic root	[10]	4	1	4	0.85s
petter1	power sum	[27]	2	1	1	.5s
petter2	power sum	[27]	2	1	1	.8s
petter3	power sum	[27]	2	1	1	4.2s
petter4	power sum	[27]	2	1	1	t/o
petter5	power sum	[27]	2	1	1	t/o
readers	simulation	[33]	6	1	3	1.95s
illinois	protocol	[8]	4	1	5	7.68s
mesi	protocol	[8]	3	1	2	2.65s
moesi	protocol	[8]	4	1	5	4.28s
berkeley	protocol	[8]	4	1	4	2.74s
firefly	protocol	[8]	4	1	5	5.01s

Example 4. **var** $a1, a2, b1, b2, c1, c2$: integer **end var**
$\quad a1 := 0;\ a2 := 0;\ b1 := 1;\ b2 := f(1);\ c1 := 3;\ c2 := f(4);$
$\quad$ **while** $a1 < 100$ **do**
$\qquad a1 := a1 + 1;\ a2 := a2 + 2;\ b1 := f(b1);\ b2 := f(b2);$
$\qquad c1 := f(c1 + 1);\ c2 := f(c2 + 1)$
end while

A parameterized formula in this combined theory can be a linear inequality (or equality) over program variables and expressions built using uninterpreted function symbols which can have linear polynomials as arguments (to stand for an index expression or location expression in case f as an array, for example).

It is thus of the form $A_0 + A_1 t_1 + \cdots \ldots + A_k t_k = 0$ or ≤ 0, where A_i are parameters and t_i is either a variable or a term with an uninterpreted symbol whose arguments either have uninterpreted symbols or $+$ as the outermost symbols.[10]

Associate a parametric formula as an inductive assertion at the loop entry of the above program and generate verification conditions. For the above loop, let us hypothesize an invariant of the form

$$I : A_1 \ a1 + A_2 \ a2 + B_1 \ b1 + B_2 \ b2 + C_1 \ c1 + C_2 \ c2 + E+$$

$$F_1 \ f(A_1' \ a1 + A_2' \ a2 + B_1' \ b1 + B_2' \ b2 + C_1' \ c1 + C_2' \ c2 + E') = 0,$$

where $A_1, A_2, B_1, B_2, C_1, C_2, E, F_1, A_1', A_2', B_1', B_2', C_1', C_2', E'$ are parameters and $a1, a2, b1, b2, c1, c2$ are program variables. Assuming that f is an array, then the above formula expresses a relation between program variables and a single array access.

The verification condition at the loop entry has two parts:

$$VC_0 : B_1 + B_2 \ f(1) + 3C_1 + C_2 \ f(4) + E + F_1 f(B_1' + B_2' \ f(1) + 3C_1' + C_2' \ f(4) + E') = 0,$$

when the loop is entered for the first time, and

$$VC_1 : (I \wedge a1 < 100) \implies (A_1 \ (a1 + 1) + A_2 \ (a2 + 2) + B_1 \ f(b1) + B_2 \ f(b2)+$$

$$C_1 \ f(c1 + 1) + C_2 \ f(c2 + 1) + E + F_1 f(A_1' \ (a1 + 1) + A_2' \ (a2 + 2)+$$

$$B_1' \ f(b1) + B_2' \ f(b2) + C_1' \ f(c1 + 1) + C_2' \ f(c2 + 1) + E') = 0)$$

for an arbitrary iteration of the loop. If a postcondition had been specified, then $I \wedge a1 \geq 100$ should also imply that postcondition; further, the postcondition could have been used to impose restrictions on the template, particularly in terms of program variables likely to appear in I.

The goal once again is to find parameters values which make the above verification conditions valid for all possible values of program variables. To generate constraints on parameters that ensure the validity of the verification conditions over the combined theory of linear arithmetic and equality theory of uninterpreted symbols is equivalent to generating parameter constraints which make the negation of the conjunction of the verification conditions unsatisfiable. In general, the problem is then to generate parameter constraints which make a parameterized quantifier-free formula over a combined theory unsatisfiable. This can be done as follows.

1. A mixed parameterized formula expressed over arithmetic and uninterpreted symbols is purified by introducing new constant symbols to stand for pure terms in arithmetic and expressions built using uninterpreted symbols (see [23] for the purification step).

---

[10] Notice that a formula of the form $f(...) = g(...)$ also has the above form $f(...) - g(....) = 0$.

The output of this step is a conjunction of two pure parameterized sub-formulas — one over arithmetic and another over quantifier-free theory of equality over uninterpreted symbols, with these subformulas sharing variables/constants and the equality symbol.

2. The result can, in principle, be converted into disjunctive normal form even though there may be better heuristics which do not involve explicit conversion to disjunctive normal form. Each conjunction of literals in arithmetic or equality theory is then considered as discussed below.

3. As in Nelson-Oppen's method for combining decision procedures of quantifier-free theories [26], for every possible equivalence relation equating shared constant symbols between pure formulas and disequating otherwise, it is checked whether there exist parameter values which make every conjunction from the disjunctive normal form unsatisfiable. If the answer is affirmative, then those parameter values yield an invariant.

4. If there are infinitely many parameter values which make every conjunction unsatisfiable, a finite description of these parameter values is then generated, if possible, to obtain the strongest possible invariant.

Since an example illustrating this combined theory is not discussed in any of our papers, we provide more details in the next subsection.

Generating Constraints on Parameters for a Combined Theory after Quantifier Elimination. From the negation of the verification conditions, after purification and conversion to disjunctive normal form, we have the following conjunctions (expressed as a set of literals) after introduction of new constants (represented by w_i's). We discuss below an incomplete heuristic for generating constraints on parameters from which invariants for the above loop can be derived.

It is easy to see that each of these conjunctions can be separated into two parts: a set of literals in Presburger arithmetic and another set of literals in the theory of equality over uninterpreted symbols.

$$NVC_0 : \{w_1 = 1, w_2 = 4, w_3 = f(w_1), w_4 = f(w_2),$$
$$w_5 = B_1' + B_2' \, w_3 + 3C_1' + C_2' \, w_4 + E', \ w_6 = f(w_5),$$
$$B_1 + B_2 \, w_3 + 3C_1 + C_2 \, w_4 + E + F_1 \, w_6 \neq 0\}.$$

$$NVC_1 : \{a1 < 100, w_7 = A_1' \, a1 + A_2' \, a2 + B_1' \, b1 + B_2' \, b2 + C_1' \, c1 + C_2' \, c2 + E',$$
$$w_8 = f(w_7), A_1 \, a1 + A_2 \, a2 + B_1 \, b1 + B_2 \, b2 + C_1 \, c1 + C_2 \, c2 + E + F_1 \, w_8 = 0,$$
$$w_9 = a1 + 1, w_{10} = a2 + 2, w_{11} = f(b1), w_{12} = f(b2), w_{13} = c1 + 1,$$
$$w_{14} = f(w_{13}), w_{15} = c2 + 1, w_{16} = f(w_{15}), w_{18} = f(w_{17}),$$
$$w_{17} = A_1' \, a1 + A_1' + A_2' \, a2 + 2A_2' + B_1' w_{11} + B_2' w_{12} + C_1' w_{14} + C_2' w_{16} + E',$$
$$A_1 \, a1 + A_1 + A_2 \, a2 + 2A_2 + B_1 \, w_{11} + B_2 \, w_{12} + C_1 \, w_{14} + C_2 \, w_{16} + E + F_1 \, w_{18} \neq 0\}.$$

A complete method can be obtained by considering all possible equivalence relations on shared constants w_i's and program variables among the subformulas from the two theories. For each such equivalence relation, parameter constraints are generated, if any, to make the conjunction unsatisfiable. Recent advances in SMT technology can be exploited so as to optimize parameter constraint generation without having to explicitly consider all possible equivalence relations on shared constants among pure formulas in different theories.

Below, we illustrate a heuristic on the above example by generating constraints on parameters by focusing on making the first conjunction NVC_0, the negation of the first verification condition VC_0, unsatisfiable.

An easy way to make NVC_0 unsatisfiable is to make all parameters in the negated literal to be 0; this leaves only A_1, A_2, and the primed parameters to be determined. NVC_1, the negation of the second verification condition VC_1, simplifies under these instantiations to

$$\{a1 < 100, w_7 = A_1'\ a1 + A_2'\ a2 + B_1'\ b1 + B_2'\ b2 + C_1'\ c1 + C_2'\ c2 + E', w_8 = f(w_7),$$

$$A_1\ a1 + A_2\ a2 = 0, w_9 = a1 + 1, w_{10} = a2 + 2, w_{11} = f(b1), w_{12} = f(b2),$$

$$w_{13} = c1 + 1, w_{14} = f(w_{13}), w_{15} = c2 + 1, w_{16} = f(w_{15}), w_{18} = f(w_{17}),$$

$$w_{17} = A_1'\ a1 + A_1' + A_2'\ a2 + 2A_2' + B_1' w_{11} + B_2' w_{12} + C_1' w_{14} + C_2' w_{16} + E',$$

$$A_1\ a1 + A_1 + A_2\ a2 + 2A_2 \neq 0\}.$$

This set is unsatisfiable if $A_1 = -2A_2$ because of the literals $A_1\ a1 + A_2\ a2 = 0, A_1\ a1 + A_1 + A_2\ a2 + 2A_2 \neq 0$. These parameter constraints, along with all other parameters made 0, make both conjunctions unsatisfiable, leading to $2a1 - a2 = 0$ as an invariant.

There are other ways to make NVC_0 unsatisfiable, particularly by again considering the last literal $B_1 + B_2\ w_3 + 3C_1 + C_2\ w_4 + E + F_1\ w_6 \neq 0$. Since $w_6 = f(w_5), w_3 = f(1), w_4 = f(4)$, the following two possibilities are considered by instantiating $B_1 = C_1 = E = 0$. (i) $C_2 = 0, B_2 = 1, F_1 = -1$, which simplifies the last literal to $w_3 - w_6$. If we make w_5 equal to 1, then the last literal is unsatisfiable. Making $B_1' = 1$ and all other parameters 0 leads to $w_5 = 1$. After these instantiations of parameters, NVC_1 is unsatisfiable since it includes literals $b2 - f(b1) = 0$ and $f(b2) - f(f(b1)) \neq 0$.

Substituting for the parameter values into the above template produces $b2 = f(b1)$ as an invariant.

(ii) Similarly, instantiating $B_2 = 0, C_2 = 1, F_1 = -1$ simplifies the last literal in NVC_0 to $w_4 - w_6$. If we make w_5 to be 4, by making $B_1' = 0, C_1' = 1, E' = 1$ and all other parameters 0, NVC_0 becomes unsatisfiable. NVC_1 also becomes unsatisfiable, leading to parameter values, which when used to instantiate the above template, gives the invariant $c2 = f(c1 + 1)$.

Both of these invariants relate array contents to program variables.[11] Each of these constraint sets on parameters are independent, thus leading to independent invariants. Other invariants can be generated in a similar fashion.

As this example illustrates, parameterized formulas in the combined theory of Presburger arithmetic and theory of equality of interpreted symbols can be used as candidates for invariants for programs in which assignments are expressed using addition and array accesses.

As shown in [21], the first-order theory of Boolean algebra admits quantifier-elimination. Kuncak has used this theory and its combination with Presburger arithmetic for analyzing shapes of lists and related container data structures. It will be interesting to identify parameterized formulas in this theory for specifying properties about container data structures.

In [19], we have proposed a *reduction approach* for generating decision procedures for quantifier-free theories over complex data structures. A formula expressing a property of a complex data structure can be transformed into an equivalent formula in Presburger arithmetic combined with uninterpreted function symbols. This approach has been used to generate decision procedure for quantifier-free theories over finite sets, finite multisets, finite lists, and finite arrays, by just using a combination of decision procedures for quantifier-free Presburger arithmetic and the theory of equality over uninterpreted symbols. In [17], a number of results about theories admitting quantifier elimination are discussed which can be useful for making the proposed approach more widely applicable.

4   Concluding Remarks

We have discussed two different approaches for automatically generating loop invariants. Both approaches depend upon elimination methods. While the approach based on polynomial ideal theory is exact and does not require any information other than the program, it is less likely to generalize since it relies heavily on beautiful results from algebraic geometry which have taken many years to arrive at. It is indeed the case that after all, the computer representation of all data structures are numbers, but it is less clear whether manipulations of number representations of data structures can be modeled using polynomials; so it is an intriguing issue whether this approach carries over after suitable number encodings of other data structures. Nevertheless, this approach suggests developing elegant decidable fragments and structural properties of theories over data structures used in programs.

The second approach based on knowing a priori shapes of invariants seems a lot more promising since it reduces to constraint solving in combination of theories. A challenge here is to identify relevant shapes of invariants of interest as well as to develop heuristics to determine from a loop body, the likely shapes of loop invariants. A related topic for further investigation is to use postconditions for guessing

---

[11] For the above program, straightforward dependency analysis would have suggested that array indices depend only b_i's and c_j's; this information could have been used to propose a simpler template.

shapes of loop invariants. This approach is also related to the abstract interpretation approach of Cousot for program analysis, which has been found quite effective in on commercial software in many applications for finding as well as ensuring the absence of certain kinds of bugs. The choice of an abstract domain in effect determines the shape of properties of programs which are of interest.

Acknowledgments. I am grateful to Enric Rodríguez-Carbonell for our collaboration on the topic of automatic generation of invariants starting from summer 2003 leading to his Ph.D. thesis. I also thank Matthias Forbach for proofreading the final draft and his comments.

References

1. Bressoud, D.: Factorization and Primality Testing. Springer (1989)
2. Cohen, E.: Programming in the 1990s. Springer (1990)
3. Colón, M.A.: Approximating the Algebraic Relational Semantics of Imperative Programs. In: Giacobazzi, R. (ed.) SAS 2004. LNCS, vol. 3148, pp. 296–311. Springer, Heidelberg (2004)
4. Colón, M.A., Sankaranarayanan, S., Sipma, H.B.: Linear Invariant Generation Using Non-linear Constraint Solving. In: Hunt Jr., W.A., Somenzi, F. (eds.) CAV 2003. LNCS, vol. 2725, pp. 420–432. Springer, Heidelberg (2003)
5. Cousot, P., Cousot, R.: Abstract Interpretation: a Unified Lattice Model for Static Analysis of Programs by Construction or Approximation of Fixpoints. In: Conference Record of the Fourth Annual ACM SIGPLAN-SIGACT Symposium on Principles of Programming Languages, Los Angeles, California, pp. 238–252. ACM Press, New York (1977)
6. Cousot, P., Halbwachs, N.: Automatic Discovery of Linear Restraints among Variables of a Program. In: Conference Record of the Fifth Annual ACM SIGPLAN-SIGACT Symposium on Principles of Programming Languages, Tucson, Arizona, pp. 84–97. ACM Press, New York (1978)
7. Cox, D., Little, J., O'Shea, D.: Ideals, Varieties and Algorithms. An Introduction to Computational Algebraic Geometry and Commutative Algebra. Springer (1998)
8. Delzanno, G.: Constraint-based verification of parameterized cache coherence protocols. Formal Methods in System Design 23(3), 257–301 (2003)
9. Dijkstra, E.: A Discipline of Programming. Prentice-Hall (1976)
10. Freire, P.: http://www.pedrofreire.com/crea2_en.htm
11. German, S., Wegbreit, B.: A Synthesizer of Inductive Assertions. IEEE Transactions on Software Engineering 1(1), 68–75 (1975)
12. Gulwani, S., Tiwari, A.: Assertion Checking over Combined Abstraction of Linear Arithmetic and Uninterpreted Functions. In: Sestoft, P. (ed.) ESOP 2006. LNCS, vol. 3924, pp. 279–293. Springer, Heidelberg (2006)
13. Kaldewaij, A.: Programming. The Derivation of Algorithms. Prentice-Hall (1990)
14. Kapur, D.: An approach for solving systems of parametric polynomial equations. In: Saraswat, Hentenryck, V. (eds.) Principles and Practices of Constraint Programming, pp. 217–244. MIT Press (1995)
15. Kapur, D.: Automatically Generating Loop Invariants using Quantifier Elimination. Technical report, Department of Computer Science, University of New Mexico, Albuquerque, NM, USA (2003)
16. Kapur, D.: A Quantifier Elimination based Heuristic for Automatically Generating Inductive Assertions for Programs. J. of Systems Science and Complexity 19(3), 307–330 (2006)

17. Kapur, D., Majumdar, R., Zarba, C.: Interpolation for data structures. In: Proceedings of the 14th ACM SIGSOFT Symp. on Foundations of Software Engineering (2006)
18. Kapur, D., Narendran, P.: An equational approach to theorem proving in first-order predicate calculus. In: Proceedings of the Ninth International Joint Conference on Artificial Intelligence (IJCAI 1985), pp. 1146–1153 (1985)
19. Kapur, D., Zarba, C.: A Reduction Approach to Decison Procedures. Technical Report, Department of Computer Science, UNM, (December 2006)
20. Knuth, D.E.: The Art of Computer Programming. Seminumerical Algorithms, vol. 2. Addison-Wesley (1969)
21. Kuncak, V.: Modular Data Structure Verification. PhD thesis, Department of EECS, MIT, Cambridge, MA (2007)
22. Manna, Z.: Mathematical Theory of Computation. McGraw-Hill (1974)
23. Manna, Z., Zarba, C.: Combining Decision Procedures. In: Formal Methods at the Crossroads: from Panacea to Foundational Support (2003)
24. Müller-Olm, M., Seidl, H.: Program Analysis through Linear Algebra. In: Symposium on Principles of Programming Languages, pp. 330–341 (2004)
25. Müller-Olm, M., Petter, M., Seidl, H.: Interprocedurally Analyzing Polynomial Identities. In: Durand, B., Thomas, W. (eds.) STACS 2006. LNCS, vol. 3884, pp. 50–67. Springer, Heidelberg (2006)
26. Nelson, G.: Techniques for Program Verification. PhD thesis, Department of Computer Science, Stanford University, Palo Alto, CA (1981)
27. Petter, M.: Berechnung von polynomiellen invarianten. Master's thesis, Fakultät für Informatik, Technische Universität München (2004), http://www2.cs.tum.edu/~petter/da
28. Rodríguez-Carbonell, E.: Automatic Generation of Polynomial Invariants for System Verification. PhD thesis, Universitat Politecnica de Catalunya (2006)
29. Rodríguez-Carbonell, E., Kapur, D.: Automatic Generation of Polynomial Loop Invariants: Algebraic Foundations. In: Intl. Symp. on Symbolic and Algebraic Computation (ISSAC), pp. 266–273 (July 2004)
30. Rodríguez-Carbonell, E., Kapur, D.: Automatic generation of polynomial invariants of bounded degree using abstract interpretation. J. of Science of Programming 64(1), 54–75 (2007)
31. Rodríguez-Carbonell, E., Kapur, D.: Generating all polynomial invariants in simple loops. J. of Symbolic Computation 42(4), 443–476 (2007)
32. Rodríguez-Carbonell, E., Kapur, D.: An Abstract Interpretation Approach for Automatic Generation of Polynomial Invariants. In: Giacobazzi, R. (ed.) SAS 2004. LNCS, vol. 3148, pp. 280–295. Springer, Heidelberg (2004)
33. Sankaranarayanan, S., Sipma, H., Manna, Z.: Non-linear Loop Invariant Generation using Gröbner Bases. In: Symp. on Principles of Programming Languages (2004)
34. Schrijver, A.: Theory of Linear and Integer Programming. John Wiley (1998)
35. Shelburne, B.J.: Zuse's Z3 square root algorithm, http://www4.wittenberg.edu/academics/mathcomp/bjsdir/ZuseZ3Talk.pdf
36. Shostak, R.: A Practical Decision Procedure for Arithmetic with Function Symbols. J. ACM 26(2), 351–360 (1979)
37. Wegbreit, B.: The Synthesis of Loop Predicates. Communications of the ACM 17(2), 102–112 (1974)
38. Wu, W.: Basic principles of mechanical theorem proving in geometries. J. of Automated Reasoning 2, 221–252 (1986)

Narrowing Based Inductive Proof Search

Claude Kirchner[1], Hélène Kirchner[1], and Fabrice Nahon[2]

[1] INRIA France
`first.last@inria.fr`
[2] Rectorat Nancy-Metz, France
`fabricenahon@googlemail.com`

In memory of Harald Ganzinger

Abstract. We present in this paper a narrowing-based proof search method for inductive theorems. It has the specificity to be grounded on deduction modulo and to yield a direct translation from a successful proof search derivation to a proof in the sequent calculus. The method is shown to be sound and refutationally correct in a proof theoretical way.

Keywords: deduction modulo, sequent calculus modulo, induction, Noetherian induction, induction by rewriting, equational reasoning, term rewriting.

Introduction

Proof by induction is a main reasoning principle and is of prime interest in informatics and mathematics. Typically in hardware and software verification problems, reasoning on complex data structures with infinite data or states make a prominent use of induction and most deep mathematical theorem proofs rely on induction. Two main approaches have been developed for mechanizing induction proof: explicit induction, used in proof assistants, and implicit induction by rewriting, used in automated theorem provers. This work was motivated by the need to have a better understanding of the relation between them. Thanks to the *deduction modulo* framework, explicit induction is applied to generate smaller instances of the property to be proved. These instances can then be used by the modulo part to implicitly simplify the goals, thanks to a sequent calculus modulo.

In this context, we provide a proof search mechanism for such inductive proofs. We show how the induction step can be performed by narrowing at innermost positions when the theory is axiomatized by a sufficiently complete and convergent rewrite system. This allows us to make precise the relationship between rewrite-based automated inductive theorem provers like Spike or RRL and case analysis in proof assistants like Coq or PVS.

We provide a proof theoretic foundation to the proof search procedure which is described by deduction rules that are proved valid in the sequent calculus modulo. This provides the ability to build a proof term for a proof assistant and

A. Voronkov and C. Weidenbach (Eds.): Ganzinger Festschrift, LNCS 7797, pp. 216–238, 2013.

therefore to be able to formally validate the proof search result. So, starting from the (inductive) proposition to be proved, the proof search mechanism builds a proof in the sequent calculus modulo, from which a proof term can be computed if needed.

This paper was presented at the event organized in 2005 to celebrate Harald Ganzinger's memory and research contributions.

The paper is built over the works and results on deduction modulo [13], first-order presentation of higher-order logic [12], formalization of induction in deduction modulo [7,8] and on preliminary results on narrowing for induction presented in [9]. We provide first a summary of these approaches in Section 1 to motivate the main idea of narrowing based induction proof search. Section 2 introduces two basic ingredients of the method: ordering on equalities and narrowing with sufficiently complete rewrite systems. Then Section 3 presents the proof search system for inductive proofs, which is proved sound and refutationally correct.

For the main notations and classical results on term rewriting, we refer to the books on that topics like [1] or [20].

1 Deduction Modulo and the Noetherian Induction Principle

Proofs by structural induction are of main use in proof assistants where the structural induction principle is generally automatically generated from the definition of the inductive data types. However, by using sophisticated termination orderings, proofs by Noetherian induction performed by rewriting are much more expressive than structural induction. We recall in this section how deduction modulo can provide the description, at the proof theoretical level, of proof by Noetherian induction.

1.1 Deduction Modulo

Let $\mathcal{T}(\Sigma, \mathcal{X})$ be the set of terms build over the signature Σ and the denumerable set of variables $\mathcal{X}$. We assume for simplicity Σ to be one-sorted, so that any term is of sort τ. Terms are denoted by letters s, t, u, v, l, r, variables by x, y, z, X, Y, Z, vectors of variables by $\overrightarrow{x}$, and substitutions on terms by Greek letters α, β, γ. $Subst^{\mathcal{T}(\Sigma,\mathcal{X})}$ denotes the set of substitutions on $\mathcal{T}(\Sigma, \mathcal{X})$.

Provided a Noetherian relation R and a user defined theory Th_u, we are looking for a proof of a proposition P using a Noetherian induction principle denoted $NoethInd$, in the sense of finding a derivation of the sequent:

$$NoethInd(R), Th_u \vdash P$$

The Noetherian induction principle being by essence a second order proposition, this is indeed a sequent in higher-order logic.

Since we want to make a primarily use of first-order rewrite concepts and techniques and to consider first-order theories, we need a first-order presentation of higher-order logic. We use the so-called $HOL_{\lambda\sigma}$ introduced in [12] which is based on deduction modulo [13] and reveals to be particularly well-suited for our concerns. It is clearly out of the scope of this paper to explain in detail the full approach, and we only sketch here the main ideas. The reader can refer to [7] and to [8] for a detailed exposition.

In deduction modulo, terms but also propositions can be identified modulo a congruence. We use a congruence that can typically be defined by conditional equalities and that takes into account the application context to evaluate the conditions. Furthermore, since the congruence application should be controlled closely, an appropriate notion of protective symbol is used, see [7]: actually the congruence is not allowed to act below a protective symbol. In deduction modulo, the notions of term and proposition come from many-sorted first-order logic. We consider theories described by a set of axioms Γ and a congruence, denoted $\sim$, defined on terms and propositions. This congruence takes three arguments: the two objects to be compared and a set of axioms Γ called a local context. When we want to emphasize this, we denote the congruence $\sim^\Gamma$. The deduction rules of the sequent calculus take this equivalence into account. For instance, the right rule for the conjunction is not stated as usual

$$\frac{\Gamma \vdash A, \Delta \quad \Gamma \vdash B, \Delta}{\Gamma \vdash A \wedge B, \Delta}$$

but is formulated

$$\frac{\Gamma \vdash_\sim A, \Delta \quad \Gamma \vdash_\sim B, \Delta}{\Gamma \vdash_\sim D, \Delta} \text{ if } D \sim^\Gamma A \wedge B.$$

We recall in Figure 1, the definition of the *sequent calculus modulo*. In these rules, Γ and Δ are finite multisets of propositions, P and Q denote propositions. Substituting the variable x by the term u in Q is denoted $Q\{u/x\}$. When the congruence $\sim$ is simply identity, this sequent calculus collapses to the usual one [16]. In that case, sequents are written as usual with the $\vdash$ symbol.

Proof checking decidability for the sequent calculus modulo reduces to the decidability of the relation $\sim^\Gamma$, since we can check for each rule that the conditions of application are satisfied and we provide the needed information in the quantifier rules. When $\sim^\Gamma$ is not decidable, we still can use instances for which one can check the conditions of application, typically using a constraint based approach [17,21]

We can now introduce the fundamental notion of compatibility: a theory (a set of propositions) $\mathcal{T}$ is said to be compatible with a congruence $\sim$ when:

$$\mathcal{T}, \Gamma \vdash \Delta \text{ if and only if } \Gamma \vdash_\sim \Delta.$$

As shown in [7,8], this property is modular: if $\mathcal{T}_1$ is compatible with a congruence C_1 and $\mathcal{T}_2$ is compatible with C_2 then $\mathcal{T}_1 \cup \mathcal{T}_2$ is compatible with $C_1 \cup C_2$.

Using the above equivalence, we can internalize propositions into the congruence, and we call this operation "push". We can also recover them at the level of the logic, and we call this operation "pop". Moreover, thanks to modularity,

$$\frac{}{\Gamma, P \vdash_\sim Q}\text{axiom if } P \sim^\Gamma Q \qquad\qquad \frac{\Gamma, P \vdash_\sim \Delta \quad \Gamma \vdash_\sim Q, \Delta}{\Gamma \vdash_\sim \Delta}\text{cut if } P \sim^\Gamma Q$$

$$\frac{\Gamma, Q_1, Q_2 \vdash_\sim \Delta}{\Gamma, P \vdash_\sim \Delta}\text{contr-l if } (\mathbf{A}) \qquad\qquad \frac{\Gamma \vdash_\sim Q_1, Q_2, \Delta}{\Gamma \vdash_\sim P, \Delta}\text{contr-r if } (\mathbf{A})$$

$$\frac{\Gamma \vdash_\sim \Delta}{\Gamma, P \vdash_\sim \Delta}\text{weak-l} \qquad\qquad \frac{\Gamma \vdash_\sim \Delta}{\Gamma \vdash_\sim P, \Delta}\text{weak-r}$$

$$\frac{\Gamma, P, Q \vdash_\sim \Delta}{\Gamma, R \vdash_\sim \Delta}\wedge\text{-l if } R \sim^\Gamma (P \wedge Q) \qquad\qquad \frac{\Gamma \vdash_\sim P, \Delta \quad \Gamma \vdash_\sim Q, \Delta}{\Gamma \vdash_\sim R, \Delta}\wedge\text{-r if } R \sim^\Gamma (P \wedge Q)$$

$$\frac{\Gamma, P \vdash_\sim \Delta \quad \Gamma, Q \vdash_\sim \Delta}{\Gamma, R \vdash_\sim \Delta}\vee\text{-l if } (\mathbf{B}) \qquad\qquad \frac{\Gamma \vdash_\sim P, Q, \Delta}{\Gamma \vdash_\sim R, \Delta}\vee\text{-r if } (\mathbf{B})$$

$$\frac{\Gamma \vdash_\sim P, \Delta \quad \Gamma, Q \vdash_\sim \Delta}{\Gamma, R \vdash_\sim \Delta}\Rightarrow\text{-l if } (\mathbf{C}) \qquad\qquad \frac{\Gamma, P \vdash_\sim Q, \Delta}{\Gamma \vdash_\sim R, \Delta}\Rightarrow\text{-r if } (\mathbf{C})$$

$$\frac{\Gamma \vdash_\sim P, \Delta}{\Gamma, R \vdash_\sim \Delta}\neg\text{-l if } R \sim^\Gamma \neg P \qquad\qquad \frac{\Gamma, P \vdash_\sim \Delta}{\Gamma \vdash_\sim R, \Delta}\neg\text{-r if } R \sim^\Gamma \neg P$$

$$\frac{}{\Gamma, P \vdash_\sim \Delta}\perp\text{-l if } P \sim^\Gamma \perp$$

$$\frac{\Gamma, Q\{t/x\} \vdash_\sim \Delta}{\Gamma, P \vdash_\sim \Delta}(Q, x, t)\ \forall\text{-l if } (\mathbf{D}) \qquad\qquad \frac{\Gamma \vdash_\sim Q\{y/x\}, \Delta}{\Gamma \vdash_\sim P, \Delta}(Q, x, y)\ \forall\text{-r if } (\mathbf{E})$$

$$\frac{\Gamma, Q\{y/x\} \vdash_\sim \Delta}{\Gamma, P \vdash_\sim \Delta}(Q, x, y)\ \exists\text{-l if } (\mathbf{F}) \qquad\qquad \frac{\Gamma \vdash_\sim Q\{t/x\}, \Delta}{\Gamma \vdash_\sim P, \Delta}(Q, x, t)\ \exists\text{-r if } (\mathbf{G})$$

$\mathbf{A} = P \sim^\Gamma Q_1 \sim^\Gamma Q_2$, $\mathbf{B} = R \sim^\Gamma (P \vee Q)$ $\mathbf{C} = R \sim^\Gamma (P \Rightarrow Q)$, $\mathbf{D} = P \sim^\Gamma \forall x\, Q$, $\mathbf{E} = P \sim^\Gamma \forall x\, Q, y$ fresh variable, $\mathbf{F} = P \sim^\Gamma \exists x\, Q, y$ fresh variable, $\mathbf{G} = P \sim^\Gamma \exists x\, Q$

Fig. 1. The sequent calculus modulo

this can be done dynamically during the proof. This duality between computation and deduction is very conveniently reflected by the compatibility property. In [13], internalization has been done statically and used to identify computation within the deduction process. Our aim here is to do internalization dynamically and to use it to design rules for induction by rewriting and an adequate strategy for Noetherian induction.

In what follows, we consider congruences generated by conditional class rewrite systems denoted $\mathcal{RE}$ and composed of (conditional) term rewrite rules, (conditional) term equational axioms, (conditional) proposition rewrite rules, (conditional) proposition equational axioms. Moreover, we assume that the left-hand side of a proposition rewrite rule and both sides of a proposition equational axiom have to be atomic propositions. Conditions may be arbitrary propositions. The variables in the right-hand side and condition of a rule must occur in the left-hand side. In the case of equational axioms, variables in both sides have to be the same and (free) variables in the condition have to be a subset of those.

We assume here that $\approx$ is a binary relation symbol which satisfies the axioms of equality (the classical denotation $=$ will only represent syntactical equality).

In this case, to any conditional class rewrite system $\mathcal{RE}$ is associated the theory denoted $T_{\mathcal{RE}}$ as follows: for each conditional rewrite rule $(l \rightarrow r$ if $c)$ or conditional equality $(l \approx r$ if $c)$ in $\mathcal{RE}$, $T_{\mathcal{RE}}$ contains the proposition:

- $\forall \overline{x}(c \Rightarrow (l \Leftrightarrow r))$ when l and r are propositions,
- $\forall \overline{x}(c \Rightarrow (l \approx r))$ when l and r are terms,

where all free variables of l, denoted $\overline{x}$, are universally quantified.

It is proved in [7] that $T_{\mathcal{RE}}$ is compatible with the congruence generated by $\mathcal{RE}$ (see also [11] and [13]). This allows us to freely use the "pushing and popping" operations. This also ensures that deduction modulo a congruence represented by a conditional class rewrite system is not a proper extension of first-order logic, but only a different presentation of it.

1.2   Deduction Modulo for Inductive Proofs

This short introduction to deduction modulo now allows us to give a proof theoretic understanding of induction by rewriting. In the context of deduction modulo, the induction hypotheses arising from equational goals can be (dynamically) internalized into the congruence. When doing this, the computational part of the deduction modulo appears to perform induction by rewriting as done for instance by systems like Spike [4] or RRL [19].

The powerful principle of these approaches is to allow application of rewrite rules of the theory at any position of the current goal, as well as application of induction hypotheses and current conjecture, provided that the applied formula is smaller in the Noetherian induction ordering than the current goal.

When the ordering contains the relation induced by a terminating rewrite system, a smaller formula is obtained as soon as a rewrite step is performed. Moreover, in Spike for instance, the choice of the induction variables and instantiation schemas is done using pre-calculated induction positions and schemas called test-sets. In the approach described below, we show how to use narrowing to automatically and completely perform these choices. The whole problem is formalized in $HOL_{\lambda\sigma}$.

Given a property P and a relation R defined on a sort τ, the Noetherian induction principle $NoethInd(P, R, \tau)$ is defined as follows:

$$\forall x \left((x \in \tau \wedge \forall y \left((y \in \tau \wedge R(y, x)) \Rightarrow P(y) \right)) \Rightarrow P(x) \right) \Rightarrow \forall x \left(x \in \tau \Rightarrow P(x) \right)$$

and we write $Noeth(R, \tau)$ to state that R is a Noetherian relation over τ.

Proving that P inductively holds in a user theory Th_u, denoted $Th_u \models_{Ind} P$, amounts to derive the sequent:

$$\forall R \, \forall \tau \, (Noeth(R, \tau) \Rightarrow \forall P \, NoethInd(P, R, \tau)), Th_u \vdash P.$$

Of course to finish the proof, one should also provide a proof of $Noeth(R, \tau)$. To get a better intuition, let us consider an equational goal Q of the form

$\forall x \, (x \in \tau \Rightarrow t_1(x) \approx t_2(x))$. The remainder of this section gives the main steps which are detailed in [7]. We start from the sequent:

$$\forall R \, \forall \tau \, (Noeth(R, \tau) \Rightarrow \forall P \, NoethInd(P, R, \tau)), Th_u$$
$$\vdash$$
$$\forall x \, (x \in \tau \Rightarrow t_1(x) \approx t_2(x))$$

In the following, we will denote NI the proposition:

$$\forall R \, \forall \tau \, (Noeth(R, \tau) \Rightarrow \forall P \, NoethInd(P, R, \tau))$$

Choosing a specific relation R (written $\prec$) and a type still denoted τ, we get:

$$Noeth(\prec, \tau) \Rightarrow \forall P \, NoethInd(P, \prec, \tau)), Th_u \vdash \forall x \, (x \in \tau \Rightarrow t_1(x) \approx t_2(x)).$$

From this, by the rule $\Rightarrow$-l of the sequent calculus, we get on one hand the sequent $Th_u \vdash Noeth(\prec, \tau)$ corresponding to the proof that $\prec$ is indeed Noetherian, on the other hand the sequent

$$\forall P \, NoethInd(P, \prec, \tau)), Th_u \vdash \forall x \, (x \in \tau \Rightarrow t_1(x) \approx t_2(x))$$

corresponding to the use of the induction principle to prove our goal.

We instantiate P as the equality to prove and we get:

$$\forall x \, ((x \in \tau \wedge \forall \underline{x} \, ((\underline{x} \in \tau \wedge \underline{x} \prec x) \Rightarrow t_1(\underline{x}) \approx t_2(\underline{x}))) \Rightarrow t_1(x) \approx t_2(x))$$
$$\Rightarrow \forall x \, (x \in \tau \Rightarrow t_1(x) \approx t_2(x)), Th_u \vdash \forall x \, (x \in \tau \Rightarrow t_1(x) \approx t_2(x))$$

where we have renamed y to $\underline{x}$ to emphasize that $\underline{x}$ is a smaller instance of x. A few easy steps of the sequent calculus later, we get:

$$Th_u \vdash \forall x \, ((x \in \tau \wedge \forall \underline{x} \, ((\underline{x} \in \tau \wedge \underline{x} \prec x) \Rightarrow t_1(\underline{x}) \approx t_2(\underline{x}))) \Rightarrow t_1(x) \approx t_2(x))$$

We then instantiate x by a fresh variable that we call X to emphasize this status, and we get:

$$Th_u \vdash (X \in \tau \wedge \forall \underline{x} \, ((\underline{x} \in \tau \wedge \underline{x} \prec X) \Rightarrow t_1(\underline{x}) \approx t_2(\underline{x}))) \Rightarrow t_1(X) \approx t_2(X).$$

The $\Rightarrow$-r and $\wedge$-l rules of the sequent calculus lead to the discovery of the induction hypothesis:

$$Th_u, X \in \tau, \forall \underline{x} \, ((\underline{x} \in \tau \wedge \underline{x} \prec X) \Rightarrow t_1(\underline{x}) \approx t_2(\underline{x})) \vdash t_1(X) \approx t_2(X).$$

Using what we have seen on compatible theories, this hypothesis can now be internalized as a conditional equality denoted in general $\mathcal{RE}_{ind}(Q, \prec, \tau)(X)$:

$$t_1(\underline{x}) \approx t_2(\underline{x}) \text{ if } \underline{x} \in \tau \wedge \underline{x} \prec X \qquad (1)$$

Note that because of its status of free fresh variable, X behaves like a constant, while $\underline{x}$ is universally quantified.

What is crucial in using the induction hypothesis (1) as an equality or a rewrite rule, is to check its condition. For any many-sorted theory, the $\underline{x} \in \tau$ part of the condition just expresses that the variable is sorted.

One of the main technical point handled in the paper is to justify that in most cases, the condition $\underline{x} \prec X$ is easily checked when an induction hypothesis like (1) is internalized and used as a simplification rewrite rule.

2   Ordering and Narrowing

Before describing the proof search system, we describe in this section the two main tools of the method, namely orderings on terms and equalities, and the narrowing properties in sufficiently complete rewrite systems. Most importantly, we provide the main result (Theorem 1) relating induction as deduction modulo as presented in the previous section and the Noetherian ordering induced by a terminating rewrite relation.

2.1   Orders and Quasi-Orders on Terms and Equalities

The set of positions in a term t is denoted $\mathcal{D}om(t)$, the subterm of t at position ω is denoted $t_{|\omega}$ and the symbol at position ω in t by $t(\omega)$. The notation $t[u]_\omega$ means that the term t contains the subterm u at position ω. These notations extend to goals $t_1 \approx t_2$ seen as a term with top symbol $\approx$ of arity 2. $Var(t)$ denotes the set of (free) variables of the term t and $|Var(t)|$ its cardinality. We define $\overrightarrow{Var(t)}$ as the vector of variables assumed linearly ordered by their name. These notations are extended to equalities, rewrite rules and goals.

From now on, we assume given a quasi simplification order $\leqslant$ on $\mathcal{T}(\Sigma, \mathcal{X})$ (see for example [10]). We denote $<$ its proper part, $\gtrless$ its associated equivalence (*i.e.* $\gtrless = (\leqslant \cap \geqslant)$) and $[t]$ the class of a term t for this equivalence. We assume that $<$ and $\gtrless$ are closed under substitutions and contexts. For instance, it is shown in [14] that if $\leqslant$ is a recursive path ordering (rpo) with status then $<$ and $\gtrless$ are closed under substitutions and contexts.

In order to compare n-tuple of terms, for any natural n, we will use the standard extension on the Cartesian product $\leqslant_n$ of $\leqslant$:

$$\forall \vec{u}, \vec{v} \in \mathcal{T}(\Sigma, \mathcal{X})^n \quad \vec{u} \leqslant_n \vec{v} \Leftrightarrow (\forall i\ 1 \leq i \leq n \Rightarrow u_i \leqslant v_i)$$

If we denote $<_n$ the proper part of this quasi-order, then $<_n$ is Noetherian on the set $\mathcal{T}(\Sigma, \mathcal{X})^n$ provided $<$ is Noetherian. We extend this quasi-order to equalities in the following way:

$$s \approx t \leqslant_2 s' \approx t' \text{ if } s \leqslant s' \text{ and } t \leqslant t'.$$

Definition 1. Let Q and Q' be two equational goals, $Q' \leq_e Q$ whenever there exists a finite sequence of equalities $(Q_i = s_i \approx t_i)_{0 \leq i \leq n}$ such that:

1. $Q = Q_0$ and $Q' = Q_n$,
2. for any i, $s_{i+1} \leqslant s_i$ and $t_i = t_{i+1}$ or $t_{i+1} \leqslant t_i$ and $s_i = s_{i+1}$.

Now, since $\leqslant$ is stable under substitution, we get:

Lemma 1. $\leq_e$ is stable under substitution.

Moreover, to compare goals in a finer way, we also will make use of another ordering on goals similar to the one in [7].

Definition 2. Let C be the following complexity measure on equalities, where $\{[t]\}$ denotes the multiset of terms in the equivalence class of t for $\gtrsim$.

$$C(s \approx t) = \begin{array}{ll} (\{[s]\}, \{[t]\}) & \text{if } [t] < [s] \\ (\{[t]\}, \{[s]\}) & \text{if } [s] < [t] \\ (\{[s], [t]\}, \emptyset) & \text{otherwise} \end{array}$$

We define a quasi ordering on equalities $\leqslant_e$ by

$$s \approx t \leqslant_e s' \approx t' \text{ if } C(s \approx t) \ll_{lex} C(s' \approx t') \text{ or } (s \gtrsim s' \text{ and } t \gtrsim t')$$

where $\ll_{lex}$ is the lexicographic extension of the multiset extension of $<$. We denote $<_e$ the proper part of $\leqslant_e$.

Let us remark that the order $<_e$ is well-suited for equalities, since it is invariant under symmetry of equality: for all $t, t', u, u' \in \mathcal{T}(\Sigma, \mathcal{X})$, we have:
$t \approx t' <_e u \approx u'$ if and only if $t' \approx t <_e u \approx u'$ if and only if $t \approx t' <_e u' \approx u$.
But it is not stable under substitution: for example with the substitution $\sigma = \{x \mapsto x_1, \ y \mapsto x_1, \ z \mapsto z_1\}$, we have:

1. $z \approx x + z <_e y \approx x + z$ since
   $C(z \approx x + z) = (\{[x + z]\}, \{[z]\})$ and
   $C(y \approx x + z) = (\{[x + z], [y]\}, \emptyset)$
2. but $z\sigma \approx x\sigma + z\sigma \not\leqslant_e y\sigma \approx x\sigma + z\sigma$ since
   $C(z\sigma \approx x\sigma + z\sigma) = (\{[x_1 + z_1]\}, \{[z_1]\})$ and
   $C(y\sigma \approx x\sigma + z\sigma) = (\{[x_1 + z_1]\}, \{[x_1]\})$

Notice the difference between $\leqslant_e$ and $\preceq_e$, the latter being included in the former as it can be checked by a simple case analysis. Indeed, stability by substitution is in particular needed when considering optimized version of the proof search method developed in [23].

2.2   Induction Hypothesis and Ordering on Goals

Taking into account vectors of variables, we are now in position to instantiate the Noetherian induction hypothesis $\mathcal{RE}_{ind}(Q, \prec, \tau)(X)$ defined in Section 1.2.

For any equality Q, for any integer n such that $n = |Var(Q)|$, for any $\overrightarrow{x} \in \mathcal{X}^n$ such that $\overrightarrow{x}$ is the vector of variables of Q, we have:

$$\mathcal{RE}_{ind}(Q, <_n, \mathcal{T}(\Sigma)^n) \triangleq (\overrightarrow{\underline{x}} \in \mathcal{T}(\Sigma)^n) \wedge (\overrightarrow{\underline{x}} <_n \overrightarrow{x}) \Rightarrow Q\{\overrightarrow{\underline{x}}/\overrightarrow{x}\}$$

In order to simplify the notations, and when no confusion can occur, we denote it simply $\mathcal{RE}_{ind}(Q, <)$.

In the same way, we introduce the following notations, where σ is any substitution:

- $\mathcal{RE}_{ind}(Q, <)\sigma \triangleq (\overrightarrow{\underline{x}} \in \mathcal{T}(\Sigma)^n) \wedge (\overrightarrow{\underline{x}} <_n \overrightarrow{x}\sigma) \Rightarrow Q\{\overrightarrow{\underline{x}}/\overrightarrow{x}\}$
- $\mathcal{RE}_{ind}(Q, \leqslant) \triangleq (\overrightarrow{\underline{x}} \in \mathcal{T}(\Sigma)^n) \wedge (\overrightarrow{\underline{x}} \leqslant_n \overrightarrow{x}) \Rightarrow Q\{\overrightarrow{\underline{x}}/\overrightarrow{x}\}$
- $\mathcal{RE}_{ind}(Q, \leqslant)\sigma \triangleq (\overrightarrow{\underline{x}} \in \mathcal{T}(\Sigma)^n) \wedge (\overrightarrow{\underline{x}} \leqslant_n \overrightarrow{x}\sigma) \Rightarrow Q\{\overrightarrow{\underline{x}}/\overrightarrow{x}\}$

A crucial point in inductive proofs will be to compare different instances of a same equational goal: this is the purpose of the next lemma.

Lemma 2. For any equational goal Q with $\vec{x} = \overrightarrow{Var(Q)}$ and $n = |\vec{x}|$, for all substitutions $\sigma, \mu \in Subst^{\mathcal{T}(\Sigma, \mathcal{X})}$, for all $t, t' \in \mathcal{T}(\Sigma, \mathcal{X})$:

1. If $t \leqslant t'$ then $Q[t]_\omega \leqslant_e Q[t']_\omega$
2. If $\vec{x}\sigma \leqslant_n \vec{x}\mu$ then $Q\sigma \leqslant_e Q\mu$.
3. If $Q\sigma <_e Q\mu$ and $\vec{x}\sigma \leqslant_n \vec{x}\mu$ then $\vec{x}\sigma <_n \vec{x}\mu$.

Proof. 1. Let i and ω', such that $\omega = i.\omega'$ ($i = 1, 2$ since Q is an equality). Since $t \leqslant t'$, and since $\leqslant$ is a reduction ordering, we have:

$$Q_{|i}[t]_{\omega'} \leqslant Q_{|i}[t']_{\omega'} \qquad (2)$$

Now, one can easily check the following proposition:

$$\forall s \, \forall s' \, \forall u \; s \leqslant s' \Rightarrow s \approx u \leqslant_e s' \approx u \qquad (3)$$

And (2) and (3) above lead to $Q[t]_\omega \leqslant_e Q[t']_\omega$
2. is obtained from 1 by an easy induction based on the number of occurrences of the variables x_i in Q
3. Assume $\vec{x}\sigma \leqslant_n \vec{x}\mu$ and $\vec{x}\sigma \not<_n \vec{x}\mu$. Then $\vec{x}\sigma \geqslant_n \vec{x}\mu$, hence $\vec{x}\mu \leqslant_n \vec{x}\sigma$, thus $Q\mu \leqslant_e Q\sigma$ by 2, and this contradicts the assumption $Q\sigma <_e Q\mu$. □

In other words, for any equational goal Q, for any vector of variables $\vec{x}$ of Q in $\mathcal{X}^n$, and for all $\sigma, \mu \in Subst^{\mathcal{T}(\Sigma, \mathcal{X})}$, in order to prove the proposition $\vec{x}\sigma <_n \vec{x}\mu$, and whenever $Q\sigma <_e Q\mu$, it suffices to check all inequalities $\sigma(x_i) \leqslant \mu(x_i)$ for all component x_i of $\vec{x}$. Indeed, we are going to see in next Lemma that the inequality $Q\sigma <_e Q\mu$ can be automatically checked in many cases.

The next theorem relates the strict ordering $<_e$ on goals with a rewrite relation $\rightarrow$. It is a crucial step to justify the correct use of Noetherian rewriting as the main ingredient to perform Noetherian induction.

Indeed, under technical conditions that can be syntactically checked, this result ensures that $Q\sigma <_e Q\mu$. It is therefore possible in most of the cases to use an equational goal Q to reduce an instance of itself, $Q\mu$, as soon as a rewrite step has been previously performed on $Q\mu$.

Theorem 1 (Main compatibility theorem). *Let Q_1, Q_2, Q_3 and Q_4 be equational goals, $l \rightarrow r$ a rewrite rule (thus $l > r$), κ_0 be either a rewrite rule $l_{\kappa_0} \rightarrow r_{\kappa_0}$ or an equality $l_{\kappa_0} \approx r_{\kappa_0}$.*
Let us consider the inequality $I : (l_{\kappa_0} \approx r_{\kappa_0})\sigma <_e Q_1$ and assume:

1. *$Q_1 \rightarrow_{l \rightarrow r, \; j.\omega_j, \; \theta} Q_2$*
2. *$Q_2 \geqslant_2 Q_3$.*

3. $Q_3 \rightarrow_{\kappa_0, \; i.\omega_i, \; \sigma} Q_4$
4. $Q_3 \geqslant_e Q_4$

Then:

1. I *is satisfied whenever* $\omega_i \neq \varepsilon$ *or* $i = j$
2. *If* $\omega_i = \varepsilon$ *and* $i \neq j$:
   (a) *If* $l_{\kappa_0} > r_{\kappa_0}$, *then:*

   $$I \Leftrightarrow ((Q_{1|i} \gtrsim l_{\kappa_0}\sigma) \wedge (Q_{1|j} < Q_{1|i}) \Rightarrow (Q_{1|j} > r_{\kappa_0}\sigma))$$

   (b) *If* $l_{\kappa_0} \gtrsim r_{\kappa_0}$, *then:*

   $$I \Leftrightarrow ((Q_{1|i} \gtrsim l_{\kappa_0}\sigma) \Rightarrow (Q_{1|j} > r_{\kappa_0}\sigma))$$

   (c) *Otherwise:*

   $$I \Leftrightarrow (\; ((Q_{1|i} \gtrsim l_{\kappa_0}\sigma) \wedge ((Q_{1|j} < Q_{1|i}) \vee (l_{\kappa_0}\sigma \gtrsim r_{\kappa_0}\sigma)) \wedge (r_{\kappa_0}\sigma \leqslant l_{\kappa_0}\sigma))$$
   $$\Rightarrow (Q_{1|j} > r_{\kappa_0}\sigma) \;)$$

Proof. The proof of this crucial result is given in [23]. It is based on a technical case analysis. □

A variant of this theorem is given in [7] for an ordering between goals based on a complexity C using a set ordering instead of multiset ordering as here.

2.3   Narrowing

To make precise the use of narrowing in the induction process, let us first introduce a few concepts and notations. Narrowing will be performed only with rewrite rules, i.e. formulas $l \rightarrow r$ with $l > r$, but not with equalities. Let $\mathcal{R}$ be a rewrite system on $\mathcal{T}(\Sigma, \mathcal{X})$. The signature Σ is partitioned into a set of constructors $\mathcal{C}$ and a set of defined symbols $\mathcal{D}$. Constructors are function symbols which do not occur as a head symbol of a rule left-hand side. A constructor term is a term built only with constructor symbols. $\mathcal{T}(\mathcal{C}, \mathcal{X})$ denotes the set of constructor terms. A ground substitution is a substitution mapping each variable to a ground term, i.e. a term without variables. Let $Subst^{\mathcal{T}(\Sigma)}$ be the set of all ground substitutions on $\mathcal{T}(\Sigma)$. A rewrite system is said to be *ground convergent* if it is confluent and terminating over the set of ground terms. For any ground convergent rewrite system $\mathcal{R}$, a term t is ground $\mathcal{R}$-reducible if $t\alpha$ is $\mathcal{R}$-reducible for any ground substitution α. Furthermore, a symbol $f \in \mathcal{D}$ of arity n is *completely defined* if $f(x_1, \ldots, x_n)$ is ground reducible, and a ground convergent rewrite system $\mathcal{R}$ is said to be *sufficiently complete* if all symbols in $\mathcal{D}$ are completely defined.

For ground convergent and sufficiently complete rewrite systems, it is possible to specify particular positions in terms where reductions must apply, and where case analysis by rewriting can usefully be done.

Definition 3. For any $t \in \mathcal{T}(\Sigma, \mathcal{X})$, a position ω in t is called *defined-innermost*, and we denote $\omega \in DI(t)$, if $t(\omega) \in \mathcal{D}$ and $t(\omega') \in \mathcal{C} \cup \mathcal{X}$ whenever $\omega < \omega'$.

For example, considering Peano's naturals, 0 and s are constructors, $+$ is a defined symbol and in $s((0+0)+s(0+s(x)))$ the occurrence 1.2.1 is defined-innermost but 1 is not.

Lemma 3. For any ground convergent rewrite system $\mathcal{R}$, for any term t, and for any position $\omega \in \mathcal{D}om(t)$, if $t(\omega)$ is completely defined and ω is defined-innermost in $\mathcal{D}om(t)$, then, for any irreducible ground substitution α, $t\alpha$ is reducible at position ω.

Proof. Classical and by case analysis   □

Definition 4. A goal Q is narrowed into Q' at a position ω with the rule $l \to r$ and the substitution σ, if σ is the most general unifier (mgu for short) of l and $Q_{|\omega}$, and $Q' = Q[r]_\omega \sigma$. This narrowing step is denoted $Q \rightsquigarrow_{l \to r, \omega, \sigma} Q'$.

Indeed, every defined-innermost occurrence is narrowable:

Corollary 1. For any ground convergent rewrite system $\mathcal{R}$, for any equational goal Q, for any defined-innermost position $\omega \in \mathcal{D}om(Q)$, for any ground substitution α and for any finite set V of variables such that $\mathcal{V}ar(Q) \cup \mathcal{D}om(\alpha \downarrow) \subseteq V$, there exists a rule $l \to r \in \mathcal{R}$, a unifier σ of $Q_{|\omega}$ and l, and a ground substitution μ such that $\sigma\mu_{|V} = (\alpha \downarrow)_{|V}$.

Proof. It is a consequence of the previous lemma and the classical narrowing
       lifting lemma [18,20].   □

Thanks to these settings, we present in the next section, an induction based proof search system, relying on a main induction rule that uses narrowing to choose both the induction variables and the instantiation schema.

3   A Proof Search System for Induction

The proof search system IndNarrow for inductive proofs introduced in this section is based on narrowing and rewriting. The main rule, called **Induce**, performs the induction step. This is the key point that provides a bridge between the implicit and explicit approaches of induction. Correctness and refutational completeness of this system are proved.

3.1   The Proof Search System IndNarrow

The rules in Figure 2 apply on sequents modulo of the form $\Gamma_1 | \Gamma_2 \vdash_{\mathcal{RE}_1 | \mathcal{RE}_2} Q$, where Γ_1 is the deduction part of the definitions, $\mathcal{RE}_1$ is their computational part; Γ_2 is the deduction part for other statements, $\mathcal{RE}_2$ is their computational part; Q is an equational goal.

Induce	$\Gamma_1|\Gamma_2 \vdash_{\mathcal{RE}_1|\mathcal{RE}_2} Q[t]_\omega \rightarrowtail$
	$\bigodot_{\substack{\kappa \in \mathcal{RE}_1 \\ \sigma = mgu(t,\, l)}} \quad \Gamma_1|\Gamma_2 \vdash_{\mathcal{RE}_1|\mathcal{RE}_2\sigma\cup\mathcal{RE}_{ind}(Q,<)\sigma} (Q[r]_\omega)\sigma$
	if $\kappa = l \rightarrow r$ and $\omega \in DI(Q)$
Orient	$\Gamma_1|\Gamma_2 \vdash_{\mathcal{RE}_1\cup\{\kappa\}|\mathcal{RE}_2} Q \quad \rightarrowtail \Gamma_1|\Gamma_2 \vdash_{\mathcal{RE}_1\cup\{l\rightarrow r\}|\mathcal{RE}_2} Q$
	if $\kappa = l \approx r$ or $\kappa = r \approx l$ and $l > r$
Push$_1$	$\Gamma_1, l \approx r|\Gamma_2 \vdash_{\mathcal{RE}_1|\mathcal{RE}_2} Q \quad \rightarrowtail \Gamma_1|\Gamma_2 \vdash_{\mathcal{RE}_1\cup\{l\approx r\}|\mathcal{RE}_2} Q$
Push$_2$	$\Gamma_1|\Gamma_2, l \approx r \vdash_{\mathcal{RE}_1|\mathcal{RE}_2} Q \quad \rightarrowtail \Gamma_1|\Gamma_2 \vdash_{\mathcal{RE}_1|\mathcal{RE}_2\cup\{l\approx r\}} Q$
Rewrite$_1$	$\Gamma_1|\Gamma_2 \vdash_{\mathcal{RE}_1\cup\{\kappa\}|\mathcal{RE}_2} Q[l\sigma]_\omega \rightarrowtail \Gamma_1|\Gamma_2 \vdash_{\mathcal{RE}_1\cup\{\kappa\}|\mathcal{RE}_2} Q[r\sigma]_\omega$
	if $\kappa = l \rightarrow r$ or $\kappa = l \approx r$ or $\kappa = r \approx l$
Rewrite$_2$	$\Gamma_1|\Gamma_2 \vdash_{\mathcal{RE}_1|\mathcal{RE}_2\cup\{\kappa\}} Q[l\sigma]_\omega \rightarrowtail \Gamma_1|\Gamma_2 \vdash_{\mathcal{RE}_1|\mathcal{RE}_2\cup\{\kappa\}} Q[r\sigma]_\omega$
	if $\kappa = l \approx r$ or $\kappa = r \approx l$ or
	$\kappa = \mathcal{RE}_{ind}(l \approx r)\mu$ or $\kappa = \mathcal{RE}_{ind}(r \approx l)\mu$
	and $\overrightarrow{x}\sigma <_n \overrightarrow{x}\mu$ where $\overrightarrow{x} = \overrightarrow{Var(l \approx r)}$
Trivial	$\Gamma_1|\Gamma_2 \vdash_{\mathcal{RE}_1|\mathcal{RE}_2} t \approx t \quad\quad \rightarrowtail \diamond$
Refutation	$\Gamma_1|\Gamma_2 \vdash_{\mathcal{RE}_1|\mathcal{RE}_2} Q \quad\quad \rightarrowtail$ Refutation
	when no other rules can be applied

Fig. 2. The proof search system IndNarrow

The distinction between $\Gamma_1/\mathcal{RE}_1$ and $\Gamma_2/\mathcal{RE}_2$ is needed because in the **Induce** rule, only $\mathcal{RE}_1$ is used for narrowing. For simplicity, we assume that $\mathcal{RE}_1$ contains only unconditional rules or equalities and we assume from now on, that $\mathcal{RE}_1$ is sufficiently complete.

Γ_2 is initialized with the proposition NI defined in subsection 1.2:

$$NI: \quad \forall R \, \forall \tau \, Noeth(R, \tau) \Rightarrow \forall P \, NoethInd(P, R, \tau)$$

and may contain other lemmas. $\mathcal{RE}_2$ receives the induction hypotheses provided by some application of the rule **Induce**. So $\mathcal{RE}_2$ may contain conditional equalities. $\odot$ operator that is an associative commutative operator on sequents with $\diamond$ as a neutral element.

The main rule is **Induce** as it performs the induction step. It uses narrowing to choose both the induction variable(s) and the instantiation schema. Narrowing is applied only at defined innermost positions (see Definition 3) $DI(Q)$ of the current goal Q. The other rules are doing the following: **Trivial** eliminates a trivial equation, **Push** pushes an equational hypothesis from the deduction part to the computational part, **Orient** orients an equation in the computational part into a rewrite rule, according to the term ordering, **Rewrite** (1 or 2) rewrites using a rule, an equation, or a smaller instance of a previous goal. **Push** and **Rewrite** are duplicated because of the $\Gamma_1/\mathcal{RE}_1$ and $\Gamma_2/\mathcal{RE}_2$ distinction.

3.2   A Simple Example

To get a better understanding of the way this set of rules is working, let us look at the proof of addition commutativity in Peano arithmetic. So, the goal is to prove:

$$x + 0 \approx x, x + s(y) \approx s(x+y) | NI \vdash_{\emptyset|\emptyset} X + Y \approx Y + X$$

Applying **Push**$_1$ twice, we get:

$$\emptyset | NI \vdash_{x+0\approx x, x+s(y)\approx s(x+y)|\emptyset} X + Y \approx Y + X$$

Then, applying **Orient** twice gives us:

$$\emptyset | NI \vdash_{x+0\to x, x+s(y)\to s(x+y)|\emptyset} X + Y \approx Y + X$$

We can now apply **Induce** since $\mathcal{RE}_1 = \{x+0 \to x, x+s(y) \to s(x+y)\}$ is confluent, terminating and sufficiently complete. This could be done at occurrence 1 or 2 of the goal. We arbitrary chose occurrence 1 and this leads us to prove the two sequents:

$$\emptyset | NI \vdash_{\mathcal{RE}_1 | \mathcal{RE}_{ind}(X+Y\approx Y+X, <, T^2_\Sigma)\{X\mapsto X_1; Y\mapsto 0\}} X_1 \approx 0 + X_1$$
$$\emptyset | NI \vdash_{\mathcal{RE}_1 | \mathcal{RE}_{ind}(X+Y\approx Y+X, <, T^2_\Sigma)\{X\mapsto X_1; Y\mapsto s(Y_1)\}} s(X_1 + Y_1) \approx s(Y_1) + X_1$$

We have now to prove in particular that 0 is left-neutral. The only applicable rule on that goal is **Induce** again and we get the two new subgoals:

$$\emptyset | NI \vdash_{\mathcal{RE}_1 | \substack{\mathcal{RE}_{ind}(X + Y \approx Y + X, <, T^2_\Sigma)\{X \mapsto 0; Y \mapsto 0\} \\ \mathcal{RE}_{ind}(X_1 \approx 0 + X_1, <, T_\Sigma)\{X_1 \mapsto 0\}}} 0 \approx 0$$
$$\emptyset | NI \vdash_{\mathcal{RE}_1 | \substack{\mathcal{RE}_{ind}(X + Y \approx Y + X, <, T^2_\Sigma)\{X \mapsto s(X_2); Y \mapsto 0\} \\ \mathcal{RE}_{ind}(X_1 \approx 0 + X_1, <, T_\Sigma)\{X_1 \mapsto s(X_2)\}}} s(X_2) \approx s(0 + X_2)$$

Trivial gets rid of the first one. **Rewrite**$_2$ can be applied on the second one since, because of narrowing, the goal has been reduced and therefore the induction hypothesis can now be used. We get:

$$\emptyset | NI \vdash_{\mathcal{RE}_1 | \substack{\mathcal{RE}_{ind}(X + Y \approx Y + X, <, T^2_\Sigma)\{X \mapsto s(X_2); Y \mapsto 0\} \\ \mathcal{RE}_{ind}(X_1 \approx 0 + X_1, <, T_\Sigma)\{X_1 \mapsto s(X_2)\}}} s(X_2) \approx s(X_2 + 0)$$

Applying now **Rewrite**$_1$ proves that 0 is left-neutral for addition. We are left with the goal $s(X_1 + Y_1) \approx s(Y_1) + X_1$ and we will make precise later on how the proof search finishes.

3.3 Soundness of **IndNarrow**

Soundness amounts to show that for each rule of the proof search system Ind-Narrow of the form:

$$\Gamma_1|\Gamma_2 \vdash_{\mathcal{RE}_1|\mathcal{RE}_2} Q \longmapsto \bigodot_{i \in I} \Gamma_1^i|\Gamma_2^i \vdash_{\mathcal{RE}_1^i|\mathcal{RE}_2^i} Q^i$$

then $\Gamma_1|\Gamma_2, \vec{x} \in \mathcal{T}(\Sigma)^n \vdash_{\mathcal{RE}_1|\mathcal{RE}_2} Q$ is derivable provided all the $\Gamma_1^i|\Gamma_2^i, \vec{x^i} \in \mathcal{T}(\Sigma)^{n^i} \vdash_{\mathcal{RE}_1^i|\mathcal{RE}_2^i} Q^i$ are. In what follows, we assume that all variables in Γ are universally quantified.

Let us first state a few basic rules which are needed in the soundness proof.

Lemma 4. The following rules (where P, P_1, P_2 are propositions) are derivable in the sequent calculus modulo:

1.

$$\frac{\Gamma \vdash_{\mathcal{RE}} P_1 \Rightarrow P_2, \Delta}{\Gamma, P_1 \vdash_{\mathcal{RE}} P_2, \Delta} \; imp$$

2.

$$\frac{}{\Gamma, x = y \vdash x \approx y} \; ref$$

3.

$$\frac{\Gamma \vdash_{\mathcal{RE}} \forall x \; \alpha(x) \approx \beta(x) \qquad \Gamma \vdash_{\mathcal{RE}\alpha} P\alpha}{\Gamma \vdash_{\mathcal{RE}\beta} P\beta} \; r_e$$

4.

$$\frac{\Gamma, \vec{x} \in \mathcal{T}(\Sigma)^n \vdash_{\mathcal{RE}} P, \Delta}{\Gamma \vdash_{\mathcal{RE}\alpha} P\alpha, \Delta} \; r_\alpha \quad \text{if} \begin{cases} \alpha \in Subst^\Sigma \\ \vec{x} \text{ is the vector of free variables of } \mathcal{RE} \cup P \end{cases}$$

5.

$$\frac{\bigwedge_{\alpha \in Subst^\Sigma} \Gamma \vdash_{\mathcal{RE}\alpha} P\alpha}{\Gamma, \vec{x} \in \mathcal{T}(\Sigma)^n \vdash_{\mathcal{RE}} P} \; r_{\vec{x}} \quad \text{if } \vec{x} \text{ is the vector of free variables of } \mathcal{RE} \cup P$$

6. For any proposition P and for any integer n, if $|Var(P) \cup Var(\mathcal{RE})| = n$, if the proposition P is inductive in some context $\Gamma \cup \mathcal{RE}$ with respect to the order $<_n$, and if this order is Noetherian in this context, then the proposition P is valid in the context $\Gamma \cup \mathcal{RE}$, whenever it contains the proposition $NI = \forall R \forall \tau \, (Noeth(R, \tau) \Rightarrow \forall P \, NoethInd(P, R, \tau))$ (see subsection 3.1)

7.

$$\frac{\Gamma, \vec{x} \in \mathcal{T}(\Sigma)^n \vdash_{\mathcal{RE} \cup \mathcal{RE}_{ind}(P,<)} P \qquad \Gamma \vdash_{\mathcal{RE}} Noeth(<_n, \mathcal{T}(\Sigma)^n)}{\Gamma, \vec{x} \in \mathcal{T}(\Sigma)^n \vdash_{\mathcal{RE}} P} \; r_I$$

if $\vec{x}$ is the vector of free variables of $\mathcal{RE} \cup P$

We are now ready to prove soundness of IndNarrow in the sequent calculus modulo by considering in turn each inference rule of IndNarrow.

Theorem 2. *For any contexts Γ_1, Γ_2, rewrite systems $\mathcal{RE}_1, \mathcal{RE}_2$, equational goal Q, occurrence $\omega \in DI(Q)$ and integer n, let us assume that:*

1. **Induce** *is applied on*
$$\Gamma_1 | \Gamma_2 \vdash_{\mathcal{RE}_1 | \mathcal{RE}_2} Q[t]_\omega$$
   to get
$$\bigodot_{\substack{l \rightarrow r \in \mathcal{RE}_1 \\ \sigma = mgu(t, l)}} \Gamma_1 | \Gamma_2 \vdash_{\mathcal{RE}_1 | \mathcal{RE}_2 \sigma \cup \mathcal{RE}_{ind}(Q, <)\sigma} (Q[r]_\omega)\sigma;$$

2. $\mathcal{RE}_1$ *is ground convergent and sufficiently complete;*

3. $<$ *is Noetherian, so that $\Gamma_1 \cup \Gamma_2 \vdash_{\mathcal{RE}_1 \cup \mathcal{RE}_2} Noeth(<_n, \mathcal{T}(\Sigma)^n)$;*

4. *for any rewrite rule $l \rightarrow r \in \mathcal{RE}_1$, when $\sigma = mgu(t, l)$ and $\overrightarrow{x}_\sigma \in \mathcal{X}^{n_\sigma}$ is the vector of free variables of $\mathcal{RE}\sigma \cup Q\sigma$, the sequent*
$$\Gamma_1 \cup \Gamma_2, \overrightarrow{x}_\sigma \in \mathcal{T}(\Sigma)^{n_\sigma} \vdash_{\mathcal{RE}_1 \cup \mathcal{RE}_2 \sigma \cup \{\mathcal{RE}_{ind}(Q, <)\sigma\}} (Q[r]_\omega)\sigma$$
   is derivable in the sequent calculus modulo.

Then, the sequent
$$\Gamma_1 \cup \Gamma_2, \overrightarrow{x} \in \mathcal{T}(\Sigma)^n \vdash_{\mathcal{RE}_1 \cup \mathcal{RE}_2} Q[t]_\omega$$
is derivable in the sequent calculus modulo.

Proof. First, let us introduce the following notations:

$$
\begin{array}{lll}
\Gamma & \text{denotes} & \Gamma_1 \cup \Gamma_2 \\
\mathcal{RE} & \text{denotes} & \mathcal{RE}_1 \cup \mathcal{RE}_2 \\
\mathcal{RE}' & \text{denotes} & \mathcal{RE} \cup \{\mathcal{RE}_{ind}(Q, <)\} \\
\mathcal{RE}\sigma & \text{denotes} & \mathcal{RE}_1 \cup \mathcal{RE}_2\sigma \\
\mathcal{RE}'\sigma & \text{denotes} & \mathcal{RE}\sigma \cup \{\mathcal{RE}_{ind}(Q, <)\}\sigma
\end{array}
\tag{4}
$$

Let V denote a finite set of variables and α a ground substitution, such that $Var(\mathcal{RE} \cup \{Q\}) \subseteq \mathcal{Dom}(\alpha) \subseteq V$. Let $\alpha \downarrow$ be the $\mathcal{RE}_1$-normal form of α. According to the narrowing lemma, we have:

$$\sigma\mu_{|V} = (\alpha \downarrow)_{|V} \tag{5}$$

for some substitution μ. Let us consider the following derivations.
Π_1

$$\frac{}{\forall x\ x(\alpha \downarrow) = x\sigma\mu \vdash_{\mathcal{RE}} \forall x\ x\alpha = x\sigma\mu}\ Ax$$

Π_2

$$\frac{\vdash \forall x\ x(\alpha \downarrow) = x\sigma\mu\ \ (by\ 5)}{\vdash_{\mathcal{RE}} \forall x\ x(\alpha \downarrow) = x\sigma\mu, \forall x\ x\alpha = x\sigma\mu}\ w + push$$

Π_3

$$\frac{\dfrac{\Pi_1\ \Pi_2}{\vdash_{\mathcal{RE}} \forall x\ x\alpha = x\sigma\mu}\ cut}{\Gamma \vdash_{\mathcal{RE}} \forall x\ x\alpha = x\sigma\mu, \forall x\ x\alpha \approx x\sigma\mu}\ w$$

Π_4:

$$\dfrac{\dfrac{\dfrac{\dfrac{\overline{\Gamma, x\alpha = x\sigma\mu \vdash x\alpha \approx x\sigma\mu}}{\Gamma, \forall x\ x\alpha = x\sigma\mu \vdash x\alpha \approx x\sigma\mu}\ \forall - l}{\Gamma, \forall x\ x\alpha = x\sigma\mu \vdash \forall x\ x\alpha \approx x\sigma\mu}\ \forall - r}{\Gamma, \forall x\ x\alpha = x\sigma\mu \vdash_{\mathcal{RE}} \forall x\ x\alpha \approx x\sigma\mu}\ w + push}{}$$

with ref applied at the top.

Π_5:

$$\dfrac{\Pi_3\ \Pi_4}{\Gamma \vdash_{\mathcal{RE}} \forall x\ x\alpha \approx x\sigma\mu}\ cut$$

Π_6:

$$\dfrac{\Gamma, \overrightarrow{x}_\sigma \in \mathcal{T}(\Sigma)^n \vdash_{\mathcal{RE}'\sigma} Q\sigma[r\sigma]_{|\omega}}{\Gamma, \overrightarrow{x}_\sigma \in \mathcal{T}(\Sigma)^n \vdash_{\mathcal{RE}'\sigma} Q\sigma, Q\sigma[r\sigma]_{|\omega}}\ w$$

Π_7

$$\dfrac{\dfrac{\dfrac{\overline{Q\sigma[r\sigma]_{|\omega} \vdash_{\mathcal{RE}_1} Q\sigma[l\sigma]_{|\omega}}\ Ax}{\Gamma, \overrightarrow{x}_\sigma \in \mathcal{T}(\Sigma)^n, Q\sigma[r\sigma]_{|\omega} \vdash_{\mathcal{RE}'\sigma} Q\sigma[l\sigma]_{|\omega}}\ w}{\Gamma, \overrightarrow{x}_\sigma \in \mathcal{T}(\Sigma)^n, Q\sigma[r\sigma]_{|\omega} \vdash_{\mathcal{RE}'\sigma} Q\sigma}}{}$$

(since $l\sigma = t\sigma$ and $Q = Q[t]_{|\omega}$)

$\Pi_{1,\sigma}$:

$$\dfrac{\Pi_6\quad \Pi_7}{\Gamma, \overrightarrow{x}_\sigma \in \mathcal{T}(\Sigma)^n \vdash_{\mathcal{RE}'\sigma} Q\sigma}\ cut$$

Denoting $\mathcal{PE}_{ind}(Q)$ the canonical proposition associated to $\mathcal{RE}_{ind}(Q, <)$, this leads to:

$\Pi_{2,\sigma}$

$$\dfrac{\dfrac{\Pi_{1,\sigma}}{\Gamma, \overrightarrow{x}_\sigma \in \mathcal{T}(\Sigma)^n, \mathcal{PE}_{ind}(Q)\sigma \vdash_{\mathcal{RE}\sigma} Q\sigma}\ pop}{\Gamma, \overrightarrow{x}_\sigma \in \mathcal{T}(\Sigma)^n \vdash_{\mathcal{RE}\sigma} \mathcal{PE}_{ind}(Q)\sigma \Rightarrow Q\sigma}\ \Rightarrow - r$$

Since the proposition $\mathcal{PE}_{ind}(Q)\sigma \Rightarrow_{\mathcal{RE}} Q\sigma$ is equivalent to $(\mathcal{PE}_{ind}(Q) \Rightarrow_{\mathcal{RE}} Q)\sigma$, we have:

$\Pi_{\sigma,\mu}$:

$$\dfrac{\Pi_{2,\sigma}}{\Gamma \vdash_{\mathcal{RE}\sigma\mu} (\mathcal{PE}_{ind}(Q) \Rightarrow Q)\sigma\mu}\ r_\mu$$

Π_α:

$$\dfrac{\Pi_{\sigma,\mu}\ \Pi_5}{\Gamma \vdash_{\mathcal{RE}\alpha} (\mathcal{PE}_{ind}(Q) \Rightarrow Q)\alpha}\ r_e$$

And since α is any ground substitution, we have:

$\Pi_{\overrightarrow{x}}$:

$$\dfrac{\dfrac{\dfrac{\bigwedge\limits_{\alpha \in Subst^\Sigma} \Pi_\alpha}{\Gamma, \overrightarrow{x} \in \mathcal{T}(\Sigma)^n \vdash_{\mathcal{RE}} \mathcal{PE}_{ind}(Q) \Rightarrow Q}\ r_{\overrightarrow{x}}}{\Gamma, \overrightarrow{x} \in \mathcal{T}(\Sigma)^n, \mathcal{PE}_{ind}(Q) \vdash_{\mathcal{RE}} Q}\ imp}{\Gamma, \overrightarrow{x} \in \mathcal{T}(\Sigma)^n \vdash_{\mathcal{RE} \cup \mathcal{RE}_{ind}(Q, <)} Q}\ push$$

Π:

$$\frac{\Pi_{\overrightarrow{x}} \qquad \Gamma \vdash_{\mathcal{RE}} Noeth(<_n, \mathcal{T}(\Sigma)^n)}{\Gamma, \overrightarrow{x} \in \mathcal{T}(\Sigma)^n \vdash_{\mathcal{RE}} Q} \; r_I$$

and we are done. $\qquad\qquad\qquad\qquad\qquad\qquad\qquad\qquad\qquad\qquad\qquad$ □

Soundness of **Push** is simply a consequence of soundness of the sequent calculus modulo.

Let us now look at the **Rewrite** inferences.

Theorem 3. *For all contexts Γ_1, Γ_2, for all rewrite systems $\mathcal{RE}_1, \mathcal{RE}_2$, for any equational goal Q, let us assume that:*

1. **Rewrite$_{1,2}$** *is applied on*
   $$\Gamma_1 | \Gamma_2 \vdash_{\mathcal{RE}_1 | \mathcal{RE}_2} Q$$
   to get:
   $$\Gamma_1 | \Gamma_2 \vdash_{\mathcal{RE}_1 | \mathcal{RE}_2} Q'$$
2. *The sequent $\Gamma_1 | \Gamma_2 \vdash_{\mathcal{RE}_1 | \mathcal{RE}_2} Q'$ admits a proof.*

Then, the sequent $\Gamma_1 | \Gamma_2 \vdash_{\mathcal{RE}_1 | \mathcal{RE}_2} Q$ is derivable in the sequent calculus modulo.

Proof. Let us use the same notations as in the previous theorem and detail the most elaborated case, namely the application of **Rewrite$_2$**. By assumption 1, and by definition of this rule, there exist
$\kappa \in \mathcal{RE}$, $(l, r) \in \mathcal{T}(\Sigma, \mathcal{X})^2$, $\omega \in \mathcal{D}om(Q)$, and $\sigma \in Subst^{\mathcal{T}(\Sigma, \mathcal{X})}$, such that:

- $\kappa = l \approx r$ or $\kappa = r \approx l$ or
  $\exists \mu \; (\mu \in Subst^{\mathcal{T}(\Sigma, \mathcal{X})})$ and $(\kappa = \mathcal{RE}_{ind}(l \approx r)\mu$ or $\kappa = \mathcal{RE}_{ind}(r \approx l)\mu)$
- $\overrightarrow{y} \in \mathcal{X}^m$ such that $\overrightarrow{y} = \overrightarrow{Var(l \approx r)}$ and $\overrightarrow{y}\sigma <_m \overrightarrow{y}\mu$
- $Q = Q[l\sigma]_{|\omega}$ and $Q' = Q[r\sigma]_{|\omega}$.

Let us then consider the following proof:
Π_1:

$$\frac{\Gamma \vdash_{\mathcal{RE}} \overrightarrow{y}\sigma <_m \overrightarrow{y}\mu}{\Gamma, Q[r\sigma] \vdash_{\mathcal{RE}} \overrightarrow{y}\sigma <_m \overrightarrow{y}\mu, Q[l\sigma]} \; w$$

Π_2:

$$\frac{\Gamma, Q[r\sigma], l\sigma \approx r\sigma \vdash Q[l\sigma]}{\Gamma, Q[r\sigma], l\sigma \approx r\sigma \vdash_{\mathcal{RE}} Q[l\sigma]} \begin{array}{l} r_s \\[2pt] w + push \end{array}$$

Π_3:

$$\frac{\Pi_1 \;\; \Pi_2}{\Gamma, Q[r\sigma], \overrightarrow{y}\sigma <_m \overrightarrow{y}\mu \Rightarrow l\sigma \approx r\sigma \vdash_{\mathcal{RE}} Q[l\sigma]} \; \Rightarrow_l$$

Π_4:

$$\frac{\Pi_3}{\dfrac{\Gamma, Q[r\sigma], \forall \overrightarrow{y} \; \overrightarrow{y} <_m \overrightarrow{y}\mu \Rightarrow (l \approx r)\{\overrightarrow{y}/\overrightarrow{y}\} \vdash_{\mathcal{RE}} Q[l\sigma]}{\Gamma, Q[r\sigma] \vdash_{\mathcal{RE} \cup \{\kappa\}} Q[l\sigma]}} \begin{array}{l} \forall_l \\[2pt] push \end{array}$$

Now, since $\kappa \in \mathcal{RE}$, we have:

Π_4:

$$\frac{\dfrac{\Pi_3}{\Gamma, Q[r\sigma], \forall \overrightarrow{\underline{y}} \ \overrightarrow{\underline{y}} <_m \overrightarrow{\underline{y}} \mu \Rightarrow (l \approx r)\{\overrightarrow{\underline{y}}/\overrightarrow{y}\} \vdash_{\mathcal{RE}} Q[l\sigma]}}{\Gamma, Q[r\sigma] \vdash_{\mathcal{RE}} Q[l\sigma]} \begin{array}{l} \forall_l \\ \\ push \end{array}$$

Π_5:

$$\frac{\Pi_4}{\Gamma, \overrightarrow{x} \in \mathcal{T}(\Sigma)^n, Q[r\sigma] \vdash_{\mathcal{RE}} Q[l\sigma]} \ w$$

Π_6:

$$\frac{\Gamma, \overrightarrow{x} \in \mathcal{T}(\Sigma)^n \vdash_{\mathcal{RE}} Q[r\sigma] \ \text{(assumed)}}{\Gamma, \overrightarrow{x} \in \mathcal{T}(\Sigma)^n \vdash_{\mathcal{RE}} Q[r\sigma], Q[l\sigma]} \ w$$

Π:

$$\frac{\Pi_5 \ \Pi_6}{\Gamma, \overrightarrow{x} \in \mathcal{T}(\Sigma)^n \vdash_{\mathcal{RE}} Q[l\sigma]} \ cut$$

and we are done. $\square$

We have already proved soundness of the rewrite system IndNarrow $\setminus \{\mathbf{Orient}\}$. Now, it is easy to see that, for all contexts Γ, Γ', for all rewrite systems $\mathcal{RE}$, $\mathcal{RE}'$, and for all equational goals Q, Q', one can build a derivation $\Gamma \vdash_{\mathcal{RE}} Q \overset{*}{\rightsquigarrow}_{\text{IndNarrow}\setminus\{\mathbf{Orient}\}} \Gamma' \vdash_{\mathcal{RE}'} Q'$ whenever there exists a derivation $\Gamma \vdash_{\mathcal{RE}} Q \overset{*}{\rightsquigarrow}_{\text{IndNarrow}} \Gamma' \vdash_{\mathcal{RE}'} Q'$. Therefore, soundness of IndNarrow is a consequence of soundness of IndNarrow $\setminus \{\mathbf{Orient}\}$.

3.4   Example (Continued)

Remember that we need to prove:

$\emptyset | NI \vdash_{\mathcal{RE}_1 | \mathcal{RE}_{ind}(X+Y\approx Y+X,<,T_\Sigma^2)\{X\mapsto X_1; Y\mapsto s(Y_1)\}} s(X_1 + Y_1) \approx s(Y_1) + X_1$

We can apply **Induce** at position 2, leading to:

$\emptyset | NI \vdash_{\mathcal{RE}_1 | \mathcal{RE}'_2} s(0 + Y_3) \approx s(Y_3)$

$\emptyset | NI \vdash_{\mathcal{RE}_1 | \mathcal{RE}_{ind}(X+Y\approx Y+X,<,T_\Sigma^2)\sigma_1\sigma_2} \ s(s(X_3) + Y_3) \approx s(s(Y_3) + X_3)$

$\mathcal{RE}_{ind}(s(X_1+Y_1)\approx s(Y_1)+X_1,<,T_\Sigma^2)\sigma_2$

where $\mathcal{RE}'_2$ is easy to explicit and where $\sigma_1 = \{X \mapsto X_1; Y \mapsto s(Y_1)\}$ (coming from the previous application of **Induce**) and $\sigma_2 = \{X_1 \mapsto s(X_3); Y_1 \mapsto Y_3\}$. In the same way as before, the goal $s(0 + Y_3) \approx s(Y_3)$ is solved. Reducing with the **Rewrite** rules and using Theorem 1 to check the conditions leads directly to the proof of the last goal, therefore finishing the proof.

Notice that, following the soundness proof above, the proof search developed in the example can be straightforwardly expanded into a sequent calculus proof.

3.5   Refutational Correctness

Refutational correctness amounts to show that for each rule of the proof search system IndNarrow of the form:

$$\Gamma_1|\Gamma_2 \vdash_{\mathcal{RE}_1|\mathcal{RE}_2} Q \rightarrowtail \bigodot_{i\in I} \Gamma_1^i|\Gamma_2^i \vdash_{\mathcal{RE}_1^i|\mathcal{RE}_2^i} Q^i$$

then all the $\Gamma_1^i|\Gamma_2^i, \overrightarrow{x^i} \in \mathcal{T}(\Sigma)^{n^i} \vdash_{\mathcal{RE}_1^i|\mathcal{RE}_2^i} Q^i$ are derivable provided $\Gamma_1|\Gamma_2, \overrightarrow{x} \in \mathcal{T}(\Sigma)^n \vdash_{\mathcal{RE}_1|\mathcal{RE}_2} Q$ is.

We detail here the most delicate point which is again the case of the rule **Induce**, addressed in the following theorem.

Theorem 4. *For all contexts Γ_1, Γ_2, for all rewrite systems $\mathcal{RE}_1$, $\mathcal{RE}_2$, for any equational goal Q, for any $\omega \in DI(Q)$, and for any integer n,*

If

$$\Gamma_1|\Gamma_2 \vdash_{\mathcal{RE}_1|\mathcal{RE}_2} Q[t]_\omega \overset{Induce}{\rightarrowtail} \bigodot_{\substack{l \to r \in \mathcal{RE}_1 \\ \sigma = mgu(t,l)}} \Gamma_1|\Gamma_2 \vdash_{\mathcal{RE}_1|\mathcal{RE}_2\sigma \cup \mathcal{RE}_{ind}(Q,<)\sigma} Q[r]_\omega\sigma$$

and if the sequent $\Gamma_1 \cup \Gamma_2, \overrightarrow{x} \in \mathcal{T}(\Sigma)^n \vdash_{\mathcal{RE}_1\cup\mathcal{RE}_2} Q[t]_\omega$ (where $\overrightarrow{x} \in \mathcal{X}^n$ denotes the vector of free variables of $\mathcal{RE}_2\cup Q$) admits a proof in sequent calculus modulo, then, for any $\sigma = mgu(t,l)$, for any integer n_σ, for any vector of free variables $\overrightarrow{x}_\sigma$ of $\mathcal{RE}\sigma \cup Q\sigma$ in $\mathcal{X}^{n_\sigma}$, one can build a proof of

$$\Gamma_1 \cup \Gamma_2, \overrightarrow{x}_\sigma \in \mathcal{T}(\Sigma)^{n_\sigma} \vdash_{\mathcal{RE}_1\cup\mathcal{RE}_2\sigma\cup\{\mathcal{RE}_{ind}(Q,<)\sigma\}} Q[r]_\omega\sigma$$

Proof. Recall the notations 4. Let $\sigma = mgu(t,l)$. For any ground substitution μ, we have:

$$\Pi_{\sigma,\mu}$$

$$\frac{\Gamma, \overrightarrow{x} \in \mathcal{T}(\Sigma)^n \vdash_{\mathcal{RE}} Q}{\Gamma \vdash_{\mathcal{RE}\sigma\mu} Q\sigma\mu} r_{\sigma\mu}$$

Now, let us consider the following derivations:

$$\Pi_{1,\sigma}:$$

$$\frac{\bigwedge_{\mu\in Subst^\Sigma} \Pi_{\sigma,\mu}}{\Gamma, \overrightarrow{x}_\sigma \in \mathcal{T}(\Sigma)^{n_\sigma} \vdash_{\mathcal{RE}\sigma} Q\sigma} r^{\overrightarrow{x}_\sigma}$$

$$\Pi_{2,\sigma}:$$

$$\frac{\Pi_{1,\sigma}}{\Gamma, \overrightarrow{x}_\sigma \in \mathcal{T}(\Sigma)^{n_\sigma} \vdash_{\mathcal{RE}\sigma} Q\sigma, Q\sigma[r\sigma]_{|\omega}} w$$

Denoting $Th_{\mathcal{RE}_2\sigma}$ the canonical theory associated to $\mathcal{RE}_2\sigma$, and since $\mathcal{RE}\sigma = \mathcal{RE}_1 \cup \mathcal{RE}_2\sigma$, we obtain:

$\Pi_{3,\sigma}$:

$$\dfrac{\dfrac{\overline{Q\sigma \vdash_{\mathcal{RE}_1} Q\sigma[r\sigma]_{|\omega}}\ Ax}{\Gamma, \overrightarrow{x}_\sigma \in \mathcal{T}(\Sigma)^{n_\sigma}, Q\sigma, Th_{\mathcal{RE}_2\sigma} \vdash_{\mathcal{RE}_1} Q\sigma[r\sigma]_{|\omega}}\ w}{\Gamma, \overrightarrow{x}_\sigma \in \mathcal{T}(\Sigma)^{n_\sigma}, Q\sigma \vdash_{\mathcal{RE}\sigma} Q\sigma[r\sigma]_{|\omega}}\ push$$

Denoting $\mathcal{PE}_{ind}(Q)$ the canonical proposition associated to $\mathcal{RE}_{ind}(Q, <)$, this leads to:

$\Pi_{4,\sigma}$:

$$\dfrac{\dfrac{\dfrac{\Pi_{2,\sigma}\ \Pi_{3,\sigma}}{\Gamma, \overrightarrow{x}_\sigma \in \mathcal{T}(\Sigma)^{n_\sigma} \vdash_{\mathcal{RE}\sigma} Q\sigma[r\sigma]_{|\omega}}\ cut}{\Gamma, \overrightarrow{x}_\sigma \in \mathcal{T}(\Sigma)^{n_\sigma}, \mathcal{PE}_{ind}(Q)\sigma \vdash_{\mathcal{RE}\sigma} (Q\sigma[r\sigma]_{|\omega})}\ w}{\Gamma, \overrightarrow{x}_\sigma \in \mathcal{T}(\Sigma)^{n_\sigma} \vdash_{\mathcal{RE}\sigma \cup \mathcal{RE}_{ind}(Q)\sigma} (Q\sigma[r\sigma]_{|\omega})}\ push$$

and we are done.   □

As a corollary of Theorem 4, we get:

Theorem 5. *The proof search system* IndNarrow *is refutationally correct.*

Proof. **Induce** being handled in Theorem 4, the other inference rules **Rewrite** and **Orient** are proved refutationally correct, in similar ways. Correctness of the other rules is a consequence of correctness of deduction modulo.   □

Moreover, thanks to the **Refutation** rule which applies when no other rule of IndNarrow can be applied, we can also prove that when a derivation ends with Refutation, the original sequent has no proof in deduction modulo.

Lemma 5. *For all contexts* Γ_1, Γ_2, *for all rewrite systems* $\mathcal{RE}_1$, $\mathcal{RE}_2$, *if:*

$$\Gamma_1 | \Gamma_2 \vdash_{\mathcal{RE}_1 | \mathcal{RE}_2} Q \rightarrowtail \text{Refutation}$$

then, the sequent $\Gamma_1 | \Gamma_2 \vdash_{\mathcal{RE}_1 | \mathcal{RE}_2} Q$ *has no proof.*

Proof. If Q contains a defined symbol, there exists a defined-innermost position in $Dom(Q)$, therefore one can apply the rule *Induce*, and there is a contradiction. Since the rule *Trivial* cannot be applied either, we have $Q = t \approx t'$, with t, t' constructor terms that are not syntactically equal. Therefore, the sequent $\Gamma_1 | \Gamma_2 \vdash_{\mathcal{RE}_1 | \mathcal{RE}_2} Q$ has no proof, since the constructors are assumed to be free and $\approx$ satisfies the axioms of equality.   □

Theorem 6. *For all contexts* Γ_1, Γ_2, *for all rewrite systems* $\mathcal{RE}_1$, $\mathcal{RE}_2$, *if there exists an* IndNarrow-*derivation*

$$\Gamma_1 | \Gamma_2 \vdash_{\mathcal{RE}_1 | \mathcal{RE}_2} Q \stackrel{*}{\rightarrowtail}_{\text{IndNarrow}} \text{Refutation}$$

then, the sequent $\Gamma_1 | \Gamma_2 \vdash_{\mathcal{RE}_1 | \mathcal{RE}_2} Q$ *has no proof.*

Proof. Assume: $\Gamma_1|\Gamma_2 \vdash_{\mathcal{RE}_1|\mathcal{RE}_2} Q \rightarrowtail^*_{IndNarrow}$ Refutation

There exist contexts Γ_1', Γ_2', rewrite systems $\mathcal{RE}_1'$, $\mathcal{RE}_2'$ and an equational goal Q' such that:

$$\Gamma_1|\Gamma_2 \vdash_{\mathcal{RE}_1|\mathcal{RE}_2} Q \rightarrowtail^*_{\mathsf{IndNarrow}} \Gamma_1'|\Gamma_2' \vdash_{\mathcal{RE}_1'|\mathcal{RE}_2'} Q' \rightarrowtail_{\mathsf{IndNarrow}} \text{Refutation}$$

And, by lemma 5, the sequent $\Gamma_1'|\Gamma_2' \vdash_{\mathcal{RE}_1'|\mathcal{RE}_2'} Q'$ has no proof. Therefore, by the refutation correctness of IndNarrow (Theorem 5), $\Gamma_1|\Gamma_2 \vdash_{\mathcal{RE}_1|\mathcal{RE}_2} Q$ has no proof either. □

Refutational completeness of the proof search system IndNarrow, i.e. proving that if a sequent has no proof in deduction modulo, then there is a derivation leading to Refutation, is not detailed here, but this result can be derived from the proof given in [24] in the more complex context where associative commutative theories are considered.

4   Conclusion

We have shown how narrowing can provide the inference mechanism to perform inductive proof search. Instead of pre-computing induction schemata and induction variables, this approach has the advantage to target exactly which variables should be instantiated and how. Moreover, because the method derives directly from the deduction modulo framework, we take benefit from a direct translation from a successful proof search derivation to a sequent calculus modulo proof. Last but not least, the fact that we are precisely specifying the conditions on the induction ordering allows us to narrow the search space. Although heuristics for lemma speculation, generalisation and induction rule choice are always in need for improvement in inductive proof search, it was not the aim of our work here. For instance, a suitable noetherian ordering is implicitly assumed throughout the paper, rather than discovered by the search strategy like in explicit induction methods. Finally, it is now possible to have an automated construction of inductive proofs into the sequent calculus for insertion into proof assistants.

At the proof level, the general framework of deduction modulo is quite relevant to keep at the deduction level only the true deduction steps like modus ponens and to delegate all computational steps on propositions or terms to specialized provers using equational and rewriting techniques. Then, some parts of the proofs can be deferred to aside computations, while the true skeleton of the proof is being built. At the checking level, the experiences described in [9] of translating equational and inductive proofs to proof terms for Coq should be quite useful.

If the approach is theoretically fruitful and enlightens the relationship between rewrite based induction methods and Noetherian induction, we are clearly in need of an implementation of the results presented here. Our goal will be to achieve this as a way to mechanize proof search in a proof assistant based on type theory and the rewriting calculus [2,26]. Along these lines, a first prototype has been written in collaboration with Paul Brauner and is described in [24]. Moreover our approach provides the ability to use an induction principle based on Noetherian rewrite systems, therefore strongly enhancing over the structural induction principle which is, in practice, used in most of the current proof assistants.

This narrowing based approach opens also new fundamental questions, let us mention three of them. The first one concerns its relationship with the very useful rippling [5] technique. Indeed, in a way related to rippling, narrowing makes explicit and links with a Noetherian rewrite system what we are in need for inductively proving a goal. This analogy should be deepened and possibly exploited. A second one concerns the extension of rewrite based inductive theorem proving to class rewriting. This has been explored in particular in [3] for associative-commutative theories. The genericity of narrowing modulo may enlighten and ease the use of such class rewrite systems to base inductive proof search. This has been explored in [24]. The third one concerns inductive proof by consistency which is indeed at the source of the use of rewrite techniques for induction [22,15,6,25]. The relationship between deduction modulo and such a consistency technique is worth to be better understood.

Acknowledgments. Many thanks to the members of the Protheo team in which, from 2004 to 2007, the results presented in this paper have been elaborated, benefitting of stimulating discussions on many of the subjects developed in this paper. Special thanks to Eric Deplagne whose PhD initiated the ideas on which this paper is based on and to the anonymous referees for their careful reading and useful comments.

References

1. Baader, F., Nipkow, T.: Term Rewriting and all That. Cambridge University Press (1998)
2. Barthe, G., Cirstea, H., Kirchner, C., Liquori, L.: Pure Patterns Type Systems. In: Principles of Programming Languages (POPL 2003), ACM, New Orleans (2003)
3. Berregeb, N., Bouhoula, A., Rusinowitch, M.: SPIKE-AC: A System for Proofs by Induction in Associative-Commutative Theories. In: Ganzinger, H. (ed.) RTA 1996. LNCS, vol. 1103, pp. 428–431. Springer, Heidelberg (1996)
4. Bouhoula, A., Kounalis, E., Rusinowitch, M.: SPIKE: An Automatic Theorem Prover. In: Voronkov, A. (ed.) LPAR 1992. LNCS, vol. 624, pp. 460–462. Springer, Heidelberg (1992)
5. Bundy, A., Basin, D., Hutter, D., Ireland, A.: Rippling: Meta-Level Guidance for Mathematical Reasoning. Cambridge University Press (2005)
6. Comon, H., Nieuwenhuis, R.: Induction=i-axiomatization+first-order consistency. Inf. Comput. 159(1-2), 151–186 (2000)
7. Deplagne, E.: Système de preuve modulo récurrence. Thèse de doctorat, Université Nancy 1 (November 2002)
8. Deplagne, E., Kirchner, C.: Induction as deduction modulo. Research report A04-R-468, LORIA (November 2004)
9. Deplagne, E., Kirchner, C., Kirchner, H., Nguyen, Q.-H.: Proof Search and Proof Check for Equational and Inductive Theorems. In: Baader, F. (ed.) CADE 2003. LNCS (LNAI), vol. 2741, pp. 297–316. Springer, Heidelberg (2003)

10. Dershowitz, N., Plaisted, D.A.: Rewriting. In: Robinson, A., Voronkov, A. (eds.) Handbook of Automated Reasoning, vol. I, ch. 9, pp. 535–610. Elsevier Science (2001)
11. Dowek, G.: La part du Calcul. Université de Paris 7, Mémoire d'habilitation (1999)
12. Dowek, G., Hardin, T., Kirchner, C.: HOL-$\lambda\sigma$ an intentional first-order expression of higher-order logic. Mathematical Structures in Computer Science 11(1), 21–45 (2001)
13. Dowek, G., Hardin, T., Kirchner, C.: Theorem proving modulo. Journal of Automated Reasoning 31(1), 33–72 (2003)
14. Ferreira, M.: Termination of Term Rewriting: Well foundedness, Totality and Transformations. PhD thesis, Utrecht University (1995)
15. Ganzinger, H., Stuber, J.: Inductive theorem proving by consistency for first-order clauses. In: Rusinowitch, M., Remy, J.-L. (eds.) CTRS 1992. LNCS, vol. 656, pp. 226–241. Springer, Heidelberg (1992); Published in 1993
16. Girard, J.-Y., Lafont, Y., Taylor, P.: *Proofs and Types*. Cambridge Tracts in Theoretical Computer Science, vol. 7. Cambridge University Press (1989)
17. Huet, G.: Constrained Resolution: A Complete Method for Higher Order Logic. PhD thesis, Case Western Reserve University (1972)
18. Hullot, J.-M.: Canonical Forms and Unification. In: Bibel, W., Kowalski, R. (eds.) Proceedings 5th International Conference on Automated Deduction. LNCS, vol. 87, pp. 318–334. Springer, Heidelberg (1980)
19. Kapur, D., Zhang, H.: An overview of rewrite rule laboratory (RRL). J. Computer and Mathematics with Applications 29(2), 91–114 (1995)
20. Kirchner, C., Kirchner, H.: Rewriting, solving, proving. A preliminary version of a book (1999), `http://www.loria.fr/~ckirchne/rsp.ps.gz`
21. Kirchner, C., Kirchner, H., Rusinowitch, M.: Deduction with symbolic constraints. Revue d'Intelligence Artificielle 4(3), 9–52 (1990); Special issue on Automatic Deduction
22. Musser, D.: On proving inductive properties of abstract data types. In: Proceedings, Symposium on Principles of Programming Languages, vol. 7, Association for Computing Machinery (1980)
23. Nahon, F.: Preuve par induction dans le calcul des séquents modulo. PhD thesis, Université Henri Poincaré - Nancy I, Nancy, France, October 26 (2007)
24. Nahon, F., Kirchner, C., Kirchner, H., Brauner, P.: Inductive Proof Search Modulo. Annals of Mathematics and Artificial Intelligence 55(1-2), 123–154 (2009)
25. Steel, G.: Proof by consistency - a literature survey (March 1999)
26. Wack, B.: Typage et déduction dans le calcul de réécriture. Thèse de doctorat, Université Henri Poincaré - Nancy I, October 7 (2005)

Inst-Gen – A Modular Approach
to Instantiation-Based Automated Reasoning

Konstantin Korovin[*]

The University of Manchester
School of Computer Science
korovin@cs.man.ac.uk

Abstract. Inst-Gen is an instantiation-based reasoning method for first-order logic introduced in [18]. One of the distinctive features of Inst-Gen is a modular combination of first-order reasoning with efficient ground reasoning. Thus, Inst-Gen provides a framework for utilising efficient off-the-shelf propositional SAT and SMT solvers as part of general first-order reasoning. In this paper we present a unified view on the developments of the Inst-Gen method: (i) completeness proofs; (ii) abstract and concrete criteria for redundancy elimination, including dismatching constraints and global subsumption; (iii) implementation details and evaluation.

1 Introduction

The basic idea behind instantiation-based reasoning is to interleave smart generation of instances of first-order formulae with propositional type reasoning. Instantiation-based methods can be divided into two major categories: (i) fine-grain interleaving of instantiation with efficient propositional inference rules, and (ii) modular combination of instantiation and propositional reasoning. One of the most prominent examples from the first category is the model evolution calculus (ME) [8] which interleaves instance generation with DPLL style reasoning. The model evolution calculus is implemented in a reasoning system called Darwin [6].

Our approach to instantiation-based reasoning [18] falls into the second category, where propositional reasoning is integrated in a modular fashion and was inspired by work on hyper-linking and its extensions (see, [35,43,24]). The main advantage of the modular combination of propositional reasoning is that it allows one to use off-the-shelf SAT and SMT solvers in the context of first-order reasoning. One of our main goals is to develop a flexible theoretical framework, called Inst-Gen, for modular combination of instantiation with propositional reasoning and more generally with ground reasoning modulo theories. This framework provides methods for proving completeness of instantiation calculi, powerful redundancy elimination criteria and flexible saturation strategies. All these ingredients are crucial for developing reasoning systems which can be used in practical applications. We also show that most of the powerful machinery developed in the resolution-based framework (see [3,38]) can be suitably adapted for

---

[*] Supported by a Royal Society University Research Fellowship.

A. Voronkov and C. Weidenbach (Eds.): Ganzinger Festschrift, LNCS 7797, pp. 239–270, 2013.

the Inst-Gen method. Based on these theoretical results we have developed and implemented an automated reasoning system, called iProver [31]. iProver features state-of-the-art implementation techniques such as unification and simplification indexes; semantically-guided inferences based on propositional models; redundancy elimination based on dismatching constraints, blocking of non-proper instantiations and global subsumption. For propositional reasoning iProver uses an optimised propositional SAT solver MiniSAT [15].

One of the major success stories of instantiation-based methods is in reasoning with the effectively propositional (EPR) fragment of first-order logic, also called the Bernays-Schönfinkel class. All known instantiation-based methods are decision procedures for the EPR fragment and experimental results show that instantiation-based methods considerably outperform other methods on this fragment. In particular, iProver has been winning the EPR division of the world championship for automated theorem proving (CASC)[1] for the last four years. Recently it was shown that the EPR fragment has a number of applications in areas such as bounded model checking, panning, logic programming and knowledge representation [40,39,25,16,17,49]. The importance of the EPR fragment has triggered the development of a number of dedicated methods [12,41,7], but these are yet to be extensively evaluated and compared with general-purpose instantiation-based methods.

In this paper we present a unified view on the developments of the Inst-Gen method from theoretical foundations to implementation and evaluation: (i) completeness proofs; (ii) abstract and concrete criteria for redundancy elimination; and (iii) implementation of Inst-Gen in iProver and evaluation.

This paper is structured as follows. Preliminaries are in Section 2. In Section 3 we introduce the Inst-Gen calculus which is the basis of our framework. We show how instantiation process can be guided by propositional models of ground abstractions in Section 4. Simplifications and redundancy elimination which are crucial for practical applicability of the method are described in Sections 5–7. A combination of instantiation with resolution is described in Section 8. We discuss strategies for interleaving application of inference rules, simplifications and propositional reasoning in Section 9. In Section 10 we show that Inst-Gen is a decision procedure for the EPR fragment. In Section 11 we discuss implementation of Inst-Gen in iProver. iProver is evaluated in Section 12.

2   Preliminaries

We adopt standard terminology used in first-order reasoning [3,38]. Let $\Sigma = \langle \mathcal{P}, \mathcal{F} \rangle$ be a first-order signature, where $\mathcal{P}$ is the set of predicate symbols and $\mathcal{F}$ is the set of function symbols. We assume that $\mathcal{F}$ contains a designated constant $\bot$ (not to be confused with falsum). Let $\mathcal{V}$ be a set of variables. The set of terms over $\mathcal{F}$ and $\mathcal{V}$ will be denoted as $\mathcal{T}(\mathcal{F}, \mathcal{V})$.

A *substitution* is a mapping from variables into terms which is the identity on all but finitely many variables. Substitutions will be denoted by ρ, σ, τ, and θ.

---

[1] http://www.cs.miami.edu/~tptp/CASC/

A *clause* is a possibly empty multiset of literals denoting their disjunction and is usually written as $L_1 \vee \ldots \vee L_n$, where a *literal* being either an atomic formula or the negation thereof. We say that C is a subclause of D, and write $C \subseteq D$, if C is a submultiset of D. Variables are usually denoted by x, y, and z, whereas, letters a, b and c denote constants. If L is a literal, $\overline{L}$ denotes the complement of L.

A substitution is called a *proper instantiator* of an expression (a literal or clause) if at least one variable of the expression is mapped to a non-variable term, otherwise it is called a *non-proper instantiator*. *Renamings* are injective substitutions, mapping variables to variables. Two clauses are *variants* of each other if one can be obtained from the other by applying a renaming. We will ambiguously use $\bot$ to denote also the substitution mapping all variables to the constant $\bot$. If S is a set of clauses, by $S\bot$ we denote all ground clauses obtained by applying $\bot$ to each clause in S.

We will be working with a refined notion of instances of clauses, called closures. A *closure* is a pair consisting of a clause C and a substitution σ written $C \cdot \sigma$. A closure $C \cdot \sigma$ *represents* the clause $C\sigma$. Let us note that a clause generally has more than one representation by closures. A closure is called *ground* if it represents a ground clause. In this paper we mainly consider ground closures and will implicitly assume that closures are ground unless specified otherwise. We work modulo renaming, that is, we do not distinguish between closures $C \cdot \sigma$ and $D \cdot \tau$ for which C is a variant of D and $C\sigma$ is a variant of $D\tau$. Let S be a set of clauses and C a clause in S, then a ground closure $C \cdot \sigma$ is called a *ground instance* of C in S and we also say that the closure $C \cdot \sigma$ is a *representation* of the clause $C\sigma$ in S.

Our restrictions on the instantiation calculus and completeness proofs are based on an ordering on closures defined as follows. A *closure ordering* is any ordering $\succ$ on closures that is total, well-founded and satisfies the following condition. If $C \cdot \sigma$ and $D \cdot \tau$ are such that $C\sigma = D\tau$ and $C\theta = D$ for some proper instantiator θ, then $C \cdot \sigma \succ D \cdot \tau$. In particular, more specific representations of the same ground clause are smaller in this ordering than more general representations. For example, $(A(x,y) \vee B(y)) \cdot [f(c)/x, c/y] \succ (A(f(u),v) \vee B(v)) \cdot [c/u, c/v]$. It is easy to see that any well-founded ordering on ground clauses can be extended to a total well-founded closure ordering. For the rest of this paper we assume that $\succ$ is a closure ordering.

We consider *Herbrand interpretations* which are sometimes partial, given by consistent sets I of ground literals. A ground literal L is called *undefined* in I if neither L nor $\overline{L}$ is in I. I is called *total* if for each ground literal, I either contains the literal or its complement. A clause C is *true* (or *valid*) in a partial interpretation I, written $I \models C$, if C is true in every total extension of I, and is called *false* (*not valid*) in I, otherwise. We say that an interpretation I is a *model* of a set of clauses S if all clauses in S are true in I. We say that a set of clauses S *entails* a set of clauses S', denoted by $S \models S'$, if every Herbrand model of S is a model of S'. The truth value of a closure is defined to be equal to the truth value of the clause it represents.

3   Instantiation Calculus

The basic idea behind the modular approach to instantiation-based reasoning is to approximate the unsatisfiability problem for sets of first-order clauses by a sequence of propositional problems. This can be done in the following way. Let S be a set of first-order clauses. We first abstract S by a set of propositional clauses $S\bot$, obtained by mapping all variables into a distinguished constant $\bot$. If the propositional abstraction $S\bot$ is unsatisfiable (which can be shown by any propositional solver), then S is also unsatisfiable and we are done. If $S\bot$ is satisfiable then it still possible that S is unsatisfiable and we need to add more instances of clauses to S witnessing the unsatisfiability of S at the ground level. The process continues by refining the ground abstraction adding appropriate instances of clauses to S, until either an unsatisfiable ground abstraction is obtained or, possibly in the limit, a set of clauses that can not be refined further. In the former case the initial set of first-order clauses is unsatisfiable and in the latter case we can show that the initial set clauses is satisfiable.

There are three major issues to consider:

1. how to generate instances;
2. how to interleave propositional reasoning and instantiation;
3. how to guide instance generation and reduce the number of redundant instances.

For the generation instances we use the Inst-Gen calculus and its refinements described below. In the later sections we address the rest of these issues. Informally, we instantiate clauses in S by applying the Inst-Gen inference rule or its refinements, until we either obtain: i) a set of clauses with unsatisfiable ground abstraction; or ii) a saturated set, i.e. no new instances can be derived by Inst-Gen. In the former case the soundness of the Inst-Gen calculus implies that S is unsatisfiable, in the latter case, completeness of Inst-Gen implies that S is satisfiable (Theorem 1).

Consider a set of clauses S and assume that the ground abstraction $S\bot$ of S is satisfiable.

Inst-Gen

$$\frac{L \vee C \quad \overline{L}' \vee D}{(L \vee C)\theta \; (\overline{L}' \vee D)\theta}$$

where (i) θ is the most general unifier (mgu) of L and L',
(ii) θ is a proper instantiator of L or L'.

The Inst-Gen inference rule resembles resolution but instead of resolving we instantiate the premises, leaving to propositional reasoning to deal with the obtained instances.

The soundness of Inst-Gen is obvious: conclusions of Inst-Gen logically follow from the premises. We say that a set of clauses S is *Inst-Gen saturated* if the conclusion of any Inst-Gen inference with premises in S is also in S. In other words, if a set of clauses S is Inst-Gen saturated, then we cannot refine our ground abstraction further using Inst-Gen. Our first completeness Theorem 1 implies that in this case, satisfiability of the ground abstraction $S\bot$ is equivalent to satisfiability of the set of first-order clauses S.

Theorem 1. [18] *Let S be an Inst-Gen saturated set of clauses. Then S is satisfiable if, and only if, $S\bot$ is satisfiable.*

Theorem 1 will follow from a more general Theorem 4 proved later. Let us consider a simple example.

Example 1. Let S be the following set of clauses.

S		$S\bot$
$A(f(x),b) \vee B(x,y)$	(1)	$A(f(\bot),b) \vee B(\bot,\bot)$
$\neg A(f(f(x)),y)$	(2)	$\neg A(f(f(\bot)),\bot)$
$\neg B(f(x),x)$	(3)	$\neg B(f(\bot),\bot)$

First we note that the propositional abstraction $S\bot$ of S is satisfiable. Applying Inst-Gen to (1) and (2) we obtain

$$S_1 = S \cup \{A(f(f(x)),b) \vee B(f(x),y); \neg A(f(f(x)),b)\}.$$

Now it is easy to see that $S_1\bot$ is unsatisfiable and we can use any propositional solver to show this. On the other hand, if we consider a set of clauses S' consisting of (1) and (2), then after applying Inst-Gen we obtain an Inst-Gen saturated set of clauses and Theorem 1 implies that S' is satisfiable.

One can think of Inst-Gen instantiation inferences as refinements of the ground abstraction in the following sense. Consider two closures $C \cdot \sigma$ and $D \cdot \tau$ representing the same ground clause G, i.e., $C\sigma = D\tau = G$. We say that $C \cdot \sigma$ is a finer representation of G than $D \cdot \tau$ if $D \cdot \tau \succ C \cdot \sigma$. In particular, if C is a proper instance of D then all ground closures of C are finer representations than corresponding ground closures of D. A ground abstraction $D\bot$ of a clause $D \in S$ is intended to represent all ground instances of D which do not have a finer representation in S. Such an abstraction may need to be refined if we have a clause $(L \vee C) \in S$ and a literal $\overline{L}' \in D$ such that L and L' share a common instance, i.e unifiable, but L and L' have different abstractions, i.e. $L'\bot \neq L\bot$. Such refinements are reflected by the Inst-Gen inference system.

Inst-Gen is similar to resolution but instead of producing a resolvent we generate corresponding instances of clauses, leaving the option of producing the resolvent to the propositional reasoner. There are also subtle differences between Inst-Gen and resolution. First, resolution usually produce clauses with increasing number of literals. Inst-Gen generates instances of the initial clauses and therefore the number of literals in clauses does not increase. In particular, Inst-Gen is a decision procedure for the effectively propositional fragment – the clausal fragment where the signature is restricted to contain only predicate symbols and constants (see Section 10). Second, there is no recombination of clauses which can result in repeated work in the resolution setting (see [35] and Example 5).

Let us observe that Inst-Gen uses most general unifiers to focus on relevant conflicting instances of clauses. Inst-Gen already features some restrictions on applicability imposed by unification and requiring the unifier to be a proper instantiator; nevertheless Inst-Gen is a very prolific inference system. One source of inefficiency is that any literal in a clause can participate in an Inst-Gen inference. Next, we show how to restrict Inst-Gen to only selected literals based on a semantic criterion.

4 Semantic Selection and Hyper-inferences

Semantic selection is motivated by the following observation. Let S be a set of clauses such that its propositional abstraction $S\bot$ is satisfiable. Let $I_\bot$ be a propositional model of $S\bot$. We try to extend $I_\bot$ to a first-order model of all ground instances of clauses in S by taking the truth value of a literal $L\sigma$ to be the truth value of $L\bot$ in $I_\bot$. Such an extension can rise to conflicts. Let S be the set of clauses $\{A(f(x)) \vee C(x); \neg A(y) \vee D(y)\}$ and $I_\bot$ a model of $S\bot$. A conflict arises if both $A(f(\bot))$ and $\neg A(\bot)$ are true in $I_\bot$, as, e.g., assigning true to both $A(f(a))$ and $\neg A(f(a))$ would result in an inconsistent interpretation. We can resolve this conflict by applying Inst-Gen inference obtaining $S_1 = S \cup \{A(f(x)) \vee C(x); \neg A(f(y)) \vee D(f(y))\}$. Now the propositional solver is supplied with the necessary information about instances of clauses with conflicting literals and a propositional model of $S_1\bot$ can be extended to a first-order model of S_1. This can be generalised to restrict Inst-Gen inferences to resolve only conflicts relevant to a propositional model of the propositional abstraction of the current set of clauses.

A *selection function* sel for a set of clauses S is a mapping from clauses in S to literals such that $\text{sel}(C) \in C$ for each clause $C \in S$. We say that sel is based on a model $I_\bot$ of $S\bot$, if $I_\bot \models \text{sel}(C)\bot$ for all $C \in S$. Let S be a set of clauses such that $S\bot$ is consistent and sel be a selection function based on a model $I_\bot$ of $S\bot$. Then, the instance generation calculus SInst-Gen based on sel, is defined as follows.

SInst-Gen

$$\frac{L \vee C \qquad \overline{L}' \vee D}{(L \vee C)\theta \ (\overline{L}' \vee D)\theta}$$

where (i) θ is the most general unifier of L and L', and
(ii) $\text{sel}(L \vee C) = L$ and $\text{sel}(\overline{L}' \vee D) = \overline{L}'$.

Although we have omitted the requirement on θ to be a proper instantiator, this condition always holds for SInst-Gen inferences.

Proposition 1. *In any inference by SInst-Gen, the mgu θ is a proper instantiator for at least one of the literals L or L'.*

Proof. Literals L and $\overline{L}'$ are selected by sel. Therefore $L\bot$ and $\overline{L}'\bot$ are true in the model $I_\bot$ of $S\bot$. Assume that θ is not proper for both L and L'. Then, $L\bot = L\theta\bot = L'\theta\bot = L'\bot$ contradicting that both $L\bot$ and $\overline{L}'\bot$ are true in $I_\bot$. ☐

Selection functions can dramatically restrict the applicability of the inferences.

Example 2. Let S be the following set of clauses:

$$A(x_1, x_2, y) \vee A(x_2, x_3, y) \vee \ldots \vee A(x_n, x_{n+1}, y) \qquad (1)$$
$$\neg A(c_1, d, y) \vee \neg A(c_2, d, y) \vee \ldots \vee \neg A(c_n, d, y). \qquad (2)$$

Unrestricted applications of Inst-Gen will generate exponentially many (wrt. n) different instances of the first clause. Indeed, it is easy to see that using Inst-Gen one can derive every instance of (1) where each variable x_i with an odd index i is mapped into one of the constants $c_1, \ldots, c_n$ and variables with even indexes are mapped into d. There are exponentially many such instances. Let us now consider SInst-Gen on this set of clauses. Consider a model $I_\perp$ of $S\perp$. Assume that $I_\perp \models A(\perp, \perp, \perp)$ and $I_\perp \models \neg A(c_1, d, \perp)$. Let sel be a selection function based on $I_\perp$ selecting $A(x_1, x_2, y)$ in clause (1) and $\neg A(c_1, d, y)$ in clause (2). Applying SInst-Gen to clauses (1) and (2) we obtain the conclusion:

$$A(c_1, d, y) \lor A(d, x_3, y) \lor \ldots \lor A(x_n, x_{n+1}, y). \qquad (3)$$

Now, extending the model $I_\perp$ to satisfy $A(d, \perp, \perp)$ and the selection function to select $A(d, x_3, y)$ in (3) will block all further inferences by SInst-Gen. The completeness Theorem 2, below, implies that S is satisfiable. This example is also interesting because most state-of-the-art resolution-based provers (e.g., E, Metis, SPASS and Vampire in the resolution mode) do not terminate on this set of clauses already for $n = 7$.

A natural generalisation of SInst-Gen is to consider hyper-inferences. For this we need to extend selection functions to select sets of literals from a clause rather than one literal. More formally, let S be a set of clauses such that $S\perp$ is consistent and $I_\perp$ a propositional model of $S\perp$. A *hyper-selection function* hsel for a set of clauses S is a mapping from clauses in S to multisets of literals such that $\emptyset \neq \mathsf{hsel}(C) \subseteq C$ for each clause $C \in S$. Literals L in $\mathsf{hsel}(C)$ are called *selected* in C (by hsel). For each clause $C \in S$ let us define a multiset of literals $\mathsf{sat}_\perp(C) = \{L \in C \mid I_\perp \models L\perp\}$. We say that a hyper-selection function hsel is *based* on $I_\perp$ if $\mathsf{hsel}(C) \subseteq \mathsf{sat}_\perp(C)$ for every $C \in S$. Thus, hyper-selection functions select some or all of the literals in a clause, whose $\perp$-instances are true in $I_\perp$. Let hsel be a hyper-selection function based on a model $I_\perp$ of $S\perp$. Instance generation, based on hsel, is defined as follows.

SHInst-Gen

$$\frac{\overline{L}'_1 \lor C_1 \quad \ldots \quad \overline{L}'_k \lor C_k \quad L_1 \lor \ldots \lor L_k \lor D}{(\overline{L}'_1 \lor C_1)\theta \quad \ldots \quad (\overline{L}'_k \lor C_k)\theta \quad (L_1 \lor \ldots \lor L_k \lor D)\theta}$$

where (i) θ is the most general unifier of $(L_1, L'_1), \ldots, (L_k, L'_k)$, and
(ii) $\mathsf{hsel}(L_1 \lor \ldots \lor L_k \lor D) = \{L_1, \ldots, L_k\}$, and
(iii) $\overline{L}'_i \in \mathsf{hsel}(\overline{L}'_i \lor C_i)$, for $1 \leq i \leq k$.

It is easy to see that SInst-Gen is a special case of SHInst-Gen when the hyper-selection function is restricted to select exactly one literal in each clause. As in the case of SInst-Gen, conditions on selection functions imply that θ is a proper instantiator for each pairs of literals (L_i, L'_i), $1 \leq i \leq k$.

Consider a set of clauses S such that $S\perp$ is satisfiable and a hyper-selection function hsel based on a model of $S\perp$. A set of clauses S is *SHInst-Gen saturated* wrt. hsel if the conclusion of any SHInst-Gen inference with premises in S is also in S. Now we can formulate the completeness theorem for SHInst-Gen, which also applies to SInst-Gen as a special case.

Theorem 2. [18] *Let S be a set of clauses such that $S\perp$ is satisfiable. If S is SHInst-Gen saturated wrt. a hyper-selection function based on a model of $S\perp$ then S is satisfiable.*

5   Redundancy Elimination

Redundancy elimination is crucial for practical applicability of any calculus. Our framework allows one to formulate a semantic-based notion of redundant clauses and redundant inferences. We first formulate redundancy notions for ground closures, which play a similar role to ground clauses in the resolution calculus.

Let $\succ$ be a closure ordering. Consider a set of ground closures U. A ground closure $C \cdot \sigma$ is called *redundant* in U if there exist ground closures $C_1 \cdot \sigma_1, \ldots, C_k \cdot \sigma_k$ in U such that, (1) $C_1 \cdot \sigma_1, \ldots, C_k \cdot \sigma_k \models C \cdot \sigma$ and (2) $C \cdot \sigma \succ C_i \cdot \sigma_i$ for each $0 \le i \le k$. In other words, a ground closure is redundant in U if it logically follows from smaller closures (w.r.t. $\succ$) in U.

We adapt this redundancy notion to be defined also on clauses by observing that a clause C is representing the set of all its ground closures $C \cdot \sigma$. Let S be a set of clauses and $\widehat{S}$ the set of all ground closures represented by clauses in S. A clause C (possibly non-ground) is called redundant in S if each ground closure $C \cdot \sigma$ is redundant in $\widehat{S}$. This abstract redundancy criterion can be used to justify many standard redundancies.

Tautologies. Note that tautologies are implied by the empty set of closures and therefore are redundant in any set of clauses.

Subsumption. A clause C *strictly subsumes* a clause C' if there is a substitution θ such that $C\theta \subsetneq C'$. For example, $A(x, y)$ strictly subsumes $A(x, a) \vee B(x)$. An ordering $\succ$ on ground clauses is called *strict subsumption compatible* if $C' \succ C$ for each ground clauses C and C' such that C is a strict sub-multiset of C', i.e., $C \subsetneq C'$. A closure ordering is *strict subsumption compatible* if its restriction to ground clauses is strict subsumption compatible. It is easy to see that if the closure ordering $\succ$ is strict subsumption compatible, then strict subsumption is an admissible redundancy. One can also eliminate non-strictly subsumed clauses in the case of non-proper instantiators as follows. An ordering is called *non-proper subsumption compatible* if $C' \cdot \sigma \succ C \cdot \theta\sigma$ for every closures $C' \cdot \sigma$ and $C \cdot \theta\sigma$ where $C\theta = C'$ and θ is a non-proper instantiator and not a renaming. For example, if the closure ordering $\succ$ is non-proper subsumption compatible, then $A(x, x) \vee B(x)$ is redundant w.r.t. $A(x, y) \vee B(y)$. Closure orderings which are strict and at the same time non-proper subsumption compatible are called *subsumption compatible orderings*. It is easy to see that any subsumption compatible ordering on ground clauses can be extended to a subsumption compatible closure ordering. Let us note that full subsumption is not an admissible redundancy. Indeed, all clauses derived by Inst-Gen are subsumed by the initial clauses.

Instantiation-Specific Redundancy. Our semantic redundancy criteria can also be used to define instantiation-specific redundancies. In particular, consider a clause C and a proper instance of C, $D = C\theta$. Then, all ground closures of C, which are also represented by D, are redundant. We will discuss this redundancy in detail when we consider dismatching constraints in Section 6.

An inference with premises $C_1, \ldots, C_n$ and a unifier θ (thus deriving conclusions $C_1\theta, \ldots, C_n\theta$) is *redundant* in S if for every substitution ρ grounding all the $C_i\theta$ there exists an index i_0 such that $C_{i_0} \cdot \theta\rho$ is redundant in S.

Example 3. Let the set of function symbols in Σ consists of the constants a and b and assume that $\succ$ is subsumption compatible. Consider the following set of clauses:

$$\frac{A(x, y) \lor B(y)}{\neg A(a, z) \lor C(z)} \quad \begin{matrix}(1) \\ (3)\end{matrix} \qquad \frac{B(a)}{C(b)} \quad \begin{matrix}(2) \\ (4)\end{matrix}$$

Let us show that the SInst-Gen inference between clauses (1) and (3) is redundant. Let $\theta = \{a/x; z/y\}$ be the mgu of atoms of the selected literals in clauses (1) and (3). Then, for any grounding substitution ρ, either closure $(A(x, y) \lor B(y)) \cdot \theta\rho$ is redundant (in the case $z\rho = a$), or closure $(\neg A(a, z) \lor C(z)) \cdot \theta\rho$ is redundant (in the case $z\rho = b$).

An important property of the (SH)Inst-Gen calculus is that adding the conclusion of an inference makes the inference redundant. The next proposition shows that in order to make an inference redundant it is sufficient to add to the clause set at least one properly instantiated clause from the conclusion (such a clause always exits, by Proposition 1).

Proposition 2. *Let $C\theta$ be a conclusion of an (SH)Inst-Gen inference and a proper instance of its respective premise C. If $C\theta$ is in S, or is redundant in S, then the inference is redundant.*

Proof. Immediately follows from the definition of redundant inference.

We can have additional flexibility with partial instantiations as follows. Let $C\theta$ be as in Proposition 2 and θ' any substitution which is a proper instantiator for C and more general than θ. Then, adding $C\theta'$ to S makes the inference redundant.

Example 4. Consider the following set of clauses $S = \{C, D\}$ where $C = A(x, y) \lor B(x)$ and $D = \neg A(f(a), b)$. The most general unifier of $A(x, y)$ and $A(\overline{f(a), b})$ is $\theta = \{f(a)/x, b/y\}$. Consider a proper instantiator of C which is more general than θ, for example $\theta' = \{f(z)/x\}$. Then, adding $C\theta' = A(f(z), y) \lor B(f(z))$ to S makes the inference between C and D redundant. Such partial instantiations can be useful for keeping reasoning at a more general level and can be combined with dismatching constraints (see Section 6).

The idea of partial instantiations is developed further in [18], where it is used to approximate first-order clauses by clauses from first-order fragments beyond propositional logic.

A set of clauses S is called *SHInst-Gen saturated up to redundancy* if all inferences in SHInst-Gen from premises in S are redundant in S. The next theorem shows that completeness is preserved under redundancy elimination.

Theorem 3. [18] *Let S be a set of clauses such that $S\perp$ is satisfiable. Let hsel be a hyper-selection function based on a model of $S\perp$. If S is SHInst-Gen saturated up to redundancy then S is satisfiable.*

This theorem also applies to weaker systems SInst-Gen and Inst-Gen. We show below that Theorem 3 is a consequence of a more general Theorem 4.

For a finer control over redundancy we consider the notion of inferences and saturation at the level of ground closures. For a set of ground closures U let $\overline{U}$ denote the set of clauses C such that $C \cdot \sigma$ is in U for some grounding substitution σ. Let hsel be a hyper-selection function for $\overline{U}$ based on a model $I_\perp$ of $\overline{U}\perp$. A SHInst-Gen inference on ground closures is defined as follows.

SHInst-Gen (ground closures)

$$\frac{(\overline{L}_1' \vee C_1) \cdot \sigma_1 \quad \ldots \quad (\overline{L}_k' \vee C_k) \cdot \sigma_k \quad (L_1 \vee \ldots \vee L_k \vee D) \cdot \sigma}{(\overline{L}_1' \vee C_1)\theta \cdot \tau_1 \quad \ldots \quad (\overline{L}_k' \vee C_k)\theta \cdot \tau_k \quad (L_1 \vee \ldots \vee L_k \vee D)\theta \cdot \tau}$$

where (i) θ is the most general unifier of $(L_1, L_1'), \ldots, (L_k, L_k')$,
(ii) $\mathsf{hsel}(L_1 \vee \ldots \vee L_k \vee D) = \{L_1, \ldots, L_k\}$, and
(iii) $\overline{L}_i' \in \mathsf{hsel}(\overline{L}_i' \vee C_i)$, for $1 \le i \le k$, and
(iv) $(\overline{L}_1' \vee C_1)\sigma_1 = (\overline{L}_1' \vee C_1)\theta\tau_1, \ldots, (\overline{L}_k' \vee C_k)\sigma_k = (\overline{L}_k' \vee C_k)\theta\tau_k,$
   $(L_1 \vee \ldots \vee L_k \vee D)\sigma = (L_1 \vee \ldots \vee L_k \vee D)\theta\tau$

A ground SHInst-inference with premises $C_1 \cdot \sigma_1, \ldots, C_n \cdot \sigma_n$ and conclusion $C_1\theta \cdot \tau_1, \ldots, C_n\theta \cdot \tau_n$ is redundant in a set of ground closures U if at least one of the closures $C_i \cdot \theta\tau_i = C_i \cdot \sigma_i$ is redundant in U, for $1 \le i \le n$. We say that a set of ground closures U is *SHInst-Gen saturated up to redundancy* wrt. hsel , if any ground SHInst-inference with a premise in U is redundant in U.

Theorem 4. *Let U be a set of ground closures such that $\overline{U}\perp$ is satisfiable. Let hsel be a hyper-selection function based on a model of $\overline{U}\perp$. If U is SHInst-Gen saturated up to redundancy wrt.* hsel *then U is satisfiable.*

Proof. For simplicity of exposition we first prove the theorem for a special case of binary inferences (SInst-Gen) and later show how to modify the proof for hyper-inferences (SHInst-Gen). The proof is based on an adaptation of the model-generation technique (see [3,38]).

Let U be a set of ground closures such that $\overline{U}\perp$ is satisfiable. First, we construct a candidate (partial) model I_U of U and then show that if U is SInst-saturated up to redundancy, any total extension of I_U is indeed a model of U. Let $I_\perp$ be a model of $\overline{U}\perp$ and sel a selection function on clauses in $\overline{U}$ based on $I_\perp$.

Informally, we construct the model I_U by adding literals in a way to satisfy closures in U. In order to construct I_U we construct a sequence of partial models and sets of literals by induction on closures ordered by $\succ$ as follows. Let $\widehat{C} = C \cdot \sigma$ be a ground closure. Suppose, as an induction hypothesis, we have defined sets of literals $\epsilon_{\widehat{D}}$, for all ground closures $\widehat{D}$ smaller than $\widehat{C}$ wrt. $\succ$. Let $I_{\widehat{C}}$ denote the set $\bigcup_{\widehat{C} \succ \widehat{D}} \epsilon_{\widehat{D}}$.

We define $\epsilon_{\widehat{C}}$ as follows. Assume $\widehat{C}$ is in U and define $L = \mathsf{sel}(C)$. We define $\epsilon_{\widehat{C}} = \{L\sigma\}$, if the following conditions hold:

1. $I_{\widehat{C}} \not\models C\sigma$, i.e., there is a total model extending $I_{\widehat{C}}$ in which $C\sigma$ is false, and
2. $L\sigma$ is undefined in $I_{\widehat{C}}$, i.e., neither $I_{\widehat{C}} \models L\sigma$ nor $I_{\widehat{C}} \models \overline{L}\sigma$ holds.

Otherwise, if either $\widehat{C}$ is not in U or at least one of the conditions (1)–(2) is not satisfied, we define $\epsilon_{\widehat{C}} = \emptyset$. In the case when $\epsilon_{\widehat{C}} = \{L\sigma\}$ we say that $L\sigma$ is *produced* by $\widehat{C}$. Define $I_U = \bigcup_{\widehat{C}} \epsilon_{\widehat{C}}$. It follows immediately from the construction that I_U is consistent.

Now, let us assume that U is SInst-saturated up to redundancy. Let I be any total extension of I_U. In order to prove our theorem we show that I is a model of U.

First, we note that our model construction satisfies the following:

- *monotonicity:* if a ground closure $\widehat{C}$ is true in some $I_{\widehat{C}}$ then $\widehat{C}$ true in all $I_{\widehat{C}'}$ for $\widehat{C}' \succ \widehat{C}$ and also true in I, and
- *productiveness:* if $\widehat{C}$ is a productive closure then (i) $I_{\widehat{C}} \not\models \widehat{C}$, and (ii) $\widehat{C}$ is true in $I_{\widehat{C}} \cup \epsilon_{\widehat{C}}$ and hence $\widehat{C}$ true in I.

Now, by induction on $\succ$ we show that every ground closure $\widehat{C}$ in U is true in $I_{\widehat{C}} \cup \epsilon_{\widehat{C}}$. From this and monotonicity of the model construction our theorem follows. Assume otherwise. Let $\widehat{C} = C\cdot\sigma$ be the minimal ground closure in U such that $I_{\widehat{C}} \cup \epsilon_{\widehat{C}} \not\models \widehat{C}$. Let $L = \text{sel}(C)$. As $\widehat{C}$ is not productive and $I_{\widehat{C}} \not\models \widehat{C}$ we have $\overline{L}\sigma \in I_{\widehat{C}}$. Indeed, otherwise all conditions (1)–(2) of the model construction would be satisfied and $\widehat{C}$ would be productive. Let $\widehat{D} = D \cdot \tau$ be a closure producing $\overline{L}\sigma$ into $I_{\widehat{C}}$, where $\widehat{C} \succ \widehat{D}$. We have $D = \overline{L}' \vee D'$ where $\overline{L}'$ is selected by sel and $\overline{L}'\tau = \overline{L}\sigma$. Therefore, a ground SInst-Gen inference is applicable to closures $\widehat{C}$ and $\widehat{D}$ producing $C\theta \cdot \sigma'$ and $D\theta \cdot \tau'$, where (i) θ is the most general unifier of L and L', and (ii) $C\theta\sigma' = C\sigma$ and $D\theta\tau' = D\tau$. By the assumption of the theorem U is SInst-saturated and hence this inference is redundant. Therefore, at least one of the closures $C \cdot \theta\sigma' = C \cdot \sigma = \widehat{C}$ or $D\theta \cdot \tau' = D \cdot \tau = \widehat{D}$ is redundant. Assume that $\widehat{C}$ is redundant. Then, $\widehat{C}$ follows from smaller (wrt. $\succ$) closures $\widehat{C}_1, \dots, \widehat{C}_n$ in U. By induction hypothesis, we have that each $\widehat{C}_i$ is true in $I_{\widehat{C}_i} \cup \epsilon_{\widehat{C}_i}$, and by monotonicity is true in $I_{\widehat{C}}$, for $1 \leq i \leq n$. From this it follows that $\widehat{C}$ is true in $I_{\widehat{C}}$, contradicting our assumption. Similarly, we arrive at a contradiction when we assume that $\widehat{D}$ is redundant. Indeed, if $\widehat{D}$ follows from smaller closures in U, then by induction hypothesis these closures are true in $I_{\widehat{D}}$, hence $\widehat{D}$ is true in $I_{\widehat{D}}$, contradicting productiveness of $\widehat{D}$. This concludes the proof of this theorem for the case of SInst-Gen.

The case of hyper-inferences is similar, we only need to make the following modifications: (i) consider hyper-selection hsel in place of selection sel, (ii) in the model construction, we define $\epsilon_{\widehat{C}} = \{L\sigma\}$ if $\widehat{C}$ is in U and $L \in \text{hsel}(C)$ such that conditions (1)–(2) are satisfied; if there are several such literals we can choose any of them to define $\epsilon_{\widehat{C}}$, (iii) we prove that I is a model for U in a similar way as above. ❏

Let us note that completeness Theorem 3 for clauses follows from Theorem 4 as follows. Let S be a set of clauses such that $S\perp$ is satisfiable. Assume that S is SHInst-Gen saturated up to redundancy wrt. a hyper-selection function hsel based on a model of $S\perp$. Let U be the set of all ground instances of clauses in S. We have that $\overline{U} = S$ and U is SHInst-Gen saturated up to redundancy wrt. hsel. By Theorem 4, U is satisfiable and therefore S is satisfiable.

Next we describe how our abstract redundancy criteria can be used to justify practical redundancy elimination. We start by introducing dismatching constraints which are used to discard redundant ground closures. Then we show how the reasoner for ground clauses can be used to simplify clauses. Finally we show how the resolution calculus can be combined with instantiation.

6   Dismatching Constraints

Let us consider a clause $C \in S$. As we have seen, adding a proper instance $C\theta$ of a clause C (e.g., as a result of applying an SInst-Gen inference) makes some ground closures represented by C redundant and consequently certain inferences with C redundant. In particular, all closures $C \cdot \sigma$ such that $C\sigma = C\theta\tau$ for a grounding substitution τ are redundant in the presence of $C\theta$. We can efficiently represent this information about redundant closures using dismatching constraints. Let us note that in the context of resolution and paramodulation various kinds of constraints have been considered (see e.g. [38,29,10]). Dismatching constraints are particularly attractive: on the one hand they provide powerful restrictions for the instantiation calculus, and on the other hand, checking dismatching constraints can be efficiently implemented.

An *atomic dismatching constraint* is a pair of variable disjoint tuples of terms, denoted $\langle s_1, \ldots, s_n \rangle \not\preceq \langle t_1, \ldots, t_n \rangle$, or simply $\bar{s} \not\preceq \bar{t}$. A solution to a constraint $\bar{s} \not\preceq \bar{t}$ is a substitution σ such that for every substitution γ, $\bar{s}\sigma \not\equiv \bar{t}\gamma$. For example, consider an atomic dismatching constraint $\varphi(x, y) = \langle x \rangle \not\preceq \langle f(y) \rangle$. Then, the substitution $\sigma_1 = \{a/x\}$ is a solution to $\varphi(x, y)$, but $\sigma_2 = \{f(g(a))/x\}$ is not since there is a substitution $\gamma = \{g(a)/y\}$ such that $\langle x \rangle \sigma_2 \equiv \langle f(y) \rangle \gamma$. It is easy to see that an atomic dismatching constraint $\bar{s} \not\preceq \bar{t}$ is satisfiable if and only if for all substitutions γ, $\bar{s} \not\equiv \bar{t}\gamma$. In other words, an atomic dismatching constraint $\bar{s} \not\preceq \bar{t}$ is not satisfiable if and only if there is a substitution γ such that $\bar{s} \equiv \bar{t}\gamma$, which is a familiar matching problem.

A *dismatching constraint* $ds(\bar{s}, \bar{t}) = \wedge_{i=1}^{n} \bar{s}_i \not\preceq \bar{t}_i$ is a conjunction of atomic dismatching constraints where every $\bar{t}_i$ is variable disjoint from all $\bar{s}_j$, and $\bar{t}_k$, for $i \neq k$. A substitution σ is a *solution* of a dismatching constraint $\wedge_{i=1}^{n} \bar{s}_i \not\preceq \bar{t}_i$ if σ is a solution of each $\bar{s}_i \not\preceq \bar{t}_i$, for $1 \leq i \leq n$.

Proposition 3. *The satisfiability problem for dismatching constraints can be solved in linear-time.*

Proof. As we noted above, the satisfiability problem for dismatching constraints can be reduced in linear-time to the matching problem which can be solved in linear-time (see, e.g., [2]).   ❑

A *constrained clause* $C \mid [\, \varphi \,]$ is a clause C together with a dismatching constraint φ. We will always assume that for a constrained clause $C \mid [\, \wedge_{i=1}^{n} \bar{s}_i \not\preceq \bar{t}_i \,]$, the clause C is variable disjoint from all t_i, $1 \leq i \leq n$. A constrained clause $C \mid [\, \varphi \,]$ represents the set of ground closures $\{C \cdot \sigma \mid \sigma$ is a solution to $\varphi\}$, denoted $Cl(C \mid [\, \varphi \,])$. An unconstrained clause C can be seen as a constrained clause with the empty constraint $C \mid [\,]$. For a set S of constrained clauses, $Cl(S)$ denotes the set of all ground closures represented by constrained clauses in S. Let S be a set of constrained clauses, then $\widetilde{S}$ denotes the set of all *unconstrained clauses* obtained from S by dropping all constraints. We say that a set of constrained clauses S is *well-constrained* if $Cl(S) \models Cl(\widetilde{S})$. In the following we consider only well-constrained sets of clauses.

Now we formulate an extension of SInst-Gen with dismatching constraints, called DSInst-Gen. For simplicity of the exposition we consider only binary inferences, the extension to hyper-inferences can be done in a similar way. DSInst-Gen inferences will generate new instances of clauses and also extend constraints of clauses in the premises. Let S be a set of constrained clauses such that $\widetilde{S}\perp$ is consistent and sel be a selection function based on a model $I_\perp$ of $\widetilde{S}\perp$. Then, DSInst-Gen inference system is defined as follows.

DSInst-Gen

$$\frac{L \vee C \mid [\,\varphi\,] \quad \overline{L}' \vee D \mid [\,\psi\,]}{L \vee C \mid [\,\varphi \wedge \bar{x} \not\preceq \bar{x}\theta\,] \quad (L \vee C)\theta}$$

where (i) $\bar{x}$ is a tuple of all variables in L, and

(ii) θ is the most general unifier of L and L', wlog. we assume that variables in the range of θ do not occur in $L \vee C \mid [\,\varphi\,]$ and the domain of θ contains all variable in $\bar{x}$, and

(iii) $\mathrm{sel}(L \vee C) = L$, and $\mathrm{sel}(\overline{L}' \vee D) = \overline{L}'$, and

(iv) θ is a proper instantiator for L, and

(v) $\varphi\theta$ and $\psi\theta$ are both satisfiable dismatching constraints.

DSInst-Gen is a replacement rule, that is replacing the clause in the left premise by clauses in the conclusion. The clause in the right premise can be seen as a side condition, that is no instances of this clause are produced.

We can see that in addition to semantic restrictions imposed by the selection function, instantiation rule is applicable only if dismatching constraints are satisfiable after applying θ. Let us note that applications of DSInst-Gen preserves well-constrainedness of sets of clauses.

The notion of redundancy can be easily adapted from clauses to constrained clauses as dismatching constraints can be seen as a method for discarding redundant ground closures. A constrained clause $C \mid [\,\varphi\,]$ is *redundant* wrt. a set of constrained clauses S if all closures in $Cl(C \mid [\,\varphi\,])$ are redundant in $Cl(S)$. A DSInst-Gen inference with the premises $C \mid [\,\varphi\,]$, $D \mid [\,\psi\,]$ and the conclusion $C \mid [\,\varphi \wedge \bar{x} \not\preceq \bar{x}\theta\,]$, $C\theta$ is *redundant* in S if the following holds. For any substitution ρ grounding for $C\theta$ and $D\theta$, which is a solution to $\varphi\theta$ and $\psi\theta$, either $C \cdot \theta\rho$ or $D \cdot \theta\rho$ is redundant in $Cl(S)$. A set of constrained clauses S is DSInst-Gen *saturated up to redundancy* if all inferences by DSInst-Gen from premises in S are redundant in S. The DSInst-Gen calculus can be seen as a way of lifting the (binary version of) SHInst-Gen calculus from closures to constrained clauses.

Theorem 5. *Let S be a set of constrained clauses such that $\widetilde{S}\perp$ is satisfiable. If S is DSInst-Gen saturated up to redundancy wrt. a selection function based on a model of $\widetilde{S}\perp$, then $Cl(S)$ is satisfiable.*

Proof. Indeed, if S satisfies the assumption of the theorem then $Cl(S)$ is SHInst-Gen saturated up to redundancy. Therefore the theorem follows from Theorem 4.

DSInst-Gen saturation strategies will be considered in Section 9.

Example 5. Let S be the following set of clauses where selected literals are underlined.

$$\underline{\neg A(x)} \vee C(x) \quad (0), \qquad \underline{A(f(y))} \vee D_1 \quad (1),$$
$$\underline{A(f^{i_2}(y))} \vee D_2 \quad (2),$$
$$\cdots$$
$$\underline{A(f^{i_n}(y))} \vee D_n \quad (n).$$

Where $i_k \geq 1$ for $2 \leq k \leq n$, and $f^m(t)$ denotes m applications of f: $f(\ldots f(t) \ldots)$. Applying DSInst-Gen to clauses (0) and (1) will produce $\neg A(f(x)) \vee C(f(x))$, denoted as (0″). We also replace clause (0) with $\neg A(x) \vee C(x) \mid [\, x \not\preceq f(z)\,]$, denoted as (0′), obtaining a new set of clauses S'. Assume that the new selection for S' is the same on the old clauses $(1), \ldots, (n)$ and (0′) inherits the selection from (0). This implies that $C(x)$ should be selected in (0″). Therefore S' will be as follows:

$$\underline{\neg A(x)} \vee C(x) \mid [\, x \not\preceq f(z)\,] \quad (0'), \qquad \underline{A(f(y))} \vee D_1 \quad (1),$$
$$\neg A(f(x)) \vee \underline{C(f(x))} \quad (0''), \qquad \underline{A(f^{i_2}(y))} \vee D_2 \quad (2),$$
$$\cdots$$
$$\underline{A(f^{i_n}(y))} \vee D_n \quad (n).$$

We can see that S' is DSInst-Gen saturated and therefore S is satisfiable by Theorem 5. Indeed, inferences between clauses (0′) and (1)–(n) are blocked by the dismatching constraint of the clause (0′). Let us note that without dismatching constraints, we would need to consider all inferences between clauses (0) and (1)–(n).

Let us compare DSInst-Gen to resolution, assuming that the same selected literals are eligible for resolution inferences. First we note that all inferences between (0) and (1)–(n) are applicable. Keeping in mind that a clause can be seen as a representation of all its ground instances we can note that instances represented by $C(x)$ are copied at each resolution inference and recombined with different clauses. This can result in repeated work on the same instances of $C(x)$ and is known as the recombination problem [35]. Dismatching constraints allow one to avoid such problems in the instantiation setting.

Without losing completeness of DSInst-Gen we can replace satisfiability for dismatching constraints with a stronger notion, called ground satisfiability. We say that a dismatching constraint φ is *ground satisfiable* if there is a grounding substitution σ which is a solution to φ. Obviously, if a constraint is ground satisfiable then it is satisfiable but converse need not hold. Consider a signature consisting of a constant a, a unary function symbol f and predicate symbols. Then, a constraint $x \not\preceq f(y) \wedge x \not\preceq a$ is satisfiable but not ground satisfiable. We can see that ground satisfiability is signature dependent, and two notions of satisfiability coincide in the case of signatures containing infinite number of constants. Problems related to ground satisfiability of dismatching constraints were studied in a number of works [27,34,42]. In contrast to the problem of satisfiability, which can be solved in linear-time, the problem of ground satisfiability is NP-complete.

Theorem 6. [34,27] *The ground satisfiability problem for dismatching constraints is NP-complete.*

7   Simplification by Propositional Reasoning

Having at hand a powerful propositional solver it is natural to investigate methods for redundancy elimination which utilise propositional or ground reasoning.

Let us first consider the case of simplifying ground closures. In order to apply our abstract redundancy criterion to simplify a ground closure $C \cdot \sigma$ wrt. a set of ground closures U we consider a set of closures $Sim = \{D_1 \cdot \tau_1, \ldots D_n \cdot \tau_n\}$ (not necessarily contained in U) such that:

1. $U \models D_1 \cdot \tau_1, \ldots, U \models D_n \cdot \tau_n$, and
2. $D_1 \cdot \tau_1, \ldots, D_n \cdot \tau_n \models C \cdot \sigma$, and
3. $C \cdot \sigma \succ D_1 \cdot \tau_1, \ldots, C \cdot \sigma \succ D_n \cdot \tau_n$.

We call Sim a *simplification set* for $C \cdot \sigma$ wrt. U. If Sim is a simplification set for $C \cdot \sigma$ wrt. U then we can replace $C \cdot \sigma$ in U by closures in Sim, without losing neither soundness nor completeness. There are a number of issues to consider in this general scheme:

- how to choose a candidate for a simplification set Sim,
- how to check whether conditions (1)–(3) above are satisfied.

In this paper we consider the case when a candidate for a simplification set for a closure $C \cdot \sigma$ consists of a strict subclosure of $C \cdot \sigma$. A closure $D \cdot \tau$ is a *strict subclosure* of a closure $C \cdot \sigma$, denoted by $D \cdot \tau \subsetneq C \cdot \sigma$, if $D \subsetneq C$ and $D\tau \subsetneq C\sigma$. In this case, condition (2) is trivially satisfied. In order to satisfy condition (3) we assume that $\succ$ is subsumption compatible (see Section 5). The most difficult is to check condition (1). Indeed, condition (1) is at least as complex as the initial problem of unsatisfiability of U. Fortunately, for redundancy elimination it is sufficient to consider sound approximations of the entailment relation in (1). Next we consider such approximations based on propositional reasoning.

Let us put these considerations in the context of constrained clauses. Let S be a set of (well-constrained) clauses. The notion of a simplification set can be readily adapted for clauses. Together with S, we consider a set of ground clauses S_{gr} such that $S \models S_{gr}$. For simplicity of exposition we assume that S_{gr} is an extension of $\widetilde{S}\perp$ by auxiliary ground clauses implied by S. The set S_{gr} will be used in propositional reasoning for approximating condition (1). Let us note that clauses in S_{gr} do not participate in instantiation inferences. In Section 7.1 we consider simplification of ground clauses, and in Section 7.2 simplification of clauses with variables.

7.1   Simplification of Ground Clauses

In this section we consider the case of simplifying ground clauses wrt. a set of clauses S. Let C be a ground clause to simplify. As a candidate for a simplification set we consider a set consisting of a strict subclause $D \subsetneq C$. Using the propositional solver we can check whether $S_{gr} \models D$. If this is the case, adding D to S makes C redundant wrt. to the new set $S \cup \{D\}$. We call this simplification as *global propositional subsumption* wrt. S_{gr}.

Global Propositional Subsumption

$$\frac{D \vee D'}{D}$$

where $S_{gr} \models D$ and D' is not empty.

Global propositional subsumption is a simplification rule, which allows one to remove the clause in the premise after adding the conclusion. Let us note that although the number of possible subclauses is exponential wrt. the number of literals, in a linear number of implication checks we can find a minimal wrt. inclusion subclause $D \subsetneq C$ such that $S_{gr} \models D$ or show that such a subclause does not exist.

Let us show that global propositional subsumption generalises a number of usual redundancy eliminations. First, note that global propositional subsumption generalises strict propositional subsumption. Indeed, if there is a strict subclause $D \subsetneq C$ such that $D \in S$ then $S_{gr} \models D$ and therefore C is globally subsumed by S_{gr}. Next, we consider *propositional subsumption resolution*.

Propositional Subsumption Resolution

$$\frac{L \vee D' \quad \overline{L} \vee D \vee D'}{D \vee D'}$$

Propositional subsumption resolution is a simplification rule, which allows one to remove the right premise after adding the conclusion. Let us show that global subsumption generalises subsumption resolution. Indeed, if the premise clauses $L \vee D'$ and $\overline{L} \vee D \vee D'$ of subsumption resolution are in S then $S_{gr} \models D \vee D'$ and therefore $\overline{L} \vee D \vee D'$ is globally subsumed by S_{gr}.

In general, global subsumption involves reasoning with the whole set S_{gr}. For example, let S_{gr} contain the following clauses

$$A(f(\bot)) \vee B(g(c)); \quad \neg B(g(c)) \vee A(c); \quad \neg A(f(\bot)) \vee A(c)$$

Then, a clause $A(c) \vee B(f(c))$ can be simplified to $A(c)$ wrt. to S_{gr}. In the cases we consider here, the clauses we try to simplify always follow from the set S (e.g. obtained by sound derivations from the initial set of clauses). Therefore, the clause we simplify, itself can be added to S_{gr} before simplification. For example, if we want to simplify a clause $C = \neg A(c) \vee B(f(c))$ wrt. S_{gr} above, we can first add C to S_{gr} obtaining $S'_{gr} = S_{gr} \cup \{C\}$ and then C can be simplified to $B(f(c))$ wrt. S'_{gr}.

7.2   Simplification of Non-ground Clauses

In this section we consider the case of simplifying non-ground clauses wrt. a set of clauses S, utilising propositional reasoning. For this we need soundly approximate semantic entailment. The approximation of entailment we use will be based on the following proposition.

Proposition 4. *Let $\varphi(\bar{x})$ and $\psi(\bar{x})$ be first-order formulas over a signature Σ and $\bar{c}$ a tuple of pairwise different constants not in Σ. Then, $\varphi(\bar{c}) \models \psi(\bar{c})$ implies $\forall \bar{x} \varphi(\bar{x}) \models \forall \bar{x} \psi(\bar{x})$.*

Proof. We have the following sequence of equivalences and implications:

$$\varphi(\bar{c}) \models \psi(\bar{c}) \Leftrightarrow$$
$$\models \varphi(\bar{c}) \rightarrow \psi(\bar{c}) \Leftrightarrow$$
$$\models \forall \bar{x}(\varphi(\bar{x}) \rightarrow \psi(\bar{x})) \Rightarrow$$
$$\models (\forall \bar{x}\varphi(\bar{x})) \rightarrow (\forall \bar{x}\psi(\bar{x})) \Leftrightarrow$$
$$\forall \bar{x}\varphi(\bar{x}) \models \forall \bar{x}\psi(\bar{x}).$$

❏

We can use Proposition 4 as follows. Let Σ_C be a signature consisting of an infinite number of constants not occurring in Σ. Let Ω be a set of injective substitutions mapping variables to constants in Σ_C. We call C' an Ω-instance of a clause C if $C' = C\gamma$ where $\gamma \in \Omega$. With each clause $C \in S$ we associate a set of Ω instances of C, denoted C_Ω. Let us assume that for every clause $C \in S$, $C_\Omega \subseteq S_{gr}$. Then, if we show that some Ω-instance of a given clause D is implied by S_{gr}, from Proposition 4 it follows that S implies D. Now we can formulate extension of global subsumption to the non-ground case:

Global Subsumption (Non-ground)

$$\frac{(D \vee D')\theta}{D}$$

where (i) θ is a (possibly identity) substitution, and
(ii) $S_{gr} \models D\gamma$ for some $\gamma \in \Omega$, and
(iii) D' is not empty.

As in the ground case, global subsumption is a simplification rule. Informally, in order to simplify a clause C using global subsumption it is sufficient to find a clause D strictly subsuming C, (i.e., $D\theta \subsetneq C$ for a substitution θ), such that an Ω-instance $D\gamma$ of D follows from S_{gr}. Then, adding D into S makes C redundant in S. There are several non-trivial issues to consider when we try to apply global subsumption. These are:

1. which Ω-instances of clauses in S to add to S_{gr},
2. which clause D to use as a candidate for the conclusion, and
3. which Ω-instances of the candidate clause D to check for entailment.

Since there are infinitely many possible Ω-instances of a clause, we restrict ourselves to some heuristics. Let us describe one of them. Assume that constants in Σ_C are ordered: $c_1, \ldots, c_k, \ldots$. For a given clause C, fix an ordering on variables occurring in C: $x_1, \ldots, x_n$. We define a substitution $\gamma_C : \{x_i \mapsto c_i \mid 1 \leq i \leq n\}$. Trivially $C\gamma_C$ is an Ω-instance of C. To address issue (1) above we assume that for a clause $C \in S$, $C\gamma_C$ is in S_{gr}. For (2), we choose candidates for the conclusion of global subsumption among strict subclauses of a given clause. For (3), we use $D\gamma_D$ as an Ω-instance of the candidate clause D.

Example 6. Consider the following example where S consists of the first four clauses of SYN-832 problem from the TPTP library [50]. For readability we rename predicate symbols.

$$A \qquad (1) \qquad\qquad \neg A \vee B(x_1) \qquad\qquad (2)$$
$$\neg B(x_1) \vee \neg A \vee C(x_1, x_2) \quad (3) \quad \neg C(x_1, x_2) \vee \neg B(x_1) \vee \neg A \vee D(x_1, x_2, x_3) \quad (4)$$

These clauses come from translations of modal formulae [26]. The set S_{gr}, in addition to clauses from $S\bot$ will contain Ω-instances $G\gamma_G$ for $G \in S$:

$$A \qquad (1) \qquad\qquad \neg A \vee B(c_1) \qquad\qquad (2)$$
$$\neg B(c_1) \vee \neg A \vee C(c_1, c_2) \quad (3) \quad \neg C(c_1, c_2) \vee \neg B(c_1) \vee \neg A \vee D(c_1, c_2, c_3) \quad (4)$$

Now, using global subsumption we can simplify clauses in S to the following set of unit clauses S':

$$A \quad (1) \quad B(x_1) \quad (2)$$
$$C(x_1, x_2) \quad (3) \quad D(x_1, x_2, x_3) \quad (4)$$

Let us emphasise that pure propositional reasoning suffices for these simplifications. In practice, we can employ efficient propositional solvers for such simplifications in a black-box fashion. One can exploit incrementality of state-of-the-art propositional solvers such as MiniSAT [15] which allow one to check satisfiability of sets of propositional clauses under assumed sets of literals. In order to check whether an Ω-instance $C\gamma = L_1\gamma \vee \ldots \vee L_n\gamma$ follows from a set of ground clauses S_{gr} it is sufficient to check unsatisfiability of S_{gr} under the assumption consisting of literals $\overline{L}_1\gamma, \ldots, \overline{L}_n\gamma$. Using linear search, one can find a minimal wrt. inclusion sub-clause of $C\gamma$ which follows from the set of ground clauses in less than n implications checks. Another approach for obtaining minimal implied sub-clauses can be based on minimal unsatisfiability cores returned by propositional solvers. Since in practice it is sufficient to approximate simplifications one can use efficient incomplete tests for checking propositional implications based, e.g., unit propagation or restricting the number of backjumps.

Let us note that global subsumption can be used not only in instantiation-based calculi, but in any calculi where strict subsumption is an admissible redundancy elimination such as, e.g., resolution. Simplifications by ground reasoning have been independently investigated in different settings (see, e.g., [30,31,1,22]).

Generating Implied Clauses by Propositional Reasoning. Using propositional reasoning we can generate clauses implied by S_{gr}. Let $C\gamma$ be an Ω-instance of a clause C, such that $C\gamma$ is implied by S_{gr}. Then, from Proposition 4 it follows that C is implied by S. Therefore we can add C to S and use C for simplifications of clauses in S. In particular, we can use implied clauses for simplifications such as strict subsumption.

Let us note the main difference with global subsumption: in global subsumption we check implications of given clauses (e.g., strict subclauses of a clause to be simplified). Here we generate implied clauses on the fly, e.g., when we check consistency of S_{gr} and use obtained clauses later for simplifications. Most state-of-the-art propositional reasoners generate such clauses, called learnt clauses or lemmas, during the proof search. If a propositional lemma $C\gamma$ is generated then $C\gamma$ is implied by S_{gr} and the corresponding first-order clause C is implied by S. We can use the obtained first-order lemma C for further simplifications.

To conclude, we have shown that propositional reasoning can be used not only to guide the instantiation process but also for simplification of clauses.

8   Combination of Instantiation with Resolution

One of the attractive properties of the instantiation calculus is that the number of literals in clauses does not increase during instantiation. On the other hand, if we consider the instantiation calculus without simplifications, the number of literals in the generated clauses does not decrease. Consequently, instantiation is not well-suited for generating clauses which can be used in simplifications, such as strict subsumption. We can overcome this limitation by combining instantiation with the (ordered) resolution calculus. There are different ways to combine instantiation with resolution, (see, e.g., [20,36]), here we consider a simple one. We run resolution simultaneously with instantiation to generate additional clauses that can be used for simplifications. Let us note that clauses generated by resolution are used only for simplifications and do not participate in instantiation inferences. In addition, we can add Ω-instances of clauses generated by resolution to S_{gr} which in turn can be used for propositional-based simplifications discussed above.

Example 7. Consider the following set of clauses S:

$$\begin{array}{ll} \neg A(x) \quad \vee H(x) & (1) \\ A(f(x)) \quad \vee B(x) & (2) \\ \neg H(f(x)) \vee B(x) & (3) \end{array}$$

Assume that in each clause (1)–(3) the first literal is eligible for resolution. Then, applying resolution to (1) and (2) we obtain $H(f(x)) \vee B(x)$ (4). Applying resolution to (4) and (3) and factoring the result we obtain $B(x)$. Now $B(x)$ can be used to simplify clauses (2) and (3). Therefore, on the instantiation side we can also simplify S into $\{\neg A(x) \vee H(x); B(x)\}$.

9   Saturation Strategies

Up to now we referred to the notion of a saturation process only informally. In this section we formalise this notion, and show that saturated sets can be achieved via fair saturation processes. First we define the notion of a saturation process for sets of ground closures. For a set of ground closures U, let $\overline{U}$ denote the set of clauses C such that $C \cdot \sigma$ is in U. An *Inst-Gen saturation process* is a sequence of triples, called *states*, $\{\langle U^i, I_\perp^i, \text{hsel}^i \rangle\}_{i=1}^\infty$, where for every i, U^i is a set of ground closures, $I_\perp^i$ a model of $\overline{U}^i \perp$ and hsel^i a selection function based on that model. In addition we assume $U^1 \models \overline{U}^1$. Given a state $\langle U^i, I_\perp^i, \text{hsel}^i \rangle$, a *successor state* $\langle U^{i+1}, I_\perp^{i+1}, \text{hsel}^{i+1} \rangle$ is obtained by one of these steps:

- *(generation step)* $U^{i+1} = U^i \cup N$, where N is a set of ground closures such that $U^i \models N$; or
- *(elimination step)* $U^{i+1} = U^i \setminus N$, where every closure in N is redundant in U^i.

If for some i, $\overline{U}^i \bot$ is unsatisfiable the process terminates with the result "unsatisfiable". It immediately follows from the definition of a saturation process that in this case the initial set of clauses U^1 is unsatisfiable. Define $U^\cup = \cup_{i=1}^\infty U^i$. The set of *persistent closures* is defined as the low limit $U_\infty = \cup_{i \geq 1} \cap_{j \geq i} U^j$. We will use auxiliary lemmas about redundant sets of closures, these lemmas are similar to the corresponding lemmas in resolution setting [3]. For a set of ground closures U, let $\mathcal{R}(U)$ denote the set of all closures redundant in U.

Lemma 1. *Let U be a set of ground closures. Then, if a closure $C \cdot \sigma$ is redundant in U then $C \cdot \sigma$ is redundant in $U \setminus \mathcal{R}(U)$. In particular, $U \setminus \mathcal{R}(U) \models U$.*

Proof. Consider a closure $C \cdot \sigma \in \mathcal{R}(U)$. Let $M = \{C_1 \cdot \sigma_1, \ldots, C_n \cdot \sigma_n\}$ be the least subset of U, wrt. the multiset extension of $\succ$, such that $M \models C \cdot \sigma$. Then, all closures in M are non-redundant in U. Therefore, $M \subseteq U \setminus \mathcal{R}(U)$, and hence $C \cdot \sigma$ is redundant in $U \setminus \mathcal{R}(U)$. ❑

Lemma 2. *Let $\{\langle U^i, I_\bot^i, \mathsf{hsel}^i \rangle\}_{i=1}^\infty$ be a saturation process. Then, (i) $U^\cup \setminus \mathcal{R}(U^\cup) = U_\infty \setminus \mathcal{R}(U_\infty)$ and (ii) $\mathcal{R}(U^\cup) = \mathcal{R}(U_\infty)$.*

Proof. Let us prove (i).

($\subseteq$) If a ground closure $C \cdot \sigma \in U^\cup$ is not redundant in $U^\cup$ then $C \cdot \sigma$ is also not redundant in U^k for any k and therefore $C \cdot \sigma \in U_\infty$. Moreover, $C \cdot \sigma$ is not redundant in U_∞. Therefore $U^\cup \setminus \mathcal{R}(U^\cup) \subseteq U_\infty \setminus \mathcal{R}(U_\infty)$.

($\supseteq$) If a closure $C \cdot \sigma \in U_\infty$ is not redundant in U_∞, then by ($\subseteq$) direction, $C \cdot \sigma$ is not redundant in $U^\cup \setminus \mathcal{R}(U^\cup)$ and by Lemma 1 is not redundant in $U^\cup$. Therefore $U_\infty \setminus \mathcal{R}(U_\infty) \subseteq U^\cup \setminus \mathcal{R}(U^\cup)$.

Let us prove (ii). From Lemma 1 it follows that $\mathcal{R}(U^\cup) = \mathcal{R}(U^\cup \setminus \mathcal{R}(U^\cup))$ and similar $\mathcal{R}(U_\infty) = \mathcal{R}(U_\infty \setminus \mathcal{R}(U_\infty))$. Therefore, (i) implies $\mathcal{R}(U^\cup) = \mathcal{R}(U_\infty)$. ❑

First we note that a saturation process preserves (un)satisfiability of sets of clauses.

Lemma 3. *Let $\{\langle U^i, I_\bot^i, \mathsf{hsel}^i \rangle\}_{i=1}^\infty$ be a saturation process. Then, U^1 is satisfiable if and only if U_∞ is satisfiable.*

Proof. Implication from left to right follows trivially from the definition of a saturation process. In order to show implication from right to left, assume that U^1 is unsatisfiable. Then, $U^\cup$ is also unsatisfiable. Lemma 1 implies $U^\cup \setminus \mathcal{R}(U^\cup)$ is unsatisfiable. Since $U^\cup \setminus \mathcal{R}(U^\cup) \subseteq U_\infty$ we have U_∞ is unsatisfiable. ❑

In order to ensure that we obtain an Inst-Gen saturated set in the limit of the saturation process we need a notion of a fair saturation. For this we consider inference system SHInst-Gen on ground closures (see Section 5). Informally, a saturation process is fair if all non-redundant inferences between persisting closures are eventually applied or otherwise shown to be redundant. Let $\{\langle U^i, I_\bot^i, \mathsf{hsel}^i \rangle\}_{i=1}^\infty$ be a saturation process. An SHInst-Gen inference between persistent closures $(\overline{L}_1' \vee C_1) \cdot \sigma_1, \ldots, (\overline{L}_k' \vee C_k) \cdot \sigma_k$ and $(L_1 \vee \ldots \vee L_k \vee D) \cdot \sigma$ is called *SHInst-persistent* if there are an infinite number of indexes $j_1, \ldots j_i, \ldots$ such that these closures are in U^{j_i} and the inference is eligible (upon the same literals) at the state $\langle U^{j_i}, I_\bot^{j_i}, \mathsf{hsel}^{j_i} \rangle$ for all $i \geq 1$, that is, conditions (i)–(iv) on applicability of SHInst-Gen are satisfied. An Inst-Gen saturation process is *SHInst-fair* if every SHInst-Gen persisting inference in U_∞ is redundant wrt. $U^\cup$. Let us note that our redundancy criterion is *effective* in the sense of [3], that is adding the conclusion of the inference makes the inference redundant. Therefore, we can ensure fairness of a saturation process by adding conclusions of non-redundant SHInst-Gen persistent inferences.

Now we need to show that in the limit U_∞ of an SHInst-Gen fair saturation process we obtain a saturated set wrt. to a model of $U_\infty\bot$. If we compare our notion of saturation to saturation in the resolution framework (e.g., [3]), one of the key differences is that the literal selection can change at each step of the saturation. In particular, we need to construct a model $I_\top^\infty$ of $U_\infty\bot$ and a selection hsel^∞ based on $I_\top^\infty$ such that U_∞ is saturated wrt. hsel^∞. Although, compactness implies $U_\infty\bot$ is satisfiable if all $U^i\bot$ are satisfiable, not every model of $U_\infty\bot$ is suitable. Indeed, it is possible to construct an example of an SHInst-Gen fair saturation process with the limit U_∞ and a model I such that U_∞ is not saturated wrt. any selection function based on I. Another obstacle in constructing the required model $I_\top^\infty$ is that a literal can be true in a model $I_\bot^i$ and its complement true in a model $I_\bot^j$ for $i \neq j$. Nevertheless, the following theorem shows that it is possible to construct a model $I_\top^\infty$ of U_∞ and a selection function hsel^∞ based on $I_\top^\infty$ such that U_∞ is saturated wrt. hsel^∞.

Lemma 4. [19] *Let U_∞ be a set of persistent clauses of a SHInst-Gen fair saturation process $\{\langle U^i, I_\bot^i, \mathsf{hsel}^i\rangle\}_{i=1}^\infty$, and $U^i\bot$ is satisfiable for every i, $i \geq 1$. Then, there exists a model $I_\bot$ of $U_\infty\bot$ and a selection function hsel based on $I_\bot$ such that U_∞ is SHInst-Gen saturated wrt. hsel.*

Proof. Let $\{C_i \cdot \sigma_i\}_{i=1}^\infty$ be an enumeration of closures in U_∞. For each $n \geq 1$ we construct a partial interpretation J^n in which all $\{C_i\bot\}_{i=1}^n$ are true and a selection function hsel_J^n for $\{C_i\}_{i=1}^n$, based on J^n (meaning that all literals in $\mathsf{hsel}_J^n(C_i)\bot$ are true in J^n, i.e., true in all total consistent extensions of J^n, for $1 \leq i \leq n$) by induction on n. For each n the following invariants will be satisfied.

1. J^n is consistent and hsel_J^n is a selection function for clauses $\{C_i\}_{i=1}^n$ based on J^n.
2. $J^{n-1} \subseteq J^n$ and hsel_J^n coincides with hsel_J^{n-1} on clauses $\{C_i\}_{i=1}^{n-1}$.
3. There are infinitely many k such that for the model $I_\bot^k$ of $U^k\bot$ we have $J^n \subseteq I_\bot^k$ and for all $1 \leq i \leq n$, $\mathsf{hsel}^k(C_i) = \mathsf{hsel}_J^n(C_i)$.

If $n = 1$, then it is easy to see that there is a multiset M_1 of literals in $C_1\bot$ such that for infinitely many k, $\mathsf{hsel}^k(C_1) = M_1$. We take $J^1 = \bigcup_{L \in M_1}\{L\bot\}$ and $\mathsf{hsel}_J^1(C_1) = M_1$. It is immediate that all invariants (1–3) on J^1, hsel_J^1 are satisfied.

Let $n \geq 1$ and assume that we have a model J^n and hsel_J^n for $\{C_i\}_{i=1}^n$ such that invariants (1–3) are satisfied. Since $(C_{n+1} \cdot \sigma_{n+1}) \in U_\infty$ we have that for some m and every $p \geq m$, $(C_{n+1} \cdot \sigma_{n+1}) \in U^p$. From this and invariant (3) it follows that for some $M_{n+1} \subseteq C_{n+1}$ there are infinitely many k such that: (i) $J^n \subseteq I_\bot^k$, and (ii) $\mathsf{hsel}^k(C_i) = \mathsf{hsel}_J^n(C_i)$ for all $1 \leq i \leq n$, and (iii) $\mathsf{hsel}^k(C_{n+1}) = M_{n+1}$. Define $J^{n+1} = J^n \cup \bigcup_{L \in M_{n+1}}\{L\bot\}$ and $\mathsf{hsel}_J^{n+1}(C_i) = \mathsf{hsel}_J^n(C_i)$ for $1 \leq i \leq n$, and $\mathsf{hsel}_J^{n+1}(C_{n+1}) = M_{n+1}$. It is easy to see that all invariants (1–3) are satisfied for J^{n+1} and hsel_J^{n+1}.

We define $J = \cup_{i=1}^{\infty} J^i$ and $\mathsf{hsel}(C_i) = \mathsf{hsel}_J^i(C_i)$ for $i \geq 1$. From compactness and invariants (1) and (2), it follows that J is consistent, and hsel is a selection function based on J. We define $I_\perp$ as a total consistent extension of J, (note that hsel is also based on $I_\perp$).

Now we need to show that U_∞ is SHInst-Gen saturated wrt. hsel. Consider a SHInst-Gen inference from closures $C_1 \cdot \sigma_1, \ldots, C_n \cdot \sigma_n$ in U_∞. Then, from the construction of hsel and in particular from the invariant (3) it follows that for infinitely many indexes k we have $\mathsf{hsel}^k(C_i) = \mathsf{hsel}(C_i)$, for all $1 \leq i \leq n$. Since the SHInst-Gen saturation process is fair, this inference is redundant in $U^\cup$ and by Lemma 2 is redundant in U_∞. Therefore, U_∞ is SHInst-Gen saturated wrt. hsel.   □

We summarise the obtained results in the following theorem.

Theorem 7. *Let* $\{\langle U^i, I_\perp^i, \mathsf{hsel}^i \rangle\}_{i=1}^\infty$, *be a SHInst-Gen fair saturation process. Then, either:*

1. *for some i, $\overline{U}^i \perp$ is unsatisfiable and therefore U^1 is unsatisfiable, or*
2. *for every i, $\overline{U}^i \perp$ is satisfiable and therefore (by Lemmas (3,4) and Theorem 4) U^1 is satisfiable.*

Moreover, if for some i, U^i is SHInst-Gen saturated then at this stage we can conclude that U^1 is satisfiable.

In particular, Theorem 7 implies that if a set of closures U is unsatisfiable, then any SHInst-Gen fair saturation process $\{\langle U^i, I_\perp^i, \mathsf{hsel}^i \rangle\}_{i=1}^\infty$ with the initial set $U^1 = U$ terminates in a finite number of steps, proving unsatisfiability of U.

Saturation for sets of constrained clauses. In practice, we do not deal with closures directly, but rather with constrained clauses and inference systems such as DSInst-Gen (see Section 6). In this case a saturation process for clauses naturally corresponds to an Inst-Gen saturation process for closures. For a set of constrained clauses S, let $\widetilde{S}$ denote the set of all unconstrained clauses obtained from S by dropping all constraints. A *DSInst-Gen saturation process* is a sequence of triples $\{\langle S^i, I_\perp^i, \mathsf{sel}^i \rangle\}_{i=1}^\infty$, where S^1 is well-constrained, S^i is a set of constrained clauses such that $I_\perp^i$ a model of $\widetilde{S}^i \perp$ and sel^i a selection function based on $I_\perp^i$, for $i \geq 1$. Given $\langle S^i, I_\perp^i, \mathsf{sel}^i \rangle$, a *successor state* $\langle S^{i+1}, I_\perp^{i+1}, \mathsf{sel}^{i+1} \rangle$ is obtained by one of these steps:

- *(generation step)* $S^{i+1} = S^i \cup N$, where N is a set of constrained clauses such that $S^i \models Cl(N)$; or
- *(elimination step)* $S^{i+1} = S^i \setminus N$, where every constrained clause in N is redundant in S^i; or
- *(constraint extension step)* $S^{i+1} = (S^i \setminus \{C \mid [\, \varphi \,]\}) \cup \{C \mid [\, \varphi \wedge \psi \,]\}$, where $C \mid [\, \varphi \,]$ is in S^i and closures in $Cl(C \mid [\, \varphi \,]) \setminus Cl(C \mid [\, \varphi \wedge \psi \,])$ are redundant in $Cl(S^i)$.

Let us note that an inference by DSInst-Gen can be split into two saturation steps: generation and constraint extension steps. For simplicity, we assume that for every i and every clause $C \in \widetilde{S}^i$ there is only one constrained clause $C \mid [\, \varphi \,] \in S^i$. If there are several constrained clauses corresponding to the same unconstrained clause, we can replace them with one constrained clause by merging the constraints. Let $\widetilde{S}_\infty = \cup_{i \geq 1} \cap_{j \geq i} \widetilde{S}^j$. Consider two persistent clauses $C, D \in \widetilde{S}_\infty$. Let p be such that for all $q \geq p$ we have $C, D \in \widetilde{S}^q$, and corresponding constrained clauses are $C \mid [\, \varphi^q \,], D \mid [\, \psi^q \,] \in S^q$. We say that an DSInst-Gen inference associated with C and D is *DSInst-Gen persistent* if there is an infinite number of indexes $j \geq q$, such that the inference is eligible on clauses $C \mid [\, \varphi^j \,], D \mid [\, \psi^j \,] \in S^q$ at the stage j (upon the same selected literals), that is conditions (i)–(v) on applicability of DSInst-Gen are satisfied. A DSInst-Gen saturation process is *DSInst-Gen fair* if every DSInst-Gen persisting inference, associated with clauses in $\widetilde{S}_\infty$, is redundant in S^i for some i.

Theorem 7 can be applied to show completeness of fair DSInst-Gen saturation processes.

Theorem 8. *Let $SP = \{\langle S^i, I^i_\perp, \mathsf{sel}^i \rangle\}_{i=1}^\infty$, be a DSInst-Gen fair saturation process. Then, either:*

1. *for some i, $\widetilde{S}^i \perp$ is unsatisfiable and therefore S^1 is unsatisfiable, or*
2. *for every i, $\widetilde{S}^i \perp$ is satisfiable and therefore S^1 is satisfiable.*

Moreover, if for some i, S^i is DSInst-Gen saturated, then at this stage we can conclude that S^1 is satisfiable.

Proof. If for some i, $\widetilde{S}^i \perp$ is unsatisfiable then from the definition of DSInst-Gen saturation process it immediately follows that S^1 is unsatisfiable.

Let us assume that for every i, $\widetilde{S}^i \perp$ is satisfiable. With the DSInst-Gen saturation process SP we associate an Inst-Gen saturation process on ground closures $\widehat{SP} = \{\langle \widehat{S}^i, I^i_\perp, \mathsf{sel}^i \rangle\}_{i=1}^\infty$, where $\widehat{S}^i = Cl(S^i)$. It is straightforward to check that if SP is DSInst-Gen fair then $\widehat{SP}$ is Inst-Gen fair. Now, Theorem 7 implies that $\widehat{S}^1$ is satisfiable. Since S^1 is equivalent to $\widehat{S}^1$ we conclude that S^1 is also satisfiable. ❏

10 The Effectively Propositional Fragment

Let us consider *the effectively propositional fragment (EPR)*, also called *the Bernays-Schönfinkel fragment*. The EPR is a clausal fragment of first-order logic where the signature is restricted to contain only predicate symbols and constants. This fragment is decidable and recently has been shown to have a number of applications ranging from hardware verification [40,17,28] to ontological reasoning [49], see [4] for more examples. Let us show that DSInst-Gen is a decision procedure for the EPR fragment.

We call a fair DSInst-Gen saturation process *pure* if all generation and constraint extension steps are results of application of DSInst-Gen inferences. For a set of constrained clauses S, let $\widehat{S}$ denote the set of ground closures represented by S. Consider a pure DSInst-Gen saturation process $\{\langle S^i, I^i_\perp, \mathsf{sel}^i \rangle\}_{i=1}^\infty$ with a finite set of initial clauses $S = S^1$. First, it is easy to see that any inference step is strictly reductive, that is if S' is obtained from S by application of a DSInst-Gen inference, then $\widehat{S} \succ_m \widehat{S}'$ (where $\succ_m$ is the multiset extension of $\succ$). Likewise, any elimination step is either strictly reductive or does not change the set of clauses. Since the initial set of clauses S is finite and

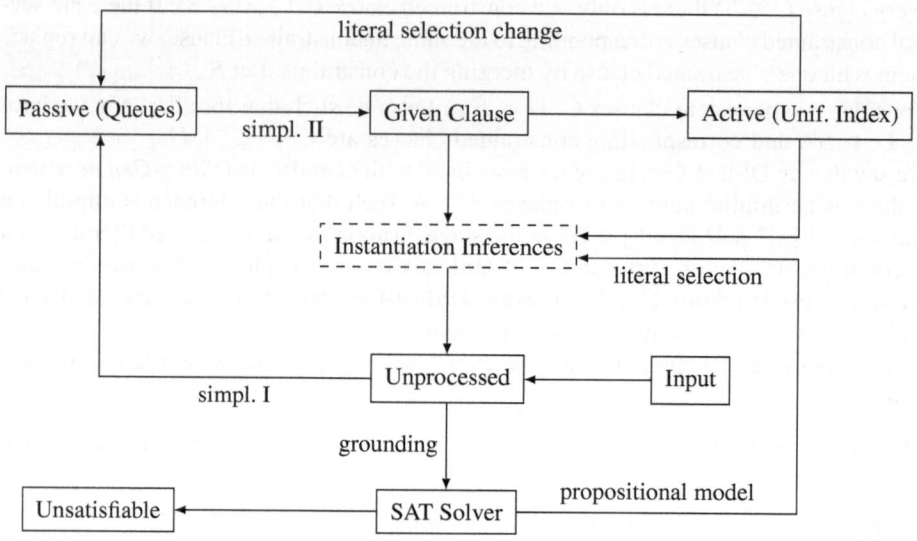

Fig. 1. Inst-Gen loop

all functional symbols in our signature are constants, the set $\widehat{S}$ is also finite. Therefore, after a finite number of steps n, the set of clauses will be stabilised, i.e., $S^n = S^{n+k}$ for $k \geq 0$. Then, Theorem 8 implies S is unsatisfiable if and only if $\widetilde{S}_n \perp$ is unsatisfiable. We summarise this in the following theorem.

Theorem 9. *DSInst-Gen is a decision procedure for the effectively propositional fragment.*

Experimental results presented in Section 12 show that instantiation-based methods and in particular DSInst-Gen are currently leading on the EPR problems.

11   Implementation of Inst-Gen in iProver

In previous sections we considered instantiation calculi, redundancy criteria and complete saturation strategies. Now we are ready to discuss implementation issues based on our implementation called iProver. iProver is a reasoning system for first-order logic based on the DSInst-Gen calculus. iProver incorporates a class of complete strategies and concrete redundancy elimination methods which we have discussed in the previous sections. At the core of iProver is the *Inst-Gen loop* (see Fig. 1) which governs the instantiation strategy.

Let us informally describe the Inst-Gen loop and its major components. The Inst-Gen loop is a modification of a well-known given clause algorithm which is a basis for all state-of-the-art resolution-based theorem provers. One of the main ideas of the given clause algorithm is to separate clauses into two sets, called *active* and *passive* with the following properties. The set of active clauses is such that all non-redundant inferences between clauses in this set are performed. The set of passive clauses are the clauses waiting to participate in inferences. Let us consider the simplest version of the given clause algorithm for inference systems such as resolution, where for each clause, the set of literals eligible for inferences is fixed. Initially, the passive set consists of the input clauses and the active set is empty. The given clause algorithm consists of a loop and at each loop iteration the following actions are executed. First, a clause is taken from the passive set, called the *given clause*. Then, all inferences between the given clause and clauses in the active set are performed. Finally, all newly derived clauses are moved to passive and the given clause is moved to the active set. If the calculus is sound and at some stage the inconsistency is found, then the input set of clauses is inconsistent. If the calculus is complete and the selection strategy for the given clauses is fair, then the given clause algorithm will find an inconsistency in a finite number of steps. Moreover, if the calculus is complete and the given clause algorithm terminates with an empty passive set, then the active set of clauses is saturated and we can conclude that the input set of clauses is satisfiable. Redundancy elimination can be integrated into the given clause algorithm in various ways: passive and active clause sets are completely simplified at each iteration of the algorithm (the Otter loop [37]), or only active clauses are kept inter-simplified (the DISCOUNT loop [13]). In addition, preprocessing can be applied to the generated clauses such as splitting without backtracking (see [45]).

In order to adapt the standard given clause algorithm for instantiation strategies we need to: (i) accommodate propositional reasoning, and (ii) reflect dynamic literal selection (based on a propositional model of the ground abstraction), which can result in moving clauses from active to passive sets. On Fig. 1 we present such an adaptation of the given clause algorithm to the Inst-Gen framework: the Inst-Gen loop. Let us overview key components of the Inst-Gen loop and how they are implemented in iProver.

Passive. The passive set are the clauses waiting to participate in inferences. It is well-known that in the resolution-based setting, the order in which clauses are selected for inferences from the passive set is an important parameter. Usually, preference is given to clauses which are heuristically more promising to derive the contradiction, or to the clauses on which basic operations are easier to perform. In iProver, the passive clauses are represented by a sequence of priority queues. In order to define priorities we consider numerical/Boolean parameters of clauses such as: the number of symbols, the number of variables, the age of the clause, the number of literals, whether the clause is ground, the conjecture distance, whether the clause contains a symbol from the conjecture (other than equality or a theory symbol), whether the clause is Horn or in the EPR. Then, each queue is ordered by a lexicographic combination of orders defined on parameters. For example, if a user specifies an iProver option:

--inst_pass_queue1 [+age;-num_symb;+ground]

then in the first queue priority is given to clauses generated at the earlier iterations of the Inst-Gen loop (older clauses), then to clauses with fewer number of symbols and finally to ground clauses. The user can also specify the ratio between the number of clauses taken from each queue.

Active. After the given clause is selected from the passive set all eligible inferences between the given clause and clauses in the active set should be performed. A unification index is used for efficient selection of clauses eligible for inferences. In particular, clauses in the active set are indexed by selected literals. The unification index implemented in iProver is based on non-perfect discrimination trees [21,44]

Let us note that since the literal selection is based on a propositional model of the ground abstraction of the current set of clauses, selection can be changed during the Inst-Gen loop iterations. This can result in moves of clauses from active to passive sets, as shown in Fig. 1 (literal selection change). Changes in selection function and moves of clauses from active to passive sets result in a number of nontrivial technical issues such as ensuring fairness, and minimising the number of moves and repeated work, which are beyond the scope of this paper.

Instantiation Inferences. Instantiation inferences in iProver are based on the DSInst-Gen calculus. In particular, constrained clauses, dismatching constraint checking and model-based literal selections are implemented. Dismatching constraints are implemented using a discrimination-type index on atomic constraints to facilitate efficient satisfiability checking.

Redundancy Elimination. The following redundancy eliminations are implemented: blocking non-proper instantiations, dismatching constraints, tautology elimination and global subsumption for both ground and non-ground clauses. The user can select whether to simplify all newly generated clauses (simpl. I in Fig. 1) or only the given clause (simpl. II in Fig. 1) or apply simplifications at both stages.

Grounding and SAT Solver. Newly derived clauses are grounded and added to the propositional solver. Although, in our theoretical considerations we used the designated constant $\perp$ for grounding, it is easy to see that all our arguments remain valid if we use any ground term in place of $\perp$. In particular, for grounding, iProver selects a constant with the greatest number of occurrences in the input set of clauses, other heuristics for selecting the term for grounding are also interesting to investigate. After grounding, clauses are added to the propositional solver. Currently, iProver integrates MiniSAT [15] for propositional reasoning.

Learning Restarts. It can happen that the Inst-Gen loop fails to terminate due to a poor choice of the literal selection on the initial set of clauses. Indeed, initially the propositional solver contains only few instances of the input clauses, and therefore selection based on the corresponding propositional model can be inadequate. Although the model and selection can be changed at the later iterations, by that time, the prover can consume most of the available resources. In order to overcome this, iProver implements restarts of the saturation process, keeping generated propositional clauses in the propositional solver. After each restart, the propositional solver will contain more instances of clauses, this can help to find a better literal selection. In addition, after each restart, global subsumption becomes more powerful.

Equality. iProver integrates equality by adding (internally) the necessary axioms of equality with an option of using Brand's transformation [9]. Our experiments show that even this naive approach of equality integration works reasonably well in the instantiation-based setting, most likely due to the semantic literal selection and absence of recombination of clauses with equality axioms. For more advanced treatment of equality based on combination of ordered unit superposition with Inst-Gen and the corresponding system iProver-Eq we refer to [33,32].

Model Representations. Consider a state in which the passive set is empty and the ground abstraction is satisfiable. Then by the completeness Theorem 8, the set of input clauses is satisfiable. Let us also assume that for each inference by DSInst-Gen between active clauses (including redundant inferences) the corresponding dismatching constraint is added to the premise according to the application of the DSInst-Gen inference rule. This can be easily achieved during or after saturation. In this case we can extract a model representation based on the selected literals in the active set of clauses and accumulated dismatching constraints. Since dismatching constraints can be naturally expressed in the language of the ground term algebra we can represent models using first-order definitions of predicates in the ground term algebra. A detailed treatment of model representations is beyond the scope of this paper, let us only mention that iProver supports several model outputs based on positive/negative predicate definitions in the ground term algebra.

Finite Models. iProver has a finite model finding mode inspired by translation of finite model finding into the EPR fragment [5], see also [11]. Since instantiation-based methods are very efficient on the EPR fragment this approach is particularly promising. The method is complete for finite model finding: if there is a finite model of the given set of clauses, then such a model will be eventually found in a finite number of steps.

Combination with Resolution. In addition to the Inst-Gen loop, iProver implements a complete saturation algorithm for ordered resolution. In this paper, we will not discuss our implementation of resolution in detail. Let us only mention that the saturation algorithm is based on the same data structures as the Inst-Gen loop and implements a number of simplifications such as forward and backward subsumption, forward and backward subsumption resolution, tautology deletion and global subsumption. We implemented a compressed feature vector index (an extension of the feature vector index [48]) for efficient forward/backward subsumption and subsumption resolution.

Resolution is combined with instantiation by sharing the propositional solver. In particular, Ω-instances of clauses generated by resolution and instantiation are added to the propositional solver and propositional solver is used for global subsumption in both resolution and instantiation saturation loops.

12 Evaluation

In this section we evaluate iProver v0.9 on the standard benchmark for first-order theorem provers: the TPTP library [50] with the current version 5.2.0. Currently, iProver does not have a built-in clausifier and we used Vampire [23] for clausification. iProver has also an interface for clausification using E prover [47] or any user provided clausifier which can output clauses in the TPTP format. Experiments were run on a cluster of

Dell rack servers under Linux v2.6.30 with cpu 2.3GHz, memory 2GB and time limit 300s.

The TPTP library contains 15386 first-order problems, out of which 12420 are unsatisfiable, 1949 satisfiable and 1017 with unknown status. iProver in the default mode solves 8554 problems: 7524 unsatisfiable and 1030 satisfiable. Problems in the TPTP are rated from 0 to 1, where problems with the rating 0 are easy and problems with the rating 1 can not be solved by any automated reasoning system, including older versions of iProver, at the time of evaluating the corresponding version of the TPTP library. In the current version of the TPTP, iProver solved 24 problems with the rating 1, and 157 with rating $\geq$ 0.9. This indicates that there is a large number of problems in the TPTP that can only be solved by iProver. In the satisfiability mode, which features finite model finding, iProver can show satisfiability of 1301 problems out of 1949 known to be satisfiable in the TPTP.

It is interesting to compare an instantiation-based prover with an ordered resolution prover. iProver implements both on the same data structures and allows user to select combination of instantiation with resolution, pure instantiation and pure ordered resolution. Let us note that in iProver equality reasoning is integrated only in an axiomatic way in both instantiation and resolution parts, we refer to iProver-Eq [32] for a superposition-based integration. Results are presented in Table 1. We can see that instantiation considerably outperforms ordered resolution in this setting and the combination of instantiation and resolution leads to further improvements.

Table 1. iProver v0.9

TPTP v5.2.0	Combination Inst. & Res.	Instantiation	Resolution
Solved	8554	7680	5724
Unsat.	7524	6731	5160
Sat.	1030	949	564

We compare iProver v0.9 with other state-of-the-art automated reasoning systems based on the results of the CASC-23 competition, held in 2011 [51]. Tables are reproduced from the competition site[2], among different versions of the same system we take one with the best result. In the major FOF division, Table 2, iProver is in the top three provers along with established leaders Vampire [46,23] and E [47].

In the EPR division, shown in Table 3, iProver considerably outperforms resolution/superposition based systems. The EPR fragment is of a particular interest since, as mentioned in the introduction, it has a wide range of applications.

Table 4 shows results in the first-order non-theorems (FNT) division. The FNT division corresponds to satisfiable first-order problems. Efficient methods for showing satisfiability are usually based on finite model finding techniques. iProver capitalises on the translation of the finite model finding problem into the EPR fragment which helped to place iProver amongst top three system in this division.

To summarise, iProver performs well on both unsatisfiable and satisfiable problems over the whole TPTP and is leading in the EPR division.

---

[2] http://www.cs.miami.edu/~tptp/CASC/23/

Table 2. CASC-23 (FOF division, 300 problems)

FOF 300	Vampire 0.6	EP 1.4	iProver 0.9	leanCoP 2.2	iProver-Eq 0.7	EKRHyper 1.2	EDarwin 1.4	Metis 2.3	LEOII 1.2.8	Otter 3.3	Muscadet 4.1
Solved	269	232	192	136	135	109	103	101	97	62	42
av. time	12.95	22.55	9.22	46.80	8.68	8.93	6.97	24.75	25.18	5.84	8.99

Table 3. CASC-23 (EPR division, 150 problems)

EPR 150	iProver 0.9	Vampire 1.8	iProver-Eq 0.7	E 1.4	Metis 2.3	E-Darwin 1.4	FIMO 0.2	E-KHyper 1.2
Solved	145	127	121	91	78	70	62	60
av. time	12.70	15.79	24.78	7.90	20.85	12.64	1.81	10.02

Table 4. CASC-23 (FNT division: first-order non-theorems, 200 problems)

FNT 200	Paradox 3.0	FIMO 0.2	iProver 0.9	Nitrox 0.2	iProver-Eq 0.7	EKRHyper 1.2	EP 1.4	EDarwin 1.4
Solved	169	162	159	140	86	85	78	57
av. time	3.33	14.43	34.93	17.42	7.52	15.92	2.40	7.23

13 Conclusions

In this paper we have presented a development of the Inst-Gen framework from theoretical foundations to a working implementation. We considered the Inst-Gen calculus, semantic selection, hyper-inferences, redundancy elimination, dismatching constraints, simplifications by propositional reasoning, saturation strategies and finally implementation issues and evaluation. There are number of further extensions, that were not considered in this paper, such as integration of equational [19,33] and theory reasoning in the black-box style [20]. These extensions open novel opportunities to utilise efficient solvers modulo theories, SMT solvers, which have recently gained great popularity due to demand in applications such as software and hardware verification.

Although our implementation is relatively new, iProver is amongst the leading systems and shows great potential of the Inst-Gen framework. We expect that integration of theory reasoning will greatly enhance applicability of iProver in domains such as verification of software and hardware.

To conclude, we believe that instantiation-based theorem proving, backed by theoretical foundations and state-of-the-art implementation techniques, is a promising approach which can be developed to be utilised in real-world applications.

Acknowledgements. I am very grateful to Harald Ganzinger who introduced me to the area of instantiation-based reasoning and with whom I had the great pleasure of investigating this area. I thank Andrei Voronkov for his encouragement, support and helpful suggestions. I thank Yevgeny Kazakov and an anonymous reviewer for many useful suggestions and Christoph Sticksel for providing the scripts used in the evaluation.

References

1. Akbarpour, B., Paulson, L.C.: Extending a Resolution Prover for Inequalities on Elementary Functions. In: Dershowitz, N., Voronkov, A. (eds.) LPAR 2007. LNCS (LNAI), vol. 4790, pp. 47–61. Springer, Heidelberg (2007)
2. Baader, F., Nipkow, T.: Term Rewriting and All That. Cambridge University press, Cambridge (1998)
3. Bachmair, L., Ganzinger, H.: Resolution theorem proving. In: Robinson, A., Voronkov, A. (eds.) Handbook of Automated Reasoning, vol. I, ch. 2, pp. 19–99. Elsevier Science (2001)
4. Baumgartner, P.: Logical Engineering with Instance-Based Methods. In: Pfenning, F. (ed.) CADE 2007. LNCS (LNAI), vol. 4603, pp. 404–409. Springer, Heidelberg (2007)
5. Baumgartner, P., Fuchs, A., de Nivelle, H., Tinelli, C.: Computing finite models by reduction to function-free clause logic. J. Applied Logic 7(1), 58–74 (2009)
6. Baumgartner, P., Fuchs, A., Tinelli, C.: Implementing the model evolution calculus. International Journal on Artificial Intelligence Tools 15(1), 21–52 (2006)
7. Baumgartner, P., Schmidt, R.A.: Blocking and Other Enhancements for Bottom-Up Model Generation Methods. In: Furbach, U., Shankar, N. (eds.) IJCAR 2006. LNCS (LNAI), vol. 4130, pp. 125–139. Springer, Heidelberg (2006)
8. Baumgartner, P., Tinelli, C.: The Model Evolution Calculus. In: Baader, F. (ed.) CADE 2003. LNCS (LNAI), vol. 2741, pp. 350–364. Springer, Heidelberg (2003)
9. Brand, D.: Proving theorems with the modification method. SIAM J. Comput. 4(4), 412–430 (1975)
10. Caferra, R., Zabel, N.: A method for simultaneous search for refutations and models by equational constraint solving. Journal of Symbolic Computation 13(6), 613–641 (1992)
11. Claessen, K., Sorensson, N.: New techniques that improve mace-style finite model finding. In: Baumgartner, P., Fermueller, C. (eds.) Proceedings of the CADE-19 Workshop: Model Computation - Principles, Algorithms, Applications (MODEL 2003) (2003)
12. de Moura, L., Bjørner, N.S.: Deciding Effectively Propositional Logic Using DPLL and Substitution Sets. In: Armando, A., Baumgartner, P., Dowek, G. (eds.) IJCAR 2008. LNCS (LNAI), vol. 5195, pp. 410–425. Springer, Heidelberg (2008)
13. Denzinger, J., Kronenburg, M., Schulz, S.: DISCOUNT - A distributed and learning equational prover. Journal of Automated Reasoning 18(2), 189–198 (1997)
14. Eén, N., Biere, A.: Effective Preprocessing in SAT Through Variable and Clause Elimination. In: Bacchus, F., Walsh, T. (eds.) SAT 2005. LNCS, vol. 3569, pp. 61–75. Springer, Heidelberg (2005)
15. Eén, N., Sörensson, N.: An Extensible SAT-solver. In: Giunchiglia, E., Tacchella, A. (eds.) SAT 2003. LNCS, vol. 2919, pp. 502–518. Springer, Heidelberg (2004)
16. Eiter, T., Faber, W., Traxler, P.: Testing Strong Equivalence of Datalog Programs - Implementation and Examples. In: Baral, C., Greco, G., Leone, N., Terracina, G. (eds.) LPNMR 2005. LNCS (LNAI), vol. 3662, pp. 437–441. Springer, Heidelberg (2005)
17. Emmer, M., Khasidashvili, Z., Korovin, K., Voronkov, A.: Encoding industrial hardware verification problems into effectively propositional logic. In: Bloem, R., Sharygina, N. (eds.) The 10th International Conference on Formal Methods in Computer-Aided Design (FMCAD 2010), pp. 137–144. IEEE (2010)
18. Ganzinger, H., Korovin, K.: New directions in instantiation-based theorem proving. In: Proc. 18th IEEE Symposium on LICS, pp. 55–64. IEEE (2003)
19. Ganzinger, H., Korovin, K.: Integrating Equational Reasoning into Instantiation-Based Theorem Proving. In: Marcinkowski, J., Tarlecki, A. (eds.) CSL 2004. LNCS, vol. 3210, pp. 71–84. Springer, Heidelberg (2004)

20. Ganzinger, H., Korovin, K.: Theory Instantiation. In: Hermann, M., Voronkov, A. (eds.) LPAR 2006. LNCS (LNAI), vol. 4246, pp. 497–511. Springer, Heidelberg (2006)
21. Graf, P.: Term Indexing. LNCS, vol. 1053. Springer, Heidelberg (1996)
22. Heule, M., Järvisalo, M., Biere, A.: Clause Elimination Procedures for CNF Formulas. In: Fermüller, C.G., Voronkov, A. (eds.) LPAR-17. LNCS, vol. 6397, pp. 357–371. Springer, Heidelberg (2010)
23. Hoder, K., Kovács, L., Voronkov, A.: Interpolation and Symbol Elimination in Vampire. In: Giesl, J., Hähnle, R. (eds.) IJCAR 2010. LNCS, vol. 6173, pp. 188–195. Springer, Heidelberg (2010)
24. Hooker, J.N., Rago, G., Chandru, V., Shrivastava, A.: Partial instantiation methods for inference in first order logic. Journal of Automated Reasoning 28, 371–396 (2002)
25. Hustadt, U., Motik, B., Sattler, U.: Reducing SHIQ-description logic to disjunctive datalog programs. In: The Ninth International Conference on Principles of Knowledge Representation and Reasoning, pp. 152–162. AAAI Press (2004)
26. Hustadt, U., Schmidt, R.: MSPASS: Modal Reasoning by Translation and First-Order Resolution. In: Dyckhoff, R. (ed.) TABLEAUX 2000. LNCS, vol. 1847, pp. 67–71. Springer, Heidelberg (2000)
27. Kapur, D., Narendran, P., Rosenkrantz, D., Zhang, H.: Sufficient-completeness, ground-reducibility and their complexity. Acta Informatica 28(4), 311–350 (1991)
28. Khasidashvili, Z., Kinanah, M., Voronkov, A.: Verifying equivalence of memories using a first order logic theorem prover. In: The 9th International Conference on Formal Methods in Computer-Aided Design (FMCAD 2009), pp. 128–135. IEEE (2009)
29. Kirchner, C., Kirchner, H., Rusinowitch, M.: Deduction with symbolic constraints. Revue Francaise d'Intelligence Artificielle 4(3), 9–52 (1990); Special issue on automated deduction
30. Korovin, K.: iProver v0.2. In: Sutcliffe, G. (ed.) The CADE-21 ATP System Competition (CASC-21) (2007), see also [31]
31. Korovin, K.: iProver – An Instantiation-Based Theorem Prover for First-Order Logic (System Description). In: Armando, A., Baumgartner, P., Dowek, G. (eds.) IJCAR 2008. LNCS (LNAI), vol. 5195, pp. 292–298. Springer, Heidelberg (2008)
32. Korovin, K., Sticksel, C.: iProver-Eq: An Instantiation-Based Theorem Prover with Equality. In: Giesl, J., Hähnle, R. (eds.) IJCAR 2010. LNCS, vol. 6173, pp. 196–202. Springer, Heidelberg (2010)
33. Korovin, K., Sticksel, C.: Labelled Unit Superposition Calculi for Instantiation-Based Reasoning. In: Fermüller, C.G., Voronkov, A. (eds.) LPAR-17. LNCS, vol. 6397, pp. 459–473. Springer, Heidelberg (2010)
34. Lassez, J.-L., Marriott, K.: Explicit representation of terms defined by counter examples. Journal of Automated Reasoning 3(3), 301–317 (1987)
35. Lee, S.-J., Plaisted, D.: Eliminating duplication with the Hyper-linking strategy. Journal of Automated Reasoning 9, 25–42 (1992)
36. Lynch, C., McGregor, R.E.: Combining Instance Generation and Resolution. In: Ghilardi, S., Sebastiani, R. (eds.) FroCoS 2009. LNCS, vol. 5749, pp. 304–318. Springer, Heidelberg (2009)
37. McCune, W.: OTTER 3.0 reference manual and guide. Technical Report ANL-94/6, Argonne National Laboratory (1994)
38. Nieuwenhuis, R., Rubio, A.: Paramodulation-based theorem proving. In: Robinson, A., Voronkov, A. (eds.) Handbook of Automated Reasoning, vol. I, pp. 371–443. Elsevier (2001)
39. Navarro Pérez, J.A.: Encoding and Solving Problems in Effectively Propositional Logic. PhD thesis, University of Manchester (2007)
40. Navarro-Pérez, J.A., Voronkov, A.: Encodings of Bounded LTL Model Checking in Effectively Propositional Logic. In: Pfenning, F. (ed.) CADE 2007. LNCS (LNAI), vol. 4603, pp. 346–361. Springer, Heidelberg (2007)

270   K. Korovin

41. Navarro, J.A., Voronkov, A.: Proof Systems for Effectively Propositional Logic. In: Armando, A., Baumgartner, P., Dowek, G. (eds.) IJCAR 2008. LNCS (LNAI), vol. 5195, pp. 426–440. Springer, Heidelberg (2008)
42. Pichler, R.: Explicit versus implicit representations of subsets of the Herbrand universe. Theor. Comput. Sci. 290(1), 1021–1056 (2003)
43. Plaisted, D., Zhu, Y.: Ordered semantic hyper-linking. J. Autom. Reasoning 25(3), 167–217 (2000)
44. Ramakrishnan, I.V., Sekar, R.C., Voronkov, A.: Term indexing. In: Robinson, J.A., Voronkov, A. (eds.) Handbook of Automated Reasoning, pp. 1853–1964. Elsevier and MIT Press (2001)
45. Riazanov, A., Voronkov, A.: Splitting without backtracking. In: Proc. of the 17 International Joint Conference on Artificial Intelligence (IJCAI 2001), pp. 611–617. Morgan Kaufmann (2001)
46. Riazanov, A., Voronkov, A.: The design and implementation of VAMPIRE. AI Communications 15(2-3), 91–110 (2002)
47. Schulz, S.: E - a brainiac theorem prover. AI Commun. 15(2-3), 111–126 (2002)
48. Schulz, S.: Simple and Efficient Clause Subsumption with Feature Vector Indexing. In: Sutcliffe, G., Schulz, S., Tammet, T. (eds.) Proc. of the IJCAR-2004 Workshop on Empirically Successful First-Order Theorem Proving, Cork, Ireland. ENTCS. Elsevier Science (2004)
49. Suda, M., Weidenbach, C., Wischnewski, P.: On the saturation of YAGO. In: Giesl, J., Hähnle, R. (eds.) IJCAR 2010. LNCS, vol. 6173, pp. 441–456. Springer, Heidelberg (2010)
50. Sutcliffe, G.: The TPTP Problem Library and Associated Infrastructure: The FOF and CNF Parts, v3.5.0. Journal of Automated Reasoning 43(4), 337–362 (2009)
51. Sutcliffe, G.: CASC-23 proceedings of the CADE-23 ATP system competition (2011), http://www.cs.miami.edu/~tptp/CASC/23/Proceedings.pdf

Common Knowledge Logic
in a Higher Order Proof Assistant

Pierre Lescanne

Laboratoire de l'Informatique du Parallélisme,
École Normale Supérieure de Lyon
46, Allée d'Italie, 69364 Lyon 07, France
Pierre.Lescanne@ens-lyon.fr

To my old friend and colleague Harald Ganzinger.

Abstract. This paper presents experiments on common knowledge logic, conducted with the help of the proof assistant CoQ. The main feature of common knowledge logic is the eponymous modality that says that a group of agents shares a knowledge about a certain proposition in a inductive way. This modality is specified by using a fixpoint approach. Furthermore, from these experiments, we discuss and compare the structure of theorems that can be proved in specific theories that use common knowledge logic. Those structures manifest the interplay between the theory (as implemented in the proof assistant CoQ) and the metatheory.

1 Introduction

In a previous paper [14], I have presented an implementation of the common knowledge logic in CoQ. There I have shown how this applies to prove mechanically popular puzzles as prolegomenon of other potential applications. In these experiments I have shown in particular that in the literature (mostly devoted to study *model theory* of common knowledge logic) some concepts of proof theory are not clearly brought out and statements made at the meta-level, i.e., in the meta-theory, are not sorted out from statements made at the level of the language, i.e., in the theory. In the deep embedding in a proof assistant (where the logic is fully implemented into the meta-language) the distinction between meta-theory and theory is made explicit, by construction. The proof assistant cannot accept ill-formed expressions and forces the user to specify the level of statements he makes, namely *inside* the theory or *outside* the theory. Thus the kind of implication or quantification or even statement, e.g., axiom or premise of a logical implication, has to be made precise. On the opposite, in the handwritten treatments of the puzzles, it is not clear whether a statement is made an axiom stated as such in the meta-theory or a proposition stated as the premise of a logical implication. This confusion is especially present in the literature on

A. Voronkov and C. Weidenbach (Eds.): Ganzinger Festschrift, LNCS 7797, pp. 271–284, 2013.

economic games [23,8]. Using a quantification in the meta-theory vs a quantification in the theory can change dramatically the strength of a statement and its scope.

In this paper, my approach is this of a proof theorist with inclination to experiments. My goal is twofold. First I present a new axiomatization of common knowledge logic (axiom **FB** and rule **LFB**). Second I discuss a specific problem of common knowledge logic, namely the dilemma between internalizing or externalizing implication. Here one needs some explanation. In a proof theoretic approach there are two kinds of implications: an internal implication (the implication of the object theory) written here $? \Rightarrow ?$, and the external implication (the implication of the meta-theory) written $\frac{\vdash ?}{\vdash ?}$. Here , $\vdash \varphi$ means *"φ is a theorem"*. This discussion about the two views of the same problem in common knowledge logic will be made first through examples and at this exploratory state no meta-theorem is proved. There are two approaches when solving a puzzle. In the first approach, a statement is made an axiom, say $\vdash \varphi$, this axiom leads to the proof of $\vdash \psi$, proving the meta implication $\frac{\vdash \varphi}{\vdash \psi}$. In the second approach, one proves $\vdash C_G(\varphi) \Rightarrow \psi$, where C_G is the *common knowledge* modality. From experiments, I have drawn the following statements. These two approaches seem to be equivalent and show the interplay between the theory and the meta-theory. An interesting meta-theorem could be to prove that equivalence (see Section 5). I call *external vs internal* the equivalence of $\frac{\vdash \varphi}{\vdash \psi}$ with $\vdash C_G(\varphi) \Rightarrow \psi$. In this paper all the discussion is based on experiments made in the proof assistant CoQ and the paper can be seen as the description of those experiments. I discovered in [5] that the correspondence between $\frac{\vdash \varphi}{\vdash \psi}$ and $\vdash C_G(\varphi) \Rightarrow C_G(\psi)$ is known, but it is not the one I am looking for. In what follows, the typewriter font is for code taken from the CoQ implementation. Most of the development in CoQ is available on the WEB at http://perso.ens-lyon.fr/pierre.lescanne/COQ/epistemic_logic.v (see [14] or a presentation). The rest can be found in [21].

2   Presentation of Common Knowledge Logic

Historical Facts

The concept of common knowledge has been introduced by the philosopher Lewis [16] and since is used in several context namely distributed systems [13,20], artificial intelligence [18] and game theory [1].

Epistemic Logic

The basis of common knowledge logic is epistemic logic. In my experiments in CoQ [4], epistemic logic is presented by a Hilbert-style system of rules and axioms. Since I use second order logic, I define only the (internal) implication and I derive the other connectors. There are only two rules namely **MP**, i.e., the *Modus Ponens* and **KG** also known as *Knowledge Generalization* and three

$$\frac{\vdash_K \varphi}{\vdash \varphi}\ \textit{Taut} \qquad \frac{}{\vdash (K_i\varphi \wedge K_i(\varphi \Rightarrow \psi)) \Rightarrow K_i\psi}\ \mathbf{K}_K \qquad \frac{}{\vdash K_i\varphi \Rightarrow \varphi}\ \mathbf{T}_K$$

$$\frac{\vdash \varphi \qquad \vdash \varphi \Rightarrow \psi}{\vdash \psi}\ \mathbf{MP} \qquad \frac{\vdash \varphi}{\vdash K_i\varphi}\ \mathbf{KG}_K$$

Fig. 1. The basic rules of epistemic logic: the system $\mathbb{T}$

axioms *Taut*, **K** and **T**. Actually *Taut* is an axiom scheme as it says that every classical tautology is a theorem in common knowledge logic. Such an approach requires a "deep embedding" (see appendix A). The main reason is that modal logic cannot be easily implemented with natural deduction without changing its basic philosophy[1]. Epistemic logic is based on modal logic and in this paper only the system $\mathbb{T}$ (see Figure 1) is considered. Since there is much flexibility in the terminology, I decided to stick to the terminology of [5]. Epistemic logic introduces one modality for each agent: it expresses that that agent "knows" the proposition that follows the modality. More specifically, if φ is a proposition, $K_i(\varphi)$ is the proposition φ modified by the modality K_i which means *"Agent i knows φ"*. In Figure 1, the statement $\vdash_K \varphi$ means that φ is a theorem in classical propositional logic (this time, K stands for the German adjective "klassisch" [9]). Knowing whether classical logic is relevant is a topics of research [24].

Common Knowledge Logic

Now let us suppose that we have a group G of agents. The knowledge of a fact φ can be shared by the group G, i. e., *"each agent in G knows φ"*. We write $E_G(\varphi)$ and the meaning of E_G is easily axiomatized by the equivalence given in Figure 2 which can also be seen as the definition of E_G; it is called *shared knowledge*.

In common knowledge logic, there is another modality, called *common knowledge* which is much stronger than shared knowledge. It is also associated with a group G of agents and is written C_G. Given φ, $C_G(\varphi)$ is the least solution of the equation

---

[1] The reason why one cannot use a natural deduction of a sequent calculus approach is essentially due to the rule **KG**. If one accepts such a rule in natural deduction, one gets

$$\frac{\Gamma \vdash \varphi}{K_i(\Gamma) \vdash K_i(\varphi)}$$

This requires to extend the operator K_i to contexts like Γ. If instead of K_i one uses a modality $\Box$, one says that $\Box(\Gamma)$ is a *"boxed context"*. Actually *linear logic* [10] is perhaps the archetypical modal logic and the equivalent of K_i is the modality *of course* written "!". The equivalent of **KG** is a rule called also *of course*. Without that rule the proof net presentation is somewhat simple [12]. Its introduction requires a machinery of boxes which increases its complexity.

$$\boxed{\dfrac{}{\vdash E_G(\varphi) \Leftrightarrow \bigwedge_{i \in G} K_i\varphi}\ \mathbf{E}}$$

Fig. 2. Shared knowledge

$$x \Leftrightarrow \varphi \wedge E_G(x).$$

"Least" should be taken w.r.t. the order induced by $\Rightarrow$. A proposition ψ is *less than* a proposition ρ if $\rho \Rightarrow \psi$. As well known in the fixed point theory, the least solution of the above equation is also the least solution of the inequation:

$$x \Rightarrow \varphi \wedge E_G(x).$$

The axiomatization of Figure 3 characterizes $C_G(\varphi)$ by two properties. Together with the system $\mathbb{T}$ and the definition of E_G it forms the system $\mathbb{CK}_G$. It asserts two things.

1. $C_G(\varphi)$ is a solution of the inequation $x \Rightarrow \varphi \wedge E_G(x)$, axiom **FB**,
2. If ρ is another solution of the inequation, then ρ implies $C_G(\varphi)$, which means that ρ is greater than $C_G(\varphi)$). This is rule **LFB**.

One can prove that C_G satisfies axioms and rules of $\mathbb{T}$, where K_i is replaced by C_G even when $G = \emptyset$. Thus we prove

$$\dfrac{}{\vdash (C_G\varphi \wedge C_G(\varphi \Rightarrow \psi)) \Rightarrow C_G\psi}\ \mathbf{K}_C \qquad \dfrac{}{\vdash C_G\varphi \Rightarrow \varphi}\ \mathbf{T}_C \qquad \dfrac{\vdash \varphi}{\vdash C_G\varphi}\ \mathbf{KG}_C$$

$\mathbf{KG}_C$ stands for *Common Knowledge Generalization*. Notice that $\mathbf{T}_C$ and $\frac{\vdash \varphi}{\vdash \varphi}$ on one side and $\vdash C_G\varphi \Rightarrow C_G\varphi$ and $\mathbf{KG}_C$ on the other side form the two first instances of *external vs internal*. Actually one can prove more, namely that C_G satisfies axiom $\mathbf{4}_C$, namely $\vdash C_G(\varphi) \Rightarrow C_G(C_G(\varphi))$. It is a variant for common knowledge logic of the axiom $\vdash K_i(\varphi) \Rightarrow K_i(K_i(\varphi))$ of epistemic logic known as *Positive Introspection* or $\mathbf{4}_K$. The proof of $\mathbf{4}_C$ does not requires this of $\mathbf{4}_K$[2].

Notice that the presentation of common knowledge given in Figure 3 is somewhat new in logic of knowledge. It is more robust than this of Fagin et al. [5] which itself formalizes this of Aumann [1]. Our axiomatization works even for an empty set of agents and this is crucial, as starting with an empty set of agents is the key of a recursive definition of E_G and C_G. However, as pointed out by a reader of this paper, this presentation is well known in modal logic and dynamic logic [11], since C_G is just the reflexive and transitive closure[3] of E_G and

---

[2] This seems to show that **4**, which is a controverted axiom in general, should be stated more appropriately for the common knowledge of a group of agents rather than for the knowledge of an individual agent.

[3] From a model theory point of view, i.e., if one sees as relations the modality which are proposition transformers in proof theory.

$$\frac{}{\vdash C_G(\varphi) \Rightarrow \varphi \wedge E_G(C_G(\varphi))} \; \textbf{FB}$$

$$\frac{\vdash \rho \Rightarrow \varphi \wedge E_G(\rho)}{\vdash \rho \Rightarrow C_G(\varphi)} \; \textbf{LFB}$$

Fig. 3. The rules for common knowledge

$(A7)$	$C_G(\varphi) \Rightarrow \varphi$
$(A8)$	$C_G(\varphi) \Rightarrow E_G(C_G(\varphi))$
$(A9)$	$C_G(\varphi) \wedge C_G(\varphi \Rightarrow \psi) \Rightarrow C_G(\psi)$
$(A10)$	$C_G(\varphi \Rightarrow E_G(\varphi)) \Rightarrow \varphi \Rightarrow C_G(\varphi)$
$(R3)$	$\dfrac{\varphi}{C_G(\varphi)}$

Fig. 4. Meyer and van der Hoek axioms $\mathbb{TEC}_G$

a presentation by fixpoint is well-known in this framework. Amazingly, Aumann and Fagin et al. consider only the transitive closure of E_G not the reflexive and transitive which seems more natural whereas the reflexive and transitive closure seems more natural.

Two Presentations of Common Knowledge Logic

This presentation should be compared with this given by Meyer and van der Hoek on page 46 of [19] (see Figure 4). The system $\mathbb{T} \cup \{A7, A8, A9, A10, R3\}$, together with the definition of E_G, is called $\mathbb{TEC}_G$. One notices that axioms $(A7)$ and $(A8)$ are just a splitting of axiom *Fixpoint*, i.e., one splits the conclusion $\varphi \wedge E_G(C_G(\varphi))$. Axiom $(A9)$ is axiom $\mathbf{K}_C$ mentioned above and $(R3)$ is $\mathbf{KG}_C$ also mentioned above. As said, both $(A9)$ and $(R3)$ can be proved as theorems in $\mathbb{CK}_G$. $(A10)$ is more interesting and requires specific consideration. Figure 5 sketches a proof of $(A10)$ as a theorem in $\mathbb{CK}_G$. Therefore $\mathbb{CK}_G$ implies $\mathbb{TEC}_G$.

$\mathbb{TEC_G}$ *implies* $\mathbb{CK_G}$. Indeed axiom **FB** is an obvious consequence of $\mathbb{TEC}_G$ and we prove that rule **LFB** is a consequence of $\mathbb{TEC}_G$ as follows.

$$\frac{\dfrac{\dfrac{\dfrac{\rho \Rightarrow \varphi \wedge E_G(\rho)}{\rho \Rightarrow E_G(\rho)}}{C_G(\rho \Rightarrow E_G(\rho))}\,(R3)}{\rho \Rightarrow C_G(\rho)}\,(A10+\mathbf{MP}) \qquad \dfrac{\dfrac{\dfrac{\rho \Rightarrow \varphi \wedge E_G(\rho)}{\rho \Rightarrow \varphi}}{C_G(\rho \Rightarrow \varphi))}\,(R3)}{C_G(\rho) \Rightarrow C_G(\varphi)}\,(A9+\mathbf{MP})}{\rho \Rightarrow C_G(\varphi)}\,(Transitivity\,of \Rightarrow)$$

$$C_G(\varphi \Rightarrow E_G(\varphi)) \Rightarrow (\varphi \Rightarrow E_G(\varphi)) \quad \text{[A7]}$$
$$\overline{C_G(\varphi \Rightarrow E_G(\varphi)) \wedge \varphi \Rightarrow E_G(\varphi)}$$

$$C_G(\varphi \Rightarrow E_G(\varphi)) \Rightarrow E_G(C_G(\varphi \Rightarrow E_G(\varphi))) \quad \text{[A8]}$$
$$\overline{C_G(\varphi \Rightarrow E_G(\varphi)) \wedge \varphi \Rightarrow E_G(C_G(\varphi \Rightarrow E_G(\varphi))) \wedge E_G(\varphi)}$$
$$\overline{C_G(\varphi \Rightarrow E_G(\varphi)) \wedge \varphi \Rightarrow E_G(C_G(\varphi \Rightarrow E_G(\varphi)) \wedge \varphi)} \quad \textbf{LFB}$$

$$C_G(\varphi \Rightarrow E_G(\varphi)) \wedge \varphi \Rightarrow \varphi \quad\quad \text{Transitivity of } \Rightarrow$$

$$C_G(\varphi \Rightarrow E_G(\varphi)) \wedge \varphi \Rightarrow \varphi \wedge E_G(C_G(\varphi \Rightarrow E_G(\varphi)) \wedge \varphi)$$
$$\overline{C_G(\varphi \Rightarrow E_G(\varphi)) \wedge \varphi \Rightarrow C_G(\varphi)}$$
$$\overline{C_G(\varphi \Rightarrow E_G(\varphi)) \Rightarrow \varphi \Rightarrow C_G(\varphi)}$$

Fig. 5. A proof of Meyer and van der Hoek's axiom (A10)

$$C_G(\varphi \Rightarrow E_G(\varphi)) \Rightarrow E_G(C_G(\varphi \Rightarrow E_G(\varphi))) \quad \boxed{\text{A8}}$$

$$C_G(\varphi \Rightarrow E_G(\varphi)) \Rightarrow (\varphi \Rightarrow E_G(\varphi)) \quad \boxed{\text{A7}}$$
$$\overline{C_G(\varphi \Rightarrow E_G(\varphi)) \wedge \varphi \Rightarrow (\varphi \Rightarrow E_G(\varphi)) \wedge \varphi \quad (\varphi \Rightarrow E_G(\varphi)) \wedge \varphi \Rightarrow E_G(\varphi)}$$
$$\overline{C_G(\varphi \Rightarrow E_G(\varphi)) \wedge \varphi \Rightarrow E_G(\varphi)}$$

$$A \wedge \varphi \Rightarrow E_G(A)$$
$$\frac{A \wedge \varphi \Rightarrow E_G(A \wedge \varphi)}{A \wedge \varphi \Rightarrow C_G(A \wedge \varphi)} \ (R10)$$

Fig. 6. A proof of $A \wedge \varphi \Rightarrow C_G(A \wedge \varphi)$

(R10) *Implies* (A10). In the above proof, we should notice that instead of axiom (A10), we use rule

$$\frac{C_G(\varphi \Rightarrow E_G(\varphi))}{\varphi \Rightarrow C_G(\varphi)}\ (R10)$$

which is a direct consequence of (A10) by **MP**. By analogy with (A10), we call that rule (R10). A closer look shows that we use the derived rule

$$\frac{\varphi \Rightarrow E_G(\varphi)}{\varphi \Rightarrow C_G(\varphi)}\ (R10')$$

which is the above rule combined with (R3). See section *Discussion* below to understand why we are interested in that rule. Let us come back to (R10) and let us call $\mathbb{TEC}'_G$ the system $\mathbb{T} \cup \{A7, A8, A9, R10, R3\}$. Since we have a proof of $\mathbb{CK}_G$ in $\mathbb{TEC}'_G$ and a proof of $\mathbb{TEC}_G$, in particular of (A10), in $\mathbb{CK}_G$, we have an indirect proof of $\mathbb{TEC}_G$ in $\mathbb{TEC}'_G$ or, in short, of (R10) implies (A10). Here is a direct proof.

Let us state $A \equiv C_G(\varphi \Rightarrow E_G(\varphi))$ in this proof. First, let us prove $A \wedge \varphi \Rightarrow C_G(A \wedge \varphi)$ (see Figure 6).

The rest is easy. First, we notice that we have $C_G(A \wedge \varphi) \Rightarrow C_G(\varphi)$.

$$\frac{\dfrac{A \wedge \varphi \Rightarrow \varphi}{C_G(A \wedge \varphi \Rightarrow \varphi)}\ (R3)}{C_G(A \wedge \varphi) \Rightarrow C_G(\varphi)}\ (A9) + \mathbf{MP}$$

By transitivity of $\Rightarrow$, we get $A \wedge \varphi \Rightarrow C_G(\varphi)$. But clearly $A \wedge \varphi \Rightarrow C_G(\varphi)$ is equivalent to $A \Rightarrow \varphi \Rightarrow C_G(\varphi)$ which is $C_G(\varphi \Rightarrow E_G(\varphi)) \Rightarrow \varphi \Rightarrow C_G(\varphi)$, e.g., (A10).

Discussion

The equivalence between (A10) and (R10') is a third instance of *external vs internal*. Indeed, we have shown that a proposition of the form $\vdash C_G(\rho) \Rightarrow \psi$ is equivalent to a rule of the form $\frac{\vdash \rho}{\vdash \psi}$.

3   The Three Wise Men

The first example we address is the well-known example of the three wise men. See [14] for a more detailed presentation. It is stated usually as follows ([5], Exercise 1.3): *"There are three wise men. It is common knowledge that there are three red hats and two white hats. The king puts a hat on the head of each of the three wise men and asks them (sequentially) if they know the color of the hat on their head. The first wise man says that he does not know; the second wise man says that he does not know; then the third man says that he knows"*. Let us call the three wise persons Alice, Bob and Carol. Let us write white Alice for *"Alice wears a white hat"* and red Alice for *"Alice wears a red hat"*. The puzzle is based on a function which says whether an agent knows the color of her (his) hat:

```
Definition Kh := fun i => (K i (white i)) V (K i (red i)).
```

Clearly one has to prove that Kh Carol holds under some assumptions. To make clear theses assumptions, we define in addition a few propositions namely

```
Definition One_hat := \-/(fun i:nat => white i | red i).
```

which says that every agent wears a red hat or a white hat. If P is a predicate, \-/P is the logical quantification, i.e., the quantification in the theory not this in the meta-theory.

```
Definition Two_white_hats := white Bob & white Carol ==> red Alice.
```

which says that there are two white hats. Notice that this is stated in a weak form, indeed it is only when Bob and Carol wear white hats that one can deduce that Alice wears a red hat. Moreover there are three concepts which say that each agent sees the hat of the other agents and therefore knows the color of the hat.

```
Definition K_Alice_white_Bob := white Bob ==> K Alice (white Bob).
Definition K_Alice_white_Carol := white Carol ==> K Alice (white Carol).
Definition K_Bob_white_Carol := white Carol ==> K Bob (white Carol).
```

A First Result

In a first attempt [14], the five above propositions were stated as axioms and I was able to prove:

```
|- K Carol (K Bob (¬ Kh Alice) & ¬ Kh Bob)
           ==> K Carol (red Carol).
```

In COQ this would give a statement like

```
|- One_hat &
   K_Alice_white_Bob &
   K_Alice_white_Carol &
   K_Bob_white_Carol &
   Two_white_hats  ->
|- K Carol (K Bob (¬ Kh Alice) & ¬ Kh Bob)
           ==> K Carol (red Carol).
```

where -> is the meta-implication, i.e., this of COQ and as usual $|-\varphi$ says that proposition φ is a theorem.

A Second Result

In the second attempt one proves:

```
|- K Carol (K Bob (One_hat &
                   K_Bob_white_Carol &
                   K_Alice_white_Bob &
                   K_Alice_white_Carol &
                   (K Alice Two_white_hats) &
                   ¬ Kh Alice) &
            ¬ Kh Bob)
   ==> Kh Carol.
```

This tells exactly the amount of knowledge which Carol requires to deduce that she knows the color of her hat, actually red. Let us call Alice_Bob_Carol the group made of Alice, Bob and Carol. From the above statement, one derives the corollary:

```
|- C Alice_Bob_Carol (Two_white_hats &
                      One_hat &
                      K_Bob_white_Carol &
                      K_Alice_white_Bob &
                      K_Alice_white_Carol)
   ==> K Carol (K Bob (¬ Kh Alice) & ¬ Kh Bob) ==> Kh Carol.
```

which is weaker. But if we state

```
φ ≡ Two_white_hats &
    One_hat &
    K_Bob_white_Carol &
    K_Alice_white_Bob &
    K_Alice_white_Carol
```

and

```
ψ ≡ K Carol (K Bob (¬ Kh Alice) & ¬ Kh Bob) ==> Kh Carol
```

we notice that we have exhibited a fourth instance of *external vs internal* since $\vdash C_G(\varphi) \Rightarrow \psi$ and $\frac{\vdash \varphi}{\vdash \psi}$ are equivalent.

4   The Muddy Children

This problem had many variants [17,7,6,8]. It is a typical example of how a community of agents acquires knowledge. In its politically correct version [5,19], a group of children have mud on their head after playing during a birthday party. The kids do not know they have mud on their head. The father of the kid who organized the party asked the children to come around him in a circle for the kids to see each other and he tells them that there is at least one child who has mud on his face so that they clearly all hear him. Then Father asks the kids who have mud to step forward. He repeats this last sentence until all the kids step forward.

Philosophers have been puzzled by the fact that the first sentence of Father namely *"There is at least one child with mud on his face"* is absolutely necessary. This fact is known by the children, but by doing so, Father makes it a common knowledge. In [14], we have identified that the key lemma is

```
Lemma Progress :
    forall n p : nat,
    |- C ([:n+1:]) (At_least (n+1) p) &
       E ([:n+1:]) (¬ Exactly (n+1) p)
       ==> C ([:n+1:]) (At_least (n+1) (p+1)).
```

In other words, if the fact that there is at least p muddy children is a common knowledge and all the children know that there is not exactly p muddy children, then the fact that there is at least $p+1$ muddy children is a common knowledge. Together with the first statement of Father:

```
Axiom First_Father_Statement :
    |- C ([:nb_children:]) (At_least n 1).
```

we are able to prove after n steps C ([:n:]) (At_least n n) which means that *the fact that there is at least n muddy children is common knowledge*. This is the final result. Common knowledge is important here because one can "progress" in common knowledge and not in shared knowledge. Thus the first statement that provides a first common knowledge allows initialization. The proof of Progress relies on a statement

```
Knowledge_Diffusion :
  forall n p i : nat,
    |- E ([:n:]) (At_least n p) ==>
       E ([:n:]) (¬ Exactly n p) ==>
       K i (E ([:n:]) (¬ Exactly n p)).
```

This statement is here to translate what children see after Father has asked the muddy ones to step forward and none did. They all know that there is at least p muddy children and they all know that there is not exactly p muddy children otherwise those with muddy face would have stepped forward, but now each one knows that all the others know that there is not exactly p muddy children.

Knowledge_Diffusion as an Axiom

In a first experiment, we made Knowledge_Diffusion an axiom and we were able to prove Progress in its above form.

Knowledge_Diffusion as a Common Knowledge

In the second experiment, we consider that proposition Knowledge_Diffusion should not be made an axiom, i.e., an immutable principle, but it should be made just a rule of a game upon everyone agrees. Therefore the rules of the game are common knowledge that everyone accepts; agreeing on these rules makes everyone to act and reason according to them, i.e., "rationally". In this version *Progress* becomes:

```
 Lemma Progress :
forall n p : nat,
|- C ([:n+1:])(Knowledge_Diffusion) ==>
    (C ([:n+1:]) (At_least (n+1) p) &
     E ([:n+1:]) (¬ Exactly (n+1) p))
    ==> C ([:n+1:]) (At_least (n+1) (p+1)).
```

Discussion

Again we show that we can change an statement of the form $\frac{\vdash \varphi}{\vdash \psi}$ into a statement of the form $\vdash C_G(\varphi) \Rightarrow \psi$. Here

```
φ ≡ C ([:n+1:]) (At_least (n+1) p) &
    E ([:n+1:]) (¬ Exactly (n+1) p))
```

and

```
ψ ≡ C ([:n+1:]) (At_least (n+1) (p+1)).
```

This is a fifth instance of *external vs internal*.

5   The Equivalence between Internal and External Implication

Fagin et al [5] in exercise 3.29 notice, with no reference, that $\frac{\vdash \varphi}{\vdash \psi}$ and $\vdash C_G(\varphi) \Rightarrow C_G(\psi)$ are equivalent. One notice by $\mathbf{T}_C$, i.e., $\vdash C_G(\rho) \Rightarrow \rho$, that this statement is stronger than *external vs internal*, which states[4] the equivalence between $\frac{\vdash \varphi}{\vdash \psi}$ and $\vdash C_G(\varphi) \Rightarrow \psi$. The proof of that result cannot be readily implemented in CoQ in our current implementation of common knowledge logic since this requires a deeper embedding of the theory. In short, in order to mechanize that proof, one needs not only internalize the object implication, which we called internal implication, but also what we called the external implication, since a meta-proof of the equivalence requires an induction on the proof of $\frac{\vdash \varphi}{\vdash \psi}$. In a first step, one can prove in CoQ that all the rules of common knowledge logic, namely **MP**, **KG** and **LFB** have their equivalent in the form $\vdash C_G(\varphi) \Rightarrow C_G(\psi)$, namely:

$$\vdash C_G((\varphi \Rightarrow \psi) \wedge \varphi) \Rightarrow C_G(\psi) \qquad \vdash C_G(\varphi) \Rightarrow C_G(K_i(\varphi))$$
$$\vdash C_G(\rho \Rightarrow \varphi \wedge E_G(\rho)) \Rightarrow C_G(\rho \Rightarrow C_G(\varphi))$$

---

[4] Provided that ψ does not contain any knowledge modality relative to an agent outside the set G.

The first one is a variant, by the means of $\vdash C_G(\chi \wedge \rho) \Leftrightarrow C_G(\chi) \wedge C_G(\rho)$, of $\mathbf{K}_C$ or $(A9)$. The second one is a basic result of common knowledge logic. The third theorem has no equivalent in the literature and has been proved in CoQ for that purpose. Then we get the following interesting result:

$$\vdash C_G(\varphi) \Rightarrow C_G(\psi) \quad\longrightarrow\quad \vdash C_G(\varphi) \Rightarrow \psi \quad\longrightarrow\quad \frac{\vdash \varphi}{\vdash \psi}$$

The back arrow is proved by induction of the length of the deduction $\vdash \varphi \to \vdash \psi$. Therefore, one notices three levels of implications: the implication $\Rightarrow$ in the theory, the implication $\frac{\vdash ?}{\vdash ?}$ in the metatheory and the implication $\longrightarrow$ in the meta-metatheory. From the above diagram one gets

$$\vdash C_G(\varphi) \Rightarrow \psi \quad\longrightarrow\quad \vdash C_G(\varphi) \Rightarrow C_G(\psi) \ .$$

Actually we have

$$\frac{\vdash C_G(\varphi) \Rightarrow \psi}{\vdash C_G(\varphi) \Rightarrow C_G(\psi)}$$

as follows

$$\frac{\dfrac{\vdash C_G(\varphi) \Rightarrow \psi \qquad \vdash C_G(\varphi) \Rightarrow E_G(C_G(\varphi))}{\vdash C_G(\varphi) \Rightarrow \psi \wedge E_G(C_G(\varphi))}}{\vdash C_G(\varphi) \Rightarrow C_G(\psi)} \text{ LFB}$$

since $\vdash C_G(\varphi) \Rightarrow E_G(C_G(\varphi))$ is a theorem of common knowledge logic.

6   Conclusion

On another hand, it is worth to mention the study on combining common knowledge logic and dynamic logic we have done with Jérôme Puisségur [22,15]. The dynamic logic is used to describe changes in the world, but those changes are *purely epistemic* (an idea we borrow from Baltag, Moss and Solecki [3,2]). This means that they affect only knowledge of the agents and nothing else. The muddy children puzzle has been axiomatized in this framework and a proof of its results has been fully mechanized in CoQ. We can draw already two lessons form those experiences. First when merging two modal logics it seems that internalizing common knowledge is more appropriate. In other words, an approach like $\vdash C_G(\varphi) \Rightarrow \psi$ should be preferred to setting the axiom $\vdash \varphi$ to prove $\vdash \psi$, as one does not know which metatheory a specific statement belongs to: dynamic logic or common knowledge logic? Second a formalization of predicate logic, allows expressing easily arbitrary depth of shared logic according to the number of agents. More precisely, common knowledge is not a priori necessary in the muddy children example and just a specific number of imbricated shared knowledge modalities corresponding to the number of children. This fact was already noticed by authors [8].

Acknowledgment. I would like to thank Bertrand Prémaillon who made part of the experiments in CoQ and René Vestergaard for stimulating discussions.

References

1. Aumann, R.J.: Backward induction and common knowledge of rationality. Games and Economic Behavior 8, 6–19 (1995)
2. Baltag, A.: A logic of epistemic actions. In: van der Hoek, W., Meyer, J.-J., Witteveen, C. (eds.) Proceedings of the ESSLLI 1999 workshop on Foundations and Applications of Collective Agent-Based Systems. Utrecht University (1999)
3. Baltag, A., Moss, L., Solecki, S.: The logic of public announcements, common knowledge and private suspicion. In: Proc. of TARK, pp. 43–56. Morgan Kaufmann Publishers (1998)
4. Bertot, Y., Castéran, P.: Interactive Theorem Proving and Program Development Coq'Art: The Calculus of Inductive Constructions. Springer (2004)
5. Fagin, R., Halpern, J.Y., Moses, Y., Vardi, M.Y.: Reasoning about Knowledge. The MIT Press (1995)
6. Gamow, G., Stern, M.: Forthy unfaithful wives. In: Puzzle Math., pp. 20–23. The Viking Press, New York (1958)
7. Gardner, M.: Puzzles from other worlds. Vintage (1984)
8. Geanakoplos, J.: Common knowledge. In: Aumann, R., Hart, S. (eds.) Handbook of Game Theory, vol. 2, pp. 1437–1496. Elsevier, Amsterdam (1994)
9. Gentzen, G.: Untersuchungen über das logische Schließen. Mathematische Zeitschrift 210, 405–431 (1935)
10. Girard, J.-Y.: Linear logic. Theoretical Computer Science 50, 1–102 (1987)
11. Harel, D., Kozen, D., Tiuryn, J.: Dynamic Logic. MIT Press, Cambridge (2000)
12. Lafont, Y.: From proof nets to interaction nets. In: Girard, J.-Y., Lafont, Y., Regnier, L. (eds.) Advances in Linear Logic, pp. 225–247. Cambridge University Press (1995)
13. Lehmann, D.: Knowledge, common knowledge and related puzzles (extended summary). In: PODC 1984: Proceedings of the Third Annual ACM Symposium on Principles of Distributed Computing, pp. 62–67. ACM Press, New York (1984)
14. Lescanne, P.: Mechanizing epistemic logic with Coq. Annals of Mathematics and Artificial Intelligence 48, 15–43 (2006)
15. Lescanne, P., Puisségur, J.: Dynamic logic of common knowledge in a proof assistant, http://hal-ens-lyon.archives-ouvertes.fr/ensl-00198782
16. Lewis, D.: Convention: A philosophical study. Harvard University Press, Cambridge (1969)
17. Littlewood, J.E.: Littlewood's miscellany. Cambridge University Press, Cambridge (1986)
18. McCarthy, J., Sato, M., Hayashi, T., Igarashi, S.: On the model theory of knowledge. Technical Report AIM-312, Stanford University (1977)
19. Meyer, J.-J.C., van der Hoek, W.: Epistemic Logic for Artificial Intelligence and Computer Science. Cambridge Tracts in Theoretical Computer Science, vol. 41. Cambridge University Press (1995)
20. Moses, Y.O., Dolev, D., Halpern, J.Y.: Cheating husbands and other stories: a case study in knowledge, action, and communication. Distributed Computing 1(3), 167–176 (1986)

21. Prémaillon, B.: Logique épistémique, modélisation dans un assistant de preuve. Master's thesis, Master Ingénierie Mathématique, Université Claude Bernard, Lyon (2005)
22. Puisségur, J.: Eléments de construction d'une logique épistémique et dynamique. Rapport de stage de licence de l'École normale supérieure de Lyon (2005)
23. Samet, D.: Hypothetical knowledge and games with perfect information. Games and Economic Behavior 17, 230–251 (1996)
24. Vestergaard, R., Lescanne, P., Ono, H.: The inductive and modal proof theory of Aumann's theorem on rationality. Technical Report IS-RR-2006-009, JAIST (2006), http://www.jaist.ac.jp/ vester/Writings/ vestergaard-IS-RR-2006-009.pdf

A   Deep Embedding

A logic $\mathcal{L}$, the object logic or the object theory, is said to be *deeply embedded* in another logic $\mathcal{M}$, the meta-theory, or in a proof assistant if one considers the logic $\mathcal{M}$ to be this of the proof assistant, if all the constituents of the logic $\mathcal{L}$ are made objects of the logic $\mathcal{M}$ and all the connectors and the rules of $\mathcal{L}$ are defined inside the logic $\mathcal{M}$. This is opposed to shallow embedding where $\mathcal{L}$ and $\mathcal{M}$ may share connectors and rules. A *shallow embedding* is usually more concise, but in a deep embedding a clear distinction is made between the connectors of the object theory and those of the meta-theory. In a deep embedding the connector and the corresponding meta-connector can be somewhat connected, but they cannot match completely. For instance, it could happen that the meta-disjunctions of two propositions meta-implies the proposition made as the conjunction of the two propositions and not vice-versa, in a sense made precise in formalizing the object theory.

Moreover not all the logics can be shallowly embedded. This is the case for common knowledge logic which cannot be formalized easily in a natural deduction framework.

Constructing Bachmair-Ganzinger Models*

Christopher Lynch

Department of Mathematics and Computer Science Box 5815,
Clarkson University, Potsdam, NY 13699-5815, USA
clynch@clarkson.edu

Abstract. We give some algorithms for constructing models from sets
of clauses saturated by Ordered Resolution (with Selection rules). In the
ground case, we give an efficient algorithm for constructing a minimal
model. Then we generalize minimal models to preferred models, which
may be useful for verification. For the ground case, we also show how to
construct all models for a set of clauses saturated by Ordered Resolution,
in time polynomial in the number of models. We also generalize our
results to nonground models, where we add a restricted splitting rule
to our inference rules, and show that for any set of clauses saturated
by Ordered Resolution (with Selection), a query about the truth of a
particular atom in the model can be decided.

1   Introduction

It is generally believed that a major drawback of Resolution-based theorem proving methods is that a model is not constructed when the set of clauses is satisfiable. If the inference system halts without producing the empty clause, then the
set of clauses is determined to be satisfiable. But there is no model constructed.
The set of clauses produced by the inference system can be considered to represent a model in some sense. In fact, it is possible to theoretically construct
a model in this case. But in the practical sense, there is no known method for
determining if a ground atom is true in this theoretically constructed model.
This problem has received some attention[9,6,5], and methods have been given
in some restricted cases. The main goal of this paper is to determine a more
general way to accomplish this.

Interestingly, the method of Bachmair and Ganzinger[1] for proving completeness of the resolution inference system actually constructs a model for a set of
clauses saturated by Resolution when the empty clause cannot be produced. But
this is only a theoretical construction. It is difficult to use this practically. In the
ground case (no variables), it can be done. But not in the nonground case.

In this paper, we first define a notion called a Preferred Model for ground
clauses. For each atom, the user defines a preference for that predicate of either
true or false. A model of a set of clauses is a Preferred Model if each atom
receives the preferred truth value whenever that is consistent with the truth

---

* This work was supported by NSF grant number CCR-0098270.

A. Voronkov and C. Weidenbach (Eds.): Ganzinger Festschrift, LNCS 7797, pp. 285–301, 2013.

value of all smaller atoms. For example, if each atom is preferred to be false, then the Preferred Model is the Minimal Model. Each set of clauses has a unique Preferred Model. We show that if a set of ground clauses S is saturated by Ordered Resolution, then the Preferred Model of S can be constructed in time $O(|S|lg(|S|))$. Preferred Models could be useful in verification. For example if a program does not meet its specifications, then the programmer would like to see a counterexample. Since all counterexamples might not make sense, it would be useful for the programmer to express some preferences.

We then give an algorithm to show that if a set of clauses S has exactly k models and if S is saturated by Ordered Resolution, then all models of S can be constructed in time $O(|S|lg(|S|) + |S|k)$. In other words, the time needed to construct all the models of S is just the time it takes to write out all the models, plus an initialization time to sort the clauses. In general, a set of clauses may have exponentially many models. But this result shows that if there are only polynomially many models, then they can all be constructed in polynomial time.

We extend our results on Preferred Models to nonground clauses saturated by Ordered Resolution (possibly with selection rules). This is useful, because Ordered Resolution is an inference rule that often halts, the only model construction results of which we are aware which handles clauses saturated by Ordered Resolution is the one of Peltier[9], but that method only handles some sets of saturated clauses. Of course, models of nonground clauses may be infinite. We do not try to schematize all the models. Instead, we are interested in developing an algorithm which will decide if a given atom is true in the Preferred Model. The notion of Preferred Model can be extended to nonground clauses by defining it for the ground instances.

The first result for nonground clauses is related to results for Local Theories. Given an ordering $<$, we can define the order type $ot(n)$ to be the number of atoms smaller than any atom of size n. If S is a set of clauses saturated by Ordered Resolution, and if A is a ground atom, then it can be decided in time polynomial in $ot(|A|)$ whether A is true in the Preferred Model of S. We can extend the result so that if N is a set of ground clauses, then it is decidable in time exponential in $ot(|N| + |A|)$ whether A is true in the Preferred Model of $S \cup N$. The interest of this last result is that rather than just deciding whether atoms are true in a model of S, we are asking whether atoms are true in a model of any set of ground clauses modulo the theory of S.

The above results can only work if the order type is finite, and it is not finite for some orderings. Therefore, we address the problems using a different technique. First, we add a Splitting rule to the Resolution inference system, which is only applicable in a restricted number of cases. Our major result is to show that if S is a set of clauses saturated by Ordered Resolution (plus Selection) with Splitting, then it is decidable whether A is in the Preferred Model of S. The Splitting rule is especially restrictive if the Ordering satisfies some simple conditions, which hold for most standard orderings.

After some preliminaries in Section 2, and a definition of the inference system in Section 3.1, we give some algorithms for constructing the minimal model for a set of ground clauses in Section 3.2. We then define preferences and generalize those algorithms for Resolution with preferences in Section 3.3. The results on preferences are used to show that if a set of ground clauses is saturated by Resolution, then all the models can be constructed in time polynomial in the size of the set of clauses. After that, we extend the results to nonground clauses by considering queries on clauses, first we give results related to local theories in Section 4.1, then to all sets of clauses where a Splitting rule is used in Section 4.2. Finally we give some conclusions in Section 5.

2   Preliminaries

We follow standard definitions for Resolution theorem proving.[1]

We assume we are given a set of variables and a set of uninterpreted function symbols of various arities. An arity is a non-negative integer. *Terms* are defined recursively in the following way: each variable is a term, and if $t_1, \cdots, t_n$ are terms, and f is of arity $n \geq 0$, then $f(t_1, \cdots, t_n)$ is a term. If P is a predicate symbol of arity n, and if $t_1, \cdots, t_n$ are terms, then $P(t_1, \cdots, t_n)$ is an *atom*. Any atom or negation of an atom is a *literal*. A literal is called *positive* if it has no negation. It is called *negative* if it has a negation. A clause is *positive* if all its literals are positive. For all literal L, we define $\bar{L}$ so that $\bar{A} = \neg A = A$ for each atom A. A *clause* is a disjunction of literals. Any object without variables is called *ground*. We will use $\top$ to represent true, and $\bot$ to represent false.

A *substitution* is a mapping from the set of variables to the set of terms, such that it is almost everywhere the identity. We identify a substitution with its homomorphic extension. If θ is a substitution then $Dom(\theta) = \{x \mid x\theta \neq x\}$, and $Ran(\theta) = \{x\theta \mid x \in Dom(\theta)\}$. A substitution θ is a *unifier* of A and B, if $A\theta = B\theta$. σ is a *most general unifier* of A and B, written $\sigma = mgu(A, B)$ if σ is a unifier of A and B, and for all unifiers θ of A and B, there is a substitution ρ such that $\sigma\rho = \theta$.

Given a clause C, define $Gr(C) = \{C\theta | C\theta \text{ is ground }\}$. Given a set of clauses S, let $Gr(S) = \bigcup_{C \in S} Gr(C)\}$. Let $|S|$ be number the number of occurrences of symbols in S.

We assume an ordering $<$ which is *substitution monotonic*, meaning that $s < t$ implies $s\theta < t\theta$, and total on all ground terms and atoms. It can be extended to literals in any way such that $A < \neg A$ for all atoms A, but there is no literal in between A and $\neg A$ in the ordering. We consider a clause as the multiset of its literals, and compare clauses using the multiset ordering. A literal L is said to be *maximum* in a clause if it is larger than all other literals in the clause, and *maximal* in a clause if no other literal in the clause is larger than it. We will use "−" to denote set difference.

Define $Vars(A)$ as the set of all variables in A. We will call an ordering $<$ *variable monotonic* if $A < B$ implies $Vars(A) \subseteq Vars(B)$ for all atoms A and B. Most orderings, such as LPO and RPO[4] are variable monotonic on its terms. But if they are extended to atoms in a way such that $P(s_1, \cdots, s_n) < Q(t_1, \cdots, t_m)$ for given P and Q and all s_i and t_j then they are not variable monotonic in general. So, in practice orderings may or may not be variable monotonic.

An *interpretation* M is defined to be a set of ground atoms. For a ground atom A, we write $M \models A$ if and only if $A \in M$. Then, as usual for ground formulas F_1 and F_2

- $M \models \neg F_1$ if and only if $M \not\models F_1$,
- $M \models F_1 \wedge F_2$ if and only if $M \models F_1$ and $M \models F_2$, and
- $M \models F_1 \vee F_2$ if and only if $M \models F_1$ or $M \models F_2$.

If M is an interpretation, and A is an atom, then let $M_A = \{B \in M \mid B < A\}$. We can compare two interpretations M and N, and say that $M < N$ if there is an atom A such that $M_A = N_A$ but $A \in N$ and $A \notin M$. Note that this does not say that M is smaller than N as a multiset. For example, if $M = \{A, C\}$ and $N = \{A, B\}$ and $A < B < C$, then $M < N$, but M is larger than N as a multiset.

If M is an interpretation and S is a set of clauses, then M is a *model* of C if $M \models C$ for all $C \in S$. If M is a model of S, then we call M a *minimal model* of S if there is no model N of S such that $N < M$. A clause is a *tautology* if it is true in all interpretations.

3 Ground Models

3.1 Resolution Inference System

In this paper, we will be concerned with the Resolution inference system. This inference system involves an ordering $<$. Based on that ordering, we have a selection rule.. A *selection rule* is a function Sel such that for each clause C, $Sel(C)$ is a nonempty set of literals in C. If $A \in Sel(C)$, then A is said to be *selected in* C. A selection rule is called *correct* if for each clause C, (i) $Sel(C)$ is a set of positive literals that contains all maximal literals in C or (ii) $Sel(C)$ contains a negative literal and nothing else. Only selected literals are required to be involved in inferences, although inferences on other literals are allowed. If all maximal literals are selected in each clause, then the inference system is called Ordered Resolution. In Ordered Resolution, inferences are only allowed on maximal literals. That restriction is useful, because it causes the inference system to halt in many more cases than the unrestricted case. Figure 1 gives the *Resolution Inference System*.

For efficiency, the Resolution Inference System generally uses *Redundancy Deletion* rules to delete redundant clauses. A clause is called *redundant* if it is implied by smaller clauses, where a clause is viewed as a multiset of its literals and clauses are compared using the multiset extension of the literal ordering. Examples of redundancy deletion rules are Subsumption and Tautology Deletion.

The Resolution inference system is obviously sound. It is also *complete* in the sense that if a set of clauses is satisfiable then the empty clause can be

---

Resolution:

$$\frac{\Gamma \vee A \quad \neg A' \vee \Delta}{(\Gamma \vee \Delta)\sigma}$$

where $\sigma = mgu(A, A')$, A is selected in its clause, and $\neg A'$ is selected in its clause.

Factoring:

$$\frac{\Gamma \vee L \vee L'}{(\Gamma \vee L)\sigma}$$

where $\sigma = mgu(L, L')$, and L is selected in $\Gamma \vee L \vee L'$.

Fig. 1. Resolution Inference System

deduced from it. We say that a set S of clauses is *saturated* if every inference on nonredundant clauses of S produces a clause that is either in S or redundant in S. A saturated set of clauses corresponds in practice to a set of clauses for which the inference rules have been performed exhaustively. Completeness is expressed by the following theorem[1].

Theorem 1. *Let Sel be a correct selection rule. Let S be a set of clauses. saturated by the Resolution inference system. Then the empty clause is in S if and only if S is unsatisfiable.*

3.2 Minimal Model

The proof of the completeness theorem is given in [1] by contradiction. The proof assumes that S does not contain the empty clause, and then constructs a minimal model of $Gr(S)$. We use that construction in this paper. Therefore, we need to define it. It is a recursive definition. For each clause C, we will define $MM_{<C}$ to be the model which has been created so far using clauses smaller than C, and then $MM_{\leq C}$ will be the updated model depending on C. So the definitions of $MM_{<C}$ and $MM_{\leq C}$ will be mutually recursive. The final model created will be called MM_S, for some set of clauses S.

Definition 1. *Let S be a set of ground clauses. Let $MM_{<C} = \bigcup_{D<C} MM_{\leq D}$. Let C be a clause, where L is the largest literal in C. If L is a maximum, positive, selected literal in C, and $MM_{<C} \not\models C$ then $MM_{\leq C} = MM_{<C} \cup \{L\}$. Otherwise $MM_{\leq C} = MM_{<C}$. In the first case, we say that C is productive and that C produces L. Let $Prod(S)$ be the set of all productive clauses in S. Define $MM_S = \bigcup_{C \in S} MM_{\leq C}$.*

We can now restate the completeness theorem so that it refers to the constructed model. We will call this a *model completeness* theorem.

Theorem 2. *Let Sel be a correct selection rule. Let S be a set of clauses. saturated by the Resolution inference system. Suppose that the empty clause is not in S. Then $MM_{Gr(S)}$ is the minimal model of $Gr(S)$.*

The proof in [1] actually proves the model completeness theorem. This model can actually be constructed in $O(nlg(n))$ time, if S is ground.

Theorem 3. *Let Sel be a correct selection rule. Let S be a set of ground clauses. saturated by the Resolution inference system. Suppose that the empty clause is not in S. Then MM_S can be constructed in $O(|S|lg(|S|)$ time.*

Proof. We sort each clause from smallest literal to largest. Then we sort all the clauses from smallest clause to largest. We have an array or a hash table, representing whether each atom is true or false. Initially, all atoms are false. Then we work our way from smallest to largest clause, checking the current values of each atom in the clause, and updating the largest atom when necessary.

The sorting part of this algorithm can be done in time $O(|S|lg(|S|)$, and the rest can be done in $O(|S|)$.

There is an obvious dynamic programming algorithm to compute a minimal model of S, given in Figure 2. We suppose that the clauses have been sorted, and that they are ordered C_1 to C_m from smallest to largest.

---

function Dyn
$\overline{MM = \emptyset}$
for $i = 1$ to m
    let L be the maximal literal in C_i
    if L is maximum, positive and selected and $MM \not\models C_i$
       $MM = MM \cup \{L\}$
    return MM

Fig. 2. Dynamically Computing Minimal Model

3.3 Preferred Models

We have shown how minimal models can be efficiently constructed for ground clauses saturated the Resolution Inference System However, in a particular verification problem we may not be interested in minimal models. Some other model may be preferable. In this section, we show that if a ground set of clauses is saturated by Ordered Resolution then any model at all can be constructed.

First we introduce the notion of a *preference predicate*. A preference predicate tells whether we prefer an atom to be true($\top$) or false($\bot$). The preference predicate will be used when constructing a model. For an atom A, we denote $Pref(A)$ as the preferred value of atom A, either $\top$ or $\bot$. Based on the preference function, we also define a *polarity function Pol*, such that $Pol(A) = A$ if $Pref(A) = \top$, and $Pol(A) = \neg A$ if $Pref(A) = \bot$. We extend $Pref$ and Pol to negative literals, so that $Pref(\neg A) = Pref(A)$ and $Pol(\neg A) = Pol(A)$. A literal L is said to be preferred if $Pol(L) = L$. Given a preference function $Pref$ a selection rule Sel is $Pref$-*correct* if for all C, (i) $Sel(C)$ is a set of non-preferred literals that contains all maximal literals in C or (ii) $Sel(C)$ contains a preferred literal in C and nothing else.

Definition 2. *Given a set of clauses S and a selection function Sel, define $Cl(L) = \{C\theta \mid C \in S$ and $C\theta$ is a non-tautological clause in S containing L as a maximal and selected literal $\}$. Note that $Cl(L)$ is empty if no clause contains L as maximal literal.*

Given a set of clauses S and a preference predicate $Pref$, we define a *preferred model* of S, as follows.

Definition 3. *Let S be a set of ground clauses and $Pref$ be a preference predicate. Suppose that A is an atom. Define $PM_{<A} = \bigcup_{B<A} PM_{\leq B}$. Then define $PM_{\leq A} = PM_{<A} \cup \{A\}$ if and only if either*

1. *$Pref(A) = \bot$ and there is a clause $C \in Cl(A)$ such that $PM_{<A} \not\models C$ in which case C is called* productive *and we say that C produces A, or*
2. *$Pref(A) = \top$ and for all $C \in Cl(\neg A)$, $PM_{<A} \models C$. If there is a clause C in $Cl(\neg A)$ where $PM_{<A} \not\models C$, then we say that the smallest such C produces $\neg A$, and that the smallest such C is productive.*

Otherwise $PM_{\leq C} = PM_{<C}$.
Define $PM_S = \bigcup_{C \in S} PM_{\leq C}$.

The point of the preference predicate is that, as the model is constructed some atoms are forced to have a particular value. But when the value is not forced, then the preference predicate will decide what the value will be. Note that if $Pref(A) = \bot$ for all predicates A, then the preferred model is the minimal model.

Now we prove that if a set of clauses is saturated by Resolution under a $Pref$-correct selection rule, and does not contain the empty clause, then it determines a preferred model. A consequence of this is that if a set of clauses is saturated by Ordered Resolution and does not contain the empty clause, then any preference predicate determines a model.

Lemma 1. *Let A and B be atoms such that $A > B$. Then $PM_S \models B$ if and only if $PM_{\leq A} \models B$ if and only if $PM_{<A} \models B$ if and only if $PM_{\leq B} \models B$.*

Proof. This is trivially true, since no larger atom can affect the truth value of a smaller one.

Theorem 4. *Let $Pref$ be a preference predicate. Let Sel be a $Pref$-correct selection rule. Let S be a set of clauses. saturated by Resolution. Suppose that the empty clause is not in S. Then $PM_{Gr(S)} \models Gr(S)$.*

Proof. The proof is by induction on the ordering clause ordering. We prove by induction that $PM_S \models C$ for all $C \in Gr(S)$. Note that if C is a tautology then obviously $PM_S \models C$. Suppose that L is the largest literal in C. Then L is either of the form A or $\neg A$. First we assume that L is selected in C.

If $C \in Cl(L)$ but L is not maximum, then C is of the form $D \lor L \lor L$. So there is a Factoring inference in $Gr(S)$ which gives $D \lor L$, and this inference is an instance of an inference in S. $D \lor L$ is smaller than $D \lor L \lor L$. So $PM_S \models D \lor L$ by the induction hypothesis, and therefore $PM_S \models D \lor L \lor L$.

Suppose that $C \in Cl(A)$ and $Pref(A) = \bot$. Then either $PM_{<A} \models A$ or $PM_{<A} \not\models A$. If $PM_{<A} \models A$, then $PM_{\leq A} \models A$. If $PM_{<A} \not\models A$, then by definition $A \in PM_{\leq A}$ so $M_{\leq A} \models C$.

A similar argument holds if $C \in Cl(\neg(A))$ and $Pref(A) = \top$.

Now suppose that $C \in Cl(\neg A)$ and $Pref(A) = \bot$. If $A \notin PM_{\leq A}$ then $PM_{\leq A} \models C$. So suppose that $A \in PM_{\leq A}$. That means there is some clause D of the form $D' \lor A$ responsible for adding A to the interpretation. Let C be the clause $C' \lor \neg A$. Then there must be a resolution inference between C and D, whose conclusion is $E = C' \lor D'$. This inference is an instance of an inference between two clauses in S. E is smaller than C. Let B be the maximum literal in E. Then B is smaller than A. Therefore, by the induction hypothesis, $PM_{\leq B} \models E$. If $PM_{<A} \not\models D' \lor A$, then $PM_{<A} \not\models D'$, and therefore $PM_{\leq B} \not\models D'$, which means that $PM_{\leq B} \models C'$ and therefore $PM_{<A} \models C$. On the other hand, if $PM_{<A} \models D' \lor A$, then, by definition, $PM_{<A} \models C$.

A similar argument holds if $C \in Cl(A)$ and $Pref(C) = \top$.

The other case is where L is maximum but not selected. This implies that there is another literal in C which is selected and preferred. By the same argument as above, there is a smaller clause and an inference which can be done, which implies by induction that C is true.

Just like the minimal model, the preferred model can also be constructed in $O(|S|lg(|S|)$ time. Note that the above theorem could also be proved by renaming literals so that the preferred model is minimal.

Theorem 5. *Let $Pref$ be a preference predicate. Let Sel be a $Pref$-correct selection rule. Let S be a set of ground clauses saturated by Resolution. Suppose that the empty clause is not in S. Then PM_S can be constructed in $O(|S|lg(|S|)$ time.*

Proof. The proof is the same idea as for the minimal model.

Given the right preference predicate, every model of S can be constructed. In particular, given a model M of S, we can define a preference predicate that assigns every atom to the truth value given in M. Then PM_S will be M, because the only time an atom is given a value that is not preferred is if it is forced to have that value in order to satisfy some clause.

Theorem 6. *Let M be a model of S. Define a preference predicate $Pref$ such that, for all atoms A, $Pref(A) = \top$ if and only if $A \in M$. Then $PM_S = M$.*

Proof. The proof is by contradiction. Suppose that $PM_S \neq M$. Then let A be the smallest atom such that $A \in PM_S$ and $A \notin M$, or $A \in M$ and $A \notin PM_S$.

We take each possibility separately. Suppose that $A \in PM_S$ and $A \notin M$. Suppose there is a clause $C \in Cl(A)$ such that $PM_{<A} \not\models C$. Let $C = C' \vee A$. Then $PM_{<A} \not\models C'$. Since $A \notin M$ and $M \models C$, it must be true that $M \models C'$. But this is a contradiction, because A is the smallest atom where PM_S and M differ.

We also need to consider the case where for all $C \in Cl(\neg A)$, $PM_{<A} \models C$ and $PM_{<A} \models Pref(A)$. But this gives a contradiction, because $A \notin M$, so $Pref(A) = \bot$.

Now suppose that $A \in M$ but $A \notin PM_S$. Since $A \notin PM_S$, this means that there is a $C \in Cl(\neg A)$ such that $PM_{<A} \not\models C$ or $PM_{<A} \not\models Pref(A)$. The second condition is clearly false, since $A \in M$ and therefore $Pref(A) = \top$. So consider the first condition. Let $C = C' \vee \neg A$. Then $PM_{<A} \not\models C'$. But PM_S agrees with M on everything smaller than S, and $M \models C'$, so $PM_S \models C'$.

Because every preference predicate determines a model, we can actually give an algorithm that constructs all the models of a set of ground clauses saturated by Ordered Resolution. We call our algorithm, the Preferred Model Construction (PMC) Algorithm. Of course, there is a trivial algorithm to construct all models of a set of clauses. The trivial algorithm just enumerates all the truth values, and then checks if each truth value satisfies all the clauses. In the trivial algorithm, one may spend an exponential amount of time looking for a model, when the set of clauses has only one model. In the PMC Algorithm, no effort will be wasted. Every truth value will lead to a model. Therefore, we get the nice result that the running time of the PMC Algorithm is proportional to the number of models. In other words, if a set of clauses has only polynomially many models, then the PMC Algorithm will find all those models in polynomial time. The PMC Algorithm is based on the preferred model construction. We initiate the PMC algorithm by calling $PMC(\emptyset, 1)$. The PMC Algorithm is given in Figure 3.

The PMC Algorithm is reminiscent of the DPLL Algorithm [3], However, the PMC Algorithm never has any false paths.

We now prove the correctness and the complexity of the PMC Algorithm, but we need a few lemmas first. First we need to say that everything the algorithm outputs is correct.

Lemma 2. *Let S be a set of ground clauses saturated by Ordered Resolution, such that S does not contain the empty clause. If PMC prints an interpretation PM, then $PM \models S$.*

Proof. We define a preference predicate $Pref$ corresponding to PM, such that for all atoms A, $Pref(A) = \top$ if $A \in PM$ and $Pref(A) = \bot$ if $A \notin PM$. We will prove that that PM will be the model PM_S constructed for the preference predicate $Pref$, and therefore $PM \models S$

```
function PMC(PM, i)
if (i == n + 1)
    print PM
else
    if for all clauses C ∈ Cl(¬A), PM_<A ⊨ C
        PMC(PM ∪ {A_i}, i + 1)
    if for all clauses C ∈ Cl(A), PM_<A ⊨ C
        PMC(PM, i + 1)
```

Fig. 3. Preferred Model Construction Algorithm

The proof is by contradiction. Suppose $PM \neq PM_S$. Then let A be the smallest atom such that $A \in PM_S$ and $A \notin PM$, or $A \in PM$ and $A \notin PM_S$.

We take each possibility separately. Suppose that $A \in PM_S$ and $A \notin PM$. Suppose there is a clause $C \in Cl(A)$ such that $PM_{<A} \not\models C$. But $A \notin PM$, therefore for all clauses $C \in Cl(A)$, $PM_{<A} \models C$. Contradiction

We also need to consider the case where for all $C \in Cl(\neg A)$, $PM_{<A} \models C$ and $PM_{<A} \models Pref(A)$. But $A \notin PM$ implies that $Pref(A) = \bot$. Contradiction.

Now suppose that $A \in M$ but $A \notin PM_S$. Since $A \notin PM_S$, this means that there is a $C \in Cl(\neg A)$ such that $PM_{<A} \not\models C$ or $PM_{<A} \not\models Pref(A)$. The second condition is clearly false, since $A \in PM$ and therefore $Pref(A) = \top$. So consider the first condition. Let $C = C' \vee \neg A$. Then $PM_{<A} \not\models C'$. But PM_S agrees with M on everything smaller than S, and $M \models C'$, so $PM_S \models C'$.

Now a lemmas to say that the algorithm never outputs the same models twice.

Lemma 3. *The PMC algorithm never outputs the same interpretation twice.*

Proof. This is clear from the algorithm, since the recursive calls always give a different value to A_i, and that is never revisited.

Finally, we need to prove that every model of S is eventually output.

Lemma 4. *Let S be a set of ground clauses. Suppose that M is a model of S. Then PMC will eventually output M.*

Proof. The proof is by contradiction. Suppose that PMC does not output M. Then let PM be the interpretation output by PMC with the largest value i such that M and PM disagree on A_i but M and PM agree on all A_j with $j < i$. Suppose that $A_i \in M$ but $A_i \notin PM$. Then there cannot be a clause $C \in Cl(\neg A)$ such that $PM_{<A} \not\models C$. Therefore the PMC algorithm add A_i to PM. And since

all paths output something, PMC will eventually output a model which agrees on M for all $j \leq i$.. Contradiction. A symmetric argument can be made for the case where $A_i \notin M$ and $A_i \in PM$.

Those lemmas immediately give us the required theorem.

Theorem 7. *Let S be a set of ground clauses saturated by Ordered Resolution, such that S does not contain the empty clause. The output of PMC is exactly the set of models of S.*

Proof. We have shown that everything output is a model of S, and that all models of S are output exactly once.

Now we examine the complexity of PMC, and show that it is proportional to the number of models output.

Theorem 8. *PMC runs in $O(|S|lg(|S|) + |S|k)$, where k is the number of models of S.*

Proof. We have shown that each model of S is output exactly once. It takes time $O(|S|lg(|S|))$ to sort each clause, and the set of clauses. In order to produce each model, each clause is examined once. The amount of time to test the truth of each clause is linear in the size of the clause, because we can store the truth of each atom as it is established. Therefore, it takes $O(|S|)$ time to output a single model, and $O(|S|k)$ time to output all of them.

A verification algorithm could use the PMC algorithm to run for a period of time to produce several models, and then examine those models. Or a verification algorithm could create a preference predicate to find a model that meets certain specifications. This could be more valuable than just constructing a minimal model.

If we want to know the truth value of a particular atom, it would be simpler to do that in a recursive algorithm. Also, in the nonground case, we will not be able to construct the entire model, but we still may be able to determine the truth value of a given atom. Therefore, here we give a recursive algorithm to compute the value of a given atom A in the preferred model. The algorithm is given in Figure 4. It is initialized by calling $Rec(A)$. It will return a Boolean value.

The algorithm for could be simplified for the minimal model. This recursive algorithm can run in exponential time. However, if memoization is used, then we get linear running time, just like the dynamic programming algorithm for constructing the minimal model. But the memoized algorithm can be more efficient in practice for determining if a particular atom is true, because it only examines the atoms whose truth value is necessary in order to know the queried atom. There may be far fewer of these atoms than there are atoms in the language.

```
function Rec(A)
t = Pref(A)
for all C ∈ Cl(¬Pol(A))
    u = ¬Pref(A)
    for all non-preferred literals B in C − {¬Pol(A)}
        if Rec(B)
            u = Pref(A)
    for all preferred literals B in C − {¬Pol(A)}
        if ¬Rec(B)
            u = Pref(A)
    if Pref(A) = ⊥
        t = t ∨ u
    else
        t = t ∧ u
return t
```

Fig. 4. Recursive Preferred Model

4   Nonground Models

In this section, we examine model construction in the context of nonground clauses saturated by Resolution. The methods in the previous section for constructing models apply to the ground and the nonground case. But there is a problem in the nonground case. In that case, the model may be infinite. Therefore, it is impossible to construct the model. Verification procedures then cannot count on seeing the whole model. The only thing we can hope is that the algorithm can ask queries to find out if particular ground atoms are true in that model. This may be enough in practice, since the programmer probably cares about the values of certain atoms. If the clauses are saturated by any Resolution with any complete selection rule, then the programmer can ask queries about the minimal model. The programmer can additionally give a preference predicate and ask questions about the preferred model. In this section, we look for criteria to determine in which cases the programmer can be guaranteed an answer to those queries.

In this section, we consider theories saturated by Ordered Resolution or Resolution with Selection Rules (which we have simply called *Resolution*), since these inference rules are used a lot in practice, since they may be more likely to terminate. We try to find if a ground atom is true in a certain model. But we also want to be able to decide if we can find the truth of a ground atom, when the saturated theory has again been saturated by some ground clauses. Such a result would be useful for verification problems

4.1   Local Theories

First we consider Local Theories, as in [8,2,7]. We are assuming an ordering on the atoms that is total on all ground clauses. For the results of Local Theories, we also need to assume certain facts about the ordering.

Definition 4. *Let $<$ be an ordering such that every atom has only finitely many smaller atoms. Then there must be some function $ot(n)$ such that every atom of size n has no more than $ot(n)$ smaller atoms. Then the function $ot(n)$ is called the order type of $<$. For a clause C, let $n(C)$ be the number of literals in C. For a set of clauses S, let $n(S) = \{max(n(C)) \mid C \in S\}$.*

Basin and Ganzinger[2] have shown the following complexity result.

Theorem 9. *Let $<$ be an ordering, such that a set of clauses S is closed under Ordered Resolution, and S does not contain the empty clause. Let $ot(n)$ be the order type of $<$. Let C be a ground clause. Then it can be decided whether $S \models C$ in co-nondeterministic time $O(ot(C)^{n(S)})$. If S contains only Horn Clauses and if C is a Horn clause, then it can be decided in time $O(ot(C)^{n(S)})$ whether $S \models C$.*

In this theorem, there are several things to note. If $ot(n)$ is polynomial, then decidability for Horn Clauses is in polynomial time. But for general clauses, it becomes co-NP, the same complexity as unsatisfiability for ground clauses. The other thing to note is that, since $<$ is required to be a total order, $ot(n)$ must be at least exponential unless the signature contains only one function symbol. In addition, that function symbol must be unary. In other words, $ot(n)$ is almost always at least exponential. Basin and Ganzinger get around that problem by showing that the ordering can be partial, and then the clauses must be saturated for Ordered Resolution under all total extensions of the partial ordering

We can get a similar theorem for determining if an atom is in the constructed model.[1]

Theorem 10. *Let $Pref$ be a preference function. Let Sel be a $Pref$-correct selection rule. Let $<$ be an ordering, such that a set of clauses S is closed under Resolution, and S does not contain the empty clause. Let $ot(n)$ be the order type of $<$. Let A be a ground atom. Let N be a set of ground clauses such that $S \cup N$ is satisfiable.*

1. *It can be decided in time $O(ot(A)^n(S))$ whether $PM_S \models A$*
2. *If S is saturated by Ordered Resolution, then let S' be the saturation of $S \cup N$. It can be decided in $O(2^{ot(N \cup \{A\})})$ whether $PM_{S'} \models A$*

Proof. In order to determine if $PM_S \models A$, we only need to examine instances of S whose literals are smaller than A. Each clause in S has at most $n(S)$ literals, and each instance of one of those literals will be a literal smaller than A. Therefore the size of the set of all those instances is $O(ot(A)^n(S))$. This

---

[1] For simplicity, we are assuming in this theorem that the clauses have already been sorted.

is ground, so we apply the procedure Rec from the previous section to decide whether $PM_S \models A$.

Now we consider the case of deciding whether $PM_{S \cup N} \models A$. First we saturate $S \cup N$, and then calculate the preferred model of that. In this saturation, we select all the maximal literals in each clause of N. The only instances we need for the saturation and for checking whether $PM_{S \cup N}$ is a model of A are those instances that are smaller than A or some literal in N. So when we saturate those instances of $S \cup N$, we get $O(2^{ot(N \cup \{A\})})$ instances of clauses smaller than A and N, and then we apply the procedure Rec from the previous section to see if this implies A.

There are several differences between the case from [2] where they are interested in a decision procedure and our case of deciding if a clause is in the model. Just for deciding a model, it is not necessary that the clauses are closed under Ordered Resolution. Any selection rule will do. Also, in the case of just constructing a model, the complexity for the general case is not worse than the complexity for Horn Clauses. But there is one big disadvantage to the model construction case. That is that it is not good enough to have partial orders. We insist on total orders, and we have not been able to prove this theorem if we only require that it is saturated under all extensions of a partial order. This means that the complexity will almost always be exponential.

4.2   Covered Clauses

In the last subsection, we considered Local Theories, and we say that it is possible to decide if an atom is true in the minimal model or preferred model. In this subsection we consider an alternative method, which does not give any requirements on the order type of the ordering.

First we define what it means for a clause to be covered. Basically, it means that the maximal literals of that clause must contain all the variables, unless that literal is not needed for the construction of the preferred model. Then we show that if a clause is saturated by Resolution, and all the clauses in the set are covered, then, given an atom A, it can be determined if A is true in the preferred model. Peltier [9] has a similar result for minimal models.

In addition, we show that it is still decidable to determine if A is in the preferred model if we further saturate S with any set of ground clauses N. This is better than the previous section, when it is required that the initial saturation is by Ordered Resolution.

Definition 5. *Let C be a clause. Then C is said to be* covered *if one of the following is true for all maximal and selected literals L in C:*

1. *L contains all the variables in C,*
2. *$L = \neg A$ and $Pref(A\theta) = \bot$ for all ground substitutions θ, or*
3. *$L = A$ and $Pref(A\theta) = \top$ for all ground substitutions θ.*

A set of clauses S is covered if all C in S are covered.

Another way to word this is to say that a clause is covered if every maximal and selected and not preferred literal in the clause contains all the variables in the clause.

Theorem 11. *Let $Pref$ be a preference predicate. Let Sel be a $Pref$-correct selection rule. Let S be a set of clauses saturated by Resolution, which does not contain the empty clause. Suppose that S is covered. Let A be a ground atom. Then it is decidable whether $PM_S \models A$. If N is a set of ground clauses such that $S \cup N$ is satisfiable, let S' be the result of the saturation of $S \cup N$, then it is also decidable whether $PM_{S'} \models A$.*

Proof. To decide if $PM_S \models A$, we only need to call $Rec(A)$ on $Gr(S)$, as given earlier in this paper. The algorithm was given for ground clauses earlier, however if S is covered then it will still work. Note that the algorithm loops through all clauses $C \in Cl(\neg Pol(A))$. By definition of covered, each such clause must be ground. By induction, we see that the algorithm is repeatedly called on smaller atoms. Therefore the algorithm will halt.

For the case of $S \cup N$, we just need to show that the saturation of $S \cup N$ will halt. We select the maximum literal of each clause in N and clauses produced in the saturation. Each clause will only have finitely many inferences with a clause from S. The conclusion of each inference will be a ground clause, whose literals are all smaller than the maximum literal in the premise. This process must halt. In addition, all the clauses produced are ground. So all the clauses are covered.

Now we want to deal with the general case, where clauses are not necessarily covered. We add a new redundancy deletion rule called Splitting to our inference system. This is a rule which will take a single clause as a premise. We need to apply it when there is a literal K in a clause which contains a variable not contained in a maximal literal L. In this case, it is necessary to split the clause into two smaller clauses which imply the original clause. If K is maximal and the ordering is variable monotonic, then this is only required to be performed when K is not preferred. This is an important restriction on the splitting rule. For example, if the ordering is variable monotonic which many orderings are, and if we use the usual preference which prefers negative literals, then the splitting inference only needs to be performed on positive literals containing an extra variable.

Splitting:

$$\frac{\Gamma \vee K \vee L}{\Gamma \vee K \vee \neg p(x_1, \cdots, x_n) \quad p(x_1, \cdots, x_n) \vee L}$$

where

1. L is maximal, selected, and not preferred,
2. K is not preferred if the ordering is variable monotonic,
3. K contains a variable which is not in L,
4. $x_1, \cdots, x_n$ are the variables in common between $\Gamma \vee K$ and L, and
5. p is a new predicate symbol, defined so that $p(x_1, \cdots, x_n) < L$.

After this inference is performed, the premise must be deleted. The premise will be redundant because the two conclusions are smaller than the premise, and together they imply the premise.

Now we show that if S is saturated by Resolution plus the Splitting rule, then S is covered.

Lemma 5. *Let S be saturated by the Resolution inference system with Splitting. Then S is covered.*

Proof. Let C be a clause in S. Suppose C is of the form $\Gamma \vee L$, where L is a maximal and selected literal in C, that is not preferred. We want to show that L contains all the variables in C.

Suppose there is another literal K in C that contains a variable not in L. If K is not preferred, or if the ordering is not variable monotonic, then C would have been removed by Splitting.

So suppose that K is preferred, and the ordering is variable monotonic. By definition of correct selection function, K cannot be maximal in C. Since the ordering is variable monotonic, $Vars(K) \subseteq Vars(L)$.

Finally, we get the main theorem.

Theorem 12. *Let $Pref$ be a preference predicate. Let Sel be a $Pref$-correct selection rule. Let S be a set of clauses saturated by the Resolution Inference System with Splitting, which does not contain the empty clause. Let A be a ground atom. Then it is decidable whether $PM_{Gr(S)} \models A$.*

Proof. We have shown that S is covered. Therefore, it is decidable if $PM_{Gr(S))} \models A$. We just apply Rec on S.

5   Conclusion

We have clarified some practical questions about constructing models in Resolution. For the ground case, the theoretical model construction technique[1] can be easily expressed as an efficient algorithm to construct the minimal model.

We generalized minimal models to preferred models, where a user is allowed to suggest a preferred value for each atom. We give an efficient algorithm to construct a preferred ground model, which is basically equivalent to the minimal model construction, but we believe preferred models have some interest in verification problems. For example, in software verification, a model represents a bug in the program, and a programmer may be interested in finding a bug of a particular type.

We also show a result that is new, as far as we are concerned, to construct all models for a set of ground clauses saturated by Ordered Resolution in time polynomial in the number of models. This could also be used by a programmer to find all bugs in a program. This algorithm can be viewed as a kind of DPLL procedure [3] without any backtracking.

The problem of finding nonground models has been studied[9,6,5]. In [6,5], models are constructed for certain classes of clauses. In [9] is given a method to construct a model for a set of clauses saturated by Ordered Resolution when the clauses are covered.

The first question for nonground models is what do we mean by a model? In this paper, a model in the nonground case means it is possible to determine if a particular atom is true or false in the preferred model. We add a restricted splitting rule to the Resolution inference system, and we show that if a set of clauses is saturated by Ordered Resolution (with selection), with a set of preference rules, then any query to the preferred model can be decided. As far as we know, this is the first such result for Ordered Resolution, aside from the result in [9] about covered clauses.

The most interesting piece of future work is to extend this result to equality. It would also be interesting to make the splitting rule more restrictive.

Acknowledgments. I would like to thank Nicolas Peltier and Christian Fermüller for pointers to related work.

References

1. Bachmair, L., Ganzinger, H.: Resolution theorem proving. In: Robinson, A., Voronkov, A. (eds.) Handbook of Automated Reasoning, pp. 19–99. North-Holland (2001)
2. Basin, D., Ganzinger, H.: Automated complexity analysis based on ordered resolution. J. Association for Computing Machinery 48(1), 70–109 (2001)
3. Davis, M., Logemman, G., Loveland, D.: A Machine Program for Theorem Proving. Communications of the ACM 5, 394–397 (1962)
4. Dershowitz, N.: Termination of Rewriting. Journal of Symbolic Computation 3, 69–116 (1987)
5. Fermüller, C., Leitsch, A., Tammet, T., Zamov, N.: Resolution Methods for the Decision Problem. LNCS, vol. 679. Springer, Heidelberg (1993)
6. Fermüller, C., Moser, G.: Have Spass with OCC1Ng=. LPAR 7, 114-130 (2000)
7. Ganzinger, H.: Relating Semantic and Proof-Theoretic Concepts for Polynomial Time Decidability of Uniform Word Problems. In: Proceedings 16th IEEE Symposium on Logic in Computer Science, LICS 2001, Boston (2001)
8. McAllester, D.: Automated Recognition of Tractability in Inference Relations. Journal of the ACM 40(2), 284–303 (1993)
9. Peltier, N.: Building Infinite Models for Equational Clause Sets: Constructing Non-Ambiguous Formulae. Logic Journal of the IGPL 11(1), 97–129 (2003)

Planning with Effectively Propositional Logic

Juan Antonio Navarro-Pérez and Andrei Voronkov

The University of Manchester

Abstract. We present a fragment of predicate logic which allows the use of equality and quantification but whose models are limited to finite Herbrand interpretations. Formulae in this logic can be thought as syntactic sugar on top of the Bernays-Schönfinkel fragment and can, therefore, still be effectively grounded into a propositional representation. We motivate the study of this logic by showing that practical problems from the area of planning can be naturally and succinctly represented using the added syntactic features. Moreover, from a theoretical point of view, we show that this logic allows, when compared to the propositional approach, not only more compact encodings but also exponentially shorter refutation proofs.

1 Introduction

Planning has been the focus of attention of many researchers in the field of artificial intelligence, where it was originally conceived as a formalisation of deduction processes [7]. Alternatively, the problem of finding a sequence of actions to reach, from an initial state, a set of desired goals, has also been reduced to the problem of finding a satisfying truth assignment for a propositional logic formula [9, 10].

In this paper we follow a similar approach but, instead of a propositional encoding, we use a fragment of predicate logic which allows some limited use of equality and quantification. This fragment, which we call *finite domain predicate logic*, allows a much more succinct and natural representation of problems. The size of the resulting formula is linear in the size of, for example, a STRIPS description [5] of the original planning problem.

We show, moreover, that any formula in the proposed logic can be translated to an equisatisfiable formula in the Bernays-Schönfinkel fragment of predicate logic. Formulae in this fragment have an $\exists^*\forall^*$ prefix when written in prenex normal form and do not allow the use of function symbols. This makes their Herbrand universe finite and, therefore, to test satisfiability one can effectively replace a formula by all its propositional ground instances. This is why formulae in this class are also referred to as *effectively propositional* (EPR), such as in one of the categories of the CASC system competitions [16].

Another motivation for using this logic as a formalism to represent problems is the fact that, as we show in this paper, not only descriptions can be much more concise, but inference steps can also be exponentially more efficient than in the propositional case. It is a well known fact that resolution proofs in first order logic can be exponentially shorter than those possible when restricted to

A. Voronkov and C. Weidenbach (Eds.): Ganzinger Festschrift, LNCS 7797, pp. 302–316, 2013.

propositional inferences, see e.g. [1]; in this paper we probe that our reduced fragment of first order logic also maintains this property.

On the other hand, our encoding may also turn out to be useful for propositional, SAT-based, approaches to planning. Indeed, it preserves the structure of the original planning problem in the obtained effectively propositional formula and reduces the problem of finding an optimised propositional encoding to the problem of finding an optimised propositional instantiation of the EPR description. Thinking in this more general fragment of first order logic, often allows one to find simplifications or alternative encodings that one might miss if only focused in the propositional case.

Reasoning with effectively propositional theories is a relatively new area of research, which seems to offer a language with a good compromise between expressibility and complexity. There are many computer scientists currently developing ideas and procedures in order to more efficiently deal with this kind of formulae, including the efforts of Claessen and Sörensson [4]; Baumgartner and Tinelli [3]; as well as Ganzinger and Korovin [6].

Unfortunately, at the time there is also a lack of benchmarks for researchers to experiment and test their systems. An important contribution of this paper is to aid filling in this gap by providing a new and rich source of problems with close links to real-life applications. Such problems are now accessible to the community through the TPTP Library [15].

Our paper is structured as follows: In Section 2 we introduce the syntax and semantics of the finite domain predicate logic and show that it can be reduced to the Bernays-Schönfinkel fragment of predicate logic. We also present an example of a family of effectively propositional unsatisfiable formulae, whose refutation proofs are exponentially shorter than those possible in the propositional setting. Then in Section 3 we formally introduce the notions of planning to later give, in Section 4, the encoding of planning problems in terms of our finite domain predicate logic.

2   Finite Domain Predicate Logic

In this section we introduce the finite domain predicate logic. It allows the use of equality, evaluated under the unique name assumption, and quantification over finite domains. We will also later show that formulae in this logic can be reduced to the Bernays-Schönfinkel fragment of predicate logic. The added syntactic sugar will be useful in later sections to describe our encodings of planning problems more naturally.

Definition 1. The language of finite domain predicate logic consists of a set of *predicate symbols* $\mathcal{P}$, a finite set of *constant symbols* $\mathcal{D}$, and a set of *variables* $\mathcal{V}$. Predicate symbols are, moreover, associated with a positive integer which we call its *arity*. The set $\mathcal{D}$ is also referred to as the *domain* of the logic. A *term* is either a variable or a constant symbol. A *predicate atom* is an expression of the form $p(t_1, \ldots, t_n)$ where $p \in \mathcal{P}$ is a predicate symbol of arity n and each t_i is a term. An *equality atom* is an expression of the form $t = t'$ where both t and t'

are terms. An *atom* is either a predicate or an equality atom. A *ground atom* is an atom all whose terms are constant symbols.

We consider the following as primitive connectives of the logic: *falsity* ($\bot$), *negation* ($\neg\phi$), *conjunction* ($\phi \wedge \psi$) and *quantification* ($\forall X \in C. \phi$); where ϕ and ψ are formulae, X a variable and $C \subseteq \mathcal{D}$ a set of constant symbols. Duals of these operators and additional connectives can be introduced as abbreviations:

$$\top \equiv \neg\bot \qquad\qquad \exists X \in C. \phi \equiv \neg(\forall X \in C. \neg\phi)$$
$$\phi \vee \psi \equiv \neg(\neg\phi \wedge \neg\psi) \qquad\qquad \phi \to \psi \equiv \neg\phi \vee \psi$$

The standard notion of *free* and *bound* variables with respect to the scope of quantifiers also applies here. A *closed formula* is a formula with no free variables. We will often use $\overline{X}$ to denote a sequence of variables $X_1, \ldots, X_n$ whose length is specified in the context where it is used. This allows, for example, to write $\exists \overline{X} \in C^n. \phi$ instead of the longer expression $\exists X_1 \in C \ldots \exists X_n \in C. \phi$. Similarly we will write $\overline{X} = \overline{Y}$ as a shorthand for $\bigwedge_{i=1}^n X_i = Y_i$.

A *substitution* is a function σ that maps variables to terms, and behaves like the identity function almost everywhere. We denote by $\phi\sigma$ the result of applying a substitution σ to a formula ϕ, i.e. the formula obtained after uniformly replacing every free variable X in ϕ with the term $X\sigma$. We also say that ϕ' is an *instance* of ϕ if there is a substitution σ such that $\phi' = \phi\sigma$; and that σ is a *unifier* of the formulae ϕ and ϕ' if $\phi\sigma = \phi'\sigma$. A substitution is often denoted by explicitly enumerating its mappings, e.g.: $\{X_1 \to t_1, \ldots, X_n \to t_n\}$.

A *Herbrand interpretation* is a set of ground predicate atoms. The notion of whether a Herbrand interpretation $\mathcal{I}$ is a *model* of a closed formula ϕ, denoted by $\mathcal{I} \models \phi$, is defined as follows:

$$
\begin{aligned}
&\mathcal{I} \not\models \bot \\
&\mathcal{I} \models p(\bar{c}) && \text{iff} \quad p(\bar{c}) \in \mathcal{I}, \\
&\mathcal{I} \models c = c' && \text{iff} \quad c \text{ coincides with } c', \\
&\mathcal{I} \models \neg\phi && \text{iff} \quad \mathcal{I} \not\models \phi, \\
&\mathcal{I} \models \phi \wedge \psi && \text{iff} \quad \mathcal{I} \models \phi \text{ and } \mathcal{I} \models \psi, \\
&\mathcal{I} \models \forall X \in C. \phi && \text{iff} \quad \mathcal{I} \models \phi\{X \to c\} \text{ for every constant } c \in C,
\end{aligned}
$$

where $\bar{c}$ denotes a tuple of constant symbols of the length equal to the arity of p. When we we speak about models of non-closed formulae, we assume the free variables of these formulae to be implicitly universally quantified. A formula is said to be *satisfiable* if it has at least one model. ∎

In the sequel we assume to deal with a logic having a fixed domain $\mathcal{D}$. For example, all formulae may only use constants from $\mathcal{D}$. Observe that equality is evaluated syntactically with respect to the constant symbol names, i.e. using the unique name assumption, and does not depend on the interpretation $\mathcal{I}$. We will now show how this restricted kind of equality can be removed from formulae while preserving its satisfiability status.

We will also call formulae *constraints* and assume that a finite set of constraints represents the conjunction of all its elements. A *clause* is a simple disjunction of literals, that is, atoms or their negations. A formula is said to be in *clause normal form* if it is a conjunction of clauses. Although we do not always write sets of constraints in clause normal form, they can often be easily rewritten in such form using simple logical identities (e.g. changing implication for disjunction).

Definition 2. Let $C = \{c_1, \ldots c_k\}$ be a set of constant symbols. We introduce the fresh new predicate symbols succ_C, less, in_C, and eq and define the set of constraints Ord_C using these symbols as follows:

$$\text{succ}_C(c_1, c_2) \wedge \cdots \wedge \text{succ}_C(c_{k-1}, c_k)$$
$$\text{succ}_C(X, Y) \rightarrow \text{in}_C(X) \wedge \text{in}_C(Y)$$

also the set of constraints EQ is defined as:

$$\text{succ}_{\mathcal{D}}(X, Y) \rightarrow \text{less}(X, Y)$$
$$\text{less}(X, Y) \wedge \text{less}(Y, Z) \rightarrow \text{less}(X, Z)$$
$$\text{less}(X, Y) \rightarrow \neg\text{eq}(X, Y) \wedge \neg\text{eq}(Y, X)$$
$$\text{eq}(X, X)$$
∎

The intuition behind the set Ord_C is to enumerate all constant symbols in the set C by providing a predicate succ_C that allows one to iterate over them. The intended meaning of $\text{in}_C(X)$ is to represent that $X \in C$. Note that Ord_C defines only the positive polarity of the predicate symbols succ_C, less and in_C. In other words, if $c \in C$ then the predicate $\text{in}_C(c)$ should be true in models of Ord_C, but the converse does not necessarily have to hold.

When we use this construction to enumerate all the elements in the domain, i.e. $\text{Ord}_{\mathcal{D}}$, then the set EQ defines an additional predicate $\text{eq}(X, Y)$ that can be used to replace the built-in equality $X = Y$.

Theorem 1. *Let ϕ be a closed formula, and let ϕ^{eq} be the formula obtained by replacing all equality atoms $t = t'$ in ϕ with $\text{eq}(t, t')$. The pair of formulae ϕ and $\text{Ord}_{\mathcal{D}} \wedge \text{EQ} \wedge \phi^{\text{eq}}$ are equisatisfiable.*

Proof. The result follows from the fact that, if an interpretation $\mathcal{I}$ is a model of the formula $\text{Ord}_{\mathcal{D}} \wedge \text{EQ}$ then $i < j$ implies $\mathcal{I} \models \text{less}(c_i, c_j)$ and, using the rest of the constraints in EQ, we have $\mathcal{I} \models \text{eq}(c_i, c_j)$ iff $i = j$ iff $c_i = c_j$ (from the unique name assumption). □

Also note that, since quantification is done with respect to a fixed finite set of constant symbols, a quantified subformula $\forall X \in C. \phi(X)$ can actually be unfolded into the conjunction $\bigwedge_{c \in C} \phi\{X \rightarrow c\}$. Although naively unfolding quantifiers this way could produce an exponential blow-up in the size of the formula, we now show an alternative approach that only incurs in a linear increase. It follows the style of structural clause form translations as proposed by Plaisted and Greenbaum [13].

In order to simplify the exposition, and avoid dealing with the polarity of subformulae, we assume that formulae are first put in *negation normal form*. This can be easily achieved by pushing negation inwards and replacing implications with disjunctions. The resulting logic formulae can therefore use any of the connectives: $\bot, \top, \wedge, \vee, \forall, \exists$; and negation is restricted to the front of atoms only.

Definition 3. Let Γ be a set of constraints. The set Γ^{ea} is defined as the result of iterating the following procedure to remove all explicit quantifiers in Γ

- If there is a subformula $\psi = \forall X \in C. \phi(X, \overline{Y})$, where $X, \overline{Y}$ are all the free variables in ϕ and $C = \{c_1, \ldots, c_d\}$, then replace the subformula ψ with the atom $\text{forall}_\psi(\overline{Y})$ and add the constraint:

$$\text{in}_C(X) \wedge \text{forall}_\psi(\overline{Y}) \rightarrow \phi(X, \overline{Y})$$

- Similarly, replace a subformula of the form $\psi = \exists X \in C. \phi(X, \overline{Y})$ with the atom $\text{exists}_\psi(\overline{Y})$ and add the constraints:

$$\text{exists}_\psi(\overline{Y}) \rightarrow \text{find}_\psi(c_0, \overline{Y})$$
$$\text{find}_\psi(X, \overline{Y}) \rightarrow \phi(X, \overline{Y}) \vee \text{xfind}_\psi(X, \overline{Y})$$
$$\text{succ}_C(X, Z) \wedge \text{xfind}_\psi(X, \overline{Y}) \rightarrow \text{find}_\psi(Z, \overline{Y})$$
$$\text{xfind}_\psi(c_d, \overline{Y}) \rightarrow \bot$$

The set of constraints Ord_C is also appended to Γ^{ea} for each set C originally appearing in a quantifier. ∎

Theorem 2. *The sets of constraints Γ and Γ^{ea} are equisatisfiable.*

Proof. The argument is similar to the one used in structural clause form translations where subformulae are replaced by fresh new atoms and constraints are added to give a meaning to those atoms.

In particular it can be shown that if $\mathcal{I} \models \psi^{\text{ea}} \wedge \text{forall}_\psi(\overline{Y})$ for a given interpretation $\mathcal{I}$, then $\mathcal{I} \models \forall X \in C. \psi$ and, for the converse, that if $\mathcal{I} \models \forall X \in C. \psi$ then one can always find an interpretation $\mathcal{I}'$ such that $\mathcal{I}' \models \psi^{\text{ea}} \wedge \text{forall}_\psi(\overline{Y})$. And analogously for the existential quantifier. □

Using the previous two results, it is then possible to eliminate equality and quantifiers from finite domain predicate formulae thus leaving formulae in the Bernays-Schönfinkel fragment. Moreover, the resulting formula is of linear size with respect to the original input. Additionally, these results complement the translation of Plaisted and Greenbaum [13] allowing one to write arbitrary finite domain predicate formulae in clause normal form. In the following we will then freely use equality and finite quantification knowing that they do not add any complexity to the logic.

2.1   Compact Proofs

In order to further motivate the use of Bernays-Schönfinkel formulae as a formal language to represent problems, we prove in this section that reasoning within this fragment can also be exponentially more efficient than in propositional logic. This shows that the language not only provides means for creating more compact encodings, but that the actual solving time could also be reduced by the use of this approach.

We consider, in particular, proofs using the resolution inference system which operates on sets of clauses. It consists of two inference rules: resolution and factoring. We refer to the work of Bachmair and Ganzinger [2] for the definitions.

Given a set of clauses Γ, a *proof of* ϕ from Γ is a sequence of clauses $\phi_1, \ldots, \phi_l = \phi$ such that each ϕ_i is either an instance of a clause in Γ or the result of applying resolution to two previous clauses. If one can obtain a proof of the empty clause from Γ, then the set Γ is unsatisfiable and the proof is known as a *refutation* of Γ. A *propositional proof* is a proof where all the clauses in the sequence are ground.

The following example shows that there is a family of sets of clauses Γ_m with respective unsatisfiability proofs Φ_m, where the shortest propositional refutation of Γ_m is exponentially larger than Φ_m.

Theorem 3. *There is a sequence of sets of clauses $S_1, S_2, \ldots$ of increasing sizes such that each S_i has a refutation of a size quadratic in i and the shortest propositional refutation of S_i has a size exponential in i.*

Proof. In the set S_i we will use two constants: 0 and 1 and a single predicate symbol s of arity i. We will denote by $\bar{0}$, $\bar{1}$, $\bar{x}$ etc. sequences of constants 0, 1 and variables, respectively, whose length will be clear from the context. The set S_i consists of the following clauses:

$$s(\bar{0}). \tag{1}$$

i clauses of the form:

$$\neg s(\bar{x}, 0, \bar{1}) \vee s(\bar{x}, 1, \bar{0}). \tag{2}$$

The clause

$$\neg s(\bar{1}). \tag{3}$$

This set of clauses is unsatisfiable and its size is quadratic in i.

Note that every ground atom is of the form $s(\bar{b})$, where $\bar{b}$ is a sequence of bits representing a number between 0 and $2^i - 1$ written in binary notation. For a number n such that $0 \leq n < 2^i$ let us denote by $\underline{n}$ the sequence of bits denoting this number. Then (1) asserts $s(\underline{0})$ and (3) asserts $\neg s(\underline{2^i - 1})$, while the ground instances of clauses in (2) assert $\neg s(\underline{n}) \vee s(\underline{n+1})$. Using this observation it is not hard to argue that every unsatisfiable set of ground instances of clauses in S_i contains all ground instances of (2), and so all propositional refutations of this set have a size exponential in i.

Let us show that S_i has a non-ground refutation of a quadratic size. To this end, we will show, by induction on the length of a non empty sequence of constants $\bar{1}$, resolution proofs of the clauses

$$\neg s(\bar{x}, \bar{0}) \vee s(\bar{x}, \bar{1}), \tag{4}$$

having a number of steps linear in the length of $\bar{1}$.

When the length is 1, then (4) is an instance of (2). When the length is greater than 1, we can assume, by induction, that there is such a refutation of a clause

$$\neg s(\bar{x}, y, \bar{0}) \vee s(\bar{x}, y, \bar{1}). \tag{5}$$

From this and (2) we can derive by a resolution inference the clause

$$\neg s(\bar{x}, 0, \bar{0}) \vee s(\bar{x}, 1, \bar{0}).$$

From this and (5) we can derive by a resolution inference the clause

$$\neg s(\bar{x}, 0, \bar{0}) \vee s(\bar{x}, 1, \bar{1}).$$

and we are done.

This implies that there is a resolution proof of the clause

$$\neg s(\bar{0}) \vee s(\bar{1})$$

having a number of steps linear in i, and hence a refutation having a number of steps linear in i. Moreover, the size of each clause in the refutation is linear in i, so the size of the refutation is quadratic in i. $\qquad\square$

3   Planning

In this section we formally introduce several notions and concepts related to planning. We first introduce the notion of a planning domain where applicable actions, their preconditions and consequences, are described. We then proceed to define what a planning problem and its solutions are. Our formalism corresponds to STRIPS style planning as introduced by Fikes and Nilsson [5].

Definition 4. The language of a planning domain consists of a triple of finite sets of symbols $(\mathcal{O}, \mathcal{F}, \mathcal{A})$ which are respectively called *object*, *fluent* and *action symbols*. Fluent and action symbols have, moreover, an associated natural number which we call the *arity* of the symbol. If f is a fluent symbol of arity m, then an expression of the form $f(t_1, \ldots, t_m)$, where each t_i is either a variable or an object symbol, is called a *fluent*.

An *action* is a triple $(\alpha_{\mathrm{req}}, \alpha_{\mathrm{add}}, \alpha_{\mathrm{del}})$ where $\alpha = a(X_1, \ldots, X_n)$, for an action symbol $a \in \mathcal{A}$ of arity n, is the *signature* of the action. Each element in the triple is a set of fluents of the form $f(t_1, \ldots, t_m)$ where each t_i is either an object symbol or a variable X_j with $1 \leq j \leq n$. We say that these are the fluents that, respectively, the action *requires*, *adds* and *deletes* when it is executed. A *planning domain* $\mathcal{D}om$ is simply a set of actions and its size, denoted $|\mathcal{D}om|$, is defined as the number of symbols occurring in the description of all its actions.

An *action instance* $\alpha' = \alpha\sigma$, where σ is any substitution, corresponds to the triple of sets of fluent instances $(\alpha'_{\mathrm{req}}, \alpha'_{\mathrm{add}}, \alpha'_{\mathrm{del}})$, where $\alpha'_{\mathrm{req}} = \alpha_{\mathrm{req}}\sigma$, etc. $\blacksquare$

Example 1. We will consider as a running example for this section, a planning domain in the context of logistics. This domain has, among others, an action load-truck that takes three parameters: a package X_1 to load, a truck X_2 where to load the package, and a location X_3 where the loading takes place. The definition of such an action would probably look like:

> load-truck(X_1, X_2, X_3)
> > Req: at(X_1, X_3), at(X_2, X_3)
> > Del: at(X_1, X_3)
> > Add: in(X_1, X_2)

where at and in are binary fluent symbols. In words, the load-truck action requires both the package, represented by the variable X_1, and the truck, represented by X_2, to be at the same location, represented by X_3. The action removes the package from the location and places it, instead, in the truck. A ground instance of this action, say load-truck(pk3, w238, man), would load the particular package pk3 into the truck with license plate w238 when both items are in Manchester (man).

The size of such definition is 16 (1 action symbol + 4 fluent symbols + 11 variable occurrences). We can imagine that the planning domain also contains other actions to unload the truck and drive it from one location to another; as well as more object symbols to identify different packages, trucks and locations.

Definition 5. Let α and β be two distinct ground actions. We say that α *interferes with* β, if the action α deletes fluents that are either required or added by β (i.e. $\alpha_{\text{del}} \cap (\beta_{\text{req}} \cup \beta_{\text{add}}) \neq \emptyset$). We say that a pair of ground actions is *interfering* if one of them interferes with the other. ∎

Example 2. The ground action load-truck(pk3, w238, man) interferes with the other ground action load-truck(pk3, y659, man) since the former deletes the fluent at(pk3, man) while the later requires it. Note that this is how, implicitly, the functionality of the fluent at is preserved, i.e. no object is allowed to end up at two different places simultaneously.

Definition 6. Given a set of ground fluents $\mathbf{S}$ and a set of ground actions $\mathbf{A}$, we say that $\mathbf{A}$ *is executable in* $\mathbf{S}$ *and produces* $\mathbf{S}'$, denoted by $\mathbf{S} \xrightarrow{\mathbf{A}} \mathbf{S}'$, if:

- $\mathbf{A}$ does not contain interfering actions,
- $\mathbf{A}_{\text{req}} \subseteq \mathbf{S}$,
- $\mathbf{S}' = \mathbf{S} \setminus \mathbf{A}_{\text{del}} \cup \mathbf{A}_{\text{add}}$.

where $\mathbf{A}_{\text{req}} = \bigcup_{\alpha \in \mathbf{A}} \alpha_{\text{req}}$, etc. ∎

Definition 7. A *planning problem* is given as a pair $\mathbf{I}, \mathbf{G}$ of sets of ground fluents, respectively known as the *initial* and *goal states* of the problem.

A *solution plan* for the problem is a sequence $\mathbf{A}_1, \ldots, \mathbf{A}_k$ of sets of ground actions such that the sequence $\mathbf{S}_1 \xrightarrow{\mathbf{A}_1} \mathbf{S}_2 \xrightarrow{\mathbf{A}_2} \cdots \xrightarrow{\mathbf{A}_k} \mathbf{S}_{k+1}$ holds, the set $\mathbf{I} = \mathbf{S}_1$ and $\mathbf{G} \subseteq \mathbf{S}_{k+1}$. ∎

The kind of plans just defined are often known as *plans with parallel actions*. The semantics of such plans is that, at each step, the actions in a set $\mathbf{A}_i$ can be executed in any order (even simultaneously) while still reaching the same outcome. In our example one could simultaneously execute both load-truck(pk3, w238, man) and load-truck(pk4, w238, man) in order to load both packages pk3 and pk4 into the truck w238. Alternatively, a *linear plan* is a plan where each $\mathbf{A}_i$ is a singleton. Trivially, any plan with parallel actions can be converted into a linear plan just by sequencing parallel actions into an arbitrary order, e.g. first load package pk3, then load pk4.

4 Encoding of Planning Problems

In this section we will consider an encoding of planning problems into finite domain predicate logic. Given a planning domain and a bound k, we construct a set of constraints Γ_k whose models correspond to plans of length k. Linear plans of shorter lengths $(< k)$ can also be encoded by allowing the use of a nop action that does nothing or, in plans with parallel actions, having steps where no action is executed (i.e. an empty $\mathbf{A}_i$).

Although fluents and actions were already defined as atoms in predicate logic, these predicate symbols will now play the role of constant symbols so that we can quantify over them in our encoding. For example, if $f(\overline{Y})$ is a fluent in a planning domain then the predicate holds$(f, \overline{Y}, T)$ will be used to denote the fact that an instance of the fluent $f(\overline{Y})$ holds at a step T of the plan.

Note that this sort of encoding requires, however, all fluents (resp. actions) to have the same arity. This can be easily achieved by padding actions with additional variables (which will be unused in its fluents), and padding fluents in actions with some dummy constant symbol $o \in \mathcal{D}$.

We will split the encoding of a planning domain into four groups of clauses. The first group Bound_k specifies the length of the plans to be considered, the second group $\mathsf{Act}_{\mathcal{D}om}$ encodes the definitions of actions, the third $\mathsf{Prob}_{\mathbf{I},\mathbf{G}}$ encodes the initial and goal states of a particular problem instance, and the fourth and last one $\mathsf{Frame}_{\mathcal{D}om}$ encodes the frame conditions. Frame conditions are the ones responsible to state that all fluents whose status is not changed by the actions executed must remain unmodified. We will, actually, show two different encodings for frame conditions which can be used to obtain plans which are either linear or with parallel actions.

In the following we will use A, B as variables that stand for actions and F as a variable to represent a fluent. Also T is a variable that represents the *current step* in the plan, and U the *next step*. A number of constant symbols $\{s_0, \ldots, s_k\} \subset \mathcal{D}$ are used to denote the actual steps in the plan.

Definition 8. Given a positive number k, the set Bound_k is simply defined as the set containing next(s_i, s_{i+1}) for every $i \leq 0 < k$. ∎

This simple set with a size of $O(k)$ is used to define an order among steps in the plan and to determine, from each step, which is the next one. The following set encodes the actions available in the domain.

Definition 9. Given a planning domain $\mathcal{D}om$, the *domain definition* $\mathsf{Act}_{\mathcal{D}om}$ is the set that contains, for each action in the domain, the constraints:

$$\mathsf{reqs}(a, \overline{X}, f, \overline{Y}\sigma) \qquad \text{for each } f(\overline{Y})\sigma \text{ required by } a(\overline{X})$$
$$\mathsf{dels}(a, \overline{X}, f, \overline{Y}\sigma) \qquad \text{for each } f(\overline{Y})\sigma \text{ deleted by } a(\overline{X})$$
$$\mathsf{adds}(a, \overline{X}, f, \overline{Y}\sigma) \qquad \text{for each } f(\overline{Y})\sigma \text{ added by } a(\overline{X})$$

together with the following three constraints that make actions have their corresponding preconditions and effects:

$$\mathsf{reqs}(A, \overline{X}, F, \overline{Y}) \wedge \neg\mathsf{holds}(F, \overline{Y}, T) \to \neg\mathsf{executes}(A, \overline{X}, T)$$
$$\mathsf{next}(T, U) \wedge \mathsf{adds}(A, \overline{X}, F, \overline{Y}) \wedge \mathsf{executes}(A, \overline{X}, T) \to \mathsf{holds}(F, \overline{Y}, U)$$
$$\mathsf{next}(T, U) \wedge \mathsf{dels}(A, \overline{X}, F, \overline{Y}) \wedge \mathsf{executes}(A, \overline{X}, T) \to \neg\mathsf{holds}(F, \overline{Y}, U) \quad \blacksquare$$

Example 3. In our running example, the action load-truck would be encoded as:

$$\mathsf{reqs}(\text{load-truck}, X_1, X_2, X_3, \text{at}, X_1, X_3)$$
$$\mathsf{reqs}(\text{load-truck}, X_1, X_2, X_3, \text{at}, X_2, X_3)$$
$$\mathsf{dels}(\text{load-truck}, X_1, X_2, X_3, \text{at}, X_1, X_3)$$
$$\mathsf{adds}(\text{load-truck}, X_1, X_2, X_3, \text{in}, X_1, X_2)$$

Similar constraints are added for other actions in the domain. The last few constraints of $\mathsf{Act}_{\mathcal{D}om}$ would ensure that an action is not executed when one of its requirements does not hold or, if the action is executed, that fluents are added or deleted accordingly. It is also easy to see that $\mathsf{Act}_{\mathcal{D}om}$ has a size of $O(|\mathcal{D}om|)$.

We now move to the encoding of a problem instance using the set of constraints $\mathsf{Prob}_{\mathbf{I}, \mathbf{G}}$. Typically, in propositional encodings of a planning problem, one has to completely specify the initial state $\mathbf{I}$ stating, for every ground fluent, whether $f(\bar{c})$ or $\neg f(\bar{c})$ should hold. To avoid this, we define a special action setup that adds all the ground fluents to be true at the initial state and does not require or delete anything. Quantifying over all fluents it is easy to express that "initially nothing holds" and then make the setup action execute at the step zero of the plan, the frame conditions will then ensure that everything not added by setup remains false.

Definition 10. Given a planning problem defined by an initial state $\mathbf{I}$ and goals $\mathbf{G}$, the encoding of the problem instance $\mathsf{Prob}_{\mathbf{I},\mathbf{G}}$ is defined as the set of constraints:

$$\neg\mathsf{holds}(F, \overline{Y}, s_0)$$
$$\mathsf{adds}(\text{setup}, \overline{X}, f, \bar{c}) \qquad\qquad \text{for every } f(\bar{c}) \text{ in } \mathbf{I}$$
$$\mathsf{executes}(\text{setup}, \bar{o}, s_0)$$
$$\mathsf{next}(T, U) \to \neg\mathsf{executes}(\text{setup}, \overline{X}, U)$$
$$\mathsf{holds}(f, \bar{c}, s_k) \qquad\qquad \text{for every } f(\bar{c}) \text{ in } \mathbf{G}$$

where $\bar{o}$ simply represents the sequence $o, \dots, o$ of dummy constant symbols of the required length. $\qquad \blacksquare$

Example 4. Suppose that initially we have two packages in Manchester, a truck in London, and our goal is to get the packages to Edinburgh. This corresponds to $\mathbf{I} = \{\text{at}(\text{pk3}, \text{man}), \text{at}(\text{pk4}, \text{man}), \text{at}(\text{w238}, \text{lon})\}$, $\mathbf{G} = \{\text{at}(\text{pk3}, \text{edn}), \text{at}(\text{pk4}, \text{edn})\}$ and would be encoded in the component $\text{Prob}_{\mathbf{I},\mathbf{G}}$ as:

$$\neg\text{holds}(F, Y_1, Y_2, s_0)$$
$$\text{adds}(\text{setup}, X_1, X_2, X_3, \text{at}, \text{pk3}, \text{man})$$
$$\text{adds}(\text{setup}, X_1, X_2, X_3, \text{at}, \text{pk4}, \text{man})$$
$$\text{adds}(\text{setup}, X_1, X_2, X_3, \text{at}, \text{w238}, \text{lon})$$
$$\text{executes}(\text{setup}, o, o, o, s_0)$$
$$\text{next}(T, U) \rightarrow \neg\text{executes}(\text{setup}, X_1, X_2, X_3, U)$$
$$\text{holds}(\text{at}, \text{pk3}, \text{edn}, s_k)$$
$$\text{holds}(\text{at}, \text{pk4}, \text{edn}, s_k)$$

The first constraint makes all fluents false at time s_0, then we have the definition of the setup action. A pair of constraints follow that make **setup** to execute at the first state, and only at that state. Finally we specify that the goals should hold at the final state s_k. Note again that we do not have to specify where packages *are not*, such as $\neg\text{at}(\text{pk3}, \text{lon})$, or that the truck is empty (because there is nothing in it).

We finally proceed to describe the rules that actually encode the frame conditions and, at the same time, to disallow the execution of interfering actions. The following sections consider two alternatives that correspond to plans that are either linear or with parallel actions.

4.1   Linear Plans

One possibility is to allow only one action to execute at a time, and the frame conditions can be directly expressed stating that the truth value of fluents not added or deleted by an action do not change. Moreover, in order to allow plans whose length is shorter than the bound k, a nop action that does nothing should be added to the definition of the planning domain.

Definition 11. Given a planning domain $\mathcal{Dom}$, the *linear frame encoding* of the domain, denoted by $\text{LFrame}_{\mathcal{Dom}}$, is the set containing, for each action symbol $a \in \mathcal{A}$ and fluent $f \in \mathcal{F}$, the constraint

$$\text{next}(T, U) \wedge \text{executes}(a, \overline{X}, T) \wedge \bigwedge_{\sigma \in \Xi_{a,f}} \overline{Y} \neq \overline{Y}\sigma \rightarrow$$
$$\text{holds}(f, \overline{Y}, T) \leftrightarrow \text{holds}(f, \overline{Y}, U)$$

and the pair of constraints

$$\exists A, \overline{X} \in \mathcal{A} \times \mathcal{O}^n. \, \text{executes}(A, \overline{X}, T)$$
$$\text{executes}(A, \overline{X}, T) \wedge \text{executes}(B, \overline{Z}, T) \rightarrow A = B \wedge \overline{X} = \overline{Z}$$

where the set $\varXi_{a,f}$ contains all substitutions σ for which the fluent $f(\overline{Y})\sigma$ is either added or deleted by $a(\overline{X})$. ∎

Example 5. In our example the linear frame conditions for the load-truck action would be expressed as follows:

$$\mathsf{next}(T, U) \land \mathsf{executes}(\text{load-truck}, X_1, X_2, X_3, T) \land$$
$$\neg(Y_1 = X_1 \land Y_2 = X_3) \rightarrow \mathsf{holds}(\text{at}, Y_1, Y_2, T) \leftrightarrow \mathsf{holds}(\text{at}, Y_1, Y_2, U)$$

$$\mathsf{next}(T, U) \land \mathsf{executes}(\text{load-truck}, X_1, X_2, X_3, T) \land$$
$$\neg(Y_1 = X_2 \land Y_2 = X_3) \rightarrow \mathsf{holds}(\text{in}, Y_1, Y_2, T) \leftrightarrow \mathsf{holds}(\text{in}, Y_1, Y_2, U)$$

In words these constraints state that, except for the package X_1 moved by the action, all other objects remain at their same locations and in their same containers. The last few constraints of LFrame_{Dom} encode the fact that one, and only one, ground action executes at any given time.

Note that this encoding requires $|\mathcal{A}||\mathcal{F}|$ constraints to represent the frame conditions, where $|\mathcal{A}|$ (resp. $|\mathcal{F}|$) denotes the number of action (resp. fluent) symbols. Additionally, each fluent added or deleted by actions must appear represented as a substitution in the set $\varXi_{a,f}$ for one of such constraints. Therefore the set of constraints LFrame_{Dom} has a size of $O(|\mathcal{A}||\mathcal{F}| + |Dom|)$.

4.2   Plans with Parallel Actions

Alternatively, several actions could be executed at once as long as they do not interfere with each other. We consider an *explanatory* encoding following ideas proposed by Haas [8], Schubert [14] and later applied in the propositional case by Kautz et al. [10]; where it is expressed that, if a fluent changes its value from one step to another, then one of the actions that modify it must have been executed.

Definition 12. Given a planning domain Dom, the *parallel frame encoding* of the domain, denoted by PFrame_{Dom}, is the set containing, for each fluent $f \in \mathcal{F}$, the constraints:

$$\mathsf{added}(f, \overline{Y}, T) \rightarrow \bigvee_{(a,\sigma)\in\Delta_f} \exists \overline{X} \in \mathcal{O}^n.(\mathsf{executes}(a, \overline{X}, T) \land \overline{Y} = \overline{Y}\sigma)$$
$$\mathsf{deleted}(f, \overline{Y}, T) \rightarrow \bigvee_{(a,\sigma)\in\nabla_f} \exists \overline{X} \in \mathcal{O}^n.(\mathsf{executes}(a, \overline{X}, T) \land \overline{Y} = \overline{Y}\sigma)$$

together with the three constraints

$$\mathsf{next}(T, U) \land \neg\mathsf{holds}(F, \overline{Y}, T) \land \quad \mathsf{holds}(F, \overline{Y}, U) \rightarrow \mathsf{added}(F, \overline{Y}, T)$$
$$\mathsf{next}(T, U) \land \quad \mathsf{holds}(F, \overline{Y}, T) \land \neg\mathsf{holds}(F, \overline{Y}, U) \rightarrow \mathsf{deleted}(F, \overline{Y}, T)$$
$$\mathsf{dels}(A, \overline{X}, F, \overline{Y}) \land \mathsf{reqs}(B, \overline{Z}, F, \overline{Y}) \land$$
$$\mathsf{executes}(A, \overline{X}, T) \land \mathsf{executes}(B, \overline{Z}, T) \rightarrow A = B \land \overline{X} = \overline{Z}$$

where the set Δ_f (resp. ∇_f) contains the pair (a, σ) whenever the fluent $f(\overline{Y})\sigma$ is added (resp. deleted) by the action $a(\overline{X})$. ∎

Example 6. In this case, the predicates added and deleted are defined for each fluent. Consider for instance the following constraint that encodes the frame conditions for the fluent $at(Y_1, Y_2)$:

$$added(at, Y_1, Y_2, T) \rightarrow$$
$$\exists \overline{X} \in \mathcal{O}^3.(executes(\text{unload-truck}, \overline{X}) \land Y_1 = X_1 \land Y_2 = X_3)$$
$$\lor \exists \overline{X} \in \mathcal{O}^3.(executes(\text{drive-truck}, \overline{X}) \land Y_1 = X_1 \land Y_2 = X_3)$$

If a fluent $at(Y_1, Y_2)$ is added at some state, then it must be the case that either a package $Y_1 = X_1$ was unloaded at a location $Y_2 = X_3$ (from some truck X_2) or, similarly, a truck was driven to that location from another.

The last few constraints trigger the predicates added and deleted, whenever a change in the truth value of a fluent occurs, in order to search for an explanation of such change. The final constraint disables the execution of two actions when one deletes a requirement of the other and, therefore, they are interfering. It is also not possible to execute two actions such that one deletes the fluent added by the other, a contradiction will occur in $\mathsf{Act}_{\mathcal{D}om}$ when both actions try to assign contradictory values to the fluent.

Note that, in this case, the number of clauses in $\mathsf{PFrame}_{\mathcal{D}om}$ is linear with respect to the number of fluent symbols in $\mathcal{F}$. Moreover, the size of the clauses only depends on the number of actions that could add or delete a given fluent. Overall, $\mathsf{PFrame}_{\mathcal{D}om}$ has only a size of $O(|\mathcal{D}om|)$ and does not directly depend on the number of actions or fluents as in the previous case.

Theorem 4. *Given a planning domain $\mathcal{D}om$, a problem $\mathbf{I}, \mathbf{G}$ and a bound k, the finite domain predicate formula $\mathsf{Bound}_k \land \mathsf{Act}_{\mathcal{D}om} \land \mathsf{Prob}_{\mathbf{I},\mathbf{G}} \land \mathsf{Frame}_{\mathcal{D}om}$, where $\mathsf{Frame}_{\mathcal{D}om}$ is either $\mathsf{LFrame}_{\mathcal{D}om}$ or $\mathsf{PFrame}_{\mathcal{D}om}$, is satisfiable if and only if the planning problem has a solution plan, respectively linear or with parallel actions, of length $\leq k$.*

Proof. It can be shown that if an interpretation $\mathcal{I}$ is a model of the encoding, then the plan where $\mathbf{A}_i = \{a(\bar{c}) \mid \mathcal{I} \models executes(a, \bar{c}, s_i)\}$, for $1 \leq i \leq k$, is a valid solution to the planning problem.

Conversely it can be shown that, if $\mathbf{A}_1, \ldots, \mathbf{A}_{k'}$ is a solution plan (linear or with parallel actions) with $k' < k$, then an interpretation $\mathcal{I}$ can be built, giving appropriate values to predicates, such that $\mathcal{I}$ is a model of the encoding. $\square$

5   Conclusions

In this paper we have introduced the finite domain predicate logic, which corresponds to a decidable fragment of first order logic with features such as equality and finite quantification. Formulae in this logic are non-propositional, but its models can be interpreted in a finite Herbrand universe. We also show that formulae in this logic can be linearly translated to the Bernays-Schönfinkel class of formulae, which also corresponds to the category of effectively propositional problems of the CASC system competition [16].

The motivation for developing such a logic is that it enables us to succinctly and naturally encode problems from applications. In particular we show how planning problems, including their frame conditions, can be easily encoded within the proposed logic. Moreover, the size of the generated formula is linear with respect to size of a standard description, e.g. in the STRIPS language, of the original planning problem. This is in contrast with propositional encodings where the size of the resulting formula is often exponential in the size of the input.

Furthermore, we also show that reasoning with effectively propositional formulae can be exponentially more efficient than in the propositional setting. We show in particular a family of unsatisfiable formulae whose refutation proofs using first order resolution can be exponentially shorter than any propositional resolution proof. This serves to suggest that, in principle, the use of a finite domain predicate encoding can be useful both to obtain more compact representations of problems and to solve them more efficiently.

On the other hand, the ideas presented here might also turn out to be useful for propositional SAT-based approaches. Since the problem of finding optimised propositional encodings, including but not limited to planning, is reduced to finding an appropriate instantiation of the obtained finite domain formula.

We think that our work is of great value to the automated reasoning community since it provides a new and relevant source of benchmarks for developers of first order reasoners, particularly those geared towards the effectively propositional fragment. Specifically, problem instances derived from the work of this paper have been contributed and are now part of the TPTP Library in the planning domain (PLA) since v3.5.0 [15]. Furthermore, follow up research work has demonstrated the use of finite domain predicate logic to encode problems from a wide range of domains, including temporal logics and software/hardware verification [11, 12].

References

[1] Baaz, M., Leitsch, A.: Complexity of resolution proofs and function introduction. Annals of Pure and Applied Logic 57(3), 181–215 (1992)

[2] Bachmair, L., Ganzinger, H.: Resolution theorem proving. In: Robinson, J.A., Voronkov, A. (eds.) Handbook of Automated Reasoning, vol. I, ch. 2, pp. 19–99. Elsevier (2001)

[3] Baumgartner, P., Tinelli, C.: The Model Evolution Calculus with Equality. In: Nieuwenhuis, R. (ed.) CADE 2005. LNCS (LNAI), vol. 3632, pp. 392–408. Springer, Heidelberg (2005)

[4] Claessen, K., Sörensson, N.: New techniques that improve MACE-style model finding. In: MODEL 2003: Proceedings of the Workshop on Model Computation (2003)

[5] Fikes, R., Nilsson, N.J.: STRIPS: A new approach to the application of theorem proving to problem solving. Artificial Intelligence 2, 189–208 (1971)

[6] Ganzinger, H., Korovin, K.: Theory Instantiation. In: Hermann, M., Voronkov, A. (eds.) LPAR 2006. LNCS (LNAI), vol. 4246, pp. 497–511. Springer, Heidelberg (2006)

[7] Green, C.: Application of theorem proving to problem solving. In: IJCAI 1969: Proceedings of the 1st International Joint Conference on Artificial Intelligence, Washington, DC, USA, pp. 219–239 (1969)

[8] Haas, A.R.: The case for domain specific frame axioms. In: Brown, F.M. (ed.) Proceedings of the 1987 Workshop on The Frame Problem in Artificial Intelligence, pp. 343–348. Morgan Kaufmann, Lawrence (1987)

[9] Kautz, H., Selman, B.: Planning as satisfiability. In: ECAI 1992: Proceedings of the 10th European Conference on Artificial Intelligence, pp. 359–363. John Wiley & Sons, Inc, Vienna (1992)

[10] Kautz, H., McAllester, D., Selman, B.: Encoding plans in propositional logic. In: KR 1996: Proceedings of the 5th International Conference on Principles of Knowledge Representation and Reasoning, Boston, MA, USA (1996)

[11] Navarro Pérez, J.A.: Encoding and Solving Problems in Effectively Propositional Logic. PhD thesis, The University of Manchester (2007)

[12] Navarro-Pérez, J.A., Voronkov, A.: Encodings of Bounded LTL Model Checking in Effectively Propositional Logic. In: Pfenning, F. (ed.) CADE 2007. LNCS (LNAI), vol. 4603, pp. 346–361. Springer, Heidelberg (2007)

[13] David, A.: Plaisted and Steven Greenbaum. A structure-preserving clause form translation. Journal of Symbolic Computation 2(3), 747–7171 (1986) ISSN: 0747-7171

[14] Schubert, L.K.: Monotonic solution of the frame problem in the situation calculus: An efficient method for worlds with fully specified actions. In: Kyburg, H., Loui, R., Carlson, G. (eds.) Knowledge Representation and Defeasible Reasoning, pp. 23–67. Kluwer Academic Publishers, Dordrecht (1990)

[15] Sutcliffe, G.: The TPTP problem library and associated infrastructure: The FOF and CNF parts, v3.5.0. Journal of Automated Reasoning 43(4), 337–362 (2009)

[16] Sutcliffe, G., Suttner, C.B.: The state of CASC. AI Communications 19(1), 35–48 (2006)

The Relative Power of Semantics and Unification

David A. Plaisted and Swaha Miller*

Department of Computer Science
UNC Chapel Hill
Chapel Hill, NC 27599-3175
plaisted@cs.unc.edu

Abstract. The *OSHL* theorem proving method is an attempt to extend propositional theorem proving techniques to first-order logic by working entirely at the ground level. A disadvantage of this approach is that *OSHL* does not perform unifications between non-ground literals, as resolution does. However, *OSHL* has the capability to use natural semantics to guide the proof search. The question arises whether the advantage of proof guidance using semantics can make up for the loss of unification between non-ground literals that other methods employ. This question is studied and some evidence is given that a properly chosen semantics causes *OSHL* to implicitly perform unifications between non-ground levels, suggesting that *OSHL* may have some of the advantages of theorem proving methods based on unification as well as some of the efficiencies of propositional theorem provers. Some implementation results of *OSHL* with and without nontrivial semantics are also presented to illustrate its properties.

Keywords: Theorem proving, propositional calculus, semantics, unification, *OSHL*.

1 Introduction

Techniques for deciding the satisfiability of propositional calculus formulas are advancing rapidly. The announcement of the Special issue of the Journal of Automated Reasoning for SAT 2005 [1] stated, "Systematic methods can now routinely solve verification problems with thousands or tens of thousands of variables, whilst local search methods can solve hard random 3SAT problems with millions of variables." It would be desirable to incorporate some of these propositional techniques into first-order theorem provers to improve their efficiency.

The *OSHL* theorem proving method [2] is one of several propositional methods for first order logic that have been developed. Others include FDPLL [3], DCTP [4], model evolution[5–8], the method of Ganzinger and Korovin [9–11], and clause linking [12]. A recent survey[13] of instance-based methods gives many more references. *OSHL* differs from other instance-based methods in two main

---

* This research was partially supported by the National Science Foundation under grant CCR-9972118.

A. Voronkov and C. Weidenbach (Eds.): Ganzinger Festschrift, LNCS 7797, pp. 317–344, 2013.
© Springer-Verlag Berlin Heidelberg 2013

respects: 1. It works entirely at the ground level, and makes no use of true unification between non-ground literals. 2. It permits the use of very general semantics to guide the proof search, in this respect reminiscent of the geometry theorem prover of Gelernter [14]. In particular, *OSHL* can make use of any semantics that is decidable on ground literals. The method of Ganzinger and Korovin also makes use of semantics; this method grounds a set of clauses by replacing variables by constants and tests the ground set for satisfiability. If the set is unsatisfiable, a refutation has been found; otherwise, a model of the ground set is found, and this model guides the generation of new instances of the clauses. So Ganzinger and Korovin's method uses semantics, but the model they obtain is the one that a satisfiability checker returns, and not one that a user may have input at the beginning.

  OSHL was implemented [15], and even without sophisticated semantics, special methods for equality, or efficient data structures it had a performance that came within a factor of two of a respectable resolution prover, and in some cases exceeded it, though it was still far behind the best provers in existence at the time. The natural question is whether the disadvantage of lacking true unification can be compensated for by the advantage of using semantics. In this paper we attempt to gain a better understanding of the relative power of semantics and unification. Also, we sketch the state of the implementation and its performance on the TPTP problem set [16] at the time the tests were run. The performance of *OSHL* on some examples run with a nontrivial semantics is also presented. This work was begun while the first author was a visitor at Max Planck Institute in 1994-95.

1.1 Terminology

The *arity* of a function or predicate symbol is the number of arguments it takes. A *first-order language* L(P,F,X) consists of a finite set F of function symbols of various arities, a countably infinite set X of variable names, and a finite set P of predicate symbols of various arities. A function symbol of arity zero is also called a *constant* symbol. It is assumed that F contains at least one constant symbol, even if this symbol does not appear in the set S of clauses being considered. A *term* over L is a well-formed expression composed of function symbols in F, including constant symbols in F, and variables in X. An *atom* over L is a predicate symbol in P followed by a list of terms over L as arguments. A *literal* over L is an atom or an atom preceded by a negation sign. If L is an atom then the literals L and $\neg L$ are said to be *complementary* and L is called a *positive* literal and $\neg L$ a *negative* literal. If L is a literal then $at(L)$ is its atom, defined by $at(A) = A$ and $at(\neg A) = A$ for atoms A. If L is a negative literal then $\neg L$ is sometimes identified with $at(L)$.

  If L is an atom then $||L||_{lin}$ is the number of occurrences of function, constant, and predicate symbols in L when it is written out as a string, so that $||P(a, f(x))|| = 4$. Also, $||L||_{dag}$ is the length of L when it is expressed as a directed acyclic graph, so that repeated subterms are only counted once. For this,

L is assumed to be represented as a sequence of symbols with repeated subterms represented by pointers, so that $P(f(a), f(a))$ would be represented by the sequence $P, f, a, 2$ where the 2 indicates a pointer to the second symbol, an f. Then $||P(f(a), f(a))||_{dag} = 4$ because the sequence $P, f, a, 2$ is of length four. These measures are extended to literals by $||\neg L||_{lin} = ||L||_{lin}$ and $||\neg L||_{dag} = ||L||_{dag}$.

A *clause* over L is a set of literals over L representing their disjunction. If C is a clause then $at(C) = \{at(L) : L \in C\}$. A clause is a *unit clause* if it contains exactly one literal and it is a *Horn clause* if it contains at most one positive literal. Variables in a clause are assumed to be universally quantified. A term, literal, or clause without variables is said to be *ground*. If C is a clause then $||C||_{lin}$ is the sum of $||L||_{lin}$ for all literals L in C, and similarly for $||C||_{dag}$.

A set S of clauses represents the conjunction of the clauses in the set. S is called a *Horn set* if all clauses in S are Horn clauses. It is assumed that a set S of clauses over L(P,F,X) is given, F is the set of constant and function symbols appearing in S, with a new constant symbol added if F has none, and P is the set of predicate symbols appearing in S.

A *substitution* is a mapping from variables in X to terms over F and X, in which only finitely many variables are changed. If t is a term and ρ is a substitution then $t\rho$ indicates the application of ρ to the term t, and similarly for literals and clauses; this represents t with all variables systematically replaced as specified by ρ. The term $t\rho$ is called an *instance* of t and similarly for literals and clauses. Note that this definition restricts instances to terms over L(P,F,X). A substitution is a *variable renaming* if all variables are mapped to variables, and no two variables are mapped to the same variable. If ρ is a variable renaming and A is an atom then $A\rho$ is called a *variant* of A, and similarly for terms and clauses.

An interpretation gives meanings to function symbols as functions over some domain, and interprets predicate symbols as relations over the same domain. Using these meanings, ground atoms can be mapped to {**true, false**}. The domain may also contain elements that do not correspond to ground atoms. A *Herbrand interpretation I* over L is a mapping from ground atoms over L to {**true, false**}. One can think of non-Herbrand interpretations as augmenting the list F of symbols by an arbitrary set of constant symbols representing elements of some domain of objects. We only consider Herbrand interpretations in this discussion. If $I(A) = $ **true** for ground atom A then one writes $I \models A$ or I satisfies A, and otherwise $I \not\models A$, I contradicts A, or A contradicts I. I is extended to literals by $I \models \neg A$ iff $I \not\models A$. I is extended to clauses by $I \models C$ iff $\exists L \in C(I \models L)$. I is extended to non-ground clauses in a standard way. For our purposes, if C is a non-ground clause then $I \models C$ iff for all ground instances D of C, $I \models D$; this is a property of Herbrand interpretations, but other interpretations may not satisfy this property. An interpretation I is extended to sets of clauses so that $I \models S$ iff $I \models C$ for all C in S. If $I \models S$ then I is called a *model* of S. If S has a model then S is *satisfiable*, else it is *unsatisfiable*. If I is an interpretation and $L_1 \ldots L_n$ are literals then $I[L_1 \ldots L_n]$ is the interpretation defined by $I[L_1 \ldots L_n] \models L$ if $L = L_i$ for some i, or $I \models L$ and $at(L) \notin \{at(L_1), \ldots, at(L_n)\}$.

If I and J are two interpretations, then $I \leq_{pos} J$ iff for all atoms A, $I \models A$ implies $J \models A$. A model I is a $\leq_{pos}$ minimal model of a set S of clauses if I is a model of S and there is no model J of S distinct from I such that $J \leq_{pos} I$.

1.2   Exhaustive Enumeration Methods

OSHL is similar to some of the early enumeration-based methods for first-order theorem proving. The idea of exhaustive enumeration is as follows:

If S is a set of clauses let H_S be the set of ground instances of clauses in S, where all symbols appearing in clauses in H_S appear in S, except for one additional constant symbol in H_S if S has no constant symbols. Let S be a set of first order clauses. Then the exhaustive enumeration method for first-order theorem proving is the following:

> **procedure enumerate**(S)
> $T_0 \leftarrow \{\}$
>   **for** $i = 1$ **step** 1 **until** ∞ **do**
>   **if** $T_{i-1} = H_S$ **then return** "satisfiable"
>   **let** D be an element of $H_S - T_{i-1}$ chosen fairly
> $T_i \leftarrow T_{i-1} \cup \{D\}$;
>   **If** T_i is unsatisfiable **then return** "unsatisfiable"
>   **od**
> **end** enumerate;

This procedure is *complete* in the sense that if S is unsatisfiable, the procedure will eventually return "unsatisfiable." If H_S is finite then this procedure will eventually return "satisfiable." Otherwise the procedure will run forever. The completeness of this procedure is a straightforward application of what is commonly known as Herbrand's theorem.

The paper [17] by Davis and Putnam in 1960 was the first one to apply this blind enumeration algorithm to clause form first-order theorem proving, and in addition, this paper used a reasonably efficient decision procedure (the original Davis and Putnam procedure, involving ground resolution) to test the sets T_i for unsatisfiability. Others had used enumeration procedures before this, but none had used Skolem functions together with clause form and none had used as efficient a propositional decision procedure.

Later Robinson [18] developed the resolution procedure which avoids blind enumeration of ground instances by use of the unification algorithm. Since then many other strategies have been developed that also use the unification algorithm in various ways.

Recently there has been a resurgence of interest in propositional approaches to first-order theorem proving. However, *OSHL* differs from most instance-based methods in that it works strictly at the ground level. This feature enables sophisticated semantic guidance to be used with *OSHL*. Thus *OSHL* does not perform true unification between non-ground literals. This lack of unification is a potential handicap to *OSHL*, so there is a question whether the ability to use semantics can compensate for the lack of unification. This paper presents some evidence in the affirmative.

2   OSHL

OSHL has the following general features. It enumerates H_S and tests the sets T_i for unsatisfiability. However, *OSHL* uses an enumeration procedure that differs from the above one in that it guarantees that no ground instance will be a logical consequence of previously generated instances. It also uses a backtracking procedure similar to DPLL[19] as a decision procedure instead of the original Davis and Putnam method. If T_i is unsatisfiable, then *OSHL* reports "unsatisfiable." Otherwise, *OSHL* continues generating ground instances. Also, *OSHL* does not perform separate satisfiability tests on each T_i but interleaves these tests with the generation of the successive T_i to avoid repeated work.

The following version of *OSHL* is very general but is still complete. A more specialized version of *OSHL* that more closely approximates the actual implementation will be presented later.

> **procedure** $OSHL_{general}(S)$
> $T \leftarrow \phi$;
> **for** $i = 0$ **step** 1 **until** ∞ **do**
>   if T is unsatisfiable then return "unsatisfiable"
>   pick interpretation I_i that satisfies all clauses in T;
>   if no clause in H_S contradicts I_i then return "satisfiable"
>   pick a clause D_i in H_S that contradicts I_i;
> $T \leftarrow T \cup \{D_i\}$;
> **od**;
> **end** $OSHL_{general}$;

Definition 1. *The sequence $D_0, D_1, D_2 \ldots$ is an* instance sequence *of OSHL for input S. This sequence is not unique for a given S.*

The actual implementation of *OSHL* differs from the given procedure; the implementation sometimes performs resolutions on clauses in the instance sequence to detect when this sequence is unsatisfiable.

Definition 2. *Let $A_1, A_2, A_3 \ldots$ be an enumeration of all ground literals over* L(P,F,X). *Suppose I and J are two interpretations over* L. *Then I and J are* k-similar *if I and J agree on A_j for all j, $1 \le j \le k$, that is, $I \models A_j$ iff $J \models A_j$ for all such j.*

Theorem 1. *Assuming that the clauses D_i are chosen fairly, the procedure $OSHL_{general}$ is complete.*

Proof. Suppose S is unsatisfiable. Let S' be an unsatisfiable set of ground instances of S. Suppose that the procedure $OSHL_{general}$ runs forever. Then there must be some limiting interpretation I having the property that for all k there are infinitely many i such that I is k-similar to I_i. I can be constructed by noting that at least one of the literals A_1, $\neg A_1$ is satisfied by infinitely many I_i; choose I to satisfy this literal. Then among the I_i that are 1-similar to I, there must be infinitely many that satisfy A_2 or $\neg A_2$; choose I to satisfy this literal, too. Continuing in this way, I can be completely specified.

Because S is unsatisfiable, some clause in S has a ground instance that I contradicts. By fairness, eventually some such clause D_k will be chosen and will become a member of T. Let m be the maximum integer such that the atom A_m in the enumeration $A_1, A_2, A_3 \ldots$ appears either positively or negatively in D_k. Then any I_i that is m-similar to I must contradict D_k. Because I is a limiting interpretation, there are infinitely many i such that I is m-similar to I_i. All such I_i contradict D_k, in particular, some I_i must contradict D_k. This cannot be so because all I_i must satisfy all clauses in T, and $D_k \in T$. Therefore such a limiting interpretation I does not exist, so the procedure $OSHL_{general}$ does not run forever. The only way that this procedure can halt on an unsatisfiable input is if it detects unsatisfiability. This argument shows that the procedure $OSHL_{general}$ is complete.

$OSHL_{general}$ is further constrained to obtain "$OSHL_{specific}$," which lets the user choose I_0 and then chooses each I_j as a minimal model of T in a certain ordering on interpretations. This version of $OSHL$ can employ an interpretation I_0 as its initial semantics if I_0 is *ground decidable*.

Definition 3. *An interpretation I is* ground decidable *if the following question is decidable: Given a ground literal L, does I satisfy L? Here I is fixed but L varies.*

Not all semantics are ground decidable; any interpretation having ground literals expressing the halting of arbitrary Turing machines, for example, is not. $OSHL_{specific}$ assumes that I_0 is ground decidable, and it then follows that all succeeding I_i are also ground decidable.

Also, in $OSHL_{specific}$, D_i is chosen as a clause that I_i contradicts and is minimal in a certain ordering on clauses, subject to this condition. The orderings on interpretations and clauses guarantee fairness and therefore completeness of $OSHL_{specific}$.

In particular, $OSHL_{specific}$ orders clauses by an ordering $>_c$ such that for every ground clause C there are only finitely many ground clauses D such that $C >_c D$. This ordering satisfies the following property: If C_1 and C_2 are clauses then $(at(C_1) \neq at(C_2)) \equiv (C_1 >_c C_2 \vee C_2 >_c C_1)$. Thus only clauses with different sets of atoms are ordered in this ordering. Also, $<_c$ is defined by $C_1 <_c C_2$ iff $C_2 >_c C_1$. If $at(C_1) = at(C_2)$ then C_1 and C_2 are treated as identical by the ordering, so that for all clauses D, $C_1 >_c D$ iff $C_2 >_c D$ and $C_1 <_c D$ iff $C_2 <_c D$. $OSHL$ also orders atoms L and M by a well-founded total ordering $>_t$. This ordering is extended to interpretations as follows: Say that two interpretations I and J *agree on* atom L if $(I \models L) \equiv (J \models L)$, that is, both I and J satisfy L or I and J contradict L. Suppose the interpretation I_0 has been specified. Let

I and J be arbitrary distinct interpretations. Let L be the $>_t$-smallest atom such that I and J do not agree on L. Then $J >_t I$ if I and I_0 agree on L and $I >_t J$ otherwise. This ordering $>_t$ on interpretations is not well-founded if H_S is infinite, it turns out. The procedure $OSHL_{specific}$ is a version of $OSHL_{general}$ in which I_i is always chosen to be the $>_t$ minimal interpretation that satisfies T and D_i is chosen to be the $>_c$ minimal ground clause in H_S that contradicts I_i. Even though the ordering $>_t$ on interpretations is not well-founded, such a minimal interpretation I_i and minimal clause D_i always exist.

Our implementations of $OSHL$ are based on $OSHL_{specific}$. The current implementation is augmented by "U rules"[15] that permit a more intelligent choice of ground instances in many cases. From now on the term $OSHL$ refers either to $OSHL_{specific}$ or the current $OSHL$ implementation unless otherwise specified.

For purposes of analyzing complexity, it will be assumed that $>_c$ is defined so that $C_1 >_c C_2$ if $||C_1||_{lin} > ||C_2||_{lin}$, unless otherwise specified.

Proposition 4. *For $OSHL_{specific}$, there is a unique instance sequence.*

Proof. Each interpretation I_j is uniquely determined by minimality in the ordering $>_t$, it turns out. Also, the ordering $>_c$ on clauses is well-founded and always orders clauses having different sets of atoms, so there is always a unique minimal ground instance contradicting I_j.

This result means that $OSHL_{specific}$ is deterministic and there is no backtracking. In [2] it is shown that in the procedure $OSHL_{specific}$, the interpretations I_i all have a special form. Recall the following definition:

Definition 5. *If I is an interpretation and $L_1 \ldots L_m$ are literals no two of which are complementary, then $I[L_1 \ldots L_m]$ is the interpretation such that $I[L_1 \ldots L_m] \models L$ iff $at(L) \notin \{at(L_1), \ldots, at(L_m)\}$ and $I \models L$, or $L = L_j$ for some j. Thus the L_j are "exceptions" to I that define $I[L_1 \ldots L_m]$.*

Theorem 2. *[2] In the procedure $OSHL_{specific}$, all interpretations I_i are of the form $I_0[L_1 \ldots L_m]$ where for all i, $1 \le i \le m$, there exists $j < i$ such that $L_i \in D_j$.*

Literals L_i as in the theorem will be called *exception literals* or *eligible literals*.

Corollary 1. *Suppose D is a clause in the instance sequence of $OSHL_{specific}$ and L is a literal of D. Then either L is the complement of an exception literal or I_0 contradicts L.*

One advantage of semantics as utilized by $OSHL$ (that is, by $OSHL_{specific}$) is that a properly chosen semantics guarantees that only "relevant" instances D_i of clauses in S are chosen. In the following definition, and from now on, T refers to a subset of S and not the set of D_i as before.

Definition 6. *Suppose S is a set of clauses and T is a subset of S consisting of clauses from the negation of the particular theorem, so that $S - T$ consists* *of general axioms and is satisfiable. Then the set R of* relevant instances *of the clauses in S is the smallest subset of H_S satisfying the following properties:*

1. All ground instances of clauses in T are in R.

2. If D_1 and D_2 are two clauses in H_S, and L_1 and L_2 are literals in D_1 and D_2, respectively, and L_1 and L_2 are complementary, and D_1 is in R, then D_2 is in R.

Note that R depends on both S and T.

The idea here is that clauses containing complementary literals are related to each other. Thus a relevant clause is either part of the particular theorem T, or related to a clause in T, or related to a clause that is related to a clause in T, et cetera. Relevance is especially important for very large clause sets.

If the initial model I_0 is a model of $S-T$, then the instance sequence generated by $OSHL$ (that is, $OSHL_{specific}$) consists entirely of relevant instances [2]. The reason for this is that any clause D_i that contradicts I_0 is relevant by definition. Other clauses D_i contain literals that are complementary to an exception literal from a previously chosen clause D_j, so such clauses D_i are also relevant.

However, this relevance property is not true of $OSHL_{general}$, and it is not true of $OSHL_{specific}$ if I_0 is not chosen in this way. This is one evidence of the influence of semantics and of the importance of choosing an appropriate semantics.

It is possible[20] to formulate $OSHL$ as a set of rules on "ascending sequences" of ground clauses. These rules can be viewed as constructing an infinite semantic tree.

3   Complexity

The asymptotic time complexity of a theorem prover is a useful measure of its performance. This measure helps in understanding the comparative performance of $OSHL$ and resolution. For this purpose, the complexity of $OSHL$ without semantics, that is, with a trivial semantics, is compared to the complexity of resolution. It turns out that with a trivial semantics, for some problems $OSHL$ is two exponentials slower than resolution. However, on many practical problems, this slowdown is not observed. A modification of $OSHL$ without semantics reduces the complexity handicap by one exponential. The question remaining is whether semantics can overcome the resulting single exponential complexity handicap. There is some evidence in the affirmative.

Consider first the simple case where $S = \{\{L\}, \{\neg M\}\}$ consists of two unit clauses, L and $\neg M$ are literals, and L and M are unifiable. For this clause set, a single resolution produces the empty clause. If $OSHL$ is run with a *positive* semantics that interprets all atoms to **true** or a *negative* semantics that interprets all atoms to **false** this problem can be much harder because $OSHL$ must generate a common ground instance G of L and M and this ground instance can be exponential in size compared to L and M. Because the ordering $>_c$ on clauses is by linear size, $OSHL$ would have to enumerate all ground instances of size less than G, which is a double exponential number, before generating G. Resolution requires only a time polynomial in the lengths of L and M to obtain the proof.

Now, the complexity of *OSHL* on this example can be reduced by one exponential by representing terms as directed acyclic graphs (dags) in which common subterms are represented only once. Recall that $||t||_{dag}$ is the dag complexity of t, namely, the number of distinct subterms of t, and $||t||_{lin}$ is the length of t when t is written out as a linear sequence of symbols. These size measures are defined for literals and clauses in a similar way. The dag representation of a term can be smaller than the linear representation by an exponential amount. In fact, unification only increases dag complexity by a linear amount, it turns out, so the dag complexity of G is proportional to the sum of that of L and M. Suppose $OSHL_{specific}$ is implemented with $>_c$ defined by $C_1 >_c C_2$ if $||C_1||_{dag} >_c ||C_2||_{dag}$ rather than the more usual definition $C_1 >_c C_2$ if $||C_1||_{lin} >_c ||C_2||_{lin}$. (On clauses of the same size but with different sets of atoms, $>_c$ must be defined in some other way.) Then *OSHL* only has to enumerate all ground literals whose dag complexity is less than or equal to $||G||_{dag}$ in order to obtain a proof. How many literals are there in all to enumerate? Suppose that dags are represented as linear sequences of function and constant symbols containing also integer pointers to other symbols in the sequence, the integer i being a pointer to the i-th symbol in the sequence. Such a data structure represents dags efficiently because common subterms need only be represented once, with other occurrences represented by pointers. Then a sequence of length n can only have pointers bounded by n with a fixed number c of other function and constant symbols, so there are $c + n$ choices for each element in all, and at most $(c + n)^n$ or $O(2^{n \log n})$ such sequences of length n, which is single exponential in n. Even adding in the number of sequences of length less than n, the total complexity is still single exponential.

Thus this dag representation yields one exponential of improvement in the complexity of *OSHL*, but *OSHL* is still an exponential slower than resolution on this example. Such an analysis on large terms is reasonable because large terms do arise during theorem proving; see [21] for a natural example where literals of size 2,940 arise by unification during theorem proving.

To get better performance from *OSHL* it is necessary to use semantics, that is, to choose I_0 carefully. The speedup that can be obtained in this way will be considered next.

4   Semantics

Gelernter [14] obtained a significant increase in power in his geometry theorem prover using semantics. Gelernter's prover drew diagrams of theorems in geometry. By examining these diagrams, the prover was able to discard certain conjectures as false and thereby not waste effort attempting to prove them. His prover essentially applied to Horn clause problems. Since Gelernter's work, the application of semantics to first-order theorem provers has been comparatively neglected, despite the importance of diagrams and semantics to humans in proving theorems. The goal of *OSHL* is to make use of semantics in a similar way to

Gelernter's prover for general first-order Horn clause problems, not necessarily about geometry, and also to generalize this use of semantics to non-Horn clauses.

In order to compare the performance of *OSHL* and resolution or unification in a formal way, it is helpful to approximate the set of instances generated by resolution proofs. This is done as follows, assuming that all clauses in S have disjoint sets of variables:

Definition 7. *Suppose $C = \{L_1, \ldots, L_m\}$ is a clause in S. Let $Unif(C)$ be $\{C\Theta : $ there exist clauses $C_1 \ldots C_n \in S$ and literals $M_1, \ldots M_n$ such that the complement of M_i is in C_i for all i and Θ is a simultaneous most general unifier of L_i and $M_i \rho_i$ for all i, where ρ_i are renamings of variables of M_i such that for all i, L_i and M_i have no common variables, and for all $i \neq j$, M_i and M_j have no common variables$\}$. Let $Unif(S)$ be $\{Unif(C) : C \in S\}$.*

The idea is that if a clause C appears in a resolution refutation, then each literal of C has to participate in a resolution at some point, and thus must unify with the complement of a literal in some other clause. $Unif(S)$ represents the set of instances C' of clauses in S obtained by unification of all literals of C' with literals of other clauses in S. These instances C' correspond, roughly speaking, to instances of clauses that can appear in resolution proofs. In fact, they are instances obtained by a sequence of resolutions involving clauses C of S, but without deleting the literals of C. The set $Unif(S)$ therefore represents instances of clauses in S obtained by the unifications that might appear in a resolution proof. Note that if S' is a minimal unsatisfiable set of ground instances of S, then all elements of S' are instances of clauses in $Unif(S)$.

Definition 8. *If S is a set of clauses and I is an interpretation then $Inst_I(S)$ is the set of clauses appearing in the instance sequence of OSHL with initial semantics I.*

It is of interest to know the relationship between $Unif(S)$ and $Inst_I(S)$. In particular, for which I does $Inst_I(S)$ consist entirely of clauses that are all instances of clauses in $Unif(S)$? The analysis contained here has not previously appeared in the literature.

4.1   Two Complementary Literals

The case of two complementary unit clauses is easiest to analyze. Recall the behavior of *OSHL* in this case; with a trivial *positive* or *negative* semantics, the performance of *OSHL* is worse than resolution by one or two exponentials. However, a better choice of semantics can lead to a significant speedup for *OSHL*.

Theorem 3. *Suppose $S = \{\{L\}, \{\neg M\}\}$ consists of two unit clauses $\{L\}$ and $\{\neg M\}$ where L and M are atoms and L and M are unifiable. Let I_0 be a model of L that is minimal in the ordering $\leq_{pos}$ subject to this condition. That is, for atoms A over L(P,F,X), $I_0 \models A$ iff A is a ground instance of L. Then for all D in $Inst_{I_0}(S)$ there is a clause D' in $Unif(S)$ such that D is an instance of D'.*

Proof. Let $D_0, D_1, D_2 \ldots$ be the instance sequence for *OSHL* with initial interpretation I_0 and set S of input clauses. Then D_0 is a ground instance of a clause in S such that D_0 is not satisfied by I_0. For convenience assume that L and M have no common variables. Because I_0 satisfies L, D_0 cannot be an instance of $\{L\}$, so D_0 must be an instance of $\{\neg M\}$. Because $\neg M$ is negative, all ground instances of $\neg M$ are negative literals, but I_0 satisfies all negative literals except those that are instances of L since I_0 is a minimal model of L. Because I_0 does not satisfy D_0, D_0 must be an instance of $\{\neg L\}$. Now D_0 is already an instance of $\{\neg M\}$, so D_0 is an instance of $\neg M \; mgu(L, M)$. In fact, because the ordering $>_c$ is by linear size, D_0 is a minimal (linear) size instance of $\neg M \; mgu(L, M)$. Among clauses having the same size as D_0, one of them, namely D_0, is the smallest in the ordering $>_c$. The clause $\neg M \; mgu(L, M)$ or a variant of it is in *Unif*(S) and D_0 is an instance of this clause.

Suppose $D_0 = \{\neg M'\}$. The clause D_1 must be a $>_c$ minimal ground instance of a clause in S contradicting the interpretation $I_1 = I_0[\neg M']$. D_1 is either another instance of $\{\neg M\}$ or an instance of $\{L\}$. The clause $\{M'\}$ is an instance of $\{L\}$ that contradicts I_1 and will be chosen as D_1 unless some other instance of L or $\neg M$ contradicting I_1 is smaller. However, no other equally small ground instance of a clause in S contradicts I_1 because it either contradicts I_0, and D_0 is the minimal instance of a clause in S contradicting I_0, or it contradicts $\neg M'$, and $\{M'\}$ is the minimal instance of a clause in S contradicting $\neg M'$.

Thus D_1 is $\{M'\}$, which is an instance of $\{L\}$. Also, D_1 is an instance of $L \; mgu(L, M)$, and either this clause or a variant of it is in *Unif*(S). Because D_0 and D_1 are contradictory, $\{D_0, D_1\}$ is unsatisfiable and *OSHL* will stop after generating D_1. Thus all clauses in the instance sequence are instances of clauses in *Unif*(S). $\quad\blacksquare$

The use of semantics with *OSHL* in this case eliminates the exponential or double exponential gap in complexity compared to resolution, regardless of whether the clause ordering is based on a linear or dag complexity measure.

4.2   Horn Problems

The preceding result shows that with an appropriate semantics, *OSHL* is implicitly performing unifications even though it works entirely at the ground level and never explicitly unifies non-ground literals. This result will be extended in several ways, beginning with an extension to Horn sets. Recall the ordering $\leq_{pos}$ on interpretations defined by $I \leq_{pos} J$ if for all atoms A, if $I \models A$ then $J \models A$. If S is a set of Horn clauses, define the *axioms* of S to be the clauses of S containing a positive literal, and possibly some negative literals. Thus the axioms of S are all clauses other than the all-negative clauses of S.

Now, for Horn sets S, each logical consequence of the axioms of S is an instance of a clause derivable by resolution. Also, the positive literal, if any, of D must be the complement of an exception literal, because for Horn sets with axioms defined in this way the exception literals will always be negative and all the negative literals of D must be false in I_0. From these facts it easily follows that for all elements D of the instance sequence there is a clause D' in $Unif(S)$ such that D is an instance of D'. This implies the following result:

Theorem 4. *Suppose that S is an unsatisfiable set of Horn clauses and I_0 is a ground decidable $\leq_{pos}$ minimal model of the axioms of S. Then for all clauses D in the instance sequence of S there is a clause D' in $Unif(S)$ such that D is an instance of D'.*

Proof. Note that all positive literals that are true in I_0 are logical consequences of the axioms of S. It was shown[2] that if S is an unsatisfiable Horn set and I_0 is a $\leq_{pos}$ minimal model of the axioms of S then all clauses D in the instance sequence of $OSHL$ have the following property: For all negative literals $\neg L$ in D, L is a logical consequence of the axioms of S, and the positive literal L in D, if it exists, is also a logical consequence of the axioms of S.

This can be seen as follows: Let D_0 be the first instance chosen by $OSHL$. The complements of negative literals in D_0 must be logical consequences of the axioms of S, because I_0 satisfies all other negative literals. Therefore the positive literal of D_0, if any, must also be a logical consequence of the axioms of S. Therefore this positive literal of D_0 is satisfied by I_0, which cannot be. So D_0 must be an all-negative clauses, and all exception literals immediately after D_0 is chosen are negative literals. (In fact, there will be only one exception literal then.) The complements of negative literals of D_1 must also be consequences of the axioms of S, because they are false in I_1 and these negative literals cannot be the complements of negative exception literals. The positive literal, if any, of D_1 is also a consequence of the axioms of S, and is therefore satisfied by I_0, so it must be the complement of an exception literal. After D_1 is chosen, all exception literals will still be negative. Continuing in this way, for all clauses D_i in the instance sequence, the complements of the negative literals of D_i will be consequences of the axioms of S and the positive literal will be the complement of an exception literal.

Suppose $\neg L$ is a negative literal of D_i. Because the complements of negative literals of D_i are consequences of the axioms of S, L is a consequence of the axioms of S and is therefore an instance of a literal derivable from the axioms of S by resolution. Also, the positive literal of D_i, if any, is the complement of an exception literal. Thus all the literals of D_i are unifiable with the complements of literals in other clauses of S, so D_i is an instance of a clause in $Unif(S)$.

However, it is easy to construct examples where $Unif(S)$ contains clauses that do not have any instances in $Inst_I(S)$. This seems to give evidence that for Horn sets, $OSHL$ is in some sense superior to resolution. But this argument does not take into account that $OSHL$ needs semantics, while resolution does not. This also does not take into account that clauses generated by resolution can be more general than clauses in $Inst_I(S)$, so there may be fewer of them altogether. On the other hand, $OSHL$ generates clauses in order of size, that is, a clause minimal in the ordering $>_c$ is found each time. This will tend to make the instances found by $OSHL$ small and may reduce their number. Another issue is that in practice the interpretations used for $OSHL$ may not be minimal models of the axioms of S.

Instead, the semantics will probably be obtained from general mathematical knowledge of the properties of the axioms. In such cases one hopes that the power of the semantics approximates the power obtained by a minimal model, but this may not always be so.

If S is an unsatisfiable Horn set and I_0 is as above, and I_0 is ground decidable, then it is not necessary to construct a proof at all. Let T be the set of all-negative clauses of S; then $S - T$ is the axioms of S and I_0 models $S - T$. Then if there is a ground instance D of a clause in T such that D is false in I_0, one knows that S is unsatisfiable without constructing a proof, because D must be an all-negative clause, and the complements of all literals in D must be logical consequences of the axioms of S. Thus we have the following modified $OSHL$ procedure in this case:

procedure $OSHL_{Horn}(S,T)$
  for $i = 0$ **step** 1 **until** ∞ **do**
    pick a new ground instance D of a clause in T, if such exists;
    if no such instance exists then return "satisfiable"
    if D contradicts I_0 then return "unsatisfiable"
  od;
  end $OSHL_{Horn}$;

It may be possible to find such ground instances D faster than by a brute force search. Of course, such instances can be enumerated by a theorem prover generating all unit consequences of $S - T$, and enumeration is all that is required for $OSHL_{Horn}$. However, there may be faster ways than this to find them.

Definition 9. *A semantic instantiation procedure for an interpretation I is a procedure which, given a clause C, returns a ground instance D of C such that $I \not\models D$, if such exists, else loops. A semantic instantiation test for I, given C, returns "true" if such a ground instance D exists, and "false" otherwise.*

Note that any ground decidable interpretation has a semantic instantiation procedure based on exhaustive enumeration. If I_0 has a semantic instantiation procedure more efficient than this, then this procedure can be used in $OSHL_{Horn}$ to reduce the search; in fact, $OSHL_{Horn}$ could simply call such a procedure on all clauses of T and return "unsatisfiable" if the semantic instantiation procedure for I_0 halts for some C in T. If there is a semantic instantiation test for I_0, then by calling it on all clauses in T one obtains a procedure to decide whether S is unsatisfiable. If a clause C is non-ground, then a semantic instantiation test for I can be used to find all ground instances of C that contradict I by creating a set of possibly non-ground instances of C, applying the test to them, and further processing those that are non-ground and pass the test.

If S is not a Horn set but I_0 is chosen as an $\leq_{pos}$-minimal model of a set H of Horn clauses that is a subset of S, and D is a ground instance in the instance sequence of S, then any negative literals of D that contradict I_0 can simply be deleted from D, because their complements are logical consequences of H. Detecting such literals is possible because I_0 is ground decidable. In this way one can combine computation and theorem proving in the general case.

4.3   Unique Model

It is possible to generalize the above results.

Definition 10. *A satisfiable set S of clauses has a* unique Herbrand model *if there is only one Herbrand interpretation that satisfies S.*

Theorem 5. *Suppose S is an unsatisfiable set of clauses and T is a subset of S. Suppose $S - T$ has a unique Herbrand model and this model is ground decidable. If I_0 is chosen as this unique Herbrand model of $S - T$, then for all elements D of $Inst_{I_0}(S)$ there is a clause D' in $Unif(S)$ such that D is an instance of D'.*

Proof. Suppose D_i is an arbitrary clause in the instance sequence for S, and L is a literal in D_i. By Corollary 1, either L is the complement of an exception literal or I_0 contradicts L. (a) If L is the complement of an exception literal, then $\neg L$ is a member of D_j for some $j < i$, and D_j is an instance of a clause in S. (b) Suppose I_0 contradicts L. Then $(S - T) \cup \{L\}$ is unsatisfiable because I_0 is the only model of $S - T$ and I_0 does not satisfy L. Therefore there is a finite unsatisfiable set G of ground instances of $(S - T) \cup \{L\}$, by Herbrand's theorem. Some clause D in G must contain the literal $\neg L$; if not then $G - \{L\}$ would be unsatisfiable, which contradicts the fact that $S - T$ is satisfiable. Thus L unifies with the complement of a literal in some clause in $S - T$. In both cases (a) and (b), L is the complement of a literal in an instance of a clause of S. This is true for all literals L in D_i, so D_i is an instance of a clause in $Unif(S)$.

This gives another condition under which semantics in some sense simulates unification for first-order theorem proving. However, if there is a unique Herbrand model, then it is not necessary to find the proof at all. After the first ground instance of T contradicting I_0 is found, one knows by the fact that I_0 is the unique Herbrand model of $S - T$, and is ground decidable, that S is unsatisfiable. This yields the following modified *OSHL* procedure in this case, where I_0 is the unique Herbrand model of $S - T$:

    procedure $OSHL_{unique}(S,T)$
      for $i = 0$ **step** 1 **until** ∞ **do**
        pick a new ground instance D of a clause in T, if such exists;
        if no such instance exists then return "satisfiable"
        if D contradicts I_0 then return "unsatisfiable"
      od;
    end $OSHL_{unique}$;

This procedure is actually identical to $OSHL_{Horn}$. As before, $OSHL_{unique}$ can be implemented by calling a semantic instantiation procedure for I_0, if one exists, and returning "unsatisfiable" if the procedure halts on some clause of T. If there is a semantic instantiation test for I_0, then one obtains a procedure to decide whether S is unsatisfiable by calling the test on all clauses of T.

    There is an optimization that can be applied to *OSHL* for clause sets having a unique Herbrand model. Let $D_0 = \{L_1 \ldots L_n\}$ be a minimal size ground instance of a clause of T that is falsified by I_0. Then $I_0 \not\models L_i$ for all i, $1 \leq i \leq n$. Also, $(S - T) \cup \{L_i\}$ is unsatisfiable because I_0 is the only model of $S - T$ and I_0 does not satisfy L_i. Therefore one can prove separately for each literal L_i that $(S - T) \cup \{L_i\}$ is unsatisfiable, which should be easier than proving that S is unsatisfiable, because this is in effect splitting up the original problem into a number of easier problems. Thus for the separate problems, one has $D_0 = \{L_i\}$ for various i. Consider the next clause D_1 in the instance sequence for one such subproblem. The clause D_1 contradicts $I_0[L_i]$. If D_1 contradicts I_0, then a similar technique can be applied to split the subproblem into simpler problems. Otherwise, D_1 contains the literal $\{\neg L_i\}$. Then $D_1 - \{\neg L_i\}$ contradicts I_0, which is the only model of $S - T$. Therefore the set of clauses $(S - T) \cup (D_1 - \{\neg L_i\})$ is unsatisfiable, but the clause $(D_1 - \{\neg L_i\})$ is derivable from D_1 and the unit clause $\{L_i\}$ by ground unit resolution. Instead of refuting the original subproblem, it is then only necessary to refute the clause set $(S - T) \cup (D_1 - \{\neg L_i\})$. Because the clause $(D_1 - \{\neg L_i\})$ contradicts I_0, this clause can again be split into unit clauses. This process can be continued. Thus considerable simplification of the problem can be obtained if $S - T$ has a unique Herbrand model.

It may be that $S - T$ does not have a unique Herbrand model, but part of the model is unique, that is, it may be known that many ground literals L are logical consequences of $S - T$. In this case, whenever these ground literals L or their complements appear in a proof, the proof attempt can be simplified by proving separately that L is a consequence of $S - T$ and then assuming L and proving the rest of the theorem. Some of these proofs that L is a consequence of $S - T$ may only require a subset of $S - T$ that has a unique Herbrand model, and then these proofs can be done by the procedure $OSHL_{unique}$, thus combining deduction and computation.

4.4   General Case

What if $S - T$ is non-Horn and does not have a unique Herbrand model? What can one say then about the advantage of semantics? In this case it is still possible to obtain a partial result along the lines of Theorem 4. For this, a more restricted version of $Unif(S)$ is necessary.

Definition 11. *Suppose C is a clause in S and $\{L_1, \ldots, L_m\}$ are the negative literals in C. Let $Unif^{neg}(C)$ be $\{C\Theta$: there exist clauses $C_1 \ldots C_n$ in S and literals $M_1, \ldots M_n$ such that the complement of M_i is in C_i for all i, and Θ is a simultaneous most general unifier of L_i and $M_i \rho_i$ for all i where ρ_i are renamings of variables of M_i such that for all i, L_i and M_i have no common variables, and for all $i \neq j$, M_i and M_j have no common variables\}$. Let $Unif^{neg}(S)$ be $\{Unif^{neg}(C) : C \in S\}$.*

Recall that the *axioms* of a Horn set H are the clauses of H having a positive literal.

Theorem 6. *Suppose S is an unsatisfiable set of clauses and T is a subset of S. Suppose $S - T$ is satisfiable. Let H be a set of Horn clauses such that for all C*

in H, there is a clause C' in $S - T$ such that C is a subset of C'. If I_0 is chosen as a $\leq_{pos}$ minimal model of the axioms of H, and I_0 is ground decidable, then for all elements D of $Inst_{I_0}(S)$ there is a clause D' in $Unif^{neg}(S)$ such that D is an instance of D'.

Proof. Suppose D_i is an arbitrary clause in the instance sequence for S and L is a negative literal in D_i. By Corollary 1, either L is the complement of an exception literal or I_0 contradicts L. If L is the complement of an exception literal, then $\neg L$ is a member of D_j for some $j < i$, and D_j is an instance of a clause in S. Suppose I_0 contradicts L. Then $\neg L_i$ is a positive literal satisfied by I_0. Because I_0 is a minimal model of H, $\neg L$ must appear in some instance of a clause in H and therefore $\neg L$ appears in some instance of a clause in S. In either case, L is the complement of a literal in an instance of a clause of S. This is true for all negative literals L in D_i, so D_i is an instance of a clause in $Unif^{neg}(S)$.

In particular, H can be chosen as a set of clauses containing only negative literals; in this case, H has no axioms so I_0 is the model making all the positive literals false. It is also possible to choose H having more positive literals than this. For general clause sets, it may be desirable to choose I_0 to be a minimal model of H where H is chosen so that for each C in $S - T$ there is a clause C' in H containing all the negative literals of C and one of the positive literals, if any, of C because this choice of H approximates S as closely as possible. A problem with this approach is that I_0 only models the clauses of $S - T$ having at least one positive literal. Thus I_0 does not satisfy the negative clauses of S, and this weakens the relevance property of $OSHL$; the instances D_i generated by $OSHL$ need not be related to T at all, but may be related to one of the negative clauses of $S - T$. The following result overcomes this objection.

Theorem 7. *Suppose S is an unsatisfiable set of clauses and T is a subset of S. Suppose $S - T$ is satisfiable. Let I_0 be a model of $S - T$ that is $\leq_{pos}$ minimal; that is, there does not exist any other model of $S - T$ that is strictly smaller than I_0 in the ordering $\leq_{pos}$. Suppose I_0 is ground decidable. Then for all elements D of $Inst_{I_0}(S)$ there is a clause D' in $Unif^{neg}(S)$ such that D is an instance of D'.*

Proof. If L is a positive ground literal satisfied by I_0, then L is an instance of a literal appearing in a clause C of $S - T$. For, consider the model I' that is identical to I_0 but fails to satisfy L. This model is strictly smaller than I_0 in the ordering $\leq_{pos}$. Because I_0 is minimal in this ordering, I' must not be a model of $S - T$, so there is some ground instance C' of a clause of $S - T$ that is not satisfied by I'. The clause C' is satisfied by I_0 because I_0 is a model of $S - T$. Because these two models only differ in their interpretation of L, C' must contain L.

Now, consider a negative literal M that appears in a clause D_i in the instance sequence of $OSHL$. Either I_0 contradicts M or M is the complement of an exception literal, by Corollary 1. If I_0 contradicts M then I_0 satisfies $\neg M$ which is a positive literal, so $\neg M$ is a member of an instance of some clause of $S - T$ as shown above. If M is the complement of an exception literal $\neg M$ then $\neg M$

is a member of a clause of S previously chosen in the instance sequence. In all cases, M is the complement of a literal contained in some ground instance of a clause of S. Because this is true for all such literals M, D_i is an instance of some clause in $Unif^{neg}(S)$.

This theorem suggests that $\leq_{pos}$ minimal models may be good choices for the semantics of $OSHL$ for non-Horn clauses. A possible problem with this choice of semantics is that such models may be difficult to construct.

In general, for clause sets without unique Herbrand models, it is necessary to choose a model. For this, it is possible to give some guidelines and some theoretical justification for which models should work best as semantics for $OSHL$. Many sets of clauses are nearly Horn sets, which means that the clauses have many negative literals and few positive literals. In this case, it is reasonable to choose a semantics that makes as many positive literals false as possible, because this semantics maximizes the probability that a negative literal will be true. The clauses D_i are chosen to be false in the models I_i, which implies that all literals of D_i are false in I_i. If D_i has many negative literals, then the probability that I_i will contradict D_i is minimized by choosing I_i to satisfy as many negative literals as possible. This will minimize the number of clauses D_i that can be chosen, and in this way will reduce the search space.

There is another way in which semantics can be used in $OSHL$. If one has many models of $S-T$, then clauses or subsets of clauses that are true in all these models can be conjectured to be true and a proof attempt can be performed on them. If a proof is found, then these clauses may be helpful to simplify the original proof.

5 Lifting $OSHL$

Because $OSHL$ works at the ground level, it is natural to ask if there is a method of lifting $OSHL$ to the non-ground level. One problem with this is the use of semantics; a non-ground version of $OSHL$ would need a procedure that, given a clause C, would produce possibly non-ground instances $C\Theta$ of C such that all ground instances of $C\Theta$ contradict the semantics I. Another problem is that $OSHL$ needs to know whether literals are identical or complementary to exception literals when deciding whether D_i contradicts I_i; this can be difficult to determine for non-ground literals, because some of their instances may be identical and some of them may not be. Thus some method of constraint handling or disunification would be needed.

In particular, for evaluating semantics on non-ground literals, one needs to lift the semantic instantiation procedure of Definition 9 for interpretations I to the non-ground level, obtaining a procedure which, given a clause C, enumerates a set X of (possibly non ground) instances $C\Theta$ of C such that I contradicts all ground instances of $C\Theta$, and such if D is a ground instance of C false in I, then D is an instance of some element of X. In this way, a non-ground clause can represent all of its ground instances, and it will be known that I contradicts all of them. One would hope that such a procedure exists that is more efficient than exhaustive enumeration of ground instances of C, which can always be done if I is ground decidable. Semantic instantiation appears to be closely related to constraints, equational unification, and possibly to Stickel's theory unification [22]. Although many details remain to be worked out, it may be possible to use this approach to extend *OSHL* to the non-ground level. This idea may also permit FDPLL, DCTP, and other propositional style provers to utilize nontrivial semantics.

Note that this use of semantic instantiation does not make it possible to remove any axioms, it just helps *OSHL* to instantiate at the non-ground level. A problem with this approach is that some interpretations may not have an efficient lifting of the semantic instantiation procedure. Thus there is an interest in seeing how well *OSHL* can perform at the ground level.

6   Implementation

OSHL was implemented by Zhu [2] but this implementation did not entirely conform to the method as described in the paper. A more faithful implementation was done by Das [15] and tested. This implementation is capable of using any ground decidable semantics, as was Zhu's. Also, if the set T of ground instances D_i is found to be satisfiable, then in the current implementation an additional test is performed on each satisfying interpretation I of the atoms appearing in T_i to see if additional intelligently generated ground instances of S contradict I. The implementation was tested on the TPTP problem set, version 2.5.0. The basic *OSHL* method obtained only 228 of the TPTP problems [16, 23] in 30 seconds with a trivial (all positive or all negative) semantics. However, with the addition of U rules [15] and various optimizations, the prover was able to get 1027 of the TPTP problems in 30 seconds with a trivial semantics. It is interesting that *OSHL* could have this level of performance even with a trivial semantics, working at the ground level, and without any special methods for equality or any efficient data structures for representing terms and performing unifications.

This implementation was compared with Otter [24] using the "auto" flag. In 30 seconds, Otter obtained 1697 of the TPTP problems. Also, the number of inferences used by *OSHL* and Otter was compared on TPTP problems for which both provers found proofs. It turned out that *OSHL* obtained more proofs than Otter in a given number of inferences on non-Horn clause sets, but Otter obtained more proofs in a given number of inferences on Horn sets. For Otter, each resolution or hyper-resolution was counted as an inference, and for *OSHL*, each generation of an instance of a clause or a resolution of two clauses, was counted. Also, *OSHL* actually outperformed Otter in terms of total proofs found on the groups FLD (field theory) and SET (set theory) of the TPTP problem set; both groups are highly non-Horn.

These results raise the possibility that *OSHL* with a more efficient implementation and natural semantics may outperform resolution and similar theorem proving methods such as model elimination on non-Horn sets. The results also suggest that different strategies should be used on Horn and non-Horn clause sets; hyper-resolution actually works very well on Horn sets. In fact, it would be helpful to have a hybrid strategy that operates differently on the Horn part of a problem than on the non-Horn part. However, with a natural semantics, *OSHL* might perform much better on Horn problems. There are other propositional style provers such as DCTP[4], FDPLL[3], model evolution[5], Equinox[25], and iProver[10] that obtain more proofs than *OSHL* with a trivial semantics on the TPTP problem set. Equinox is actually very similar in philosophy to *OSHL*, and operates at the ground level, but has a better equality mechanism and performs respectably well in the CASC competitions[26]. In fact, the performance of Vampire[27] on the FOF division improved dramatically between 2009 and 2010 in the CASC competition, possibly because in 2010 Vampire added some special facilities for handling ground clauses. Because *OSHL* operates at the ground level, it can use any ground decidable semantics. This paper attempts to compare the use of such sophisticated semantics with the use of unification.

7 Examples of Natural Semantics in *OSHL*

OSHL combines efficient propositional proof methods and semantic guidance during proof search. The semantics provides the prover with guidance specific to the problem. The *OSHL* algorithm was originally intended to be used only in conjunction with semantic guidance to avoid blind enumeration. This accounts for the relatively poor performance of the *OSHL* strategy using trivial semantics. In general, natural semantics – that is, a semantics that corresponds to the mathematical or physical meaning of the symbols and satisfies all the axioms – could help the proof search by providing to the automated theorem prover the same kind of information that is available to a human mathematician. Standard semantics are known for many domains, and it seems reasonable to allow the prover to take advantage of this knowledge. The following results demonstrate that semantics can indeed be used to better guide instance generation. We measure the search space, i.e., the number of clauses generated, and execution times to show that the performance of *OSHL* can be improved with the use of non-trivial semantics.

7.1 An Example: "Who Killed Aunt Agatha?"

We give an example of the use of semantics on the problem PUZ001-2 from the PUZ (puzzles) domain of the TPTP problems. This problem has 15 clauses, three of which are non-Horn, and five involving equality. This problem is easy for many current theorem provers, which solve it with a small number of inferences. Even Otter 3.3 solved it in half a second, generating 34 clauses. This problem is harder for *OSHL* because *OSHL* does not have special methods for equality. However, on this example, *OSHL* performs considerably better with a natural semantics than without.

The logic puzzle, stated in English, is as follows:

Someone who lives in Dreadbury Mansion killed Aunt Agatha. Agatha, the butler, and Charles live in Dreadbury Mansion, and are the only people who live therein. A killer always hates his victim, and is never richer than his victim. Charles hates no one that Aunt Agatha hates. Agatha hates everyone except the butler. The butler hates everyone not richer than Aunt Agatha. The butler hates everyone Aunt Agatha hates. No one hates everyone. Agatha is not the butler. Therefore, Agatha killed herself.

The input consists of 26 clauses, with the equality axioms added, and 53 literals. The predicates in the problem are $equal(X,Y)$, $lives\_at\_dreadbury(X)$, $hates(X,Y)$, $richer(X,Y)$ and $killed\ (X,Y)$. The constants are $aunt\_agatha$, $butler$, $charles$ and $someone$; $everyone\_\ but\ (X)$ is a Skolem function that arises from the statement – No one hates everyone.

A human is able to reason about the puzzle and solve it, even without the use of formal logic. But if one were to present the same problem, replacing all the predicates, functions, and constants with names such as $pred_1$, $pred_2$, $func_1$, and so on, then it would become a lot more difficult for the human to solve. This is because a human is able to interpret the semantics of the problem in a certain way, which helps him or her solve the problem. For example, a human "knows" that there are only 3 persons and one of those 3 persons is the killer. This means that the domain of definition to consider in solving this problem should have 3 elements. A human also "knows" that a person can not be richer than himself/herself, and interprets the $richer(X,Y)$ predicate accordingly. However, with a purely syntactic formulation of the problem, such additional semantic information is lost, making it harder to solve the problem. Because an automated theorem prover lacks this kind of human "knowledge" of the problem, a human user can supply this extra information to the prover through a semantic model. The semantic model provides the prover with an initial interpretation that incorporates extra information that the human user knows about the problem.

In order to solve this problem, $OSHL$ was supplied with a non-trivial semantic model consisting of 3 elements. We did not provide a fully natural semantics. Some of the input clauses are not modeled by our initial semantics, which maps the $killed$ predicate such that Charles is the killer. Also, it may not be apparent to a human user how the function $everyone\_but$ (arising from Skolemization) should be interpreted. We mapped the function to be consistent with the mapping for the $hates$ predicate. The domain of definition $D = \{1, 2, 3\}$. The mappings of the constants, function, and predicates are as follows.

aunt_agatha $\mapsto 1$
butler $\mapsto 2$
charles $\mapsto 3$
someone $\mapsto 1$

everyone_but : $D \mapsto D$

                $1 \mapsto 2$

                $2 \mapsto 2$

                $3 \mapsto 3$

equal : $D \times D \mapsto$ {True, False}

            $(X, Y) \mapsto$ True, if $X = Y$

            $(X, Y) \mapsto$ False, otherwise

lives_at_dreadbury : $D \mapsto$ {True, False}

                $1 \mapsto$ True

                $2 \mapsto$ True

                $3 \mapsto$ True

hates : $D \times D \mapsto$ {True, False}

                $(1, 1) \mapsto$ True

                $(1, 2) \mapsto$ False

                $(1, 3) \mapsto$ True

                $(2, 1) \mapsto$ True

                $(2, 2) \mapsto$ False

                $(2, 3) \mapsto$ True

                $(3, 1) \mapsto$ False

                $(3, 2) \mapsto$ True

                $(3, 3) \mapsto$ False

richer : $D \times D \mapsto$ {True, False}

              $(1, 1) \mapsto$ False

              $(1, 2) \mapsto$ False

              $(1, 3) \mapsto$ True

              $(2, 1) \mapsto$ True

              $(2, 2) \mapsto$ False

              $(2, 3) \mapsto$ True

              $(3, 1) \mapsto$ False

              $(3, 2) \mapsto$ False

              $(3, 3) \mapsto$ False

killed : $D \times D \mapsto$ {True, False}

            $(X, Y) \mapsto$ True, if $X = 3$ and $Y = 1$.

            False, otherwise

With the non-trivial semantics described, *OSHL* found the proof in 5 minutes 49 seconds, generating 1795 clauses. On changing the described semantics to model Aunt Agatha as the killer, *OSHL* found the proof in 5 minutes 48 seconds, generating 1632 clauses. On changing the described semantics by using different mappings for the *hates* and the *richer* predicates, *OSHL* still obtained the proof in about 6 minutes. With an all-positive or all-negative semantics,

OSHL ran for over 3 hours generating more than 50,000 clauses, without finding a proof. Therefore, in this case, a user-specified semantics produces significant improvement in *OSHL* performance over a trivial semantics. Even a semantics that does not model all of the axioms and gives a false answer to the question "Who killed Aunt Agatha?" helps significantly. The version of *OSHL* used for this was *OSHL-U*[15], which has *U* rules added.

7.2 Semantics in Group Theory Problems

We also tested the use of user-specified semantics on some group theory (GRP) problems from TPTP. Table 1 shows the results obtained with *OSHL* using a non-trivial semantics compared to those with *OSHL* using trivial semantics and with Otter in the "auto" mode, on these problems. Cases when a prover timed out without generating a proof are marked with "fail" and the execution time allotted to the proof attempt is noted.

In mathematics, a group is a set, with a binary operation on elements of the set, such as multiplication or addition, satisfying certain axioms. We used a non-trivial natural semantics that models a finite group of size 4. The domain elements were mapped to the integers 0, 1, 2, 3 and the binary operation was addition modulo 4. The semantics chosen was suitable for all the problems in Table 1 except GRP008-1. These problems are theorems about identity and inverse functions in a group and have only Horn clauses; problem GRP008-1 is stated to be a theorem of "unknown meaning" and has one non-Horn clause. On some of the problems, use of this semantics gives the proof faster and with the generation of fewer clauses than using either of the trivial semantics. Use of the semantics also helps to obtain proofs of some problems that could not be proved with trivial semantics. Problems in GRP are mostly all Horn, so Otter exhibits good performance on these problems. However, there are a couple of problems proved by the semantics that even Otter, in the autonomous mode, could not prove.

We also tested non-natural semantics on some GRP problems. In these cases, the groups were sets of integers of size 2 ({0,1}) and 4 ({0,1,2,3}). However, the binary operation was selected to be such that the axioms of group theory are not all satisfied by the model. Table 2 shows the result of these tests. These indicate that even a non-natural semantics can perform better than trivial semantics on some problems.

We performed the experiments with natural semantics of larger sizes using groups of sizes 16, 24, and 40. The results were similar to those with groups of size 4. Using larger semantics, proofs of the same problems were found as with semantics of size 4 generating the same number of clauses in similar execution times. Adding more elements did not increase the information conveyed by the semantics; proofs of the same problem were not found any faster and no new proofs were found. At the same time, an increase in the number of terms did not result in more clauses being generated.

Table 1. Execution time and number of clauses generated with *OSHL* and a non-trivial natural semantics, with *OSHL* and trivial semantics (all-positive and all-negative), and with Otter in the "auto" mode. The number of clauses generated and the execution time in seconds are shown. 300+ (600+) means that the prover timed out in 300 (600) seconds without finding a proof.

Problem	Natural		All-pos		All-neg		Otter	
	gen.	time(sec)	gen.	time(sec)	gen.	time(sec)	gen.	time(sec)
GRP003-1	140	119.20	fail	300+	fail	300+	116	0.01
GRP004-1	53	28.00	fail	300+	fail	300+	129	0.00
GRP004-2	222	716.50	fail	300+	fail	300+	335	0.01
GRP007-1	17	0.38	18	1.99	58	3.8	85	0.01
GRP008-1	396	226.30	fail	600+	fail	600+	fail	600+
GRP017-1	241	16.05	fail	300+	fail	300+	210	0.02
GRP018-1	15	0.48	36	6.40	108	6.14	266	0.01
GRP019-1	14	0.24	39	7.90	fail	300+	267	0.01
GRP020-1	20	1.55	68	33.80	fail	300+	265	0.02
GRP021-1	18	0.87	45	5.55	fail	300+	264	0.01
GRP022-1	36	17.90	fail	600+	fail	600+	448	0.02
GRP023-1	16	0.50	15	0.33	fail	300+	79	0.01
GRP023-2	36	1.91	23	0.69	fail	300+	fail	300+

Table 2. Execution time and number of clauses generated with *OSHL* and a non-trivial non-natural semantics, with *OSHL* and trivial semantics (all-positive and all-negative), and with Otter in the "auto" mode. The domain size is given for the non-trivial semantics. The number of clauses generated and the execution time in seconds are shown. 300+ (600+) means that the prover timed out in 300 (600) seconds without finding a proof.

Problem	Non-natural			All-pos		All-neg		Otter	
	size	gen.	time(sec)	gen.	time(sec)	gen.	time(sec)	gen.	time(sec)
GRP005-1	2	6	0.02	6	0.02	6	0.02	57	0.02
GRP008-1	2	90	16.6	fail	600+	fail	600+	fail	600+
GRP018-1	2	21	0.97	36	6.40	108	6.14	266	0.01
GRP019-1	2	22	1.570	39	7.920	fail	300+	267	0.01
GRP034-3	4	25	2.242	44	4.183	84	10.185	141	0.01

Table 3. Timing of FOLPLAN and OTTER on a set of test examples. Times are in seconds. — means no proof in 1000 secs. Both programs are run on a SPARC-20 model 612.

	FOLPLAN	OTTER
blocksworld	12.7	—
briefcase	9.7	0.5
monkey	69.4	—
weather	0.7	0.4
pinball	1.2	0.5
maze	157.6	—

7.3 Planning Problems

Zhu's implementation of *OSHL*[2] was run on some planning problems[28]. This discussion is largely taken from that work. The application of *OSHL* to planning problems was done in a system called FOLPLAN. Input axioms were expressed in first-order clause format. For each problem an input semantics was given to approximate the reachability predicate of the planning problem. The semantics was expressed in PROLOG.

We illustrate the axiomatization used for planning problems with a simple example. It contains a car at location $l0$, and two gas stations at $l1$ and $l2$; these are individual constants. The variable S is a *situation variable*. There is a traffic light which is either green or red at any moment. The car can only go straight at the green light and can only turn right at the red right.[1] The problem is to show that the car can always get to a gas station. The axioms are listed in Figure 1. Figure 7.3 lists the set of unsatisfiable instances of the axioms in Figure 1.

$\neg canFillTank(car, S).$
$canFillTank(car, S) :- at(car, l1, S).$
$canFillTank(car, S) :- at(car, l2, S).$
$at(car, l1, drive(straight, S)) :-$
$\qquad at(car, l0, S), greenlight(S).$
$at(car, l2, drive(turn, S)) :-$
$\qquad at(car, l0, S), redlight(S).$
$greenlight(S) \lor redlight(S).$
$at(car, l0, s0).$

Fig. 1. Axioms for the traffic light example

1. $\neg canFillTank(car, drive(straight, s0)).$
2. $\neg canFillTank(car, drive(turn, s0)).$
3. $canFillTank(car, drive(straight, s0)) :-$
$\qquad at(car, l1, drive(straight, s0)).$
4. $canFillTank(car, drive(turn, s0)) :-$
$\qquad at(car, l2, drive(turn, s0)).$
5. $at(car, l1, drive(straight, s0)) :-$
$\qquad at(car, l0, s0), greenlight(s0).$
6. $at(car, l2, drive(turn, s0)) :-$
$\qquad at(car, l0, s0), redlight(s0).$
7. $greenlight(s0) \lor redlight(s0).$
8. $at(car, l0, s0).$

Fig. 2. An unsatisfiable set of instances for the traffic light example

We ran a number of well known examples such as blocks world, monkey and bananas, briefcase problems, et cetera. Some examples were also tested containing states with incomplete information. "weather" is the problem of finding a

---

[1] The car is not allowed to turn right at the green light.

path between two cities. Depending on the weather and the season, different paths are needed. "pinball" is the problem of showing a pinball will eventually fall into a pocket, where at every step, the ball might roll to two possible positions. "maze" describes an 8 by 8 maze where the state of some intersections is not completely known. Input semantics were manually generated by using approximate finite automata representations of the problems. Non-ground decision procedures were constructed based on breath-first traversal of the finite automata states. These procedures test if a non-ground clause has any instances that contradict the semantics; thus they are the same as the semantic instantiation test presented in Definition 9. Such tests can be used to find ground instances of a clause C that contradict the semantics, as indicated earlier. This helps the efficiency of *OSHL*. These planning problems are probably difficult to represent naturally using STRIPS[29, 30] and ADL[31, 32], neither of which allows disjunctive postconditions. Domain axioms are used to represent the commutativity of the connection between rooms in the maze problem and the monkey and bananas problem. In Table 3, the performance of our planner and that of OTTER, a well known resolution-based theorem prover, are listed. OTTER is slightly faster than FOLPLAN on the simpler problems due to its efficient implementation. FOLPLAN is faster on the more difficult examples. Its better performance can be attributed to the effective use of semantics to guide the search and the utilization of an efficient propositional procedure in *OSHL* to handle non-Horn clauses.

8   Discussion

The instantiation mechanism of *OSHL* has been compared to the instantiation produced by simultaneous unification of all the literals or all the negative literals of a clause with complementary literals in other clauses. An example is given to show that *OSHL* with a trivial semantics is two exponentials slower than resolution. With a modified clause ordering, this complexity handicap can be reduced to one exponential. However, with a better choice of the semantics, the performance of *OSHL* is improved relative to unification and resolution. For Horn sets or clause sets having a unique Herbrand model, if the semantics is chosen properly then *OSHL* will only generate instances that could have been generated by simultaneous unifications. For the general case, this property can only be guaranteed for simultaneous unification of the negative literals of a clause, and this also requires a proper choice of semantics. This gives some evidence that *OSHL* is capable of performing simultaneous unifications even though it works entirely at the ground level, and suggests that with an appropriate choice of semantics *OSHL* may have performance comparable to that of resolution and other first-order strategies using unification. This also gives some evidence of the value of semantic guidance for a theorem prover. There are some resolution strategies[33] that could theoretically be adapted to the use of semantics, and it would be interesting to study their properties as well.

For propositional calculus, especially for non-Horn clauses, DPLL[19] is generally understood to be much more efficient than resolution. *OSHL* can be viewed as an extension of DPLL to first-order logic. Therefore, if *OSHL* can overcome the disadvantage of not performing unification, it may also benefit from the efficiency of DPLL and have the potential to be superior to methods based on resolution. The results presented here give evidence that *OSHL* does in fact have much of the power of unification in its operation, posing the question whether *OSHL* can become more efficient than resolution for first-order clause sets, with a comparable implementation.

Some implementation results suggest that *OSHL* obtains more proofs with a comparable number of inferences than Otter does on non-Horn clause sets, and in many cases obtains proofs of the same theorem with many fewer inferences than Otter. This also suggests the possibility that *OSHL* might be superior to resolution if it were implemented with comparable efficiency.

The theoretical results presented in this paper assume a specially chosen "ideal" semantics. This semantics may be difficult to supply in many cases. Instead, a natural semantics based on common mathematical knowledge may be used. It remains to be seen how well *OSHL* with such a semantics will perform, but one would expect that the performance of such natural semantics will improve as it more closely approximates the ideal semantics required by the previously stated theorems. Some examples have been given to show how the performance of *OSHL* improves with a natural semantics. The improvement should be more marked for much larger clause sets, in which relevance to the theorem will be much more important.

In addition to the ability to simulate unification, another feature of semantics suggests that the performance of *OSHL* may be superior to that of resolution and related methods. This is the fact that a model of a set $S - T$ of clauses is a global property that depends on all the clauses in the set. On the other hand, unification as performed in resolution is a local property that only depends on the two clauses being resolved. Because semantics is a global property, it may give superior performance. One way to see this is that *OSHL* with semantics not only essentially performs a unification between literals of C and complementary literals of other clauses C_i, it also requires that these clauses C_i permit unifications of their literals with complementary literals of yet other clauses, et cetera. Thus the instances generated by *OSHL* with semantics entail a multitude of unifications among many clauses of S.

In order to better assess the potential of *OSHL* with semantics it will be necessary to obtain a much more efficient implementation in a language such as C or C++, and also implement special methods for equality. The task of implementing *OSHL* is not as easy as it may seem, because choosing a clause C contradicting I such that C is minimal in the ordering $>_c$ is not a trivial task. Thus a more efficient implementation of *OSHL* may entail more work than it appears at first glance.

9   Conclusion

The relative performance of *OSHL* and unification-based theorem proving strategies for first-order logic has been studied, and some results show that *OSHL* with a properly chosen semantics implicitly performs simultaneous unifications. These results suggest that *OSHL* may perform as well or better than conventional unification-based strategies for first-order logic with a comparable implementation and appropriate semantics. Some preliminary implementation results also give limited evidence of the properties of *OSHL* and the value of a natural semantics. It will be interesting to see how other propositional approaches to first-order logic develop as their implementations also improve. A suggestion for extending *OSHL* to the non-ground level, while still permitting the use of natural semantics, has been presented. This idea may also apply to other methods such as FDPLL and DCTP.

References

1. Giunchiglia, E., Walsh, T.: SAT 2005 (January 2004)
2. Plaisted, D.A., Zhu, Y.: Ordered semantic hyper linking. Journal of Automated Reasoning 25(3), 167–217 (2000)
3. Baumgartner, P.: FDPLL – A First-Order Davis-Putnam-Logeman-Loveland Procedure. In: McAllester, D. (ed.) CADE 2000. LNCS, vol. 1831, pp. 200–219. Springer, Heidelberg (2000)
4. Letz, R., Stenz, G.: DCTP - A Disconnection Calculus Theorem Prover - System Abstract. In: Goré, R.P., Leitsch, A., Nipkow, T. (eds.) IJCAR 2001. LNCS (LNAI), vol. 2083, pp. 381–385. Springer, Heidelberg (2001)
5. Baumgartner, P., Tinelli, C.: The Model Evolution Calculus. In: Baader, F. (ed.) CADE 2003. LNCS (LNAI), vol. 2741, pp. 350–364. Springer, Heidelberg (2003)
6. Baumgartner, P., Tinelli, C.: Model Evolution with Equality Modulo Built-in Theories. In: Bjørner, N., Sofronie-Stokkermans, V. (eds.) CADE 2011. LNCS, vol. 6803, pp. 85–100. Springer, Heidelberg (2011)
7. Baumgartner, P., Tinelli, C.: The Model Evolution Calculus as a First-Order DPLL Method. Artificial Intelligence 172(4-5), 591–632 (2008)
8. Baumgartner, P., Tinelli, C.: The Model Evolution Calculus with Equality. In: Nieuwenhuis, R. (ed.) CADE 2005. LNCS (LNAI), vol. 3632, pp. 392–408. Springer, Heidelberg (2005)
9. Ganzinger, H., Korovin, K.: New directions in instantiation-based theorem proving. In: Proc. 18th IEEE Symposium on Logic in Computer Science, pp. 55–64. IEEE Computer Society Press (2003)
10. Korovin, K., Sticksel, C.: iProver-Eq: An Instantiation-Based Theorem Prover with Equality. In: Giesl, J., Hähnle, R. (eds.) IJCAR 2010. LNCS, vol. 6173, pp. 196–202. Springer, Heidelberg (2010)
11. Ganzinger, H., Korovin, K.: Integrating Equational Reasoning into Instantiation-Based Theorem Proving. In: Marcinkowski, J., Tarlecki, A. (eds.) CSL 2004. LNCS, vol. 3210, pp. 71–84. Springer, Heidelberg (2004)
12. Lee, S.-J., Plaisted, D.: Eliminating duplication with the hyper-linking strategy. Journal of Automated Reasoning 9(1), 25–42 (1992)

13. Baumgartner, P., Thorstensen, E.: Instance based methods — a brief overview. KI - Künstliche Intelligenz 24, 35–42 (2010)
14. Gelernter, H., Hansen, J.R., Loveland, D.W.: Empirical explorations of the geometry theorem proving machine. In: Feigenbaum, E., Feldman, J. (eds.) Computers and Thought, pp. 153–167. McGraw-Hill, New York (1963)
15. Das, S., Plaisted, D.: An improved propositional approach to first-order theorem proving. In: Baumgartner, P., Fermueller, C. (eds.) CADE-19 Workshop W4 Model Computation - Principles, Algorithms, Applications, Miami, Florida, USA (2003)
16. Suttner, C.B., Sutcliffe, G.: The TPTP problem library (TPTP v2.0.0). Technical Report AR-97-01, Institut für Informatik, Technische Universität München, Germany (1997)
17. Davis, M., Putnam, H.: A computing procedure for quantification theory. Journal of the Association for Computing Machinery 7, 201–215 (1960)
18. Robinson, J.: A machine-oriented logic based on the resolution principle. Journal of the Association for Computing Machinery 12, 23–41 (1965)
19. Davis, M., Logemann, G., Loveland, D.: A machine program for theorem-proving. Communications of the ACM 5, 394–397 (1962)
20. Yahya, A., Plaisted, D.A.: Ordered semantic hyper tableaux. Journal of Automated Reasoning 29(1), 17–57 (2002)
21. McCune, W.: Fascinating XCB inference. AAR Newsletter 66 (February 2005)
22. Stickel, M.E.: Automated deduction by theory resolution. Journal of Automated Reasoning 1, 333–355 (1985)
23. Sutcliffe, G.: The TPTP Problem Library and Associated Infrastructure: The FOF and CNF Parts, v3.5.0. Journal of Automated Reasoning 43(4), 337–362 (2009)
24. McCune, W.: Otter 2.0 (theorem prover). In: Stickel, M.E. (ed.) CADE 1990. LNCS, vol. 449, pp. 663–664. Springer, Heidelberg (1990)
25. Claessen, K.: Equinox, a new theorem prover for full first-order logic with equality. In: Dagstuhl Seminar 05431 on Deduction and Applications (October 2005)
26. Sutcliffe, G., Suttner, C.: The State of CASC. AI Communications 19(1), 35–48 (2006)
27. Riazanov, A., Voronkov, A.: The design and implementation of VAMPIRE. AI Commun. 15(2-3), 91–110 (2002)
28. Zhu, Y., Plaisted, D.: FOLPLAN: A semantically guided first-order planner. In: Proceedings of the 10th International FLAIRS Conference (1997)
29. Fikes, R., Nilsson, N.J.: STRIPS: A new approach to the application of theorem proving to problem solving. Artif. Intell. 2(3/4), 189–208 (1971)
30. Lifschitz, V.: On the semantics of STRIPS. In: Reasoning about Actions and Plans: Proceedings of the 1986 Workshop, pp. 1–9. Morgan Kaufmann (1987)
31. Penberthy, J.S., Weld, D.S.: UCPOP: A sound, complete, partial order planner for ADL. In: The Third International Conference on Knowledge Representation and Reasoning (KR 1992), pp. 103–114 (1992)
32. Edwin, P.D.: Pednault. ADL and the state-transition model of action. J. Log. Comput. 4(5), 467–512 (1994)
33. Bonacina, M., Hsiang, J.: On semantic resolution with lemmaizing and contraction and a formal treatment of caching. New Generation Computing 16(2), 163–200 (1998)

First-Order Resolution Methods for Modal Logics

Renate A. Schmidt[1] and Ullrich Hustadt[2]

[1] The University of Manchester, UK
Renate.Schmidt@manchester.ac.uk
[2] University of Liverpool, UK
U.Hustadt@csc.liv.ac.uk

Abstract. In this paper we give an overview of results for modal logic which can be shown using techniques and methods from first-order logic and resolution. Because of the breadth of the area and the many applications we focus on the use of first-order resolution methods for modal logics. In addition to traditional propositional modal logics we consider more expressive *PDL*-like dynamic modal logics closely related to description logics. Without going into too much detail, we survey different ways of translating modal logics into first-order logic, we explore different ways of using first-order resolution theorem provers to solve a range of reasoning problems for modal logics, and we discuss a variety of results which have been obtained in the setting of first-order resolution.

1 Introduction

The main motivation for reducing problems in one logic (the source logic) to 'equivalent' problems in another logic (the target logic) is to exploit results of the target logic to draw some conclusions about the initial problems and use existing methods and tools of the target logic for the purpose of solving problems in the source logic. Reduction of modal logic problems to first-order logic is the pertinent case considered in this paper. There are good reasons for following this approach. First, a plethora of results on first-order logic and subclasses of it are available, including (un)decidability results, complexity results, correctness results for a wide range of calculi for first-order logic, and results on practical aspects and optimisation of the implementation of these calculi. Second, over the years a number of first-order logic theorem provers have been developed, and the current generation of provers has reached a high level of sophistication and has been extensively tuned for efficiency. These two points together make first-order logic a natural choice as a target logic, in particular, for source logics reducible to first-order logic. A wide range of non-classical logics, either in the guise of modal logics or description logics, fall into this category. For these logics, the advantage of using a translation approach is that no major implementation effort is necessary, most often all that is required is the implementation of translation routines. This contrasts with special-purpose approaches for which either an implementation needs to be developed from scratch or requires an existing implementation to be adapted and extended for each new logic. In the

A. Voronkov and C. Weidenbach (Eds.): Ganzinger Festschrift, LNCS 7797, pp. 345–391, 2013.
© Springer-Verlag Berlin Heidelberg 2013

case of modal logic a number of translation approaches are already implemented in MSPASS [64, 104] so that in this case no implementation overhead is needed, because MSPASS can be used directly as a modal logic theorem prover.

There are however not only practical advantages to using translation-based approaches. There are also significant theoretical advantages. By using translations it is often possible to transfer results and insights about one logic to another logic, similarly it is possible to transfer knowledge about certain classes of problems to other classes of problems. For example, in logic and computer science decidability and undecidability results are often shown by methods of translation, usually referred to as methods of interpretation or reduction methods. Complexity theory is another example where translations play a key role. In this case reductions are used for obtaining worst-case complexity results. This allows for the classification of decidable problems into broad complexity classes. Mathematicians and logicians usually just use interpretation methods and reductions as tools for proving, say, decidability, undecidability or complexity results, but are not normally interested in developing algorithms or proof procedures which could exploit these methods. Often the reductions are indeed not practically feasible, but when they are constructive then there is a possibility that these can be turned into efficient, implemented algorithms. There are few examples where such possibilities have been seriously explored. It is therefore perhaps not surprising that some authors are put off by the idea of using a translation approach for automated deduction. Such attitudes are however completely unjustified. From the perspective of computer science, adopting the translation approach is like using compilers to convert programs into machine code instructions for execution (or like converting text files into dvi files). In programming it is generally acceptable to use compilers and interpreters and we see no reason why the use of translation approaches for reasoning should not be equally acceptable. If we think about it then all inference steps of any deduction calculus are just transformation steps anyway.

In this paper it is our intention to give an overview of some of the many uses of translation approaches and techniques at the heart of automated reasoning. Over the years a powerful and versatile framework of first-order resolution has evolved, which is increasingly applied to obtain strong results in numerous fields, both inside as well as outside of automated reasoning. Recent results suggest that the modern framework of (first-order) resolution provides perhaps the most successful, current approach for developing practical decision procedures, certainly within the scope of first-order logic. Very many modal logics and expressive description logics are decidable by resolution. Moreover, the same refinements of resolution that decide these logics can be seen to decide very expressive fragments of first-order logic (guarded fragments, the two-variable fragment, fluted logic, Maslov's class K, and the Bernays-Schönfinkel class). It can be shown that there is a one-to-one correspondence between most tableau methods for modal logics, including description logics, and a certain refinement of first-order resolution. This simulation by resolution has a number of fundamental consequences. It provides valuable insight into the similarities and differences of resolution and tableau methods. Since for present day modal logic and description logic systems simulations in the other direction are currently absent this also shows that resolution-based methods are very powerful, and in many cases provably more powerful. Simulation results show a close connection between different styles of proof methods and can also be used as a basis for systematically developing specialised reasoning methods. In this way it has been possible to develop completely new tableau-like calculi for expressive modal and description logics within the resolution framework. Many results which are traditionally proved using model-theoretical constructions can in fact be proved within the resolution framework (soundness and completeness of special-purpose proof systems, the finite model property, correspondence properties, interpolation, etc). First-order logic theorem proving tools are therefore not only useful for solving reasoning problems in modal logics, but can be exploited for realising and testing theoretical results about modal logics. In contrast to special-purpose approaches no major implementation effort is necessary; often all that is required is the implementation of translation routines. Decision procedures and simulations of other styles of deduction can then be obtained by simply selecting a correct set of parameters for the first-order prover. All this makes the combination of the translation approach and resolution very attractive for solving all kinds of problems requiring reasoning within and about modal logics (but not just modal logics).

Without going into too much detail the purpose of this paper is to give a high-level overview of the application of first-order resolution methods to modal logic. We focus on a large class of modal logics, including traditional propositional modal logics and more expressive *PDL*-like dynamic modal logics which are closely related to description logics. We review a variety of the different uses of first-order resolution for these logics. In particular, we focus on the development of practical inference methods, for studying specific issues such as decidability, the finite model property, the automatic generation of models, automated correspondence theory, and the relationships to other deduction approaches such as tableaux.

The paper is structured as follows. In Section 2 we recall standard definitions of resolution-based first-order theorem proving. Section 3 defines the essential concepts of the modal logics considered in this paper, namely syntax, the standard relational semantics and the corresponding relational translation method. These are defined for two kinds of modal logics: traditional style modal logics (Section 3.1) and dynamic modal logics (Section 3.2). Section 4 describes numerous alternative translations methods which are classified as syntactic approaches (Section 4.1), semantic approaches (in particular, approaches based on functional translations, Section 4.2), and approaches combining syntactic and semantic elements (in particular, the axiomatic translation approaches, Section 4.3). Section 5 reviews solvable first-order fragments and solvable clausal classes to which modal logics can be mapped using these different translation approaches. Fragments and classes relevant to the relational translation (Section 5.2), the semi-functional translation (Section 5.3), the optimised functional translation (Section 5.4), and the axiomatic translation methods (Section 5.5) are discussed in turn. The topic of Section 6 is decision procedures. Various kinds of resolution decision procedures ranging from decision procedures not relying on any kind of refinements (Section 6.1), decision procedures based on ordering refinements (Section 6.2) and selection-based refinements (Section 6.3) are considered. Section 7 focusses on the connection between resolution and tableaux, and how this connection has been exploited to simulate, develop and study modal tableau proof approaches. Resolution-based methods are also suitable for automatically generating Herbrand models. The application of such methods to modal logics is discussed in Section 8. Section 9 discusses resolution-based algorithms capable of transforming modal logic axioms into their corresponding first-order frame properties. Finally, in the Conclusion we give pointers to survey papers on related topics and summarise the direct contributions of Harald Ganzinger to modal logic theorem proving.

2   The Modern Resolution Framework

The resolution calculus operates on sets of clauses. Clauses are quantifier free disjunctions of literals which may contain function symbols. The variables in clauses are implicitly assumed to be universally quantified. Any first-order formula can be transformed into a satisfiability equivalent set of clauses.

Theorem 1. *There is a polynomial or linear reduction* Cls *of any first-order formula to a set of clauses such that φ is valid in first-order logic iff* Cls$(\neg\varphi)$ *is unsatisfiable.*

The clausal form is obtained by transformation to conjunctive normal form, Skolemisation and crucially involves structural transformation which introduces new predicate symbols and definitions. Since resolution is a refutation calculus, instead of proving theoremhood, resolution attempts to refute the negation of a given formula.

The (unrefined) propositional resolution calculus is very simple and consists of two inference rules, the resolution rule and the factoring rule, and no axioms. For propositional logic the resolution rule is just the operation that infers a clause $C \vee D$ from two clauses $C \vee A$ and $D \vee \neg A$. The factoring rule is a form of simplification rule which eliminates multiple copies of the same literal from one clause, that is, it infers $C \vee A$ from $C \vee A \vee A$. These two rules suffice to give us a sound and complete calculus for propositional logic and sets of ground clauses. We obtain a sound and complete inference system for full first-order logic and first-order clause sets, if we augment the rules with unification. This calculus, the *basic resolution calculus*, due to Robinson [100], is sound and complete for full first-order logic and first-order clause sets. It is however hopelessly inefficient. This was already noticed in the very early stages of the development of first-order resolution methods (by Robinson and others). The first papers on refinements of resolution appeared in the same year that Robinson published his famous paper which introduced resolution. Since the mid-sixties the advances have been impressive. The current generation of theorem provers, which include SPASS [120, 121], E [114] and

VAMPIRE [98] (in order of creation), are based on the modern framework of resolution and superposition to whose development Harald Ganzinger has made important contributions. In the following, when we refer to *resolution* we mean the resolution (and superposition) framework described in a series of papers by Bachmair and Ganzinger [7–9], see also for example [82].

The main ingredients of this framework are refinements of the inference rules which restrict their applicability and a general notion of redundancy. Refinements of inference rules are defined in terms of two parameters: an ordering $\succ$ and a selection function S. The idea is that inferences do not need to be performed (but can) unless they are on literals maximal under the given ordering or on (negative) literals selected by the selection function S. The selection function can override the ordering. That is, if a literal is selected then it is the preferred candidate for an inference step even though there may be 'larger' literals in the clause. The ordering and selection function are used to limit the number of possible inferences. It is clear that, in general, if we can reduce the number of possible inferences without losing completeness then a proof can be found more quickly as the search space for the proof is reduced. There is a general completeness proof due to Bachmair and Ganzinger which requires only weak conditions for the admissibility of orderings and selection functions.

Simplification and deletion rules are important regardless of the style of deduction one uses. In the resolution framework these are based on a general notion of redundancy, which is based on considerations of the model construction which is at the centre of the completeness proof of the framework. Standard simplification rules like elimination of duplicate literals within a clause, tautology deletion, subsumption deletion (forward and backward subsumption deletion) and condensing are instances of this notion [9].

Let $R_{\text{sp}}^{\text{red}}$ be the resolution calculus defined by the rules of Figure 1. (The meaning of 'red' in the notation is 'with redundancy' and the meaning of 'sp' is 'with splitting'.) In our presentation we distinguish four kinds of rules. The Deduce rules are the ordered resolution and positive factoring rules. The ordering $\succ$ is a parameter which can be any admissible ordering and S is any selection function of negative literals.

The Delete and Simplify rules are deletion and replacement rules compatible with the general notion of redundancy of [9, 10]. Essentially, a ground clause is redundant with respect to a set N and the ordering $\succ$ if it follows from smaller instances of clauses in N, and a non-ground clause is redundant in N if all its ground instances are redundant in N. Tautology deletion is a familiar instance of the Delete rule. Other examples are the forward and backward subsumption deletion rules. A clause D *subsumes* a clause C iff there exists a substitution σ such that $D\sigma \subseteq C$ (strictly speaking, in the framework $D\sigma \subset C$ has to hold). Condensing is an instance of the Simplify rule. The *condensation* cond(C) of a clause C is a minimal multiple (positive or negative) factor of C which subsumes C (minimality is with respect to the number of literals in the clause). A clause C is *condensed* if there is no proper subclause of C which is a factor of C. Testing for redundancy in its general form is an expensive operation; in

Deduce: $\dfrac{N}{N \cup \{C\}}$ if C is a factor or resolvent of premises in N.

Delete: $\dfrac{N \uplus \{C\}}{N}$ if C is redundant with respect to N.

Simplify: $\dfrac{N}{(N \backslash M) \cup M'}$ if $(N \backslash M) \cup M'$ is satisfiable when N is satisfiable and every clause in M is redundant with respect to $(N \backslash M) \cup M'$.

Split: $\dfrac{N \uplus \{C \vee D\}}{N \cup \{C\} \mid N \cup \{D\}}$ if C and D are variable-disjoint.

Resolvents and factors are computed with:

Ordered resolution: $\dfrac{C \vee A \quad \neg B \vee D}{(C \vee D)\sigma}$

provided (i) σ is the most general unifier of A and B, (ii) no literal is selected in C, and $A\sigma$ is strictly $\succ$-maximal with respect to $C\sigma$, and (iii) $\neg B$ is either selected, or $\neg B\sigma$ is maximal with respect to $D\sigma$ and no literal is selected in D.

Ordered factoring: $\dfrac{C \vee A \vee B}{(C \vee A)\sigma}$

provided (i) σ is the most general unifier of A and B, and (ii) no literal is selected in C and $A\sigma$ is $\succ$-maximal with respect to $C\sigma$.

Fig. 1. The calculus $R_{\mathrm{sp}}^{\mathrm{red}}$

first-order logic general redundancy elimination is undecidable. For this reason one does not find theorem provers that implement redundancy elimination in its full generality. Only effectively computable instances of the Delete and Simplify rules are normally implemented in theorem provers.

The Split rule is a rule familiar from DPLL algorithms and tableau calculi. Instead of refuting $N \cup \{C \vee D\}$ one refutes both $N \cup \{C\}$ and $N \cup \{D\}$ [18]. Alternatively, it is possible to use the complement splitting rule, which means that instead of refuting $N \cup \{C \vee D\}$ one refutes both $N \cup \{C\}$ and $N \cup \{\neg C, D\}$. The splitting rule is don't know non-deterministic and usually requires backtracking. However, in the resolution framework splitting can be simulated by transformation steps that introduce new propositional symbols. If $C \vee D$ is a clause that can be split into two split components C and D, then it is possible to replace $C \vee D$ by two clauses $C \vee q$, and $\neg q \vee D$. The new symbol q is made minimal in the ordering $\succ$, and $\neg q$ is selected [23, 99].

The calculus without the splitting rule is denoted by R^{red} and R is the calculus with just Deduce rules.

Theorem 2 ([9, 10]). *(i)* $R_{\mathrm{sp}}^{\mathrm{red}}$ *is a sound and complete refutation system for clause sets. (ii)* R^{red} *(without splitting) is a sound and complete refutation system for clause sets.*

Corollary 1. *R is a sound and complete refutation system for clause sets.*

Ordered hyperresolution: $\dfrac{C_1 \vee A_1 \quad \ldots \quad C_n \vee A_n \quad \neg B_1 \vee \ldots \vee \neg B_n \vee D}{(C_1 \vee \ldots \vee C_n \vee D)\sigma}$

provided (i) σ is the most general unifier such that $A_i\sigma = B_i\sigma$ for every i, $1 \leq i \leq n$, (ii) $A_i\sigma$ is strictly $\succ$-maximal with respect to $C_i\sigma$, and the C_i are positive clauses, for every i, $1 \leq i \leq n$, and (iii) for every i, $1 \leq i \leq n$, $\neg B_i$ is selected and D is a positive clause.

Ordered factoring: $\dfrac{C \vee A \vee B}{(C \vee A)\sigma}$

provided (i) σ is the most general unifier of A and B, and (ii) C is positive and $A\sigma$ is $\succ$-maximal with respect to $C\sigma$.

Fig. 2. The Deduce rules of ordered hyperresolution

The *(ordered) hyperresolution calculus* is based on maximal selection of negative literals. This means the selection function selects exactly the set of all negative literals in any non-positive clause. Let $OH^{\mathrm{red}}_{\mathrm{sp}}$ be the calculus based on maximal selection and an ordering $\succ$, where the Deduce rules are given by the rules in Figure 2. This means the rules are the above hyperresolution rule, positive factoring, redundancy elimination and splitting. Similar as above, OH^{red}, respectively OH, denotes the calculus $OH^{\mathrm{red}}_{\mathrm{sp}}$ but without the splitting rule, respectively the calculus just consisting of Deduce rules. For completeness an ordering refinement is optional. We use the notation $H^{\mathrm{red}}_{\mathrm{sp}}$, H^{red}, and H for the unordered versions.

Corollary 2. $OH^{\mathrm{red}}_{\mathrm{sp}}$, OH^{red}, OH, $H^{\mathrm{red}}_{\mathrm{sp}}$, H^{red} *and* H *are sound and complete refutation systems for clause sets.*

3   Modal Logic and the Classical Relational Translation

We are interested in a broad class of modal logics. These include the *traditional modal logics* which have been extensively studied since the 1960ies and even well before then. There are also PDL-like modal logics, which we refer to as *dynamic modal logics*, because they have a dynamic component (that is, relational operators) that traditional modal logics do not have. Dynamic modal logics are of particular interest because of the close relationship to description logics. Description logics are popular in the area of knowledge representation and have become a topic of much interest in connection with the semantic web and ontologies.

3.1   Traditional Modal Logics

The language of modal logic is an extension of the language of propositional logic with a family of unary modal operators $\square_i$ (the box operators). More precisely, given a countably infinite set of propositional variables $p, p_1, p_2, \ldots$, modal formulae are defined inductively as follows. Every propositional variable

Axiom $\mathcal{A}$		Correspondence property	
T	$\Box_i p \to p$	reflexivity	$\forall x\, R_i(x,x)$
B	$\Diamond_i \Box_i p \to p$	symmetry	$\forall xy\, (R_i(x,y) \to R_i(y,x))$
D	$\Box_i p \to \Diamond_i p$	seriality	$\forall x \exists y\, R_i(x,y)$
4	$\Box_i p \to \Box_i \Box_i p$	transitivity	$\forall xyz\, (R_i(x,y) \wedge R_i(y,z) \to R_i(x,z))$
alt_1	$\Diamond_i p \to \Box_i p$	functionality	$\forall xyz\, (R_i(x,y) \wedge R_i(x,z) \to y \approx z)$
5	$\Diamond_i \Box_i p \to \Box_i p$	Euclideanness	$\forall xyz\, (R_i(x,y) \wedge R_i(x,z) \to R_i(y,z))$

Fig. 3. Axioms and relational background theories

is a modal formula. If ϕ and ψ are modal formulae, then so are $\neg\phi$, $(\phi \wedge \psi)$, and $\Box_i\phi$. Other familiar connectives such as $\bot$, $\top$, $\vee$, $\to$ and $\leftrightarrow$ can then be defined as expected. As usual we let $\Diamond_i\phi =^{\mathrm{def}} \neg\Box_i\neg\phi$. A *substitution* σ is a mapping from propositional variables to modal formulae that can be lifted to modal formulae in the standard way. The application of σ to a modal formula ϕ is denoted by $\phi\sigma$ and $\phi\sigma$ is called an *instance* of ϕ. A *modal axiom (schema)* is a modal formula ϕ representing the set of all instances of ϕ.

A *(normal) modal logic* is defined by a set of modal formulae which includes all propositional tautologies and the axiom $\Box_i(p \to q) \to (\Box_i p \to \Box_i q)$, called the axiom K, for each $\Box_i$ modality in the language. In addition this set is closed under the rule of uniform substitution (if $\vdash p$ and σ is a substitution, then $\vdash p\sigma$), modus ponens (if $\vdash p$ and $\vdash p \to q$ then $\vdash q$) and the rule of necessitation (if $\vdash p$ then $\vdash \Box_i p$). $K_{(m)}$ is the weakest multi-modal logic, that is, the logic given by the smallest set of modal formulae constituting a normal modal logic. Other modal logics commonly considered in the literature and used in applications are extensions of the logic $K_{(m)}$ with additional axioms such as those listed in Figure 3. In this paper we refer to these logics as *traditional modal logics* to distinguish them from the dynamic modal logics considered in the next section. Let Δ denote a finite set of formulae. By $K_{(m)}\Delta$ we denote the smallest modal logic extending $K_{(m)}$ that includes all substitution instances of formulae in Δ (the formulae in Δ are the extra axioms) and is closed under the inference rules. A modal formula φ is a *theorem* of $K_{(m)}$ or one of its extensions iff φ can be derived by using the axioms and the rules of the logic.

The standard semantics of propositional modal logics, known as the *Kripke semantics* or *possible world semantics*, is given in terms of relational structures called *frames*. A frame of a modal logic is a pair $\mathcal{F} = (W, \{R_i\}_i)$ of a non-empty set of worlds W and a family of binary accessibility relations R_i over W. The defining class of frames of a modal logic determines, and is determined by, a corresponding class of models. A *(relational) model* is a pair $\mathcal{M} = (\mathcal{F}, v)$ of a frame $\mathcal{F}$ and a *valuation* function v. v assigns subsets of W to atomic propositional variables. The model $\mathcal{M}$ is therefore said to be *based on the frame* $\mathcal{F}$. *Truth* in any model $\mathcal{M}$ and any world $x \in W$ is defined inductively by:

$$\mathcal{M}, x \models p \text{ iff } x \in v(p) \qquad \mathcal{M}, x \models \neg\phi \text{ iff } \mathcal{M}, x \not\models \phi$$

$$\mathcal{M}, x \models (\phi \wedge \psi) \text{ iff both } \mathcal{M}, x \models \phi \text{ and } \mathcal{M}, x \models \psi$$

$$\mathcal{M}, x \models \Box_i\phi \text{ iff } (x,y) \in R_i \text{ implies } \mathcal{M}, y \models \phi, \text{ for any } y \in W$$

If $\mathcal{M}, x \models \varphi$ holds then we say φ is true at x in $\mathcal{M}$ and $\mathcal{M}$ *satisfies* φ. A modal formula φ is *satisfiable* iff there exists a model $\mathcal{M}$ and a world x in $\mathcal{M}$ such that $\mathcal{M}, x \models \varphi$. A modal formula is *valid in a frame* iff it is valid in all models based on the frame. The basic multi-modal logic $K_{(m)}$ is completely determined by the class of all frames.

Normal modal logics can be studied systematically by considering the classes of frames they define. In general, these are subclasses of the class of all frames that define the basic modal logic $K_{(m)}$. A modal logic $K_{(m)}\Delta$ is said to be *sound* (respectively *complete*) *with respect to a class of frames* iff for any modal formula φ, any frame in the class validates φ if (respectively iff) φ is a theorem in $K_{(m)}\Delta$. A modal logic is said to be *complete* iff it is complete with respect to some class $\mathfrak{F}$ of frames. Given a modal logic $K_{(m)}\Delta$ and a class $\mathfrak{F}$ of frames for which it is sound and complete, $\mathfrak{F}$ can be characterised by a second-order formula Ψ, that is, there is a second-order formula Ψ such that a frame $\mathcal{F}$ is in $\mathfrak{F}$ iff Ψ is true for $\mathcal{F}$. In some cases, but not always, the second-order formula Ψ is equivalent to a first-order formula ψ and ψ is then called a *first-order correspondence property* for $K_{(m)}\Delta$. A class of frames comprising of all frames satisfying a set of first-order conditions is an *elementary* class. Figure 3 lists the first-order correspondence properties satisfied by classes of frames for extensions $K_{(m)}\Delta$ for a selection of common axioms.

When given a modal formula φ, the problem of determining whether there exists a model $\mathcal{M}$ and a world x in $\mathcal{M}$ such that φ is true at x in $\mathcal{M}$ is also called the *local satisfiability problem*. By contrast, the *global satisfiability problem* is the problem of determining whether there exists a model $\mathcal{M}$ such that for every world x in $\mathcal{M}$, the given φ is true at x in $\mathcal{M}$.

We are also interested in inference problems relative to finite sets of assumptions or *background theories*. We use the notation Γ for background theories. The modal formulae in Γ are referred to as *non-logical axioms*, because by definition they are formulae true in every world of a model but are not logical axioms which are required to be true in every world in every model of a class. A model $\mathcal{M}$ *(globally) satisfies* a background theory Γ if, for each world x in $\mathcal{M}$ and each $\rho \in \Gamma$, it is the case that $\mathcal{M}, x \models \rho$. We can then consider the local satisfiability of a modal formula φ with respect to a background theory Γ, that is, whether there exists a model $\mathcal{M}$ and a world x in this model so that φ is true in x and Γ is globally true in $\mathcal{M}$. Global satisfiability with respect to a background theory is defined as expected.

The standard interpretation of (first-order definable) modal logics inside first-order logic is given by the *classical (relational) translation* mapping, here denoted by π_r. It maps modal formulae to first-order formulae by uniquely associating each propositional variable p with a unary predicate symbol Q_p and simply mimicking the semantic definitions of the operators.

$$\pi_r(p, x) = Q_p(x) \qquad \pi_r(\phi \wedge \psi, x) = \pi_r(\phi, x) \wedge \pi_r(\psi, x)$$
$$\pi_r(\neg\phi, x) = \neg\pi_r(\phi, x) \qquad \pi_r(\Box_i\phi, x) = \forall y\,(R_i(x, y) \to \pi_r(\phi, y))$$

Let $\mathrm{Corr}(\Delta)$ denote the set of first-order frame properties of the axioms in Δ.

Theorem 3. *Let L be a first-order definable propositional multi-modal logic $K_{(m)}\Delta$ which is complete with respect to the class of frames satisfying $\mathrm{Corr}(\Delta)$. Then, for any formula φ and any finite set Γ of non-logical axioms, (i) π_r can be computed in linear time, (ii) φ is locally satisfiable in L iff $\mathrm{Corr}(\Delta) \wedge \bigwedge_{\rho \in \Gamma} \forall x\, \pi_r(\rho, x) \wedge \exists x\, \pi_r(\varphi, x)$ is satisfiable in first-order logic, and (iii) φ is globally satisfiable in L iff $\mathrm{Corr}(\Delta) \wedge \bigwedge_{\rho \in \Gamma} \forall x\, \pi_r(\rho, x) \wedge \forall x\, \pi_r(\varphi, x)$ is satisfiable in first-order logic.*

3.2   Dynamic Modal Logics

Dynamic modal logics provide another kind of extension of the basic modal logic $K_{(m)}$. They are *PDL*-like modal logics in which the modal operators are parametrised by relational formulae. These can be used to formalise dynamic notions such as actions or programs and are useful in linguistic or AI applications. Logics which belong to this family of logics, or are closely related, are propositional dynamic logic *PDL* itself, but also Boolean modal logic *BML* [42], tense logic, information logics [28], dynamic modal logic [25], logics expressing inaccessibility and sufficiency [43, 55, 56] as well as a large class of description logics.

The strongest logic in the class of dynamic modal logics we consider in this paper is called *Peirce logic*. Peirce logic subsumes all the logics mentioned in the previous paragraph except for *PDL* (but can be easily extended to also subsume *PDL*). Peirce logic is a logical formalisation of representable Peirce algebras [80, 112] and is closely related to de Rijke's dynamic modal logic [25].

Formally, Peirce logic is the modal logic defined over relations which form a relation algebra. The language of Peirce logic consists of two syntactic types: dynamic modal formulae and relational formulae. The logical connectives are (i) the connectives of the modal logic $K_{(m)}$, with the difference that the modal operators are indexed with relational formulae, instead of just numbers, (ii) the standard connectives of relational logics, namely: ; (composition), $\smile$ (converse), *id* (identity), and (iii) a left cylindrification operator ^{c}. (Instead of the left cylindrification operator one could have chosen the test operator of *PDL*, domain restriction, range restriction, or cross product, cf. [19]; the symbol *id* is a logical constant which is interpreted as the identity relation.) Given countably many propositional variables denoted by p_j as before, and countably many relational variables, denoted by r_i, *dynamic modal formulae* and *relational formulae* are defined inductively as follows. Every propositional variable is a dynamic modal formula and every relational variable is a relational formula. If ϕ, ψ are dynamic modal formulae and α, β are relational formulae, then $\neg\phi$, $(\phi \wedge \psi)$, $[\alpha]\phi$ are dynamic modal formulae and *id*, $\neg\alpha$, $(\alpha \wedge \beta)$, $(\alpha\,;\beta)$, $\alpha^\smile$, ϕ^c are relational formulae.

We define the set of *formulae* of Peirce logic to be the set of dynamic modal formulae. The definition in [112] allows also relational formulae as first-class citizens, but these can be expressed in terms of dynamic modal formulae (see below). This variation in the definition is thus inconsequential.

The semantics of Peirce logic is defined in terms of frames, where a frame is a tuple (W, R) of a non-empty set W (of worlds) and a mapping R from relational formulae to binary relations over W satisfying:

$$R_{\neg \alpha} = W^2 \backslash R_\alpha \qquad R_{\alpha \wedge \beta} = R_\alpha \cap R_\beta \qquad R_{\alpha ; \beta} = R_\alpha ; R_\beta$$
$$R_{\alpha^\smile} = R_\alpha^\smile \qquad R_{id} = Id_W \qquad R_{\phi^c} = \{(x, y) \in W^2 \mid x \in v(\phi)\}.$$

Here and in the rest of the paper we prefer to use the notation R_α instead of $R(\alpha)$. Id_W denotes the identity relation on the set W, while $R^\smile$ denotes the converse (or inverse) of a relation R. A model is now given by a triple $\mathcal{M} = (W, R, v)$, where (W, R) is a frame and v is a mapping from propositional variables to subsets of W satisfying the same conditions as before with the following change.

$$\mathcal{M}, x \models [\alpha]\phi \text{ iff } (x, y) \in R_\alpha \text{ implies } \mathcal{M}, y \models \phi, \text{ for any } y \in W$$

The definitions of the notions of satisfiability and validity remain the same. The notions of local satisfiability, global satisfiability and satisfiability with respect to a set of non-logical axioms are also defined as for traditional modal logics.

There is a natural hierarchy of dynamic modal logics in which $K_{(m)}$ forms the weakest logic and Peirce logic forms the strongest logic. It is not difficult to see that $K_{(m)}$ is just the reduct of Peirce logic in which relational formulae are limited to m relational variables r_j. *Dynamic modal logics* are defined over the language of $K_{(m)}$ but include in addition to the operators of $K_{(m)}$ and relational variables also finitely many relational operators $\star_1, \ldots, \star_k$. By *relational operators* we mean relation formula forming operators, namely those of Peirce logic: relational $\neg$, $\vee$, $\wedge$, $;$, $\smile$, id, ^{c} plus relational operators definable in terms of the operators of Peirce logic. A logic $K_{(m)}(\star_1, \ldots, \star_k)$ is then defined to be the multi-modal logic defined over relations closed under the set-theoretic operations corresponding to the relational operators $\star_1, \ldots, \star_k$. The class of dynamic modal logics forms therefore a lattice in which $K_{(m)}$ is the weakest logic and every other logic is obtained by enhancing the language with one or more relational operators $\star_i$. Clearly some of the logics in this lattice are expressively equivalent. Peirce logic is equivalent to the top element in the lattice. Tense logic coincides with the logic $K_{(m)}(\smile)$, *BML* coincides with $K_{(m)}(\neg, \wedge)$, and the description logic $\mathcal{ALB}$ [63] coincides with $K_{(m)}(\neg, \wedge, \smile, 1)$. The operator $\upharpoonright$ is the domain restriction operator, that is, $\alpha \upharpoonright \phi =^{\text{def}} (\alpha \wedge \phi^c)$. Range restriction may be defined by $\alpha \downharpoonright \phi =^{\text{def}} (\alpha^\smile \upharpoonright \phi)^\smile$.

Relational formulae as 'independent' formulae are implicit in all dynamic modal logics with relational negation and relational conjunction or disjunction. For example, implication between relational formulae can be defined by $(\alpha \rightarrow \beta) =^{\text{def}} (\top \rightarrow [\alpha \wedge \neg \beta]\bot)$. Then it is also possible to specify properties of the underlying accessibility relations. Figure 4 gives some properties of the accessibility relation associated with r which can be specified by relational formulae in Peirce logic. If r is a relational variable then the universal modality

Property of R_r	Relational formula	Property of R_r	Relational formula
reflexivity	$id \to r$	transitivity	$r \,;\, r \to r$
symmetry	$r \to r^{\smile}$	functionality	$r^{\smile} \,;\, r \to id$
seriality	$\top \to r \,;\, \top$ or $\top \to \langle r \rangle \top$	Euclideanness	$r \,;\, r^{\smile} \to r$

Fig. 4. Relational properties expressed as relational formulae. (The relational operators are assumed to have higher priority than $\to$.).

can be defined by either $[\top]\phi =^{\text{def}} [r \vee \neg r]\phi$ or $[\top]\phi =^{\text{def}} [\neg(r \wedge \neg r)]\phi$. The test operator of PDL can be defined by $\phi? =^{\text{def}} (id \wedge \phi^c)$. We also define the operator $id(\cdot)$ by $id(\alpha) =^{\text{def}} (\alpha \wedge id)$.

The standard (relational) translation of Peirce logic into first-order logic is specified by the following.

For dynamic modal formulae:

$$\pi_r(p, x) = Q_p(x) \qquad \pi_r(\phi \wedge \psi, x) = \pi_r(\phi, x) \wedge \pi_r(\psi, x)$$

$$\pi_r(\neg\phi, x) = \neg\pi_r(\phi, x) \qquad \pi_r([\alpha]\phi, x) = \forall y\, (\tau(\alpha, x, y) \to \pi_r(\phi, y))$$

For relational formulae:

$$\tau(r, x, y) = Q_r(x, y) \qquad \tau(\alpha \wedge \beta, x, y) = \tau(\alpha, x, y) \wedge \tau(\beta, x, y)$$

$$\tau(\neg\alpha, x, y) = \neg\tau(\alpha, x, y) \qquad \tau(\alpha\,;\,\beta, x, y) = \exists z\, (\tau(\alpha, x, z) \wedge \tau(\beta, z, y))$$

$$\tau(\alpha^{\smile}, x, y) = \tau(\alpha, y, x) \qquad \tau(\phi^c, x, y) = \pi_r(\phi, x)$$

$$\tau(id, x, y) = x \approx y$$

Theorem 4. *Let L be a logic in the lattice of dynamic modal logics and let Σ be a (possibly empty) set of first-order relational frame properties. Then, for any formula φ, (i) $\pi_r(\varphi, x)$ can be computed in linear time, and (ii) φ is satisfiable in L with respect to Σ iff $\Sigma \wedge \exists x\, \pi_r(\varphi, x)$ is first-order satisfiable.*

4   Different Translation Methods

The standard translation of propositional modal logics and dynamic modal logics presented in the previous section is just one among many other reductions of these logics to first-order logic. A variety of non-standard translation mappings have been developed and studied. Experience shows that the performance of a first-order logic prover depends heavily on the translation chosen as well as subsequent transformations. Choosing a suitable translation mapping for a particular modal logic is therefore an important decision to make.

Broadly there are three types of translation methods: (i) syntactic translation methods, (ii) semantic translation methods, and (iii) a mixture of both.

4.1   Syntactic Translation

If a sound and complete axiomatisation exists for a logic then it is normally straightforward to interpret the logic inside first-order logic. Take for example the

Hilbert-style axiomatisations of the modal logic $S4$. This consists of an axiomatisation of propositional logic, the axioms K, T and 4, and uniform substitution, modus ponens and necessitation. This can be straightforwardly embedded in first-order logic by encoding formulae as terms and using a special T predicate representing the truth (entailment) relation. Each axiom $\mathcal{A}$ is then encoded as a universally quantified formula of the form $\forall \overline{p}\, T(\pi_t(\mathcal{A}))$, for example the axiom 4 is encoded as the following term, $\pi_t(4) = i(b(p), b(b(p)))$, where i and b are designated function symbols representing implication and box. The rules are encoded as $\forall p_1 p_2 ((T(p_1) \wedge T(i(p_1, p_2))) \rightarrow T(p_2))$ for modus ponens and $\forall p\, (T(p) \rightarrow T(b(p)))$ for necessitation. This kind of *syntactic translation* is quite old and is regularly used by Wos, McCune and others in their investigations into the existence of small axiom bases for algebras and other mathematical problems. Syntactic translations, or *T-encodings* as Ohlbach [89] calls them, are quite widely applicable. For instance, in contrast to semantics-based encodings they are readily applicable to a great many modal logics and algebras including second-order (modal) logics for which no first-order semantic characterisations are known.

4.2   Semantic Translations

In modal logic *semantic translations* are more often used than syntactic translations. The main reason for this is that it is easier to control the theorem proving processes and reduce the search space of a theorem prover, and it is easier and more natural to prove interesting properties of the logics. In the previous section we gave the definitions of the classical translation of modal logics into first-order logic. Because the translation just follows the standard definition of the standard semantic definition in terms of accessibility relations this translation is often referred to the *relational translation* approach.

Functional Translations. The semantics of modal logics can also be specified as structures based on accessibility *functions* rather than accessibility relations. Corresponding translations to first-order logic, so-called *functional translations*, have been introduced and studied by a variety of authors, including [6, 32, 87, 103]. In this paper we want to highlight some results obtained in Saarbrücken and therefore confine ourselves to the semi-functional translation method due to Nonnengart [83] as well as the optimised functional translation method studied by Ohlbach and others [52, 92, 122].

Semi-functional Translation. The semi-functional translation approach [83, 85] combines the advantages of the relational and functional translation approach and tries to avoid their disadvantages. For an elaboration of the considerations leading to the development of the semi-functional translation approach please refer to Nonnengart [84]. The translation is called *semi-functional* as it translates box modalities in the standard way, while diamond modalities are translated functionally. In the following we focus on the modal logic K and its extensions by a set of axiom schemas Δ, because in the case of just one modality, the semi-functional translation provides an elegant encoding of Δ which in turn allows us to obtain strong decidability results.

The semi-functional translation maps modal formulae to many-sorted first-order formulae. We distinguish between the sorts W and AF for worlds and accessibility functions. Unary predicate symbols have sort W, the binary predicate symbol R associated with the accessibility relation has sort $W \times W$, the constant symbol ϵ has sort W, and the binary (left-associative) function $[\cdot, \cdot]$ has sort $W \times AF \to W$. Then the semi-functional translation π_{sf} is defined as follows.

$$\pi_{sf}(p, s) = Q_p(s) \qquad \pi_{sf}(\phi \wedge \psi, s) = \pi_{sf}(\phi, s) \wedge \pi_{sf}(\psi, s)$$
$$\pi_{sf}(\neg\psi, s) = \neg\pi_{sf}(\psi, s) \qquad \pi_{sf}(\Box\psi, s) = \forall y(R(s, y) \to \pi_{sf}(\psi, y))$$
$$\pi_{sf}(\Diamond\psi, s) = \mathrm{def}(s) \wedge \exists\alpha\pi_{sf}(\psi, [s\alpha])$$

Note that $\forall y$ quantifies over a variable of sort W while $\exists\alpha$ quantifies over a variable of sort AF. The expression $[s\alpha]$ is of sort W. Since the semi-functional translation incorporates both the relational representation and the functional representation of the accessibility relation, it is necessary to relate the two representations by means of the following formula.

$$\mathrm{Sim}_{sf} = \forall x\forall\alpha(\mathrm{def}(x) \to R(x, [x\alpha])) \wedge \forall xy(R(x, y) \to \mathrm{def}(x))$$

The two conjuncts of Sim_{sf} are called the *simulator axioms* for R. The following theorem states that the translation preserves the satisfiability and unsatisfiability of modal formulae.

Theorem 5 (Nonnengart [84]). *Let $K\Delta$ be a complete modal logic with first-order definable relational frame properties $\mathrm{Corr}(\Delta)$. A modal formula φ in negation normal form is satisfiable iff $\pi_{sf}(\varphi, \epsilon) \wedge \mathrm{Sim}_{sf} \wedge \mathrm{Corr}(\Delta)$ is satisfiable.*

Note that for any modal formula φ in negation normal form, $\pi_{sf}(\varphi, \epsilon)$ only contains negative R-literals, that is, negative literals with predicate symbol R. Consequently, positive R-literals can only come from Sim_{sf} and from $\mathrm{Corr}(\Delta)$, the set of first-order frame properties associated with a set of axioms Δ. This allows us to compute the consequences $\mathcal{C}$ of Sim_{sf} and $\mathrm{Corr}(\Delta)$ without the need to take $\pi_{sf}(\varphi, \epsilon)$ into account. In fact, we are not interested in all consequences $\mathcal{C}$ of Sim_{sf} and $\mathrm{Corr}(\Delta)$, but only in the subset $\mathcal{C}_R$ of positive R-literals of $\mathcal{C}$. Then, $\pi_{sf}(\varphi, \epsilon) \wedge \mathrm{Sim}_{sf} \wedge \mathrm{Corr}(\Delta)$ is satisfiable iff $\pi_{sf}(\varphi, \epsilon) \wedge \mathrm{Sim}_{sf} \wedge \mathcal{C}_R$ is satisfiable. This approach can be taken further. Instead of $\mathcal{C}_R$, which might be infinite, we may use any (finite) set of first-order formulae $\mathcal{C}'$ which has as logical consequences the same set $\mathcal{C}_R$ of positive R-literals, that is, $\pi_{sf}(\varphi, \epsilon) \wedge \mathrm{Sim}_{sf} \wedge \mathrm{Corr}(\Delta)$ is satisfiable iff $\pi_{sf}(\varphi, \epsilon) \wedge \mathrm{Sim}_{sf} \wedge \mathcal{C}'$ is satisfiable. The set $\mathcal{C}'$ can be seen as an alternative representation of $\mathcal{C}_R$. Figure 5 lists the formulae we obtain following this approach for a variety of well-known extensions of K by the axiom schemas 4, 5, B, D, and T. While the set of consequences of a set of first-order formulae can be computed automatically, for example, using resolution, there is as yet no way to automatically compute its alternative representation.

$K4$	$\forall xy\forall\alpha((\mathrm{def}(x)\to R(x,[x\alpha]))\wedge$ $((\mathrm{def}(x)\wedge R(x,y))\to R(x,[y\alpha])))$	KD	$\forall x\forall\alpha(\mathrm{def}(x)\wedge$ $R(x,[x\alpha]))$
$K45$	$\forall xy\forall\alpha((\mathrm{def}(x)\to\mathrm{def}(y))\wedge$ $(\mathrm{def}(y)\to R(x,[y\alpha])))$	$KD45$	$\forall xy\forall\alpha(\mathrm{def}(x)\wedge$ $R(x,[y\alpha]))$
KB	$\forall xy\forall\alpha((\mathrm{def}(x)\to\mathrm{def}(y))\wedge$ $(\mathrm{def}(x)\to R(x,[x\alpha]))\wedge$ $(\mathrm{def}(x)\to R([x\alpha],x)))$	KDB	$\forall x\forall\alpha(\mathrm{def}(x)\wedge$ $R(x,[x\alpha])\wedge$ $R([x\alpha],x))$
$KD4$	$\forall xy\forall\alpha(\mathrm{def}(x)\wedge$ $R(x,[x\alpha])\wedge$ $(R(x,y)\to R(x,[y\alpha])))$	KT	$\forall x\forall\alpha(\mathrm{def}(x)\wedge$ $R(x,x)\wedge$ $R(x,[x\alpha]))$
$S4$	$\forall xy\forall\alpha(\mathrm{def}(x)\wedge$ $R(x,x)\wedge$ $(R(x,y)\to R(x,[y\alpha])))$	$S5$	$\forall xy(\mathrm{def}(x)\wedge$ $R(x,y))$
$K5$	$\forall xy\forall\alpha\beta((\mathrm{def}(x)\to\mathrm{def}(y))\wedge$ $(\mathrm{def}(\epsilon)\to R(\epsilon,[\epsilon\alpha]))\wedge$ $((\mathrm{def}(x)\wedge\mathrm{def}(y))\to R([x\alpha],[y\beta])))$	$KD5$	$\forall xy\forall\alpha\beta(\mathrm{def}(x)\wedge$ $R(\epsilon,[\epsilon\alpha])\wedge$ $R([x\alpha],[y\beta]))$

Fig. 5. Logics and semi-functional frame properties

Theorem 6 (Nonnengart [84]). *Let Δ be a subset of $\{4,5,B,D,T\}$. Let $\mathrm{SF}(\Delta)$ be the first-order formula representing the frame properties of $K\Delta$ according to Figure 5. Then a modal formula φ in negation normal form is satisfiable iff $\pi_{sf}(\varphi,\epsilon)\wedge\mathrm{SF}(\Delta)$ is satisfiable.*

Optimised Functional Translation. The *(monadic) optimised functional translation* is as the name suggests an improvement of the functional translation. It maps the basic modal logic $K_{(m)}$ to many-sorted first-order logic, more precisely, to a monadic fragment of sorted first-order logic, called *basic path logic*, and maps extensions of $K_{(m)}$ with axioms to extensions of the basic path logic by equational theories [92, 103]. Basic path logic has a sort S_W for the set of worlds W and a sort S_i for each modality $\Box_i$ in the logic. For each i there is a binary, left-associative function $[\cdot,\cdot]_i$ of sort $S_W\times S_i\to W$. Also there are special unary predicates def_i of sort S_W representing subsets of W. Each propositional variable p is uniquely associated with a unary predicate symbols Q_p of sort S_W.

Commonly, the (monadic) optimised functional translation π_{of} is defined as a two step process: (i) the application of the functional translation to a modal formula which translates it to basic path logic, followed by (ii) the application of a quantifier exchange operation which converts the first-order formula obtained from the functional translation into prenex normal form and moves all existential quantifiers outwards as far as possible (or inwards, depending on one's point of view). Since we focus here only on the satisfiability problem, we can give a simplified presentation of the optimised functional translation obtained in just one step.

Axiom $\mathcal{A}$		Functional correspondence property
D	$\Box_i p \to \Diamond_i p$	$\forall x{:}S_W \; \mathrm{def}_i(x)$
T	$\Box_i p \to p$	$\forall x{:}S_W \; \exists y{:}S_i \; (\mathrm{def}_i(x) \wedge x \approx [x\,y])$
B	$p \to \Box_i \Diamond_i p$	$\forall x{:}S_W \; \forall y{:}S_i \; \exists z{:}S_i \; (\mathrm{def}_i(x) \to \mathrm{def}_i[x\,y]) \wedge$
		$(\mathrm{def}_i(x) \to x \approx [x\,y\,z])$
4	$\Box_i p \to \Box_i \Box_i p$	$\forall x{:}S_W \; \forall y,z{:}S_i \; \exists u{:}S_i \; (\mathrm{def}_i(x) \wedge \mathrm{def}_i[x\,y]) \to$
		$[x\,y\,z] \approx [x\,u]$
5	$\Diamond_i p \to \Box_i \Diamond_i p$	$\forall x{:}S_W \; \forall y,z{:}S_i \; \exists u{:}S_i \; (\mathrm{def}_i(x) \to \mathrm{def}_i[x\,z]) \wedge$
		$(\mathrm{def}_i(x) \to [x\,y] \approx [x\,z\,u])$
G	$\Diamond_i \Box_i p \to \Box_i \Diamond_i p$	$\forall x{:}S_W \; \forall y,z{:}S_i \; \exists u,u'{:}S_i \; (\mathrm{def}_i(x) \to (\mathrm{def}_i[x\,y] \wedge \mathrm{def}_i[x\,z] \wedge$
		$[x\,y\,u] \approx [x\,z\,u']))$
alt_1	$\Diamond_i p \to \Box_i p$	$\forall x{:}S_W \; \forall y,z{:}S_i \; (\mathrm{def}_i(x) \to [x\,y] \approx [x\,z])$

Fig. 6. Axiom schemas and functional correspondence properties

$$\pi_{of}(p,s) = Q_p(s) \qquad \pi_{of}(\varphi \wedge \psi, s) = \pi_{of}(\varphi, s) \wedge \pi_f(\psi, s)$$
$$\pi_{of}(\neg\varphi, s) = \neg\pi_{of}(\varphi, s) \qquad \pi_{of}(\Box_i\varphi, s) = \forall y{:}S_i(\mathrm{def}_i(s) \to \pi_{of}(\varphi, [s\,y]_i))$$
$$\pi_{of}(\Diamond_i\varphi, s) = \mathrm{def}_i(s) \wedge \pi_{of}(\varphi, [s\,y]_i)$$

The symbol s denotes a path and y denotes a variable of sort S_i. The intuition of the term $[s\,y]_i$ is that it represents an i-successor world which is reached via the path s to its predecessor world followed by a y transition of type S_i. This means $[s\,y]_i$ represents both a world and the path via which it is reached from the initial world. The inclusion of a specification for diamond formulae in the above definition is intentional and so is the omission of the quantifiers. The optimised functional translation of a modal formula φ is given by $\pi_{of}(\varphi, x)$, where x is an arbitrary variable of sort S_W, and x as well as the y from $\pi_{of}(\Diamond_i\varphi, s)$, are free variables that are implicitly existentially quantified.

Similar as for the relational semantics, the functional semantics of extensions of $K_{(m)}$ can be characterised by frame properties, this time they are formulated over accessibility functions. Figure 6 gives a selection of modal axioms and equivalent first-order formulae of the functional frames. For some schemas (such as D, T and 4) these properties may be simplified by a form of globalisation; see [92, 103] for details.

Theorem 7 ([92]). *Let $K_{(m)}\Delta$ be a complete modal logic such that the functional frame properties corresponding to the axioms in Δ are a set Σ of first-order formulae. Then, a modal formula φ is satisfiable in $K_{(m)}\Delta$ iff the formula $\Sigma \wedge \exists x{:}S_W \; \exists\overline{y{:}S_i} \; \pi_{of}(\varphi, x)$ is first-order satisfiable.*

An important advantage of the optimised translation is that a wider class of modal logics can be embedded into first-order logic than can be done with the relational translation method, cf. [92, 102].

If we are only interested in establishing the satisfiability of formulae in the basic modal logic $K_{(m)}$ or extensions of $K_{(m)}$ by the axiom D for some or all modalities, then the use of sorted first-order logic and binary function symbols can be avoided by using k-ary predicates where the sort information is coded into the predicate names [60], see also [53]. The k-ary predicate symbols are $Q_{p,\sigma}$ and $\text{def}_{i,\sigma}$ where p denotes a propositional symbol, and σ is a sequence of length k of natural numbers. We use $\overline{x}$ to denote a sequence of variables $x_1, \ldots, x_k$, and we denote by 'ϵ' and '$.$' the empty sequence and the concatenation operation on sequences, respectively. Then the *polyadic optimised functional translation* π'_{of} is given by the following.

$$\pi'_{of}(p, \overline{x}, k, \sigma) = \begin{cases} Q_{p,\epsilon} & \text{if } \sigma = \epsilon \text{ and } k = 0 \\ Q_{p,\sigma}(x_1, \ldots, x_k) & \text{otherwise} \end{cases}$$

$$\pi'_{of}(\neg\varphi, \overline{x}, k, \sigma) = \neg\pi'_{of}(\varphi, \overline{x}, k, \sigma)$$
$$\pi'_{of}(\varphi \wedge \psi, \overline{x}, k, \sigma) = \pi'_{of}(\varphi, \overline{x}, k, \sigma) \wedge \pi'_{of}(\psi, \overline{x}, k, \sigma)$$
$$\pi'_{of}(\Box_i\varphi, \overline{x}, k, \sigma) = \forall x_{k+1}\,(\text{def}_{i,\sigma}(\overline{x}) \to \pi'_{of}(\varphi, \overline{x}.x_{k+1}, k+1, \sigma.i))$$
$$\pi'_{of}(\Diamond_i\varphi, \overline{x}, k, \sigma) = \text{def}_{i,\sigma}(\overline{x}) \wedge \pi'_{of}(\varphi, \overline{x}.x_{k+1}, k+1, \sigma.i)$$

In this definition the variable sequence in the argument position two of π'_{of} represents the world, and its path from the initial world, where the formula in argument position one is true. The translation of a modal formula φ is given by $\pi'_{of}(\varphi, \epsilon, 0, \epsilon)$. In the case of the modal logic KD, and for any modal logic where an accessibility relation R_i is serial, all occurrences of $\text{def}_{i,\sigma}$ can be replaced by the logical constant $\top$. The following is an easy consequence of the previous theorem.

Theorem 8. *For any multi-modal logic L with K-modalities and D-modalities only, a modal formula φ is satisfiable in L iff $\exists\overline{x}\,\pi'_{of}(\varphi, \epsilon, 0, \epsilon)$ is first-order satisfiable.*

4.3   Mixed Syntactic-Semantic Translations

The *axiomatic translation* method has a mixed syntactic-semantic flavour, because it is based on the standard semantic translation method, but instead of using correspondence properties it incorporates some or all of the additional modal axioms into the first-order translation [110, 111]. The method can be viewed as an almost semantic approach obtained by partially reducing the Hilbert-style syntactic encoding according to the definitions of the logical operators. The general motivation of this approach is to substitute the first-order theory expressed as correspondence properties by a theory with better computational and mathematical properties. Of course it must be a minimal requirement that satisfiability and unsatisfiability are preserved by the substitute theory.

It is necessary to define some extra notation before proceeding with a formal definition of the axiomatic translation mapping. Let $\text{Sf}(\varphi)$ denote the set of all subformulae of φ. If ψ denotes a modal formula then let $\sim\psi$ denote the complement of ψ, that is, $\sim\psi =^{\text{def}} \phi$ if $\psi = \neg\phi$, and $\sim\psi =^{\text{def}} \neg\psi$ otherwise. For any subformula ψ of φ, let the following represent the *definition* of Q_ψ.

$$\text{Def}(\psi) = \forall x\, (Q_\psi(x) \to \pi(\psi, x))$$
$$\wedge\, \forall x\, (Q_\psi(x) \to \neg Q_{\sim\psi}(x)) \wedge \forall x\, (Q_{\sim\psi}(x) \to \pi(\sim\psi, x))$$

Q_ψ is a new predicate symbols uniquely associated with the modal formula ψ, and $\pi(\psi, x)$ is a first-order formula (with one free variable x) given by:

$$\pi(p, x) = \top \qquad\qquad\qquad \pi(\neg p, x) = \neg Q_p(x)$$
$$\pi(\psi \wedge \phi, x) = Q_\psi(x) \wedge Q_\phi(x) \qquad \pi(\neg(\psi \wedge \phi), x) = Q_{\sim\psi}(x) \vee Q_{\sim\phi}(x)$$
$$\pi(\Box_i\psi, x) = \forall y\, (R_i(x, y) \to Q_\psi(y)) \qquad \pi(\neg\Box_i\psi, x) = \exists y\, (R_i(x, y) \wedge Q_{\sim\psi}(y))$$

Theorem 9. *Let L be a first-order definable propositional multi-modal logic $K_{(m)}\Delta$ which is sound and complete. For any modal formula φ, (i) φ is satisfiable in L iff $\text{Corr}(\Delta) \wedge \exists x\, Q_\varphi(x) \wedge \bigwedge\{\text{Def}(\psi) \,|\, \psi \in \text{Sf}(\varphi)\}$ is first-order satisfiable, and (ii) the translation can be computed in linear time.*

The definition of the encoding in this theorem is based on the standard relational semantics and structural transformation which introduces new symbols for each modal subformula. In the axiomatic translation the correspondence properties are replaced by a set of instances of so-called *schema clauses*. Figure 7 lists the schema clauses of some common axioms. They can be easily read off from the axioms or can be automatically computed from the modal axioms with the theorem prover MSPASS. The clauses are assumed to be closed under universal quantification of the free (first-order) variables. For each $\mathcal{A} \in \Delta$, let $\mathfrak{X}_\mathcal{A}$ be a predetermined set of modal formulae. The intention is that each $\mathfrak{X}_\mathcal{A}$ is the instantiation set for the axiom $\mathcal{A}$. Let $\text{Ax}^\mathcal{A}(\psi)$ be the conjunction of (the universal closure of) all clauses $C\{p/\psi\}$, where C is a schema clause in the schema clause set associated with $\mathcal{A}$. Further, let $X =^{\text{def}} \{\text{Ind}^\mathcal{A}(\psi) \,|\, \mathcal{A} \in \Delta,\ \psi \in \mathfrak{X}_\mathcal{A}\}$, where $\text{Ind}^\mathcal{A}(\psi)$ denotes the set of modal formulae occurring in the indices of the instances of the clauses associated with $\mathcal{A}$ as determined by the instance set $\mathfrak{X}_\mathcal{A}$. Then, if φ is a modal formula, the *axiomatic translation* of φ for $K_{(m)}\Delta$, relative to $\{\mathfrak{X}_\mathcal{A} \,|\, \mathcal{A} \in \Delta\}$, is the following conjunction.

$$\exists x\, Q_\varphi(x) \wedge \bigwedge\{\text{Def}(\psi) \,|\, \psi \in \text{Sf}(\varphi)\}$$
$$\bigwedge\{\text{Ax}^\mathcal{A}(\psi) \,|\, \mathcal{A} \in \Delta,\ \psi \in \mathfrak{X}_\mathcal{A}\}$$
$$\bigwedge\{\text{Def}(\psi) \,|\, \psi \in \text{Sf}(X)\}$$
$$\bigwedge\{\forall x\, (\neg Q_{\sim\psi}(x) \to Q_\psi(x)) \,|\, \psi \in \text{Sf}(X) \cup \text{Sf}(\varphi)\}$$

There is an implicit restriction in this definition to axioms with one free variable, but the definition can be generalised for modal axioms in more than one variable.

In [110, 111] we have proved the following soundness and completeness results.

Theorem 10. *Let L be a consistent propositional modal logic $K_{(m)}\Delta$ with Δ a finite set. Let φ be any L-formula and assume $\bigcup\{\mathfrak{X}_\mathcal{A} \,|\, \mathcal{A} \in \Delta\}$ is a (finite) set of L-formulae. If φ is L-satisfiable then the axiomatic translation of φ for L relative to $\{\mathfrak{X}_\mathcal{A} \,|\, \mathcal{A} \in \Delta\}$ is first-order satisfiable.*

Axiom $\mathcal{A}$		Schema clause $\text{Ax}^{\mathcal{A}}(p)$
T	$\Box_i p \to p$	$\neg Q_{\Box_i p}(x) \vee Q_p(x)$
B	$\neg \Box_i \neg \Box_i p \to p$	$\neg R_i(x,y) \vee \neg Q_{\Box_i p}(y) \vee Q_p(x)$
D	$\Box_i p \to \neg \Box_i \neg p$	$\neg Q_{\Box_i p}(x) \vee Q_{\neg \Box_i \neg p}(x)$
4	$\Box_i p \to \Box_i \Box_i p$	$\neg Q_{\Box_i p}(x) \vee \neg R_i(x,y) \vee Q_{\Box_i p}(y)$
alt_1	$\neg \Box_i \neg p \to \Box_i p$	$\neg Q_{\neg \Box_i p}(x) \vee Q_{\Box_i \neg p}(x)$
5	$\neg \Box_i \neg \Box_i p \to \Box_i p$	$\neg R_i(x,y) \vee \neg Q_{\Box_i p}(y) \vee Q_{\Box_i p}(x)$

Fig. 7. Schema clauses for the axiomatic translation

Theorem 11. *For each of the modal logics $K4$, KT, KD, KB, $Kalt_1$, $KT4$, KTB, KDB, $KD4$, $K5$, $K4B$, $KT4B$, or their fusions, and any modal formula φ, there is an effectively computable set $\mathfrak{X} =^{\text{def}} \{\mathfrak{X}_{\mathcal{A}} \mid \mathcal{A} \in \Delta\}$ such that (i) φ is satisfiable in $K_{(m)}\Delta$ iff the axiomatic translation of φ relative to $\mathfrak{X}$ is first-order satisfiable, and (ii) the translation can be computed in linear time.*

In [111] we also show that the axiomatic translation can be applied to extensions of K with some generalised axioms ($alt_1^{\kappa_1,\kappa_2}$, 4^κ, 5^κ).

In addition, we show that the classical translation using correspondence properties and the axiomatic translation can be used together. We refer to this as the *combined axiomatic-relational translation*.

Theorem 12. *Let L be a consistent propositional modal logic $K_{(m)}\Delta$ with Δ a finite set. Suppose Δ can be partitioned into two sets, Δ' and Δ'', so that all axioms occurring in Δ' are first-order definable. Further suppose $\bigcup\{\mathfrak{X}_{\mathcal{A}} \mid \mathcal{A} \in \Delta''\}$ is a finite set, and φ is any L-formula. If φ is L-satisfiable then the conjunction of $\text{Corr}(\Delta')$ and the axiomatic translation of φ relative to $\{\mathfrak{X}_{\mathcal{A}} \mid \mathcal{A} \in \Delta''\}$ is first-order satisfiable.*

This theorem gives a general soundness result for the combined axiomatic-relational translation method. Completeness can be proved for $S5$ where the correspondence properties are used for the axioms T and B, while for the axiom 4 instantiations of the schema clause for 4 with all box subformulae of the input problem are sufficient. Other completeness results can be given for the logics KDB and $KD4$, and their fusions with any of the logics in Theorem 11. The axiomatic translation has the advantage that it can reduce also second-order modal logics to first-order logic. We expect it can be shown that any modal logic complete via the filtration construction can be reduced to first-order logic by this method. All the results are also true in the presence of non-logical axioms and for global satisfiability.

4.4 Other Translations

There are many more ways of interpreting modal logics in other logics. Due to space restrictions we were forced to be selective about which translation methods to discuss. Other translations worth mentioning are the following. First, Areces et al [5] introduced a tree layered translation for the basic modal logic into first-order logic. It can be shown that there is a one-to-one correspondence between this translation and the (optimised) functional translation. Methods based on this translation can therefore be linearly simulated with the (optimised) functional translation method.

Second, with the translation of Demri and De Nivelle [27] all modal regular grammar logics with converse $RGL(\breve{\ })$ can be reduced to GF^2, the two-variable guarded fragment, and decided by decision procedures for GF^2. This is a strong result because many of the common modal logics belong to $RGL(\breve{\ })$. In some instances it can be easily seen that the axiomatic translation is equivalent to the translation of Demri-De Nivelle. In other instances the connection appears to be less immediate and deserves further investigation.

Third, translations to logics other than first-order logic exist as well. There is also a close relationship between modal logics and particularly the family of dynamic modal logics to description logics. Although their origins and motivations are different mathematically modal logics and description logics are the same. This means modal logic problems can be encoded as description logic problems, and vice versa. Further, it is easy to see that many traditional modal logics can be embedded into suitably expressive dynamic modal logics, for example, Peirce logic and $K_{(m)}(\neg)$ or $K_{(m)}(\top)$, or even just $K_{(m)}$ possibly with serial modalities. In order to exploit fast SAT procedures we might even prefer to translate modal logics into propositional logic. The possibilities are endless.

5   Modal Fragments, First-Order Fragments and Clausal Classes

Where do the different translations take us? Every translation described in the previous section associates a particular fragment of first-order logic to the modal source logic. Since the translations are all sound and complete it is immediate that any first-order logic theorem prover can be used as a prover for the considered source logic. All the translations for the modal logics considered here are linear time computable and the different target fragments inherit all the essential properties of the source modal logic, for example, decidability, the finite model property, and computational complexity. Our aim is to use existing first-order logic provers and we want decision procedures for the fragments of first-order logic which correspond to decidable modal logics. For this reason we take a closer look at the decidability of the target logics of the different translations and review the most important decidable clausal classes that are relevant.

5.1   Syntactic Translation

Syntactic translations, that is, encodings of Hilbert-style axiomatisations, take us to fragments of first-order logic with function symbols. Very few papers can be found in the literature on this kind of translation for modal logics. Consequently there are currently more open questions than answers. For example, since the 'syntactic modal fragments' are decidable for decidable modal logics, are there resolution methods for deciding these fragments, or can such methods be developed? Are solvable first-order fragments known which subsume these fragments?

5.2   Relational Translation

First-Order Target Logics. The target logic of the basic modal logic $K_{(m)}$ obtained via the classical relational translation is the *(relational) modal fragment* of first-order logic [119]. The modal fragment is the monadic fragment of first-order logic but the quantifiers are replaced by conditional quantifiers of the form $\forall y\, R(\cdot, y) \to \dots$ and $\exists y\, R(\cdot, y) \land \dots$ involving binary predicate symbols. A generalisation of this fragment is the *guarded fragment* and its many extensions [3, 4, 50, 49]. The guarded fragment has many of the same good properties as modal logics. It is decidable, it has the finite model property, it has the tree model property, etc. Thus, since its introduction the guarded fragment has taken over the role of the *two-variable fragment* of first-order logic (FO^2) as being regarded as a good generalisation of the modal fragment. FO^2 is decidable but Craig interpolation, Beth definability, and invariance for bisimulation fail. The guarded fragment subsumes more than just the (relational) modal fragment, it is also the target logic of a number of extensions of $K_{(m)}$, for example, it encompasses the dynamic modal logic $K_{(m)}(\land, \lor, \breve{\ }, id, ?)$ via the relational translation (cf. [111]). The standard translation of any formula with relational negation is not a guarded formula however.

FO^2, by contrast, has the advantage that it subsumes the relational fragment associated with dynamic modal logics with relational negation, for example Boolean modal logic, that is, the logic $K_{(m)}(\neg, \land)$. It seems that the most expressive dynamic modal logic subsumed by $FO^2(\approx)$, the two-variable fragment with equality, is the logic $K_{(m)}(\neg, \land, \breve{\ }, id,^c)$.

There are other solvable first-order fragments that encompass modal logics via the relational translation method. One is the class $\overline{DK}$ containing conjunctions of formulae in the dual of *Maslov's class K* [77]. This logic contains a variety of classical, solvable fragments, including the monadic class MON, the initially extended Skolem class $[\exists^*\forall\exists^*, \forall^*]$, and the Gödel class $\exists^*\forall^2\exists^*$. FO^2 (without equality) can also be embedded into $\overline{DK}$ in a satisfiability-equivalence preserving way. Perhaps the most expressive dynamic modal logic subsumed by $\overline{DK}$ is the extension $K_{(m)}(\neg, \land, \breve{\ }, ;^{pos},^c)$, where $;^{pos}$ means that occurrences of composition are restricted to positive occurrences only.

Another solvable first-order fragment that encompasses modal logics via the relational translation is *fluted logic* (*FL*). Fluted logic was introduced by Quine as part of the definition of predicate functor logic [96, 97]. Fluted logic and extensions of fluted logic with binary converse and equality were shown to be decidable by Purdy [94, 95]. Fluted logic is actually quite closely related to modal logic, because the *dyadic fluted fragment*, that is, the set of fluted formulae over unary and binary predicate symbols, is in fact the target logic of $K_{(m)}(\neg, \land)$ via the relational translation. One can prove [66] the following:

Theorem 13. *(i) For any formula φ in $K_{(m)}(\neg, \wedge)$, the formula $Qx\,\pi_r(\varphi, x)$, where $Q \in \{\forall, \exists\}$, is a dyadic fluted formula. (ii) For any closed dyadic fluted formula ψ there is a formula φ in $K_{(m)}(\neg, \wedge)$ such that ψ is logically equivalent to $Qx\,\pi_r(\varphi, x)$, where $Q \in \{\forall, \exists\}$.*

From a modal logic perspective, this result states that the dyadic fragment of fluted logic is the *relational modal fragment* of first-order logic associated with Boolean modal logic $K_{(m)}(\neg, \wedge)$. Analogous statements are respectively true for $K_{(m)}(\neg, \wedge, \smile)$ and $FL(\smile)$, that is, fluted logic with converse, and $K_{(m)}(\neg, \wedge, \smile, id)$ and $FL(\smile, \approx)$, that is, fluted logic with converse and equality.

More frame correspondence properties belong to $FO^2(\approx)$, $\overline{DK}$ and the fluted logic $FL(\smile, \approx)$ than the guarded fragments, but there are correspondence properties which do not belong to any of these fragments. Most notable examples are: transitivity and Euclideanness, the correspondence properties of the axioms *4* and *5*, respectively. Transitivity and Euclideanness are formulae which belong to the Bernays-Schönfinkel class, that is, the $\exists^*\forall^*$ prefix class, which is decidable. Unfortunately, this is not of general use, because few modal formulae reduce to this class by the relational translation mapping; local satisfiability problems of modal formulae in which no existential modal operators occur below universal modal operators do. Here, by existential (universal) modal operators we mean positive (negative) occurrences of diamond operators and negative (positive) occurrences of box operators.

Solvable Clausal Classes. It is usually the case that the class of clauses corresponding to a solvable first-order fragment can be defined more generally. Two clausal clauses important in connection with modal logics are the class of guarded clauses and a class called DL^*.

The class of *guarded clauses* is a generalisation of the clausal class corresponding to the guarded fragment introduced by Ganzinger and De Nivelle [37]. The definition of this class makes use of the notions of shallow terms, simple literals and simple clauses, which are defined as follows. A term is *shallow* iff either it is a variable or a term $f(t_1, \ldots, t_n)$ such that each t_i is a variable or a constant $(0 \leq n, 1 \leq i \leq n)$. A literal L is *simple* iff each term in L is shallow, and a clause C is *simple* iff all literals in C are simple. A simple clause C is *guarded* iff it satisfies one of the following conditions:

1. C is a positive, non-functional, single-variable clause.
2. Every functional subterm of C contains all the variables of C, and, if C is non-ground, then C contains a non-functional negative literal, called a *guard*, that contains all the variables of C.

The class of all guarded clauses over the first-order language without equality is denoted by GC, with equality the class is denoted by $GC(\approx)$. The class $GC(\approx)$ is in fact slightly more general than the class of guarded formulae. In the next theorem the notation ^{cpos} means that occurrences of cylindrification are restricted to positive occurrences.

Theorem 14. *The (global) satisfiability problem in $K_{(m)}(\wedge, \vee, \smile, ;^{\text{pos}}, id, ?,^{c\,\text{pos}})$ with respect to a set of non-logical axioms of a formula φ is linearly reducible via the relational translation mapping to $GC(\approx)$.*

The class DL^* [24] is a variation of the class of DL-clauses, which was introduced in [63] with the purpose of handling expressive description logics. For reasons of simplicity we assume that all clauses are maximally split (that is, the clauses cannot be partitioned into distinct variable-disjoint subclauses). A maximally split clause C is a DL^*-*clause* iff the following conditions are satisfied.

1. All literals are unary or binary.
2. There is no nesting of function symbols.
3. Every functional term in C contains all the variables of C.
4. Every binary literal (even if it has no functional terms) contains all the variables of C.

Theorem 15. *The (global) satisfiability problem of a formula φ in the logic $K_{(m)}(\neg, \wedge, \smile, ;^{\text{pos}},^c)$ with respect to a set of non-logical axioms is linearly reducible via the relational translation mapping to a set of clauses in DL^*.*

It is still the case that the clausal form of some relational correspondence properties including transitivity and Euclideanness do not belong to either GC or DL^*. The clausal classes associated with fluted logic [108] or Maslov's class $\overline{DK}$ [61] are no help here either.

5.3 Semi-functional Translation

According to Theorem 6, a modal formula ϕ is $K\Delta$-satisfiable iff $\pi_{sf}(\phi, \epsilon) \wedge SF(\Delta)$ is satisfiable, where $SF(\Delta)$ is a first-order formula representing the frame properties of $K\Delta$ according to Figure 5, where Δ is a subset of $\{4, 5, B, D, T\}$. First, looking just at the translation mapping π_{sf}, we can see that the resulting first-order formulae do not belong to the guarded fragment, fluted logic, nor to the two-variable fragment due to the presence of the binary function symbol $[\cdot, \cdot]$. For the same reason, the clauses corresponding to the semi-functional translation of a modal formula do not belong to the clausal classes associated with these three decidable fragments of first-order logic. However, the clauses belong the clausal class $\overline{DKC}$ [61, 57] corresponding to the decidable class $\overline{DK}$. Inspecting the formulae in Figure 5, one can see that the same is true for the clauses we obtain from the axioms D, T, B, and their combinations.

Theorem 16 ([57]). *Let Δ be any combination of the axiom schemas D, T, and B. Let φ be a modal formula and let N be the clausal form of $\pi_{sf}(\varphi, \epsilon) \wedge SF(\Delta)$. Then N belongs to the clausal class $\overline{DKC}$.*

By contrast, the first-order formulae and clauses corresponding to the axiom schemas *4* and *5*, and their combination with other axiom schemas do not belong to $\overline{DKC}$. In [57] two decidable clausal classes are defined, the class of *small SF-clauses* and the class of *SF-clauses*.

Theorem 17 ([57]). *Let Δ be the axiom schema 5, or its combination with 4, D, and T. Let φ be a modal formula in negation normal form and N be the clausal form of $\pi_{sf}(\varphi, \epsilon) \wedge \mathrm{SF}(\Delta)$. Then N consists only of small SF-clauses.*

Theorem 18 ([57]). *Let Δ be any combination of the axiom schemas 4, D, and T. Let φ be a modal formula and N be the clausal form of $\pi_{sf}(\varphi, \epsilon) \wedge \mathrm{SF}(\Delta)$. Then N consists only of SF-clauses.*

5.4   Optimised Functional Translation

The target logics of the optimised functional translation is a class of *path logics* of which the basic path logic is the weakest logic. Basic path logic corresponds to the basic modal logics which in this case are $K_{(m)}$ and $K(D)_{(m)}$, that is, $K_{(m)}$ adjoined with serial modalities. Basic path logic is a fragment of the monadic Bernays-Schönfinkel class with one designated two-place function symbol and a constant. It is possible to prove that the monadic class with one binary function symbol is undecidable. Still, if we consider translations obtained via the polyadic optimised functional translation π'_{of}, then we can observe the following.

Theorem 19. *The polyadic optimised functional translation π'_{of} of any modal formula is equivalent to a formula in the Bernays-Schönfinkel class.*

In fact, the target logic of the π'_{of} variation of the optimised functional translation for $K_{(m)}$ (possibly adjoined with serial modalities) is a fragment of the Bernays-Schönfinkel class (and predicate symbols are not limited to monadic predicate symbols). Formulae in the π'_{of} fragment of $K(D)_{(m)}$ and formulae in path logics satisfy an interesting syntactic restriction called *prefix-stability*. Prefix stability says that every variable in $\pi_{of}(\varphi, x{:}S_W)$ (and $\pi'_{of}(\varphi, \epsilon, 0, \epsilon)$) has a unique prefix. This property is due to a characteristic ordering of variables in the path terms determined by the structure of modal formulae and is a reflection of the property of modal logic that the truth of a formula in a world depends only on the truth of subformula in the world and does not depend on predecessor worlds. Prefix stability is fundamental to the optimised functional translation, because it provides justification for the non-standard exchange of quantifiers (step (ii) in the transformation described on page 359). As a consequence the clausal classes corresponding to path logics have two important properties: (i) their input clauses do not contain any Skolem terms other than Skolem constants, and (ii) every occurrence of a variable or constant in an input clause has a unique prefix. These properties are preserved by inference steps in essentially any resolution procedure for those path logics for which the background theory does not include equational literals [102, 103].

Although we are focussing in this section on the optimised functional translation there is an interesting observation worth making about the (non-optimised) functional translation. Suppose we take the variation of the functional translation, used in the definition of π'_{of}, where the paths are encoded by k-ary argument sequences rather than path terms. We refer to it here as the π'_f translation.

It can be shown that the π'_f translation of any modal formula is a fluted formula [66, 102]. It therefore turns out that, besides dyadic fluted logic, there is another natural fragment of fluted logic relevant to modal logic. This is the *functional modal fragment*, a logic defined by Herzig in [53] with the original name 'ordered first-order logic'. This fragment is the target logic of the mentioned π'_f variation of the functional translation mapping for local satisfiability in $K(D)_{(m)}$. As a consequence all of the properties of $K(D)_{(m)}$ carry over to the functional modal fragment, in particular also the applicability of the non-standard quantifier exchange operator which is used in the optimised functional translation mapping. With this operator the functional modal fragment can be mapped into the Bernays-Schönfinkel class [60]. The transformed fragment coincides with the target logic of the optimised functional translation given by π'_{of}.

5.5 Axiomatic Translation

A drawback of the guarded fragments when using the relational translation is that the correspondence properties such as transitivity, Euclideanness and functionality are not guarded formulae, and the guarded fragment extended with transitivity of binary predicates is undecidable [50] (but the monadic two-variable guarded fragment with transitive guards is decidable as shown by Ganzinger, Meyer, and Veanes [40]). Therefore a number of common modal logics apparently lie beyond the scope of the guarded fragment. Similar observations can be made for the other solvable fragments. Are important logics like *S4*, *S5*, *KD45* therefore outside the reach of decision procedures based on translation methods? The answer is no, the situation changes when using the axiomatic translation instead of the relational translation.

Theorem 20 ([111]). *For each of the modal logics $K4$, KT, KD, KB, $K\,alt_1$, $KT4$, KTB, KDB, $KD4$, $K5$, $K4B$, $KT4B$, or their fusions, we have: (i) The axiomatic translation of any modal formula is equivalent to a GF^2 formula. (ii) The axiomatic translation of any modal formula can be linearly reduced to a set of DL^* clauses. (iii) The axiomatic translation of any modal formula can be linearly reduced to the modal fragment.*

Thus, the axiomatic translation always reduces (local and global satisfiability) problems (with non-logical axioms) in any of the traditional modal logics, for which completeness of the axiomatic translation can be proved, to GF^2 as well as DL^* and there are standard methods to reduce them to the modal fragment. This is the case for all the logics given in Theorem 11. The mixed axiomatic and relational translation, where some axioms are represented by correspondence properties while others are represented by an internalisation of axioms, might of course cross the boundaries of GF^2 and/or DL^*; this depends on whether the correspondence properties can be expressed in GF^2 (DL^*) or not.

5.6 Summary

We have seen that the basic modal logic $K_{(m)}$ can be embedded in one way or another into all the important decidable first-order fragments. This is summarised

	GF	$\exists^*\forall^*$	FL	$FL(\breve{\ })$	$\overline{DK}$	GC	DL^*	$\overline{DKC}$
$[\exists^*\forall\exists^*,\forall^*]$					•		•	•
$\exists^*\forall^2\exists^*$					•		•	•
FO^2			•		•		•	•
π_r fragment for $K_{(m)}$ (1)	•		•	•	•	•	•	•
π_r fragment for $K_{(m)}(\neg,\wedge)$ (2)		•	•	•	•		•	•
π'_f fragment for $K_{(m)}$ (3)		•	•	•				
π'_{of} fragment for $K_{(m)}$ (4)		•						
π_{sf} fragment for $K_{(m)}$								•

(1) π_r fragment for $K_{(m)}$
(2) π_r fragment for $K_{(m)}(\neg,\wedge)$
(3) π'_f fragment for $K_{(m)}$
(4) π'_{of} fragment for $K_{(m)}$

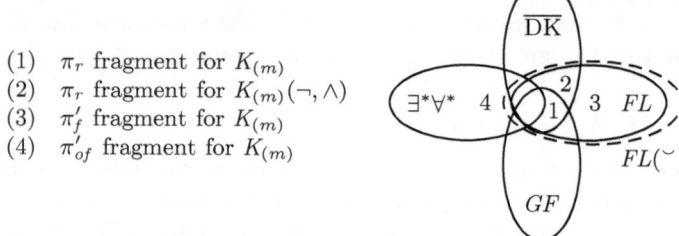

Fig. 8. Modal fragments, decidable first-order fragments and clausal classes

	GF	FO^2	$\overline{DK}$	FL	$FL(\breve{\ })$	GC	DL^*	$\overline{DKC}$
$K_{(m)}(\wedge,\vee,\breve{\ },^{c\,pos})$	•	•	•	•	•	•	•	•
$K_{(m)}(\wedge,\vee,\breve{\ },;^{pos},^{c\,pos})$			•			•	•	•
$K_{(m)}(\wedge,\vee,\breve{\ },^{c})$		•	•		•		•	•
$K_{(m)}(\wedge,\vee,\breve{\ },;^{pos},^{c})$		•	•				•	•
$K_{(m)}(\neg,\wedge)$		•	•	•	•		•	•
$K_{(m)}(\neg,\wedge,\breve{\ },^{c})$		•	•		•		•	•
$K_{(m)}(\neg,\wedge,\breve{\ },;^{pos},^{c})$			•				•	•

Fig. 9. Dynamic modal logics and decidable fragments

in Figure 8. A dot means that the fragment associated with the row is subsumed by the fragment or clausal class associated with the column. Figures 9 and 10 summarise the relationship between dynamic modal logics and decidable first-order fragments with and without equality into which they can be embedded by the relational translation method.

6   Decision Procedures

From the previous section a number of decidability results can be formulated for modal logics as consequences of the decidability of the first-order fragments into which they can be reduced. We can also use the decision procedures available for these fragments as decision procedures for the modal logics they incorporate.

	$GF(\approx)$	$FO^2(\approx)$	$FL(\check{\ },\approx)$	$GC(\approx)$
$K_{(m)}(\wedge,\vee,\check{\ },id,?)$	•	•	•	•
$K_{(m)}(\wedge,\vee,\check{\ },;^{\mathrm{pos}},id,?)$				•
$K_{(m)}(\wedge,\vee,\check{\ },id,^c)$		•	•	
$K_{(m)}(\neg,\wedge,\check{\ },id,^c)$		•	•	

Fig. 10. Dynamic modal logics and decidable fragments with equality

In this section we review results that have been obtained with different instances of the resolution framework.

Before we go on we want to note that most modern first-order logic theorem provers are implementations based on the Bachmair-Ganzinger framework of resolution. All of the ordering and selection-based refinements described in this section and subsequent sections are actually implemented in theorem provers such as (M)SPASS, VAMPIRE and E. Consequently, these provers immediately provide practical decision procedures for all the modal logics and solvable fragments covered by the decidability results stated in this section. Since the majority of the refinements are specified in general ways and can be realised in a number of ways also outside the framework of Bachmair-Ganzinger, it is possible to use resolution provers as decision procedures as well. Sometimes some modest implementation effort is necessary for implementing the required translation mapping, but many of translation mappings are already implemented in the theorem prover MSPASS. MSPASS [64, 104] has served as the experimental platform for much of our research. It is an extension of SPASS and differs from SPASS in that it accepts also formulae as input from (traditional and dynamic) modal logics, description logic and relational logic. We have also extended the converter of first-order logic formulae to clausal form. MSPASS supports non-logical axioms and global satisfiability/validity. In addition, it is possible to specify additional frame properties, or other first-order restrictions on the translated formulae. A converter to TPTP syntax is also available so that other first-order theorem provers can be used.

6.1 Unrefined Resolution

First we consider whether decision procedures can be based on unrefined resolution, that is, there is no ordering restriction and the selection function S is empty.

Using the Optimised Functional Translation. The basic unrefined resolution calculus R plus condensing provides a decision procedure for propositional logic, but it does not decide the standard (relational) modal fragment of the basic modal logic [102, 103]. The latter may appear surprising given the great variety of other proof methods (tableaux, sequent systems, natural deduction) that decide the modal logic $K_{(m)}$. However, on the one hand, modal tableau decision procedures can be regarded as *refinements* of resolution that are decision procedures for $K_{(m)}$ (see Section 7). On the other hand, it has been shown that the basic modal logics *can* be decided by unrefined resolution when the optimised functional translation, or essentially equivalent translations, are used.

Theorem 21 ([102, 103]). *R with condensing is a decision procedure for (i) the clausal form of the basic path logic, and (ii) the clausal form of the $\pi_{of'}$ fragment for $K(D)_{(m)}$.*

This result can be formulated as giving general criteria under which unrefined resolution with condensing, theory unification and theory normalisation provides a decision procedure for path logics extended with equational theories and consequences for modal logics that meet these conditions; see [102, 103] for details. These results are interesting both from a theoretical and practical perspective because Theorem 21 says that no special refinements are required and, in fact:

Theorem 22 ([102, 103]). *Any refinement of resolution with condensing is a decision procedure for basic path clauses and the local satisfiability of problems in $K(D)_{(m)}$.*

Corollary 3. *For any admissible ordering and any selection function any resolution procedure based on R^{red} or $R^{\mathrm{red}}_{\mathrm{sp}}$ with condensing are decision procedures for basic path clauses and local satisfiability problems in $K(D)_{(m)}$.*

Since condensing is explicitly present in many resolution provers, or if not, can be simulated by factoring and subsumption deletion, which are present in all state-of-the-art resolution provers, Theorem 22 means that *any complete and fair* use of a first-order resolution prover is a decision procedure for $K(D)_{(m)}$, when the (monadic or polyadic) optimised functional translation is used. This gives essentially complete freedom in the way the theorem provers can be used for these logics without sacrificing guaranteed (normal) termination. In other words, unrestricted use and fine-tuning of ordering restrictions, selection functions and redundancy criteria is possible. This implies that, for example, (M)SPASS, VAMPIRE and E are decision procedures for the translation of $K(D)_{(m)}$. What about tableaux-based theorem provers for first-order logic? Since basic path logic is a fragment of the Bernays-Schönfinkel class and this class can be decided by almost all tableaux provers, it follows that these tableaux-based theorem provers (and instantiation-based methods, for example, DCTP [117], first-order DPLL [12], the model evolution approach [16], the INST-GEN approach [39]) are also decision procedures for $K(D)_{(m)}$.

6.2   Ordered Resolution

Using the Semi-functional Translation. According to Theorem 17 the clausal form of the semi-functional translation of a formula φ in *K5* and its extensions by an arbitrary combination of the axiom schemas *4*, *D*, and *T* is a set of small SF-clauses. The satisfiability of a set of small SF-clauses can be decided by ordered resolution based on a general class of atom orderings [57]. Namely, let $\succ_{cov}$ be any atom ordering compatible with the multiset extension $\succ^s_{mul}$ of the strict subterm ordering $\succ^s$ on the complexity measure c_L on literals, where for any literal L, c_L is the multiset of arguments of L.

Theorem 23 ([57]). *Let Δ be a combination of the axiom schema 4, D, and T plus the axiom schema 5. Let φ be a modal formula in negation normal form and let N be the clausal form of $\pi_{sf}(\varphi, \epsilon) \wedge \mathrm{SF}(\Delta)$. Any derivation from N by ordered resolution and ordered factoring based on the ordering $\succ_{cov}$ terminates.*

In analogy, according to Theorem 18 the clausal form of the semi-functional translation of a formula φ in K extended by an arbitrary combination of the axiom schemas 4, D, and T is a set of SF-clauses. In contrast to the class of small SF-clauses, we need a selection function in addition to an atom ordering to ensure termination of derivations from sets of SF-clauses. We also need to be more restrictive concerning the atom ordering that we are allowed to use.

Let $\succ$ be any total reduction ordering on ground terms in which the constant ϵ is the minimal term. For every ground literal L, let $c'_L = (\max_L, \mathrm{ar}_L, \mathrm{pol}_L, s_L)$ where (i) $\max_L$ is the maximal argument of L with respect to $\succ$, (ii) ar_L is the arity of L, (iii) pol_L is 1, if L is negative, and 0 otherwise, and (iv) s_L is 1, if L is a dyadic literal $\neg r(s, t)$ and $s \succ t$, and 0 otherwise, The ordering $\succ_c$ over the complexity measure is then the lexicographic combination of $\succ$, $>_N$, $>_N$, and $>_N$. For example, if $s \succ t$, then the complexity of $r(s, t)$ is $(s, 2, 0, 1)$, whereas the complexity of $\neg r(t, s)$ is $(s, 2, 1, 0)$. Observe that the maximal term is the main criterion, and a negative literal is considered more complex than a positive literal with the same maximal term. Note that $\succ_c$ represents a strict partial and well-founded ordering on ground literals. Any total and well-founded extension (again denoted by $\succ$) of $\succ_c$ is an admissible ordering in the sense of [7]. Let $\succ_{\mathcal{ML}}$ be any such ordering. The ordering $\succ_{\mathcal{ML}}$ is lifted to non-ground expressions in the standard manner.

In addition, we make use of a selection function $S_{\mathcal{ML}}$ which is defined as follows. If a ground clause C contains a negative dyadic literal of the form $\neg r(s, t)$ such that s is an occurrence of a $\succ$-maximal term in C, then S selects one such literal. No other literals are selected by $S_{\mathcal{ML}}$. A literal L is *selected* in a non-ground clause C, $L\sigma$ is selected in $C\sigma$, for all ground instances, by a substitution σ, of an inference with $C\sigma$ by ordered resolution or ordered factoring such that the ordering constraints are satisfied.

Theorem 24 ([57]). *Let Δ be any combination of the axiom schemas 4, D, and T. Let φ be a modal formula in negation normal form and let N be the clausal form of $\pi_{sf}(\varphi, \epsilon) \wedge \mathrm{SF}(\Delta)$. Any derivation from N by ordered resolution and ordered factoring with selection based on the ordering $\succ_{\mathcal{ML}}$ and the selection function $S_{\mathcal{ML}}$ terminates.*

Using the Relational Translation. We have seen that using the relational translation method many of the modal logics we consider reduce to the two decidable clausal classes, $GC(\approx)$ and DL^*.

Let $>_d$ be an ordering on terms defined as follows: $s >_d t$ if s is deeper than t, and every variable that occurs in t, occurs deeper in s. This ordering is lifted to atoms using a multiset extension. Let S be the selection function which selects all guard literals in each non-ground guarded clause. Let $R^{\succ, S}$ denote any resolution procedure with condensing based on an ordering $\succ$ compatible

Axiom		Correspondence property
Det	$[\beta]p \to \langle\gamma\rangle p$	$\forall x \exists y \, (R_\beta(x,y) \wedge R_\gamma(x,y))$
Sym	$\langle\alpha\rangle[\beta]p \to p$	$\forall x \forall y \, (R_\alpha(x,y) \to R_\beta(y,x))$
Gr	$[\beta]p \to [\alpha]p$	$\forall x \forall y \, (R_\alpha(x,y) \to R_\beta(x,y))$
Conf	$\langle\alpha\rangle[\beta]p \to \langle\gamma\rangle p$	$\forall x \forall y \, (R_\alpha(x,y) \to \exists z \, (R_\gamma(x,z) \wedge R_\beta(y,z)))$

Fig. 11. Modal axioms and their relational correspondence properties

with $>_d$, and the selection function S. In $S^{\succ,S}$ the rules are those of $R^{\succ,S}$, and for equality, ordered paramodulation is added.

Theorem 25 (Ganzinger and De Nivelle [37]). *(i) $R^{\succ,S}$ is a decision procedure for GC. (ii) $S^{\succ,S}$ is a decision procedure for $GC(\approx)$.*

Corollary 4. *Let L be a dynamic modal logic in the sublattice bounded by $K_{(m)}$ and $K_{(m)}(\wedge, \vee, \smile, ;^{\text{pos}}, id, ?, ^c{}^{\text{pos}})$, let φ be an L-formula, and let Σ be a finite set of relational properties expressible in $GC(\approx)$. Then, (i) there is a linear transformation of $\Sigma \wedge \exists x \, \pi_r(\varphi, x)$ into a set N of $GC(\approx)$ clauses, (ii) any derivation from N in $S^{\succ,S}$ terminates, and (iii) φ is unsatisfiable in L iff there is a refutation of N in $S^{\succ,S}$. (Analogously, for global satisfiability and non-logical axioms.)*

The clausal class DL^* can be decided by standard ordering refinements of resolution based on the ordering $>_d$, without the need for a specific selection function. In particular, let $R^{\succ}$ denote any resolution procedure with condensing based on an ordering $\succ$ compatible with $>_d$, and the empty selection function.

Theorem 26 ([24, 63]). *$R^{\succ}$ is a decision procedure for DL^*.*

This theorem has the following consequences for modal logics [109].

Corollary 5. *Let L be a dynamic modal logic in the sublattice bounded by $K_{(m)}$ and $K_{(m)}(\neg, \wedge, \smile, ;^{\text{pos}}, ^c)$, and let φ be an L-formula, let Σ be a finite set of relational properties expressible in DL^*. Then, (i) there is a linear transformation of $\Sigma \wedge \exists x \, \pi_r(\varphi, x)$ into a set N of DL^* clauses, (ii) any derivation from N in $R^{\succ}$ terminates, and (iii) φ is unsatisfiable in L iff there is a refutation of N in $R^{\succ}$. (Analogously, for global satisfiability and non-logical axioms.)*

Corollary 6. *Let Δ be any finite set of instances of formulae in Figure 11, where α is a relational formula built from relational variables and disjunction only, while β and γ denote either a relational variable or a relational formula built from relational variables using disjunction and composition. Then, (i) the satisfiability problem in $K_{(m)}\Delta$ is decidable, and (ii) it can be decided by reduction to DL^* (via the relational translation) and $R^{\succ}$. (Analogously, for global satisfiability and non-logical axioms.)*

The above results are not stated in the most general form possible, because in fact a slight extension of DL^* can be decided by resolution (cf. [109]). However Corollary 5 cannot be strengthened further by removing the restriction on occurrences of composition. From the undecidability result of the equational theory of Boolean algebras with composition in [72] it follows that allowing arbitrary occurrences of composition leads to undecidability.

Theorem 27. *The satisfiability problem in $K_{(m)}(\neg, \wedge, ;)$ and every logic in the family of dynamic modal logics extending $K_{(m)}(\neg, \wedge, ;)$ is undecidable.*

Using the Axiomatic Translation. Some of the common traditional modal logics which escape embedding into decidable fragments by the other translation methods can be decided when using the axiomatic translation method. The results stated here have been formulated and proved for local satisfiability without any non-logical axioms in [111], but are also true for global satisfiability and non-logical axioms.

Theorem 28 ([111]). *Let L be a (sound and) complete modal logic $K_{(m)}\Delta$. Then, L is decidable, whenever the following conditions are satisfied. (i) Δ is finite. (ii) For any L-formula φ, there are effectively computable sets $\mathfrak{X}_{\mathcal{A}}$ for each $\mathcal{A} \in \Delta$ such that, if the axiomatic translation of φ for L relative to $\{\mathfrak{X}_{\mathcal{A}} \mid \mathcal{A} \in \Delta\}$ is first-order satisfiable, then φ is satisfiable in L.*

Corollary 7 ([111]). *Each of the modal logics $K4$, KT, KD, KB, $K\,alt_1$, $KT4$, KTB, KDB, $KD4$, $K5$, $K4B$, $KT4B$, and their fusions are decidable.*

The decidability of the logics $K4^\kappa$, $K5^\kappa$ and $K\,alt_1^{\kappa_1, \kappa_2}$ can also be shown using the axiomatic translation method.

Theorem 29. *Both $R^\succ$ and $R^{\succ, S}$ decide the axiomatic translation of satisfiability problems in all modal logics satisfying the conditions of Theorem 28.*

Theorem 30 ([111]). *Let L be a (sound and) complete propositional modal logic $K_{(m)}\Delta$ and suppose Δ is partitioned into two sets Δ' and Δ''. Then, L is decidable, whenever the following conditions are satisfied. (i) Δ is finite. (ii) For each axiom $\mathcal{A}$ in Δ', $\mathrm{Corr}(\mathcal{A})$ is expressible in DL^*. (iii) For any L-formula φ, there are effectively computable sets $\mathfrak{X}_{\mathcal{A}}$ for each axiom $\mathcal{A}$ in Δ'' such that, if ψ is the axiomatic translation of φ relative to $\{\mathfrak{X}_{\mathcal{A}} \mid \mathcal{A} \in \Delta''\}$ then $\mathrm{Corr}(\Delta') \wedge \psi$ is satisfiable in first-order logic then φ is satisfiable in L.*

Theorem 31 ([111]). *$R^\succ$ decides the encoding of satisfiability problems in all modal logics satisfying the conditions of Theorem 30.*

For example, $R^\succ$ decides the combined axiomatic-relational translation of problems in the logics $KT4$, KDB and $KD4$.

The ideas and principles underlying the axiomatic translation are quite general and are applicable not just to traditional modal logics. For example, the principle can be used to obtain decision procedures for the monadic two-variable guarded fragment with transitivity studied in Ganzinger, Meyer and Veanes [40].

6.3   Selection-Based Resolution

The logic $K_{(m)}(\wedge, \vee, \breve{\ }, {}^{c\,\mathrm{pos}})$, and dynamic modal logics below it, have the property that they can be decided by a refinement of resolution that is defined solely by a selection function of negative literals, and as a particular case hyperresolution. The results stated here are (in some cases slightly strengthened results) from [24, 63]. Let $H_{\mathrm{sp}}^{\mathrm{taut}}$ denote the (unordered) hyperresolution calculus $H_{\mathrm{sp}}^{\mathrm{red}}$ with splitting and at least tautology deletion. All results hold also for positive resolution and ordered hyperresolution $OH_{\mathrm{sp}}^{\mathrm{red}}$ (the latter is more restrictive and means that the search space is smaller).

Theorem 32. *Let L be a dynamic modal logic in the sublattice bounded by $K_{(m)}$ and $K_{(m)}(\wedge, \vee, \breve{\ }, {}^{c\,\mathrm{pos}})$. Let φ be any L-formula. Then, φ can be reduced via the relational translation into a clause set N such that, (i) any $H_{\mathrm{sp}}^{\mathrm{taut}}$-derivation from N terminates, and (ii) φ is unsatisfiable in L iff there is a refutation of N by $H_{\mathrm{sp}}^{\mathrm{taut}}$.*

Theorem 33. *Let L be a dynamic modal logic in the sublattice bounded by $K_{(m)}$ and $K_{(m)}(\wedge, \vee, \breve{\ }, {}^{c\,\mathrm{pos}})$. Let Σ be a finite $H_{\mathrm{sp}}^{\mathrm{taut}}$-saturated set of clauses consisting of two kinds of split components.*

1. *Clauses with at most two free variables, which are built from finitely many binary predicate symbols R_j, no function symbols, and containing at least one guard literal (that is, this literal is negative and includes all the variables of the clause).*
2. *Clauses built from one variable, finitely many function symbols (including constants), and finitely many binary predicate symbols R_j, with the restriction that (a) the argument multisets of all non-ground literals coincide, and (b) each literal which contains a constant is ground.*

Suppose φ is an L-formula. Then, φ can be reduced via the relational translation into a clause set N such that, (i) any $H_{\mathrm{sp}}^{\mathrm{taut}}$-derivation from $N \cup \Sigma$ terminates, and (ii) φ is unsatisfiable in L with respect to Σ iff there is a refutation of $N \cup \Sigma$ by $H_{\mathrm{sp}}^{\mathrm{taut}}$.

Ordered resolution and hyperresolution are refinements of resolution which traverse the search space in different manners. Ordering refinements are designed to prevent term depth growth, whereas in general in hyperresolution derivations terms get larger for translated modal formulae. An important technical problem therefore is to find criteria and mechanisms for preventing unbounded growth of terms. Our studies in [45, 46] have shown that, in general, terms do not grow indefinitely and hyperresolution procedures terminate when the clauses satisfy a certain acyclic dependency relation. This acyclicity condition is satisfied for the logics for which positive results are stated above. In the absence of this property hyperresolution ($H_{\mathrm{sp}}^{\mathrm{taut}}$ or $OH_{\mathrm{sp}}^{\mathrm{red}}$) is in general *not* a decision procedure for (the relational translation of) modal logics. What would be required is an additional mechanism for detecting repetitions. In many cases the use of a blocking deduction rule [62] combined with equality reasoning suffices. At certain points during

Relational property	GC	DL^*	Thm 33
$\forall x \forall y\,(R_\alpha(x,y) \rightarrow R_\beta(x,y))$	•	•	•
$\forall x \forall y\,(R_\alpha(x,y) \rightarrow R_\gamma(x,y))$	•	•	
$\forall x \exists y\, R_\beta(x,y)$		•	•
$\forall x \exists y\, R_\delta(x,y)$		•	
$\exists x \exists y\, R_\delta(x,y)$	•	•	
$\exists x \exists y\, R_\epsilon(x,y)$	•	•	•

α is built from relational variables and $\wedge$, $\vee$, $\smile$

β is built from relational variables and $\wedge$, $\vee$, $\smile$, $\bot$

γ is built from relational variables and $\wedge$, $\vee$, $\smile$, $;$, ^{c}, 1, $\llcorner$, $\bot$

δ is built from relational variables and $\wedge$, $\vee$, $\smile$, $;$, ^{c}, 1, $\llcorner$
  or $\neg$, $\wedge$, $\vee$, $\smile$, ^{c}, 1, $\llcorner$

ϵ is built from relational variables and $\wedge$, $\vee$, $\smile$, $;$

Fig. 12. Categorisation of some relational properties

a derivation this rule adds equations $t_1 \approx t_2$ between ground terms t_1 and t_2 to the clause set, rendering inferences on literals involving the greater of the two terms redundant. The methods introduced in [14] provide related, alternative solutions.

6.4 Categorisation of Relational Properties

In Figure 12, we give a non-exhaustive categorisation of the expressibility of some relational frame properties in the mentioned classes to give the reader a glimpse into the scope of the results stated in this section.

7 Relationship to Tableaux

It is possible to show that many forms of modal tableau calculi can be linearly simulated with standard techniques in resolution-based theorem proving. For example, in [65] we give details of how to simulate the single-step prefixed tableau calculi of [78] using the hyperresolution calculus $H_{\mathrm{sp}}^{\mathrm{taut}}$ (see also [24, 54, 109]). Simulation results of tableau procedures for description logics can be found in [62, 63], see also [33].

From the proofs of these simulation results the view emerges that labelled semantic tableau algorithms are just hyperresolution with on-the-fly translation to first-order logic. The same can be said for many tableau algorithms without the use of labels and without explicit representation of accessibility, but this is less obvious, cf. [54]. The following question arises as a consequence: Is it possible to develop new tableau inference calculi within the resolution framework? The answer is: yes. In [24] we show how the relationship between hyperresolution and tableau can be exploited for systematically developing sound, complete and terminating tableau procedures for dynamic modal logics. The tableau calculus

$$(\bot) \; \frac{s:\psi, \; s:\neg\psi}{s:\bot} \qquad (\wedge) \; \frac{s:\psi \wedge \phi}{s:\psi, \; s:\phi} \qquad (\vee) \; \frac{s:\psi \vee \phi}{s:\psi \; \mid \; s:\phi}$$

$$(\Diamond) \; \frac{s:\langle a\rangle\psi}{(s,t):\alpha, \; t:\psi} \; \text{with } t \text{ new to the branch} \qquad (\Box) \; \frac{(s,t):\alpha, \; s:[\alpha]\psi}{t:\psi}$$

$$(\smile) \; \frac{(s,t):\alpha^{\smile}}{(t,s):\alpha} \qquad (\wedge^r) \; \frac{(s,t):\alpha \wedge \beta}{(s,t):\alpha, \; (s,t):\beta} \qquad (\vee^r) \; \frac{(s,t):\alpha \vee \beta}{(s,t):\alpha \; \mid \; (s,t):\beta}$$

$$(\smile_I) \; \frac{(t,s):\alpha}{(s,t):\alpha^{\smile}} \qquad (\wedge^r_I) \; \frac{(s,t):\alpha, \; (s,t):\beta}{(s,t):\alpha \wedge \beta} \qquad (\vee^r_I) \; \frac{(s,t):\alpha}{(s,t):\alpha \vee \beta}$$

Fig. 13. Tableau calculus for $K_{(m)}(\wedge, \vee, {}^{\smile})$. For the rules $(\smile_I)$, $(\wedge^r_I)$ and $(\vee^r_I)$ the side conditions are that the relational formulae in the denominator, that is, $\alpha^{\smile}$, $\alpha \wedge \beta$ or $\alpha \vee \beta$, occur as subformulae of the relational formula γ of a box formula $s : [\gamma]\psi$ on the current branch. It is assumed that in a derivation no rule is applied twice to the same instance of the nominator.

extracted for $K_{(m)}(\wedge, \vee, {}^{\smile})$ is defined in Figure 13 (the formulae are w.lo.g. assumed to be in negation normal form). It follows from Theorem 32 that:

Theorem 34 ([24]). *The tableau calculus defined in Figure 13 is sound, complete and terminating for local satisfiability in* $K_{(m)}(\wedge, \vee, {}^{\smile})$.

The calculus in Figure 13 is unusual in that it requires the rules for the relational operators to be applied in two directions. Thus, the calculus comprises both elimination rules and introduction rules. Consequently the calculus can also be viewed as a restricted form of natural deduction calculus. While introduction rules could jeopardise decidability, the side conditions specify restrictions which imply that any procedure based on this calculus is a decision procedure. This means in particular that blocking mechanisms are not required. To our knowledge the calculus in Figure 13 was the first non-resolution calculus to be defined for local satisfiability in $K_{(m)}(\wedge, \vee, {}^{\smile})$. Standard methods can be used to extend this calculus for testing global satisfiability and handling non-logical axioms.

It is actually possible to derive sound and complete tableau-like calculi via any of the translation methods we have discussed. When $H_{\text{sp}}^{\text{taut}}$ is a decision procedure for the appropriate clause forms then decidability follows also immediately.

Let us take the axiomatic translation. Figure 14 gives examples of tableau calculi that can be more or less immediately read off from the combination of the axiomatic translation and hyperresolution [109, 111]. It follows from Corollary 7 that:

Theorem 35 ([111]). *The tableau calculi defined in Figure 14 are sound and complete for local satisfiability in the logics specified in the figure.*

Similarly sound and complete tableau calculi can be derived for the logics: $K4^\kappa$, $K\mathit{alt}_1^{\kappa_1,\kappa_2}$, $K5^\kappa$, $K4B$ and $KT4B$. Again, standard methods can be used to extend these calculi for testing global satisfiability and handling non-logical axioms.

$$(\bot)\ \frac{s:\psi,\ s:\neg\psi}{s:\bot} \quad (\neg)\ \frac{s:\neg\neg\psi}{s:\psi} \quad (\wedge)\ \frac{s:\psi\wedge\phi}{s:\psi,\ s:\phi} \quad (\neg\wedge)\ \frac{s:\neg(\psi\wedge\phi)}{s:\sim\psi\ \mid\ s:\sim\phi}$$

$$(\neg\Box)\ \frac{s:\neg\Box\psi}{(s,t):R,\ t:\sim\psi}\ \text{where } t \text{ is new to the branch} \quad (\Box)\ \frac{(s,t):R,\ s:\Box\psi}{t:\psi}$$

$$(T)\ \frac{s:\Box\psi}{s:\psi} \qquad\qquad (D)\ \frac{s:\Box\psi}{s:\neg\Box\neg\psi} \qquad (B)\ \frac{(s,t):R,\ t:\Box\psi}{s:\psi}$$

$$(4)\ \frac{s:\Box\psi,\ (s,t):R}{t:\Box\psi} \qquad\qquad (alt_1)\ \frac{s:\neg\Box\psi}{s:\Box\sim\psi}$$

$$
\begin{array}{llll}
K: & (K) & KD: & (K),(D) & KT: & (K),(T)\\
KB: & (K),(B) & K4: & (K),(4) & K\,alt_1: & (K),(alt_1)\\
KTB: & (K),(T),(B) & KDB: & (K),(D),(B) & KD4: & (K),(D),(4)\\
S4: & (K),(T),(4)
\end{array}
$$

Fig. 14. Tableau calculi obtained via the axiomatic translation. It is assumed that in a derivation no rule is applied twice to the same instance of the nominator.

Interestingly the calculi in Figure 14 either coincide with or are equivalent to labelled semantic tableau calculi developed in [21, 48, 78] for example. This means that our implementation of the axiomatic translation and any first-order logic theorem prover supporting hyperresolution can be used as a tableau prover for these logics. Moreover, MSPASS can essentially be used as a tableau theorem prover for $K_{(m)}(\wedge,\vee,\breve{\ })$ by just choosing the appropriate combination of flag settings that simulate the tableau inference steps for $K_{(m)}(\wedge,\vee,\breve{\ })$. This shows that in resolution, not only do we have a theoretical framework for studying and developing tableau methods, but also that we can get fully operational tableau provers essentially for free.

8 Automated Model Generation

A problem closely related to satisfiability problems is the problem of generating (counter-)models. Hyperresolution can be used for constructing Herbrand models (and representations of Herbrand models) [33]. A *Herbrand interpretation* is a set of ground atoms. By definition a ground atom A is *true* in an interpretation H iff $A \in H$ and it is *false* in H iff $A \notin H$. The definition extends as expected to (non-)ground clauses, and sets of clauses.

The results below are consequences of properties of classes of range restricted clause sets. For range restricted clause sets hyperresolution procedures implicitly generate Herbrand models [20, 44, 46]. For a class of solvable range restricted clauses, if hyperresolution terminates on a clause set N without having produced a refutation then a model can be extracted from any complete, open branch in the derivation. The model is given by the set of ground unit clauses in the limit of the branch. In general the generated Herbrand model can be infinite, but using Theorems 32 and 33 we get (cf. [24, 65]):

Theorem 36. *The combination of the relational translation and $H_{\mathrm{sp}}^{\mathrm{taut}}$ can be used as a Herbrand model generator for the local satisfiability in any dynamic modal logic in the ideal generated by $K_{(m)}(\wedge, \vee, \breve{})$.*

Theorem 37. *Let L and Σ be as in Theorem 33. For any modal formula locally satisfiable in L with respect to Σ a finite modal model can be effectively constructed on the basis of hyperresolution and the relational translation.*

This implies the finite model property for the relevant modal logics. By the simulation results in the previous section these results extend also to the corresponding tableau calculi.

Corollary 8 ([24]). *If L is a dynamic modal logic in the ideal generated by $K_{(m)}(\wedge, \vee, \breve{})$, and φ is locally satisfiable in L then a finite modal model can be effectively constructed on the basis of the tableau calculus for L given by the appropriate subset of inference rules in Figure 13.*

With the exception of non-serial and non-functional modal logics it can be inferred from the completeness proofs in [111] that the model constructed by hyperresolution (with a blocking deduction rule) for the axiomatic encoding of a modal formula φ is a tree model. This model can be easily mapped into a corresponding modal (tree) model. In general this model is however not a model of the considered formula φ, but can be viewed as a skeleton model which can be completed with respect to the appropriate correspondence properties to a model of φ. Thus:

Theorem 38 ([111]). *Let L be any of following logics or their fusions: $K4$, KT, KB, $KT4$, KTB, , $K5$, $K4B$, $KT4B$. If a modal formula φ is L-satisfiable then (i) it is satisfiable in a model with at most $2^{\mathcal{O}(|\varphi|)}$ elements, that is, L has the small model property, and (ii) resolution can be used to construct an L-model for φ.*

The result holds also for the logics $K4^{\kappa}$ and $K5^{\kappa}$.

In general Herbrand models are not unique and can be large. Methods for generating 'small' Herbrand models are therefore of interest. Various approaches to generating minimal Herbrand models with hyperresolution are known [13, 20, 51, 81]. An interpretation H is a *minimal Herbrand model* for a set N of clauses iff H is a Herbrand model of N and for no Herbrand model H' of N, $H' \subset H$ holds. With a moderate extension of hyperresolution $H_{\mathrm{sp}}^{\mathrm{taut}}$ it is possible to guarantee the generation of all and only minimal Herbrand models for any modal and description logics reducible to a decidable class of range restricted clauses. This follows from [20] and investigations of a fragment of the guarded fragment and the class $\mathcal{BU}$ [44, 45]. An alternative approach proposed in [44, 45] uses a variant of a local minimality test developed for propositional logic.

It is not difficult to see that model generation procedures and the mentioned minimal Herbrand model generation procedures can be developed by using hyperresolution, or ordered resolution with maximal selection, and any of the other translation methods. Because of the close connection to tableau, corresponding tableau procedures can be defined and all results carry over to this setting.

9   Automated Correspondence Theory

Modal correspondence theory is concerned with the study of the characteristic properties of Kripke frames in the semantics of traditional modal logics, see [119] and also [17, 71] for example. One of the most general results in correspondence theory is Sahlqvist's theorem [101] where two facts are proved for a large, syntactically defined class of modal formulae, now called Sahlqvist formulae: (i) All Sahlqvist formulae define first-order conditions on (standard relational) frames and these properties can be effectively computed (correspondence result), and (ii) all Sahlqvist formulae are canonical, that is, valid in their canonical (relational) frames and hence axiomatise completely the classes of frames satisfying the corresponding first-order properties (completeness result). Sahlqvist and others have developed a variety of methods for reducing individual axioms to relational first-order correspondence properties [71, 101, 119]. While these methods are specific to modal correspondence theory (in the form described), there are also two generalised methods that can be used for computing correspondence properties from modal axioms and have been automated: SCAN [31, 35, 90] and DLS [29, 30, 118]. Both these methods provide algorithms for eliminating second-order quantifiers from second-order formulae. Interestingly both algorithms are based on a form of resolution. Here we focus just on the SCAN algorithm, but more details of DLS and other quantifier elimination algorithms can be found in [29, 36, 86, 118].

Computing the first-order equivalents of modal formulae (if they exists) amounts to the elimination of universal or existential monadic second-order quantifiers. For example, if we are interested in establishing the relational frame properties corresponding to a modal axiom φ, then we either have to eliminate the universal monadic second-order quantifiers from $\forall \overline{Q_{p_i}} \forall x \, \pi_r(\varphi, x)$, or, equivalently, the existential monadic second-order quantifiers from

$$\Psi = \exists \overline{Q_{p_i}} \exists x \, \pi_r(\neg \varphi, x).$$

There can be no algorithm which is guaranteed to find a first-order equivalent formula if there exists one, that is, no algorithm can be complete in general, but still SCAN (and DLS) provide a partial solution to the quantifier elimination problem. SCAN basically uses a special kind of constraint (or hierarchical) first-order resolution to generate logical consequences of the initial formula Ψ, eventually keeping from the resulting set of clauses only those in which none of the second-order variables occur. In general, termination cannot be guaranteed. If the saturation process terminates then SCAN attempts to restore first-order quantifiers from the Skolem functions by reversing Skolemisation. If the reversal of Skolemisation succeeds then SCAN produces an equivalent first-order formula. This last step is not always possible, and in this case SCAN outputs an equivalent formula involving second-order Henkin quantifiers.

Experiences with SCAN are very positive. For example, it can compute the frame correspondence properties for very many well-known axioms such as T, 4, 5, and the others from Figure 3. In fact, recent work has shown:

Theorem 39 ([47]). *The* SCAN *algorithm is complete for the class of Sahlqvist formulae, in the sense that, when given a Sahlqvist formula, it successfully computes an equivalent first-order formula for it.*

Because of their generality the applicability of algorithms such as SCAN and DLS is not limited to correspondence theory with respect to the classical relational semantics. These algorithms, and in particular SCAN, which has a dedicated interface for modal logic, have proved useful in the investigations of nonstandard translation methods, see for example [84, 89, 102], but the algorithms have also other numerous other applications, see [36].

10   Conclusion

Because we are interested in the big picture brought to view by the results and methods surveyed in this paper, and also due to lack of space and time, we have omitted many details and could not cover all important topics in the area. We therefore want to point the interested reader to a selected list of survey papers and books: [32, 88, 89, 91] on various translation approaches for non-classical logics, [32] surveys also other methods including resolution methods; [36, 86] on second-order quantifier elimination; [54] on resolution and tableau approaches to modal logic; [66] on decidable first-order fragments relevant to description and modal logics; and [8, 9, 82] on the modern framework of resolution.

Let us conclude this survey with some remarks on the contributions of Harald Ganzinger to automated reasoning in modal logic. His *direct* contributions to modal logic include decision procedures for transitive modal logics based on the ordered chaining calculus [38] (cf. also [41]), and a generalisation of the SCAN algorithm of [35] as an instance of hierarchical theorem proving for first-order logic [11]. Also relevant is his work on solvable first-order fragments [10], and especially the work on the solvability of the guarded fragment and extensions with transitivity [37, 40]. For us the development and presentation of a uniform framework of resolution (and ultimately automated reasoning), together with Leo Bachmair [7–9] and Uwe Waldmann [10], was, above anything, the most important contribution of Harald Ganzinger. Within this framework it is actually possible to obtain more general results than presented here, and the application and potential of the underlying principles and methods clearly go beyond just modal logics and related logics. The underlying principles and methods are quite general—universal even, as is more than amply demonstrated by past and present research in the area of automated reasoning.

About This Paper/Postscript

For us there was no doubt that the topic of this paper should be about automated reasoning and specifically resolution. We could have made this an overview paper of automated reasoning and resolution for solvable first-order classes, for description logics or for modal logics. We decided on an overview of automated reasoning and resolution for modal logics because a significant part of the research carried out in Harald Ganzinger's research group, to which we had the privilege of belonging from 1991 to 1997/8, has been in this area. In addition, because of the close relationship between modal logics and description logics all results and observations about modal logics carry over to description logics.

Since this volume is a dedication to Harald this survey is intentionally biased towards work that originated at the Max-Planck Institute in Saarbrücken. We apologise for this bias, because important results have also been obtained elsewhere, but due to a lack of space, reference to other work has been kept to a minimum.

The paper was written in 2005–2006. Since then various new results have been obtained that could have been included in the paper. We have decided to preserve the paper in the original form except for addressing the comments of the reviewer (for which we are thankful), making minor additional improvements and updating some of the references. However to further illustrate the power of resolution and explain our optimism about the applicability and potential of the methods that Harald has been working on, we mention examples of relevant work published in the meantime.

The features and facilities for supporting automated reasoning in traditional and dynamic modal logics and related logics implemented in MSPASS have been upgraded and integrated into SPASS since Version 3.0 [121]. This means that many of the translation methods and decision procedures described in this paper are available in the latest version of SPASS. An extension of SPASS 3.0 with the axiomatic translation is described in [115, 116]. An adaptation of SPASS 3.5, which translates resolution proofs back into modal tableau proofs and first-order models into modal models is presented in [1, 2]. This provides a new and slightly unusual implementation of a modal tableau prover. Currently it caters for the dynamic modal logic $K_{(m)}(\wedge, \vee, \breve{\ }, \uparrow)$ and extensions with first-order frame correspondence properties.

In Section 7 we discussed that it is possible to linearly simulate many forms of modal or description logic tableau calculi with techniques of first-order resolution theorem proving and mentioned that the simulations can be exploited to read off tableau rules from the clausal forms of the translations used. This has been turned into the so-called 'develop via first-order resolution approach' to devising various deduction calculi, not only tableau calculi, in [106]. The approach allows us to develop different calculi and directly compare them in a common framework. A short overview of two methods for synthesising deduction calculi from the semantic specification of a logic is given in [107].

Though blocking has so far mainly been used in conjunction with tableau methods for non-classical logics, we mentioned in Section 6.3 that blocking can be used in a first-order setting. We have defined and experimented with a technique, called unrestricted blocking [113], and various restricted forms of blocking as enhancements of bottom-up model generation methods for first-order logic [15]. Bottom-up model generation methods are closely related to hyperresolution and hypertableau methods. Using these methods in combination with the unrestricted blocking mechanism, it should be possible to devise new decision procedures for a wide range of logics and solvable first-order fragment.

The paper [105] introduces refined calculi and procedures for solving the problem of second-order quantifier elimination in modal logic. The approach is used to compute first-order frame correspondence properties for modal axioms and modal rules. It is shown to solve two new classes of formulae wider in scope than the Sahlqvist class and other existing classes known to be solvable by second-order quantifier elimination methods.

As mentioned earlier, description logics are closely related to the modal logics considered in this paper and consequently resolution decision procedure exist for a variety of description logics. In recent work, decision procedures based on the basic superposition calculus for the description logics $\mathcal{SHIQ}$ and $\mathcal{SHOIQ}$ were presented in [59] and [68], respectively. Both procedures require auxiliary decomposition rules that introduce new predicate and constant symbols combined with redundancy elimination to prevent unbounded term depth growth in a derivation.

In [79] an alternative decision procedure based on hypertableau is introduced for the description logic $\mathcal{SHOIQ}^+$ that extends $\mathcal{SHOIQ}$ with local reflexivity and disjoint, reflexive, irreflexive, symmetric, and asymmetric roles. This approach is closely related to hyperresolution with the splitting rule H_{sp} combined with blocking. In [67] a saturation procedure for ontologies in the Horn fragment of $\mathcal{SHIQ}$ is described where the deduction rules combine several resolution inferences into meta inference rules.

A resolution-based method for reducing queries with respect to a TBox and an ABox to queries with respect to the ABox for a class of decidable description logics expressible in Horn logic has been introduced in [93]. Experiments of an implementation have shown that this approach is significantly better than other (non-first-order) approaches available. Further performance improvements have been obtained by [22] based on a sophisticated implementation of an input resolution approach.

There is now extensive work on resolution calculi for propositional linear time and branching time temporal logics as well as monodic first-order linear time temporal logic [26, 34, 58, 70, 73, 75, 124, 125]. In these discrete temporal logics, reasoning about the interaction between the □-operator (meaning always in the future) and the ○-operator (meaning in the next moment in time) requires a form of induction. This inductive reasoning can be realised by a series of saturation processes using ordered resolution. While resolution calculi for temporal logics are typically presented as direct resolution calculi operating on temporal logic formulae in a clausal normal form, the basic inference steps map to inferences in ordered first-order resolution with selection. This correspondence forms the basis for implementations of a number of theorem provers, including TRP++ for propositional linear time temporal logic [58, 69], CTL-RP for computation tree logic [123, 126], and TSPASS for monodic first-order linear time temporal logic over expanding domains [74, 76], the latter two being obtained by modifying and extending SPASS 3.0.

References

1. AlBarakati, R.G.: Development of a tableaux resolution prover. Master's thesis, The University of Manchester, UK (2009)
2. AlBarakati, R.G.: SPASS-TAB (2009),
   http://www.cs.man.ac.uk/~schmidt/spass-tab/
3. Andréka, H., Németi, I., van Benthem, J.: Modal languages and bounded fragments of predicate logic. Journal of Philosophical Logic 27(3), 217–274 (1998)
4. Andréka, H., van Benthem, J., Németi, I.: Back and forth between modal logic and classical logic. Bulletin of the IGPL 3(5), 685–720 (1995)
5. Areces, C., Gennari, R., Heguiabehere, J., de Rijke, M.: Tree-based heuristics in modal theorem proving. In: Proc. ECAI 2000, pp. 199–203. IOS Press (2000)
6. Auffray, Y., Enjalbert, P.: Modal theorem proving: An equational viewpoint. Journal of Logic and Computation 2(3), 247–297 (1992)
7. Bachmair, L., Ganzinger, H.: Rewrite-based equational theorem proving with selection and simplification. Journal of Logic and Computation 4(3), 217–247 (1994)
8. Bachmair, L., Ganzinger, H.: Equational reasoning in saturation-based theorem proving. In: Bibel, W., Schmitt, P.H. (eds.) Automated Deduction—A Basis for Applications, vol. I, pp. 353–397. Kluwer (1998)
9. Bachmair, L., Ganzinger, H.: Resolution theorem proving. In: Robinson, A., Voronkov, A. (eds.) Handbook of Automated Reasoning, pp. 19–99. Elsevier (2001)
10. Bachmair, L., Ganzinger, H., Waldmann, U.: Superposition with Simplification as a Decision Procedure for the Monadic Class with Equality. In: Mundici, D., Gottlob, G., Leitsch, A. (eds.) KGC 1993. LNCS, vol. 713, pp. 83–96. Springer, Heidelberg (1993)
11. Bachmair, L., Ganzinger, H., Waldmann, U.: Refutational theorem proving for hierarchic first-order theories. Applicable Algebra in Engineering, Communication and Computing 5(3/4), 193–212 (1994)
12. Baumgartner, P.: A First-order Davis-Putnam-Logeman-Loveland Procedure. In: McAllester, D. (ed.) CADE-17. LNCS (LNAI), vol. 1831, pp. 200–219. Springer, Heidelberg (2000)
13. Baumgartner, P., Horton, J.D., Spencer, B.: Merge Path Improvements for Minimal Model Hyper Tableaux. In: Murray, N.V. (ed.) TABLEAUX 1999. LNCS (LNAI), vol. 1617, pp. 51–66. Springer, Heidelberg (1999)
14. Baumgartner, P., Schmidt, R.A.: Blocking and Other Enhancements for Bottom-Up Model Generation Methods. In: Furbach, U., Shankar, N. (eds.) IJCAR 2006. LNCS (LNAI), vol. 4130, pp. 125–139. Springer, Heidelberg (2006)
15. Baumgartner, P., Schmidt, R.A.: Blocking and other enhancements for bottom-up model generation methods. Manuscript (2008)
16. Baumgartner, P., Tinelli, C.: The Model Evolution Calculus. In: Baader, F. (ed.) CADE 2003. LNCS (LNAI), vol. 2741, pp. 350–364. Springer, Heidelberg (2003)

17. Blackburn, P., de Rijke, M., Venema, V.: Modal Logic. Cambridge Tracts in Theoretical Computer Science, vol. 53. Cambridge University Press (2001)
18. Bledsoe, W.W.: Splitting and reduction heuristics in automatic theorem proving. Artificial Intelligence 2, 55–77 (1971)
19. Brink, C., Britz, K., Schmidt, R.A.: Peirce algebras. Formal Aspects of Computing 6(3), 339–358 (1994)
20. Bry, F., Yahya, A.: Positive unit hyperresolution tableaux for minimal model generation. Journal of Automated Reasoning 25(1), 35–82 (2000)
21. Castilho, M.A., Fariñas del Cerro, L., Gasquet, O., Herzig, A.: Modal tableaux with propagation rules and structural rules. Fundamenta Informaticae 32(3-4), 281–297 (1997)
22. Chortaras, A., Trivela, D., Stamou, G.: Optimized Query Rewriting for OWL 2 QL. In: Bjørner, N., Sofronie-Stokkermans, V. (eds.) CADE 2011. LNCS (LNAI), vol. 6803, pp. 192–206. Springer, Heidelberg (2011)
23. de Nivelle, H.: Splitting through New Proposition Symbols. In: Nieuwenhuis, R., Voronkov, A. (eds.) LPAR 2001. LNCS (LNAI), vol. 2250, pp. 172–185. Springer, Heidelberg (2001)
24. de Nivelle, H., Schmidt, R.A., Hustadt, U.: Resolution-based methods for modal logics. Logic Journal of the IGPL 8(3), 265–292 (2000)
25. de Rijke, M.: Extending Modal Logic. PhD thesis, University of Amsterdam, The Netherlands (1993)
26. Degtyarev, A., Fisher, M., Konev, B.: Monodic temporal resolution. ACM Transactions in Computational Logic 7(1), 108–150 (2006)
27. Demri, S., de Nivelle, H.: Deciding regular grammar logics with converse through first-order logic. Journal of Logic, Language and Information 14(3), 289–329 (2005)
28. Demri, S., Gabbay, D.: On modal logics characterized by models with relative accessibility relations: Part II. Studia Logica 66(3), 349–384 (2000)
29. Doherty, P., Lukaszewicz, W., Szalas, A.: Computing circumscription revisited: A reduction algorithm. Journal of Automated Reasoning 18(3), 297–336 (1997)
30. Doherty, P., Lukaszewicz, W., Szalas, A., Gustafsson, J.: DLS (1996), http://www.ida.liu.se/labs/kplab/projects/dls/
31. Engel, T.: Quantifier elimination in second-order predicate logic. Diplomarbeit, Fachbereich Informatik, Universität des Saarlandes, Saarbrücken, Germany (1996)
32. Fariñas del Cerro, L., Herzig, A.: Modal deduction with applications in epistemic and temporal logics. In: Gabbay, D.M., Hogger, C.J., Robinson, J.A. (eds.) Handbook of Logic in Artificial Intelligence and Logic Programming: Epistemic and Temporal Reasoning, pp. 499–594. Clarendon Press (1995)
33. Fermüller, C., Leitsch, A., Hustadt, U., Tammet, T.: Resolution decision procedures. In: Robinson, A., Voronkov, A. (eds.) Handbook of Automated Reasoning, pp. 1791–1849. Elsevier (2001)
34. Fisher, M., Dixon, C., Peim, M.: Clausal temporal resolution. ACM Transactions on Computational Logic 2(1), 12–56 (2001)
35. Gabbay, D.M., Ohlbach, H.J.: Quantifier elimination in second-order predicate logic. South African Computer Journal 7, 35–43 (1992)
36. Gabbay, D.M., Schmidt, R.A., Szałas, A.: Second-Order Quantifier Elimination: Foundations, Computational Aspects and Applications. Studies in Logic: Mathematical Logic and Foundations, vol. 12. College Publications (2008)
37. Ganzinger, H., de Nivelle, H.: A superposition decision procedure for the guarded fragment with equality. In: Proc. LICS-14, pp. 295–303. IEEE (1999)

38. Ganzinger, H., Hustadt, U., Meyer, C., Schmidt, R.A.: A resolution-based decision procedure for extensions of K4. In: Advances in Modal Logic. Lecture Notes, vol. 2, 119, pp. 225–246. CSLI Publications (2001)
39. Ganzinger, H., Korovin, K.: New directions in instantiation-based theorem proving. In: Proc. LICS-18, pp. 55–64. IEEE (2003)
40. Ganzinger, H., Meyer, C., Veanes, M.: The two-variable guarded fragment with transitive relations. In: Proc. LICS-14, pp. 24–34. IEEE (1999)
41. Ganzinger, H., Sofronie-Stokkermans, V.: Chaining techniques for automated theorem proving in finitely-valued logics. In: Proc. ISMVL 2000, pp. 337–344. IEEE (2000)
42. Gargov, G., Passy, S.: A note on Boolean modal logic. In: Mathematical Logic: Proceedings of the 1988 Heyting Summerschool, pp. 299–309. Plenum Press (1990)
43. Gargov, G., Passy, S., Tinchev, T.: Modal environment for Boolean speculations. In: Mathematical Logic and its Applications: Proceedings of the 1986 Gödel Conference, pp. 253–263. Plenum Press (1987)
44. Georgieva, L., Hustadt, U., Schmidt, R.A.: Computational Space Efficiency and Minimal Model Generation for Guarded Formulae. In: Nieuwenhuis, R., Voronkov, A. (eds.) LPAR 2001. LNCS (LNAI), vol. 2250, pp. 85–99. Springer, Heidelberg (2001)
45. Georgieva, L., Hustadt, U., Schmidt, R.A.: A New Clausal Class Decidable by Hyperresolution. In: Voronkov, A. (ed.) CADE 2002. LNCS (LNAI), vol. 2392, pp. 260–274. Springer, Heidelberg (2002)
46. Georgieva, L., Hustadt, U., Schmidt, R.A.: Hyperresolution for guarded formulae. Journal of Symbolic Computation 36(1–2), 163–192 (2003)
47. Goranko, V., Hustadt, U., Schmidt, R.A., Vakarelov, D.: SCAN is Complete for all Sahlqvist Formulae. In: Berghammer, R., Möller, B., Struth, G. (eds.) RelMiCS 2003. LNCS, vol. 3051, pp. 149–162. Springer, Heidelberg (2004)
48. Goré, R.: Tableau methods for modal and temporal logics. In: D'Agostino, M., Gabbay, D., Hähnle, R., Posegga, J. (eds.) Handbook of Tableau Methods, pp. 297–396. Kluwer (1999)
49. Grädel, E.: Decision Procedures for Guarded Logics. In: Ganzinger, H. (ed.) CADE 1999. LNCS (LNAI), vol. 1632, pp. 31–51. Springer, Heidelberg (1999)
50. Grädel, E.: On the restraining power of guards. Journal of Symbolic Logic 64, 1719–1742 (1999)
51. Hasegawa, R., Fujita, H., Koshimura, M.: Efficient Minimal Model Generation using Branching Lemmas. In: McAllester, D. (ed.) CADE-17. LNCS (LNAI), vol. 1831, pp. 184–199. Springer, Heidelberg (2000)
52. Herzig, A.: Raisonnement automatique en logique modale et algorithmes d'unification. PhD thesis, University Paul-Sabatier, Toulouse, France (1989)
53. Herzig, A.: A new decidable fragment of first order logic. In: Abstracts of 3rd Logical Biennial, Summer School & Conf. in honour of S. C. Kleene, Bulgaria (1990)
54. Horrocks, I., Hustadt, U., Sattler, U., Schmidt, R.A.: Computational modal logic. In: Blackburn, P., van Benthem, J., Wolter, F. (eds.) Handbook of Modal Logic. Studies in Logic and Practical Reasoning, pp. 181–245. Elsevier (2007)
55. Humberstone, I.L.: Inaccessible worlds. Notre Dame Journal of Formal Logic 24(3), 346–352 (1983)
56. Humberstone, I.L.: The modal logic of 'all and only'. Notre Dame Journal of Formal Logic 28(2), 177–188 (1987)

57. Hustadt, U.: Resolution-Based Decision Procedures for Subclasses of First-Order Logic. PhD thesis, Universität des Saarlandes, Saarbrücken, Germany (1999)

58. Hustadt, U., Konev, B.: TRP++: A temporal resolution prover. In: Collegium Logicum, pp. 65–79. Kurt Gödel Society (2004)

59. Hustadt, U., Motik, B., Sattler, U.: Deciding expressive description logics in the framework of resolution. Information and Computation 206(5) (2008)

60. Hustadt, U., Schmidt, R.A.: An empirical analysis of modal theorem provers. Journal of Applied Non-Classical Logics 9(4), 479–522 (1999)

61. Hustadt, U., Schmidt, R.A.: Maslov's Class K Revisited. In: Ganzinger, H. (ed.) CADE 1999. LNCS (LNAI), vol. 1632, pp. 172–186. Springer, Heidelberg (1999)

62. Hustadt, U., Schmidt, R.A.: On the relation of resolution and tableaux proof systems for description logics. In: IJCAI 1999, pp. 110–115. Morgan Kaufmann (1999)

63. Hustadt, U., Schmidt, R.A.: Issues of Decidability for Description Logics in the Framework of Resolution. In: Caferra, R., Salzer, G. (eds.) FTP 1998. LNCS (LNAI), vol. 1761, pp. 191–205. Springer, Heidelberg (2000)

64. Hustadt, U., Schmidt, R.A.: MSPASS: Modal Reasoning by Translation and First-Order Resolution. In: Dyckhoff, R. (ed.) TABLEAUX 2000. LNCS (LNAI), vol. 1847, pp. 67–71. Springer, Heidelberg (2000)

65. Hustadt, U., Schmidt, R.A.: Using resolution for testing modal satisfiability and building models. Journal of Automated Reasoning 28(2), 205–232 (2002)

66. Hustadt, U., Schmidt, R.A., Georgieva, L.: A survey of decidable first-order fragments and description logics. Journal of Relational Methods in Computer Science 1, 251–276 (2004)

67. Kazakov, Y.: Consequence-driven reasoning for horn $\mathcal{SHIQ}$ ontologies. In: Proc. IJCAI 2009, pp. 2040–2045 (2009)

68. Kazakov, Y., Motik, B.: A resolution-based decision procedure for $\mathcal{SHOIQ}$. Journal of Automated Reasoning 40(2-3), 89–116 (2008); Erratum in Journal of Automated Reasoning 40(4), 357 (2008)

69. Konev, B.: TRP++ 2.1, (2010)
    http://www.csc.liv.ac.uk/~konev/software/trp++/

70. Konev, B., Degtyarev, A., Dixon, C., Fisher, M., Hustadt, U.: Mechanising first-order temporal resolution. Information and Computation 199(1–2), 55–86 (2005)

71. Kracht, M.: Tools and Techniques in Modal Logic. Studies in Logic, vol. 142. Elsevier (1999)

72. Kurucz, Á., Németi, I., Sain, I., Simon, A.: Undecidable varieties of semilattice-ordered semigroups, of Boolean algebras with operators and logics extending lambek calculus. Bulletin of the IGPL 1(1), 91–98 (1993)

73. Ludwig, M.: Advancing Formal Verification: Resolution-Based Methods for Linear-Time Temporal Logics. PhD thesis, University of Liverpool, UK (2010)

74. Ludwig, M.: TSPASS 0.94 (2010),
    http://www.csc.liv.ac.uk/~michel/software/tspass/

75. Ludwig, M., Hustadt, U.: Fair Derivations in Monodic Temporal Reasoning. In: Schmidt, R.A. (ed.) CADE-22. LNCS (LNAI), vol. 5663, pp. 261–276. Springer, Heidelberg (2009)

76. Ludwig, M., Hustadt, U.: Implementing a fair monodic temporal logic prover. AI Communication 23(2-3), 69–96 (2010)

77. Maslov, S.J.: The inverse method for establishing deducibility for logical calculi. In: Orevkov, V.P., Petrovskiĭ, I.G., Nikol'skiĭ, S.M. (eds.) Proc. of the Steklov Institute of Mathematics, vol. 98, pp. 25–96. Amer. Math. Soc., Providence (1968)

78. Massacci, F.: Single step tableaux for modal logics: Computational properties, complexity and methodology. Journal of Automated Reasoning 24(3), 319–364 (2000)
79. Motik, B., Shearer, R., Horrocks, I.: Hypertableau reasoning for description logics. Journal of Artifical Intelligence Research 36, 165–228 (2009)
80. Nellas, K.: Reasoning about sets and relations: A tableaux-based automated theorem prover for Peirce logic. Master's thesis, The University of Manchester, UK (2001)
81. Niemelä, I.: A Tableau Calculus for Minimal Model Reasoning. In: Miglioli, P., Moscato, U., Ornaghi, M., Mundici, D. (eds.) TABLEAUX 1996. LNCS (LNAI), vol. 1071, pp. 278–294. Springer, Heidelberg (1996)
82. Nieuwenhuis, R., Rubio, A.: Paramodulation-based theorem proving. In: Robinson, A., Voronkov, A. (eds.) Handbook of Automated Reasoning, pp. 371–443. Elsevier (2001)
83. Nonnengart, A.: First-order modal logic theorem proving and functional simulation. In: Proc. IJCAI 1993, pp. 80–85. Morgan Kaufmann (1993)
84. Nonnengart, A.: A Resolution-Based Calculus For Temporal Logics. PhD thesis, Universität des Saarlandes, Saarbrücken, Germany (1995)
85. Nonnengart, A.: Resolution-Based Calculi for Modal and Temporal Logics. In: McRobbie, M.A., Slaney, J.K. (eds.) CADE 1996. LNCS (LNAI), vol. 1104, pp. 598–612. Springer, Heidelberg (1996)
86. Nonnengart, A., Ohlbach, H.J., Szałas, A.: Elimination of predicate quantifiers. In: Ohlbach, H.J., Reyle, U. (eds.) Logic, Language and Reasoning. Essays in Honor of Dov Gabbay, pp. 159–181. Kluwer (1999)
87. Ohlbach, H.J.: Semantics based translation methods for modal logics. Journal of Logic and Computation 1(5), 691–746 (1991)
88. Ohlbach, H.J.: Translation methods for non-classical logics: An overview. Bulletin of the IGPL 1(1), 69–89 (1993)
89. Ohlbach, H.J.: Combining Hilbert Style and Semantic Reasoning in a Resolution Framework. In: Kirchner, C., Kirchner, H. (eds.) CADE 1998. LNCS (LNAI), vol. 1421, pp. 205–219. Springer, Heidelberg (1998)
90. Ohlbach, H.-J., Engel, T.: SCAN (1994), http://www.mpi-inf.mpg.de/departments/d2/software/SCAN/
91. Ohlbach, H.J., Nonnengart, A., de Rijke, M., Gabbay, D.: Encoding two-valued nonclassical logics in classical logic. In: Robinson, A., Voronkov, A. (eds.) Handbook of Automated Reasoning, pp. 1403–1486. Elsevier (2001)
92. Ohlbach, H.J., Schmidt, R.A.: Functional translation and second-order frame properties of modal logics. Journal of Logic and Computation 7(5), 581–603 (1997)
93. Pérez-Urbina, H., Motik, B., Horrocks, I.: Tractable query answering and rewriting under description logic constraints. Journal of Applied Logic 8(2), 186–209 (2010)
94. Purdy, W.C.: Decidability of fluted logic with identity. Notre Dame Journal of Formal Logic 37(1), 84–104 (1996)
95. Purdy, W.C.: Quine's 'limits of decision'. Journal of Symbolic Logic 64(4), 1439–1466 (1999)
96. Quine, W.V.: Variables explained away. In: Proc. American Philosophy Society, vol. 104, pp. 343–347 (1960)
97. Quine, W.V.: Algebraic logic and predicate functors. In: Rudner, R., Scheffler, I. (eds.) Logic and Art: Esssays in Honor of Nelson Goodman. Bobbs-Merrill (1971)
98. Riazanov, A., Voronkov, A.: Vampire. In: Ganzinger, H. (ed.) CADE 1999. LNCS (LNAI), vol. 1632, pp. 292–296. Springer, Heidelberg (1999)

99. Riazanov, A., Voronkov, A.: Splitting without backtracking. In: Proc. IJCAI 2001, pp. 611–617. Morgan Kaufmann (2001)
100. Robinson, J.A.: A machine-oriented logic based on the resolution principle. Journal of the ACM 12(1), 23–41 (1965)
101. Sahlqvist, H.: Completeness and correspondence in the first and second order semantics for modal logics. In: Proc. 3rd Scandinavian Logic Symposium, pp. 110–143. North-Holland (1973-1975)
102. Schmidt, R.A.: Optimised Modal Translation and Resolution. PhD thesis, Universität des Saarlandes, Saarbrücken, Germany (1997)
103. Schmidt, R.A.: Decidability by resolution for propositional modal logics. Journal of Automated Reasoning 22(4), 379–396 (1999)
104. Schmidt, R.A.: MSPASS (1999), http://www.cs.man.ac.uk/~schmidt/mspass/
105. Schmidt, R.A.: Improved Second-Order Quantifier Elimination in Modal Logic. In: Hölldobler, S., Lutz, C., Wansing, H. (eds.) JELIA 2008. LNCS (LNAI), vol. 5293, pp. 375–388. Springer, Heidelberg (2008)
106. Schmidt, R.A.: A new methodology for developing deduction methods. Annals of Mathematics and Artificial Intelligence 55(1–2), 155–187 (2009)
107. Schmidt, R.A.: Simulation and synthesis of deduction calculi. Electronic Notes in Theoretical Computer Science 262, 221–229 (2010)
108. Schmidt, R.A., Hustadt, U.: A Resolution Decision Procedure for Fluted Logic. In: McAllester, D. (ed.) CADE 2000. LNCS (LNAI), vol. 1831, pp. 433–448. Springer, Heidelberg (2000)
109. Schmidt, R.A., Hustadt, U.: Mechanised Reasoning and Model Generation for Extended Modal Logics. In: de Swart, H., Orłowska, E., Schmidt, G., Roubens, M. (eds.) Theory and Applications of Relational Structures as Knowledge Instruments. LNCS, vol. 2929, pp. 38–67. Springer, Heidelberg (2003)
110. Schmidt, R.A., Hustadt, U.: A Principle for Incorporating Axioms into the First-Order Translation of Modal Formulae. In: Baader, F. (ed.) CADE 2003. LNCS (LNAI), vol. 2741, pp. 412–426. Springer, Heidelberg (2003)
111. Schmidt, R.A., Hustadt, U.: The axiomatic translation principle for modal logic. ACM Transactions on Computational Logic 8(4), 1–55 (2007)
112. Schmidt, R.A., Orlowska, E., Hustadt, U.: Two Proof Systems for Peirce Algebras. In: Berghammer, R., Möller, B., Struth, G. (eds.) RelMiCS 2003. LNCS, vol. 3051, pp. 238–251. Springer, Heidelberg (2004)
113. Schmidt, R.A., Tishkovsky, D.: Using Tableau to Decide Expressive Description Logics with Role Negation. In: Aberer, K., Choi, K.-S., Noy, N., Allemang, D., Lee, K.-I., Nixon, L.J.B., Golbeck, J., Mika, P., Maynard, D., Mizoguchi, R., Schreiber, G., Cudré-Mauroux, P. (eds.) ASWC 2007 and ISWC 2007. LNCS, vol. 4825, pp. 438–451. Springer, Heidelberg (2007)
114. Schulz, S.: E: A brainiac theorem prover. Journal of AI Communications 15(2–3), 111–126 (2002)
115. Smith, K.J.: The axiomatic translation of modal logic into first order logic. Master's thesis, The University of Manchester, UK (2008)
116. Smith, K.J.: Downloads for project in Axiomatic Translation of Modal Logic 2007/8 Manchester (2008), http://project.kjsmith.net/
117. Stenz, G.: DCTP 1.2 - System Abstract. In: Egly, U., Fermüller, C. (eds.) TABLEAUX 2002. LNCS (LNAI), vol. 2381, pp. 335–340. Springer, Heidelberg (2002)
118. Szałas, A.: On the correspondence between modal and classical logic: An automated approach. Journal of Logic and Computation 3(6), 605–620 (1993)

119. van Benthem, J.: Correspondence theory. In: Gabbay, D., Guenther, F. (eds.) Handbook of Philosophical Logic, pp. 167–247. Reidel, Dordrecht (1984)
120. Weidenbach, C., Brahm, U., Hillenbrand, T., Keen, E., Theobald, C., Topic, D.: SPASS Version 2.0. In: Voronkov, A. (ed.) CADE 2002. LNCS (LNAI), vol. 2392, pp. 275–279. Springer, Heidelberg (2002)
121. Weidenbach, C., Schmidt, R.A., Hillenbrand, T., Rusev, R., Topic, D.: System Description: SPASS Version 3.0. In: Pfenning, F. (ed.) CADE 2007. LNCS (LNAI), vol. 4603, pp. 514–520. Springer, Heidelberg (2007)
122. Zamov, N.K.: Modal resolutions. Soviet Mathematics 33(9), 22–29 (1989); Translated from Izv. Vyssh. Uchebn. Zaved. Mat. 9(328), 22–29 (1989)
123. Zhang, L.: CTL-RP 00.25 (2010), http://www.csc.liv.ac.uk/~lan/softwares.html
124. Zhang, L.: Clausal Reasoning for Branching-Time Logics. PhD thesis, University of Liverpool, UK (2011)
125. Zhang, L., Hustadt, U., Dixon, C.: A Refined Resolution Calculus for CTL. In: Schmidt, R.A. (ed.) CADE-22. LNCS (LNAI), vol. 5663, pp. 245–260. Springer, Heidelberg (2009)
126. Zhang, L., Hustadt, U., Dixon, C.: CTL-RP: A computation tree logic resolution prover. AI Communication 23(2-3), 111–136 (2010)

On Combinations of Local Theory Extensions

Viorica Sofronie-Stokkermans

Max-Planck-Institut für Informatik, Stuhlsatzenhausweg 85, Saarbrücken, Germany
sofronie@mpi-inf.mpg.de

Abstract. In this paper we study theory extensions in which efficient reasoning is possible. We study local extensions (in which hierarchical reasoning is possible) and give several examples from computer science or mathematics in which such extensions occur in a natural way. We then identify situations in which combinations of local extensions of a theory are again local extensions of that theory. We thus obtain criteria both for recognizing wider classes of local theory extensions, and for modular reasoning in combinations of theories over non-disjoint signatures.

1 Introduction

Many problems in mathematics and computer science can be reduced to proving the satisfiability of conjunctions of literals in a background theory (which can be the extension of a base theory with additional functions – e.g., free, monotone, or recursively defined – or a combination of theories). It is therefore very important to identify situations where reasoning in complex theories can be done efficiently and accurately. Efficiency can be achieved for instance by:

(1) reducing the search space (preferably without losing completeness);
(2) modular reasoning, i.e., delegating some proof tasks which refer to a specific theory to provers specialized in handling formulae of that theory.

We are interested in identifying situations in which both these goals can be achieved without loss of completeness.

Controlling the Search Space. The quest for identifying theories where the search space can be controlled without loss of completeness led McAllester and Givan to define *local theories*, that is sets N of Horn clauses with the property that for any ground clause G, $N \models G$ iff G can already be proved using only those instances $N[G]$ of N containing only ground terms occurring in G or in N. For local theories, validity of ground Horn clauses can be checked in polynomial time. In [BG96, BG01], Ganzinger and Basin defined the more general notion of *order locality* and showed how to recognize (order-)local theories and how to use these results for automated complexity analysis.

Similar ideas also occurred in algebra, where the main interest was to identify classes of algebras for which the uniform word problem is decidable in polynomial time. In [Bur95], Burris proved that if a quasi-variety axiomatized by a set $\mathcal{K}$ of Horn clauses has the property that *every finite partial algebra which is a partial*

A. Voronkov and C. Weidenbach (Eds.): Ganzinger Festschrift, LNCS 7797, pp. 392–413, 2013.

model of the axioms in $\mathcal{K}$ *can be extended to a total algebra model of* $\mathcal{K}$ then the uniform word problem for $\mathcal{K}$ is decidable in polynomial time. In [Gan01], Ganzinger established a link between proof theoretic and semantic concepts for polynomial time decidability of uniform word problems. He defined two notions of locality for equational Horn theories, and established relationships between these notions of locality and corresponding semantic conditions, referring to embeddability of partial algebras into total algebras.

Modular Reasoning. When reasoning in extensions or combinations of theories it is very important to find ways of delegating some proof tasks which refer to a specific theory to provers specialized in handling formulae of that theory. Of particular interest are situations when reasoning can be done:

- in a hierarchical way (that is, for reasoning in a theory extension a prover for the base theory can be used as a black-box), or
- in a modular way (that is, for reasoning in a combination of theories reasoning in the component theories is "decoupled", i.e., the information about the component theories is never combined and only formulae in the joint signature are exchanged between provers for the components).

In [GSSW04, GSSW06] we analyzed possibilities of modular reasoning (using special superposition calculi) in combinations of first-order theories involving both total and partial functions. The calculi are shown to be complete provided that functions that are not in the intersection of the component signatures are declared as partial. Cases where the partial models can always be made total are identified: in such cases modular superposition is also complete with respect to the standard (total function) semantics of the theories. Inspired by the link between embeddability and locality established by Ganzinger in [Gan01], such extensions were called *local*.

Reasoning in Local Theory Extensions and Their Combinations. In [GSSW04], [GSSW06] and, later, in [SS05] we showed that for *local theory extensions* efficient hierarchic reasoning is possible. For such extensions the two goals previously mentioned can be addressed at the same time: the locality of an extension allows to reduce the search space, but at the same time (as a by-product) it allows to perform an easy reduction to a proof task in the base theory (for this, a specialized prover can be used as a black box).

Many theories important for computer science or mathematics are local extensions of a base theory: theories of data structures, theories of monotone functions or of functions satisfying the Lipschitz conditions at a given point. However, often it is necessary to consider complex extensions, with various types of functions (such as, for instance, extensions of the theory of real numbers with free, monotone and Lipschitz functions). It is important to have efficient methods for hierarchic and/or modular reasoning for such combinations as well. Finding methods for reasoning in combinations of extensions of a base theory is far from trivial: as these are usually combinations of theories over non-disjoint signatures, classical combination results such as the Nelson-Oppen combination method [NO79] cannot be applied; methods for reasoning in combinations of theories over non-disjoint signatures – as studied by Ghilardi et al. [Ghi04, BG07] – may also not always be applicable (unless the base theory is universal and the extensions satisfy certain model-theoretic compatibility conditions required in [Ghi04, BG07]).

In this paper we identify situations in which a combination of local extensions of a base theory is guaranteed to be itself a local extension of the base theory. We thus obtain criteria for recognizing complex local theory extensions, and for efficient reasoning in such combinations of theories (over non-disjoint signatures) in a modular way.

Structure of the paper: The paper is structured as follows: Section 2 contains generalities on partial algebras, weak validity and embeddability of partial algebras into total algebras. In Section 3 the notion of local theory extension is introduced. In Section 4 links between embeddability and locality of an extension are established. In Section 5, examples of local theory extensions are given. In the following two sections we identify situations under which a combination of local extensions of a base theory is guaranteed to be itself a local extension of the base theory, under stronger (Section 6) or weaker (Section 7) embeddability conditions for the components. Some ideas on hierarchical and modular reasoning in such combinations are discussed in Section 8. Section 9 contains conclusions and plans for future work.

Many of the results presented here are a natural continuation of joint work with Harald Ganzinger. His work on locality and especially the links he established between locality and embeddability [Gan01] were a source of inspiration for the similar criteria for local theory extensions. In addition, the results on combinations of local extensions of a base theory presented in this paper generalize results on combinations of local theories obtained in [GSS01].

2   Preliminaries

This section contains the main notions and definitions necessary in the paper.

2.1   Partial Structures

Let $\Pi = (\Sigma, \mathsf{Pred})$ be a signature where Σ is a set of function symbols and Pred a set of predicate symbols.

Definition 1. *A partial Π-structure is a structure $(A, \{f_A\}_{f \in \Sigma}, \{P_A\}_{P \in \mathsf{Pred}})$, where A is a non-empty set and for every $f \in \Sigma$ with arity n, f_A is a partial function from A^n to A. The structure is a (total) structure if all functions f_A are total.*

In what follows we usually denote both an algebra and its support with the same symbol. Details on partial algebras can be found in [Bur86].

The notion of evaluating a term t with respect to a variable assignment β : $X \to A$ for its variables in a partial algebra A is the same as for total algebras, except that this evaluation is undefined if $t = f(t_1, \ldots, t_n)$ and either one of $\beta(t_i)$ is undefined, or else $(\beta(t_1), \ldots, \beta(t_n))$ is not in the domain of f_A.

Definition 2. *We define* weak validity *in structures* $(A, \{f_A\}_{f \in \Sigma}, \{P_A\}_{P \in \mathsf{Pred}})$, *where* Pred *is a set of predicate symbols and* $(A, \{f_A\}_{f \in \Sigma})$ *is a partial Σ-algebra. Let $\beta : X \to A$.*

(1) $(A, \beta) \models_w t \approx s$ if and only if (a) $\beta(t)$ and $\beta(s)$ are both defined and equal; or (b) at least one of $\beta(s)$ and $\beta(t)$ is undefined.

(2) $(A, \beta) \models_w t \not\approx s$ if and only if (a) $\beta(t)$ and $\beta(s)$ are both defined and different; or (b) at least one of $\beta(s)$ and $\beta(t)$ is undefined.

(3) $(A, \beta) \models_w P(t_1, \ldots, t_n)$ if and only if (a) $\beta(t_1), \ldots, \beta(t_n)$ are all defined and $(\beta(t_1), \ldots, \beta(t_n)) \in P_A$; or (b) at least one of $\beta(t_1)$, $\ldots$, $\beta(t_n)$ is undefined.

(4) $(A, \beta) \models_w \neg P(t_1, \ldots, t_n)$ if and only if (a) $\beta(t_1)$, $\ldots$, $\beta(t_n)$ are all defined and $(\beta(t_1), \ldots, \beta(t_n)) \notin P_A$; or (b) at least one of $\beta(t_1), \ldots, \beta(t_n)$ is undefined.

(A, β) weakly satisfies a clause C (notation: $(A, \beta) \models_w C$) if $(A, \beta) \models_w L$ for at least one literal L in C. A weakly satisfies C (notation: $A \models_w C$) if $(A, \beta) \models_w C$ for all assignments β. A weakly satisfies a set of clauses $\mathcal{K}$ (notation: $A \models_w \mathcal{K}$) if $A \models_w C$ for all $C \in \mathcal{K}$.

Example 1. *Let A be a partial Σ-algebra, where $\Sigma = \{\mathsf{car}/1, \mathsf{nil}/0\}$. Assume that nil_A is defined and $\mathsf{car}_A(\mathsf{nil}_A)$ is not defined. Then $A \models_w \mathsf{car}(\mathsf{nil}) \approx \mathsf{nil}$ and $A \models_w \mathsf{car}(\mathsf{nil}) \not\approx \mathsf{nil}$ (because one term is not defined in A).*

Definition 3. *A weak Π-embedding between the partial structures $(A, \{f_A\}_{f \in \Sigma}, \{P_A\}_{P \in \mathsf{Pred}})$ and $(B, \{f_B\}_{f \in \Sigma}, \{P_B\}_{P \in \mathsf{Pred}})$ is a total map $i : A \to B$ such that*

- *whenever $f_A(a_1, \ldots, a_n)$ is defined then $f_B(i(a_1), \ldots, i(a_n))$ is defined and $i(f_A(a_1, \ldots, a_n)) = f_B(i(a_1), \ldots, i(a_n))$;*
- *i is injective;*
- *i is an embedding w.r.t. Pred, i.e. for every $P \in \mathsf{Pred}$ with arity n and every $a_1, \ldots, a_n \in A$, $P_A(a_1, \ldots, a_n)$ if and only if $P_B(i(a_1), \ldots, i(a_n))$.*

In this case we say that A weakly embeds into B.

2.2   Theories and Extensions of Theories

Theories can be regarded as sets of formulae or as sets of models. Let $\mathcal{T}$ be a Π-theory and ϕ, ψ be Π-sentences. We say that $\mathcal{T} \wedge \phi \models \psi$ (written also $\phi \models_\mathcal{T} \psi$) if ψ is true in all models of $\mathcal{T}$ which satisfy ϕ.

In what follows we consider extensions of theories, in which the signature is extended by new *function symbols* (i.e. we assume that the set of predicate symbols remains unchanged in the extension). If a theory is regarded as a set of formulae, then its extension with a set of formulae is set union. If $\mathcal{T}$ is regarded as a collection of models then its extension with a set $\mathcal{K}$ of sentences (in the extended signature) consists of all structures (in the extended signature) which are models of $\mathcal{K}$ and whose reduct to the signature of $\mathcal{T}_0$ is in $\mathcal{T}_0$. In this paper we regard theories as sets of models. All the results of this paper can easily be reformulated to a setting in which $\mathcal{T}_0$ is a collection of formulae (but then the remarks on compactness in Theorem 1 become superfluous).

Let $\mathcal{T}_0$ be an arbitrary theory with signature $\Pi_0 = (\Sigma_0, \mathsf{Pred})$, where the set of function symbols is Σ_0. We consider extensions $\mathcal{T}_1$ of $\mathcal{T}_0$ with signature $\Pi = (\Sigma, \mathsf{Pred})$, where the set of function symbols is $\Sigma = \Sigma_0 \cup \Sigma_1$. We assume that $\mathcal{T}_1$ is an extension of $\mathcal{T}_0$ with a set $\mathcal{K}$ of (universally quantified) clauses.

Definition 4. *A partial Π-algebra A is a* weak partial model *of $\mathcal{T}_1$ with totally defined Σ_0-function symbols if (i) $A_{|\Pi_0}$ is a model of $\mathcal{T}_0$ and (ii) A weakly satisfies all clauses in $\mathcal{K}$.*

If the base theory $\mathcal{T}_0$ and its signature are clear from the context, we will refer to *weak partial models* of $\mathcal{T}_1$. We will use the following notation:

- $\mathsf{PMod}_w(\Sigma_1, \mathcal{T}_1)$ is the class of all weak partial models of $\mathcal{T}_1$ in which the Σ_1-functions are partial and all the other function symbols are total;
- $\mathsf{PMod}_w^f(\Sigma_1, \mathcal{T}_1)$ is the class of all finite weak partial models of $\mathcal{T}_1$ in which the Σ_1-functions are partial and all the other function symbols are total;
- $\mathsf{PMod}_w^{fd}(\Sigma_1, \mathcal{T}_1)$ is the class of all weak partial models of $\mathcal{T}_1$ in which the Σ_1-functions are partial and their definition domain is a finite set, and all the other function symbols are total;
- $\mathsf{Mod}(\mathcal{T}_1)$ denotes the class of all models of $\mathcal{T}_1$ in which all functions in $\Sigma_0 \cup \Sigma_1$ are totally defined.

Embeddability. For theory extensions $\mathcal{T}_0 \subseteq \mathcal{T}_1 = \mathcal{T}_0 \cup \mathcal{K}$, where $\mathcal{K}$ is a set of clauses, we consider the following condition:

(Emb$_w$)   Every $A \in \mathsf{PMod}_w(\Sigma_1, \mathcal{T}_1)$ weakly embeds into a total model of $\mathcal{T}_1$.

We also define a stronger notion of embeddability, which we call *completability*:

(Comp$_w$)   Every $A \in \mathsf{PMod}_w(\Sigma_1, \mathcal{T}_1)$ weakly embeds into a total model B of $\mathcal{T}_1$ such that $A_{|\Pi_0}$ and $B_{|\Pi_0}$ are isomorphic.

Weaker conditions, which only refer to embeddability of *finite* partial models, will be denoted by (Emb$_w^f$), resp. (Comp$_w^f$). Conditions which refer to embeddability of partial models in $\mathsf{PMod}_w^{fd}(\Sigma_1, \mathcal{T}_1)$ will be denoted by (Emb$_w^{fd}$), resp. (Comp$_w^{fd}$).

3   Locality

The notion of *local theory* was introduced by Givan and McAllester [GM92, McA93].

Definition 5 (Local theory). *A local theory is a set of Horn clauses $\mathcal{K}$ such that, for any ground Horn clause C, $\mathcal{K} \models C$ only if already $\mathcal{K}[C] \models C$ (where $\mathcal{K}[C]$ is the set of instances of $\mathcal{K}$ in which all terms are subterms of ground terms in either $\mathcal{K}$ or C).*

The notion of locality in *equational* theories was studied by Ganzinger [Gan01], who also related it to a semantical property, namely embeddability of partial algebras into total algebras. In [GSSW04, GSSW06, SS05] the notion of locality for Horn clauses is extended to the notion of *local extension* of a base theory.

Let $\mathcal{K}$ be a set of clauses in the signature $\Pi = (\Sigma_0 \cup \Sigma_1, \mathsf{Pred})$. In what follows, when we refer to sets G of ground clauses we assume that they are in the signature $\Pi^c = (\Sigma \cup \Sigma_c, \mathsf{Pred})$, where Σ_c is a set of new constants. If Ψ is a set of ground $\Sigma_0 \cup \Sigma_1 \cup \Sigma_c$-terms, we denote by $\mathcal{K}_\Psi$ the set of all instances of $\mathcal{K}$ in which all terms starting with a Σ_1-function symbol are ground terms in the set Ψ. If G is a set of ground clauses and $\Psi = \mathsf{st}(\mathcal{K}, G)$ is the set of ground subterms occurring in either $\mathcal{K}$ or G then we write $\mathcal{K}[G] := \mathcal{K}_\Psi$.

We will focus on the following type of locality of a theory extension $\mathcal{T}_0 \subseteq \mathcal{T}_1$, where $\mathcal{T}_1 = \mathcal{T}_0 \cup \mathcal{K}$ with $\mathcal{K}$ a set of (universally quantified) clauses:

(Loc) For every set G of ground clauses $\mathcal{T}_1 \cup G \models \perp$ iff $\mathcal{T}_0 \cup \mathcal{K}[G] \cup G$ has no weak partial model in which all terms in $\mathsf{st}(\mathcal{K}, G)$ are defined.

A weaker notion (Loc^f) can be defined if we require that the respective conditions hold only for *finite* sets G of ground clauses. An intermediate notion of locality (Loc^{fd}) can be defined if we require that the respective conditions hold only for sets G of ground clauses containing only a finite set of terms starting with a function symbol in Σ_1.

Definition 6. *An extension $\mathcal{T}_0 \subseteq \mathcal{T}_1$ is local if it satisfies condition* (Loc^f).

A local theory [Gan01] is a local extension of the empty theory (i.e. of the pure theory of equality).

4   Locality and Embeddability

There is a strong link between locality of a theory extension and embeddability of partial models into total ones. Links between *locality of a theory* and *embeddability* were established by Ganzinger in [Gan01]. We show that similar results can also be obtained for *local theory extensions*.

In what follows we say that a non-ground clause is Σ_1-*flat* if function symbols (including constants) do not occur as arguments of function symbols in Σ_1. A Σ_1-flat non-ground clause is called Σ_1-*linear* if whenever a variable occurs in two terms in the clause which start with function symbols in Σ_1, the two terms are identical, and if no term which starts with a function in Σ_1 contains two occurrences of the same variable.

We first show that for sets of Σ_1-flat clauses locality implies embeddability. This generalizes results presented in the case of local theories in [Gan01].

Theorem 1. *Assume that $\mathcal{K}$ is a family of Σ_1-flat clauses in the signature Π.*

(1) If the extension $\mathcal{T}_0 \subseteq \mathcal{T}_1 := \mathcal{T}_0 \cup \mathcal{K}$ satisfies (Loc) *then it satisfies* (Emb_w).

(2) If the extension $\mathcal{T}_0 \subseteq \mathcal{T}_1 := \mathcal{T}_0 \cup \mathcal{K}$ satisfies (Loc^f) then it satisfies (Emb$_w^f$).
(3) If the extension $\mathcal{T}_0 \subseteq \mathcal{T}_1 := \mathcal{T}_0 \cup \mathcal{K}$ satisfies (Loc^{fd}) then it satisfies (Emb$_w^{fd}$).
(4) If $\mathcal{T}_0$ is compact and the extension $\mathcal{T}_0 \subseteq \mathcal{T}_1$ satisfies (Loc^f), then $\mathcal{T}_0 \subseteq \mathcal{T}_1$ satisfies (Emb$_w$).

Proof: We prove (4) and show how the proof can be changed to provide proofs for (1), (2) and (3). Let A be a partial Π-algebra with totally defined Σ_0-functions, which is a model of $\mathcal{T}_0$ and weakly satisfies $\mathcal{K}$. Let

$$\Delta(A) = \{f(a_1, \ldots a_n) \approx a \mid \text{if } f_A(a_1, \ldots, a_n) \text{ is defined and equal to } a\}$$
$$\cup \{f(a_1, \ldots a_n) \not\approx a \mid \text{if } f_A(a_1, \ldots, a_n) \text{ is defined and not equal to } a\}$$
$$\cup \{P(a_1, \ldots, a_n) \mid P \in \mathsf{Pred} \text{ and } (a_1, \ldots, a_n) \in P_A\}$$
$$\cup \{\neg P(a_1, \ldots, a_n) \mid P \in \mathsf{Pred} \text{ and } (a_1, \ldots, a_n) \notin P_A\}$$
$$\cup \{a \not\approx a' \mid a \neq a', a, a' \in A\}$$

We prove that $\mathcal{T}_0 \cup \mathcal{K} \cup \Delta(A)$ is consistent, where the elements of A are regarded as new constants. Assume $\mathcal{T}_0 \cup \mathcal{K} \cup \Delta(A) \models \bot$. By compactness of $\mathcal{T}_0$, $\mathcal{T}_0 \cup \mathcal{K} \cup \Gamma \models \bot$, for some finite subset Γ of $\Delta(A)$. We know that A is a model of $\mathcal{T}_0$. Every term starting with a function symbol in Σ_1 contained in the clauses in $\mathcal{K}[\Gamma]$ is either a ground (subterm of a) term occurring in Γ (and, hence, a constant $a \in A$, or a term $f(a_1, \ldots, a_n)$, where $f_A(a_1, \ldots, a_n)$ is defined), or is a ground subterm in $\mathcal{K}$, i.e. a constant, and hence, again defined in A. Therefore, all terms occurring in the clauses in $\mathcal{K}[\Gamma]$ are defined in A, so A satisfies all these clauses, i.e. A is a model of $\mathcal{T}_0 \cup \mathcal{K}[\Gamma]$. Since $\Delta(A)$ is obviously true in A and $\Gamma \subseteq \Delta(A)$, A is a partial model of $\mathcal{T}_0 \cup \mathcal{K}[\Gamma] \cup \Gamma$, in which all ground terms occurring in $\mathcal{K}$ or Γ are defined. This contradicts the fact that $\mathcal{T}_1$ is a local extension of $\mathcal{T}_0$. Hence, the assumption that $\mathcal{T}_0 \cup \mathcal{K} \cup \Delta(A) \models \bot$ was false, so $\mathcal{T}_0 \cup \mathcal{K} \cup \Delta(A)$ has a model A' in which, therefore, A weakly embeds.

(1) If (Loc) holds then we can choose $\Gamma = \Delta(A)$. (2) If A is finite we can choose $\Gamma = \Delta(A)$, so the compactness of $\mathcal{T}_0$ is not needed. (3) If all functions in Σ_1 have a finite domain of definition in A, then $\Delta(A)$ contains only finitely many terms starting with a Σ_1-function. Therefore also in this case we can choose $\Gamma = \Delta(A)$. $\qquad\square$

Conversely, embeddability implies locality. The following results appear in [SS05] and [SSI07a, SSI07b]. This result allows to give several examples of local theory extensions.

Theorem 2 ([SS05, SSI07a, SSI07b]). *Let $\mathcal{K}$ be a set of Σ_1-flat and Σ_1-linear clauses.*

(1) If the extension $\mathcal{T}_0 \subseteq \mathcal{T}_1$ satisfies (Emb$_w$) then it satisfies (Loc).
(2) Assume that $\mathcal{T}_0$ is a locally finite universal theory, and that $\mathcal{K}$ contains only finitely many ground subterms. If the extension $\mathcal{T}_0 \subseteq \mathcal{T}_1$ satisfies (Emb$_w^f$), then $\mathcal{T}_0 \subseteq \mathcal{T}_1$ satisfies (Loc^f).
(3) $\mathcal{T}_0 \subseteq \mathcal{T}_1$ satisfies (Emb$_w^{fd}$). Then $\mathcal{T}_0 \subseteq \mathcal{T}_1$ satisfies (Loc^{fd}).

5   Examples of Local Theory Extensions

We present several examples of theory extensions for which embedding conditions among those mentioned above hold and are thus local. For details cf. [SS05, SS06a, SSI07a, SSI07b].

Extensions with free functions. Any extension $\mathcal{T}_0 \cup \mathsf{Free}(\Sigma)$ of a theory $\mathcal{T}_0$ with a set Σ of free function symbols satisfies condition $(\mathsf{Comp_w})$.

Extensions with selector functions. Let $\mathcal{T}_0$ be a theory with signature $\Pi_0 = (\Sigma_0, \mathsf{Pred})$, let $c \in \Sigma_0$ with arity n, and let $\Sigma_1 = \{s_1, \ldots, s_n\}$ consist of n unary function symbols. Let $\mathcal{T}_1 = \mathcal{T}_0 \cup \mathsf{Sel}_c$ (a theory with signature $\Pi = (\Sigma_0 \cup \Sigma_1, \mathsf{Pred})$) be the extension of $\mathcal{T}_0$ with the set Sel_c of clauses below. Assume that $\mathcal{T}_0$ satisfies the (universally quantified) formula Inj_c (i.e. c is injective in $\mathcal{T}_0$) then the extension $\mathcal{T}_0 \subseteq \mathcal{T}_1$ satisfies condition $(\mathsf{Comp_w})$ [SS05].

$$(\mathsf{Sel}_c) \qquad s_1(c(x_1, \ldots, x_n)) \approx x_1$$
$$\ldots$$
$$s_n(c(x_1, \ldots, x_n)) \approx x_n$$
$$x \approx c(x_1, \ldots, x_n) \to c(s_1(x), \ldots, s_n(x)) \approx x$$
$$(\mathsf{Inj}_c) \qquad c(x_1, \ldots, x_n) \approx c(y_1, \ldots, y_n) \to (\bigwedge_{i=1}^{n} x_i \approx y_i)$$

Extensions with functions satisfying general monotonicity conditions. In [SS05] and [SSI07a, SSI07b] we analyzed extensions with monotonicity conditions for an n-ary function f w.r.t. a subset $I \subseteq \{1, \ldots, n\}$ of its arguments:

$$(\mathsf{Mon}_f^I) \quad \bigwedge_{i \in I} x_i \leq_i y_i \wedge \bigwedge_{i \notin I} x_i = y_i \to f(x_1, .., x_n) \leq f(y_1, .., y_n).$$

Here, $\mathsf{Mon}_f^{\emptyset}$ is equivalent to the congruence axiom for f. If $I = \{1, \ldots, n\}$ we speak of monotonicity in all arguments; we denote $\mathsf{Mon}_f^{\{1, \ldots, n\}}$ by Mon_f. Monotonicity in some arguments and antitonicity in other arguments is modeled by considering functions $f : \prod_{i \in I} P_i^{\sigma_i} \times \prod_{j \notin I} P_j \to P$ with $\sigma_i \in \{-, +\}$, where $P_i^+ = P_i$ and $P_i^- = P_i^{\partial}$, the order dual of the poset P_i. The corresponding axioms are denoted by Mon_f^{σ}, where for $i \in I$, $\sigma(i) = \sigma_i \in \{-, +\}$, and for $i \notin I$, $\sigma(i) = 0$. The following hold [SS05, SSI07a, SSI07b]:

1. Let $\mathcal{T}_0$ be a class of (many-sorted) bounded semilattice-ordered Σ_0-structures. Let Σ_1 be disjoint from Σ_0 and $\mathcal{T}_1 = \mathcal{T}_0 \cup \{\mathsf{Mon}^{\sigma}(f) | f \in \Sigma_1\}$. Then the extension $\mathcal{T}_0 \subseteq \mathcal{T}_1$ satisfies $(\mathsf{Comp_w^{fd}})$, hence is local.

2. Any extension of the theory of posets with functions in a set Σ_1 satisfying $\{\mathsf{Mon}_f^{\sigma} \mid f \in \Sigma_1\}$ satisfies condition $(\mathsf{Emb_w})$, hence is local.

This provides us with a large number of concrete examples. For instance the extensions with functions satisfying monotonicity axioms Mon_f^{σ} of the following (possibly many-sorted) classes of algebras are local:

- any class of algebras with a bounded (semi)lattice reduct, a bounded distributive lattice reduct, or a Boolean algebra reduct (($\mathsf{Comp_w^{fd}}$) holds);
- any extension of a class of algebras with a semilattice reduct, a (distributive) lattice reduct, or a Boolean algebra reduct, with monotone functions into an infinite numeric domain (($\mathsf{Comp_w^{fd}}$) holds);
- $\mathcal{T}$, the class of totally-ordered sets; $\mathcal{DO}$, the theory of dense totally-ordered sets (($\mathsf{Comp_w^{fd}}$) holds);
- the class $\mathcal{P}$ of partially-ordered sets (($\mathsf{Emb_w}$) holds).

Similarly, it can be proved that any extension of the theory of reals (integers) with functions satisfying Mon_f^σ into a fixed infinite numerical domain is local (condition ($\mathsf{Comp_w^{fd}}$) holds).

Boundedness conditions. Any extension of a theory for which $\leq$ is reflexive with functions satisfying (Mon_f^σ) and boundedness (Bound_f^t) conditions is local [SS06a, SSI07a, SSI07b].

(Bound_f^t) $\forall x_1, \ldots, x_n(f(x_1, \ldots, x_n) \leq t(x_1, \ldots, x_n))$

where $t(x_1, \ldots, x_n)$ is a term in the base signature Π_0 with variables among $x_1, \ldots, x_n$ (such that in any model the associated function has the same monotonicity as f).

Similar results can be given for *guarded monotonicity conditions* with mutually disjoint guards [SS06a].

Extensions with Lipschitz functions. The extension $\mathbb{R} \subseteq \mathbb{R} \cup (\mathsf{L}_f^\lambda)$ of $\mathbb{R}$ with a unary function which is λ-Lipschitz in a point x_0 (for $\lambda > 0$) satisfies condition ($\mathsf{Comp_w}$).

(L_f^λ) $\forall x \; |f(x) - f(x_0)| \leq \lambda \cdot |x - x_0|$

The results described before can easily be extended to a many-sorted framework. Therefore various additional examples of (many-sorted) theory extensions related to data structures can be given cf. e.g. [SS06b].

6   Combinations of Local Extensions Satisfying ($\mathsf{Comp_w}$)

In this and the following sections we study the locality of combinations of local theory extensions. In the light of the results in Section 4 we concentrate on studying which embeddability properties are preserved under combinations of theories. For the sake of simplicity, in what follows we only consider the conditions ($\mathsf{Emb_w}$) and ($\mathsf{Comp_w}$). Analogous results can be given for the conditions ($\mathsf{Emb_w^f}$), ($\mathsf{Comp_w^f}$), resp. ($\mathsf{Emb_w^{fd}}$), ($\mathsf{Comp_w^{fd}}$) and combinations thereof.

We start with a simple case of combinations of local extensions of a base theory: we consider the situation when both components satisfy the embeddability condition ($\mathsf{Comp_w}$). We first analyze the simple case of combinations of local extensions of a base theory $\mathcal{T}_0$ by means of sets of mutually disjoint function symbols. Then some results on combining extensions with non-disjoint sets of function symbols are discussed.

Theorem 3. *Let $\mathcal{T}_0$ be a first-order theory with signature $\Pi_0 = (\Sigma_0, \mathsf{Pred})$ and $\mathcal{T}_1 = \mathcal{T}_0 \cup \mathcal{K}_1$ and $\mathcal{T}_2 = \mathcal{T}_0 \cup \mathcal{K}_2$ two extensions of $\mathcal{T}_0$ with signatures $\Pi_1 = (\Sigma_0 \cup \Sigma_1, \mathsf{Pred})$ and $\Pi_2 = (\Sigma_0 \cup \Sigma_2, \mathsf{Pred})$, respectively. Assume that both extensions $\mathcal{T}_0 \subseteq \mathcal{T}_1$ and $\mathcal{T}_0 \subseteq \mathcal{T}_1$ satisfy condition (Comp$_\mathsf{w}$), and that $\Sigma_1 \cap \Sigma_2 = \emptyset$. Then the extension $\mathcal{T}_0 \subseteq \mathcal{T} = \mathcal{T}_0 \cup \mathcal{K}_1 \cup \mathcal{K}_2$ satisfies condition (Comp$_\mathsf{w}$). If, additionally, in $\mathcal{K}_i$ all terms starting with a function symbol in Σ_i are flat and linear, for $i = 1, 2$, then the extension is local.*

Proof: Let $P \in \mathsf{PMod}_\mathsf{w}(\Sigma_1 \cup \Sigma_2, \mathcal{T})$. Then $P_{|\Pi_1} \in \mathsf{PMod}_\mathsf{w}(\Sigma_1, \mathcal{T}_1)$, hence $P_{|\Pi_1}$ weakly embeds into a total model B of $\mathcal{T}_1$, such that $P_{|\Pi_0}$ and $B_{|\Pi_0}$ are isomorphic. Let $i : P_{|\Pi_0} \to B_{|\Pi_0}$ be the isomorphism between these two Π_0-structures. We use the isomorphism i to transfer also the Σ_2-structure from P to B. That is, for every $f \in \Sigma_2$ with arity n, and every $b_1, \ldots, b_n \in B$, we define:

$$f_B(b_1, \ldots, b_n) = \begin{cases} i(f_P(i^{-1}(b_1), \ldots, i^{-1}(b_n))) & \text{if } f_P(i^{-1}(b_1), \ldots, i^{-1}(b_n)) \\ & \text{is defined in } P \\ \text{undefined} & \text{otherwise} \end{cases}$$

With these definitions of Σ_2-functions, $B_{|\Pi_2} \in \mathsf{PMod}_\mathsf{w}(\Sigma_2, \mathcal{T}_2)$. Therefore, $B_{|\Pi_2}$ weakly embeds into a total model C of $\mathcal{T}_1$, such that $B_{|\Pi_0}$ and $C_{|\Pi_0}$ are isomorphic. Let $j : B_{|\Pi_0} \to C_{|\Pi_0}$ be the isomorphism between these two structures. We use this isomorphism to transfer, as explained above, the (total) Σ_1-structure from B to C. The algebra A obtained this way from C is a total model of $\mathcal{T}$, and $j \circ i : P_{|\Pi_0} \to A_{|\Pi_0}$ is an isomorphism. Thus, the extension $\mathcal{T}_0 \subseteq \mathcal{T} = \mathcal{T}_0 \cup \mathcal{K}_1 \cup \mathcal{K}_2$ satisfies condition (Comp$_\mathsf{w}$). The last claim is an immediate consequence of Theorem 2. $\qquad\square$

Example 2. *The following combinations of theories (seen as extensions of a first-order theory $\mathcal{T}_0$) satisfy condition (Comp$_\mathsf{w}$) (or in case (4) condition (Comp$_\mathsf{w}^{\mathsf{fd}}$)):*

(1) $\mathcal{T}_0 \cup \mathsf{Free}(\Sigma_1)$ and $\mathcal{T}_0 \cup \mathsf{Sel}_c$ if $\mathcal{T}_0$ is a theory and $c \in \Sigma_0$ is injective in $\mathcal{T}_0$.
(2) $\mathbb{R} \cup \mathsf{Free}(\Sigma_1)$ and $\mathbb{R} \cup \mathsf{Lip}_c^\lambda(f)$, where $f \notin \Sigma_1$.
(3) $\mathbb{R} \cup \mathsf{Lip}_{c_1}^{\lambda_1}(f)$ and $\mathbb{R} \cup \mathsf{Lip}_{c_2}^{\lambda_2}(g)$, where $f \neq g$.
(4) $\mathcal{T}_0 \cup \mathsf{Free}(\Sigma_1)$ and $\mathcal{T}_0 \cup \mathsf{Mon}_f^\sigma$, where $f \notin \Sigma_1$ has arity n, $\sigma : \{1, \ldots, n\} \to \{-1, 1, 0\}$, if $\mathcal{T}_0$ is, e.g., a theory of algebras with a bounded semilattice reduct.

A more general result holds, which allows to prove locality also for extensions which share non-base function symbols.

Theorem 4. *Let $\mathcal{T}_0$ be an arbitrary first-order theory, and $\mathcal{T}_1 = \mathcal{T}_0 \cup \mathcal{K}_1$ and $\mathcal{T}_2 = \mathcal{T}_0 \cup \mathcal{K}_2$ two extensions of $\mathcal{T}_0$ with functions in Σ_1 and Σ_2 respectively, which satisfy condition (Comp$_\mathsf{w}$). Assume that there exists a set $\mathcal{K}$ of clauses in signature $\Sigma_0 \cup \Sigma$, where $\Sigma = \Sigma_1 \cap \Sigma_2 \subset \Sigma_i$, $i = 1, 2$, such that every model of $\mathcal{T}_0 \cup \mathcal{K}_i$ is a model of $\mathcal{T}_0 \cup \mathcal{K}$ for $i = 1, 2$. Then the extension $\mathcal{T}_0 \cup \mathcal{K} \subseteq (\mathcal{T}_0 \cup \mathcal{K}) \cup \mathcal{K}_1 \cup \mathcal{K}_2$ again satisfies condition (Comp$_\mathsf{w}$) and hence is a local extension.*

Proof: Note that if $\mathcal{T}_0 \subseteq \mathcal{T}_0 \cup \mathcal{K}_i$ satisfies condition (Comp$_w$) then the extension $\mathcal{T}_0 \cup \mathcal{K} \subseteq (\mathcal{T}_0 \cup \mathcal{K}) \cup \mathcal{K}_i$ also satisfies condition (Comp$_w$). The conclusion now follows from Theorem 3, taking into account the fact that the signatures $(\Sigma_1 \setminus \Sigma)$ and $(\Sigma_2 \setminus \Sigma)$ are disjoint. □

Example 3. *The following theory extensions satisfy condition* (Comp$_w$):

(1) $\mathcal{T}_0 \cup \mathsf{Free}(\Sigma) \subseteq (\mathcal{T}_0 \cup \mathsf{Free}(\Sigma \cup \Sigma_1)) \cup (\mathcal{T}_0 \cup \mathsf{Free}(\Sigma) \cup \mathsf{Sel}_c)$, *provided that* $\mathcal{T}_0$ *is a theory containing an injective function* c.
(2) $\mathbb{R} \cup \mathsf{Free}(f) \subseteq (\mathbb{R} \cup \mathsf{Mon}_f \cup \mathsf{Mon}_g) \cup (\mathbb{R} \cup \mathsf{Free}(f) \cup \mathsf{Lip}_c^\lambda(h))$, *where* f, g, h *are different function symbols.*
(3) $\mathbb{R} \cup \mathsf{Lip}_c^{\lambda_2}(f) \subseteq (\mathbb{R} \cup \mathsf{Lip}_c^{\lambda_1}(f) \cup \mathsf{Mon}(g)) \cup (\mathbb{R} \cup \mathsf{Lip}_c^{\lambda_2}(f) \cup \mathsf{Free}(h))$, *where* f, g, h *are different function symbols and* $\lambda_1 \leq \lambda_2$.

Proof: Immediate consequences of Theorem 4. (1) is obvious; for (2) note that every model of $\mathbb{R} \cup \mathsf{Mon}_f \cup \mathsf{Mon}_g$ is a model of $\mathbb{R} \cup \mathsf{Free}(f)$; for (3) note that, as $\lambda_1 \leq \lambda_2$, every model of $\mathbb{R} \cup \mathsf{Lip}_c^{\lambda_1}(f) \cup \mathsf{Mon}(g)$ is a model of $\mathbb{R} \cup \mathsf{Lip}_c^{\lambda_2}(f)$. □

7 More General Combinations of Local Theory Extensions

The result above can be extended to the more general situation in which one of the extensions, say $\mathcal{T}_0 \subseteq \mathcal{T}_1 = \mathcal{T}_0 \cup \mathcal{K}_1$, satisfies condition (Emb$_w$) and the other extension $\mathcal{T}_0 \subseteq \mathcal{T}_2 = \mathcal{T}_0 \cup \mathcal{K}_2$ satisfies condition (Comp$_w$), or if both extensions satisfy condition (Emb$_w$). The natural analogon of the proof of Theorem 3 would be the following: Start with a partial model P of $\mathcal{T}_0 \cup \mathcal{K}_1 \cup \mathcal{K}_2$; extend it, using property (Emb$_w$), to a total model A of $\mathcal{T}_1$. The technical problem which occurs when we now try to use the embedding property for $\mathcal{T}_2$ is that we need to be sure that A remains also a partial model of $\mathcal{T}_2$, with the operations inherited from P. Unfortunately this may not always be the case, as shown below.

Example 4. *Let* $\Pi_0 = (\{f\}, \mathsf{Pred})$ *and let* $\mathcal{T}_0$ *be a* Π_0-*theory (we assume here that* $\mathsf{Pred} = \emptyset$*). Let* $\mathcal{T}_1 = \mathcal{T}_0 \cup \mathcal{K}_1$, *and* $\mathcal{T}_2 = \mathcal{T}_0 \cup \mathcal{K}_2$ *be two theories over extensions of* Π_0 *with function symbols in* Σ_1, Σ_2. *Assume that* $\Sigma_2 = \{g\}$, $\Sigma_1 \cap \Sigma_2 = \emptyset$, *and* $\mathcal{K}_2 = \{x = f(x) \rightarrow g(y) = y\}$ *(f and g are unary function symbols).*

Let $P = (\{a, b\}, f_P, g_P, \{\sigma_P\}_{\sigma \in \Sigma_1})$ *be a partial* $\Sigma_0 \cup \Sigma_1 \cup \Sigma_2$- *algebra, where:*

> f_P *is total with* $f_P(a) = b$ *and* $f_P(b) = a$;
> g_P *is partial with* $g_P(a) = b$ *and* $g_P(b)$ *is undefined.*

P weakly satisfies $\mathcal{K}_2$ *because the premise of the clause in* $\mathcal{K}_2$ *is always false in P. Assume that P weakly embeds into a total model A of* $\mathcal{T}_1$ *via a* Π_1-*embedding* $h : P \hookrightarrow A$, *and that A contains an element* $c \notin \{h(a), h(b)\}$, *such that* $f_A(c) = c$. *The algebra A "inherits" the* Σ_2-*operation g from P via h, in the sense that:*

- *we can define* $g_A(h(a)) := h(g_P(a)) = h(b)$ *and*
- *we assume that* g_A *is undefined in everywhere else.*

However, with the Σ_2-operation defined this way A does not weakly satisfy $\mathcal{K}_2$:
Let $\beta : X \to A$ with $\beta(x) = c$ and $\beta(y) = h(a)$. (A, β) does not weakly satisfy
the clause in $\mathcal{K}_2$, since:

$$\beta(f(x)) = f_A(\beta(x)) = f_A(c) = c, \ \ \textit{whereas}$$
$$\beta(g(y)) = g_A(\beta(y)) = g_A(h(a)) = h(g_P(a)) = h(b) \neq h(a) = \beta(y).$$

This happens because the variable x in the clause in $\mathcal{K}_2$ does not occur below any
function symbol in Σ_2.

In what follows we identify conditions which ensure that an extension A of a
partial algebra P which weakly satisfies $\mathcal{K}_2$ remains a partial model of $\mathcal{K}_2$ with
the Σ_2-operations inherited from P.

7.1   Preservation of Truth under Extensions

Lemma 5. *Let $\mathcal{T}_0$ be a theory with signature $\Pi_0 = (\Sigma_0, \mathsf{Pred})$, and let $\mathcal{T}_0 \subseteq$*
$\mathcal{T} := \mathcal{T}_0 \cup \mathcal{K}$ be a theory extension by means of a set $\mathcal{K}$ of Σ-flat clauses over the
signature $\Pi = (\Sigma_0 \cup \Sigma, \mathsf{Pred})$. Assume that for each clause C of $\mathcal{K}$ all occurrences
of variables in C are below some Σ-function symbol.
Let $P \in \mathsf{PMod}_w(\Sigma, \mathcal{T})$, $A \in \mathsf{Mod}(\mathcal{T}_0)$, and $h : P \hookrightarrow A$ be a Π_0-embedding.
Then a partial Σ-structure can be defined on A such that A weakly satisfies $\mathcal{K}$,
and h is a weak Π-embedding.

Proof: For every $a_1, \ldots, a_n \in A$ and every $f \in \Sigma$ define

$$f_A(a_1, \ldots, a_n) := \begin{cases} a & \begin{array}{l} \text{if } \exists p_1, \ldots, p_n \in P \text{ such that all } a_i = h(p_i), \\ f_P(p_1, \ldots, p_n) \text{ is defined in } P, \\ \text{and } a = h(f_P(p_1, \ldots, p_n)) \end{array} \\ \text{undefined} & \text{otherwise.} \end{cases}$$

As h is injective, f_A is well-defined. By hypothesis, h is a Π_0-embedding. With
the definition of operations in Σ given above, h is also a weak Σ-homomorphism.
Let $p_1, \ldots, p_n \in P$ and $f \in \Sigma$ be such that $f_P(p_1, \ldots, p_n)$ is defined. Then, by the
definition of f_A, $f_A(h(p_1), \ldots, h(p_n))$ is defined and equal to $h(f_P(p_1, \ldots, p_n))$.
We now prove that with the operations defined as shown before A weakly
satisfies $\mathcal{K}$. Let $C \in \mathcal{K}$ and let $\beta : X \to A$ be an assignment of elements in
A to the variables in C. Assume that for every term t occurring in C, $\beta(t)$ is
defined in A (otherwise, due to the definition of weak satisfiability, $(A, \beta) \models_w C$
trivially). In order to show that $(A, \beta) \models_w C$, we construct an assignment α of
elements in P to the variables in C, and use the fact that $(P, \alpha) \models_w C$.
Let $t = f(t_1, \ldots, t_k)$ be an arbitrary term occurring in C, with $f \in \Sigma$. As $\beta(t)$
is defined, $f_A(\beta(t_1), \ldots, \beta(t_k))$ is defined in A, hence there exist $p_1, \ldots, p_k \in P$
such that $h(p_i) = \beta(t_i)$, $f_P(p_1, \ldots, p_k)$ is defined, and $f_A(\beta(t_1), \ldots, \beta(t_k)) =$
$h(f_P(p_1, \ldots, p_n))$. As all clauses in $\mathcal{K}$ are Σ-flat, all terms t_i are variables. In
this way we can associate with every variable x occurring as argument in a term
$f(t_1, \ldots, t_n)$ of C with $f \in \Sigma$ an element $p_x \in P$ such that $h(p_x) = \beta(x)$. Assume

that for some such (variable) subterm x, two elements of P, say p_x and q_x, can be associated in this way. Then $h(p_x) = \beta(x) = h(q_x)$, and the injectivity of h guarantees that $p_x = q_x$. This shows that an assignment $\alpha : X \to P$ can be defined, such that for all variables in C occurring below a function symbol in Σ (hence for all variables in C) $\alpha(x) := p_x$. It is easy to see that for every term t occurring in C, $h(\alpha(t)) = \beta(t)$. As $(P, \alpha) \models C$ and h is a weak Π-embedding it follows that $(A, \beta) \models C$. $\qquad\square$

The result above will be applied in Theorems 7 and 8 in the following form:

Corollary 6. *Let $\mathcal{T}_0$ be a first-order theory with signature $\Pi_0 = (\Sigma_0, \mathsf{Pred})$. Let Σ_1, Σ_2 be two disjoint sets of function symbols, and let $\Pi_i = (\Sigma_0 \cup \Sigma_i, \mathsf{Pred})$, $i = 1, 2$, and $\Pi = (\Sigma_0 \cup \Sigma_1 \cup \Sigma_2, \mathsf{Pred})$. Let $\mathcal{K}_2$ be a set of Σ_2-flat clauses over Π_2. Assume that for each clause C of $\mathcal{K}_2$ all variables in C occur below some function symbol in Σ_2.*

Let P be a partial Π-structure such that $P_{|\Pi_0}$ is a total model of $\mathcal{T}_0$, and P weakly satisfies $\mathcal{K}_2$. Let A be a total Π_1-structure, and let $h : P \hookrightarrow A$ be a weak Π_1-embedding. Then a partial Σ_2-structure can be defined on A such that A weakly satisfies $\mathcal{K}_2$, and h is a weak Π-embedding.

7.2   Combining Local Extensions, One of Which Satisfies (Comp$_w$)

We now analyze the case of combinations of theories in which one component satisfies condition (Comp$_w$) and the other component satisfies condition (Emb$_w$).

Theorem 7. *Let $\mathcal{T}_0$ be a first-order theory with signature $\Pi_0 = (\Sigma_0, \mathsf{Pred})$, and let $\mathcal{T}_1 = \mathcal{T}_0 \cup \mathcal{K}_1$ and $\mathcal{T}_2 = \mathcal{T}_0 \cup \mathcal{K}_2$ be two extensions of $\mathcal{T}_0$ with signatures $\Pi_1 = (\Sigma_0 \cup \Sigma_1, \mathsf{Pred})$ and $\Pi_2 = (\Sigma_0 \cup \Sigma_2, \mathsf{Pred})$, respectively. Assume that:*

(1) $\mathcal{T}_0 \subseteq \mathcal{T}_1$ satisfies condition (Comp$_w$),
(2) $\mathcal{T}_0 \subseteq \mathcal{T}_2$ satisfies condition (Emb$_w$),
(3) $\mathcal{K}_1$ is a set of Σ_1-flat clauses in which all variables occur below a Σ_1-function.

Then the extension $\mathcal{T}_0 \subseteq \mathcal{T}_0 \cup \mathcal{K}_1 \cup \mathcal{K}_2$ satisfies (Emb$_w$). If, additionally, in $\mathcal{K}_i$ all terms starting with a function symbol in Σ_i are flat and linear, for $i = 1, 2$, then the extension is local.

Proof: Let $P \in \mathsf{PMod}_w(\Sigma_1 \cup \Sigma_2, \mathcal{T}_0 \cup \mathcal{K}_1 \cup \mathcal{K}_2)$. Then $P_{|\Pi_2} \in \mathsf{PMod}_w(\Sigma_2, \mathcal{T}_2)$, hence $P_{|\Pi_2}$ weakly embeds into a total model B of $\mathcal{T}_2$. By (3), in $\mathcal{K}_1$ all variables occur below some function symbol in Σ_1, and all clauses in $\mathcal{K}_1$ are Σ_1-flat. Then, by Lemma 5, we can transform B into a weak partial model B' of $\mathcal{T}_1$ (with the Σ_2-structure inherited from B and the Σ_1-structure inherited from P). But then B' weakly embeds into a total model C of $\mathcal{T}_1$ such that $B'_{|\Pi_0}$ and $C_{|\Pi_0}$ are Π_0-isomorphic. We can use this isomorphism to transfer the (total) Σ_2-structure from B to C. This way, we obtain a total model A of $\mathcal{T}_0 \cup \mathcal{K}_1 \cup \mathcal{K}_2$ in which P weakly embeds. The last claim is an immediate consequence of Theorem 2. $\qquad\square$

Example 5. *The following theory extensions satisfy* (Emb$_w$), *hence are local:*

(1) $\mathcal{E}q \subseteq \mathsf{Free}(\Sigma_1) \cup \mathcal{L}$, *where* $\mathcal{E}q$ *is the pure theory of equality, without function symbols, and* $\mathcal{L}$ *the theory of lattices.*

(2) $\mathcal{T}_0 \subseteq (\mathcal{T}_0 \cup \mathsf{Free}(\Sigma_1)) \cup (\mathcal{T}_0 \cup \mathsf{Mon}(\Sigma_2))$, *where* $\Sigma_1 \cap \Sigma_2 = \emptyset$, *and* $\mathcal{T}_0$ *is, e.g., the theory of posets.*

An analogon of Theorem 4 holds also in this case.

7.3   Combinations of Theory Extensions Satisfying (Emb$_w$)

We identify conditions under which embeddability conditions for the component theories imply embeddability conditions for the theory combination.

Theorem 8. *Let* $\mathcal{T}_0$ *be an arbitrary theory in signature* $\Pi_0 = (\Sigma_0, \mathsf{Pred})$. *Let* $\mathcal{K}_1$ *and* $\mathcal{K}_2$ *be two sets of clauses over signatures* $\Pi_i = (\Sigma_0 \cup \Sigma_i, \mathsf{Pred})$, *where* Σ_1 *and* Σ_2 *are disjoint. We make the following assumptions:*

(A1) *The class of models of* $\mathcal{T}_0$ *is closed under direct limits of diagrams in which all maps are embeddings (or, equivalently,* $\mathcal{T}_0$ *is a* $\forall\exists$ *theory).*

(A2) $\mathcal{K}_i$ *is* Σ_i-*flat and* Σ_i-*linear for* $i = 1, 2$, *and* $\mathcal{T}_0 \subseteq \mathcal{T}_0 \cup \mathcal{K}_i$, $i = 1, 2$ *are both local extensions of* $\mathcal{T}_0$.

(A3) *For all clauses in* $\mathcal{K}_1$ *and* $\mathcal{K}_2$, *every variable occurs below some extension function.*

Then $\mathcal{T}_0 \cup \mathcal{K}_1 \cup \mathcal{K}_2$ *is a local extension of* $\mathcal{T}_0$.

Proof: The proof uses the semantical characterization of locality in Theorems 1 and 2. Assumption (A2) guarantees that the extensions $\mathcal{T}_0 \subseteq \mathcal{T}_0 \cup \mathcal{K}_i$, $i = 1, 2$ are both local and that, by Theorem 1, they satisfy condition (Emb$_w$). We show that $\mathcal{T}_0 \subseteq \mathcal{T}_0 \cup \mathcal{K}_1 \cup \mathcal{K}_2$ satisfies condition (Emb$_w$), hence, by Theorem 2, is local.

Let $\Pi = (\Sigma_0 \cup \Sigma_1 \cup \Sigma_2, \mathsf{Pred})$ and let P be a partial Π-algebra which weakly satisfies $\mathcal{K}_1 \cup \mathcal{K}_2$ and whose Π_0-reduct is a total model of $\mathcal{T}_0$. By the locality of the extension $\mathcal{T}_0 \subseteq \mathcal{T}_0 \cup \mathcal{K}_1$, there exists a total Π_1-model of $\mathcal{T}_0 \cup \mathcal{K}_1$, which we denote P_1^1, and a weak embedding $\pi_1^1 : P \hookrightarrow P_1^1$. By Lemma 5 and Corollary 6, a partial Σ_2-structure can be defined on P_1^1 such that P_1^1 weakly satisfies $\mathcal{K}_2$ and π_1^1 is a weak Π-embedding.

Thus, P_1^1 becomes a partial Π_2-algebra which weakly satisfies $\mathcal{K}_2$, and is a total Π_0-model of $\mathcal{T}_0$. By the locality of the extension $\mathcal{T}_0 \subseteq \mathcal{T}_0 \cup \mathcal{K}_2$, there exists a total Π_2-model of $\mathcal{T}_0 \cup \mathcal{K}_2$, which we denote P_2^1, and a weak embedding $\pi_2^1 : P_1^1 \hookrightarrow P_2^1$. Again, a partial Σ_1-structure can be defined on P_2^1 such that P_2^1 weakly satisfies $\mathcal{K}_1$ and π_2^1 is a weak Π-embedding.

By iterating this process we obtain a sequence of partial Π-structures P_1^i, P_2^i, $i \geq 1$, all of whose reducts to Π_0 are total models of $\mathcal{T}_0$, which weakly satisfy $\mathcal{K}_1 \cup \mathcal{K}_2$, and have the property that, for every $i \geq 1$, P_1^i is a total Σ_1-algebra, P_2^i is a total Σ_2-algebra, and there are weak Π-embeddings $\pi_1^i : P_1^i \to P_2^i$ and $\pi_2^i : P_2^i \to P_1^{i+1}$.

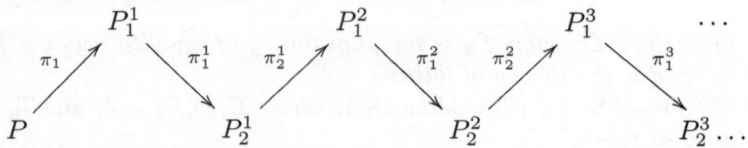

If P_l^i precedes P_k^j in the chain above (where $k, l \in \{1, 2\}$ and $i, j \geq 1$), let $g_{li}^{kj} : P_l^i \to P_k^j$ be the composition of the corresponding weak embeddings from P_l^i to P_k^j. Being a composition of weak embeddings, g_{li}^{kj} is itself a weak embedding.

Let $P \coprod (\coprod_{i \geq 1} (P_1^i \coprod P_2^i))$ be the disjoint union of all partial Π-structures constructed this way. In this disjoint union we identify all elements that are images of the same element in some P_k^i. This is, we define an equivalence relation $\equiv$ on this disjoint union by $x \equiv y$ if $x \in P_l^i$, $y \in P_k^j$ and either

(i) P_l^i precedes P_k^j in the chain above and $g_{li}^{kj}(x) = y$, or
(ii) P_k^j precedes P_l^i in the chain above and $g_{kj}^{li}(y) = x$.

As for every $l \in \{1, 2\}, i \geq 1$, g_{li}^{li} is the identity map, if $x \equiv y$ for $x, y \in P_l^i$ then $x = y$. It is easy to see that $\equiv$ is an equivalence relation.

Let $A_0 := P \coprod (\coprod_{i \geq 1} (P_1^i \coprod P_2^i)) / \equiv$. We show that total functions in $\Sigma_0 \cup \Sigma_1 \cup \Sigma_2$ and predicates in Pred can be defined on A_0 such that the expansion A of A_0 obtained this way is a (total) model of $\mathcal{T}_0 \cup \mathcal{K}_1 \cup \mathcal{K}_2$, and that the map $g : P \to A$ defined by $g(p) = [p]$ (the equivalence class of p in A) is a weak Π-embedding.

A Π-structure on A can be defined in a canonical way (the usual way of constructing direct limits). For the sake of completeness, we present the details of the construction in what follows:

- *Interpretation of signature Π_0.* We first define the Σ_0-functions. Let $f \in \Sigma_0$ with arity n, and let $[a_1], \ldots, [a_n] \in A$. Then, for every $1 \leq j \leq n$, there exist $i_j \geq 1$ such that $a_j \in P_1^{i_j} \coprod P_2^{i_j}$. Let $m = \max\{i_j \mid 1 \leq j \leq n\}$. Let $b_1, \ldots, b_n$ be the images of $a_1, \ldots, a_n$ in P_1^{m+1}. By the definition of $\equiv$, $[b_j] = [a_j]$ for every $1 \leq j \leq n$. P_1^{m+1} is a total Σ_0-algebra, so $b = f_{P_1^{m+1}}(b_1, \ldots, b_n)$ exists in P_1^{m+1}. The fact that the definition does not depend on the representatives follows from the fact that all embeddings in the diagram are Σ_0-homomorphisms.

  The predicates in Pred are defined in a similar way. The fact that the definitions do not depend on the choice of representatives in the equivalence classes follows from the fact that all the maps in the diagram are Π_0-embeddings.

- *Interpretation of the signature $\Sigma_1 \cup \Sigma_2$.* We define the Σ_1-functions (the Σ_2-functions can be defined similarly). Let $f \in \Sigma_1$ with arity n, and let $[a_1], \ldots, [a_n] \in A$. Then, for every $1 \leq j \leq n$, there exist $i_j \geq 1$ such that $a_j \in P_1^{i_j} \coprod P_2^{i_j}$. Let $m = \max\{i_j \mid 1 \leq j \leq n\}$. Let $b_1, \ldots, b_n$ be the images of $a_1, \ldots, a_n$ in P_1^{m+1}. By the definition of $\equiv$, $[b_j] = [a_j]$ for every $1 \leq j \leq n$.

P_1^{m+1} is a total Σ_1-algebra, so $b = f_{P_1^{m+1}}(b_1, \ldots, b_n)$ exists in P_1^{m+1}. The equivalence class of b does not depend on the choice of representatives of the equivalence classes $[a_1], \ldots, [a_n]$. Indeed, assume that $c_1, \ldots, c_n$ are images of $a_1, \ldots, a_n$ in P_1^{k+1}, with e.g. $k \geq m$. By the definition of $g_{1,m+1}^{1,k+1}$: $P_1^{m+1} \to P_1^{k+1}$, $c_j = g_{1,m+1}^{1,k+1}(b_j)$. As $f_{P_1^{m+1}}(b_1, \ldots, b_n)$ is defined in P_1^{m+1}, we know that $g_{1,m+1}^{1,k+1}(f_{P_1^{m+1}}(b_1, \ldots, b_n)) = f_{P_1^{k+1}}(g_{1,m+1}^{1,k+1}(b_1), \ldots, g_{1,m+1}^{1,k+1}(b_n))$ $= f_{P_1^{k+1}}(c_1, \ldots, c_n)$. It follows therefore that $b \equiv f_{P_1^{k+1}}(c_1, \ldots, c_n)$, so the equivalence class of b does not depend on the choice of the representatives of $[a_1], \ldots, [a_n]$. We can define $f_A([a_1], \ldots, [a_n]) := [b]$. f_A is well-defined for every $f \in \Sigma_1$.

The Π-structure A is the direct limit of the diagram defined by the partial structures P_j^i and the corresponding Π-embeddings π_j^i, $i \in \mathbb{N}$, $j \in \{1, 2\}$.

It can be seen that for every k, i, the map $g_k^i : P_k^i \to A$ defined by $g(x) := [x]$ is a weak Π-embedding.

- *The fact that g_k^i is a Σ_0-homomorphism* is obvious.
- *We show that g_k^i is a weak Σ_1-homomorphism.* Let $f \in \Sigma_1$ of arity n and $x_1, \ldots, x_n \in P_k^i$ be such that $f_{P_k^i}(x_1, \ldots, x_n)$ is defined. Then, by the definition of f_A, $f_A([x_1], \ldots, [x_n]) = [f_{P_k^i}(x_1, \ldots, x_n)] = g_k^i(f_{P_k^i}(x_1, \ldots, x_n))$.

  The fact that g_k^i is a Σ_2-homomorphism can be proved analogously.
- *We prove that g_k^i is injective.* Assume that $g_k^i(x) = g_k^i(y)$ for $x, y \in P_k^i$. Then $x \equiv y$, hence $g_{ki}^{ki}(x) = y$, i.e. $x = y$ (since g_{ki}^{ki} is the identity map). This also shows that $g : P \to A$, $g(p) = [p]$ is an injective weak homomorphism.
- *We prove that g_k^i is an embedding w.r.t.* **Pred**. Let $Q \in$ **Pred** be an n-ary predicate symbol, and let $x_1, \ldots, x_n \in P_k^i$. We show that $Q_{P_k^i}(x_1, \ldots, x_n)$ if and only if $Q_A(g_k^i(x_1), \ldots, g_k^i(x_n))$. By the way Q_A is constructed it is obvious that if $Q_{P_k^i}(x_1, \ldots, x_n)$ then $Q_A([x_1], \ldots, [x_n])$. Conversely, assume that $Q_A([x_1], \ldots, [x_n])$. By definition, there exists m and $b_1, \ldots, b_n \in P_1^{m+1}$ such that $[x_1] = [b_1], \ldots, [x_n] = [b_n]$ and $Q_{P_1^{m+1}}(b_1, \ldots, b_n)$. The conclusion now follows from the fact that the composition of all maps in the diagram leading from P_k^i to P_1^{m+1} (or vice versa) is a weak Π-embedding, and hence also $Q_{P_k^i}(x_1, \ldots, x_n)$.

The reduct to Π_0 of A is the direct limit of a diagram of models of $\mathcal{T}_0$, in which all maps are embeddings. Therefore, if $\mathcal{T}_0$ is closed under such direct limits (i.e. it is a $\forall\exists$ theory) then A is a model of $\mathcal{T}_0$.

Finally, we show that A satisfies all clauses in $\mathcal{K}_1 \cup \mathcal{K}_2$. Let $C \in \mathcal{K}_1$ (the case $C \in \mathcal{K}_2$ is similar). Let $\beta : X \to A$. We know that every variable of C occurs below a function symbol in Σ_1, and that all terms of C containing a function symbol in Σ_1 are of the form $f(x_1, \ldots, x_n)$. For every variable x occurring in C, $\beta(x) = [a_x]$, where $a_x \in P_k^{j_x}$ for some $j_x \geq 1$. Let $m = \max\{j_x \mid x \text{ variable of } C\}$, and let b_x

be the image of a_x in P_1^{m+1} for each variable x of C. Then $\beta(f(x_1, \ldots, x_n))$ is defined in P_1^{m+1} for every term of C of the form $f(x_1, \ldots, x_n)$. In fact, it is easy to see that for every term occurring in C, $\beta(t) = [b_t]$ for some $b_t \in P_1^{m+1}$. Let $\alpha : X \to P_1^{m+1}$ with $\alpha(x) := b_x$ for every variable x of C. It can be seen that $g_1^{m+1}(\alpha(t)) = \beta(t)$ for every subterm t of C. As P_1^{m+1} satisfies C and all terms in C are defined under the assignment α it follows that there exists a literal L in C such that $(P_1^{m+1}, \alpha) \models_w L$. We know that $g_1^{m+1} : P_1^{m+1} \hookrightarrow A$ is a weak embedding w.r.t. Π_1. It therefore preserves the truth of positive and negative Π_1-literals. Therefore, as $g_1^{m+1}(\alpha(t)) = \beta(t)$ for every term t of C, $(A, \beta) \models L$.

$\square$

Example 6. *The following combinations of theories (seen as extensions of the theory $\mathcal{T}_0$) satisfy condition* (Emb$_w$):

(1) The combination of the theory of lattices and the theory of integers with injective successor and predecessor is local (local extension of the theory of pure equality).

(2) $\mathcal{T}_0 \subseteq \mathcal{T}_0 \cup \mathrm{Mon}(\Sigma)$, where $\mathrm{Mon}(\Sigma) = \bigwedge_{f \in \Sigma} \mathrm{Mon}_f^{\sigma(f)}$, and $\mathcal{T}_0$ is one of the theories of posets, (dense) totally-ordered sets, (semi)lattices, distributive lattices, Boolean algebras, $\mathbb{R}$.

8   Hierarchical and Modular Reasoning

In what follows we discuss some issues related to modular reasoning in combinations of local theory extensions. By results in [SS05], hierarchical reasoning is always possible in local theory extensions. In this section we analyze possibilities of modular reasoning, and, in particular, the form of information which needs to be exchanged between provers for the component theories when reasoning in combinations of local theory extensions.

8.1   Hierarchical Reasoning in Local Theory Extensions

Consider a local theory extension $\mathcal{T}_0 \subseteq \mathcal{T}_0 \cup \mathcal{K}$, where $\mathcal{K}$ is a set of clauses in the signature $\Pi = (\Sigma_0 \cup \Sigma_1, \mathrm{Pred})$. The locality condition requires that, for every set G of ground clauses, $\mathcal{T}_1 \cup G$ is satisfiable if and only if $\mathcal{T}_0 \cup \mathcal{K}[G] \cup G$ has a weak partial model with additional properties. All clauses in $\mathcal{K}[G] \cup G$ have the property that the function symbols in Σ_1 only occur at the root of ground terms. We can therefore flatten and purify $\mathcal{K}[G] \cup G$:

Flattening and Purification. $\mathcal{K}[G] \cup G$ can be flattened and purified (i.e. the function symbols in Σ_1 are separated from the other symbols) by introducing, in a bottom-up manner,

- new constants c_t for subterms $t = f(g_1, \ldots, g_n)$ with $f \in \Sigma_1$, g_i ground $\Sigma_0 \cup \Sigma_c$-terms (where Σ_c is a set of constants which contains the constants introduced by flattening, resp. purification), together with
- corresponding definitions $c_t \approx t$.

The process clearly terminates. It transforms the class of formulae $\mathcal{K}[G] \cup G$ into:

- a class $\mathcal{K}_0 \cup G_0$ of $\Pi_0 \cup \Sigma_c$-clauses obtained from $\mathcal{K}[G] \cup G$ by replacing all Σ_1-terms with new constants; and
- a set D of equalities of the form $c_{f(g_1,\ldots,g_n)} \approx f(g_1,\ldots,g_n)$ obtained in the purification process, where $f \in \Sigma_1$ and $g_1,\ldots,g_n$ are ground $\Sigma_0 \cup \Sigma_c$-terms.

Example 7. *Assume that $\mathcal{T}_0$ is the theory $\mathbb{R}$ of real numbers.*

(1) Let $\Sigma_1 = \{f\}$ and $\mathcal{K} = \{\forall x, y(x \leq y \rightarrow f(x) \leq f(y))\}$. Let G consist of the following ground clauses $\{a = b + 1, f(a) < f(b)\}$. Then $\mathcal{K}[G]$ consists of all instances of $\mathcal{K}$ in which the terms starting with the extension function f are among the subterms in G, i.e.:

$$\mathcal{K}[G] = \{a \leq a \rightarrow f(a) \leq f(a), a \leq b \rightarrow f(a) \leq f(b),$$
$$b \leq a \rightarrow f(b) \leq f(a), b \leq b \rightarrow f(b) \leq f(b)\}$$

To flatten $\mathcal{K}[G] \cup G$ we introduce new subterms c_1 and c_2 for the ground terms $f(a)$ resp. $f(b)$, together with definitions $D = \{c_1 \approx f(a), c_2 \approx f(b)\}$. We thus transform $\mathcal{K}[G] \cup G$ into $\mathcal{K}_0 \cup G_0 \cup D$ where D is as above, $G_0 = \{a = b + 1, c_1 < c_2\}$ and:

$$\mathcal{K}_0 = \{a \leq a \rightarrow c_1 \leq c_1, a \leq b \rightarrow c_1 \leq c_2, b \leq a \rightarrow c_2 \leq c_1, b \leq b \rightarrow c_2 \leq c_2\}$$

Since $\leq$ is reflexive, the presentation of $\mathcal{K}[G]$ and $\mathcal{K}_0$ can be simplified by omitting the redundant clauses (in this case the first and last clause).

(2) Assume now that $\mathcal{K}$ has the form:

$$\forall x, y, z(x \leq z \wedge z \leq y \wedge z \leq 100 \rightarrow f(x) \leq f(y)).$$

Let $G = \{a = b + 1, f(a) < f(b)\}$ as above. Since there are variables in $\mathcal{K}$ which do not occur below function symbols $\mathcal{K}[G]$ is of the form:

$$\{\forall z(a \leq z \wedge z \leq a \wedge z \leq 100 \rightarrow f(a) \leq f(a)), \forall z(a \leq z \wedge z \leq b \wedge z \leq 100 \rightarrow f(a) \leq f(b)),$$
$$\forall z(b \leq z \wedge z \leq a \wedge z \leq 100 \rightarrow f(b) \leq f(a)), \forall z(b \leq z \wedge z \leq b \wedge z \leq 100 \rightarrow f(b) \leq f(b))\}$$

i.e. contains universally quantified variables. The flattening of $\mathcal{K}[G] \cup G$ proceeds as before, and transforms $\mathcal{K}[G] \cup G$ into $\mathcal{K}_0 \cup G_0 \cup D$ where D and G_0 are as above and:

$$\mathcal{K}_0 = \{\forall z(a \leq z \wedge z \leq a \wedge z \leq 100 \rightarrow c_1 \leq c_1), \forall z(a \leq z \wedge z \leq b \wedge z \leq 100 \rightarrow c_1 \leq c_2),$$
$$\forall z(b \leq z \wedge z \leq a \wedge z \leq 100 \rightarrow c_2 \leq c_1), \forall z(b \leq z \wedge z \leq b \wedge z \leq 100 \rightarrow c_2 \leq c_2)\}$$

(3) Let $\Sigma_1 = \{f, g, h\}$, $\mathcal{K} = \{\forall x \ f(g(x)) > x\}$, $G = \{h(f(g(a))) = b\}$, where a, b are constants. Then $\mathcal{K}[G] = \{f(g(a)) > a\}$; $\mathcal{K}_0$ is obtained by first replacing $g(a)$ with a new constant c_1, then replacing $f(c_1)$ with c_2, and finally replacing $h(c_2)$ with c_3 (and adding $c_1 \approx g(a), c_2 \approx f(c_1)$, and $c_3 \approx h(c_2)$ to D). The purified set of clauses consists of:

$$\mathcal{K}_0 = \{c_2 > a\}, \quad G_0 = \{c_3 = b\}, \quad D = \{c_1 \approx g(a), c_2 \approx f(c_1), c_3 \approx h(c_2)\}.$$

Assume now that G is $h(g(a)) = b$. There are no instances of $\mathcal{K}$ which only contain extension subterms occurring in G. Thus, in this case $\mathcal{K}[G] = \emptyset$.

These flattening and purification transformations preserve both satisfiability and unsatisfiability with respect to total algebras, and also with respect to partial algebras in which all ground subterms which are flattened are defined [SS05].

For the sake of simplicity in what follows we will always flatten and then purify $\mathcal{K}[G] \cup G$. Thus we ensure that D consists of ground unit clauses of the form $f(c_1, \ldots, c_n) \approx c$, where $f \in \Sigma_1$, and $c_1, \ldots, c_n, c$ are constants.

Lemma 9 ([SS05]). *Let $\mathcal{K}$ be a set of clauses and G a set of ground clauses, and let $\mathcal{K}_0 \cup G_0 \cup D$ be obtained from $\mathcal{K}[G] \cup G$ by flattening and purification, as explained above. Assume that $\mathcal{T}_0 \subseteq \mathcal{T}_0 \cup \mathcal{K}$ is a local theory extension. Then the following are equivalent:*

(1) $\mathcal{T}_0 \cup \mathcal{K}[G] \cup G$ has a partial model in which all terms in $\mathsf{st}(\mathcal{K}, G)$ are defined.
(2) $\mathcal{T}_0 \cup \mathcal{K}_0 \cup G_0 \cup D$ has a partial model with all terms in $\mathsf{st}(\mathcal{K}_0, G_0, D)$ defined.
(3) $\mathcal{T}_0 \cup \mathcal{K}_0 \cup G_0 \cup N_0$ has a (total) model, where

$$N_0 = \{\textstyle\bigwedge_{i=1}^{n} c_i \approx d_i \rightarrow c \approx d \mid f(c_1, \ldots, c_n) \approx c, f(d_1, \ldots, d_n) \approx d \in D\}.$$

Example 8. *Let $\mathcal{T}_0$ be the theory $\mathbb{R}$ of real numbers, $\Sigma_1 = \{f\}$, $\mathcal{K} = \{\forall x, y(x \leq y \rightarrow f(x) \leq f(y))\}$ and $G = \{a = b + 1, f(a) < f(b)\}$ as in Example 7(1). Any extension of $\mathbb{R}$ with a monotone function f is local. Hence, by Lemma 9, $\mathcal{T}_0 \cup \mathcal{K} \cup G \models \perp$ iff $\mathcal{T}_0 \cup \mathcal{K}_0 \cup G_0 \cup N_0 \models \perp$, where $G_0 = \{a = b + 1, c_1 < c_2\}$,*

$$\mathcal{K}_0 = \{a \leq a \rightarrow c_1 \leq c_1, a \leq b \rightarrow c_1 \leq c_2, b \leq a \rightarrow c_2 \leq c_1, b \leq b \rightarrow c_2 \leq c_2\}$$
$$N_0 = \{a \approx a \rightarrow c_1 \approx c_1, a \approx b \rightarrow c_1 \approx c_2, b \approx a \rightarrow c_2 \approx c_1, b \approx b \rightarrow c_2 \approx c_2\}$$

Since $\leq$ and $\approx$ are reflexive, the presentation can be simplified by omitting the first and last clause in $\mathcal{K}_0$ and N_0. It is easy to check that $\mathbb{R} \cup \mathcal{K}_0 \cup G_0 \cup N_0 \models \perp$.

8.2 Modular Reasoning in Local Combinations of Theory Extensions

Let $\mathcal{T}_1$ and $\mathcal{T}_2$ be theories with signatures $\Pi_1 = (\Sigma_1, \mathsf{Pred})$ and $\Pi_2 = (\Sigma_2, \mathsf{Pred})$, and G a set of ground clauses in the joint signature with additional constants $\Pi^c = (\Sigma_0 \cup \Sigma_1 \cup \Sigma_2 \cup \Sigma_c, \mathsf{Pred})$. We want to decide whether $\mathcal{T}_1 \cup \mathcal{T}_2 \cup G \models \perp$.

The set G of ground clauses can be flattened and purified as explained above. For the sake of simplicity, everywhere in what follows we will assume w.l.o.g. that $G = G_1 \wedge G_2$, where G_1, G_2 are flat and linear sets of clauses in the signatures Π_1, Π_2 respectively, i.e. for $i = 1, 2$, $G_i = G_i^0 \wedge G_0 \wedge D_i$, where G_i^0 and G_0 are clauses in the base theory and D_i a conjunction of unit clauses of the form $f(c_1, \ldots, c_n) = c, f \in \Sigma_i$.

Corollary 10. *Assume that $\mathcal{T}_1 = \mathcal{T}_0 \cup \mathcal{K}_1$ and $\mathcal{T}_2 = \mathcal{T}_0 \cup \mathcal{K}_2$ are local extensions of a theory $\mathcal{T}_0$ with signature $\Pi_0 = (\Sigma_0, \mathsf{Pred})$, where $\Sigma_0 = \Sigma_1 \cap \Sigma_2$, and that the extension $\mathcal{T}_0 \subseteq \mathcal{T}_0 \cup \mathcal{K}_1 \cup \mathcal{K}_2$ is local. Let $G = G_1 \wedge G_2$ be a set of flat, linear and purified ground clauses, such that $G_i = G_i^0 \wedge G_0 \wedge D_i$ are as explained above. Then the following are equivalent:*

(1) $\mathcal{T}_1 \cup \mathcal{T}_2 \cup (G_1 \wedge G_2) \models \perp$,

(2) $\mathcal{T}_0 \cup (\mathcal{K}_1 \cup \mathcal{K}_2)[G_1 \wedge G_2] \cup (G_1^0 \wedge G_0 \wedge D_1) \wedge (G_2^0 \wedge G_0 \wedge D_2) \models \perp$,

(3) $\mathcal{T}_0 \cup \mathcal{K}_1[G_1] \cup \mathcal{K}_2[G_2] \cup (G_1^0 \wedge G_0 \wedge D_1) \wedge (G_2^0 \wedge G_0 \wedge D_2) \models \perp$,

(4) $\mathcal{T}_0 \cup \mathcal{K}_1^0 \cup \mathcal{K}_2^0 \cup (G_1^0 \cup G_0) \cup (G_2^0 \cup G_0) \cup N_1 \cup N_2 \models \perp$, *where*

$$N_1 = \{\bigwedge_{i=1}^{n} c_i \approx d_i \rightarrow c = d \mid f(c_1, \ldots, c_n) \approx c, f(d_1, \ldots, d_n) \approx d \in D_1\}$$

$$N_2 = \{\bigwedge_{i=1}^{n} c_i \approx d_i \rightarrow c = d \mid f(c_1, \ldots, c_n) \approx c, f(d_1, \ldots, d_n) \approx d \in D_2\}$$

and $\mathcal{K}_i^0$ *is the formula obtained from* $\mathcal{K}_i[G_i]$ *after purification and flattening, taking into account the definitions from* D_i.

Proof: Direct consequence of Lemma 9. The fact that $(\mathcal{K}_1 \cup \mathcal{K}_2)[G_1 \wedge G_2] = \mathcal{K}_1[G_1] \cup \mathcal{K}_2[G_2]$ is a consequence of the fact that G_i are flattened and for $i = 1, 2$, $\mathcal{K}_i$ contains only function symbols in Σ_i. The equivalence of (3) and (4) follows from the fact that Σ_1 and Σ_2 only have function symbols in Σ_0 in common. $\square$

The method for hierarchic reasoning described in Corollary 10 is modular, in the sense that once the information about $\Sigma_1 \cup \Sigma_2$-functions has been separated into a Σ_1-part and a Σ_2-part, it does not need to be recombined again. For reasoning in the combined theory one can proceed as follows:

- Purify (and flatten) the goal G, and thus transform it into an equisatisfiable conjunction $G_1 \wedge G_2$, where G_i consists of clauses in the signature Π_i, for $i = 1, 2$, and $G_i = G_i^0 \wedge G_0 \wedge D_i$, as above.
- The formulae containing extension functions in the signature Σ_i, $\mathcal{K}_i[G_i] \wedge G_i$ are "reduced" (using the equivalence of (3) and (4)) to the formula $\mathcal{K}_i^0 \wedge G_i^0 \wedge G_0 \wedge N_i$ in the base theory.
- The conjunction of all the formulae obtained this way, for all component theories, is used as input for a decision procedure for the base theory.

Remark 11. *Let* $\mathcal{T}_0 \subseteq \mathcal{T}_0 \cup \mathcal{K}_i$ *be local extensions for* $i = 1, 2$. *Assume that* $\mathcal{K}_i$ *are* Σ_i-*flat and* Σ_i-*linear and all variables in clauses in* $\mathcal{K}_i$ *occur below a* Σ_i-*symbol, and that the extension* $\mathcal{T}_0 \subseteq \mathcal{T}_0 \cup \mathcal{K}_1 \cup \mathcal{K}_2$ *is local. Let* $G = G_1 \wedge G_2$ *be as constructed before. Assume that* $\mathcal{T}_0 \cup (\mathcal{K}_1 \wedge G_1) \wedge (\mathcal{K}_2 \wedge G_2) \models \perp$. *Then we can construct a ground formula* I *which contains only function symbols in* $\Sigma_0 = \Sigma_1 \cap \Sigma_2$ *such that* $(\mathcal{T}_0 \cup \mathcal{K}_1) \wedge G_1 \models I$ *and* $(\mathcal{T}_0 \cup \mathcal{K}_2) \wedge G_2 \wedge I \models \perp$.

Proof: We assumed that the goal is flat and linear, i.e. $G_i = G_i^0 \wedge G_0 \wedge D_i$ where G_i^0, G_0 contains only function symbols in Σ_0 and D_i is a set of definitions of the form $c \approx f(c_1, \ldots, c_n)$ with $f \in \Sigma_i$. If $\mathcal{T}_0 \cup (\mathcal{K}_1 \wedge G_1) \wedge (\mathcal{K}_2 \wedge G_2) \models \perp$ then, by Corollary 10 (with the notations used there):

$$\mathcal{T}_0 \cup \mathcal{K}_1^0 \cup \mathcal{K}_2^0 \cup (G_1^0 \cup G_0) \cup (G_2^0 \cup G_0) \cup N_1 \cup N_2 \models \perp.$$

Obviously, every model of $\mathcal{T}_0$ which satisfies $\mathcal{K}_1 \wedge G_1^0 \wedge G_0 \wedge D_1$ is also a model of $\mathcal{T}_0 \cup \mathcal{K}_1^0 \cup G_1^0 \cup G_0 \cup N_1$, and every model of $\mathcal{T}_0$ which satisfies $\mathcal{K}_2 \wedge G_2^0 \wedge G_0 \wedge D_2$

is also a model of $\mathcal{T}_0 \cup \mathcal{K}_2^0 \cup G_2^0 \wedge G_0 \cup N_2$. Let $I = \mathcal{K}_1^0 \cup G_1^0 \cup G_0 \cup N_1$. Then

$$\mathcal{T}_1 \wedge G_1^0 \wedge G_0 \wedge D_1 \models I,$$
$$I \wedge \mathcal{T}_2 \wedge G_2^0 \wedge G_0 \wedge D_2 \models \mathcal{T}_0 \cup (\mathcal{K}_1^0 \cup G_1^0 \cup G_0 \cup N_1) \cup (\mathcal{K}_2^0 \cup G_2^0 \cup G_0 \cup N_2) \models \bot.$$

All variables in clauses in $\mathcal{K}_i$ occur below a Σ_i-symbol, so $\mathcal{K}_i[G_i]$ (hence also $\mathcal{K}_i^0$) is ground for $i = 1, 2$, i.e. I is quantifier-free.   □

If the goal is not flattened, then we can flatten and purify it first and use Theorem 11 to construct an interpolant I_1. We can now construct I from I_1 by replacing each constant c_t introduced in the purification process (and therefore contained in a definition $c_t \approx t$ in $D_1 \cup D_2$) with the term t. It is easy to see that I satisfies the required conditions. We can in fact prove that only information over the shared signature (i.e. shared functions and constants) is necessary.

Theorem 12 ([SS06a]). *With the notations above, assume that $G_1 \wedge G_2 \models_{\mathcal{T}_1 \cup \mathcal{T}_2} \bot$. Then there exists a ground formula I, containing only constants shared by G_1 and G_2, with $G_1 \models_{\mathcal{T}_1 \cup \mathcal{T}_2} I$ and $I \wedge G_2 \models_{\mathcal{T}_1 \cup \mathcal{T}_2} \bot$.*

9   Conclusions

We presented criteria for recognizing situations in which combinations of theory extensions of a base theory are again local extensions of the base theory. We showed, for instance, that if both component theories satisfy the embeddability condition ($\mathsf{Comp_w}$), which guarantees that we can always embed a partial model into one with isomorphic support, then the combination of the two theories again satisfies condition ($\mathsf{Comp_w}$). The main problem which we needed to overcome when considering more general combinations of local theory extensions was the preservation of truth of clauses when extending partial operations to total operations in a partial algebra. We identified some conditions which guarantee that this is the case. These results allow to recognize wider classes of local theory extensions, and open the way for studying possibilities of modular reasoning in such extensions. From the point of view of modular reasoning in such combinations of local extensions of a base theory, it is interesting to analyze the exact amount of information which needs to be exchanged between provers for the component theories. We showed that if we start with a goal in purified form $G = G_1 \wedge G_2$, it is sufficient to exchange only ground formulae containing only constants and function symbols common to $G_1 \wedge \mathcal{T}_1$ and $G_2 \wedge \mathcal{T}_2$. We would like to understand whether there are any links between the results described in this paper and other methods for reasoning in combinations of theories over non-disjoint signatures e.g. by Ghilardi [Ghi04].

References

[BG96]   Basin, D.A., Ganzinger, H.: Complexity analysis based on ordered resolution. In: Proc. 11th IEEE Symposium on Logic in Computer Science (LICS 1996), pp. 456–465. IEEE Computer Society Press (1996)

[BG01]   Basin, D., Ganzinger, H.: Automated complexity analysis based on ordered resolution. Journal of the ACM 48(1), 70–109 (2001)

[BG07]   Baader, F., Ghilardi, S.: Connecting many-sorted theories. The Journal of Symbolic Logic 72(2), 535–583 (2007)

[Bur86]   Burmeister, P.: A Model Theoretic Oriented Approach to Partial Algebras: Introduction to Theory and Application of Partial Algebras, Part I. Mathematical Research, vol. 31. Akademie-Verlag, Berlin (1986)

[Bur95]   Burris, S.: Polynomial time uniform word problems. Mathematical Logic Quarterly 41, 173–182 (1995)

[Gan01]   Ganzinger, H.: Relating semantic and proof-theoretic concepts for polynomial time decidability of uniform word problems. In: Proc. 16th IEEE Symposium on Logic in Computer Science (LICS 2001), pp. 81–92. IEEE Computer Society Press (2001)

[Ghi04]   Ghilardi, S.: Model theoretic methods in combined constraint satisfiability. Journal of Automated Reasoning 33(3-4), 221–249 (2004)

[GM92]   Givan, R., McAllester, D.: New results on local inference relations. In: Principles of Knowledge Representation and Reasoning: Proceedings of the Third International Conference (KR 1992), pp. 403–412. Morgan Kaufmann Press (1992)

[GSS01]   Ganzinger, H., Sofronie-Stokkermans, V.: Combining local equational Horn theories. Unpublished manuscript (2001)

[GSSW04]   Ganzinger, H., Sofronie-Stokkermans, V., Waldmann, U.: Modular Proof Systems for Partial Functions with Weak Equality. In: Basin, D., Rusinowitch, M. (eds.) IJCAR 2004. LNCS (LNAI), vol. 3097, pp. 168–182. Springer, Heidelberg (2004)

[GSSW06]   Ganzinger, H., Sofronie-Stokkermans, V., Waldmann, U.: Modular proof systems for partial functions with Evans equality. Information and Computation 204(10), 1453–1492 (2006)

[McA93]   McAllester, D.: Automatic recognition of tractability in inference relations. Journal of the Association for Computing Machinery 40(2), 284–303 (1993)

[NO79]   Nelson, G., Oppen, D.C.: Simplification by cooperating decision procedures. ACM Transactions on Programming Languages and Systems (1979)

[SS05]   Sofronie-Stokkermans, V.: Hierarchic Reasoning in Local Theory Extensions. In: Nieuwenhuis, R. (ed.) CADE 2005. LNCS (LNAI), vol. 3632, pp. 219–234. Springer, Heidelberg (2005)

[SS06a]   Sofronie-Stokkermans, V.: Interpolation in Local Theory Extensions. In: Furbach, U., Shankar, N. (eds.) IJCAR 2006. LNCS (LNAI), vol. 4130, pp. 235–250. Springer, Heidelberg (2006)

[SS06b]   Sofronie-Stokkermans, V.: Local reasoning in verification. In: Autexier, S., Mantel, H. (eds.) IJCAR 2006 Workshop: VERIFY 2006: Verification Workshop. IJCAR 2006 Workshop Proceedings, pp. 128–145, Seattle, USA (2006)

[SSI07a]   Sofronie-Stokkermans, V., Ihlemann, C.: Automated reasoning in some local extensions of ordered structures. In: Proceedings of ISMVL 2007, paper 1. IEEE Computer Society (2007)

[SSI07b]   Sofronie-Stokkermans, V., Ihlemann, C.: Automated reasoning in some local extensions of ordered structures. Journal of Multiple-Valued Logics and Soft Computing 13(4–6), 397–414 (2007)

Interprocedural Shape Analysis
for Effectively Cutpoint-Free Programs

J. Kreiker[1], T. Reps[2,*], N. Rinetzky[3,**], M. Sagiv[3],
Reinhard Wilhelm[4], and E. Yahav[5,***]

[1] Technical University of Munich
joba@model.in.tum.de
[2] University of Wisconsin
reps@cs.wisc.edu
[3] Tel Aviv University
{maon,msagiv}@tau.ac.il
[4] University des Saarlandes
wilhelm@cs.uni-sb.de
[5] Technion, Haifa, Israel
yahave@cs.technion.ac.il

Abstract. We present a framework for local interprocedural shape analysis that computes procedure summaries as transformers of procedure-local heaps (the parts of the heap that the procedure may reach). A main challenge in procedure-local shape analysis is the handling of *cutpoints*, objects that separate the input heap of an invoked procedure from the rest of the heap, which—from the viewpoint of that invocation—is non-accessible and immutable.

In this paper, we limit our attention to *effectively cutpoint-free* programs—programs in which the only objects that separate the callee's heap from the rest of the heap, when considering *live* reference fields, are the ones pointed to by the actual parameters of the invocation. This limitation (and certain variations of it, which we also describe) simplifies the local-reasoning about procedure calls because the analysis needs not track cutpoints. Furthermore, our analysis (conservatively) verifies that a program is effectively cutpoint-free,

1 Introduction

Shape-analysis algorithms statically analyze a program to determine information about the heap-allocated data structures that the program manipulates. The algorithms are *conservative* (sound), i.e., the discovered information is true for every input. Handling the heap in a precise manner requires strong pointer updates [3]. However, performing

---

* Supported by NSF under grants CCF-0540955, CCF-0810053, and CCF-0904371, by ONR under grant N00014-09-1-0510, by ARL under grant W911NF-09-1-0413, and by AFRL under grant FA9550-09-1-0279.
** Supported in part by a Royal Academy of Engineering research fellowship, and in part by EPSRC.
*** Deloro Fellow.

A. Voronkov and C. Weidenbach (Eds.): Ganzinger Festschrift, LNCS 7797, pp. 414–445, 2013.

strong pointer updates requires a flow-sensitive and context-sensitive analysis and expensive heap abstractions, which may be doubly-exponential in the program size [25]. The presence of procedures escalates the problem because of interactions between the program stack and the heap [22] and because recursive calls may introduce additional exponential factors in an analysis. This makes interprocedural shape analysis a challenging problem.

This paper introduces a new approach for *local* [10, 18] interprocedural shape analysis for a class of imperative programs. The main idea is to restrict the aliasing between live access paths at procedure calls. This allows procedure invocations to be analyzed ignoring *non-relevant* parts of the heap, more specifically, the parts of the heap not reachable from actual parameters. Moreover, shape analysis verifies that the above restrictions are satisfied.

The restricted class of programs is chosen based on observations made in [20]. There, Rinetzky et al. present a non-standard semantics in which procedures operate on procedure-local heaps containing only the objects reachable from actual parameters. The most complicated aspect of [20] is the treatment of sharing from the global heap and local variables of pending calls into the procedure-local heap. The problem is that the local heap can be accessed via access paths that bypass actual parameters. Therefore, objects in the local heap are treated differently when they separate the local heap (accessible by a procedure) from the rest of the heap (which—from the viewpoint of that procedure—is non-accessible and immutable). These objects are referred to as *cutpoints* [20].

Example 1. Fig. 1 illustrates the notions of local heaps and cutpoints. To gain intuition, Fig. 1 shows these notions using the familiar *store-based* semantics. (See, e.g., [18]). The figure depicts a memory state of a program comprised of four procedures: main, foo, bar, and zoo. The figure depicts a memory state that may occur at the entry to zoo. The stack of activation records is depicted on the left side of the diagram. Each activation record is labeled with the name of the procedure it is associated with. Thus, as we can see, zoo was invoked by bar; procedure bar was invoked by foo; and foo was invoked by the main procedure. The activation record at the top of the stack pertains to the *current* procedure (zoo). All other activation records pertain to *pending* procedure calls. Thus, for example, the access paths $z1.f1.f1$, $y9$, and $x5.f2$ are pending access paths.

Heap-allocated objects are depicted as rectangles labeled with their location. The value of a reference variable (resp. field) is depicted by an edge labeled with the name of the variable (resp. field). The shaded cloud marks the part of the heap that zoo can access (i.e., the part of the heap containing the relevant objects for the invocation). The cutpoints for the invocation of zoo ($u8$ and $u9$) are heavily shaded. Note that $u7$ is not a cutpoint because it is also pointed to by $h7$, zoo's formal parameter.

Cutpoints present a major challenge for shape abstractions: Procedure-local heaps together with special handling of cutpoints was found to be key in obtaining efficient and precise interprocedural shape-analysis algorithms [28]. Thus, the shape abstraction cannot abstract away the sharing patterns induced by cutpoints between the procedure-local heap of the procedure and the rest of the heap. These sharing patterns may lack any regular shape. However, the regularity of the sharing pattern is, in fact, what enables the effective shape abstraction of unbounded linked data structures.

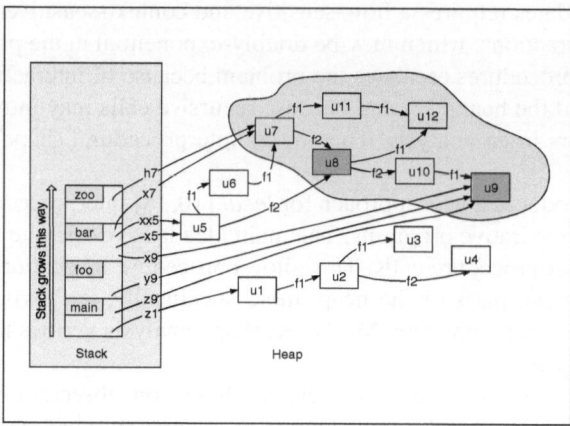

Fig. 1. An illustration of the cutpoints for an invocation in a store-based small-step (stack-based) operational semantics at the entry to zoo. We assume that $h7$ is zoo's formal parameter.

We observe that cutpoints need special treatment in the analysis of a procedure because the caller may use its direct references to the cutpoint after the procedure returns. We develop an interprocedural shape analysis in which such direct usages are forbidden. We refer to a reference that, at the time when a procedure is invoked, points to a cutpoint and does not come from an object in the callee's local heap as a *piercing reference* for that invocation. An execution is *effectively cutpoint-free* if in every invocation that occurs during the execution, all the piercing references for that invocation are not *live* [26] at the time of the invocation, i.e., their r-values are not used later on in the execution before being set. A program is effectively cutpoint-free if all its executions are. When analyzing effectively cutpoint-free programs, there is no need to give special care to cutpoint objects. However, to verify that a program is effectively cutpoint-free, special care needs to be taken regarding future usages of piercing references.

In this paper we present $\mathcal{ECPF}$, a small-step operational semantics [16] that handles *effectively cutpoint-free* programs. This semantics is interesting because procedures operate on local heaps, i.e., every procedure invocation starts executing on a memory state in which *parts of the heap not relevant to the invocation are ignored*. Thus, $\mathcal{ECPF}$ supports the notion of *heap-locality* [10,18] while permitting the usage of a global heap and destructive updates. Moreover, the absence of cutpoints drastically simplifies the meaning of procedure calls. $\mathcal{ECPF}$ tracks the set of piercing references and checks that their values are never used, thus dynamically verifying that the program execution is indeed effectively cutpoint-free. As a result, $\mathcal{ECPF}$ is applicable to arbitrary programs, and does not require an a priori classification of a program as effectively cutpoint-free. We show that for effectively cutpoint-free programs, $\mathcal{ECPF}$ is observationally equivalent to the standard global heap semantics.

$\mathcal{ECPF}$ gives rise to a functional [6,27] interprocedural shape analysis for effectively cutpoint-free programs. The analysis tabulates abstractions of memory states before and after procedure calls. Mimicking the semantics, memory states are represented in a procedure-local way *ignoring parts of the heap not relevant to the procedure with no special abstraction for cutpoints.* This reduces the complexity of the analysis because the analysis of procedures does not represent information about references and the heap from calling contexts. Indeed, this makes the analysis local in the heap and thus allows reusing the summarized effect of a procedure at different calling contexts.

Technically, our algorithm is built on top of the 3-valued logical framework for program analysis of [13, 25]. Thus, it is parametric in the heap abstraction and in the concrete effects of program statements, which allows experimenting with different instances of interprocedural shape analyzers. For example, we can employ different abstractions for singly-, doubly-linked lists, and trees. Also, a combination of theorems in Appendix A.2 and [25] guarantees that every instance of our *interprocedural* framework is sound (see Sec. 5).

Main Results. The contributions of this paper can be summarized as follows:
1. We define the notion of effectively cutpoint-free programs, in which the context not reachable from a procedure's actual parameters can be ignored when reasoning about the procedure's possible effect.
2. We define an operational semantics for a simple imperative language with references and procedures. The semantics dynamically checks that a program execution is effectively cutpoint-free. Procedures operate on procedure-local heaps, thus supporting the notion of heap-locality while permitting the usage of a global heap and destructive updates.
3. We present an interprocedural shape analysis for effectively cutpoint-free programs. The analysis is local in the heap and thus allows reusing the effect of a procedure at different calling contexts and at different call-sites.
4. We describe several extensions to our approach that allow its efficiency, precision, and applicability to be improved by utilizing a limited form of user-supplied annotations.

Outline. The rest of the paper is organized as follows. Sec. 2 presents an informal overview of our approach. Sec. 3 introduces our programming model. Sec. 4 defines our new local heap semantics, which checks whether a program is effectively cutpoint-free. Sec. 5 conservatively abstracts this semantics and provides the semantic foundation of the local interprocedural shape analysis algorithm described in Sec. 6. Sec. 7 describes certain efficiency-oriented extensions of our approach and certain relaxations of our restrictions aimed at increasing the class of effectively cutpoint-free programs. Sec. 8 describes related work, and Sec. 9 concludes.

2 Overview

This section provides an overview of our framework for interprocedural shape analysis using procedure-local heaps. The presentation is at an intuitive level; a more detailed treatment of this material is presented in the later sections of the paper.

2.1 Motivating Example

Fig. 2 shows a simple Java program that splices three non-shared, disjoint, acyclic singly-linked lists using a recursive `splice` procedure. This program serves as a running example in this paper.

```
public class List{                          public static List splice(List p, List q) {
  List n = null;                              List w = q;
  int data;                                   if (p != null) {
                                                List pn = p.n;
  public List(int d){                           p.n = null;
    this.data = d;                              p.n = splice(q, pn);
  }                                             w = p;
                                              }
  static public List create3(int k) {        return w;
    List t1 = new List(k);                  }
    List t2 = new List(k+1);
    List t3 = new List(k+2);                public static void main(String[] argv) {
    t1.n = t2; t2.n = t3;                     List x = create3(1);
    return t1;                                List y = create3(4);
  }                                           List z = create3(7);
                                              List t = splice(x, y);
  static public int getData(List w) {        List s = splice(t, z);
    assert(w != null);                        int i = 0;
    int d = w.data;                           ℓ₀ : // if (y == null) i++;
    return d;                                 ℓ₁ : // if (y == x) i++;
  }                                           ℓ₂ : // int i = getData(y);
                                              print(i);
                                            }

                                          }
```

Fig. 2. An effectively-cutpoint-free program written in Java

2.2   Procedure-Local Heaps

In our semantics, procedures operate on local heaps. The local heap contains only the part of the program's heap accessible to the procedure. Thus, procedures are invoked on local heaps containing only objects reachable from actual parameters. We refer to these objects as the *relevant* objects for the invocation.

Example 2. Fig. 3 shows the concrete memory states that occur at the call t=splice(x,y). S_3^c shows the state at the point of the call, and S_3^e shows the state on entry to splice. Here, splice is invoked on local heaps containing the (relevant) objects reachable from either x or y.

The fact that the local heap of the invocation t=splice(x,y) contains only the lists referenced by x and y guarantees that destructive updates performed by splice can only affect access paths that pass through an object referenced by either x or y.

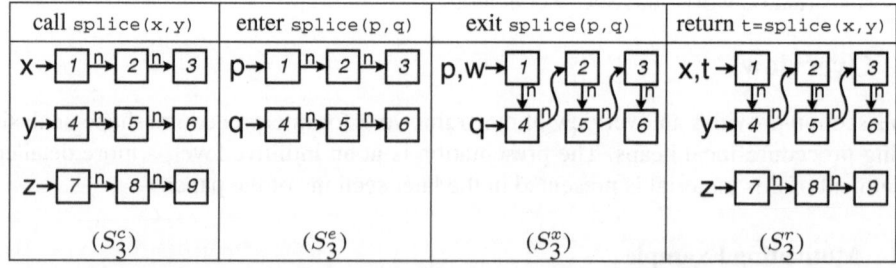

Fig. 3. Concrete states for the invocation t = splice(x, y) in the running example

2.3 Cutpoints and Cutpoint-Freedom

Obviously, this is not always the case. In particular, consider the second call in the example program, s=splice(t,z). Fig. 4(a) shows the concrete states when s=splice(t,z) is invoked. $S_4^{c_{cp}}$ shows the state on invocation, and $S_4^{r_{cp}}$ the state when the call returns. As shown in the figure, the destructive updates of the splice procedure change not only paths from t and z, but also change the access paths from y.

To emphasize the effect of this invocation, consider a variant of the example program in which the invocation s=splice(t,z) has been replaced with an invocation s=splice(y,z), as shown in Fig. 4(b). In this variant, the invocation can only affect access paths that pass through an object referenced by either y or z.

We capture the difference between these invocations by introducing the notion of a cutpoint [20]. A cutpoint for an invocation is an object that is: (i) reachable from an actual parameter, (ii) not pointed-to by an actual parameter, and (iii) reachable without going through an object that is pointed-to by an actual parameter (that is, it is either pointed-to by a variable or by an object not reachable from the parameters). In other words, a cutpoint is a relevant object that separates the part of the heap that is reachable for the invocation from the rest of the heap, but not pointed-to by a parameter.

For example, the object pointed-to by y at the call s=splice(t,z) (Fig. 4(a)) is a *cutpoint*, thus this invocation is not *cutpoint-free* [23]. In contrast, in the invocation s=splice(y,z) (Fig. 4(b)) no object is a cutpoint, and thus this invocation is *cutpoint-free* [23].

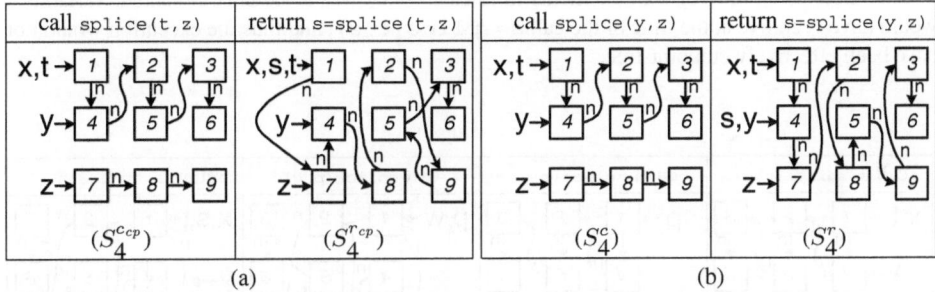

Fig. 4. Concrete states for: (a) the invocation s=splice(t,z) in the program of Fig. 2; (b) a variant of this program with an invocation s=splice(y,z).

2.4 Effective Cutpoint-Freedom

The importance of cutpoints is that they allow the analysis to handle more precisely the notion of procedure local variables: No invocation of splice can modify the local variables of main. Thus, when control returns to main, it is guaranteed that the local variable y points to the same object that it pointed to before the invocation, and the main procedure can use the y reference to access directly that object. In general, it is very challenging to design a shape analysis that can track relations between arbitrary objects across the execution of procedure calls. However, if the caller does not use its direct references to the cutpoints after the procedure returns, the analysis does not need to track this relation.

For example, note that after `main` regains control, it does not use the value of the y variable. Thus, although the invocation `s=splice(t,z)` has a cutpoint, and is thus not cutpoint-free, in the context of the whole execution this invocation is *effectively cutpoint free*.

The semantics utilizes the above observation and instead of giving special treatment to the cutpoint objects, it assigns a special *inaccessible* value to all piercing references. The inaccessible value is used to track references which should not be used. It is a simple mechanism which the semantics uses to check (in runtime) whether a piercing pointer is used , e.g., in a dereference operation or during the evaluation of a condition, and if such a usage occurs to abort the execution and report that the program is not effectively cutpoint-free. (See Sec. 4).

Example 3. Fig. 5 shows the concrete memory states that occur at the call `s=splice(t,z)`. S_5^c shows the state at the point of the call, in which the object pointed to by y is a cutpoint. In S_5^r, the return state of that call, y no longer points to an object, instead it has the inaccessible value, depicted by a black bullet. The semantics intentionally does not utilize the information it has regarding the identity of objects. It acts as if it "forgets" that the object referenced by y at the call state is the third node in the returned list, mimicking in the concrete semantics the loss of information that occurs in the analysis. Note that the cutpoint object is not treated differently during the execution of `splice`, e.g., S_5^e and S_5^x show the states on entry to `splice` of the call and at its exit, respectively.

Also note that if any of the statements in lines $\ell_0 - \ell_2$ was to be uncommented, variable y would have been live at the time of the call `s=splice(t,z)`, and thus the execution would not have been effectively cutpoint-free.

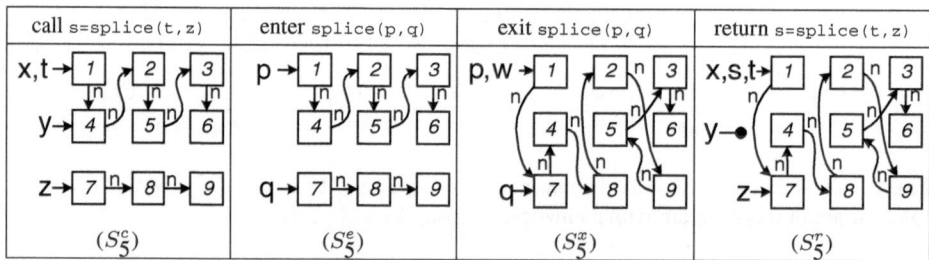

Fig. 5. Concrete states for the invocation s = splice(t, z) in the running example

2.5   Interprocedural Shape Analysis

The algorithm computes procedure summaries by tabulating pairs of abstract input memory-states and abstract output memory-states. The tabulation is restricted to abstract memory-states that occur in the *analyzed* program. The tabulated abstract memory-states represent procedure-local heaps, but do not keep track of cutpoints. However, they do record the inaccessible values. Therefore, these abstract states are independent of the context in which a procedure is invoked. As a result, the summary computed for a procedure could be used at different calling contexts and at different call-sites while sustaining enough information to verify effective cutpoint freedom.

3   Programming Model

For expository reasons we limit our attention to a small imperative programming language. It has references to objects. Objects have fields, which can be either references to other objects or integers. The analyses developed here can be applied to Java-like languages and other imperative pointer languages alike (unless pointer arithmetic is used).

We abstract from specific control-flow statements and simply assume the presence of one control-flow graph per procedure. Control-flow graph edges are annotated with any one of the following statements below, where $x.f$ denotes the f field of the object referenced by x. The statement $x = \text{alloc}()$ returns a reference to a newly created object. Conditionals are implemented using assume statements.

$$stms ::= x = \text{null} \mid x = y \mid x = y.f \mid$$
$$x.f = y \mid x = \text{alloc}() \mid \text{assume}(x \bowtie y) \mid$$
$$y = p(x_1, \ldots, x_k) \mid \text{return}$$

In our running example we take the liberty to use integer variables and fields as well.

In the rest of the paper, we assume that we are working with a fixed arbitrary program P. For a procedure p, V_p denotes the set of its local variables and $F_p \subseteq V_p$ denotes the set of its formal parameters. A procedure returns a value by assigning it to a designated variable ret. We assume that parameters are passed by value and that formal parameters cannot be assigned to. The set of all local variables of P is written $\mathcal{V}$. We write $\mathcal{F}$ to denote the set of all field names in P.

We assume a standard store-based operational semantics for our language, very much like $\mathcal{GSB}$ defined previously in [19, 20]. $\mathcal{GSB}$ treats live cutpoints properly.

4   Concrete Semantics

In this section, we define $\mathcal{ECPF}$ (*effectively cutpoint-free*), a non-standard semantics that checks whether a program execution is effectively cutpoint-free. $\mathcal{ECPF}$ defines the execution traces that are the foundation of our analysis.

$\mathcal{ECPF}$ is a *store-based* semantics (see, e.g., [18]). A traditional aspect of a store-based semantics is that a memory state represents a heap comprised of all the allocated objects. $\mathcal{ECPF}$, on the other hand, is a *procedure-local heap* semantics [20]: A memory state that occurs during the execution of a procedure does not represent objects that, at the time of the invocation, are not reachable from the actual parameters.

$\mathcal{ECPF}$ is a small-step operational semantics [16]. Instead of encoding a stack of activation records inside the memory state, as is traditionally done, $\mathcal{ECPF}$ maintains a *stack of program states* [12, 21]: Every program state consists of a program point and a memory state. The program state of the *current procedure* is stored at the top of the stack, and it is the only one that can be manipulated by intraprocedural statements. We refer to this memory state as the *current memory state*. When a procedure is invoked, the *entry memory state* of the callee is computed by a $Call$ operation according to the caller's current memory state, and pushed onto the stack. When a procedure returns, the stack is popped, and the caller's *return memory state* is updated using a Ret operation according to its memory state before the invocation (the *call memory state*) and the callee's (popped) *exit memory state*. The $Call$ and Ret operations of $\mathcal{ECPF}$ are defined in Fig. 8.

The use of a stack of program states allows us to represent in every memory state the (values of) local variables and the local heap of just one procedure. The *lifting* of an intraprocedural semantics to an interprocedural semantics, that uses a stack of program states, is formally defined in [19].

An execution trace of a program P always begins with P's main executing on an *initial memory state* in which all its reference variables have the value *null* and the heap is empty. We say that a memory state is *reachable* in a program P if it occurs as the current memory state in an execution trace of P.

$\mathcal{ECPF}$ is a procedure-local heap semantics [20]: when a procedure is invoked, it starts executing on an *input heap* containing only the set of *relevant objects for the invocation*. An object is *relevant for an invocation* if it is a *parameter object*, *i.e.*, either referenced by an actual parameter or reachable from one.

A procedure-local heap semantics and its abstractions benefit from not having to represent irrelevant objects. However, in general, the semantics needs to take special care of cutpoints. In this paper, we avoid the need to take special care of cutpoint objects by assuming and verifying that a program is *effectively cutpoint free*: We refer to a reference that at invocation time points to a cutpoint and does not come from an object in the callee's local heap as a *piercing reference* for that invocation. An execution is *effectively cutpoint-free* if in every of its invocations during an execution all the piercing references for that invocation are *dead* at the time of the invocation, i.e., their r-values are not used before being set. A program is *effectively cutpoint-free* if all of its executions are.

For effectively cutpoint-free programs, there is no need to give special care to cutpoint objects. However, to verify that a program is effectively cutpoint-free, special care needs to be taken regarding the piercing references. In this section, we describe the way $\mathcal{ECPF}$ validates at runtime that an execution is effectively cutpoint-free.

4.1 Memory States

Fig. 6 defines the concrete semantic domains and the meta-variables ranging over them. We assume Loc to be an unbounded set of locations. A value $v \in Val$ is either a location, *null*, or $\bullet$, the inaccessible value used to represent references to locations that should not be accessed.

$$
\boxed{\begin{array}{l}
l \in \mathit{Loc} \\
v \in \mathit{Val} = \mathit{Loc} \cup \{\mathit{null}\} \cup \{\bullet\} \\
\hline
\rho \in \mathcal{E} = \mathcal{V} \rightharpoonup \mathit{Val} \\
h \in \mathcal{H} = \mathit{Loc} \rightharpoonup \mathcal{F} \rightharpoonup \mathit{Val} \\
\sigma \in \Sigma = \mathcal{E} \times 2^{\mathit{Loc}} \times \mathcal{H}
\end{array}}
$$

Fig. 6. Semantic domains

A memory state in the $\mathcal{ECPF}$ semantics is, essentially, a 2-level store. Formally, a memory state is a 3-tuple $\sigma = \langle \rho, L, h \rangle$: $\rho \in \mathcal{E}$ is an environment assigning values for the variables of the *current* procedure. $L \subset \mathit{Loc}$ is the set of allocated locations. (A dynamically allocated object is identified by its location. We interchangeably use the terms object and location.) $h \in \mathcal{H}$ assigns values to fields of allocated objects.

In $\mathcal{ECPF}$, reachability is defined with respect to relevant objects: Informally, an object l_2 is *reachable from* an object l_1 in a memory state σ if there is a directed path in the heap of σ from l_1 to l_2. An object l is *reachable* in σ if it is reachable from a location that is pointed-to by some variable. Note that $\bullet$-valued references do not point to any object.

4.2 Operational Semantics of Intraprocedural Statements

The meaning of atomic statements is described by a transition relation $\overset{i}{\rightsquigarrow} \subseteq (\Sigma \times \mathit{stms}) \times \Sigma \uplus \{\sigma_\bullet\}$, where $\sigma_\bullet$ is a special error state indicating a forbidden usage of the inaccessible value.

Fig. 7 defines the axioms for atomic intraprocedural statements. These are handled as in a standard 2-level store semantics like $\mathcal{GSB}$.[7] The main difference between the $\mathcal{ECPF}$ semantics and $\mathcal{GSB}$ with respect to the meaning of intraprocedural statements is captured by the side-conditions of the form $\rho(x) = \bullet$ or $\rho(y) = \bullet$, which prevent usage of the inaccessible locations.

4.3 Operational Semantics of Interprocedural Statements

Fig. 8 defines the meaning of the $Call$ and Ret operations pertaining to an arbitrary procedure call $y = p(x_1, \ldots, x_k)$ assuming p's formal parameters are $z_1, \ldots, z_k$, the memory state at the call site is $\sigma_c = \langle \rho_c, L_c, h_c \rangle$, and the memory state at the exit of p is $\sigma_x = \langle \rho_x, L_x, h_x \rangle$. The $Call$ operation is used to compute the state update along a call edge in the control-flow graph; the Ret operation computes the state update along a return edge. As defined in Sec. 3, variable `ret` is used to communicate the return value. We use the function $R_h(L)$ to compute the locations that are reachable in heap h from the set of locations L. This function is formally defined in Appendix A.1.

Procedure Calls. The $Call$ operation computes the callee's *entry memory state* (σ_e) from the state at the call-site (σ_c). The entry memory state is computed by binding the values of the formal parameters in the callee's environment to the values of the corresponding actual parameters (ρ_e) and restricting the caller's heap to the relevant objects for the invocation (L_{rel}).

$$\langle \mathtt{x = null}, \sigma\rangle \overset{i}{\leadsto} \langle \rho[x \mapsto null], L, h\rangle$$

$$\langle \mathtt{x = y}, \sigma\rangle \overset{i}{\leadsto} \langle \rho[x \mapsto \rho(y)], L, h\rangle$$

$$\langle \mathtt{x = y.f}, \sigma\rangle \overset{i}{\leadsto} \langle \rho[x \mapsto h(\rho(y), f)], L, h\rangle \qquad \rho(y) \in Loc$$

$$\langle \mathtt{y.f = x}, \sigma\rangle \overset{i}{\leadsto} \langle \rho, L, h[(\rho(y), f) \mapsto \rho(x)]\rangle \qquad \rho(y) \in Loc$$

$$\langle \mathtt{x = alloc()}, \sigma\rangle \overset{i}{\leadsto} \langle \rho[x \mapsto l], L\cup\{l\}, h[l \mapsto I]\rangle \qquad l \in Loc \setminus L$$

$$\langle \mathtt{assume(x \bowtie y)}, \sigma\rangle \overset{i}{\leadsto} \sigma \qquad \rho(x) \bowtie \rho(y)$$

$$\langle \mathtt{x = y}, \sigma\rangle \overset{i}{\leadsto} \sigma_\bullet \qquad \rho(y) = \bullet$$

$$\langle \mathtt{x = y.f}, \sigma\rangle \overset{i}{\leadsto} \sigma_\bullet \qquad \rho(y) = \bullet \text{ or } h(\rho(y)) = \bullet$$

$$\langle \mathtt{y.f = x}, \sigma\rangle \overset{i}{\leadsto} \sigma_\bullet \qquad \rho(y) = \bullet \text{ or } \rho(x) = \bullet$$

$$\langle \mathtt{assume(x \bowtie y)}, \sigma\rangle \overset{i}{\leadsto} \sigma_\bullet \qquad \rho(x) = \bullet \text{ or } \rho(y) = \bullet$$

Fig. 7. Axioms for intraprocedural statements, where in each line σ is understood as a shorthand for $\langle \rho, L, h\rangle$. I denotes the function $\lambda f \in \mathcal{F}.null$. $\bowtie$ stands for either $=$ or $\neq$. When convenient, we sometimes treat h as an uncurried function, i.e., as a function from $Loc \times \mathcal{F}$ to Val.

$$Call_{y=p(x_1,\dots,x_k)}(\sigma_c) = \sigma_e \qquad\qquad Ret_{y=p(x_1,\dots,x_k)}(\sigma_c, \sigma_x) = \sigma_r$$

$$\sigma_e = \langle \rho_e, L_c, h_c|_{L_{rel}}\rangle \qquad\qquad\quad \sigma_r = \langle \rho_r, L_x, h_r\rangle$$

$$\rho_e = [z_i \mapsto \rho_c(x_i) \mid 1 \leq i \leq k] \qquad\quad \rho_r = (block \circ \rho_c)[y \mapsto \rho_x(ret)]$$

$$h_r = (block \circ h_c|_{L_c \setminus L_{rel}}) \cup h_x$$

where:

$$L_{parameters} = \{\rho_c(x_i) \in Loc \mid 1 \leq i \leq k\}$$

$$L_{rel} = R_{h_c}(L_{parameters})$$

$$L_{cutpoints} = (L_{rel} \setminus L_{parameters}) \cap$$
$$(\{\rho_c(z) \mid z \in V_q\} \cup \{h_c(l)f \in Loc \mid l \in L_c \setminus L_{rel}, f \in \mathcal{F}\})$$

$$block = \lambda v \in Val. \begin{cases} \bullet & v \in L_{cutpoints} \\ v & \text{otherwise} \end{cases}$$

$$Call_{y=p(x_1,\dots,x_k)}(\sigma_c) = \sigma_\bullet \qquad \rho_c(x_1) = \bullet \text{ or } \cdots \text{ or } \rho_c(x_k) = \bullet$$

$$Ret_{y=p(x_1,\dots,x_k)}(\sigma_c, \sigma_x) = \sigma_\bullet \qquad \rho_x(ret) = \bullet$$

Fig. 8. $Call$ and Ret operations for an arbitrary procedure call $y = p(x_1, \dots, x_k)$ by an arbitrary procedure q, where it is understood that $\sigma_c = \langle \rho_c, L_c, h_c\rangle$, $\sigma_x = \langle \rho_x, L_x, h_x\rangle$, and V_q denotes the set of local variables of procedure q.

Example 4. Fig. 3 shows the entry state S_3^e that results from applying the *Call* operation pertaining to the invocation t=splice(x, y) to the call memory state S_3^c. Fig. 5 shows the entry state S_5^e that results from applying the *Call* operation pertaining to the invocation s=splice(t, z) to the call memory state S_5^c.

Procedure Returns. The *Ret* operation maps the memory state at the exit of a procedure (σ_x) together with the state at call-site (σ_c) to the return state σ_r from which the caller resumes its computation. *Ret* updates the caller's memory state by carving out the input heap passed to the callee from the caller's heap ($h_c|_{L_c \setminus L_{rel}}$) and replacing it with the callee's (possibly) mutated heap (h_x).

In $\mathcal{ECPF}$, an object never changes its location, and locations are never reallocated. Thus, any pointer to a relevant object in the caller's memory state (either by a field of an irrelevant object or a variable) points after the replacement to an up-to-date version of the object.

Blocking Piercing References. $\mathcal{ECPF}$ detects forbidden accesses that violate the effective-cutpoint-freedom condition, and aborts the program in an error state if such an access is detected. Technically, when a procedure invocation returns, $\mathcal{ECPF}$ assigns the special value • to all piercing references, an operation which we refer to as *blocking*, and uses this special value to detect forbidden accesses. (Recall that in an effectively cutpoint-free execution, every live reference that points to an object which separate the callee's heap from the caller's heap should point to a parameter object, i.e., to one of the objects in $L_{parameters}$.)

Example 5. Fig. 3 shows the return state S_3^r, that results from applying the *Ret* operation pertaining to the invocation t=splice(x, y) to the call memory state S_3^c and the exit memory state S_3^x. Fig. 5 shows the return state S_5^r, that results from applying the *Ret* operation pertaining to the invocation s=splice(t, z) to the call memory state S_5^c and the exit memory state S_5^x. The second node in the list pointed to by t at the call state S_5^c is a cutpoint. Thus, variable y gets blocked when computing S_5^r.

4.4   Observational Soundness

We say that two values are *comparable* in $\mathcal{ECPF}$ if neither one is •. We say that a $\mathcal{ECPF}$ memory state σ is *observationally sound* with respect to a standard semantics σ_G if for every pair of access paths that have comparable values in σ, they have equal values in σ iff they have equal values in σ_G. $\mathcal{ECPF}$ *simulates* the standard 2-level store semantics: Executing the same sequence of statements in the $\mathcal{ECPF}$ semantics and in the standard semantics either results in a $\mathcal{ECPF}$ memory states that is observationally sound with respect to the resulting standard memory state, or the $\mathcal{ECPF}$ execution gets to an *error state* due to a constraint breach (detected by $\mathcal{ECPF}$). A program is *effectively cutpoint-free* if it does not have an execution trace that gets to an error state. (Note that the initial state of an execution in $\mathcal{ECPF}$ is observationally sound with respect to its standard counterpart).

Our goal is to detect structural invariants that are true according to the *standard semantics*. $\mathcal{ECPF}$ acts like the standard semantics as long as the program's execution satisfies certain constraints. $\mathcal{ECPF}$ enforces these restrictions by blocking references that a program should not access. Similarly, our analysis reports an invariant concerning equality of access paths only when these access paths have comparable values.

An invariant concerning equality of access paths in $\mathcal{ECPF}$ for an effectively cutpoint-free program is also an invariant in the standard semantics. This makes abstract interpretations of $\mathcal{ECPF}$ suitable for verifying data-structure invariants, for detecting memory access violations, and for performing compile-time garbage collection.

5   Abstract Interpretation

In this section, we present $\mathcal{ECPF}^{\#}$, an abstract interpretation [5] of the $\mathcal{ECPF}$ semantics. $\mathcal{ECPF}^{\#}$ is the basis of our static-analysis algorithm which uses the 3-valued logic-based framework of [25]. The soundness of the abstract semantics with respect to $\mathcal{GSB}^{1}$ is guaranteed by the combination of the theorems in Appendix A.2 and [25]:

- In Appendix A.2, we show that for effectively cutpoint-free programs, $\mathcal{ECPF}$ is observationally equivalent to $\mathcal{GSB}$.
- In [25], it is shown that every program-analyzer that is an instance of the 3-valued logic-based framework is sound with respect to the concrete semantics it is based on.

5.1   Abstract States

We conservatively represent unbounded sets of unbounded memory states using a bounded set of bounded 3-valued logical structures, which we refer to as *abstract states*. Note that there are actually three different notions of *concrete states*. The most concrete states are those in $\mathcal{GSB}$, containing full information including integer variables and fields. Integers are already abstracted away when we talk about $\mathcal{ECPF}$, which, on top of that, also yields errors when cutpoint references are illegally used. $\mathcal{ECPF}$ states are equivalently encoded into *two-valued* logical structures by viewing objects as individuals in a logical structure and references as binary predicates (see below). Note, however, that location identifiers play no role in the logical structure encoding. Indeed, the semantics does not distinguish between isomorphic structures.

We use the term *concrete state* whenever we talk about a state that is not a 3-valued logical structure. We believe that, despite the resulting imprecision, our intentions are clear. In drawings, we use the same graphical notations to depict concrete states in all of the aforementioned semantics. (Integer values, when drawn, should be ignored when considering a figure to be a graphical depiction of a state in $\mathcal{ECPF}$ or of a logical structure.)

3-*Valued Logical Structures.*   A 3-valued logical structure is a logical structure with an extra truth-value $\frac{1}{2}$, which denotes values that may be 1 or may be 0. The information partial order on the set $\{0, \frac{1}{2}, 1\}$ is defined as $0 \sqsubseteq \frac{1}{2} \sqsupseteq 1$, and $0 \sqcup 1 = \frac{1}{2}$. Formally, a 3-valued logical structure is $S^{\#} = \langle U^{S^{\#}}, \iota^{S^{\#}} \rangle$ where:

---

[1] $\mathcal{GSB}$ is a standard two-level store semantics for heap-manipulating programs. It is formally defined in [20].

- $U^{S^\sharp}$ is the universe of the structure.
- $\iota^{S^\sharp}$ is an interpretation function mapping predicates to their truth-value in the structure, i.e., for every predicate $p \in \mathcal{P}$ of arity k, $\iota^S(p) \colon U^{S^{\sharp k}} \to \{0, \frac{1}{2}, 1\}$.

A 2-valued logical structure is a 3-valued logical structure where the truth-values of predicates are either 0 or 1. The set of *3-valued* logical structures is denoted by *3Struct*. The set of *2-valued* logical structures is denoted by *2Struct*.

Abstraction Function. We abstract sets of $\mathcal{ECPF}$ memory states by a point-wise application of an *extraction function* $\beta : \Sigma \rightharpoonup$ *3Struct* mapping an $\mathcal{ECPF}$ memory state to its *best representation* by an *abstract state*. The extraction function β is defined as a composition of two functions: (i) $\beta_{shape} : \Sigma \rightharpoonup$ *2Struct*, which maps an $\mathcal{ECPF}$ memory state to a 2-valued logical structure and (ii) *canonical abstraction* [25], which maps 2-valued logical structures to a bounded number of 3-valued logical structures.

Representing Memory States Using 2-Valued Logical Structures. We represent $\mathcal{ECPF}$ memory states using 2-valued logical structures. Every individual in the structure corresponds to a heap-allocated object. Predicates of the structure correspond to properties of heap-allocated objects.

Core Predicates. Tab. 1 shows the core predicates used in this paper. A binary predicate $f(v_1, v_2)$ holds when the $\mathtt{f} \in \mathcal{F}$ field of v_1 points to v_2. The designated binary predicate $eq(v_1, v_2)$ is the equality predicate, which records equality between v_1 and v_2. A unary predicate $x(v)$ holds for an object that is referenced by the reference variable $\mathtt{x} \in \mathcal{V}$ of the *current* procedure.[2] The predicate ia holds only for a unique individual, which represents the inaccessible locations. The role of the predicates $inUc$ and $inUx$ is explained in Sec. 5.2.

Instrumentation Predicates. Instrumentation predicates record derived properties of individuals, and are defined using a logical formula over core predicates. Instrumentation predicates are stored in the logical structures like core predicates. They are used to refine the abstract semantics, as we shall shortly see. Tab. 2 lists the instrumentation predicates used in this paper. We use $F(v_1, v_2)$ as a shorthand to denote that v_1 has a field $f \in \mathcal{F}$ which points to v_2 and $F^*(v_1, v_2)$ as the reflexive transitive closure of F. (For a formal definition, see Appendix B).

2-valued logical structures are depicted as directed graphs. We draw individuals as boxes. We depict the value of a reference variable x by drawing an edge from x to the individual representing the object that x references. For all other unary predicates p, we draw p inside a node u when $\iota^S(p)(u) = 1$; conversely, when $\iota^S(p)(u) = 0$ we do not draw p in u. A directed edge between nodes u_1 and u_2 that is labeled with a binary predicate symbol p indicates that $\iota^S(p)(u_1, u_2) = 1$. For clarity, we do not draw the binary equality predicate eq. The inaccessible value is depicted as a line ending with •.

---

[2] For simplicity, we use the same set of predicates for all procedures. Thus, our semantics ensures that $\iota^S(x) = \lambda u.0$ for every local variable $\mathtt{x}$ that does not belong to the current call.

Table 1. Predicates used to represent (concrete) memory states

Predicate	Intended Meaning
$f(v_1, v_2)$	the f-field of object v_1 points to object v_2
$eq(v_1, v_2)$	v_1 and v_2 are the same object
$x(v)$	reference variable x points to the object v
$ia(v)$	v is an inaccessible location
$inUc(v)$	v originates from the caller's memory state at the call site
$inUx(v)$	v originated from the callee's memory state at the exit site

Table 2. The instrumentation predicates used in this paper

Predicate	Intended Meaning	Defining Formula
$r_{obj}(v_1, v_2)$	v_2 is reachable from v_1 by some field path	$\neg ia(v_1) \wedge \neg ia(v_2) \wedge F^*(v_1, v_2)$
$ils(v)$	v is *locally* shared. i.e., v is pointed-to by a field of more than one object in the *local heap*	$\exists v_1, v_2 \colon \neg ia(v)$ $\neg eq(v_1, v_2) \wedge F(v_1, v) \wedge F(v_2, v)$
$c(v)$	v resides on a directed cycle of fields	$\exists v_1 \colon F(v, v_1) \wedge F^*(v_1, v)$
$r_x(v)$	v is reachable from variable x	$\neg ia(v) \wedge \exists v_x \colon x(v_x) \wedge F^*(v_x, v)$

Example 6. The structure S_3^c of Fig. 3 shows a *2-valued* logical structure that represents the memory state of the program at the call t=splice(x, y). The depicted numerical values are only shown for presentation reasons, and have no meaning in the logical representation.

The structure S_5^r of Fig. 5 shows a *2-valued* logical structure that represents the memory state of the program at the return of s=splice(t, y). Note that the value of y is the inaccessible value.

Bounded Abstraction. We now formally define how memory states are represented using abstract memory states. The idea is that each object from the (concrete) state is mapped to an individual in the abstract state. An abstract memory state may include *summary nodes*, i.e., individuals that correspond to one or more concrete nodes in one of the concrete states represented by the abstract state. For a summary node $u \in U^\sharp$ in abstract state $S^\sharp = \langle U^\sharp, \iota^\sharp \rangle$ it holds that $\iota(eq)(u, u) = \frac{1}{2}$.

Canonical Abstraction. A *3-valued* logical structure $S^\sharp$ is a **canonical abstraction** of a *2-valued* logical structure S if there exists a surjective function $\upsilon \colon U^S \to U^{S^\sharp}$ satisfying the following conditions: (i) For all $u_1, u_2 \in U^S$, $\upsilon(u_1) = \upsilon(u_2)$ iff for all unary predicates $p \in \mathcal{P}$, $\iota^S(p)(u_1) = \iota^S(p)(u_2)$, and (ii) for all predicates $p \in \mathcal{P}$ of arity k and for all k-tuples $u_1^\sharp, u_2^\sharp, \ldots, u_k^\sharp \in U^{S^\sharp}$,

$$\iota^{S^\sharp}(p)(u_1^\sharp, u_2^\sharp, \ldots, u_k^\sharp) = \bigsqcup_{\substack{u_1, \ldots, u_k \in U^s \\ \upsilon(u_i) = u_i^\sharp}} \iota^S(p)(u_1, u_2, \ldots, u_k).$$

3-valued logical structures are also drawn as directed graphs. Definite values (0 and 1) are drawn as for 2-valued structures. Binary indefinite predicate values ($\frac{1}{2}$) are drawn as dotted directed edges. Summary nodes are depicted by a double frame.

Example 7. Fig. 9 shows the abstract states (as *3-valued* logical structures) representing the concrete states of Fig. 3. Note that only the local variables p and q are represented inside the call to splice(p,q). Representing only the local variables inside a call ensures that the number of unary predicates to be considered when analyzing the procedure is proportional to the number of its local variables. This reduces the overall complexity of our algorithm to be worst-case doubly-exponential in the maximal number of local variables rather than doubly-exponential in their total number (as in e.g., [22]).

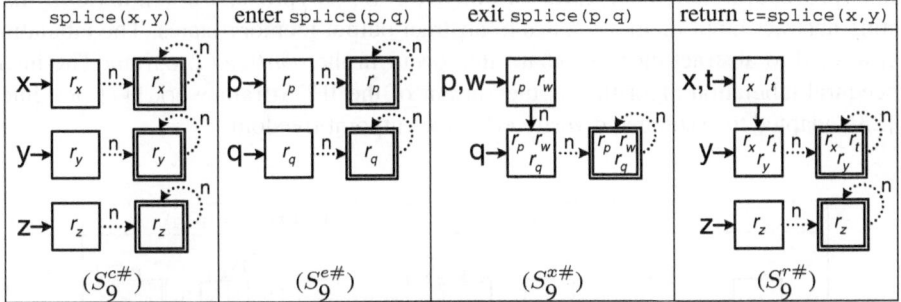

Fig. 9. Abstract states for the invocation t = splice(x, y); in the running example

The Importance of Reachability. Recording derived properties by means of *instrumentation predicates* may provide additional information that would have been otherwise lost under abstraction. In particular, because canonical abstraction is directed by unary predicates, adding unary instrumentation predicates may further refine the abstraction. This is called the *instrumentation principle* in [25]. In our framework, the predicates that record reachability from variables play a central role. They enable us to identify the individuals representing objects that are reachable from actual parameters. For example, in the *3-valued* logical structure $S_9^{c\#}$ depicted in Fig. 9, we can detect that the top two lists represent objects that are reachable from the actual parameters because either r_x or r_y holds for these individuals. None of these predicates holds for the individuals at the (irrelevant) list referenced by z. We believe that these predicates should be incorporated in any instance of our framework.

5.2 Abstract Operational Semantics

The meaning of statements is described by a transition relation $\overset{\sharp}{\leadsto} \subseteq (\mathit{3Struct} \times \mathit{stms}) \times \mathit{3Struct}$. Because our framework is based on [25], the encoding of the meaning of statements in $\mathcal{ECPF}$ (as transformers of 2-valued structures), also defines the corresponding abstract semantics (as transformers of 3-valued structures). This abstract semantics is obtained by reinterpreting logical formulae using a 3-valued logic semantics and serves as the basis for our static analysis. In particular, reinterpreting the side conditions of intraprocedural statements conservatively verifies that the *program* is effectively cutpoint-free.

For brevity, we omit the aforementioned encoding from the body of the paper and provide it in Appendix B. We wish to note that all the transformers, including the interprocedural operations *Call* and *Ret* are specified using predicate-update formulae[3] in first-order logic with transitive closure.

6   Interprocedural Static Analysis

Abstract interpretation of the $\mathcal{ECPF}$ semantics provides the semantic foundations for an interprocedural static-analysis algorithm that computes procedure summaries by tabulating abstract input memory-states to abstract output memory-states. The tabulation is restricted to abstract memory-states that occur in the *analyzed* program. The interprocedural tabulation algorithm is the variant of the IFDS-framework [17] presented in [23], adapted to assume and verify effective cutpoint freedom.

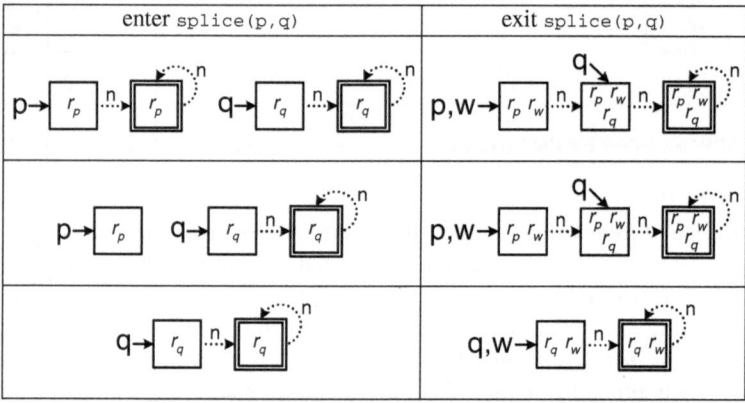

Fig. 10. Partial tabulation of abstract states for the splice procedure

Example 8. Fig. 10 shows a partial tabulation of abstract local heaps for the `splice` procedure of the running example. The figure shows 3 possible input states of the list pointed-to by p. Identical possible input states of the list pointed-to by q, and their combinations are not shown. As mentioned in Sec. 1, the splice procedure is only analyzed 9 times before its tabulation is

---

[3] Predicate-update formulae express the semantics of statements: Suppose that σ is a memory state that arises before statement st, that σ' is the store that arises after st is evaluated on σ, and that S is the 2-valued logical structure that encodes σ. A collection of predicate-update formulae—one for each predicate p in the vocabulary of S—allows one to obtain the structure S' that encodes σ'. When evaluated in structure S, the predicate-update formula for a predicate p indicates what the value of p should be in S'. See [25, Observation 2.6]. Evaluation of the predicate-update formulae in 3-valued logic captures the transfer function for st of the abstract semantics. See [25, Observation 2.9].

complete, producing a summary that is then reused whenever the effect of splice(p, q) is needed.

Note that this tabulation represents the input/output relation for any call to splice, including ones with cutpoints, e.g., the call s=splice(t, y) and all recursive calls to splice in our running example.

7   Extensions and Relaxations

In this section, we describe several extensions that use a limited form of annotations on procedures to improve the analysis algorithmic's efficiency, precision, and applicability.

7.1   Blindspots

$\mathcal{ECPF}$ records in every state the value of every formal parameter at the entry to the procedure. This is done to allow the caller to observe the (possibly mutated) part of the heap that was relevant to the callee after the callee returns. However, in certain cases, such observations are not needed or even desirable.

For example, in the program of Fig. 2, the variable y is not used after the call t=splice(x, y). Thus, the effort invested to restore its value when the call returns is, for all practical purposes, wasted. Furthermore, direct access to the list returned by splice through one of the actual parameters might be considered a form of bad programming. (A clearer example might be a merge procedure that merges two sorted lists. When an invocation of merge returns, one actual parameter references the head of the list and the other one references one of the list elements. Using the actual parameters at this point makes the code less readable and more sensitive to the implementation details of merge. Thus, it is reasonable to expect that the caller uses the returned value, but not the actual parameters.)

Blindspots (for a procedure invocation) are parameter objects for which all the variables and fields pointing to them at the time of the call, excluding fields of relevant objects for the invocation, are *dead* when the procedure returns.[4] $\mathcal{ECPF}$, and its abstract interpretations, can utilize an annotation (e.g., in the form of a subset of the actual/formal parameters) that states which of the parameter objects are blindspots. Such information can improve the efficiency of the analysis algorithim by allowing it to avoid tracking unnecessary information. It also allows verifying good programming style.

For example, Fig. 11 shows the call, entry, exit, and return states that occur in the $\mathcal{ECPF}$ during the invocation t=splice(x,y) when both parameter objects are annotated as a *blindspots*. Based on this annotation, the exit state does not record the value of the formal parameters, allowing for more compact summaries. Note that at the return state, x and y are blocked. As a result, the returned list can be accessed only through t.

7.2   Tolerance for a Bounded Number of Cutpoints

$\mathcal{ECPF}$, and its abstract interpretations, *can* allow for procedure invocations to have up to a bounded number of live cutpoints, i.e., cutpoints that are accessed directly by

---

[4] Note that a blindspot for a procedure invocation is not necessarily a dead *object*.

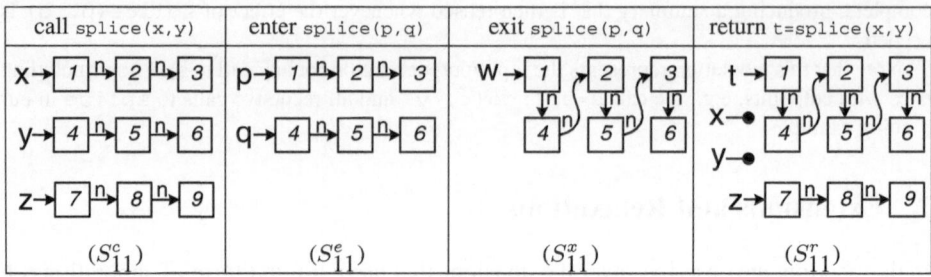

call splice(x,y)	enter splice(p,q)	exit splice(p,q)	return t=splice(x,y)

Fig. 11. Concrete states for the invocation t = splice(x, y) when both parameter objects are annotated as a *blindspots*

a piercing reference after the procedure returns. The main idea is to treat cutpoints as additional parameters: Every procedure is modified to have k additional (hidden) formal parameters (where k is the bound on the number of allowed cutpoints). When a procedure is invoked, the (modified) *semantics* binds the additional parameters with references to the cutpoints.

We can allow for a bounded number of cutpoints by having an annotation regarding the maximal number of allowed cutpoints[5] or by having the user provide a specification (using first-order formulae with transitive closure) of a distinguished set of explicitly-allowed cutpoints. For example, a cutpoint at the last element of a list can be treated differently then other cutpoints.

Fig. 12 depicts the call, entry, exit, and return states that occur in the $\mathcal{ECPF}$ during the invocation s = splice(t, z) when procedures are allowed to have at least one cutpoint, or, alternatively, when the second element of the first list is specified as an explicitly-allowed cutpoint. The hidden parameter X_1 gets bound to the cutpoint at the entry state and used to restore the value of y at the return state.

7.3   Restricted Access to the Inaccessible Value

For a program to be effectively cutpoint-free, every piercing reference must not be live at the time of the actual invocation. The reason behind this requirement is to allow the semantics/analysis to avoid maintaining certain aliasing relations, yet still maintain a certain notion of observational soundness with respect to the standard semantics. However, certain *usages* of piercing references are innocuous, i.e., our notion of observational soundness is still maintained as long as programs use piercing references in certain restricted ways. For example, statements such as x = y, as well as conditions involving comparisons between •-valued references and null, are innocuous. In the former case, the assignment neither affects the control flow of the program nor may lead to a memory fault. In the latter case, it always holds that a •-valued reference is not *null*-valued; thus the condition of the assume statement always evaluates to the same value in both semantics.

---

[5] This is the essence of the treatment of cutpoints by Gotsman et al. [8].

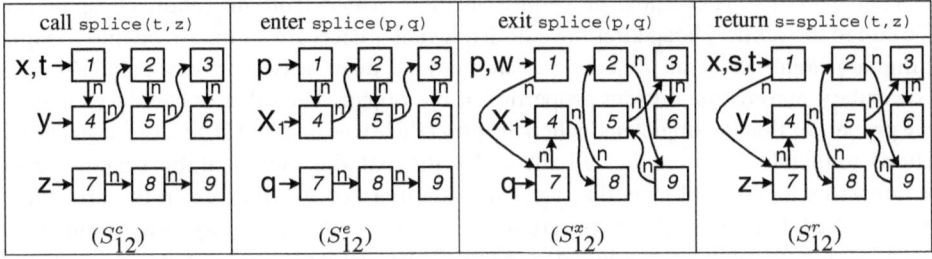

Fig. 12. Concrete states for the invocation s = splice(t, z) when one cutpoint is allowed or alternatively, when access path t.n is specified as an *explicitly-allowed* cutpoint

Effectively, the above observation allows us to relax the requirements of executions to be effectively cutpoint-free: Instead of forbidding all future usages of piercing references (i.e., requiring that they are not live when the invocation of the callee returns), we need only to forbid "effective" future usages of this pointers, i.e., we need only to forbid them from being dereferenced or compared with non-null values both in assume statements and in assertions.

7.4 Arbitrary Cutpoints in Pure Procedures

An additional relaxation regarding the requirements of a procedure invocation to be effectively cutpoint-free is possible when a procedure invocation is found to be *pure*. A pure invocation does not modify the shared state. Thus, the abstract representation of the heap at the call site can be reused at the return site. As a result, for reconstructing the layout of the heap, the number of cutpoints is irrelevant, and piercing references do not need to be blocked.

The above approach has one rather significant complication: In case the procedure's return value is a pointer to a heap-allocated object, figuring out which object in the call state corresponds to the one returned by the procedure is not simple. (This complication arises because the abstract semantics does not retain the identity of locations.)

One possible remedy is not to use this relaxation when the return value of the invoked procedure is a (non-null) reference. Another possible remedy is to apply a *meet* operator between the call state and the exit state (after certain renaming operations, similar to the ones used in [11]). We note that the framework of [25] provides an algorithmic meet operator [1]. We also note that (some) information regarding cutpoints can (potentially) make the results of the meet operator more precise.

8   Discussion and Related Work

In this section, we review closely related work.

Rinetzky and Sagiv [22] explicitly represent the runtime stack and abstract it as a linked-list. In this approach, the entire heap, and the runtime stack are represented at every program point. As a result, the abstraction may lose information about properties of the heap *for parts of the heap that cannot be affected by the procedure at all.*

Jeannet et al. [11] consider procedures as transformers from the (entire) heap before the call to the (entire) heap after the call. Irrelevant objects are summarized into a single summary node. Relevant objects are summarized using a two-store vocabulary. One vocabulary records the current properties of the object. The other vocabulary encodes the properties that the object had when the procedure was invoked. The latter vocabulary allows to match objects at the call-site and at the exit-site. Note that this scheme never summarizes together objects that were not summarized together when the procedure was invoked. For cutpoint-free programs, this may lead to needlessly large summaries. Consider for example a procedure that operates on several lists and nondeterministically replaces elements between the list tails. The method of [11] will not summarize list elements that originated from different input lists. Thus, it will generate exponentially more mappings in the procedure summary than the ones produced by our method. On the other hand, the method of [11] can establish properties of called procedures that our method cannot establish (e.g., that a procedure to reverse a list actually reverses all elements of the list).

Rinetzky et al. [20] present a procedure-local storeless concrete semantics and describe an abstract interpretation of their semantics that can be used for interprocedural shape-analysis for programs manipulating singly linked lists. Their abstract interpretation algorithm explicitly records cutpoint objects in the local heap, and may become imprecise when there is more than one cutpoint. Our algorithm can be seen as a specialization of [20] that provides a partial answer to this problem. In addition, because we restricted our attention to effectively cutpoint-free programs, our semantics and analysis are much simpler than the ones in [20].

In [23], the problem of abstracting cutpoint-induced sharing patterns is addressed by forbidding cutpoints: We developed an interprocedural shape analysis for the class of *cutpoint-free* programs, in which program invocations never generate cutpoints. In the present paper, we extend the framework developed in [23] to a larger class of programs: *effectively cutpoint-free* programs. One can see [23] as an eager form of enforcing effective cutpoint-freedom, while the present paper takes a more lazy approach.

Hackett and Rugina [9] develop a staged analysis to obtain a relatively scalable interprocedural shape analysis. Their approach uses a scalable imprecise pointer-analysis to decompose the heap into a collection of independent locations. The precision of this approach might be limited because it relies on pointer-expressions that appear in the program's text. The analysis tabulates global heaps, potentially leading to a low reuse of procedure summaries.

For the special case of singly-linked lists, another approach for modular shape analysis is presented by Chong and Rugina [4] without an implementation. The main idea there is to record for every object both its current properties and the properties it had at that time the procedure was invoked.

Gotsman et al. [8] describe a heap-modular interprocedural shape analysis for singly linked lists that can handle a bounded numbers of cutpoints. The main idea is to treat a bounded number of cutpoint-labels as, essentially, additional parameters: Every procedure can be seen as having k additional (hidden) formal parameters (where k is the bound on the number of allowed cutpoints). When a procedure is invoked, their analysis (non-deterministically) binds these additional parameters with references to the cutpoints. If the procedure has more than k cutpoint, they turn every piercing reference to a dangling pointer, which, essentially, makes the reference inaccessible. Thus, their analysis does not differentiate between dangling references and piercing references. However, every program that it manages to analyze is a k-cutpoint-tolerant effectively cutpoint-free program.

Yang et al. [28] present a heap-modular interprocedural shape analysis that, similar to [8], is based on a domain of separation-logic formulae. Their experimental results indicate that the use of local heaps provides a speedup of $2 - 3\times$ in the analysis compared to a global heap analysis. Furthermore, the use of an interprocedural analysis that passes only the reachable portion of the heap was found to be one of the three key reasons for the scalability of their analysis. (The other two key reasons being an efficient join operator and the discard of intermediate states.) In this analysis, cutpoints are passed as additional (hidden) parameters to called procedures, but their number is not bounded. This is one of the possible reasons that their analysis may not terminate (although in many interesting cases it does). In later work [2], the problem of cutpoint abstraction is reduced because the compositional nature of the analysis allows to represent only a subset of the reachable heap.

Marron et al. [14] present a context-sensitive shape analysis that is employed for automatic parallelization of sequential heap manipulating programs. The interprocedural analysis is based on an abstraction of local heaps with cutpoints. The analysis employs an abstraction of cutpoint-labels that uses two main ideas: (i) avoid summarizing cutpoints that are generated by the local variables of the *immediate* caller and (ii) abstract all other cutpoints by recording the set of roots of access paths. The analysis also uses liveness information to avoid recording as cutpoints objects that are only pointed to by dead references.

Rubinstein [24] provides a preliminary study regarding the classification of cutpoints that occur in real-life Java programs. The study is conducted by monitoring program executions. Algorithms for detecting usages of piercing references[6] are presented but not implemented. While the experimental results are non-conclusive, they do indicate that in several interesting cases the unbounded number of cutpoints occur when the program manipulates shared *immutable* data structures. This can motivate special treatment for pure (i.e., readonly) methods (see Sec. 7.4).

A local interprocedural may-alias analysis is given in [7]. The key observation there is that a procedure operates uniformly on all aliasing relationships involving variables of pending calls. This method applies to programs with cutpoints. However, the lack of *must*-alias information may lead to a loss of precision in the analysis of destructive updates. For more details on the relation between [7] and local heap shape analysis see [19].

Local reasoning [10, 18] provides a way of proving properties of a procedure independently of its calling contexts by using the "frame rule". In some sense, the approach used in this paper is in the spirit of local reasoning. The $\mathcal{ECPF}$ semantics resembles the frame rule in the sense that the effect of a procedure call on a large heap can be obtained from its effect on a subheap. Local reasoning allows for an arbitrary partitioning of the

---

[6] The term a *live cutpoint* is used in [24] to refer to an object which gets dereferenced using a piercing reference.

heap based on user-supplied specifications. In contrast, in our work, the partitioning of the heap is built into the concrete semantics, and abstract interpretation is used to establish properties in the absence of user-supplied specifications.

Another relevant body of work is that concerning *encapsulation*, also known as *confinement* or *ownership*. (A review about different encapsulation models can be found in [15]). These works allow modular reasoning about heap-manipulating (object-oriented) programs. The common aspect of these works, as described in [15], is that they all place various restrictions on the kind of sharing allowed in the heap, while pointers from the stack are generally left unrestricted. In our work, the semantics allows for arbitrary heap sharing within the same procedure, but restricts both the heap sharing and the stack *live* sharing across procedure calls.

9   Conclusions and Future Work

In this paper, we presented an interprocedural shape analysis for effectively cutpoint-free programs. The analysis is local in the heap and thus allows reusing the effect of a procedure at different calling contexts. We presented the first non-trivial solution for procedure calls with an unbounded number of cutpoints. The solution is limited because it applies only to pure (read-only) procedures; however, we believe that it opens the door for future work to address the important, and still open, problem of handling an unbounded number of live cutpoints under abstraction.

In general, we believe that the distinction between live piercing references and dead ones can benefit analyses that abstract an unbounded number of cutpoints by allowing them to focus on only abstracting cutpoints that are pointed to by live piercing references. We consider this issue to be future work.

References

1. Arnold, G., Manevich, R., Sagiv, M., Shaham, R.: Combining Shape Analyses by Intersecting Abstractions. In: Emerson, E.A., Namjoshi, K.S. (eds.) VMCAI 2006. LNCS, vol. 3855, pp. 33–48. Springer, Heidelberg (2006)
2. Calcagno, C., Distefano, D., O'Hearn, P., Yang, H.: Compositional shape analysis by means of bi-abduction. In: Symp. on Princ. of Prog. Lang. (POPL), pp. 289–300. ACM (2009)
3. Chase, D.R., Wegman, M., Zadeck, F.: Analysis of pointers and structures. In: Conf. on Prog. Lang. Design and Impl., PLDI (1990)
4. Chong, S., Rugina, R.: Static analysis of accessed regions in recursive data structures. In: Cousot, R. (ed.) SAS 2003. LNCS, vol. 2694, pp. 463–482. Springer, Heidelberg (2003)
5. Cousot, P., Cousot, R.: Abstract interpretation: A unified lattice model for static analysis of programs by construction of approximation of fixed points. In: Symp. on Princ. of Prog. Lang. (POPL), pp. 238–252. ACM Press, New York (1977)
6. Cousot, P., Cousot, R.: Static determination of dynamic properties of recursive procedures. In: Neuhold, E.J. (ed.) Formal Descriptions of Programming Concepts (IFIP WG 2.2, St. Andrews, Canada), pp. 237–277. North-Holland (August 1977)
7. Deutsch, A.: Interprocedural alias analysis for pointers: Beyond k-limiting. In: Conf. on Prog. Lang. Design and Impl. (PLDI) (1994)
8. Gotsman, A., Berdine, J., Cook, B.: Interprocedural Shape Analysis with Separated Heap Abstractions. In: Yi, K. (ed.) SAS 2006. LNCS, vol. 4134, pp. 240–260. Springer, Heidelberg (2006)

9. Hackett, B., Rugina, R.: Region-based shape analysis with tracked locations. In: Symp. on Princ. of Prog. Lang. (POPL) (2005)
10. Ishtiaq, S.S., O'Hearn, P.W.: BI as an assertion language for mutable data structures. In: Symp. on Princ. of Prog. Lang. (POPL) (2001)
11. Jeannet, B., Loginov, A., Reps, T., Sagiv, M.: A Relational Approach to Interprocedural Shape Analysis. In: Giacobazzi, R. (ed.) SAS 2004. LNCS, vol. 3148, pp. 246–264. Springer, Heidelberg (2004)
12. Knoop, J., Steffen, B.: The interprocedural coincidence theorem. In: Int. Conf. on Comp. Construct. (CC) (1992)
13. Lev-Ami, T., Sagiv, M.: . TVLA: A framework for Kleene based static analysis. In: International Static Analysis Symposium (SAS) (2000),
http://www.math.tau.ac.il/~tvla
14. Marron, M., Hermenegildo, M., Kapur, D., Stefanovic, D.: Efficient context-sensitive shape analysis with graph based heap models. In: Int. Conf. on Comp. Construct. (CC), pp. 245–259 (2008)
15. Noble, J., Biddle, R., Tempero, E., Potanin, A., Clarke, D.: Towards a model of encapsulation. In: The First International Workshop on Aliasing, Confinement and Ownership in Object-Oriented Programming (IWACO) (2003)
16. Plotkin, G.D.: A Structural Approach to Operational Semantics. Technical Report DAIMI FN-19, University of Aarhus (1981)
17. Reps, T., Horwitz, S., Sagiv, M.: Precise interprocedural dataflow analysis via graph reachability. In: Symp. on Princ. of Prog. Lang. (POPL) (1995)
18. Reynolds, J.: Separation logic: a logic for shared mutable data structures. In: Symp. on Logic in Computer Science (LICS) (2002)
19. Rinetzky, N.: Interprocedural and Modular Local Heap Shape Analysis. PhD thesis, Tel Aviv University (June 2008)
20. Rinetzky, N., Bauer, J., Reps, T., Sagiv, M., Wilhelm, R.: A semantics for procedure local heaps and its abstractions. In: Symp. on Princ. of Prog. Lang. (POPL) (2005)
21. Rinetzky, N., Poetzsch-Heffter, A., Ramalingam, G., Sagiv, M., Yahav, E.: Modular Shape Analysis for Dynamically Encapsulated Programs. In: De Nicola, R. (ed.) ESOP 2007. LNCS, vol. 4421, pp. 220–236. Springer, Heidelberg (2007)
22. Rinetzky, N., Sagiv, M.: Interprocedural shape analysis for recursive programs. In: Int. Conf. on Comp. Construct. (CC) (2001)
23. Rinetzky, N., Sagiv, M., Yahav, E.: Interprocedural Shape Analysis for Cutpoint-Free Programs. In: Hankin, C., Siveroni, I. (eds.) SAS 2005. LNCS, vol. 3672, pp. 284–302. Springer, Heidelberg (2005)
24. Rubinstein, S.: On the utility of cutpoints for monitoring program execution. Master's thesis, Tel Aviv University, Tel Aviv, Israel (2006)
25. Sagiv, M., Reps, T., Wilhelm, R.: Parametric shape analysis via 3-valued logic. Trans. on Prog. Lang. and Syst. (TOPLAS) 24(3), 217–298 (2002)
26. Shaham, R., Yahav, E., Kolodner, E.K., Sagiv, M.: Establishing Local Temporal Heap Safety Properties with Applications to Compile-time Memory Management. In: Cousot, R. (ed.) SAS 2003. LNCS, vol. 2694, pp. 483–503. Springer, Heidelberg (2003)
27. Sharir, M., Pnueli, A.: Two approaches to interprocedural data flow analysis. In: Muchnick, S.S., Jones, N.D. (eds.) Program Flow Analysis: Theory and Applications, ch.7, pp. 189–234. Prentice-Hall, Englewood Cliffs, NJ (1981)
28. Yang, H., Lee, O., Berdine, J., Calcagno, C., Cook, B., Distefano, D., O'Hearn, P.W.: Scalable Shape Analysis for Systems Code. In: Gupta, A., Malik, S. (eds.) CAV 2008. LNCS, vol. 5123, pp. 385–398. Springer, Heidelberg (2008)

A   Formal Details Pertaining to the $\mathcal{ECPF}$ Semantics

In this section, we provide the technical details that were glanced over in Sec. 4.

A.1   Reachability

In this section, we give formal definitions for the notions of *reachability*. These definitions are based on the corresponding standard notions in 2-level stores. Intuitively, location l_2 is *reachable from* a location l_1 in a memory state σ if there is a directed path in the heap of σ from l_1 to l_2. A locations l is *reachable* in σ if it is reachable from a location which is referenced by some variable. Note that the inaccessible value, similarly to the *null* value, is not a location.

Definition 1 (Heap path). *A sequence of locations $\zeta : \{0, \ldots, n \mid n \in \mathcal{N}\} \to Loc$ is a directed heap path in a heap $h \in \mathcal{H}$, if for every $0 \leq i < |\zeta| - 1$ there exists $f_i \in \mathcal{F}$ such that $h(\zeta(i), f_i) = \zeta(i+1)$. A directed heap path ζ goes from l_1, if $\zeta(0) = l_1$, it goes to l_2 if $\zeta(|\zeta| - 1) = l_2$. A heap path ζ traverses through l if there exists i such that $0 \leq i < |\zeta|$ and $l = \zeta(i)$.*

Definition 2 (Reachability). *A location l_2 is* reachable from *a location l_1 in a memory state $\sigma = \langle \rho, L, h \rangle$, if there is a directed heap path in h going from l_1 to l_2.*

Definition 3 (Reachable locations). *A locations l is* reachable *in σ if it is reachable from a location which is referenced by some variable. We denote the set of* reachable *locations in $\sigma \in \Sigma$ by $\mathcal{R}(\sigma)$, i.e., $\mathcal{R}(\sigma) = \{l \in L | x \in \mathcal{V}$ and l is reachable in σ from $\rho(x) \in Loc\}$.*

A.2   Properties of the $\mathcal{ECPF}$ Semantics

In this section, we formally define the notions of *observational soundness* and of *simulation* between the $\mathcal{ECPF}$ semantics and the standard semantics. To be precise, when referring to the standard semantics we refer to the standard store-based semantics $\mathcal{GSB}$ defined in [19, 20]. In short, memory states in $\mathcal{GSB}$ are represented in the same way as memory states in $\mathcal{ECPF}$. The main difference between $\mathcal{GSB}$ and $\mathcal{ECPF}$ is that the operational semantics never blocks references in $\mathcal{GSB}$, and thus • is not a possible value.

Access paths We introduce access paths, which are the only means by which a program can observe a state. Note that the program cannot observe location names.

Definition 4 (Field Paths). *A field path $\delta \in \Delta = \mathcal{F}^*$ is a (possibly empty) sequence of field identifiers. The empty sequence is denoted by ϵ.*

Definition 5 (Access path). *An access path $\alpha = \langle x, \delta \rangle \in AccPath = \mathcal{V} \times \Delta$ is a pair consisting of a local variable and a field path.*

Definition 6 (Access path value in the $\mathcal{ECPF}$ semantics). *The value of an access path* $\alpha = \langle x, \delta \rangle$ *in state* $\sigma = \langle \rho, L, h \rangle$ *of the* $\mathcal{ECPF}$ *semantics, denoted by* $[\![\alpha]\!]_{\mathcal{ECPF}}(\sigma)$, *is defined to be* $\hat{h}(\rho(x), \delta)$, *where*

$$\hat{h} : Val \times \Delta \rightharpoonup Val \text{ such that}$$

$$\hat{h}(v, \delta) = \begin{cases} v & \text{if } \delta = \epsilon \quad (\text{note that } v \text{ might be } \bullet \,) \\ \hat{h}(h(v, f), \delta') & \text{if } \delta = f\delta', \, v \in Loc \\ undefined & \text{otherwise} \quad (\text{note that } v \text{ might be } \bullet \,) \end{cases}$$

Note that an access to a field of the inaccessible value is not defined.

Definition 7 (Comparable values). *A pair of values of the* $\mathcal{ECPF}$ *semantics* $v_1, v_2 \in Val$ *are* comparable, *denoted by* $v_1 \overset{?}{\bowtie} v_2$, *if* $v_1 \neq \bullet$ *and* $v_2 \neq \bullet$.

Definition 8 (Access path value in the $\mathcal{GSB}$ semantics). *The value of an access path* $\alpha = \langle x, \delta \rangle$ *in state* $\sigma_G = \langle \rho, L, h \rangle$ *of the* $\mathcal{GSB}$ *semantics, denoted by* $[\![\alpha]\!]_{\mathcal{GSB}}(\sigma_G)$, *is defined to be* $\overline{h}(\rho(x), \delta)$, *where* $Val_G = Val \setminus \{\bullet\}$ *and*

$$\overline{h} : Val_G \times \Delta \rightharpoonup Val_G \text{ such that}$$

$$\overline{h}(v, \delta) = \begin{cases} v & \text{if } \delta = \epsilon \\ \overline{h}(h(v, f), \delta') & \text{if } \delta = f\delta', \, v \in Loc \\ undefined & \text{otherwise} \end{cases}$$

Observational soundness We define the notion of observational soundness between a $\mathcal{ECPF}$ memory state σ and a standard 2-level store σ_G of the $\mathcal{GSB}$ semantics as the preservations in σ_G of all equalities and inequalities which hold in σ.[7] Note that the preservation in the other direction is not required. Also note that an equality resp. inequality of values of access paths holds in σ only when the two access paths have comparable values. For simplicity, we define $[\![null]\!]_{\mathcal{ECPF}}(\sigma) = [\![null]\!]_{\mathcal{GSB}}(\sigma) = null$.

Definition 9 (Observational soundness). *The memory state* $\sigma \in \Sigma$ *is* observationally sound *with respect to memory state* $\sigma_G \in \Sigma_G$, *denoted by* $\sigma_G \leq \sigma$, *if for every* $\alpha, \beta \in AccPath \cup \{null\}$ *it holds that*

if $[\![\alpha]\!]_{\mathcal{ECPF}}(\sigma) \overset{?}{\bowtie} [\![\beta]\!]_{\mathcal{ECPF}}(\sigma)$ *then*
$$[\![\alpha]\!]_{\mathcal{ECPF}}(\sigma)) = [\![\beta]\!]_{\mathcal{ECPF}}(\sigma) \Leftrightarrow [\![\alpha]\!]_{\mathcal{GSB}}(\sigma_G) = [\![\beta]\!]_{\mathcal{GSB}}(\sigma_G)$$

We define the notion of observational soundness between two $\mathcal{ECPF}$ memory states (resp. two standard memory states) in a similar manner.

Simulation Before we define the notion of simulation we briefly review some execution traces accessing-functions (formally defined in [19]). Given an execution trace π, the initial resp. final memory state of an execution trace π, denoted by $in(\pi)$ resp. $out(\pi)$, is the current memory state in the first resp. last stack of program states. $\pi(i)$ returns the stack at the ith step of the execution and $|\pi(i)|$ returns its height. $path(\pi)$ is the sequence of program points which the execution traverses. *i.e.*, $path(\pi)(i)$ is the program point in the ith step of the execution. (We assume that every statement is labeled by a program point.)

The following theorem shows that $\mathcal{ECPF}$ simulates the standard semantics. In the lemma, we denote by $path(\pi)$ the sequence of intraprocedural statements and $Call$ and $Return$ operations executed in π. We also use $[\pi]_k$ to denote the memory state of the current procedure at $\pi(k)$, the kth program state of π

Theorem 1 (Simulation). *Let P be an effectively cutpoint-free program according to the $\mathcal{ECPF}$ semantics. Let π_S be a trace of a program P according to the standard semantics. There exists a trace π_E of P according to the $\mathcal{ECPF}$ semantics such that the folowing holds (i) $|\pi_S| = |\pi_E|$, (ii) $path(\pi_S) = path(\pi_E)$, and (iii) $[\pi_S]_k \leqq [\pi_E]_k$ for every $0 \leq k < |\pi_S|$.*

Sketch of Proof: The proof is done by induction on the length of the execution. We look at memory states as graphs. The graph nodes are the allocated objects and the graph edges are the object fields. The graph nodes may be labeled by variables. The graph edges are labeled by field names.

We prove that observational equivalence is preserved by showing a stronger property: every memory state $[\pi_E]_k$ produced by the $\mathcal{ECPF}$ can be seen as a subgraph of $[\pi_S]_k$, the corresponding memory state of the $\mathcal{GSB}$ semantics. Furthermore, that two graphs agree on the values of live references.

We maintain an injective and a surjective function ϱ from the set of objects that are reachable from the variables of the current procedure in a memory state of the $\mathcal{GSB}$ to the set of objects in the corresponding memory state of the $\mathcal{ECPF}$ semantics. Clearly when a program starts, and prior to the allocation of any object, the two memory states are isomorphic. It is easy to verify that atomic statement preserves the isomorphism: ϱ remains unchanged, except that object allocation maps the new location to the new individual.

When a procedure is invoked, the mapping ϱ is projected on the set of objects passed to the invoked procedure. When a procedure returns, the mapping of locations that were irrelevant for the invocation remains as in the call site. The mapping for locations that were relevant for the invocation, as well as those that were allocated during the invocation, are taken from the exit site. Note that the induction assumption ensures that the above scheme is well defined.

To show that the return memory state produced by the $\mathcal{ECPF}$ semantics is a subgraph of the corresponding return memory state of the $\mathcal{GSB}$ semantics agrees with it on the values of live references, we make the following argument: The computation of return states in the $\mathcal{ECPF}$ semantics blocks piercing references. The computation of the return states in the $\mathcal{GSB}$ semantics does not. Thus, it remains to show that all the references that gets blocked by the $\mathcal{ECPF}$ semantics are not live in the $\mathcal{GSB}$ semantics.

The computation of return states in the $\mathcal{ECPF}$ semantics restores all references from the caller's local heap to parameter objects which, by the induction assumption, must be in the ϱ relation. It only blocks the value of piercing references (i.e., it changes the value of every pointer field or variable pointing to a cutpoint). The execution π_S never uses a a field f of an object o such that the f-field in $\varrho(o)$ at the corresponding $\mathcal{ECPF}$ points to the inaccessible location. Otherwise, π_E is a non effectively cutpoint-free execution of P in $\mathcal{ECPF}$ which is a contradiction to the assumption that P is effectively cutpoint-free. For similar reasons, the value of a variable which gets blocked by the $\mathcal{ECPF}$ semantics does not get used by the $\mathcal{GSB}$ semantics.

Lemma 1. *Let P be an effectively cutpoint-free program. The following holds:*

[Invariants] *An invariant concerning equality of values of access paths in the $\mathcal{ECPF}$ semantics is an invariant in the standard semantics*
[Cleanness] *P does not dereferences null references in the standard semantics.*

Lemma 2. *Let P be an effectively cutpoint-free program. A reference, that at a given program point always has the inaccessible value, is not live at that program point in the standard semantics.*

Definition 10 (Observational equivalence). *The $\mathcal{ECPF}$ memory states $\sigma_1, \sigma_2 \in \Sigma$ are* observationally equivalent, *denoted by $\sigma_1 \lesseqgtr \sigma_2$, if $\sigma_1 \lesssim \sigma_2$ and $\sigma_2 \lesssim \sigma_1$.*

The following lemma shows that $\mathcal{ECPF}$ is indifferent to location names.

Theorem 2 (Indifference to location names). *Let π_1, π_2 be execution traces of a program P according to the $\mathcal{ECPF}$ semantics. If $|\pi_1(1)| = |\pi_2(1)| = 1$, $in(\pi_1) \lesssim in(\pi_2)$ and $path(\pi_1) = path(\pi_2)$ then $out(\pi_1) \lesssim out(\pi_2)$.*

B   Update Formulae

In this section, we encode the abstract transformers using the notations of [25].

B.1   Intraprocedural Statements

The meaning of assignments is specified by defining the values of the predicates in the outgoing structure using first-order logic formulae with transitive closure over the incoming structure [25]. The inference rules for assignments are rather straightforward. We encode conditional using assume() statements.

The operational semantics for assignments is specified by *predicate-update formulae*: for every predicate p and for every statement st, the value of p in the 2-valued structure which results by applying st to S, is defined in terms of a formula evaluated over S.

The predicate-update formulae of the core-predicates for assignment is given in Fig. 13. The table also specifies the side condition which enables that application of the statement. These conditions check that null-dereference is not performed and that the *inaccessible value is not used*. The value of every core-predicate p after the statement executes, denoted by p', is defined in terms of the core predicate values before the statement executes (denoted without primes). Core predicates whose update formula is not specified, are assumed to be unchanged, i.e., $p'(v_1, \ldots) = p(v_1, \ldots)$.

None of the assignments, except for object allocation, modifies the underlying universe. Object allocation is handled as in [25]: A new individual is added to the universe to represent the allocated object; the auxiliary predicate *new* is set to hold *only* at that individual; only then, the predicate-update formulae is evaluated.

The semantics transitions into the error state ($\sigma_\bullet$) under the same conditions as the $\mathcal{ECPF}$ semantics, i.e., when an inaccessible-valued variable or field are accessed. (See Fig. 7). The following side condition trigers such a transition when a variable x points to an inaccessible location $\exists v \colon x(v) \land ia(v_2)$. Similarly, the following side condition trigers such a transition when the f-field of the object pointed to by a variable x points to an inaccessible location $\exists v_1, v_2 \colon x(v_1) \land f(v_1, v_2) \land ia(v_2)$.

Statement	Predicate-update formulae	side − condition
y = null	$y'(v) = 0$	
y = x	$y'(v) = x(v)$	$\forall v_1 : \neg(x(v_1) \wedge ia(v_1))$
y = x.f	$y'(v) = \exists v_1 : x(v_1) \wedge f(v_1, v)$	$\exists v_1 : x(v_1) \wedge \neg ia(v_1) \wedge$
		$\forall v_2 : \neg(x(v_1) \wedge f(v_1, v_2) \wedge ia(v_2))$
y.f = null	$f'(v_1, v_2) = f(v_1, v_2) \wedge \neg y(v_1)$	$\exists v_1 : y(v_1) \wedge \neg ia(v_1)$
y.f = x	$f'(v_1, v_2) = f(v_1, v_2) \vee (y(v_1) \wedge x(v_2))$	$\exists v_1 : y(v_1) \wedge \neg ia(v_1) \wedge$
		$\forall v_2 : \neg(x(v_2) \wedge ia(v_2))$
y = alloc	$eq'(v_1, v_2) = eq(v_1, v_2) \vee new(v_1) \wedge new(v_2)$	
	$new'(v) = 0$	

Fig. 13. The predicate-update formulae defining the operational semantics of assignments. Note that we always assume that a reference variable is nullified before re-assigned.

B.2   Interprocedural Statements

The treatment of procedure call and return could be briefly described as follows: (i) constructing the memory state at the callee's entry site (S_e) and (ii) the caller's memory state at the call site (S_c) and the callee's memory state at the exit site (S_x) are used to construct the caller's memory state at the return site (S_r). We now formally define and explain these steps.

Fig. 14 specifies the procedure call rule for an arbitrary call statement $y = p(x_1, \ldots, x_k)$ by an arbitrary function q. The rule is instantiated for each call statement in the program.

Computing the Memory State at the Entry Site. S_e, the memory state at the entry site to p, represents the local heap passed to p. It contains only these individuals in S_c that represent objects that are relevant for the invocation. It also contains the individual representing the inaccessible value. The formal parameters are initialized by $updCall_q^{y=p(x_1,\ldots,x_k)}$, defined in Fig. 15(a). The latter, specifies the value of the predicates in S_e using a predicate-update formulae evaluated over S_c. We use the convention that the updated value of x is denoted by x'. Predicates whose update formula is not specified, are assumed to be unchanged, i.e., $x'(v_1, \ldots) = x(v_1, \ldots)$. Note that only the predicates that represent variable values are modified. In particular, field values, represented by binary predicates, remain in p's local heap as in S_c.

Computing the Memory State at the Return Site. The memory state at the return-site (S_r) is constructed as a combination of the memory state in which p was invoked (S_c) and the memory state at p's exit-site (S_x). Informally, S_c provides the information about the (unmodified) irrelevant objects and S_x contributes the information about the destructive updates and allocations made during the invocation.

The main challenge in computing the effect of a procedure is relating the objects at the call-site to the corresponding objects at the return site. The fact that the invocation is effectively cutpoint-free guarantees that the only live references into the local heap are references to objects referenced by an actual parameter. This allows us to reflect the

Table 3. Formulae shorthands and their intended meaning

Shorthand	Formula	Intended Meaning
$F(v_1, v_2)$	$\bigvee_{f \in \mathcal{F}} f(v_1, v_2)$	v_1 has a field that points to v_2
$\varphi^*(v_1, v_2)$	$(eq(v_1, v_2) \vee$ $(TC\ w_1, w_2 : \varphi(w_1, w_2))(v_1, v_2))$	the reflexive transitive closure of φ
$R_{\{x_1,\dots,x_k\}}(v)$	$\neg ia(v) \wedge$ $\bigvee_{x \in \{x_1,\dots,x_k\}} \exists v_1 : x(v_1) \wedge F^*(v_1, v)$	v is reachable from $\mathbf{x_1}$ or $\mathbf{x_2}$ or $\dots$ or $\mathbf{x_k}$
$isCP_{q,\{x_1,\dots,x_k\}}(v)$	$R_{\{x_1,\dots,x_k\}}(v) \wedge$ $(\neg x_1(v) \wedge \dots \wedge \neg x_k(v)) \wedge$ $(\bigvee_{y \in V_q} y(v) \vee$ $\exists v_1 : \neg R_{\{x_1,\dots,x_k\}}(v_1) \wedge F(v_1, v))$	v is a cutpoint

$$Call_{y=p(x_1,\dots,x_k)}(S_c) = S_e \qquad Ret_{y=p(x_1,\dots,x_k)}(S_c, S_x) = S_r$$

where

$S_e = \langle U_e, \iota_e \rangle$ where
$\quad U_e = \{u \in U^{S_c} \mid S_c \models R_{\{x_1,\dots,x_k\}}(u) \vee ia(v)\}$
$\quad \iota_e = updCall_q^{y=p(x_1,\dots,x_k)}(S_c)$

$S_r = \langle U_r, \iota_r \rangle$ where
$\quad$ Let $U' = \{u.c \mid u \in U_c\} \cup \{u.x \mid u \in U_x\}$

$$\iota' = \lambda p \in \mathcal{P}. \begin{cases} \iota_c[inUc \mapsto \lambda v.1](p)(u_1, \dots, u_m) & : \quad u_1 = w_1.c, \dots, u_m = w_m.c \\ \iota_x[inUx \mapsto \lambda v.1](p)(u_1, \dots, u_m) & : \quad u_1 = w_1.x, \dots, u_m = w_m.x \\ 0 & : \quad otherwise \end{cases}$$

$\quad$ *in* $\ U_r = \{u \in U' \mid \langle U', \iota' \rangle \models inUx(u) \vee (inUc(u) \wedge \neg ia(u) \wedge \neg R_{\{x_1,\dots,x_k\}}(u))\}$
$\qquad \iota_r = updRet_q^{y=p(x_1,\dots,x_k)}(\langle U', \iota' \rangle)$

$$Call_{y=p(x_1,\dots,x_k)}(S_c) = \sigma_\bullet \qquad S_c \models \exists v : ia(v) \wedge (x_1(v) \vee \dots \vee x_k(v))$$
$$Ret_{y=p(x_1,\dots,x_k)}(S_c, S_x) = \sigma_\bullet \qquad S_x \models \exists v : ia(v) \wedge ret(v)$$

Fig. 14. The inference rule for a procedure call $y = p(x_1, \dots, x_k)$ by a procedure q. The functions $updCall_q^{y=p(x_1,\dots,x_k)}$ and $updRet_q^{y=p(x_1,\dots,x_k)}$ are defined in Fig. 15.

effect of p into the local heap of q by: (i) replacing the relevant objects in S_c with S_x, the local heap at the exit from p; (ii) redirecting all references to an object referenced by an actual parameter to the object referenced by the corresponding formal parameter in S_x; (iii) block every piercing reference.

Technically, S_c and S_x are *combined* into an intermediate structure $\langle U', \iota' \rangle$. The latter contains a copy of the memory states at the call site and at the exit site. To distinguish between the copies, the auxiliary predicates $inUc$ and $inUx$ are set to hold for individuals that originate from S_c and S_x, respectively.

a. Predicate update formulae for $updCall_q^{y=p(x_1,\ldots,x_k)}$
$z'(v) = \begin{cases} x_i(v) & : \quad z = h_i \\ 0 & : \quad z \in \mathcal{V} \setminus \{h_1,\ldots,h_k\} \end{cases}$

b. Predicate update formulae for $updRet_q^{y=p(x_1,\ldots,x_k)}$
$z'(v) = \begin{cases} ret_p(v) & : \quad z = y \\ \begin{aligned} & inUc(v) \wedge z(v) \wedge \neg R_{\{x_1,\ldots,x_k\}}(v) \vee \\ & \exists v_1 \colon z(v_1) \wedge match_{\{\langle h_1,x_1\rangle,\ldots,\langle h_k,x_k\rangle\}}(v_1,v) \vee \\ & \exists v_1 \colon z(v_1) \wedge isCP_{q,\{x_1,\ldots,x_k\}}(v_1) \wedge inUx(v) \wedge ia(v) \end{aligned} & : \quad z \in V_q \setminus \{y\} \\ 0 & : \quad z \in \mathcal{V} \setminus V_q \end{cases}$
$\begin{aligned} f'(v_1,v_2) = \; & inUx(v_1) \wedge inUx(v_2) \wedge f(v_1,v_2) \vee \\ & inUc(v_1) \wedge inUc(v_2) \wedge f(v_1,v_2) \wedge \neg ia(v_2) \wedge \neg R_{\{x_1,\ldots,x_k\}}(v_2) \vee \\ & inUc(v_1) \wedge inUx(v_2) \wedge \exists v_{sep} \colon f(v_1,v_{sep}) \wedge match_{\{\langle h_1,x_1\rangle,\ldots,\langle h_k,x_k\rangle\}}(v_{sep},v_2) \vee \\ & inUc(v_1) \wedge inUx(v_2) \wedge \exists v_{sep} \colon f(v_1,v_{sep}) \wedge isCP_{q,\{x_1,\ldots,x_k\}}(v_{sep}) \wedge ia(v_2) \end{aligned}$
$inUc'(v) = inUx'(v) = 0$

Fig. 15. Predicate-update formulae for the core predicates used in the procedure call rule. We assume that the p's formal parameters are $h_1,\ldots,h_k$. There is a separate update formula for every local variable $z \in \mathcal{V}$ and for every field $f \in \mathcal{F}$.

Pointer redirection is specified by means of predicate update formulae, as defined in Fig. 15(b). The most interesting aspect of these update-formulae is the formula $match_{\{\langle h_1,x_1\rangle,\ldots,\langle h_k,x_k\rangle\}}$, defined below:

$$match_{\{\langle h_1,x_1\rangle,\ldots,\langle h_k,x_k\rangle\}}(v_1,v_2) \stackrel{\text{def}}{=} \begin{aligned} & inUc(v_1) \wedge ia(v_1) \wedge inUx(v_2) \wedge ia(v_2) \vee \\ & \bigvee_{i=1}^k inUc(v_1) \wedge x_i(v_1) \wedge inUx(v_2) \wedge h_i(v_2) \end{aligned}$$

This formula matches an individual that represents a (parameter) object which is referenced by an actual parameter at the call-site, with the individual that represents the object which is referenced by the corresponding formal parameter at the exit-site. The assumption that formal parameters are not modified allows us to match these two individuals as representing the same object. Once pointer redirection is complete, all individuals originating from S_c and representing relevant objects are removed, resulting with the updated memory state of the caller. In addition, the formula matches the individual representing the inaccessible value at the call site with the one representing the inaccessible value at the return site, thus preserving the value of inaccessible references from before the call.

We block piercing references using formula $isCP_{q,\{x_1,\ldots,x_k\}}(v)$, defined in Tab. 3. The formula holds when v is a cutpoint object. It is comprised of three conjuncts. The first conjunct, requires that v be reachable from an actual parameter. The second conjunct, requires that v not be pointed-to by an actual parameter. The third conjunct, requires that v be an entry point into p's local heap, i.e., is pointed-to by a local variable of q (the caller procedure) or by a field of an object not passed to p.

Predicate Update Formulae for Instrumentation Predicates. Fig. 16 provides the update formulae for instrumentation predicates used by the procedure call rule. We use $PT_X(v)$ as a shorthand for $\bigvee_{x \in X} x(v)$. The intended meaning of this formula is to specify that v is pointed to by some variable from $X \subseteq \mathcal{V}$. We use $bypass_X(v_1, v_2)$ as a shorthand for $(F(v_1, v_2) \wedge \neg R_X(v_1))^*$. The intended meaning of this formula is to specify that v_2 is reachable from v_1 by a path that does not traverse any object which is reachable from any variable in $X \subseteq \mathcal{V}$. Note that, again, formula $match_{\{\langle h_1, x_1 \rangle, \dots, \langle h_k, x_k \rangle\}}(v_1, v_2)$ again plays a central role.

---

a. Predicate update formulae for $updCall_q^{y=p(x_1,\dots,x_k)}$

$ils'(v) = ils(v) \wedge \neg(PT_{x_1,\dots,x_k}(v) \vee isCP_{q,\{x_1,\dots,x_k\}}(v)) \vee$
$\qquad\qquad \exists v_1, v_2 : R_{\{x_1,\dots,x_k\}}(v_1) \wedge R_{\{x_1,\dots,x_k\}}(v_2) \wedge$
$\qquad\qquad\qquad\qquad F(v_1, v) \wedge F(v_2, v) \wedge \neg eq(v_1, v_2))$

$r'_y(v) = \begin{cases} r_{x_i}(v) & : \quad y = h_i \\ 0 & : \quad y \in \mathcal{V} \setminus \{h_1, \dots, h_k\} \end{cases}$

b. Predicate update formulae for $updRet_q^{y=p(x_1,\dots,x_k)}$

$ils'(v) = ils(v) \wedge (inUc(v) \wedge \neg R_{\{x_1,\dots,x_k\}}(v) \vee inUx(v)) \vee$
$\qquad PT_{x_1,\dots,x_k}(v) \wedge \exists v_1, v_2, v_3 : match_{\{\langle h_1, x_1 \rangle, \dots, \langle h_k, x_k \rangle\}}(v_1, v) \wedge \neg eq(v_2, v_3) \wedge$
$\qquad\qquad inUc(v_2) \wedge \neg R_{\{x_1,\dots,x_k\}}(v_2) \wedge F(v_2, v_1) \wedge$
$\qquad\qquad (inUc(v_3) \wedge \neg R_{\{x_1,\dots,x_k\}}(v_3) \wedge F(v_3, v_1) \vee inUx(v_3) \wedge F(v_3, v))$

$r'_{obj}(v_1, v_2) = r_{obj}(v_1, v_2) \wedge inUx(v_1) \wedge inUx(v_2) \vee$
$\qquad r_{obj}(v_1, v_2) \wedge inUc(v_1) \wedge inUc(v_2) \wedge \neg R_{\{x_1,\dots,x_k\}}(v_2) \vee$
$\qquad inUc(v_1) \wedge inUx(v_2) \wedge \exists v_a, v_f : match_{\{\langle h_1, x_1 \rangle, \dots, \langle h_k, x_k \rangle\}}(v_a, v_f) \wedge$
$\qquad\qquad bypass_{\{x_1,\dots,x_k\}}(v_1, v_a) \wedge r_{obj}(v_f, v_2)$

$r'_x(v) = inUc(v) \wedge r_x(v) \wedge \neg R_{\{x_1,\dots,x_k\}}(v) \vee$
$\qquad inUx(v) \wedge \exists v_x, v_a, v_f : match_{\{\langle h_1, x_1 \rangle, \dots, \langle h_k, x_k \rangle\}}(v_a, v_f) \wedge$
$\qquad\qquad x(v_x) \wedge bypass_{\{x_1,\dots,x_k\}}(v_x, v_a) \wedge r_{obj}(v_f, v)$

Fig. 16. The predicate update formulae for the instrumentation predicates used in the procedure call rule. We give the semantics for an arbitrary function call $y = p(x_1, \dots, x_k)$ by an arbitrary function q. We assume that the p's formal parameters are $h_1, \dots, h_k$.

Author Index